PRAGUE, VIENNA & BUDAPEST

JENNIFER D. WALKER & AUBURN SCALLON

Contents

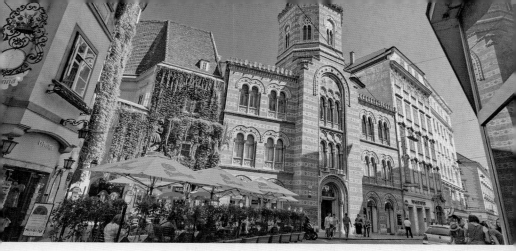

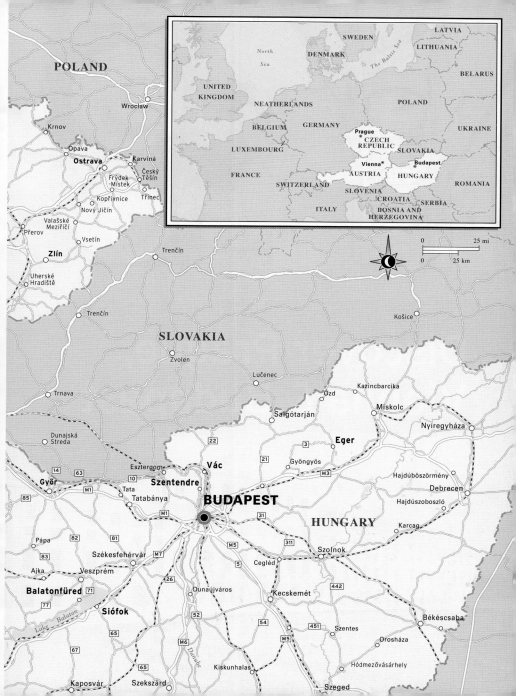

Discover Prague, Vienna & Budapest

Prague, Vienna, and Budapest offer travelers a rich tapestry of history and culture.

Before World War I, all three cities resided within the Austro-Hungarian Empire, and traces of the crumbled Habsburg dynasty, still linger in the decadent palaces and wide boulevards lined with extravagant buildings. Central Europe echoes the "World of Yesterday," with its gilded opera houses, grand hotels, and the wood-paneled cafés perfumed with percolating coffee and freshly baked cakes. Against this historic backdrop, modern (futuristic, even) innovations, from cryptocurrency-friendly cafes to eye-catching public art installations, are a delightful contrast.

Life is slow, even reflective, and flows with the seasons; locals flock to the beer gardens perched up in Letná Park in Prague escaping the summer heat, and as the leaves rust when fall arrives, the Viennese drink "this year's wine" in the Heurige beside the city's vineyards overlooking the Vienna Woods, and when the temperature drops in December the scent of spiced hot wine winds round the cities' Christmas markets. Music, art, and literature lovers can follow in the footsteps of giants, whether it's visiting Dvořak's grave in Prague, Freud's favorite café in Vienna, or Liszt's apartment in Budapest.

Clockwise from top left: The Griechengasse, a narrow alley in old town Vienna; Prague's Astronomical Clock; lion statue guarding the Chain Bridge over the Danube in Budapest; Vajdahunyad Castle in City Park, Budapest; pastry in Prague; Schönbrunn Palace in Vienna.

17 TOP
EXPERIENCES

1 Admiring **spectacular architecture,** from Prague's dramatic Gothic monuments to colorful art nouveau in Budapest to Habsburg grandeur in Vienna (page 32).

2 Soaking in one of Budapest's **thermal baths** (page 364).

3 Discovering the vast complex of Prague's **Vyšehrad,** which is no less impressive (and much less crowded) than the Prague Castle (page 80).

4 Listening to **classical music in Vienna,** the city where Mozart, Beethoven, Strauss, Schubert composed and conducted (page 244).

<<<

5 Drinking a *pálinka* or Unicum in a **ruin bar,** or *kert*, in Budapest's Jewish Quarter (page 370).

>>>

6 Taking in views over the Danube from Budapest's **Fisherman's Bastion** (page 333).

<<<

7 Boating or cycling through the **Wachau Valley,** where ruined castles, vineyards, and rolling hills line the banks of the Danube (page 298).

8 Following in the Habsburgs' footsteps at **Schönbrunn,** their summer palace in Vienna (page 231).

9 Wandering through the "bone church" at the **Sedlec Ossuary,** which contains the artfully arranged bones of more than 40,000 human skeletons (page 146).

10 Sipping a foam-topped *pivo* (beer) in one of **Prague's beer gardens** (page 92).

>>>

11 Losing yourself in centuries of art at Vienna's **Kunsthistorisches Museum** (page 204).

>>>

12 Exploring **Prague's outer neighborhoods,** where you can still get a taste of the undiscovered vibe the city was once known for (page 88).

<<<

13 Sipping a *Melange* in a cozy booth within a classic **Viennese coffeehouse** (page 258).

14 **Watching the sunset** over a spire-filled skyline in Prague (page 71).

15 Escaping city life on a hiking trail through the **Vienna Woods** (page 294).

<<<

16 Sampling local wine, from the spicy "Bull's Blood" in Hungary's **Valley of Beautiful Women** (page 442) to local vintages in rustic wine taverns or *Heurige* (page 240).

>>>

17 Browsing the stalls and enjoying a warm drink al fresco at **Prague's Christmas and Easter markets** (page 114).

<<<

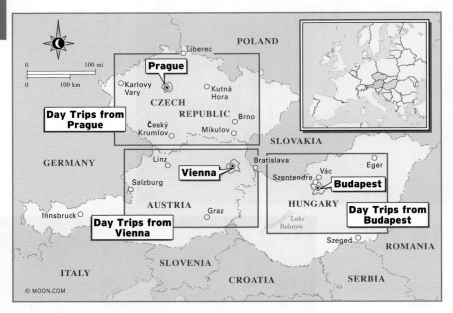

Planning Your Trip

Where to Go

Prague

Since regaining independence in the Velvet Revolution of 1989, Prague's **architectural beauty, fairy-tale atmosphere,** and **affordable nightlife** have secured the Central European capital a prominent place on travelers' lists. Postcard-worthy sights like the **Charles Bridge, St. Vitus Cathedral** at the **Prague Castle,** or the church spires and **Astronomical Clock** of **Old Town Square** draw significant crowds to admire (and photograph) their beauty. Prague's **surrounding neighborhoods** still hold plenty of **undiscovered character** to contrast the typical tourist experience of the historical city center. Head to hilltop **Vyšehrad complex** for peaceful sightseeing, enjoy a night of culture inside the old-world glamour

of Prague's **theaters and concert halls,** and pair any activity, any time of day, with a nice cold *pivo* (beer).

Day Trips from Prague

For a quick trip, head north to **Liberec** to visit the mountaintop Ještěd tower and embrace the summertime vibe at the reservoir, or reconnect with nature on a hike through the forests and sandstone rocks of **Bohemian Paradise.** The eastern town of **Kutna Hora** holds an impressive collection of churches (including one decorated in bones). Free-flowing fountains of mineral springs draw a quieter crowd to the western spa town of **Karlovy Vary.** Combine a river rafting adventure with a visit to the picturesque castle of South Bohemia's beloved **Český Krumlov.** Venture

If You Want...

Art museums: You could spend weeks in Vienna just exploring its iconic art museums.

Grand palaces: Vienna's Hofburg and Schönbrunn Palace; Lednice and Valtice chateaux.

Classical music: Concerts and opera in elegant settings in Vienna and Prague (especially during the Prague Spring festival in May).

Hiking: Vienna Woods (very accessible from the city); Bohemian Paradise outside Prague.

Other outdoor activities: Caving in Budapest; boating or cycling down the Danube in the Wachau Valley; cycling from Budapest to Szentendre or along the Danube Bend; rafting the Vltava River outside Český Krumlov.

Nightlife: Budapest's ruin bars; Prague's beer gardens; Prague's Vinohrady district for LGBTQ Nightlife.

Beer: Prague's beer gardens and craft beer pubs.

Wine: Vienna's Heurige; Eger and the Valley of the Beautiful Women; Lake Balaton; Prague's Karlín neighborhood; the National Czech Wine Salon at the Valtice Chateau.

Jewish history: Prague's medieval Jewish Quarter; Budapest's Dohány Street Synagogue; Vienna's Jewish Museums.

Communist History: Budapest's Memento Park; Prague's John Lennon Wall, Museum of Communism, and spy tower in the Town Belfry by St. Nicholas Church.

rafting the Vltava River in Český Krumlov

Street food: Try lángos (deep fried savory dough topped with cheese and sour cream) in Budapest, and sausages from the Würstelstand in Vienna.

Markets: Vienna's Nachsmarkt; Budapest's Central Market Hall.

Cheap Thrills: Prague and Budapest are affordable cities; Vienna not so much.

further east into South Moravia to discover the diverse architecture and lively nightlife scene in **Brno** or pair local wines with stately chateaux in **Mikulov, Lendnice, and Valtice.**

Vienna

Once the heart of the Austro-Hungarian Empire, Vienna still bears the grandeur of the Habsburgs with its **grand palaces,** the **Spanish Riding School,** and extravagant parkland. Trace the footsteps of **Gustav Klimt,** then while away the hours in Vienna's **world-class art museums** and galleries. Music aficionados should make

pilgrimages to **Mozart, Beethoven,** and **Strauss**'s former homes before taking in an **opera** at the world famous **Staatsoper.** Visit Freud's former home, ride a **100-year-old Ferris wheel** in the Prater, and round up the day people-watching in one of Vienna's **classic cafes.**

Day Trips from Vienna

Nestled in the Alps, **Salzburg**—home to both Mozart and the Sound of Music—is just two hours from Vienna. Closer to the capital, you can **sail up the Danube** as it winds through the **Wachau Valley** where castles

view of Prague bridges from Letná hill

and monasteries dot the landscape, or hop on a train to **Bratislava, Slovakia** to add another country to your itinerary. **Mauthausen Concentration Camp** is a poignant reminder of the horrors of the Holocaust. Right outside Vienna are the **Vienna Woods,** where you can visit the fairy-tale Liechtenstein Castle just outside Mödling, or relax in the spa town of Baden bei Wien.

Budapest

A tale of two cities, Budapest is divided by the **Danube River** with spectacular vistas wherever you look. See sights like **Buda Castle** on Castle Hill, then spend some time soaking in one of the many **thermal baths.** By night crowds flock to the famous **ruin pubs** in the Jewish Quarter. Ride back into history on the **Children's Railroad,** the retro train operated by children, as it chugs up into the Buda Hills, or head over to **Memento Park,** where communist statues go to die. Once you've seen the sites and ate your fill of goulash, delve deeper by visiting one of the city's hundreds of **caves** or ride a boat up the Danube to one of the **Danube beaches.**

Day Trips from Budapest

It's easy to escape Budapest for the day. Take the train down to **Lake Balaton,** Central Europe's largest lake, where you can explore the magical peninsula of Tihany, stroll the promenade in Balatonfüred, or sunbathe and party down in Siófok. Alternatively, you can **sail down the Danube Bend,** hike up to the citadel at Visegrád for stunning views over the Danube, or explore the former Serbian community-turned-artists-colony in picturesque **Szentendre.** Get on the bus for a couple of hours to the city of **Eger** in north eastern Hungary, famous for resisting an Ottoman siege at its historic castle and also famous for its **spicy red wines** served down in the evocatively named **"Valley of Beautiful Women."**

When to Go

There is no right or wrong time to embark on a journey through Central Europe. Prague, Vienna, and Budapest are beautiful year-round, with plenty to offer throughout the seasons.

High Season (June-Aug. and Dec.)

Summers can be scorching (sometimes rising above 40°C/104°F) and often come punctuated with flash storms. But this is when you can sail along the Vltava River, sunbathe on a beach beside the Danube, or grab a picnic in a leafy park. Skip July and August if you want to avoid the crowds, especially in Prague or Budapest, when the Sziget Festival is in full swing in the latter. December, when the Christmas markets set up shop, is also a busy time in each city.

Shoulder Season (April-May and Sept.-Nov.)

If you're outdoorsy, spring and fall may be your best bet. You get to escape intense temperatures of the summer months and the dreary cold weather of the winter. In the spring, cherry and apricot blossoms burst into bloom, and in the fall, the trees paint the landscape with a palette of rusty colors. Culinary and wine festivals take over the public spaces of the towns and cities—like the wine festival in Buda Castle—so if you're a foodie it's a good time to visit, with fewer crowds than you'll experience in summer or December.

Low Season (Jan.-Mar.)

Winters can dip down to subzero temperatures (as low as -15°C/5°F), yet Central Europe is at its most beautiful in the snow. When the temperatures plunge, you can escape the chill in a museum or a cozy café with its own curious cast of local characters. Going off season can be easier on the wallet, as hotels often have rooms available at lower prices, but many outdoor attractions close down or operate with limited opening hours.

Before You Go

Passports and Visas

Travelers from the **United States, Canada, Australia,** or **New Zealand** do not need a visa to enter the EU for visits lasting under 90 days. To enter Europe, all you need is a passport that's valid at least three months after your departure from the EU. (A visa is required for travelers from **South Africa.**) UK travelers should check for new regulations post-Brexit.

Once you arrive in Central Europe, you can usually cross the borders without having your passport or ID checked. However, in some instances, like the Budapest to Vienna train, you may need to show your passport to the border control.

Advance Reservations

In general, it's a good idea to purchase tickets for museums in advance, as you can save a lot of time skipping the lines when you arrive. Usually, you can do this before you set out in the morning—just ask your hotel to print out the ticket before you go.

However, there are some reservations that are worth making before you even get on the plane:

PRAGUE

Prague's **Strahov Library** only allows a limited number of visitors per year, so book as early in advance as possible if that sight is on your wishlist. Outside Prague, **a tour of**

Vila Tugendhat, Brno's UNESCO-protected jewel of modern architecture, requires three to four months of advance notice to experience.

VIENNA

It's a good idea to book tours for the Third Man Tour of the Vienna Sewers, which run one English language tour a day, or the Spanish Riding School in advance.

BUDAPEST

Book your ticket for the Hungarian Parliament before going. Spots are limited and fill up quickly in high season.

Transportation

GETTING TO CENTRAL EUROPE

You can get to Central Europe by flying into Prague, Vienna, or Budapest directly, although there are more frequent international flights to nearby destinations like Frankfurt, Munich, or Berlin. Vienna International Airport (VIE, Wien-Flughafen, Schwechat, tel. 01/7007-22233, www.viennaairport.com) has the most long-haul connections out of the three cities, including many cities in the US and Canada. Václav Havel Airport Prague (PRG, Aviatická, tel. 02/20-111-888, www.prg. aero) has a few seasonal connections to the US and Canada, and Budapest Ferenc Liszt International Airport (BUD, Budapest, tel. 01/296-9696, www.bud.hu) has a couple of transcontinental flights to Toronto, New York, Chicago, and Philadelphia. If you're coming from Australia, New Zealand or South Africa, you will have to change at a larger airport like Dubai or Istanbul before flying onto Central Europe. You can also get direct flights to the main airports in all three cities from London—and you also have the option of flying into Bratislava as well.

Old Town in Budapest

fiacre in old city centre in Vienna

TRAVELING BETWEEN PRAGUE, VIENNA, AND BUDAPEST

Once you reach Central Europe, traveling between the three cities is pretty straightforward. Europe has excellent rail connections, and you can go direct between Prague, Vienna, and Budapest directly.

Since Budapest and Vienna, and Vienna and Prague are fairly close to each other, it's not worth flying between the cities (it's expensive and the trains will probably get you there in the same time or less if you factor in check in and security checks). If you really have to take a plane, **Austrian Airlines** (www.austrian.com) does connect Vienna with both cities. **Czech Airlines** (www.csa.cz) runs regular flights between Budapest and Prague.

The Best of Prague, Vienna & Budapest

These three cities—and the appealing day trips beyond them—each offer a unique slice of Central Europe.

Some international travelers will need to go back to Prague at the end of their trip for their flight home. However, if you can book two one-way tickets, it would make more sense to fly back home from Budapest.

Prague

DAY 1: PRAGUE

Get an overview of Prague's cultural landscape with Art Nouveau paintings in the morning at the **Mucha Museum** and an evening of dance, opera, or classical music at one of Prague's **ornate theaters.** Walk through the **historic city center** and have a drink at **Letná Beer Garden** to round out the afternoon, followed by an evening at the theater.

DAY 2: PRAGUE

Stroll through the peaceful **Wallenstein Gardens,** find the **John Lennon Wall,** and spend an afternoon inside the **Prague Castle** complex. Then give your feet a break and treat your stomach to a decadent dinner of **Czech cuisine** before crossing the **Charles Bridge** under the stars.

DAY 3: DAY TRIP TO LIBEREC

After a one-hour bus from the Černy Most station to Liberec, hop on tram #3 at **Fugnerova** to Horní Hanychov and follow signs to catch a cable car to **Ještěd Hotel and TV Tower.** Have lunch at the retro-futuristic restaurant and take in the mountaintop view.

Cable car down again and jump on tram #3 to **Mikyna** for quality coffee. On a rainy day, hit the nearby **Lázně Regional Art Gallery.** If the

Cafe and restaurants at Old Town Square

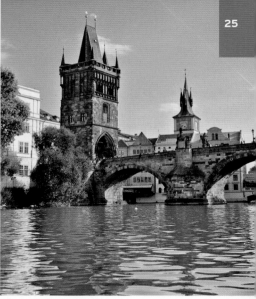

Náplavka, Prague's riverside party

Charles Bridge from the river

sun is shining, head southeast to the **Liberec Reservoir** where you can sip Svijany beer on the lawn or circle the one-mile path around this semi-secluded body of water.

Around 5pm, walk about 15 minutes to the center to admire the exteriors of the **Liberec Town Hall, FX Šalda Theatre,** and David Černý's sculptural bus stop. **Radniční Sklípek** serves traditional Czech meals underneath the town hall. Catch the last bus back to Prague at 9pm.

DAY 4: PRAGUE LIKE A LOCAL
For a taste of life outside the city center, start with brunch in the **Karlín** neighborhood before discovering the far less crowded castle complex of **Vyšehrad.** Join the locals walking along **Náplavka** and get a taste of modern architecture at the **Dancing House** and history at the **National Monument to the Heroes of the Heydrich Terror.** Return to Karlín for dinner, drinks, and innovative entertainment at **Kasárna Karlín.**

DAY 5: PRAGUE TO VIENNA
Spend a last morning soaking in Prague before boarding a 4-hour train to Vienna and settling into your hotel.

Vienna
DAY 6: VIENNA
Explore the **Hofburg** and **St. Stephen's Cathedral,** taking time for a quick **schnitzel** before seeing Klimt's iconic *The Kiss* at the Belvedere. End your day with sunset views from the **Riesenrad,** the historic Ferris wheel in the Prater.

DAY 7: VIENNA
View avant-garde art at the **Secession,** followed by a bite and browsing at the stalls of the Naschmarkt. After lunch, explore the former Habsburg residence of **Schönbrunn Palace.** End your evening with live music in the **Gürtel,** a trendy nightlife district that occupies the arches under the elevated U-Bahn rails.

Dürnstein Castle along the Danube River, in the picturesque Wachau Valley

view from St. Stephen's Cathedral

DAY 8: VIENNA LIKE A LOCAL

See some of architect **Friedensreich Hundertwasser**'s most spectacular buildings, along with the stunning art nouveau **St. Leopold Church** by Otto Wagner. Grab a *Käsekrainer*, a sausage filled with cheese, at one of Vienna's iconic sausage stands, drink coffee with the locals, and finish out your day with nightlife at a local hidden bar, like **Tür 7.**

DAY 9: DAY TRIP TO THE WACHAU VALLEY

Hop on a train heading to **Melk** from the Westbahnhof. After an hour's journey, you will already see the striking, orange **Melk Abbey** on the hill in front of you as you exit the station. Follow the signs up the hill to the abbey and spend a couple of hours exploring, then head down to town for lunch.

Take the Wachau Cruise ferry departing at 1:45pm from Melk down the Danube through the Wachau Valley. Get off at Dürnstein and hike up to the famous ruins of **Dürnstein Castle** and then take the bus on to **Krems an der Donau.**

Get the train back to Vienna to Wien Franz-Josefs-Bahnhof (1 hour).

Back in Vienna, cross the Danube Canal over to the **Augarten** for some late afternoon sun.

DAY 10: VIENNA TO BUDAPEST

Have one last *Melange* in one of Vienna's famous cafes before heading to Wien Hauptbahnhof to take the **train to Budapest Keleti.** The journey will take just under three hours and will bring you right into the heart of Budapest. Take the metro to the city center—line 2 will take you to downtown Pest and over to Buda just north of Castle Hill, whereas line 4 will take you to the southern part of Buda around the trendy Bartók Béla Avenue. Get settled in and take a **walk along the Danube** before grabbing dinner downtown.

Budapest

DAY 11: BUDAPEST

Spend your first day in Budapest exploring the Castle District. Take in the views from

---

1 the Belvedere building complex, Vienna **2** Little Princess perched by the tram rails with Buda Castle in the background.

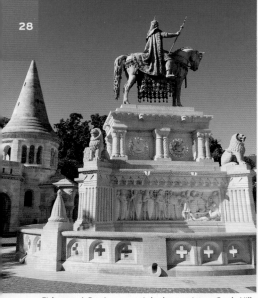

Fisherman's Bastion, a scenic lookout point on Castle Hill

Tihany Abbey at Lake Balaton

Fisherman's Bastion, making time for quirky Hospital in the Rock in the afternoon, followed by a sweet at Budapest's oldest *cukrászda* (confectionary). Visit the **Hungarian National Gallery** in the late afternoon.

DAY 12: BUDAPEST
Take in the views from the top of **St. Stephen's Basilica,** explore the **Royal Postal Savings Bank** and **Hungarian Parliament,** then kick back on a **Danube cruise.** Spend the end of your day in some of Budapest's most famous **ruin pubs.**

DAY 13: BUDAPEST LIKE A LOCAL
Head out of the city center and into the Buda Hills, taking a ride on the **Children's Railway,** a small railway run by children as a relic left over from Communist times. Take in the views from the **Elizabeth Lookout Tower,** then spend the day soaking and swimming in **Lukács Thermal Baths,** the local favorite of all of Budapest's baths.

DAY 14: DAY TRIP TO LAKE BALATON
Grab the train from Déli Pályaudvar train station to **Balatonfüred** (2 hours). Once you reach Balatonfüred hop on a bus to **Tihany** (you will find the buses go from the train station), which will take another 30 minutes. The bus will put you down in the center of the town, so head up to the **Benedictine Abbey of Tihany** for amazing views over the lake. Stop in at the **Rege Cukrászda** for a coffee and a cake—try the lavender infused custard cream cake—or grab some lunch in the village. Make sure you pick up some lavender-based gifts before heading back to Balatonfüred. Back in Balatonfüred, drink from the **Kossuth Lajos spring** before strolling down the **Tragore Prominade** along the lake side. Grab something to eat at one of the restaurants before taking the train back to Budapest.

DAY 15: GOODBYE, CENTRAL EUROPE
If your flight home leaves from Prague, you can take the train from Nyugati Pályaudvar (or the night train from Keleti Pályaudvar) back to the Czech capital and head on to the airport from there. Otherwise, head to the Budapest airport for your flight home.

Drinking in Central Europe

Drinking in Central Europe isn't just about getting drunk, it's about savoring the moment: Whether it's with a good glass of local wine in a tavern or a vineyard in Vienna, to a refreshing pint of locally brewed Czech beer. You don't have to stay up till 4am partying hard to enjoy the cities' famous bars—but you can if you want! Prague and Budapest have earned their wild nightlife reputation, while Vienna is perceived as more subdued (despite having its own microcosm of clubs and bars around the city).

Prague
BEER GARDENS
Embrace the Czech concept of *Česká pohoda*: enjoying life outdoors. Dress casually, bring cash, and slide onto a wooden bench to spend a day sipping delicious Czech *pivo* in the fresh air.

- It's hard to say whether the hilltop views or the cold brews at **Letná Beer Garden** are more likely to lighten your mood. (Good thing you don't have to choose.)
- Join the locals for some laid-back day drinking at **Hospůdka Na Hradbách** in the Vyšehrad complex.
- 1,400-seat **Reigrovy Sady** in Vinohrady wins the award for Prague's largest and rowdiest beer garden.

LGBT VINOHRADY
Prague's bar and pub scenes are largely tolerant, live-and-let-live landscapes where groups socialize with the friends that they came with, but there are areas where specific communities tend to congregate. The LGBT nightlife scene centers historically (but not exclusively) around the Vinohrady neighborhood.

- **Termix**'s tiny dance floor keeps the mostly male clientele in tight quarters dancing to Top 40 hits.

- **Termax** labels itself the Czech Republic's largest gay bar and dance club.
- **PM Club** near Vyšehrad hosts monthly Freedom Night parties attracting a largely lesbian crowd.

COCKTAILS BARS OUTSIDE THE CITY CENTER
Heading outside the city center to neighborhoods like Žižkov and Vršovice offers a more low-key local experience of Prague.

- The lights are low, the martinis are well mixed, and the staff are efficiently friendly at **Bukowski's Bar** in Žižkov.
- **Café Bar Pilotu** sets the scene of a living room party with your coolest bartending friends playing host.

Vienna
HEURIGE AND *STADHEURIGEN*
Vienna is one of the only European capitals with its own significant wine region, and the best place to sample the local wine is at a famous *Heurige* (wine tavern). Most of Vienna's *Heurigen* back onto the vineyards in the Vienna Woods outside the city center, and also serve hearty Austrian food. They're popular in summer but really come to life in the fall. If you can't make it to a *Heurige*, visit a *Stadheuirge*, which is the in-city version.

- **Weinstube Josefstadt** is one of the few *Heurige* you'll find in the center of Vienna.
- **Heuriger Sirbu** has amazing views over Vienna from its vineyard.
- **Furgassl-Huber,** in business for 40 years, is an institution on the Viennese *Heurige* scene.

BEACH BARS
In the summer, Vienna buzzes around the Danube and the Danube Canal on lazy weekend afternoons. Sunbathe by day, and enjoy the scene by the river after the sun sets.

Hohensalzburg Castle, Salzburg, Austria

Austria, the Czech Republic, and Hungary have much to offer outside their big cities, and venturing even an hour further afield can provide insight into the local culture and landscape. From Vienna, the capital of another country—Bratislava, Slovakia—is even within reach.

FROM PRAGUE

- **Liberec:** Get a peek at local life in the Czech Republic in Liberec, a less touristed city just an hour away from Prague by bus.

- **Kutná Hora:** This town is known for its "bone church" at the Sedlec Ossuary. It's an hour east of Prague, so you can take the train out and return the same day.

FROM VIENNA

- **Bratislava, Slovakia:** The Slovak capital lies one hour from Vienna and 2 hours from Budapest by train. It's easy to see the highlights of this small city (Blue Church, the Old Town, and the castle) in a day.

- **Vienna Woods:** Only 20 minutes out of Vienna by train, explore Liechtenstein Castle, sail an underground lake, or drink wine in Vienna's famous *Heurige* overlooking the vineyards for the day.

- **Wachau Valley:** The best way to experience the scenic Wachau Valley is to take the 1.5 hour Danube cruise from Melk (an hour by train from Vienna) to Krems. Expect to spend a couple of hours in Melk if you plan to visit the abbey.

- **Salzburg:** Mozart's hometown spreads out below the snowcapped Alps and is only 2.5 hours by train from Vienna. You can do Salzburg in a day but to really appreciate this historic city it's best to spend the night.

FROM BUDAPEST

- **Tihany:** The magical peninsula of Tihany juts out into Lake Balaton with undulating volcanic hills that burst with lavender in the summer. It'll take 2.5 hours to reach from Budapest by train and bus, and can be done in a day but it's better to linger for the night.

- **Eger and the Valley of Beautiful Women:** Walk the castle walls overlooking this baroque jewel box of a town that's famous for its spicy red wines. Just 2 hours from Budapest, it's good for either a day trip or an overnight excursion.

- **Visegrád:** Hike up to Visegrád fortress for stunning views over the Danube Bend. It'll take you an hour to get here either by bus or by train with a ferry crossing. It's easy to do Visegrád in a day—you can even sail back to Budapest in the afternoon.

- **Tel Aviv Beach** captures a Mediterranean beach feel with real sand, Middle Eastern food and cocktails.

- **Strandbar Herrmann** feels like the cross between a mini-festival and a day at the beach.

- **Palmar on the Danube Island** has that tropical feeling with palm trees, fairy lights, and great cocktails.

THE GÜRTEL

Vienna really takes off after dark under the arches of the Stadtbahn just outside the city center. You'll find cool clubs and bars with an alternative slant in this area.

- **The Chelsea** is a classic live music venue that doubles as a football theme bar.

- **B72** is a two-story club offering both live music and DJ nights.

- **The Loft** occupies a former factory that is now a club and alternative cultural center.

Budapest
RUIN BARS AND KERTS

Unique to Budapest, ruin pubs occupy crumbling former apartment blocks, dental laboratories, or glass factories filled with fairy lights, eclectic furniture pulled off the street, and quirky art. In the summer, locals head to *kerts* (Hungarian for a garden), which are usually abandoned plots set in the gravel under a firewall, or pop-up in a park for the summer. Most of these venues are concentrated in the city's Jewish Quarter.

- **Szimpla Kert** is Budapest's first ruin bar and a must-visit on your first trip to Budapest.

- Set in a former dental laboratory, ruin bars **Fogas Ház & Instant** joined forces to create a super club with numerous bars and dancefloors.

- **Kőleves Kert** is an outdoor ruin bar in a downtown lot-turned-garden that's popular with locals in the summer.

Vienna is one of the few capital cities in the world with its own vineyards.

Spectacular Architecture

The Golden Triangle of Central Europe is famed for its stunning architecture. Head to Prague for dramatic Gothic architecture and cubism; Budapest for baroque grandeur, intricate art nouveau, or social realism; and Vienna for Habsburg grandeur and Otto Wagner's stunning art nouveau buildings. You could lose yourself in the details of each building as you wander through the streets of these cities, and remember: Always look up!

Prague

WWII did comparably little damage to the Czech capital compared to its Central European neighbors. This has left centuries of diverse architectural styles, from dark Gothic structures to elaborate art nouveau exteriors and modern masterpieces, standing shoulder to shoulder along Prague's cobblestoned streets.

- **Náměstí Republiky:** Simply turn your head while standing on the corner of Na Příkopě street in New Town to survey the architectural mix of the Powder Tower (Gothic), Municipal House (Art Nouveau), Hybernia Theater (Empire-style), and Czech National Bank (International).

- **Basilica of Sts. Peter & Paul:** The dark, neo-Gothic silhouette of this Vyšehrad cathedral houses gorgeous Art Nouveau décor inside its doors.

- **Dancing House:** This 1990s collaboration between Canadian-American Frank Gehry and Croatian-Czech Vlado Milunić was inspired by and named after Fred Astaire and Ginger Rogers. The intertwined glass and stone towers beside the Vltava River symbolize Prague's delicate balance between its proud historical past and developing modern identity.

- **Žižkov TV Tower:** Love it or hate it, Prague's

Art Nouveau Municipal House on Republic Square, Prague

Dancing House in Prague

Secession Building in Vienna

Hundertwasser House, designed by Austrian artist and architect Friedensreich Hundertwasser

tallest building gets people talking. Built in the late 1980s, the gray, rocket-like tower dominates the skyline outside of the Old Town.

- **Cubist Architecture:** Cubism as an architectural trend never really took off, but it did make its mark in Prague. Old Town's **Grand Café Orient** incorporates right angles into every detail from the coat hooks to the coffee cups, and the world's only Cubist lamppost stands outside the pub **U Pinkasů** just off Wenceslas Square.

Outside Prague

- **Ještěd Hotel and TV Tower:** The curved walls of this unique building in Liberec slope skyward into an upside-down funnel shape, earning an International Perret Architecture Award for blending seamlessly into the mountain range it sits atop.

- **Vila Tugendhat:** Fans of Functionalist architecture should book months before visiting Brno to see the beautifully balanced simplicity in these light-filled rooms and custom-made

furniture designed by German-American architect Ludwig Mies van der Rohe in the 1930s.

Vienna

Vienna is overwhelmed with Baroque and Historicist grandeur, punctuated with Secessionist avant-garde buildings offering a breath of fresh air.

- **Kirche Am Steinhof (St. Leopold's Church):** This gold-domed church is Otto Wagner's most spectacular masterpiece. It's out of the way but worth the architectural pilgrimage.

- **Hundertwasserhaus:** A contrast to the Biedermeier and Habsburg buildings dotted around Vienna, Friedensreich Hundertwasser's multicolored house of uneven proportions and playful angles is an architectural breath of fresh air.

- **Secession:** The Secession caused a scandal when it opened in 1897, with its "Golden Cabbage" crowning the austere white cube-like structure. Today it's a symbol of Vienna's

PRAGUE

Petřín Lookout Tower: Climbing 299 steps (or taking an elevator) to the observation deck of Prague's mini-Eiffel Tower offers one of the highest viewpoints in the city.

Vyšehrad: The hilltop location of Prague's "other" castle complex is surrounded by winding paths and observation points over the Vltava River and iconic red rooftops of the Czech capital.

Vitkov Hill: The courtyard platform outside the National Memorial on the outskirts of Žižkov gives an alternative to the typical city center panoramas and an incredible vantage point to watch the sun set over the Prague Castle.

Náplavka Riverbanks: Some of Prague's prettiest views lie below street level along the boardwalks lining the Vltava River. In the summer, you can take a small ferry to Náplavka Smíchov for a Vyšehrad view with a bevy of swans and a railway bridge in the foreground.

VIENNA

St. Stephen's Cathedral: Take the elevator up to the top of the north tower or climb the 343 steps in the south tower for views of Vienna's old inner city, along with cathedral's colorful mosaic rooftop.

Prague's mini-Eiffel Tower on Petřín Hill

Donauturm (Danube Tower): Shoot up in the elevator to the top of the highest man-made point in the city for views over the Danube, the old town and hills of the Vienna Woods beyond.

Riesenrad: Hop on this iconic 100-year-old Ferris wheel for changing views over Vienna and the Prater. Catch a glimpse of the Danube, the Danube Canal as well as the historic center from its elegant carriages.

Schönbrunn Park's Gloriette: Hike up to this triumphal hilltop arch in Schönbrunn Park for sweeping vistas over brilliant yellow Schönbrunn Palace and the park's manicured hedges, with the Vienna Woods and the city rising up in the backdrop.

BUDAPEST

Fisherman's Bastion: Although any view from Pest's Castle Hill won't disappoint, for Budapest's most romantic spot stroll over to the Fisherman's Bastion, a turreted neo-Gothic lookout platform.

Gellért Hill: Hike up Gellért Hill for vistas of Budapest's most iconic sites. Just before you reach the Citadella, there is a small lookout point where you can see the Royal Palace, the Danube, and the Hungarian Parliament all from the same spot.

St. Stephen's Basilica: A platform circles this basilica's iconic domed roof allowing you to take in views of the inner city and famous landmarks. As a bonus, you get some of the basilica towers in the shot along with the stunning backdrop.

Elizabeth Lookout Tower: Either take the chairlift up to the top of János Hegy, the Children's Railway or hike up from Normafa to the Elizabeth lookout tower. This is the highest point in Budapest. Although you won't make out any of the famous landmarks easily, if the weather conditions are right, you may see a hint of the mountains in Slovakia.

DANUBE BEND

Visegrád Citadel: It's worth the hike (or taxi ride) up to the Visegrád Citadel just to see the Danube Bend from above. This is perhaps one of the most spectacular viewing points in the whole of Hungary.

modernism, and still used as a hub of contemporary art.

- **MuseumsQuartier:** The former imperial stables are now the cutting edge of the avant-garde, not only when it comes to art, but architecture too. Check out the simple lines of the mumok and Leopold museums—both of which are a stark contrast against the grander more elaborate buildings in downtown Vienna.
- **Schönbrunn Palace:** The shade of yellow of this imperial summer palace is so iconic it has a color named after it. Schönbrunn Palace is the most opulent and spectacular out of the Habsburg Palaces around Vienna, and worth the day just to revel around its splendorous wings both inside and out.

Outside Vienna

- **Blue Church in Bratislava:** This church in various hues of blue by Hungarian architect Ödön Lechner is a must visit in Bratislava if you love art nouveau architecture.

Budapest

Budapest has a lot in common architecturally with its sister cities, but there are a few nuances that set it apart. The iconic buildings found in the Hungarian capital dating from the golden age around the year 1900 have architect Miklós Ybl to thank, who built the Hungarian State Opera House and the finishing touches on St. Stephen's Basilica. And of course, there's also the work of Ödön Lechner, the architect who pioneered Hungary's own brand of art nouveau, blending orientalism with Hungarian folk art in his style with brightly colored glazed architectural ceramics.

- **Hungarian Parliament:** This piece of neo-Gothic grandeur on the Danube is one of the city's most iconic architectural legacies and impressive whether viewed from afar in Buda or up close in Pest.
- **Institute of Geology and Geophysics:** One of Ödön Lechner's most spectacular buildings is an exquisite piece of Hungarian

Hungarian Parliament Building

The Dohány Street Synagogue is Europe's largest synagogue.

art nouveau. From afar, admire its blue tiled roof topped with globes held up by Atlas statues, and from close up see how many geological references you can spot.

- **Gellért Thermal Baths:** Unimpressive on the outside, the interior of these thermal baths are a temple to the golden age of Hungary's spa culture. The baths are lined with mosaics and glazed ceramics in fifty shades of subterranean blue and turquoise.

- **Vajdahunyad Castle:** Built to celebrate architecture from Hungary and its former territories, Vajdahunyad Castle is a blend of different castles, churches and palaces from different eras, and worth the visit for an interactive introduction to Hungarian architecture.

- **Dohány Street Synagogue:** Europe's largest synagogue (and one of Budapest's most beautiful buildings) blends neo-orientalism with elements of a Christian church. Inside, a vast rose window rises above the pews, while parts of the exterior synagogue resemble a mosque, with Moorish style design.

Prague

Since the turn of the century, Prague has moved

from an undiscovered darling to a popular European destination. The city's architectural landscape, from the church spires of Old Town to repurposed industrial spaces in Holešovice, provides a visual timeline of art history, with Gothic towers, Cubist lampposts, and Communist functionalism all punctuating the pastel buildings and cobblestoned streets. These postcard-worthy structures are a perfect backdrop for romantic walks or watching the sunset from a vantage point above it all.

Along with Prague's often described fairy-tale atmosphere, Czech culture includes an affinity for whimsy and ideals of freedom and beauty, as seen in the John Lennon graffiti wall, David Černy's often controversial public art pieces, or adults wearing hoodies with animal

Highlights

Look for ★ to find recommended sights, activities, dining, and lodging.

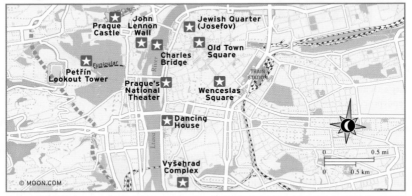

★ **Old Town Square:** Church towers to your right, a 15th-century astronomical clock to your left, and a Baroque church across the square. Old Town Square (Staroměstské náměstí) also plays host to holiday markets at Easter and Christmas (page 51).

★ **Jewish Quarter (Josefov):** One of the most intact Jewish quarters in Central Europe includes a historic cemetery, powerful Holocaust memorial, and the oldest active synagogue in Europe (page 54).

★ **Wenceslas Square:** The center of political and commercial life in Prague, this square has plenty of stories to tell (page 61).

★ **Dancing House:** A whimsically curved building from the early 1990s, inspired by Fred Astaire and Ginger Rogers, symbolizes a blend of East meets West and old and new ideas (page 65).

★ **Charles Bridge:** Take a walk along more than 650 years of history while enjoying sweeping city views from the towers, plus street musicians, and souvenir stands (page 66).

★ **John Lennon Wall:** Feel free to add to this living, breathing graffiti wall. It's been consistently covered with Beatles lyrics, John Lennon portraits, and scrawled variations of "We were here" since the 1980s (page 67).

★ **Prague Castle:** The world's largest castle complex includes the Gothic glory of St. Vitus Cathedral, expansive manicured gardens, and the royal elegance of the Lubkowicz Palace (page 70).

★ **Petřín Lookout Tower:** Prague's mini-Eiffel Tower may not be taller, but its perch on top of Petřín Hill technically makes it higher than its French inspiration (page 78).

★ **Vyšehrad Complex:** Prague's "other castle" offers a more peaceful vibe than the Prague Castle. The cemetery provides the resting place of some local legends, while today's locals enjoy the beer garden in the summer (page 80).

★ **Prague's Beer Gardens:** Czechs famously drink more *pivo* (beer) per capita than any nation in the world. A summer afternoon in one of Prague's beer gardens will show you why (page 92).

★ **Prague's National Theater:** This golden beauty, home to ballet, opera, and theater performances, was partially crowd-funded by Czech citizens in the 1800s (page 100).

ears unironically. Although to be fair, the dark humor and cautiously pessimistic local character resembles a Brothers Grimm story more closely than a light-hearted cartoon. Replace "…they all lived happily ever after" with the national motto of "truth prevails," and you'll start to get the picture.

The capital city is still defining its rapidly changing identity, maintaining an old-world charm while embracing twenty-first-century innovation. Historic exteriors often hold modern design inside restaurants, coffee shops, and office buildings. An entrepreneurial spirit has led to a wave of small businesses trying new concepts, like cafes centered around cats or cryptocurrency and computer-focused museums, all within steps of centuries-old structures.

This multi-dimensional culture can please an entire spectrum of interests: architecture, fine arts and culture, culinary curiosities, niche museums, rowdy and sophisticated nightlife options. There is a laid back, live-and-let-live attitude, and a strong sense of enjoying your free time with as much as enthusiasm as you spend striving for professional success.

HISTORY

The Prague fairy tale begins around the year 870, when the Přemyslid dynasty (Prague's earliest line of ruling families) founded the Prague Castle. This remained the seat of power until the 11th century, when Vratislav II, King of Bohemia, chose to rule from Vyšehrad instead. These two hillside fortified complexes on opposite sides of the Vltava River helped to ensure the safety and prominence of Prague's early aristocracy.

Wenceslas I (known as Vaclav in Czech), now the patron saint of the Czech Republic and inspiration for the Christmas carol "Good King Wenceslas," ruled as the Duke of Bohemia from 922-935. He was known for being a devout Christian in an era when paganism was still quite popular. Wenceslas died a martyr's death on September 28, 935, killed by his own brother, Boleslav the Cruel. You can pay your respects to the good king at his chapel inside St. Vitus Cathedral, or at the enormous statue of the saint on horseback at the top of Wenceslas Square.

Another hero of Czech history arrives centuries later. After the Přemyslid failed to produce an heir in the early 1300s, the title was passed to John of Luxembourg and then to his son Charles IV, who ruled over Prague's Golden Age during the 14th century. Charles (Karel in Czech) was named both King of Bohemia and Holy Roman Emperor, giving his seat in Prague even more importance. Charles' legacy includes the establishment of the New Town and the founding of Charles University in 1348, plus the construction of the Charles Bridge in 1357.

The early 14th century was a time of religious conflict led by Jan Hus, the religious leader behind the Hussite movement. Hus stood up to the Catholic Church by giving sermons on reformation directly to the people in their local language. This didn't go over well and he was burned at the stake in 1415. A statue of Jan Hus and his followers now dominates the center of Old Town Square, and July 6 is a public holiday in his honor.

The Habsburg dynasty took over in 1526, moving the seat of power to Vienna and solidifying Prague's connection with the surrounding regions of Austria and Hungary for the next few centuries. Prague enjoyed a brief resurgence in the late 16th century.

The Second Defenestration took place in 1618 at the Prague Castle, and is marked with a plaque both inside and outside of the tower. Tossing two officials out this window was a Protestant response to Emperor Ferdinand II attempting to impose Catholicism as the law of the land. This act led to the Thirty Years War that raged across Europe from 1618-1648.

The 18th and 19th centuries brought a

Previous: aerial view over Church of Our Lady before Týn at Old Town Square; the Royal Gardens and Summer Palace of Prague Castle; baroque decorations at the Prague Castle.

Prague

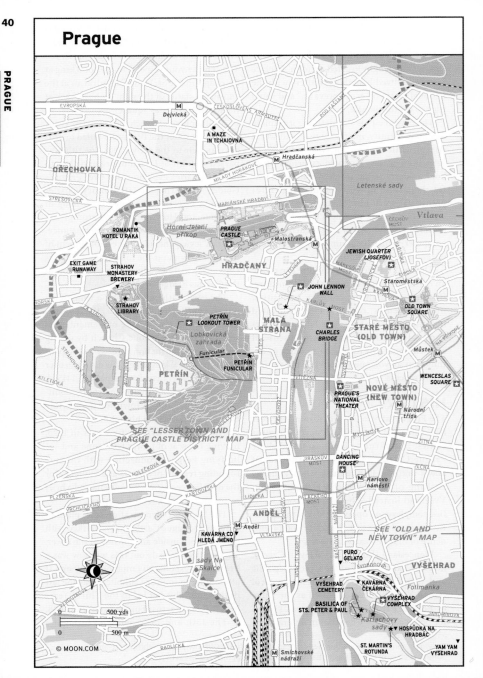

EVROPSKÁ

Dejvická

ČESKOSLOVENS ARMÁDY

BOŽÍ KASÍN

A MAZE
IN TCHAIOVNA

Hradčanská

MILADY HORÁKOVÉ

Vtlava

Letenské sady

ČECHŮV
MOST

OŘECHOVKA

STREŠOVICKÁ

MARIÁNSKÉ HRADBY

Horní Jelení
příkop

ROMANTIK
HOTEL U RAKA

PRAGUE
CASTLE

Malostranská

JEWISH QUARTER
(JOSEFOV)

Staroměstská

EXIT GAME
RUNAWAY

STRAHOV
MONASTERY
BREWERY

HRADČANY

KARLŮV MOST

JOHN LENNON
WALL

OLD TOWN
SQUARE

HORSKÁ

STRAHOV
LIBRARY

A. STAŠKOVÁ

PETŘÍN
LOOKOUT TOWER

MALÁ
STRANA

STARÉ MĚSTO
(OLD TOWN)

Můstek

ATLETICKÁ

Lobkovická
zahrada

Funicular

CHARLES
BRIDGE

WENCESLAS
SQUARE

STRAHOVSKÝ TUNEL

PETŘÍN

PETŘÍN
FUNICULAR

VÍTĚZNÁ

NOVÉ MĚSTO
(NEW TOWN)

PRAGUE'S
NATIONAL
THEATER

Národní
třída

SEE "LESSER TOWN AND
PRAGUE CASTLE DISTRICT" MAP

JIRÁSKŮV
MOST

MYSLÍKOVA

DANCING
HOUSE

ŽITNÁ

MOLÉČKOVA

DANCING
HOUSE

JEČNÁ

PLZEŇSKÁ

VRCHLICKÉHO

LIDICKÁ

ANDĚL

PALACKÉHO
MOST

NÁDRAŽNÍ

Karlovo
náměstí

KAVÁRNA CO
HLEDÁ JMÉNO

Anděl

VLTAVSKÁ

SEE "OLD AND
NEW TOWN" MAP

KARTOUZSKÁ

sady Na
Skalce

PURO
GELATO

VYŠEHRAD

RAŠÍNOVO NÁBŘEŽÍ

VYŠEHRAD
CEMETERY

KAVÁRNA
ČEKÁRNA

Folimanka

0   500 yds
0   500 m

BASILICA OF
STS. PETER & PAUL

VYŠEHRAD
COMPLEX

Karlachovy
sady

JAROMÍROVA

© MOON.COM

RADLICKÁ

Smíchovské
nádraží

ST. MARTIN'S
ROTUNDA

HOSPŮDKA NA
HRADBÁC

YAM YAM
VYŠEHRAD

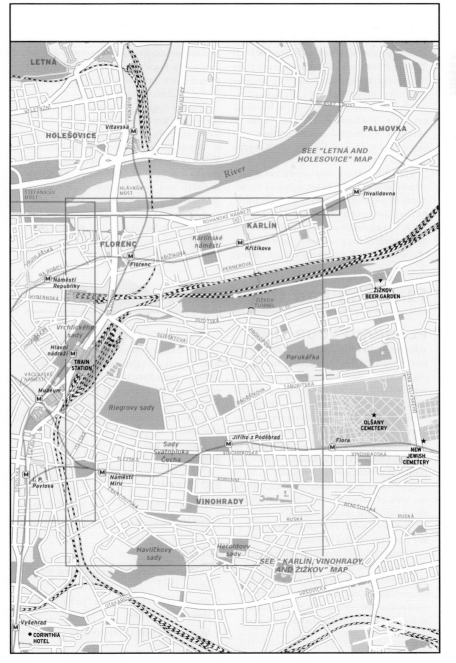

LETNÁ

VELETRŽNÍ

BUBENSKÁ

Vltavská Ⓜ

HOLEŠOVICE

PALMOVKA

SEE "LETNÁ AND
HOLEŠOVICE" MAP

River

ŠTEFÁNIKŮV
MOST

HLÁVKŮV
MOST

ROHANSKÉ NÁBŘEŽÍ

Invalidovna Ⓜ

KARLÍN

TRUHLÁŘSKÁ

FLORENC

Karlínské
náměstí

KŘIŽÍKOVA

Ⓜ Křižíkova

NA POŘÍČÍ

Ⓜ Florenc

PERNEROVA

Ⓜ Náměstí
Republiky

HYBERNSKÁ

ŽIŽKOV
TUNNEL

ŽIŽKOV
BEER GARDEN ▾

JINDŘIŠSKÁ

Vrchlického
sady

HUSITSKÁ

SEIFERTOVA

PROKOPOVA

Hlavní
nádraží Ⓜ

TRAIN
STATION

Parukářka

JANA ŽELIVSKÉHO

VÁCLAVSKÉ
NÁMĚSTÍ

TÁBORITSKÁ

Muzeum
Ⓜ

ONDŘÍČKOVA

Riegrovy sady

★
OLŠANY
CEMETERY

Jiřího z Poděbrad

Flora

SLEZSKÁ

Sady
Svatopluka
Čecha

Ⓜ

VINOHRADSKÁ

Ⓜ

VINOHRADSKÁ

★
NEW
JEWISH
CEMETERY

Ⓜ J. P.
Pavlova

Ⓜ Náměstí
Míru

KORUNNÍ

SOKOLSKÁ

TRÓJICKOVA

VINOHRADY

BĚLEHRADSKÁ

BENEŠOVSKÁ

RUSKÁ

RUSKÁ

Havlíčkovy
sady

Heroldovy
sady

SEE "KARLÍN, VINOHRADY,
AND ŽIŽKOV" MAP

VRŠOVICKÁ

OTAKAROVA

Ⓜ Vyšehrad

● CORINTHIA
HOTEL

movement of increased pride in the local language and culture known as the Czech National Revival. This led to the foundation of the National Museum (1818) the National Theater (1868), and the eventual break from the Austro-Hungarian Empire to become the independent state of Czechoslovakia on October 28, 1918. The First Republic era (1918-1938) under President Tomas G. Masaryk saw the rise of café culture, preserved today in Café Louvre and Kavárna Slávia.

The 20th century then turned to the horrors of WWII (1939-1945) followed by decades of isolation from the outside world under Communist rule from 1945-1989. There was a brief loosening of restrictions on things such as the press, travel, and freedom of speech in 1968, called the Prague Spring, but this was met with a brutal Soviet invasion and crackdown later that year. A Soviet presence remained in Prague until 1989. You can find deeper insights into these events at sights such as the Jewish Museum, the Museum of Communism, and the Town Belfry by St. Nicholas Church.

Prague's modern life began in 1989, when the Velvet Revolution marked the end of Soviet occupation and the re-establishment of an independent Czechoslovakia. This was followed by the Velvet Divorce just a few short years later in 1993, when the Czech Republic and Slovakia peacefully divided into two countries. The word "Velvet" refers to the peaceful nature of these dissolutions, and acknowledges the affinity of Czech president Václav Havel for the band the Velvet Underground.

Planning and Orientation

PLANNING YOUR TIME

You could do a whirlwind tour of Prague in a fast-paced **two days** by picking and choosing the sights most important to you. A long weekend will give you the extra time needed to explore the lesser-known sights and neighborhoods for the less crowded corners of character and culture. Add a day trip to one of the surrounding towns such as Kutna Hora or Liberec. One week in the Czech Republic is a great way to compare the cosmopolitan life of Prague with a second destination such as the spa town of Karlovy Vary or the wine region surrounding the town of Mikulov.

Summer, Easter, and Christmas holidays are peak times, you will receive an incredible festive atmosphere in exchange for longer lines at most major sights. It's best to arrange hotel reservations, tickets to performances, and even restaurant reservations as far in advance as possible for the best selection and rates.

Daily Reminders

The importance of work-life balance in Czech means that many cafes, restaurants, and independent shops have limited hours on weekends, especially Sundays. There are still plenty of restaurants focused on an international clientele where you can find a good meal. Cafes also open later in the day as opposed to early mornings, so save your coffee breaks for the afternoons.

SATURDAY

• The sights of the Jewish quarter are closed.

• Weekly farmers market is held at Náplavka.

SUNDAY

• St. Vitus Cathedral has limited hours (noon-4pm).

• Church of Our Lady Before Týn has limited hours (10am-noon).

• Many shops have limited hours.

MONDAY

The following sights are closed:

- National Museum
- Church of Our Lady Before Týn
- National Monument to the Heroes of the Heydrich Terror
- National Gallery

TUESDAY

- DOX Center for Contemporary Art is closed.

Public Holidays

There are a number of Czech public holidays that visitors may not expect: **Good Friday** and **Easter Monday** may have limited shopping hours, but the long weekend also brings Easter markets to many town squares. **May 1** and **May 8** are national holidays marking Labor Day and Victory in Europe (VE) Day. Both **July 5** and **July 6** are public holidays likely to limit access to some museums and shops. **September 28** (St. Wenceslas Day), **October 28** (the foundation of Czechoslovakia), and **November 17** (commemorating the Struggle for Freedom and Democracy) are often marked with performances, events, or protests in Wenceslas Square. Christmas is celebrated on **December 24** in the Czech Republic, with additional public holidays on **December 25** and **26,** but you'll also find Christmas markets popping up around the beginning of December.

Advance Booking and Time-Saving Tips

SIGHTS

Many of Prague's sights require buying tickets or arranging tours onsite. Two that you can book online in advance are a guided tour of the **Prague Castle** (via email at info@hrad. cz) and a guided tour of the **Strahov Library** (via email at erika@strahovskyklaster.cz). The Prague Castle availability is usually open to accommodate requests, but the Strahov Library is limited to a strict number of visitors per year, so send your request or questions as soon as (or before) you book your dates if you want to see the building's ornately painted ceilings up close.

RESTAURANTS AND NIGHTLIFE

One quirk of Prague's restaurant and café scene is a near obsession with reservations. Yes, people often book seats to meet their friends for an afternoon coffee or a drink at a pub or cocktail bar. The growing demand for high-quality dining and the response of constant restaurant openings mean that everyone (including the locals) wants to try the latest places. Some restaurants offer online reservation systems, while others require a phone call, which hotel concierges can often help with. The English-friendly website and mobile app **Restu.cz** (scroll to the bottom to choose your language) is also a good option for a middleman to arrange your reservation without any miscommunications of the time and number of guests.

Many pubs and restaurants are often booked with company holiday parties throughout the month of December, so double check availability with any place you plan to visit before arriving.

Sightseeing Passes

A **Prague Card** (www.praguecard.com) offers free admission or discounts on many of the city's attractions, including certain areas of the Prague Castle, Petřín Tower, the Jewish Museum, the Charles Bridge Towers, St. Nicholas' Town Belfry, and the Mucha Museum. It can be purchased for two-days (about 1,500 CZK), three-days (about 1,700 CZK) or four-days (about 2,000 CZK). The card also works as a valid ticket for all public transport in Prague (e.g. buses, trams, and the metro), but must be presented along with an ID if inspected. The card can be purchased in-person or ordered online and collected at Tourist Information Centers at the Prague Airport (8am-8pm) or at the two Centers in their Old Town locations (9am-7pm).

The Prague card is definitely useful, but not an essential tool for exploring the city. It provides many valuable discounts, but usually doesn't offer priority entry or exclusive access. A basic three-day public transport pass costs 310 CZK and the average entrance to Prague's sights ranges from free to around 250 CZK. However, if you combine the Jewish Museum with access to multiple tower views where you only spend half an hour, these admissions can add up. Getting value for your purchase depends on how many of the included sights are on your preferred itinerary, so peruse the list before purchasing.

One ticket that does offer faster entrance to a popular sight is the mobile ticket to the **Old Town Hall and Astronomical Clock tower** (http://prague.mobiletickets.cz, 210 CZK). This provides the combined benefit of discounted admission and allowing visitors to skip the line of tourists purchasing tickets onsite.

Exploring the City

Prague's city center is incredibly walkable (with comfortable shoes), and public transport easily connects almost every neighborhood. The most popular sights are clustered in a few areas—the condensed Old Town, the ring of New Town wrapping around it, and the Malá Strana neighborhood sitting below the Prague Castle. Most surrounding neighborhoods such as Vinohrady, Žižkov, Letná, or Karlín are just one or two metro or tram stops outside the city center, making them easy to access or even to use as your home base.

One possible pitfall is that Prague's streets are not arranged in a grid, so carry or download an offline map to avoid getting turned around, especially in Old Town.

ORIENTATION

The historic center of Prague is packed with history and interesting sights, but it can also be packed with people vying for the best photographs. For a deeper sense of the city, split your time between visiting monuments and getting to know the surrounding neighborhoods of Holešovice, Letná, Karlín, Vinohrady, Vršovice, or Žižkov.

Old Town
(Staré Město)

The **cobblestoned streets** and **century-spanning architecture** of this neighborhood inspired the UNESCO World Heritage Center to crown the entire Historic Center of Prague a protected sight in 1992. This twisted

Old Town Prague

maze of streets around **Old Town Square** can get a bit crowded. Early mornings and off-seasons are a great time to enjoy this area with a little more breathing room. The Jewish quarter known as **Josefov** sits in the northwest corner of Old Town, surrounded by the curve of the Vltava River.

New Town
(Nové Město)

The name New Town applies to a large semicircle that wraps from one edge of the Vltava River, around the Old Town to the other side of the river bend. Charles IV founded this neighborhood along with Charles University in 1348 (not exactly "new" by today's standards) in order to expand the size and influence of the city towards his grand dreams. Walking from the **Municipal House and Powder Tower** on one edge to the **National Theater** and **Dancing House** on the other could take half an hour (without stopping to sightsee). Three micro-neighborhoods are centered around New Town's main squares: **Náměstí Republiky, Václavské náměstí,** and **Karlovo náměstí.**

Lesser Town
(Malá Strana)

Malá Strana, the Czech name for the neighborhood sprawled around the base of the Prague Castle, loosely translates to "Lesser Town" or "Little Quarter", but it deserves far more credit than this nickname implies. Long before joining Hradčany, Old Town, and New Town to form a unified Prague in 1784, this eighth-century market area was **Prague's oldest settlement.** Situated between two of the city's most popular tourist attractions (**Charles Bridge** and the Prague Castle), these cobblestoned streets were an essential part of the Royal Route during the processions of newly ordained kings. These days, the area's **historic charm** is tempered with a fairly heavy presence of touristy souvenir shops and camera-wielding tourists. However, the history and beauty surrounding these cobblestoned streets are worth taking a few side

steps around the crowds to discover semi-hidden sights, such as the **Wallenstein Gardens** and **John Lennon Wall**. As you head south along the base of Petřín Park, historic Malá Strana blends into the more modern dining district of **Anděl.**

Prague Castle District
(Hradčany)

The hillside castle district of Hradčany, across the Vltava River from Old Town and above Malá Strana, is dominated by the **Prague Castle** grounds and surrounding gardens, with a few **luxury hotels** and **cafes** dotting the residential area behind it. Beware that a deceptively easy walk plotted on a map may actually take double the time you anticipate to climb stairs or find an entrance among the fortified castle walls. This area is more of a destination than a place to get lost among the streets, so choose your entry point, note your tram stops, and enjoy the view from the geographical vantage point that drew the royal residence in the first place.

Petřín and Anděl

The **massive green hillside** on the western side of the Vltava River separates the historic castle district of Hradčany to the north from the bustling cosmopolitan life around the **Anděl** neighborhood in the sprawling southern district of Smichov. Largely dominated by **Petřín Park,** this quiet side of Prague is an ideal place for an outdoor picnic, a romantic (if a bit strenuous) walk through the park, or just a chance to sprawl out on the grass and admire the city skyline.

Vyšehrad

The area around Vyšehrad (meaning "high castle") south of New Town walks a fine line— it's not quite the center of town, but not quite the suburbs—and includes **the Vyšehrad Complex,** a major tourist attraction that doubles as a locally loved destination for relaxation. The beauty and importance of the Vyšehrad Complex rivals the Prague Castle, but draws a fraction of the crowds, and the surrounding streets and restaurants showcase more **local life** than souvenir stands.

Vinohrady and Vršovice

This popular home for **international residents** is filled with **restaurants** that reflect that diversity, and **bars** that cater to the wide-ranging clientele. The surrounding **parks** such as **Havlíčkovy sady** and **Reigrovy Sady** often host food and wine festivals during warmer months, and the Christmas market at **Náměstí Miru** is a local favorite. Just southeast of Wenceslas Square, Karlovo náměstí, and the edges of New Town, these are easy baby steps off the traditional tourist path. The southeastern edge of Vinohrady blends into neighboring **Vršovice**, best known for the nightlife destination of **Krymská Street**.

Žižkov

This formerly **working-class neighborhood,** stretching from Prague's main train station (Hlavní Nádraží) in New Town along the northern edge of Vinohrady, may be rapidly changing, but it hasn't completely lost its gritty, take-it-or-leave-it spirit. Case in point: you shouldn't necessarily expect an English menu or a smiling server in every establishment. You can pinpoint Žižkov from almost anywhere in Prague thanks to the rocket-shaped **TV Tower** dominating the city skyline. The **pub-heavy neighborhood** was named for Hussite hero Jan Žižka, who sits atop neighboring Vitkov Hill.

Karlín

After massive flooding in 2002, Karlín experienced an extensive revitalization effort. Today this sophisticated neighborhood is better known for its **culinary scene, wine bars,** and prime location for house-hunting young families. The **artsy vibe** is less dance party and more conversations over Cabernet, with recently-opened **repurposed spaces** such as **Manifesto Market** and **Kasárna Karlín** adding more life to the changing landscape. Karlín stretches east from the edge of New Town and Florenc bus station along the banks of the Vltava River.

Letná and Holešovice

Letná, located across the river to the north of Old Town and west of Hradčany, is best known for the massive **Letná Park** that lines its southern edge. The **Letná beer garden** inside the park is a major summertime hot spot, and the surrounding **trendy residential streets** are lined with cafes, international restaurants, and the **National Gallery's Trade Fair Palace.**

There are no ideas too weird for the **industrial** neighborhood of Holešovice to the east of Letná. Theatrical space in a former slaughterhouse? Check. Dance club covered in pipes and gears? Sure. Crypto-anarchist coffee shop that only accepts virtual currencies? Why not? From **street art** to a **contemporary arts center** focused on socially conscious exhibitions, this neighborhood is full of surprises.

Itinerary Ideas

DAY 1

Before you set out for the day, book a mobile ticket to skip the line for the Old Town Hall Tower views above Prague's Astronomical Clock.

1 Start the day with a healthy acai bowl or hearty breakfast bagel at **Cacao,** a casual café just off Náměstí Republiky.

2 Pause to admire the architectural diversity of the Municipal House, Powder Tower, and Hybernia Theater from the corner of Na Příkopě street along your ten-minute walk to the **Alfons Mucha Museum**. Spend around ninety minutes exploring the swirling style of an Art Nouveau master before browsing the gift shop.

3 Just five minutes further west, Jindřišská Street opens up onto **Wenceslas Square**. Find the cross in bricks in front of the National Museum, stand under the horseback statue of St. Wenceslas, peruse the quotes on benches lining the center, and imagine thousands of citizens shaking their keys in the air in 1989 as then Czechoslovakia regained its independence.

4 Take a deep breath before a crowded, ten-minute, cobblestoned walk from the base of Wenceslas Square to the postcard views of **Old Town Square**. Using your mobile ticket booked in advance, skip the line to the Old Town Hall Tower and proceed straight to the 360-degree views from above the Astronomical Clock.

5 Walk ten minutes east along Dlouhá street to **Sisters Bistro** to fuel up on *chlebíčky* (open-faced sandwiches).

6 How tired are your feet? You can either walk twenty minutes across the Vltava River and uphill through the park to **Letná Beer Garden**, or jump on tram 8 or 26 from Dlouhá třída to Letenské náměstí and enjoy an easy ten-minute walk south. Either way, you'll be rewarded with a cold pilsner and panoramic views from one of Prague's most popular warm weather escapes. After a couple beers, head back to your hotel or hostel to regroup and get dressed for a night at the theater.

7 A yellow Metro line to the Národní třída stop or a tram to the Národní divadlo stop will drop you near the **National Theater**, symbolizing the importance of the arts to Czech culture as part of the National Revival in the early 20th century.

8 Make a reservation for a post-show dinner in the elegant First Republic-style of the early 1900s at **Café Louvre**, just a three-minute walk east of the National Theater. A riverside walk after dinner includes a lit view of the Prague Castle, courtesy of the Rolling Stones.

DAY 2

The Malá Strana neghborhood is home to a few lesser-known sights scattered among the most popular tourist attractions. Before you leave for the day, make reservations for dinner at U modré kachničky.

1 Start with coffee and a fluffy Benedict soufflé for breakfast at **Kavárna co hledá jméno,** a local favorite hidden inside a parking lot in the Anděl neighborhood.

2 After brunch, jump on a fifteen-minute tram from the Anděl tram stop to Malostranská to explore the **Wallenstein Gardens**—keep an eye out for free-roaming peacocks between the fountains, statues, and labyrinth-like hedges.

3 Exit the Wallenstein Gardens near Malostranská and walk along the riverfront, underneath the Charles Bridge, and across Kampa Island for about ten minutes to find the **John Lennon Wall**. Feel free to add a quote or sing a Beatles song.

4 Follow Lázeňská street north for two minutes to Mostecká Street. Instead of crossing the Charles Bridge (don't worry, you will later), spend half an hour climbing the **Lesser Town Bridge Tower** for a bird's eye view of the afternoon crowds.

5 Head a few steps back into Malá Strana to grab a coffee or beer and a bite to eat at **Roesel—Beer & Cake**, a friendly local cafe tucked just off this touristy street.

Prague Itineraries

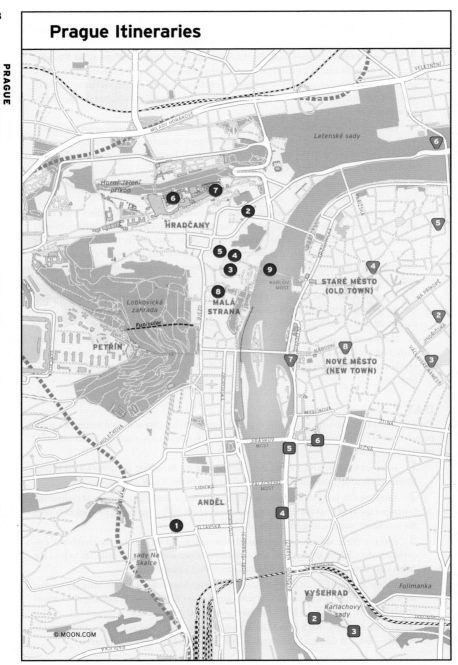

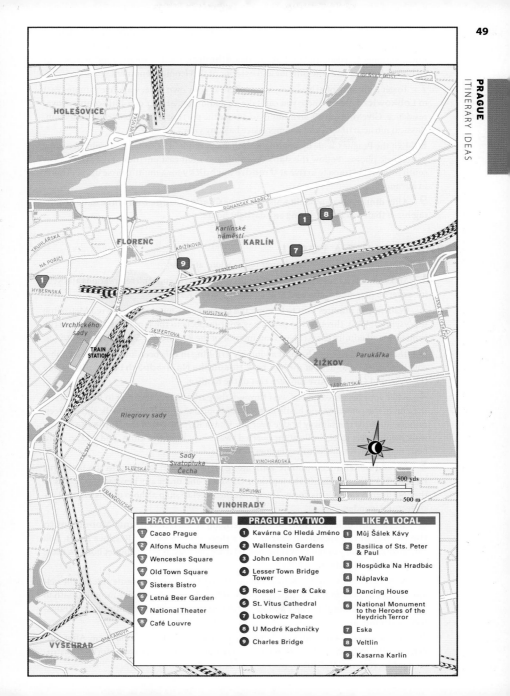

HOLEŠOVICE

ROHANSKÉ NÁBŘEŽÍ

Karlínské
náměstí

FLORENC

KARLÍN

KŘIŽÍKOVA

PERNEROVA

NA POŘÍČÍ

HYBERNSKÁ

Vrchlického
sady

TRAIN
STATION

HUSITSKÁ

SEIFERTOVA

ŽIŽKOV

Parukářka

TÁBORITSKÁ

Riegrovy sady

Sady
Svatopluka
Čecha

VINOHRADSKÁ

SLUZSKÁ

KORUNNÍ

VINOHRADY

0   500 yds
0   500 m

VYŠEHRAD

PRAGUE DAY ONE	PRAGUE DAY TWO	LIKE A LOCAL
1 Cacao Prague	1 Kavárna Co Hledá Jméno	1 Můj Šálek Kávy
2 Alfons Mucha Museum	2 Wallenstein Gardens	2 Basilica of Sts. Peter & Paul
3 Wenceslas Square	3 John Lennon Wall	3 Hospůdka Na Hradbác
4 Old Town Square	4 Lesser Town Bridge Tower	4 Náplavka
5 Sisters Bistro	5 Roesel – Beer & Cake	5 Dancing House
6 Letná Beer Garden	6 St. Vitus Cathedral	6 National Monument to the Heroes of the Heydrich Terror
7 National Theater	7 Lobkowicz Palace	7 Eska
8 Café Louvre	8 U Modré Kachničky	8 Veltlin
	9 Charles Bridge	9 Kasarna Karlín

6　After your light lunch, walk around the corner to Malostranské náměstí and catch tram 22 to the Prague Castle. Jump off at tram stop Královský letohrádek to enter through the Royal Summer Gardens and find **St. Vitus Cathedral**. You'll want to spend at least half an hour admiring both the interior and exterior of this iconic monument.

7　To get a glimpse of aristocratic atmosphere at your own pace, walk five minutes east to **Lobkowicz Palace** where you can take an audio-guided tour of a 16th-century royal residence. Give yourself 60-90 minutes to peruse the portrait gallery, porcelain collection, classical music artifacts, and an impressive balcony view.

8　Exit the Prague Castle by heading west through the South Gardens, stopping for a few panoramic photos. Follow the stairs downhill and head east on Thunovská street, then south into Malá Strana to arrive at **U modré kachničky** for a multi-course dinner (book in advance).

9　After dinner, take a moonlit walk across the **Charles Bridge** with a little more breathing room than you'll find during any daylight hours.

PRAGUE LIKE A LOCAL

Before setting out for the day, book dinner reservations at **Eska**.

1　Make a weekday reservation or arrive early on the weekends (no reservations allowed) for expertly prepared coffee and brunch at **Můj šálek kávy**.

2　Walk fifteen minutes west to Florenc and take a ten-minute ride on the red Metro line to Vyšehrad. Walk through the parks, pay your respects to the famous names inside the cemetery, and admire the Art Nouveau interior of the **Basilica of Sts. Peter & Paul**.

3　There is no need to be bashful about day drinking in this beer-loving capital. Grab a cold beverage and a snack at the laid-back **Hospůdka Na Hradbách** beer garden inside the Vyšehrad Complex, five minutes east of the basilica.

4　After your beer break, head west through the park towards the river to find the stairs in front of the cemetery and basilica entrance. Continue downhill and walk about fifteen minutes towards the railway bridge over the Vltava River to reach the **Náplavka** boardwalk below street level. Smile at the overfed swans begging for crumbs, and add an extra hour here if you hit the Saturday farmer's market.

5　An additional fifteen-minute walk along Náplavka will take you to the **Dancing House**. Take the elevator to the top-floor Glass Bar and order any beverage for access to the 360-degree viewing platform. Then cross the street to snap a photo of this unusual architectural wonder.

6　Add a touch of local history to your afternoon at the free **National Monument to the Heroes of the Heydrich Terror**, just a three-minute walk up Resslova Street. You can absorb the story of the WWII heroes, who are the reason for the bullet holes in these church walls, in less than an hour.

7　Walk two minutes to the Karlovo náměstí stop for a twenty-minute ride on the yellow Metro line back to Karlín. Exit the metro at Křižíkova and walk five minutes south to **Eska** (book in advance) to enjoy a modern take on Czech cuisine in a minimalist, industrial environment.

8　Prague may be known for beer, but Karlín is home to the Czech wine scene. After dinner, walk five minutes northeast from Eska to sample *vino* from across the former Austro-Hungarian region at **Veltlin**.

9 For more lively entertainment, walk fifteen minutes west to the edge of the neighborhood to **Kasárna Karlín**. You'll find an artsy, international crowd enjoying open-air bars, live music, an outdoor summer cinema, and a variety of effortlessly cool events.

Sights

OLD TOWN
(Staré Město)
★ Old Town Square
(Staroměstské náměstí)

Metro: Staroměstská or Můstek

If you've ever seen a postcard of Prague, there's a good chance it was taken in **Old Town Square**, a pedestrian square known for its attractive church spires, Gothic towers, and pastel palette. Stunning views and festive holiday markets make this eternally photogenic location worth a visit, especially in the quieter early mornings or late evenings. Stake out some bench space at the base of the **Jan Hus monument** to admire the architecture on all sides.

Try to avoid patronizing any plush dancing animals or floating carpet illusionists detracting from the historic significance of the area. Also, it's best to skip the food stands (beware of heaping piles of Prague ham deceptively priced by weight, not portion) and largely overpriced restaurants lining the perimeter.

Tip: For friendly service and a reasonably-priced snack in the area, venture left of the Old Town Hall, underneath the etched scenes in the Renaissance façade of the "House at the Minute" (Dum U Minuty) to find the semi-hidden entrance to the **Skautsky Institut.**

OLD TOWN HALL
(Staroměstská radnice)

Staroměstské náměstí 1, +420 775 400 052,
www.staromestskaradnicepraha.cz/en, 9am–10pm
Tues–Sat, 11am–10pm Sun, 250 CZK, metro stops
Staroměstská or Můstek

The only remaining pieces of Prague's 14th century Old Town Hall are the Gothic Tower of the Astronomical Clock and a sliver of burgundy wall across from the Church of Our Lady Before Týn. The remainder of the building was destroyed in the Prague Uprising against German occupation at the end of WWII. A series of white crosses in the bricks around the base mark the execution place of twenty-seven noblemen and followers of Jan Hus. These men led a Protestant revolt in the early 1600s with Prague's Second Defenestration (throwing someone out a window) at the Prague Castle.

Admission to the Old Town Hall includes a bird's eye view from the top of the **clock tower**—accessible via elevator—coupled with access to a few historical interior halls and the Chapel of the Virgin Mary. A pre-purchased electronic ticket (https://prague.mobiletickets.cz, 210 CZK) allows you to save some money and skip the lines. Two-hour English-language tours (250 CZK) are also available on select scheduled evenings, often on Saturdays.

ASTRONOMICAL CLOCK

Prague's Astronomical Clock (known as "Orloj" in Czech) is more than 600 years old. It's often said that clock master Hanuš was blinded so that he couldn't replicate its beauty for any other city; however, this myth has been debunked by documentation from 1410 giving actual credit to clock maker Mikuláš of Kadaň and an astronomy and math professor Jan Šindel (who each kept their eyes). The façade and machinery got a careful restorative makeover to repair some residual damage from WWII and present its best face for the 2018 celebrations of Czechoslovakia's 100th anniversary.

The amount of information held on the colorful faces is as impressive as the fact that this 15th-century timepiece is still ticking today.

Old and New Town

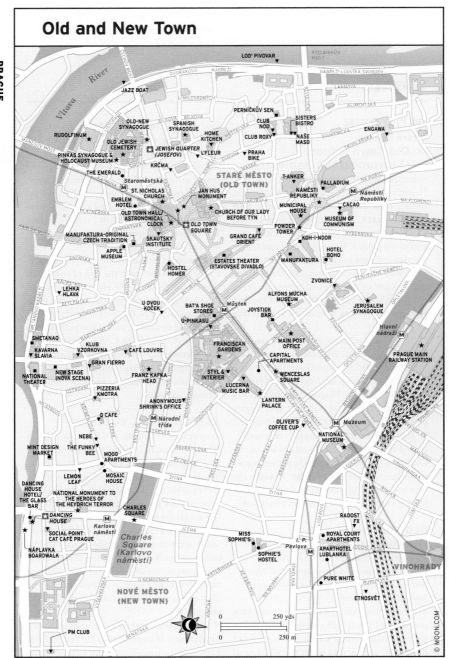

© MOON.COM

The golden swirls of the upper circle track a twelve-hour and twenty-four-hour clock, the time of sunrise and sunset, the current zodiac sign, and a variety of other historic time systems.

When the hour is approaching, crowds gather on the street in front of the clock in anticipation. When the bells chime hourly 9am-11pm, the four characters on either side come to life, with vanity staring in a mirror, greed holding a purse full of money, a skeleton (death) ringing his bell, and a musical Turk shaking his head in denial. A parade of the twelve apostles rotate through the doors above the clock face. Full disclaimer: despite its fame, many find the just-under-a-minute animation underwhelming, so feel free to skip the show and arrive between the hours. Then wait for the masses to disperse to admire the impressive external beauty of the clock faces up close.

The stationary statues flanking the lower face are known as the Philosopher, the Archangel Michael, the Astronomer, and the Chronicler. Inside the ring, a 365-day calendar fans out around the paintings of zodiac signs. If you look closely, you'll see a name or two written beside each number, representing a Czech name day (or "svátek"). That's right—most Czechs have one of these traditional names, and parents who want to deviate have to register for official government permission. As a result, Czechs get two yearly excuses to celebrate: the day they were born, and the day that their name falls on the calendar. You'll find Adam and Eva on December 24 (in connection with Christmas), and Czechs take their name for New Year's Eve, "Silvestr", from December 31.

JAN HUS MONUMENT

The dominant stone figure in the center of Old Town Square represents an early 14th century figure of rebellion against the Catholic Church. Jan Hus may not have the international name recognition of Martin Luther, but he was fighting for religious reform, roughly a century before the Protestant Reformation gained momentum. Sadly, like so many enemies of the Catholic church, Hus was burned at the stake on July 6, 1415. This statue was unveiled in 1915, exactly 500 years after his execution, and July 6 remains a Czech national holiday in his honor. The base of the statue is engraved with multiple quotes, including one from Hus himself: "Love each other, and wish the truth to everyone" (*Milujte se, pravdy každému přejte*).

CHURCH OF OUR LADY BEFORE TÝN
(Chrám Matky Boží před Týnem)

Staroměstské náměstí 604, +420 222 318 186 or +420 602 204 213, www.tyn.cz, 10am-1pm and 3pm-5pm Tues-Sat, 10am-noon Sun, by donation, metro stops Staroměstská or Můstek

The twin Gothic towers of the Church of Our Lady Before Týn, called Adam and Eve, are an iconic symbol of Old Town Square. If you look closely, you'll see that the pair are not symmetrical, an unintended result of decades-long construction delays from the mid-14th and continued renovations over the centuries.

The history of the decoration also speaks of Prague's religious turmoil. The church was adorned first with a statue of the Virgin Mary, then replaced during the Hussite era with a golden chalice and statue of the first Hussite King George of Poděbrad. When Catholics regained control, the chalice was melted down and Mary retook her place of power. Walk around the church to the right to see a replica of the Virgin Mary.

The interior of the church is visible only through a gate just inside the entryway, which serves as a small viewing area for visitors, and photography is prohibited. Architecture fans might enjoy a quick peek at the Baroque design, golden touches, and the oldest organ in all of Prague. The entrance is hidden beneath the arches below, tucked between art galleries and restaurants. Otherwise, this church is best admired from across the square, particularly when overlooking seasonal Christmas and Easter markets.

ST. NICHOLAS CHURCH
(Chrám sv. Mikuláše)

Staroměstské náměstí 1101, +420 224 190 990,
www.svmikulas.cz, 10am-4pm Mon-Sat, 12pm-4pm
Sun, free, metro and tram stop Staroměstská

The towering Baroque beauty with green domed rooftops in the corner of Old Town Square is best known for hosting nightly classical music concerts (400-500 CZK), usually at 5pm or 8pm. The tourist-friendly program focuses on international favorites such as Mozart, Vivaldi, and Pachelbel with the occasional inclusion of local names such as Antonín Dvořák. Tickets are available online through the Prague Ticket Office (www.pragueticketoffice.com) or at the Via Musika shop near the entrance of the Church of Our Lady Before Týn. Even if classical music isn't your thing, poke your head inside long enough to admire the crystal chandelier and gold details of the church interior.

To avoid confusion, note that the Church of St. Nicholas shares a name with another Church of St. Nicholas (Kostel sv. Mikuláše) across town in the Malá Strana neighborhood.

RUDOLFINUM

Alšovo nábřeží 12, +420 227 059 227,
www.rudolfinum.cz, tram or metro stop Staroměstská

This concert hall has played host to more than just incredible symphonies. After hosting classical concerts and gallery exhibitions from 1885 to 1918, the Rudolfinum became the home of the new Czechoslovakian parliament. Concert halls were renovated into meeting rooms and didn't return to a home of culture until the midst of WWII, when it housed the German Philharmonic from 1942-1945 and served as a meeting place for Nazi officials.

This period of German occupation spawned a legend around the statues lining the rooftop. In the novel, *Mendelssohn Is on the Roof*, Reinhard Heydrich (one of Hitler's high-ranking deputies) ordered the statue of Jewish composer Felix Mendelssohn-Bartholdy to be removed. The fictional plot sends two workers to the roof who don't know which one Mendelssohn is, and they almost demolish Richard Wagner, one of Hitler's favorite German composers, because of his large nose. While this story is often repeated as factual by walking tour guides, none of them are able point out the statue of Wagner on the rooftop. Wagner was never actually part of the crowd, but you can find Bach, Beethoven, Mendelssohn, and Mozart.

Today this building is home to the Czech Philharmonic Orchestra and serves as one of the premiere venues of the Prague Spring Festival. The lower floors of the building hold a free gallery space and children's interactive exhibitions, as well as a column-lined café, accessible on the lower left side of the building while facing the entrance.

★ Jewish Quarter (Josefov)

Prague's Jewish Quarter, tucked into the river bend around Old Town, has roots as early as the 10th century. This former ghetto was officially walled in after a 13th century decree requiring the separation of Jewish and Christian communities. Restrictions lightened in the 16th century under Rudolf II, who worked with many Jewish banking families, then tightened again under Maria-Theresa in the 17th century. An Edict of Tolerance was finally granted in 1781 by Emperor Josef II, namesake of the neighborhood.

One of the darker reasons that Prague's Jewish Quarter is more intact than its Central European neighbors was Hitler's affinity for Prague. The Nazi dictator's plans to establish a "monument to an extinguished race" kept the bombs of WWII from demolishing the area. This created the bittersweet result of preserving centuries-old streets and synagogues from an inhumane era of occupation, so that today's visitors can focus on the rich, vast history of the Jewish community in Prague.

The majority of sights, including the Old Jewish Cemetery, Pinkas Synagogue, and

---

1 the sun, the moon, the stars…Prague's Astronomical Clock 2 the crooked headstones of the Old Jewish Cemetery 3 Old Town Square

Spanish Synagogue, are managed by the **Jewish Museum** (www.jewishmuseum. cz), which includes packaged admission (350 CZK) to a collection of seven buildings and sites. A combination ticket to the Jewish Town of Prague (530 CZK) also includes admission to the Old-New Synagogue, which is the only sight available to purchase individually (220 CZK). Tickets may be purchased at the Spanish Synagogue, Pinkas Synagogue, Klausen Synagogue, the Information and Reservations Center located at Maiselova 15, or online.

Interested parties could easily spend multiple days exploring Josefov. There is a quiet air of reverence and remembrance around the individual sights and synagogues, but the surrounding streets are full of modern life, hotels, and some of the city's most high-end shopping on Pařížská Street. Most religious sites around the neighborhood are closed on Saturdays, but the restaurants, cafes, and designer shops remain open. The seclusion of previous centuries has faded away, with the area now existing as a part of tourist trails and daily cosmopolitan life in the city center.

Many sights below are closed on Jewish holidays. Note that shoulders should be covered, and men will be required to wear a head covering in some locations.

OLD-NEW SYNAGOGUE
(Staronová synagoga)

Červená, +420 224 800 812 or +420 224 800 813, www.synagogue.cz, Nov-Mar 9am-5pm Sun-Thurs, April-Oct 9am-6pm Sun-Thurs, open Fridays until one hour before Shabbat, closed Saturdays and Jewish holidays, 220 CZK, metro and tram stop Staroměstská

The Old-New Synagogue holds the title of oldest working synagogue in all of Europe. Originally known as "New" or "Great" when it was built in the 13th century, the ironic name developed when younger buildings popped up in the 16th century. The simplicity of the high ceilings, arched Gothic windows, and dark ironwork inside provide a contrast to the more ornate embellishments of its neighbors.

Legend surrounds the attic, which is said to house a giant clay creature created by Rabbi Löw sometime around 1590. The Rabbi supposedly created the mythical Golem to protect the Jewish community from harm, and then put him to bed every Friday night to rest for the Sabbath. When the Golem's temper began to turn more Frankenstein than friend, the Rabbi put him into long-term hibernation in the attic, where he waits to be awakened if needed again. The attic remains off limits to visitors today, so consider yourself safe. The building is also rumored to have survived for so long, through fires and wars, under the protective cover of angel wings transformed into doves.

Guided tours (80 CZK) held in English around 10:30am or 2pm (other times available upon request) can help to add context and legend to the experience. Visit the Information and Reservations Center located at Maiselova 15 in-person to confirm that day's availability.

The Old-New Synagogue is not part of the Jewish museum, but entrance can be combined with entrance to all Jewish Museum sights under the Jewish Town of Prague ticket (530 CZK). The Old-New Synagogue can also be combined with a ticket to the colorful Jerusalem (also known as "Jubilee") Synagogue near Prague's Main Train Station (Hlavní nádraží) and the Alfons Mucha Museum. The combined Old-New Synagogue and Jerusalem Synagogue ticket (270 CZK) is available for purchase from the Jerusalem Synagogue.

OLD JEWISH CEMETERY
(Starý židovský hřbitov)

Široká 3, +420 222 749 211, www.jewishmuseum. cz, 9am-4:30pm Nov-Mar, 9am-6pm April-Oct, closed Saturdays and Jewish holidays, entry covered by Jewish Museum ticket, metro and tram stop Staroměstská

Roughly 12,000 crooked headstones are crowded into the Old Jewish Cemetery, likely representing thousands more buried below. Many of the gravestones, ranging from the early 15th century to 1787, are marked with symbols connected to their occupations or family names. You're likely to find a crowd around Rabbi Löw in connection with the tale of the Golem at the Old-New Synagogue. Wandering the narrow paths through the graves is both a peaceful and powerful experience, illustrating the confinement that this community endured along with a warm reverence of maintaining the tradition of honoring these lives. Instead of flowers, you may spot evidence of the Jewish tradition of leaving small rocks on top of individual headstones. This historic resting place is tucked just off the Vltava riverbank near the Rudolfinum Concert Hall.

PINKAS SYNAGOGUE AND HOLOCAUST MUSEUM
(Pinkasova synagoga)

Široká 3, +420 222 749 211, www.jewishmuseum. cz, 9am-4:30pm Nov-Mar, 9am-6pm April-Oct, closed Saturdays and Jewish holidays, entry covered by Jewish Museum ticket, metro and tram stop Staroměstská

The second-oldest synagogue in Prague built in 1535 now functions as a somber memorial to nearly 80,000 victims of the Shoah (a Hebrew word meaning calamity or destruction, and now used as a preferred term by many in the Jewish community for "the Holocaust"). The names, grouped by both family name and the victims' Czech and Moravian hometowns, were handwritten on the synagogue's interior walls between 1992-1996 to create this moving site of remembrance.

Continue through a hall of drawings made by children who were held at the Jewish ghetto of Terezín while en route to the concentration camps at Treblinka or Auschwitz. The pictures were saved by Friedl Dicker-Brandeis, who taught art classes while also held at Terezín (1942-1944) to help the youngest residents process their emotions. She hid the drawings in two suitcases when she was transported from the premises, resulting in their preservation. The drawings are a heart-wrenching (and, for many, tear-inducing)

combination of happy memories and expressions of despair.

A visit to the Pinkas Synagogue may be emotional, but important. It embodies the notion from philosopher George Santayana that "Those who cannot remember the past are condemned to repeat it."

SPANISH SYNAGOGUE
(Španělská synagoga)

Dušní 12, +420 222 749 211, www.jewishmuseum.cz, 9am-4:30pm Nov-Mar, 9am-6pm April-Oct, closed Saturdays and Jewish holidays, entry covered by Jewish Museum ticket, metro stop Staroměstská or tram stop Dlouhá třída

The 19th-century Spanish Synagogue is one of the most ornate buildings of the Jewish Museum, and takes its name from its Moorish-style design inspired by the Alhambra Palace in Granada, Spain. The lavish golden embellishments covering the walls, balconies, and light fixtures combined with stained glass windows, and a massive collection of silver artifacts serve to remind visitors that the history of the Jewish community in Prague isn't all dark. A permanent exhibit of the History of Jews in Bohemia and Moravia covers periods from the late 1700s to post-World War II. You can also catch a classical or chamber music concert (average price 800 CZK) on most non-Saturday evenings, usually at 7pm. Tickets are available online through the Prague Ticket Office (www.pragueticketoffice.com) or at the Via Musika shop near the entrance of the Church of Our Lady Before Týn in Old Town Square. The Spanish Synagogue does hold religious services, but they are outside of opening hours so you don't have to worry about interrupting.

NEW TOWN
(Nové Město)
Republic Square
(Náměstí Republiky)

This northeastern side of New Town holds an incredible collection of original architectural styles. From the curve of Na Příkopě street you are surrounded by the dark Gothic stone of the Powder Tower, swirling Art Nouveau elegance of the Municipal House, the columned entrance of the Empire-style Hybernia Theater, the sturdy International façade of the Czech National Bank, and the stark grey cement of the KB banking building.

As a language note, while Old Town Square and Wenceslas Square have become relatively common English translations, Náměstí Republiky (and most names including "Náměstí" pronounced "NAHM-yes-tee") sound odd in any form other than Czech, even to the resident English speakers—imagine someone looking for Los Angeles asking how to get to "The Angels." Think of these square names as a chance to practice the local dialect, and remembering their original form will help you decipher maps, find the correct public transport stops, and ask directions across the city.

POWDER TOWER
(Prašná brána)

Náměstí Republiky 5, www.muzeumprahy.cz/ prasna-brana, Nov-Feb 10am-6pm, April and Oct 10am-8pm, May-Aug 10am-10pm, 100 CZK, tram or metro stop Náměstí Republiky

The Powder Tower is named for one of its many previous uses, storing gunpowder in the 18th century. Centuries before, this 1475 Gothic tower marked the historical entrance to Old Town and the beginning of the royal coronation route to the Prague Castle. Admission gains you access to a spiral staircase of 186 stone steps and an overview of the Old Town that is often less crowded and shared less often on social media than the iconic bird's eye view from Charles Bridge Towers. Otherwise, and if there are no cars coming, take a quick detour off the sidewalk and strut underneath the arch connecting New Town to Old Town with your best royal posture.

MUNICIPAL HOUSE
(Obecní dům)

Náměstí Republiky 5, www.obecnidum.cz, 10am-8pm, 250 CZK tours, tram or metro stop Náměstí Republiky

This modern-day concert hall has been instrumental in the country's political history. On October 28, 1918, the independent state of Czechoslovakia was announced from its balcony, and later Václav Havel, first president of the Czech Republic, held his early meetings with Communist-era Prime Minister Ladislav Adamec inside these halls.

The Municipal House was built on the site of the King's Court in the 14th and 15th centuries, which served as the residence of Bohemian kings during that period. The Art Nouveau exterior reflects the decadence of the early 20th century and symbolizes part of the Czech National Revival leading up to the First Republic of Czechoslovakia. The swirling exterior includes a mosaic entitled an "Homage to Prague" framed by a quote from Svatopluk Čech, proclaiming, "Hail to you Prague! Defy time and malice as you have weathered all storms throughout the ages!"

The interior holds a number of concert spaces, most notably **Smetana Hall,** which serves as home to the Prague Symphony Orchestra (FOK) and where the Prague Spring Music Festival kicks off each year. Access to the upstairs halls require concert tickets or guided tours (300-600 CZK) that you can book online (www.obecnidum.cz) or at the Municipal House box office on the left side of the ground floor between 10am-8pm. Feel free to wander the bottom floors to admire the Art Nouveau details in a pricey pair of ornately decorated restaurant and café (beers around 100 CZK).

MUSEUM OF COMMUNISM
(Muzeum Komunismu)

V Celnici 4, +420 224 212 966, www.muzeumkomunismu.cz, 9am-8pm, 290 CZK, tram or metro stop Náměstí Republiky

It can be hard for an outsider to imagine life under the Communist rule imposed from the 1940s to 1989. The personal collection inside the Museum of Communism helps put the

1 Prague's Art Nouveau Municipal House
2 Rudolfinum exterior full of legends 3 the rotating face of Franz Kafka by David Černý 4 Wenceslas Square, the cosmopolitan heart of the city

personal touches and propaganda of the era into perspective. Re-creations include a school classroom, a child's bedroom, a workshop, and an interrogation room alongside exhibits and photos chronicling decades of occupation. Give yourself time to read the descriptions along the walls to get a more nuanced picture of everyday life, from healthcare and education to local police and major military events.

This large warehouse-style exhibition space is rarely overcrowded. You'll find the building tucked just off Náměstí Republiky, behind the Hybernia Theater and the weekday farmers markets that surround the metro entrance.

JERUSALEM SYNAGOGUE
(Jeruzalémská synagoga)

Jeruzalémská 7, +420 224 800 812 or +420 224 800 813, www.synagogue.cz, 10am-5pm Sun-Fri, 80 CZK, tram stop Jindřišska

Also called the **Jubilee Synagogue** to commemorate the 50th anniversary of Franz Josef's rule, this youngest of Prague's Jewish houses of worship was built from 1905-1906. The brightly hued exterior combined Moorish structural design with an Art Nouveau interior. Visitors interested in Jewish history should head inside for a permanent exhibition, "Jewish Monuments and their Reconstruction after 1989," as well as temporary exhibitions often focused on modern, postwar history.

To find this off-the-beaten-path beauty, take the scenic route from Náměstí Republiky towards Wenceslas Square, down Senovážná street instead of Na Příkopě going toward Jindřišska Tower. You'll first see the Church of Svatý Jindřich a svatá Kunhuta near the tram stop. Behind this church on the left-hand side, you'll find Jerusalem Synagogue hiding down quiet Jeruzalemska street.

PRAGUE MAIN RAILWAY STATION
(Praha hlavní nádraží)

Wilsonova 8, +420 221 111 122, www.cd.cz, 3:15am-12:30am Mon-Thurs, 24-hours Sun-Fri, 80 CZK, metro or tram stop Hlavní nádraží

Prague's Main Railway Station is surrounded by a long stretch of green grass presided over by a statue of US president Woodrow Wilson, who supported the establishment of Czechoslovakia. This outdoor area is one of few places in Prague to avoid (or at least be alert) after dark.

The ground floor of the station is your typical, modern collection of fast food and convenience shops, but the second floor holds a few interesting sights even for travelers who don't plan to use its transport services. Look for the domed ceiling and Art Nouveau design, including a carved stone face of Prague, Mother of Cities. A more paternal figure, Sir Nicholas Winton, is memorialized on Platform 1. The bronze statue of the British hero, standing beside a suitcase and holding two young children, symbolizes Winton's efforts to save 669 Jewish children during the Holocaust by arranging transport out of the country to Britain on "kindertrains." In 2014, Winton was awarded the Order of the White Lion, the highest Czech honor, at age 105, just a few months before his death.

ALFONS MUCHA MUSEUM

Panská 7, +420 224 216 415, www.mucha.cz, 10am-6pm, 240 CZK, tram stop Jindřišska or metro stop Můstek

While the Art Nouveau movement is generally associated with Paris, one of its original innovators is an undeniably local hero, Alfons Mucha. This three-room museum offers an easy introduction to one of the most revered Czech artists, whose work contributed to the beauty of the Municipal House and St. Vitus Cathedral.

After growing up in the South Moravian region of the Czech Republic, Mucha made his name doing interior decoration for the aristocracy of the Austro-Hungarian Empire and designing theatrical posters in Paris that ultimately established his signature swirling designs. Later in life, he returned to his homeland to focus on more political works that captured the essence of the Czech character.

Admire the theatrical posters in the front of the museum, and don't miss the 30-minute video about his life tucked into the rear of the building. Before you leave, stop by the adjoining gift shop for a wide range of sophisticated souvenirs to delight the art fan in your life.

★ Wenceslas Square
(Václavské náměstí)

This center of economic activity and political change may not look like much at first glance, but the streets around this long rectangular "square" have witnessed some world-changing history. The only hints of its early 14th century days as Koňský trh (a "Horse Market") are the massive statue of St. Wenceslas, the patron saint of the Czech Republic, on horseback at the top of the square. The highway dividing the square from the National Museum was renamed Wilsonova in 1989, a symbolic departure from its previous Vítězného února ("Victorious February") that marked the Communists taking power in 1948.

Today the busy square holds pieces of past and present influences. International shopping outlets, tourist-focused restaurants, and fast food chains occupy many of the historic buildings. The city has plans to revitalize this pedestrian space and bring local life back to the center. For now, take a walk through the benches engraved with inspirational quotes that line the center islands and absorb the years of political protests that marked this space over the years. As recently as March 2018, Czech citizens packed these streets to express their discontent with their local government.

NATIONAL MUSEUM
(Národní museum)

Václavské náměstí 68, www.nm.cz, 10am-6pm Tues & Thurs-Sun, 10am-8pm Wed, 250 CZK, metro stop Muzeum

Located at the top of Wenceslas Square, the National Museum has been closed for renovations since 2011, and the date of completion, currently projected for 2019. As of January 2019, a limited number of rooms re-opened with an exhibit on Czechs and Slovaks as additional work continues. Even if you don't make it inside, do take a moment to admire the newly polished exterior of this late 19th-century Renaissance beauty, which had its place in the Czech National Revival movement. The domed rooftop and arched windows were built alongside the National Theater and Municipal House in an effort to reclaim a sense of national pride and cultural identity. This eventually led to the establishment of the glamorous First Republic of an independent Czechoslovakia in 1918. These days, the building attracts the glitterati of Hollywood, appearing in films such as *Casino Royale* and *Mission Impossible*.

The National Museum has had a long history of delays. The museum and its collection were established in 1818 and housed in Hradčany in the early 1800s. New locations were considered in the 1840s, and 1860s, but it wasn't until the late the late 1800s that the current location was approved. The current building officially opened in 1891—after half a century of discussions and negotiations!

MAIN POST OFFICE
(Hlavní pošta)

Jindřišská 14, +420 221 131 111, 2am-midnight, free, tram stop Václavské náměstí and metro stops Muzeum or Můstek

Even if you have nothing to mail, the Main Post Office is worth a look inside, but you have to look up. Swirling frescoed designs line the walls around arched windows beneath a vaulted glass ceiling. A shop in the corner sells stationary, stickers, and packing materials. Stop in almost any time—the building only closes between midnight and 2am—but stick to mental pictures to avoid a reprimand from the security staff. Photography is not allowed inside this government building.

LANTERN PALACE
(Palac Lucerna)

Štěpánská 61, +420 224 224 537, free, passage open 24 hours, tram stop Václavské náměstí

Prague's city center is filled with covered passageways, known as *pasáž* in Czech, that connect the cafes, shops, and venues housed in the buildings that surround them. In the

Student Protests and Occupations

Political demonstrations and celebrations have often centered around Wenceslas Square and the surrounding streets of New Town.

- **Celebration of Czechoslovakia's Independence (Oct. 28, 1918):** Crowds gathered on Wenceslas Square to celebrate the newfound independence of Czechoslovakia from the Austro-Hungarian Empire. This day remains a national holiday, and 2018 marked joyful celebrations of the 100th anniversary, even though Czechoslovakia doesn't technically exist today.

- **Student protests against German invasion (Oct. 28, 1939):** On October 28, 1939, student protesters marked the anniversary of Czech independence by taking to the streets, including Old Town Square and Wenceslas Square, to express outrage against the growing German occupation of Czechoslovakia. When German soldiers tried to get the crowds under control, a young medical student, Jan Opletal, was shot in the stomach and died in the hospital.

- **Anti-Nazi protests (Nov. 15, 1939):** A funeral for Jan Opletal, the man who was killed in protests just weeks earlier turned into another spontaneous anti-Nazi protest. In response, German soldiers raided the dormitories and executed nine of the student organizers behind the events on November 17, 1939. Nazi occupation continued until the end of WWII in 1945. Opletalova Street, running from Wenceslas Square to Prague's main train station (Hlavní nádraží), is named after the young man who sacrificed his life, and November 17 became known as International Students' Day.

- **Student protests against the Soviet occupation (1969):** To protest the restrictive Soviet occupation under the Communist government, young philosophy student Jan Palach lit himself on fire in Wenceslas Square, on January 16, 1969. A second act of self-immolation, by student Jan Zajíc, occurred on February 25, 1969. Despite their extreme efforts, Soviet occupation continued for another 20 years. A cross in bricks in front of the National Museum marks the spot where Palach lit himself on fire.

- **International Students' Day Anniversary (Nov. 1989):** By November 17, 1989, the Berlin Wall had crumbled and Communist regimes were falling around Europe. Students gathered at Vyšehrad for a demonstration to mark the 50th anniversary of their outspoken predecessors and express their desire for independence. Thousands of citizens joined the march along the Vltava River towards Wenceslas Square, but were stopped and brutally attacked by riot police. A memorial of hands reaching out from Národní třída street pays tribute to this massacre.

- **Celebrations of Independence from Communism (Dec. 1989):** The November demonstrations led to the formation of the Civic Forum and its elected leader Václav Havel. Demonstrations continued for weeks in Wenceslas Square with protesters jingling their keys in the air to symbolize time for the Communist government to go home. Top officials resigned within weeks, and Havel was officially elected president on December 29, 1989. Chants of "*Havel na hrad*" (Havel to the castle) marked the end of the Velvet Revolution, named for its casualty-free (if not entirely peaceful) transition of power.

early 1900s, Palac Lucerna was the first of these shopping and culture centers built in the Czech Republic. The design and construction were carried out by Václav Havel, grandfather of future president Václav Havel. Today, one of the biggest draws for visitors is the highly photographable David Černy sculpture hanging from its domed ceiling. In contrast to the proud statue of St. Wenceslas on the square outside, Černy's rider sits astride an upside-down horse, with rumors of the saint's face resembling various modern politicians.

The hallways surrounding the sculpture lead to the historic 1909 Kino Lucerna cinema, a glamorous First Republic-style café in Kavárna Lucerna, the low-key pub Kávovarna, and one of Prague's longest-running dance clubs Lucerna Music Bar.

FRANCISCAN GARDENS
(Františkánská zahrada)

Jungmannovo náměstí, +420 221 097 231,
Oct-April 8am-7pm, April-Sept 7am-10pm, Sept-Oct
7am-8pm, free, tram stop Václavské náměstí

This peaceful, relaxing outdoor garden hidden in an inner courtyard provides an escape from busy Wenceslas Square. The pace of life is slow in this little oasis, with families enjoying ice cream on benches surrounded by latticed fences covered in rose vines. The tall, arched windows and red rooftops of the massive **Church of Our Lady of the Snows** watches over the children's playground near its base. Take a moment to imagine the Prague landscape if this house of worship extended all the way to the Vltava River's edge, as originally planned. Light-hearted sculptures and a bubbling fountain round out the overall sense of calm.

The Franciscan Gardens are accessible from the Svetozor Passage on Vodičkova Street or an unmarked gate tucked into the back corner of Jungmannovo náměstí.

FRANZ KAFKA HEAD

Spálená 22, +420 221 097 231, free, tram or metro
stops Národní třída

As you head from Wenceslas Square towards Prague's National Theater, you'll come across an artistic tribute to a local literary genius from renowned local sculptor David Černy. A giant mirrored head of Franz Kafka installed in 2014 rotates in forty-two layers, slowly turning the author's profile in circles in a courtyard just off Národní třída street in front of the Quadrio shopping center. The profile moves in different patterns every few seconds, so split your group into spots around the statue and see who can snap the first picture of a completed profile. This statue also has a twin at Whitehall Technology Park in Charlotte, North Carolina.

Charles Square
(Karlovo náměstí)

The most residential part of New Town stretches from Prague's National Theater along the Vltava riverbank and around the larger rectangular park of Karlovo náměstí, yet another site named for the beloved King Charles IV. The square, established in 1348, was also known as the Cattle Market (Dobytčí trh) or the New Town Square, for its proximity to the New Town Hall (Novoměstská radnice). The Gothic Tower in the corner of the square was the site of Prague's First Defenestration (the act of throwing someone, usually an authority figure, out a window). In 1419, an angry crowd of Jan Hus' followers demanded the release of Protestant prisoners before tossing seven council members from the tower, an early act of the religious conflict that led to the Hussite Wars.

These days, the square is more likely to serve as a site of relaxation than radical protest. The two rectangular halves of green space are divided by busy streets of tram tracks and traffic, but inside the border of trees and flowered gardens a Baroque fountain, curving pathways, and benches to rest your feet cultivate a peaceful vibe.

NATIONAL MONUMENT TO THE HEROES OF THE HEYDRICH TERROR
(Národní památník hrdinů heydrichiády)

Resslova 9a, +420 973 204 951, 9am-5pm Tues-Sun,
free, tram or metro stops: Karlovo náměstí

The National Monument to the Heroes of the Heydrich Terror is a moving tribute to one brave act of WWII resistance efforts. The memorial is in the basement of the Baroque Church of Saints Cyril and Methodius, which played an important role in the story. After successfully assassinating Reinhard Heydrich, one of Hitler's top deputies, the small group of men who carried out the plan took refuge inside this church, where they hid for weeks from a city-wide manhunt. This eventually led to a standoff with the Nazi army that ended in their deaths. You'll find a plaque that describes the events (in Czech) flanked by small statues of a paratrooper and a priest outside the church above original bullet holes on the

Heroes of the Resistance: The Anthropoid Mission

the Church of Saints Cyril and Methodius holds a WWII memorial

Prague is known for its history of foreign rulers and occupations, but the local character is also defined by acts of resistance from brave, everyday citizens standing up to injustice in the face of impossible odds. The Anthropoid mission of 1942 is one of these stories, recently catching Hollywood's attention with two English-language films (the painstakingly researched *Anthropoid* in 2016 and Heydrich-focused *The Man with the Iron Heart* in 2017). Spoilers ahead, in case you want to watch them first.

A pair of paratroopers living in exile during WWII were sent back to Czechoslovakia in late 1941 with a daunting task—to assassinate Reinhard Heydrich, one of Hitler's cruelest deputies who was nicknamed "The Butcher of Prague." Josef Gabčík and Jan Kubiš teamed up with a small group of fellow dissidents, who often risked their lives to house or meet with the men. The group observed the Nazi leader's movements and concocted a plan.

On May 27, 1942, they stopped Heydrich's car in the outskirts of the city, en route to the Prague Castle. Josef Gabčík jumped in front of the car and attempted to shoot Heydrich, but his gun failed. Jan Kubiš turned to Plan B and tossed a grenade toward the car. Its blast lodged a piece of metal into Heydrich's body. The Anthropoid team retreated and Heydrich was taken to the hospital, where he died from infection roughly one week later.

A seven-man team went into hiding, eventually given sanctuary inside the Church of Saints Cyril and Methodius. Their location was given up by a fellow paratrooper, Karel Čurda, resulting in a standoff at the church on June 18, 1942. The men opened fire on the Nazi army when they entered, and took refuge in the basement, where they were attacked with tear gas and rising water. Five men saved their last bullets to take their own lives and avoid capture. Many of the families who housed them turned to cyanide capsules to avoid interrogation. Nazi retaliation for the assassination wiped out the village of Lidice and killed hundreds more.

church wall. The year 1942 is also embedded in the sidewalk below the plaque.

Inside the free memorial is a small exhibition of letters and photos in glass cases that tell the stories of the soldiers in both Czech and English. Visitors may also enter the crypt where most of the men ultimately lost their lives. The Church of Saints Cyril and Methodius is only open during Orthodox Sunday masses. The separate entrance to the memorial is located at street level beside steps to the church itself.

★ DANCING HOUSE
(Tančící dům)

Jiráskovo Náměstí 6, +420 720 983 172, www.tadu.cz, observation deck 9am-midnight, tram stop Jiráskovo náměstí

The twisted glass and stone walls of the Dancing House look like a hand reached out of clouds and squeezed one corner of the skyline, yet somehow it blends seamlessly into the city landscape. The architectural landmark stands on a site accidentally bombed by the American army in 1945 which stood empty until after the Velvet Revolution. The modern collaboration between two 20th-century architects, Canadian-American Frank Gehry and Croatian-Czech Vlado Milunić,

was inspired by the shape of famous dancing couple Fred Astaire and Ginger Rogers, after whom the top-floor restaurant is named. Its tension and intertwined embrace between the materials also represents the mid-1990s state of the Czech Republic, blending respect for the past while charging optimistically into the future, navigating cultural influences of East and West.

The ground floor houses a small gallery, with the floors above holding office space, and the boutique Dancing House Hotel. The top two levels are occupied by the fine dining Fred and Ginger restaurant, the Glass Bar, and an observation deck wrapped around the twisted metal orb on top of the building that offers with 360-degree views of the Vltava River, the Prague Castle, and city skylines. The small observation platform with binoculars on the edges and limited bench seating in the center can get crowded on summer afternoons, but is often peaceful in the morning, after dark, and during off-seasons.

NÁPLAVKA BOARDWALK

Náplavka, +420 222 013 618, www.prazskenaplavky.cz, free, tram stop Palackého náměstí or metro stop Karlovo náměstí

Whether it's for a Saturday farmers market,

The Dancing House

food festival, or midweek evening stroll, the Rašín boardwalk, better known known as Náplavka, draws locals and visitors to its cobblestoned paths year-round. This below-street-level embankment is lined with boat bars and restaurants, occasional live music or permitted buskers, and swans begging for food from anyone dangling their legs over the edge. Access is possible via ramps and stairs at various points along the street, from around the Dancing House to the railway bridge just below Vyšehrad. You can also catch a five-minute ride on one of the small wooden summer ferry boats here, included in the Prague public transport system, to the opposite riverbank of Náplavka Smíchov (another prime swan-spotting destination). Ferries run every 10-15 minutes from 8am to 8pm April through October.

LESSER TOWN
(Malá Strana)
★ Charles Bridge
(Karlův most)

Karlův most, free, tram stops Malostranské náměstí or Staroměstská

Construction of the Charles Bridge famously began in 1357 on July 9 at 5:31am based on Charles IV's beliefs in numerology and astrology that 1-3-5-7-9-7-5-3-1 would bring good luck. Whether he was right, or the rumored combination of eggs, wine, or milk mixed into the foundations kept the oldest of Prague's bridges safe for centuries, is one of the structures many secrets.

Crossing the bridge begins by passing through glorious Gothic splendor under the arches of the **Old Town Bridge Tower (Staroměstská mostecká věž)** on one side and the **Lesser Town Bridge Towers (Malostranské mostecké věže)** of Malá Strana. Entrance to either tower (www.muzeumprahy.cz, 100 CZK each) is accessible from 10am to roughly sunset, depending on the time of year, offering a coveted bird's eye view over the hordes of tourists below. Both towers offer incredible views, so decide whether you want a better view of Malá Strana or Old Town before you make the climb, or splurge on both perspectives by documenting the city with photographs of every direction.

Thirty Baroque statues along the edges of the bridge were installed between the late 17th century to 1928, upping the landmark's visual appeal. These famous figures include Saint Wenceslas in prayer on your right as you enter from Malá Strana, and Sts. Cyril and Methodius, credited for bringing Christianity

climb the Charles Bridge Towers for an incredible view

to the area, baptizing the Czechs and Slovaks on the fifth statue on your right entering from Old Town.

By far the most popular statue is **St. Jan of Napomuk,** crowned with a golden halo of five stars near the center of the bridge. St. Jan was famously martyred by King Wenceslas IV for either jealousy or politics—protecting the confessional secrets of Queen Sofia or disrespecting Wenceslas by confirming a monastery without his permission, depending on who you ask. It has become a tourist ritual to rub the image of Sofia at the base of his statue, as well as an unrelated dog engraved on the left side, to bring good luck or a return visit to Prague.

An ornate plaque of swirling iron a few steps to the right of St. Jan of Napomuk's statue marks the site where his body was thrown into the Vltava River on Wenceslas' orders. Please don't attach any "love locks" to this essential grave marker—or really any historical bridge in the city. A local preservation group removes them monthly to maintain structural integrity, and a photo is a much better way to commemorate a romantic moment.

To cross the bridge with any breathing room, you'll need to be up at dawn with the photographers, stumbling home in the early morning hours, or visiting on an off-peak weekday in questionable weather. This popular pedestrian bridge is generally packed with people jostling for a photo, browsing souvenir stands of jewelry and skyline sketches, or crowded around a tour guide explaining one of the bridge's many legends. Crossing the bridge can take anywhere from 7-20 minutes depending on your ability to dodge selfie sticks.

★ John Lennon Wall
(Zeď Johna Lennona)
Velkopřevorské náměstí, free, tram stop Malostranské náměstí or Hellichova

John Lennon never visited Czechoslovakia, but his messages of peace and rebellious spirit still managed to reach the hearts of its residents. The John Lennon Wall was born shortly after Lennon's assassination in 1980, when an unknown artist covered the wall surrounding a courtyard in Beatles lyrics alongside singer's likeness. Under Communist rule, which prohibited Western music and influences, this was a criminal act. The wall was painted over multiple times, but never stayed blank for very long.

In November of 2014, 25 years after the Velvet Revolution, the wall was completely whitewashed by a group of local art students who left only the words "Wall Is Over." The group later released a statement saying that they were opening "free space for new messages of the current generation." Prague's art community responded to the challenge and within days of the event, the interactive monument was covered again with its latest incarnation of peaceful words and political grievances.

Today, scrawled tourist messages of "we were here" mix with lyrics and occasional portraits of its namesake, and street musicians are usually present to serenade the selfie takers with Beatles covers. The living monument is constantly changing, and finding anything you've previously written can be impossible just in a matter of weeks.

Town Belfry by St. Nicholas Church
(Svatomikulášská městská zvonice)
Malostranské náměstí 556/29, +420 725 847 927, http://en.muzeumprahy.cz/the-town-belfrey-by-st-nicholas-church, 10am-6pm Nov-Feb, 10am-8pm Mar, 10am-10pm April-Sept, and 10am-8pm Oct, 150 CZK, tram stop: Malostranské náměstí

The six floors or platforms of this belfry (which is not actually part of the domed house of worship next door) spread across 215 steps take you through a decade-by-decade tour of Czech history. Climb the stairs from the bedrooms of 18th century watchmen, through a shadowy bell tower, all the way up to re-created holographic conversations of the top floor, which was used as a Communist spy center in the 1980s. A multimedia presentation just below the spy center tells the story of

Prague's Musical History

Music has long been intertwined with Czech culture, from classical composers such as Antonín Dvořák and Bedřich Smetana to the music festivals that fill the countryside each summer. The influence of music has also made its mark on modern-day politics and tourism. A few of my favorite pieces of Czech musical trivia include the following:

- Austria may be able to claim Mozart's birthplace, but the **statue outside the Estates Theater** where he premiered the opera *Don Giovanni* is a testament to his notorious love (and some would argue preference) for Prague audiences.

- The arrest of the psychedelic band **Plastic People of the Universe** for disturbing the peace under Communist Czechoslovakia helped to inspire the Charter 77 petition of 1976. These signatures became a who's who of political dissidents, many of whom received government retaliation for speaking up for personal freedoms (and the right to rock and roll).

- Two charismatic political leaders took the stage at **Reduta Jazz Club** for an impromptu saxophone jam session in 1994. A plaque marks the site where Czech President Havel joined US President Bill Clinton onstage for the joy of making music in a democratic society.

- You can thank the **Rolling Stones** for keeping the Prague Castle visible throughout the night. As one of the first rock bands to play in Prague after the fall of Communism, and friends of President Václav Havel, the band designed and financed the lighting design in 1995.

- Prague has even made its mark on MTV. The dance club at **Radost FX** was featured in Rihanna's music video for the song "Please Don't Stop the Music" in 2007.

- **Metallica** won local praise in 2018 when they performed a cover of 1970s Czech folk classic Jožin z bažin ("Jožin of the Swamp") for a packed house. A quick online search for the video with English subtitles and iconic dance moves will introduce you to one of the greatest quirky fairy tales ever told in song and a taste of Czech humor.

Lesser Town (Malá Strana's) role in resistance efforts from May 5-9, 1945 that led to the end of WWII. Take advantage of 360-degree views of the Charles Bridge and the Prague Castle on both the outdoor gallery level and covered windows of the top floor. This monument, which reopened in 2017 after the Prague City Museum took over operations and carried out renovations, is still fairly undiscovered by tourist standards, so you can enjoy some breathing room while you explore.

Vrtba Garden
(Vrtbovská zahrada)

Letenská 4, +420 272 088 350 or +420 603 233 912, www.vrtbovska.cz, 10am-6pm April-Oct only, 69 CZK, tram or metro stop Malostranské náměstí

Fans of landscape architecture should visit the Italian-style terraces of the Vrtba Garden with the added bonus of a raised viewpoint over panoramic city skylines and an almost eye-level perspective of the Prague Castle. This quiet, 18th-century oasis decorated with swirling grass, expressive statues of Roman gods, and a curved staircase leading to a hillside pavilion is a popular site for weddings and engagement photos. The entrance, down an unassuming driveway on your right while walking away from St. Nicholas Church on Karmelitská street, can be easy to miss, so keep your eyes peeled for the small sign.

Kampa Museum

U Sovových mlýnů 2, +420 257 286 147, www.museumkampa.cz, 10am-6pm, 350 CZK, tram stop Hellichova

You can spot Kampa Museum, housed in a former mill inside Park Kampa, from the opposite

1 the John Lennon Wall, a living breathing monument **2** St. Nicholas Church **3** view of the Prague Castle from Wallenstein Gardens

side of the Vltava River thanks to its line of glowing yellow penguins. The collection of modern art, curated by Jan and Meda Mládek, focuses on Central European artists expressing the struggles of working under oppression in the second half of the 20th century, as well as temporary exhibitions on modern themes. You could spend as little as one hour or an entire afternoon in this space. As you leave, don't miss a photo op with three of David Černy's creepy-but-cute bronze babies with bar codes for faces, crawling in the grass beside the museum. Discounted tickets for limited access to specific exhibitions are available.

Franz Kafka Museum

Cihelná 2b, +420 257 535 507, www.kafkamuseum. cz, 10am–6pm, 200 CZK, tram or metro stop Malostranská

Inside this museum, fans of this complicated literary legend will find letters, diaries, photographs, music, and installations that explore the connection between his most famous works and their underlying connections to the city of his birth. Kafka was raised by German-speaking Jewish parents and was educated in both German and Czech schools in the Czech Republic. Many of his novels were written in German, but he was able to speak and write both languages. A thorough read of extracts from the letters and manuscripts that have been translated into English could take a couple hours if you want to fully immerse yourself. Even if you don't step foot inside the museum, it's worth visiting the courtyard, which holds one of David Černy's many controversial sculptures—two men pissing into a pool in the shape of the Czech Republic.

To get here, take a riverside walk just north of the Charles Bridge.

PRAGUE CASTLE DISTRICT
(Hradčany)
★ Prague Castle
(Pražský hrad)

Pražský hrad, +420 224 372 423 or +420 224 371 111, www.hrad.cz, upper tram stops Královský letohrádek,

Pražský hrad, or Pohořelec, lower metro stops Malostranská or Malostranské náměstí

The name Prague Castle can be a bit misleading. The "castle" is not one building of turrets and royal residences, but actually refers to a massive fortified area of government buildings, churches, museums, and manicured gardens. This roughly 70,000 square meter area (more than 17 acres/750,000 sq ft) holds the Guinness World Record for the largest castle complex in the world.

The castle's history covers roughly a century of royal families and architectural styles. Duke of Bohemia Bořivoj I and his wife Ludmila founded the castle around the year 880. Future residents included their grandson Wenceslas I (later known as St. Wenceslas), members of the Habsburg royal family, and Thomas Garrigue Masaryk, the first president of Czechoslovakia in 1918. The Prague Castle remains the seat of the Czech president today, with the flag flying on days he (or she) is in town. The stone-faced, unmovable castle guards outside the main Matthias Gates put on a "Changing of the Guards" ceremony at noon, with a smaller version happening every hour from 7am.

The mixed-and-matched architectural style—from a Gothic-Renaissance-Baroque blend of the St. Vitus Cathedral to the Baroque exterior and Romanesque interior of St. George's Basilica—chronicles an ongoing "home improvement" project that stretched from 880 to the early 1900s. You can spot the more modern elements of Slovenian architect Josip Plečnik's 20th-century touches around the grounds.

VISITING THE PRAGUE CASTLE

The Prague Castle can easily be a multi-hour excursion, and visiting every corner would take multiple days. That said, you can pick and choose the areas that interest you most to customize your exploration, and a combination of 2-4 buildings and gardens can be enough to give you a taste of the castle experience. Those in a hurry or on a budget can take a peek inside St. Vitus Cathedral followed by

Sunset over Prague

Thanks to a spire-filled skyline, a hilly landscape, and a local affinity for nature and being out-doors, watching the sunset on a summer evening in Prague is a spectacular experience. Sunsets in Prague happen around 9pm in June and July and roughly 4pm in December or January. Grab a picnic and a partner (or go solo and peaceful) and try any of these prime viewing spots.

SIGHTS WITH VIEWS

You'll have to pay to catch views at these sights, but the memorable experience is worth the price.

- **Charles Bridge Towers:** It may require patience to get a prime spot in either the **Old Town Bridge Tower** or the **Lesser Town Bridge Towers** near Malá Strana, but these views are worth the wait. Stick to Old Town for a direct view of the Prague Castle over the River and Malá Strana for a slightly less crowded experience.

- **The Dancing House:** If you prefer an aerial perch, head to the viewing platform on the top floor of the Dancing House. Entrance fees are waived with purchase of a cocktail (125-200 CZK) or non-alcoholic drink (55-75 CZK) at the adjoining Glass Bar. An off-season evening in spring or autumn offers a more peaceful atmosphere around this popular landmark, while sunset marks the lively beginning of nightlife in summer.

PARKS AND OUTDOOR SPACES

Join the locals in a park or riverside boardwalk for a free visual feast as evening approaches.

- **Náplavka:** Dangle your legs over the edge of this riverside boardwalk between the southern edge of New Town and Vyšehrad and admire the swans on the Vltava River as the evening turns to night.

- **Reigrovy Sady:** The great sloping lawn of this Vinohrady park offers a tree-framed sunset view of the Prague Castle over a sea of red roofs. In the early evening, open space becomes scarce in between couples and families on picnic blankets, dogs curled beside their people, and the occasional Frisbee player or acoustic guitarist setting a soft soundtrack.

- **Vitkov Hill:** My personal favorite sunset spot requires a 20-minute gentle climb from the edge of Žižkov up to the courtyard outside the National Memorial on Vitkov Hill (U Památníku, www.nm.cz, free). Grab a seat on the stairs or stand underneath the massive equestrian statue of Jan Žižka and survey the lands of Old Town, New Town, Karlín, and Malá Strana. This lesser-known vantage point in the outskirts of Prague provides a quieter experience to end the day.

a walk along the South Garden's panoramic city views, both for free. Add on an hour-long visit to the Lobkowicz Palace for a single-admission entrance to explore aristocratic interiors and an enviable balcony view, plus the optional add-on of an afternoon classical music concert.

The castle grounds themselves are open from 6am–10pm, while the buildings and museums have shorter hours. Be prepared for a steady stream of tour groups from open to close in high seasons, with slightly more breathing room during off seasons and weekdays.

Ticket options include **Prague Castle—Circuit A** (350 CZK, valid for 2 days), which includes St. Vitus Cathedral, the Old Royal Palace, "The Story of Prague Castle" exhibition, St. George's Basilica, Golden Lane with the Daliborka Tower, and Rosenberg Palace. **Prague Castle—Circuit B** (250 CZK, valid for 2 days), which includes St. Vitus Cathedral, the Old Royal Palace, St. George's Basilica, and Golden Lane with the Daliborka

Lesser Town and Prague Castle District

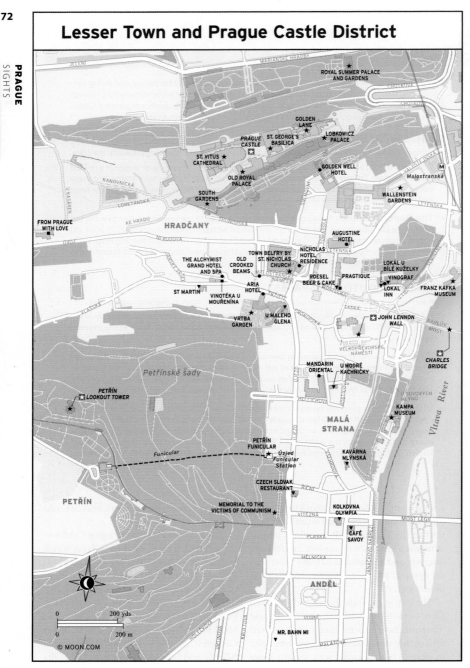

JELLENÍ

MARIÁNSKÉ HRADBY

ROYAL SUMMER PALACE
AND GARDENS

GOLDEN
LANE

PRAGUE
CASTLE ★

ST. GEORGE'S
BASILICA ★

LOBKOWICZ
PALACE ★

ST. VITUS ★
CATHEDRAL

OLD ROYAL
PALACE

GOLDEN WELL
HOTEL

M
Malostranská

KANOVNICKÁ

SOUTH
GARDENS

WALLENSTEIN
GARDENS

LORETÁNSKÁ

U KASÁREN

FROM PRAGUE
WITH LOVE

KE HRADU

HRADČANY

AUGUSTINE
HOTEL

NERUDOVA

ÚVOZ

TOWN BELFRY BY
ST. NICHOLAS
CHURCH

NICHOLAS
HOTEL
RESIDENCE

THE ALCHYMIST
GRAND HOTEL
AND SPA

OLD
CROOKED
BEAMS

LOKÁL U
BÍLÉ KUŽELKY

MALOSTRANSKÉ
NÁMĚSTÍ

ROESEL
BEER & CAKE

PRAGTIQUE

VINOGRAF

ST MARTIN

ARIA
HOTEL

LOKÁL
INN

FRANZ KAFKA
MUSEUM

VINOTÉKA U
MOUŘENÍNA

SASKÁ

VRTBA
GARDEN

U MALÉHO
GLENA

JOHN LENNON ★
WALL

KARLŮV
MOST

VELKOPŘEVORSKÉ
NÁMĚSTÍ

CHARLES
BRIDGE ★

Petřínské sady

MANDARIN
ORIENTAL

U MODRÉ
KACHNIČKY

HELLICHOVA

U SOVOVÝCH
MLÝNŮ

PETŘÍN ★
LOOKOUT TOWER

KAMPA
MUSEUM

MALÁ
STRANA

Vltava River

Funicular

PETŘÍN
FUNICULAR

Újezd
Funicular
Station

KAVÁRNA
MLÝNSKÁ

PETŘÍN

CZECH SLOVAK
RESTAURANT

ŘÍČNÍ

KOLKOVNA
OLYMPIA

MEMORIAL TO THE
VICTIMS OF COMMUNISM

VÍTĚZNÁ

MOST LEGIÍ

CAFÉ
SAVOY

PLASKÁ

MĚLNICKÁ

ANDĚL

0   200 yds
0   200 m

© MOON.COM

MR. BAHN MI

Tower. A pass to photograph the interiors of the Prague Castle requires an additional 50 CZK ticket.

An official **tour guide** in English (100 CZK per person, per hour, minimum 400 CZK) adds much more color and personalized explanations than an **audioguide** (350 CZK per device for 3 hours, 450 CZK per device per day). To book a guide, visit the information center in the Third Courtyard near the entrance to St. Vitus Cathedral or email info@hrad.cz.

Increased security measures were implemented after protest art group Ztohoven snuck onto the grounds in 2015 and replaced the Czech flag with a giant pair of red boxer shorts. Entrances now require a security checkpoint, no large bags are allowed inside, and drones are prohibited from flying overhead.

ROYAL SUMMER PALACE AND GARDENS
(Letohrádek královny Anny)

Mariánské hradby 1, +420 224 372 434 or +420 224 372 415, www.hrad.cz, 10am–6pm April–Oct only, free, tram stop Královský letohrádek

For a peaceful start to your castle tour during the warmer months, use the smaller entrance one tram stop before the main entrance at **Queen Anne's Summer Palace and Royal Gardens**. The 16th century Italian Renaissance villa is etched with scenes of love above its columned terrace arches. Sadly, the story behind that romance is tragic—King Ferdinand I of the Habsburg empire family started construction for his beloved Queen Anne, but she passed away before it was completed after giving birth to her 15th(!) child. To understand the name of the "singing fountain" in the courtyard, you have to actually crouch underneath and put your ear to the cement basin to hear the vibrations. Then peek between the trees in the corner for a first glimpse of the hilltop views over Malá Strana before a leisurely stroll through the gardens towards the castle gates.

ST. VITUS CATHEDRAL
(Katedrála sv. Víta)

Pražský hrad - III. nádvoří, +420 224 372 423, www.katedralasvatehovita.cz, April-Oct 9am-5pm Mon-Sat, 12pm-4pm Sun, Nov–Mar 9am–4pm Mon-Sat, 12pm-4pm Sun, limited free access, full access with Circuit A (350 CZK) or B (250 CZK), tram stop Pohořelec

St. Vitus Cathedral is the dominant figure of the Prague skyline. It's what most people associate with the historic castle grounds, although it wasn't entirely completed until the 20th century. Wenceslas I first built a Romanesque rotunda on this spot in the 10th century. Charles IV began construction of the Gothic beauty, whose official full name is the Cathedral of St. Vitus, Václav and Vojtěch, in 1344. The long name recognizes the man who founded it (Vaclav or Wenceslas). An arm bone of the Sicilian St. Vitus—the patron saint of dancers and performing artists, who also protects against dog bites, lightning, and oversleeping—is buried in St. Wenceslas' tomb. The third name, Vojtěch, represents a Bohemian bishop killed during missionary work and also buried on this site, although with far less name recognition and fanfare than his famous counterparts.

Construction began in the 14th century but wasn't finished for 600 years. Work on the cathedral was interrupted or damaged throughout the centuries by events like the 15th century Hussite wars, 16th century fires, the Thirty Years War in the 17th century, multiple conflicts under Maria Theresa's 18th century rule, and neglect by the Habsburgs in the 19th century. It took the spirit of the Czech National Revival and the creation of the Association for the Completion of the St. Vitus temple in 1859 to see the project through to consecration in 1929.

Exterior: The intricate façade over the western entrance to St. Vitus has a historical look, but this area was actually part of the building's finishing touches. For example, both the rose window and the decorative doors covered with images from the cathedral's storied history weren't completed until the mid-1900s. The four proud architects of this final construction era also weren't shy about adding statues of themselves just below the rose window.

Around the corner to the right of the church exterior lies the truly historical 14th-century **Golden Gate,** on the southern side of the building. The tall pointed doorways of this former entrance, no longer in use, sit underneath mosaics of the Last Judgement, made with around one million individual pieces of glass and marble around 1370.

Interior: The entrance to the cathedral is on the left-hand side of the Western façade, with lines often wrapped around the corner of the building. Both ticketed and non-ticketed visitors stand in the same line. The rear of the church just inside the entryway is as far as non-ticketed visitors are allowed to go, so waves of tour groups come inside to get one shot of the church layout bathed in the light of stained glass (and photos without ticketed permission are not technically allowed, but loosely enforced in this area).

The first perk for ticketed visitors just past the turnstiles on your left is an unobstructed view of Alfons Mucha's window scene depicting Christianity coming to the Czech lands. It's painted, not stained glass, which sets it apart from the remaining windows, all done by different Czech artists.

Continuing down the left aisle, the center of the cathedral marks the border between old and new construction, with this expansion shifting the organ to this unusual position on a side wall. The wooden relief on the right side of the aisle depicts four areas (Malá Strana, Hradčany, Old Town, and New Town) that were united in 1784 to form the city of Prague—this feature is often overlooked, but it can be fun to pick out city sights or where you're staying. Crowds generally form a bottleneck at the rear curve of the cathedral and shuffle slowly around the two-ton silver sculpture topping St. Jan of Napomuk's coffin.

St. Wenceslas Chapel lies on this opposite side of the building. It's worth craning your neck to see inside the doorways to the rectangular area that's restricted to all visitors. This chapel also serves as the entrance to the crown jewel storage area but they're on strict lock down and only displayed to the public on rare special occasions and anniversaries. Opening the door requires seven keys split between public figures including the Czech president, Prime Minister, and Archbishop.

Tickets and tours: The quick, budget-friendly way to see St. Vitus Cathedral is a free peek from just inside the neo-Gothic entryway (which requires waiting in line with ticketed visitors). Any of the sights beyond the entryway of the church require a packaged castle ticket, either Circuit A (350 CZK) or Circuit B (250 CZK). If you decide on an all-access castle ticket, splurge on a tour guide (100 CZK per person, per hour, minimum 400 CZK) for detailed stories that add color to the historic figures represented inside all of the buildings. You can book a guide in person at the information center in the Third Courtyard near the entrance to St. Vitus Cathedral or via email to info@hrad.cz.

OLD ROYAL PALACE
(Starý královský palác)
Třetí nádvoří Pražského hradu 2, +420 224 372 434, www.hrad.cz, April-Oct 9am-5pm, Nov-Mar 9am-4pm, Admission only with Circuit A (350 CZK) or B (250 CZK), tram stop Pohořelec or Pražský hrad

The Old Royal Palace, one of the castle's earliest buildings from the 12th century, is a fun stop for history buffs. The former royal residence and receiving area only retains a few small glimpses of its interior glamour, but is best known as the site of war-causing conflict. The intricately webbed ceiling of Vradislav Hall covers a long central corridor that was historically used for jousting matches and seen in the wide "Rider's Staircase" used to exit the room. The palace tower also marks the site of the Second (more famous) Defenestration of Prague in 1618. Another religious rebellion, this time in response to Catholic Emperor Ferdinand II of the Habsburgs closing Protestant chapels in

Bohemia, saw two government officials and their secretary tossed out the window. The fall was not fatal, as legend has it they landed in a pile of excrement before being taken in by Polyxena Lubkowitz at her nearby palace, but that doesn't mean it didn't have consequences. The act is credited for starting the Thirty Year's War that wreaked havoc on Central Europe. The window is marked inside and also marked by a ground-level plaque and visible free of charge from the Southern Gardens.

ST. GEORGE'S BASILICA
(Bazilika sv. Jiří)

Náměstí U Svatého Jiří, +420 224 372 434, www.
hrad.cz, April-Oct 9am-5pm, Nov-Mar 9am-4pm,
Admission only with Circuit A (350 CZK) or B (250
CZK), tram stop Pohořelec or Pražský hrad

Entrance to St. George's Basilica gives architecture buffs a chance to compare the orange-red Baroque exterior with the minimalist Romanesque arched ceilings inside (and tired tourists a seat in the pews to rest your feet). The large stone coffin in the center of the chapel holds Boleslav I, also known as Boleslav the Cruel and the younger brother of Wenceslas responsible for his murder. It also holds the chapel of St. Ludmila, grandmother of Boleslav and Wenceslas, on the right side of the central staircases. Ludmila's figure is usually depicted with a scarf or veil around her neck to symbolize her death by strangulation, rumored to be ordered by her daughter-in-law Drahomira. Ludmila raised Wenceslas as a Christian, while Drahomira was loyal to the pagans of Bohemia, yet another instance of Czech resentment over the imposition of a dominant religion.

St. George's Basilica also holds fairly regular evening concerts of classical favorites.

LOBKOWICZ PALACE
(Lobkowiczký palác)

Jiřská 3, +420 702 201 145, www.lobkowicz.com,
10am-6pm, 295 CZK, tram stops Pohořelec or
Pražský hrad, metro stop Malostranská

The 16th-century Lobkowicz Palace is the only privately owned building in the castle complex. After centuries of housing one of Prague's early noble families, the building now serves as a museum offering a taste of aristocratic elegance and an impressive collection of memorabilia showcasing the family's patronage towards artists and musicians. This is also the house where Polyxena Lobkowicz took in survivors of the 1618 Prague Defenstration from the Old Royal Palace.

Getting to the palace is possible without a castle ticket—just head downhill from St. George's Basilica on Jiřská street parallel to Golden Lane—but visitors will need to buy a ticket to enter the palace itself. Plan at least an hour to immerse yourself in the aristocratic atmosphere.

Inside, descendants of the 700-year Lobkowicz family line take great pride in describing their family collection via audio guide included with admission. The building and its elements were seized in recent decades by both the Nazis and Communists, before finally returning to the family. Twenty-two decadent rooms include a massive collection of portraits (both people and animals) and porcelain dishes, an armory of rifles, and chandelier topped rooms draped with curtains. You may want to skip past some of the detailed family descriptions of the portraits in the first two rooms, simply pausing to admire and learn more about any that catch your eye.

Classical music fans will appreciate the music room, which displays Josef František Maxmilián's patronage of composers such as Mozart, Beethoven, and Handel. Find written symphonies dedicated to the Lobkowicz prince alongside portraits of the composers and historical musical instruments. Time your visit around 1pm to join the audience for daily classical concerts (390 CZK concert or 590 CZK concert + museum) under a frescoed ceiling in the intimate Baroque concert hall, or wander the exhibitions during that hour without crowds.

The museum route ends with a panoramic balcony view of Prague.

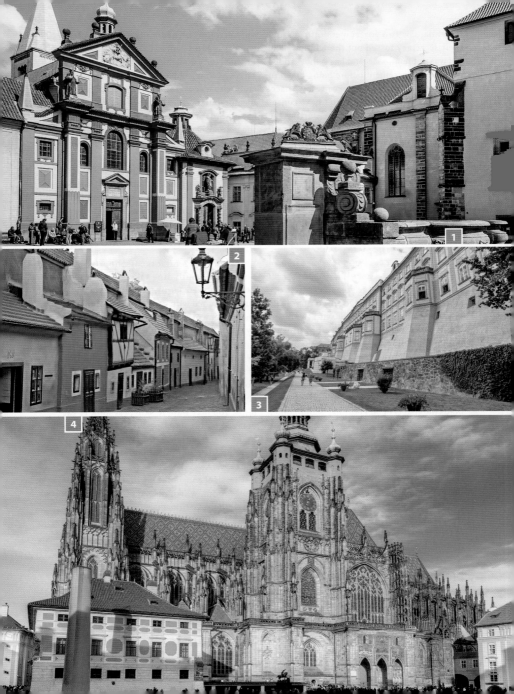

GOLDEN LANE
(Zlatá ulička)

Zlatá ulička, +420 224 372 423, www.hrad.cz,
April-Oct 9am-5pm, Nov-Mar 9am-4pm, Admission
only with Circuit A (350 CZK) or B (250 CZK),
tram stops Pohořelec or Pražský hrad, metro stop
Malostranská

For a kitschy glimpse at 16th century life in this area, choose a castle ticket that includes access to Golden Lane. The rows of 16 small houses built into the fortifying wall were inhabited by goldsmiths and members of the castle guard from the 16th century. Many tour guides offer speculation about alchemists' workshops in the area to fulfill the whims of occult enthusiast Rudolph II, but these legends should be taken a healthy dose of skepticism. The preserved and recreated residences now include Franz Kafka's former writing haunt (number 22) alongside souvenir and toy shops. Number 14 was the home of internationally renowned tarot card reader Matylda Průšová, also known as "Madame de Thebes," who was arrested and died in custody for predicting the end of the Nazi regime. Climb the stairs into the White Tower (Bílá věž) to view suits of armor and a small torture chamber of brutal instruments.

The entire street is restricted by a ticketed turnstile during opening hours. Free access to walk down Golden Lane without entry to the buildings is possible only after 6pm.

SOUTH GARDENS
(Jižní zahrady)

Pražský hrad, www.hrad.cz, 6am-10pm April-Oct
only, free, tram stops Pohořelec or Pražský hrad,
metro stops Malostranská or Malostranské náměstí

For panoramic city views with no surcharge, head to the South Gardens. This long strip of manicured lawns and rounded staircases provides an obstacle-free view (if you don't count the selfie-takers) over Malá Strana's red roofs, the Vltava River, Old Town, and the city beyond. Look along the castle walls

outside the Old Royal Palace for the plaque at the base of the tower from which the officials were tossed during the Defenestration of Prague in 1618.

Those on a free castle tour can access these gardens through the Bull Staircase from the third courtyard beside St. Vitus Cathedral, and opposite the Golden Gate, while those on a full tour can get here from the end of Golden Lane or Jiřská street after visiting the Lobkowicz Palace. These eastern end of these gardens marks the entrance to **St. Wenceslas' Vineyard,** named for the patron saint of the Czech lands, where you can recap your visit over a bottle of Riesling or Pinot Noir (500-900 CZK). You can also exit the South Gardens to the west onto Hradčanské náměstí and walk towards the Strahov Library, Strahov Brewery, or Petřín Park and Lookout Tower.

Strahov Library
(Strahovská knihovna)

Strahovské nádvoří 1, +420 233 107 752,
www.strahovskyklaster.cz, 9am-12pm and 1pm-5pm,
120 CZK, tram stop Pohořelec

The **Strahov Library,** with its ceiling murals, ornate globes, and book-lined walls, is the crown jewel of the early 12th century Strahov Monastery complex, which also includes a gallery and basilica. Inside the library, the intricately decorated Theological Hall and Philosophical Hall feature regularly on "Most Beautiful Libraries in the World" lists—and, unlike the similarly opulent library in Old Town's Klementinum, which prohibits photos, photography is allowed in Strahov Library for an extra 50 CZK. The Strahov Library is worth a stop for photography fans and architecture buffs, while less enthusiastic members of any travel group can wait patiently over a beer at the nearby Strahov Monastery Brewery.

The library accepts a limited number of visitors per year to protect the books, and visitors are not allowed to step foot inside the two halls without a guided tour reserved well in advance. (Book individually via email:

1 St. George's Basilica 2 Golden Lane in the Prague Castle 3 Prague Castle gardens 4 St. Vitus Cathedral

erika@strahovskyklaster.cz.) Admission comes with a printed guide in English to provide some history and context. During your visit, if you opt for the tour, be aware that you will likely appear in many visitors' photographs as you walk through the rooms.

The Strahov Monastery was established on this site in the 12th century, but the buildings suffered from centuries of fires and attacks. Ongoing restoration efforts have preserved the 17th-century Baroque style of the Theological Hall and the Philosophical Hall maintains brighter Classicist elements of the late 18th century.

In addition to angling for photos, you can explore the Cabinet of Curiosities, a full corridor outside the two halls that is lined with artifacts seen as exotic in previous centuries—think: unusual animals for a landlocked area (crab, turtle, and seashells) and the remains of a now-extinct Dodo bird alongside jeweled books and Asian statues of warriors and aristocrats.

PETŘÍN

★ Petřín Lookout Tower
(Petřínská rozhledna)

Petřínské sady, +420 257 320 112, www.muzeumprahy. cz, April-Sept 10am-10pm, Nov-Feb 10am-6pm, March and Oct 10am-8pm, 150 CZK, tram stop Újezd + Funicular ride

After visiting the newly unveiled Parisian Eiffel Tower in 1889, the Czech Tourist Club decided that the Prague skyline was missing something. The Petřín Lookout Tower was created for the General Land Centennial Exhibition in 1891, serving as a replica in tribute and admiration for its French inspiration. The tower also holds cheeky bragging rights as being technically higher than the Eiffel Tower due to its hilltop location. Climbing the 299 steps to the observation deck gives you one of the highest viewpoints in the city. There is an elevator (60 CZK), but it is seen more as an option for limited mobility and elderly visitors than for tired tourists.

The easiest way to reach the tower is an uphill funicular ride from the Petřín station located inside the park near the Újezd tram stop and requires the same rules as a ride on any form of Prague's public transport—have a ticket and be sure to validate it before entering. For a simple, cost-free option, you could also walk through the park from the top of the hill after a visit to the Prague Castle or Strahov Monastery, both near the Pohořelec tram stop.

Petřín Funicular

Petřínské sady, www.dpp.cz, 9am-11:30pm, brief closures in March and Oct, 24 CZK, tram stop Újezd

This land-based version of a cable car is more than just the simplest way to ascend Petřín Hill. The Petřín Funicular offers panoramic window views in between stops at two platforms from the base of the hill to the Petřín Lookout Tower. This nostalgic hillside transport first ran on a water-based system in 1891, halting operations during WWI before switching to an electrical system when it resumed in 1932. The system took another twenty-year break after a landslide in 1965. Since reopening in 1985, the ride has been part of the city's public network and included within a valid Prague transport ticket. Carriages leave every fifteen minutes from November to March and every ten minutes from April to October. Look for the Petřín funicular station just inside the grounds of the park when entering near the Újezd tram stop.

The Petřín Funicular is part of Prague's public transport system. There is a ticket machine on site, and a single ride (24 CZK) requires first buying a ticket and then stamping it in the yellow validation machines before boarding the funicular, to avoid a hefty fine from the controllers checking at either side of the ride.

---

1 Chapel of the Holy Sepulcher in the Petřín Gardens 2 expressive statues of Roman gods in the Vrtba Garden 3 a stark Memorial to the Victims of Communism by Olbram Zoubek 4 one of the oldest structures in Prague, St. Martin's Rotunda in the Vyšehrad Complex

Memorial to the Victims of Communism

Petřínské sady, free, tram stop Újezd

Seven crumbling bronze men by sculptor Olbram Zoubek line the steps to Petřín Park as a Memorial to the Victims of Communism unveiled in 2002. The first man appears whole, while successive statues are each missing parts of their bodies, symbolizing a commitment to perseverance in the face of the damage inflicted from 1948-1989. The statistics running along the stairs spell out the effects in stark numbers: 205,486 people convicted, 248 executed, 4,500 died in prison, 327 died during illegal border crossings, and 170,938 people left their homes behind to emigrate. The figures are particularly harrowing when lit from below in the evening.

TOP EXPERIENCE

VYŠEHRAD
★ Vyšehrad Complex

V Pevnosti 159/5b, +420 261 225 304,
www.praha-vysehrad.cz, free, metro stop Vyšehrad

Legend has it that this vast complex (and the city of Prague itself) was constructed after Princess Libuše looked out over the undeveloped landscape around the 8th century and declared, "Behold, I see a great city, whose fame will touch the stars."

You can enter the large grass-filled grounds of the Vyšehrad Complex after a short walk from the Vyšehrad metro, taking the exit towards the Congress Center and following the brown street signs pointing the way through a few residential streets. The grounds themselves include a maze of green spaces dotted with statues, alongside some of the city's oldest historic monuments. This quiet complex is far less crowded or touristy than the Prague Castle across the river, but filled with comparable levels of history and beauty. Wander the edges of the park complex for stunning citywide viewpoints from an alternative angle to Old Town or Malá Strana.

Visitors to both Vyšehrad (meaning "high castle") and the Prague Castle are often confused by the lack of Disneyland-style turrets and princess-worthy bedrooms. The term "castle" in Prague is not necessarily a single ornate building, but is used to describe fortified walls surrounding a seat of power, such as this royal base of King Vratislav II in the 11th century.

ST. MARTIN'S ROTUNDA (Rotunda sv. Martina)

V Pevnosti, +420 224 911 353, www.kkvys.cz, free, metro stop Vyšehrad

Shortly beyond the brick entrance of the Vyšehrad Complex you'll come upon a large circular building seemingly sprouting from the ground. St. Martin's Rotunda is arguably Prague's oldest intact building from the 11th century. It has seen its fair share of battles, after being used as gunpowder storage during the Thirty Years' War from 1618-1648 (much like the Powder Tower of New Town in later years). The rotunda still holds a cannonball in its walls from the Prussians during the Battle of Prague in 1757. These days it maintains a more peaceful existence used for occasional religious services. It is not open for tourists, but signage in English in the surrounding courtyard can add context to the view. If you're ready for a break, the entrance to the **Hospůdka Na Hradbách** beer garden is hiding just behind the rotunda.

BASILICA OF STS. PETER AND PAUL (Bazilika sv. Petra a Pavla)

Štulcova, +420 224 911 353, www.kkvys.cz, 50 CZK, metro stop Vyšehrad

The tall, neo-Gothic towers of the Basilica of Sts. Peter and Paul mirror the Prague Castle's St. Vitus Cathedral across the river. The interior of this 19th-century version (damaged and remodeled multiple times from its 11th-century roots established by King Vratislav II) contains gorgeous Art Nouveau-style depictions of saints along its columns, along with flowered ceilings and stained glass windows. Give yourself at least half an hour to browse the eye-catching decoration in soft, muted

Karlín, Vinohrady, and Žižkov

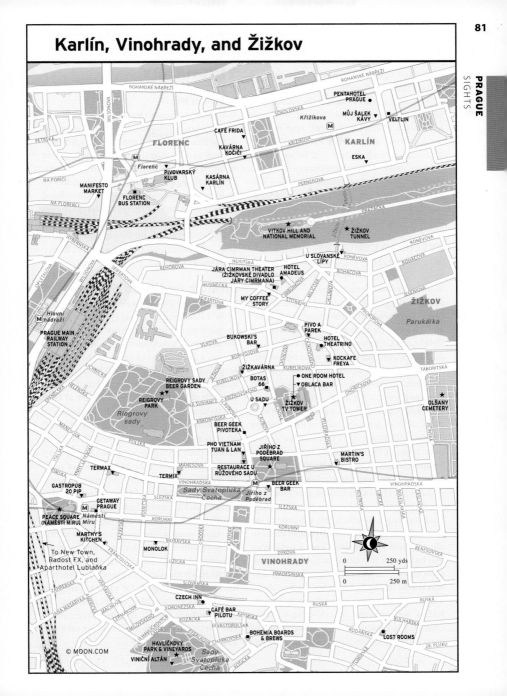

ROHANSKÉ NÁBŘEŽÍ

PENTAHOTEL PRAGUE ●

Křižíkova MŮJ ŠALEK KÁVY ▼ VELTLIN ■

CAFÉ FRIDA ▼

FLORENC KAVÁRNA KOČIČÍ ▼ KARLÍN

Florenc ESKA ▼

PIVOVARSKÝ KLUB ▼ KASÁRNA KARLÍN ▼

MANIFESTO MARKET ▼

FLORENC BUS STATION

VÍTKOV HILL AND NATIONAL MEMORIAL ★ ★ ŽIŽKOV TUNNEL

U SLOVANSKÉ LÍPY ▼

JÁRA CIMRMAN THEATER (ŽIŽKOVSKÉ DIVADLO JÁRY CIMRMANA) HOTEL AMADEUS ●

ŽIŽKOV

MY COFFEE STORY ▼ Parukářka

Hlavní nádraží PIVO A PAREK ▼

PRAGUE MAIN RAILWAY STATION HOTEL THEATRINO ● BUKOWSKI'S BAR ▼ KOCKAFE FREYA ▼

REIGROVY SADY BEER GARDEN ŽIŽKAVÁRNA ▼ BOTAS 66 ▼ ● ONE ROOM HOTEL ▼ OBLACA BAR

REIGROVY PARK U SADU ● ŽIŽKOV TV TOWER ★ OLŠANY CEMETERY ★

Riegrovy sady

BEER GEEK PIVOTEKA ■

PHO VIETNAM TUAN & LAN ▼ JIŘÍHO Z PODĚBRAD SQUARE MARTIN'S BISTRO ▼

TERMAX ▼ RESTAURACE U RŮŽOVÉHO SADU ▼

TERMIX ■ BEER GEEK BAR ▼

GASTROPUB 20 PIP ▼ Sady Svatopluka Čecha Jiřího z Poděbrad VINOHRADSKÁ

GETAWAY PRAGUE ■

PEACE SQUARE Náměstí Míru (NÁMĚSTÍ MÍRU)

MARTHY'S KITCHEN ▼

To New Town, Radost FX, and Aparthotel Lublaňka MONOLOK ▼

VINOHRADY 0   250 yds
         0   250 m

CZECH INN ●

CAFÉ BAR PILOTU ▼

© MOON.COM HAVLÍČKOVY PARK & VINEYARDS BOHEMIA BOARDS & BREWS ▼ LOST ROOMS ★

VINIČNÍ ALTÁN Sady Svatopluka Čecha

28. PLUKU

colors on every wall. The church was given the status of a "basilica minor" by Pope John Paul II, engraved in a plaque near the ornate doors, as a sign of its importance as opposed to its architectural style.

The church is accessible to the public from 10am daily except for 10:30am after mass on Sundays, and stays open until 5pm in winter and 6pm on summer evenings except Thursday, when it shuts at 5:30 to prepare for evening mass. This ornate beauty is far less crowded and more accessible than St. Vitus, drawing visitors on a tight schedule or those wanting to experience a slice of history without elbowing their way through tour groups.

VYŠEHRAD CEMETERY

Štulcova, +420 224 911 353, www.slavin.cz, May-Sept 8am-7pm, Nov-Feb 8am-5pm, Mar-April and Oct 8am-6pm free, metro stop Vyšehrad

Many of Prague's final resting places are artfully decorated with intricate headstones and designed for visitors. In fact, the aisles of Vyšehrad's Cemetery hold many of Prague's celebrities who may enjoy an audience beyond the grave as much as they did while walking the earth. You can enter the cemetery through a gate to the left of the Basilica of Sts. Peter and Paul, where a list of famous graves are detailed by number, or from the back of the cemetery after a walk from the Vyšehrad metro station. Some of the names you may recognize include classical composers Bedřich Smetana, surrounded by towering obelisks, and a bust of Antonín Dvořák behind a gate along the northern wall. Art Nouveau painter Alfons Mucha's plaque is tucked into a corner of the Slavin Tomb at the top of stairs near the eastern entrance, and romantic poet Karel Hynek Mácha's name is written in gold on a headstone among the aisles. Literary fans take note that the Kafka buried here is Czech sculptor Bohumil Kafka, and is not the writer Franz Kafka, whose grave is in the New Jewish Cemetery in Žižkov. Also, "Rodina" is not the most popular Czech surname, but it means "family," so you'll find it on many of the tombstones marking familial plots.

VINOHRADY
Peace Square
(Náměstí Míru)

Free, metro stop Náměstí Míru

This square is defined by the towering spires of the Neo-Gothic **Church of St. Ludmila** (Kostel svaté Ludmily). The church is best admired from the outside, alongside the residents reading or relaxing on the benches as pedestrians crisscross the bright, flower-lined paths. Easter and Christmas markets in this square are among the city's most popular, when wooden stands fill the air with the sweet smell of crepes (*palačinky*) and hot honey wine (*medovina*).

Jiřího z Poděbrad Square

Free, metro stop Jiřího z Poděbrad

Jiřího z Poděbrad Square is a popular outdoor hangout to enjoy a takeaway meal, browse the farmers market, admire the architecture, or toss a Frisbee in the grass in the heart of neighborhood life in Prague. The large clock face of the modern, brown and white, Catholic **Church of the Most Sacred Heart of Our Lord** (Kostel Nejsvětějšího Srdce Páně) marks the border where Vinohrady begins to blend into the neighborhood of Žižkov. Take a poll among your group to see how the majority feel about this love-it-or-hate-it piece of early 20th-century architecture. A farmers market of fresh vegetables and flowers, plus ready-to-eat snacks, covers half the square from morning to late afternoon every Wednesday through Saturday. The area is also surrounded by independent restaurants and coffee shops frequented by the neighborhood's international residents. Grab a seat on the benches lining the central path for some prime people-and-puppy watching before crossing the street to Beer Geek for a microbrew or to Pho Vietnam Tuan & Lan for some take out Vietnamese food.

Local Legends

These names are legendary among the local community, but not necessarily household names unless you're a fine arts aficionado. Here is a short rundown of some famous Czechs that locals would be shocked to hear you've never heard of.

You will be forgiven for not knowing romantic poet **Karel Hynek Mácha** (1810-1836), but he will be familiar to anyone who visited his statue in Petřín Park. Mácha's most famous work, "Maj" ("May"), uses description of nature to portray its depictions of love, and was translated in into English on the 200th anniversary of his birth in 2010.

Bedřich Smetana's (1824-1884) music is celebrated in his hometown of Litomyšl, about two hours east of Prague, with a festival every summer. The classical composer also lends his name to the great concert hall inside the Municipal House. This father of Bohemian music is best known for "Má vlast" ("My Homeland"), which opens the Prague Spring Music Festival each year and includes odes to the Vltava River and Vyšehrad.

Grave of classical music legend Bedřich Smetana

Smetana's younger contemporary, **Antonín Dvořák** (1841-1904) gained international, or you could even say intergalactic, recognition for his classical compositions infused with Czech folk influences. Dvořák's "New World Symphony" accompanied American astronauts Neil Armstrong and Buzz Aldrin on their trip to the moon in 1969.

Even if you don't immediately recognize his name, the swirling designs of Art Nouveau painter **Alfons Mucha** (1860-1939) will likely look familiar. While the artistic style is often connected to France, this hero of the movement is undeniably Czech. Mucha's work graces a window in St. Vitus Cathedral, the ceiling murals of Smetana Hall in the Municipal House, and an entire museum in New Town devoted to his posters, paintings, and interesting life story.

Jaromír Jágr (1972-present), one of the most beloved ice hockey heroes of the modern Czech nation (even though he played many years for the NHL in the US), is an artist on the ice. The Kladno-born god of the sport went pro in the Czech Republic at age 15 and won two Stanley Cup championships with the Pittsburgh Penguins. You can also thank Jágr for helping to popularize the mullet hairstyle in the early 1990s, still embraced by some older Czech men to this day.

ŽIŽKOV
Žižkov TV Tower
(Žižkovský vysílač)

Mahlerovy Sady 1, +420 210 320 081, www.towerpark.cz, 9am-midnight, observation deck 250 CZK, tram stop Lipanská or tram and metro stops Jiřího z Poděbrad

It is a fitting testament to Prague's growth and fluctuation that the defining structure of the Žižkov neighborhood offers an array of posh experiences in an area known for its rough and tumble reputation. The Žižkov TV Tower, built between 1985 and 1992, holds the title of the tallest building in Prague, at more than 700 feet (216 meters). The interior contains an observation deck with panoramic views as well as an exclusive One Room Hotel and the Oblaca fine dining restaurant and cocktail bar. From 2000 to 2018, ten of David Černy's giant baby sculptures (similar to those beside Kampa Museum in Malá Strana) could be seen climbing its walls. However, they traveled

to an exhibition in Palm Springs, California in 2018. At the time of writing, the tower was awaiting a refurbishment of the sculptures to withstand the elements of a life spent clinging to the side of a building.

Olšany Cemetery and New Jewish Cemetery
(Olšanské hřbitovy/ Nový židovský hřbitov)

tram and metro stops Želivského

Two important burial grounds serving Prague's Jewish community are located on the outside edge of Žižkov. The massive Olšany Cemetery (Vinohradská 153, www.hrbitovy.cz, May-Sept 8am-7pm, Mar-April and Oct 8am-5pm Fri, Nov-Feb 8am-4pm, free) was established in 1680 in response to the Plague epidemic sweeping Europe. Prague's oldest and largest graveyard holds the body of student protester Jan Palach. Across the road, Prague's New Jewish Cemetery (Izraelská 1, +420 224 800 812, www.synagogue.cz, April-Oct 9am-5pm Sun-Thurs, 9am-2pm Fri, Nov-Mar 9am-4pm Sun-Thurs, 9am-2pm Fri, free), established in 1890, is best known for housing the grave of writer Franz Kafka and his parents (tombstone number 21 - 14 - 21) along with a memorial to the Czechoslovak Jews killed during the Holocaust.

Vitkov Hill and National Memorial
(Národní památník na Vítkově)

U Památníku, +420 732 947 509, www.nm.cz, Nov-Mar 10am-6pm Thurs-Sun, April-Oct 10am-6pm Wed-Sun Sun, memorial 120 CZK, tram stop Biskupcova or bus stop Ohrada

One of the most beautiful places to watch the sunset over Prague is from the National Memorial at Vitkov Hill. A roughly 20-minute walk up the hill from the Žižkov beer garden on the edge of Žižkov treats visitors to an open platform around a towering statue of Jan Žižka on horseback, the Czech flag flying to your left, and the Prague Castle framed by trees directly in front of you. History fans may want to peek inside the National Memorial with an exhibition on important events in 20th-century Czech history. Otherwise, skip the entrance fee and simply enjoy the view.

Žižkov Tunnel
(Žižkovský Tunel)

Žižkovský Tunel, free, bus stop Tachovské náměstí

The nearly 1,000-foot (300-meter) long Žižkov Tunnel connects the Žižkov neighborhood with Karlín, whose residents prefer to call it the Karlín Tunnel, underneath Vitkov Hill. The lengthy path is perfectly safe, even though you can't see from one side to the other, and is limited to pedestrians and bicycles. It was originally built for shelter from a nuclear fallout. The echo is powerful, and you may often hear shouts or even music on your pilgrimage between the two very different districts of Prague. The tunnel is well lit at night, making it an easy connection for dinner at nearby U Slovanské Lípy on the Žižkov side and an evening drink at one of Karlín's sophisticated wine bars.

LETNÁ AND HOLEŠOVICE
Metronome

Nábřeží Edvarda Beneše, free, tram stop Čechův most

The giant red Metronome keeping time over Prague is a fairly modern monument, built in 1991. The largest statue of Joseph Stalin in the world previously held this perch, keeping a symbolic watchful eye over the city until the Communist-era monument was blown to bits with dynamite in 1962. If you want an up-close look these days, you'll have to dodge the skateboarders who have claimed the cement platform around the metronome and its surrounding ledges. Pop-up beverage beer stands and occasional concerts cater to the crowds of summer.

---

1 benches lining the aisles of Náměstí Míru
2 a towering statue of Jan Žižka watches over the neighborhood named after him

Letná and Holešovice

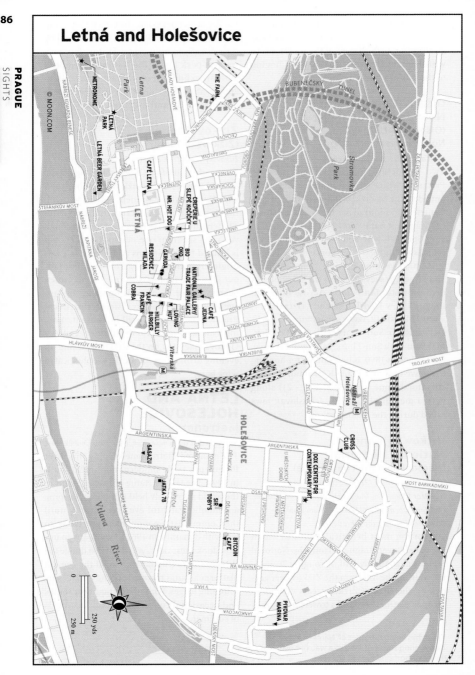

© MOON.COM

THE FARM

BUBENEČSKÝ
TUNEL

Stromovka
Park

Letná
Park

METRONOME

LETNÁ
PARK

LETNÁ BEER GARDEN

CAFÉ LETKA

CREPERIE U
SLEPÉ KOČKÝ

MR. HOT DOG

LETNÁ

BIO
OKO

RESIDENCE
MILADA

GARUDA

NATIONAL GALLERY/
TRADE FAIR PALACE

CAFÉ
JEDNA

COBRA

KAFE
FRANKIN

HILLBILLY
BURGER

LOVING
HUT

STEFÁNIKŮV MOST

HLÁVKŮV MOST

TROJSKÝ MOST

Nádraží (M)
Holešovice

ARGENTINSKA

SASAZU

HOLEŠOVICE

CROSS
CLUB

DOX CENTER FOR
CONTEMPORARY ART

MOST BARIKÁDNÍKŮ

JÁTKA 78

SIR
TOBY'S

BITCOIN
CAFE

Vltava River

PIVOVAR
MARINA

0   250 yds

0   250 m

The Notorious David Černý

If you see a public sculpture in Prague, there is a good chance that David Černý is the artist behind it. The controversial artist was born just before the Prague Spring of 1968 and grew up in the subsequent era of Communist crack down. When the Velvet Revolution opened Czechoslovakia's borders, Černý seized the opportunity to study in Switzerland and New York City.

The young artist grabbed attention in 1991 by painting a Soviet tank and war memorial bright pink. This earned him an arrest at age 23, but members of parliament re-painted the tank pink in protest. Černý didn't stay imprisoned long and the tank was removed. The artist's work (and political statements) continue to decorate and provoke the city—he sent a giant blue middle finger entitled "Gesture" down the Vltava River when President Miloš Zeman was elected in 2013. Below are some of his pieces worth seeking out:

- A seven-foot Sigmund Freud entitled **"Man Hanging Out"** grips a rooftop outside the building at Na Perštýně 14 in Old Town (don't be fooled by the similar man hanging from an umbrella in front of the Mosaic House Hotel).

Three of David Černý's "Babies" stand outside of Kampa Museum

- The **saint riding an upside-down horse** suspended from the rooftop of Palac Lucerna in Wenceslas Square is also a David Černý creation.

- **"Piss"**—two mechanical men urinating into a Czech Republic-shaped pool—embodies his cheeky, provocative style in front of the Franz Kafka Museum.

- Three of his bronze **"Babies"** with barcodes for faces sit beside the Kampa Museum. Ten of their siblings were notorious for crawling the sides of the Žižkov TV Tower until 2018, when they were removed (temporarily) for repair.

- Černý's latest installation is a rotating, mirrored **head of Franz Kafka** near the National Theater.

- A day trip to Liberec includes his **"Giant's Feast,"** a severed head and beverages decorating the top of a bus stop.

National Gallery— Trade Fair Palace
(Veletržní palác - Národní galerie)

Dukelských hrdinů 47, +420 224 301 122, www.ngprague.cz, 10am-6pm Tues-Sun, 150 CZK, free for children and visitors under 26, tram stops Strossmayerovo náměstí or Veletržní palác

Prague's National Gallery includes a collection of exposition places scattered across Prague, but most people mentioning the National Gallery mean the Trade Fair Palace. A large collection of modern and contemporary art—including work by Vincent van Gogh, Gustav Klimt, Alfons Mucha, Claude Monet, and Pablo Picasso—fill the walls and halls of this three-story exhibition space. Contemporary exhibitions often provide context for local life, such as a photography exhibit to mark the anniversary of the 1968 Soviet invasion or painted interpretations of Czech identity and national symbols. The 1920s building was the first example of Functionalist architecture

Prague Off the Beaten Path

Prague's surrounding neighborhoods are full of color and character.

Prague's major sights are worth seeing, but the central neighborhoods can be packed with tourists. A good strategy is to visit the top sights that you can't bear to miss for as long as you can stand the crowds—then head to some of the lesser-known neighborhoods for the more undiscovered vibe that backpackers often associated with Prague of the 1990s and early 2000s. This adventure into fewer English-language menus, signage, and tourist-friendly customer service can give a more authentic picture of local life in Prague when approached with patience, preparation, and respect for the space.

Here's what some of Prague's lesser-known neighborhoods have to offer:

- **Vinohrady:** International, and just baby steps off the tourist path.

- **Žižkov:** Rowdy, and rumored to have the "most bars per capita" of any European district.

- **Karlín:** Sophisticated, and known for its food and wine bars, Karlín also embodies a spirit of revitalization, with repurposed spaces holding markets and entertainment venues.

- **Holešovice:** Industrial and offbeat. Think: Theatrical space in a former slaughterhouse, or crypto-anarchist coffee shop.

in Prague, built for the Prague Sample Trade Fairs that inspired its name. Join families and art fans at the adjoining Café Jedna to relax over coffee, a glass of wine, and some of the best hummus in town.

DOX Center for Contemporary Art

Poupětova 1, +420 295 568 123, www.dox.cz, 10am-6pm Sat-Mon, 11am-7pm Wed and Fri, 11am-pm Thurs, 180 CZK, tram stop Ortenovo náměstí

The mission of DOX Center for Contemporary Art includes using a variety of art forms to "create a space for research, presentation, and debate on important social issues." Thought-provoking exhibitions provide the starting point for panel discussions, film screenings, and interactive community events on topics ranging from big data and migration to the portrayal of war-torn countries. Recent exhibitions include Chinese contemporary artist Ai Weiwei's statement on refugees and human rights. This former 19th-century industrial space was converted to its present-day incarnation in the beginning of the millennium. Come with an open mind and decompress with a post-excursion discussion at the nearby Bitcoin Café. This space embodies a modern Czech sensibility both literally and figuratively—Czechs of all ages aren't shy about talking politics or world events over a beer, and the space shows repurposed spaces and art among industry that characterizes the Holešovice neighborhood.

Bars and Nightlife

"Nightlife" is almost the wrong term to use for Prague's beverage scene, considering a cold beer with lunch or an afternoon drinking in a beer garden is as much a part of life as a night on the town. Hikes and cycling trips include multiple pub stops along the way, and a steaming adult beverage at an outdoor holiday market isn't limited to roped off areas or wristbands. Recreation with a drink in hand is integrated into all hours of daily life.

That prevalence of adult beverages doesn't necessarily translate to a rowdy, shouty landscape. Prague overall has more of a mellow pub culture than a massive club scene (but there are definitely places to dance if desired). Most wine, beer, and cocktail bars apart from the dance clubs stick to table service all night, as opposed to mingling around a bar and communicating directly with a bartender. Budget 30 CZK-65 CZK for a domestic beer, depending on the neighborhood, and 50-100 CZK for craft beer and imported microbrews. A glass of wine can vary from 35-150 CZK, and specialty cocktails generally fall into the 150-300 CZK range.

Servers often keep a tally of the drinks on a piece of paper at your table in a traditional pub or an automated system in other venues. Separate checks are expected, but it is the responsibility of the patrons to remember what they had and tell the server which food or drinks they want to pay for at the end of the night—something to note if you're the last one of your group to pay the bill! Credit cards are accepted in maybe 65 percent of venues, but many systems don't allow tips on cards, so carrying cash in the local currency is always a good backup plan. Euros may be accepted in some touristy pubs around the center, but usually at an abysmal exchange rate.

The pub scene starts in the early evening around 4-7pm. Many venues and restaurants then transition from dinner to late night drinks without much change to the atmosphere. A recent smoking ban has also put more patrons on the sidewalks in front of pubs and clubs, so noise ordinances in residential areas usually limit these hours to 11pm or midnight.

Dance clubs may ask for ID to get in the door, and non-EU residents often have to show their passport (not just a copy). Cover charges aren't prevalent, but live music venues may ask for a 50-200 CZK entry fee depending on the entertainment of the evening. Nightlife in Prague is also fairly casual, and people generally don't worry about changing clothes to go from work, school, or the park to the pub.

NIGHTLIFE DISTRICTS

The international crowd is likely to liven up most establishments around the center. **Old Town** dance clubs generally cater to a young crowd of college students, tourists, and international bachelor/bachelorette parties looking to down drinks without being 100 percent sure where they're going to wake up.

The pubs and small clubs lining **Krymská street** in the Vršovice district get a steady stream of business from the large Czech Inn hostel at the top of the hill and the local residents who live in the surrounding area. Lots of pubs spread across the **Žižkov** neighborhood make for a wide array of choices, but aren't consolidated around a single street.

Wine bars in **Karlín** and craft beer pubs in **Vinohrady** allow for conversation over a

Reservations...at the Bar?

Visitors may be surprised to find that local nightlife requires reservations. For a seat in a popular pub or a table at a wine or cocktail bar, channel your inner planner and call ahead with a name, time, and number in your party, or check the venue's website for an online reservation system. It is possible to bounce from bar to bar, but be prepared for about 50 percent of the places you try to have no seats available. Standing at the bar or in the aisles of a pub isn't generally done. But don't worry—this doesn't mean you have to spend your whole night sitting at a table. Music venues such as Cross Club, Cobra, Nebe, or Lucerna Music Bar, or alternative spaces such as Kasárna Karlín or Klub Vzorkovna, plus any of the city's beer gardens are your best chances to interact with younger locals and meet fellow international visitors.

quality beverage, while the music venues of **Holešovice**, from DJs and concerts at Sasazu to hip-hop and electronic music at Cross Club, attract an eclectic crowd.

Try a mini-pub crawl from **Letná** beer garden to Café Letka to Bio Oko's cinema bar, ending with a cocktail at Cobra to experience the walkable diversity of this neighborhood's nightlife scene.

PUBS
Old Town
(Staré Město)
★ SKAUTSKY INSTITUTE
Staroměstské náměstí 4, +420 732 947 509, www.skautskyinstitut.cz, 9am-10pm Mon to Fri, 10am-6pm Sat and Sun

Skautsky Institute is a peaceful escape from Old Town crowds. The laid-back space, run by young adult members of Prague's local Boy and Girl Scouts organization, extends from the light-filled interior with minimalist wooden furniture to the wrap-around balcony in the quiet center of the building. Coffee, craft beer on draft, and light snacks are surprisingly budget-friendly for Old Town Square. This secret hideout is popular with students and location-independent workers.

T-ANKER
Náměstí Republiky 8, +420 722 445 474, www.t-anker.cz, 11am-10pm

For a nostalgic trip through Prague's modern history, take the escalators through the 1970s Kotva Shopping Center up to the modern crowd enjoying a rooftop beer at T-Anker. Nine rotating taps and a full menu keep local office workers and international visitors coming back to this lookout on the eastern edge between Old and New Towns for lunch and after-work drinks. Elevator access direct to the pub is available on the left-hand side when facing the building.

New Town
(Nové Město)
U PINKASŮ
Jungmannovo náměstí 16, +420 221 111 152, www.upinkasu.com, 10am-11:30pm

Bartenders have kept the regulars of U Pinkasu supplied with foam-topped pints of Pilsner—well, technically half-liters—since the mid 1800s. The pub has expanded over the decades, along with the crowds, into multiple floors of arched ceilings and wooden pub furniture. Try the afternoon for a coveted seat in the Gothic Summer Beer Garden between the stone walls. Reservations strongly recommended.

KLUB VZORKOVNA
Národní 11, 5pm-3am daily

Klub Vzorkovna, near the National Theater, is easy to spot: Look for the line of young, international students crowding the entrance. This grungy, alternative space is known locally as "the dog bar" after the owner's Irish wolfhound, who often roams the underground maze of rooms. Drinks are prepaid via electronic bracelets loaded with credit when entering (50 CZK minimum) and served in jars. The furniture is movable and an anything-goes environment includes swings, pianos, and a foosball table. Live music is just as likely to be impromptu as a scheduled concert.

Lesser Town (Malá Strana) and Anděl
★ LOKÁL U BÍLÉ KUŽELKY
Míšeňská 12, +420 257 212 014, www.lokal-ubilekuzelky.ambi.cz, 11:30am-midnight Sun-Thurs, 11:30am-1am Fri-Sat

Multiple Lokál locations across the city take a traditional, casual Czech beer hall and give it a trendy, minimalist twist. Reservations are recommended for a seat in the long halls of Lokál U Bílé kuželky just off the Charles Bridge in Malá Strana. The pours of various foam-levels are largely a gimmick, so stick to a full glass of *pivo* (beer) with locally-sourced sausage or marinated cheese as a snack.

KAVÁRNA MLÝNSKÁ
Všehrdova 14, +420 257 313 222, 12pm-midnight

Kavárna Mlýnská on the edge of Park Kampa attracts a mellow, artsy crowd that occasionally includes notorious local artist David Černy. The muraled walls, cozy size, and affordable drinks create a fairly local space, so pull out a few Czech phrases, keep your conversations to a moderate volume, and pay in cash (no cards accepted) to blend in with the crowd.

Prague Castle District
(Hradčany)
STRAHOV MONASTERY BREWERY
Strahovské nádvoří 301, +420 233 353 155, www.klasterni-pivovar.cz, 10am-10pm

From the monks who brought you the gorgeous halls of the Strahov Library comes the centuries-old, but refurbished in this millennium, Strahov Monastery Brewery, known locally as "Klášterní pivovar Strahov." While admittedly a little touristy, the 230-seat restaurant and beer hall serves delicious seasonal brews and Czech food with efficient,

multi-lingual service and plenty of indoor and outdoor seating.

Vinohrady and Vršovice
GASTROPUB 20 PIP
Slezská 1, +420 773 163 394, 5pm-1am

For a broader range of beer choices than your average Czech pub, cross the street behind the Church of St. Ludmila at Náměstí Miru to Gastropub 20 PIP. The 20-plus taps of local and international microbrews that inspired the previous name—20 PIP Craft Beer Pub—expanded in 2018 to include a funky menu of bar snacks ranging from satay skewers and tartare to savory waffle combos and Italian-style *pinsa* (a small oval pizza). The two-story venue with coaster-covered walls has quickly become a local favorite. They do take credit cards, but not reservations, so shoot for early evening to claim your seat.

★ BEER GEEK BAR
Vinohradská 62, +420 776-827-068, www.beergeek.cz, 3pm-2am

Beer Geek Bar was one of the earliest purveyors of microbrew culture in Prague. The 32 rotating taps across the street from Jiřího z Poděbrad square still draw an international crowd of locals and travelers to this mid-sized, underground pub lined with banquette seating in primary colors. Order your beers and snacks (including 11 flavors of chicken wings from an American head chef) at the bar. The bottle shop of the same name two streets away (at Slavíkova 10) stocks a wide selection of souvenirs for the beer lover in your life. Reservations recommended by phone or email at rezervace@beergeek.cz.

Žižkov
PIVO A PÁREK
Bořivojova 58, +420 734 201 195, 2pm-10pm Mon-Fri, 4pm-10pm Sat-Sun

The limited menu of Pivo a Párek is as simple as translating the name "beer and hot dogs." That casual simplicity extends to the chalk-board-menu-and-wooden-table interior of this mid-sized staple. A lively summer beer garden in the inner courtyard has a residential feel in the shadow of the Žižkov TV Tower. If the 10pm closing time is early for your tastes, grab some takeaway bottles from their well-stocked beer fridges or head down the street to Bukowski's Bar for a late night cocktail.

Karlín
PIVOVARSKÝ KLUB
Křižíkova 17, +420 222 315 777,
www.pivovarskyklub.com, 11:30am-11:30pm
In a neighborhood known for wine bars and artsy spaces, Pivovarský klub keeps beer fans in good spirits. The walls of this large, two-story pub and restaurant are lined with a 200+ bottle selection to supplement six taps of local beer. No frills, no gimmicks, just classic Czech pub ambiance.

Letná and Holešovice
CAFÉ LETKA
Letohradská 44, +420 777 444 035,
www.cafeletka.cz, 8am-midnight Mon-Fri,
10am-midnight Sat, 10am-10pm Sun
Prague bars are usually split into two camps: great beer and house wine or impressive wine selection and one decent beer. Café Letka serves the best of both worlds in an intimate setting of distressed wood, pillow-lined windows, and pastel accents. Quality coffee and a breakfast menu brings a morning crowd that blends seamlessly into leisurely lunches and post-work crowds unwinding over adult beverages and late-night snacks. This is a sophisticated alternative to the nearby Letná beer garden. Cash only and weekend reservations recommended.

TOP EXPERIENCE

★ BEER GARDENS
The phrase *Česká pohoda* is one of those tricky, untranslatable ideas, but is basically used to describe enjoying life in good weather. Combine two essential elements of Czech social life—beer and being in nature—and you've got the idea. The opening of beer gardens in nearly every neighborhood is a sure

sign that the season of sunshine has arrived. Each of the city's beer gardens has a distinctive character.

Vyšehrad
HOSPŮDKA NA HRADBÁCH
V Pevnosti 2, +420 734 112 214, 2pm-midnight
Mon-Fri, noon-midnight Sat-Sun, indoor pub open
year-round with garden depending on weather
This beer garden tucked inside the Vyšehrad Complex just behind St. Martin's Rotunda is a laid-back, all-ages space popular among locals. Picnic tables lining the outer edges offer a view of the city if you peek over the hedges. The center area of the two-tiered lawn offers more tables surrounding an open play space, drawing families and the stroller set to enjoy a drink within eyesight of their young ones. Beverage stands along the edges offer a wide selection of beer, wine, cider, and *domácí limonády* (a sparkling soft drink in various fruit and herb flavors), plus grilled meats and snacks. The small indoor pub on site can provide refuge in a rainstorm, but the beer garden is the star of this space.

Vinohrady
REIGROVY SADY
Rieger 28, Prague 2, 120 00, +420 222 717 247,
www.restauraceriegrovysady.cz, noon-midnight
or 2:30am depending on weather and business
The rowdy 1,400-seat beer garden inside Reigrovy Sady park (one of the city's most popular places to watch the sunset) is the largest in the city, enclosed within a fence lined with beverage stands. Entertainment comes from a projection screen showing major sporting matches or live music and DJs on a mini-stage.

Žižkov
ŽIŽKOV BEER GARDEN
Koněvova, +420 774 567 367, 11 am-midnight daily,
usually May-Sept (depending on weather)
Žižkov beer garden, at the base of Vitkov Hill, near the Ohrada bus stop, feels more like an outdoor barbeque or family reunion. Pop music from recent decades blasts from

In Prague, the local custom is to stick to the deliciously simple beer or wine by the glass, or indulge in high-end cocktails heavy on flair and presentation. Ordering a rum and Coke in a traditional Czech pub is likely to get you a shot of rum plus a bottle of cola (charged for both), and maybe a glass of ice to mix them yourself! (If you're looking for cocktails, choose a place specializing in mixology.)

BEER

Beer is the local beverage of choice, and cheaper than water(!) on most menus. A beer in Prague can range from 30 CZK for a half-liter in small neighborhood pubs, rising to around 50 CZK in more touristy areas around the city center or Malá Strana, and up to 75-100 CZK for an imported microbrew. Most locals prefer a foam-topped **Pilsner Urquell,** although the growing microbrewery scene caters to a broadening array of tastes—**Matuška** and **Únětice** are some popular up-and-coming brands.

Homemade lemonades (*domácí limonády*) come in all kinds of flavors.

WINE

Central Europe's climate and geography favors white wines and lighter, fruit-forward reds, with the eastern region of Moravia producing some of the best domestic labels.

Burčák is a sweet young wine similar to Beaujolais nouveau. You won't find it on a lot of wine menu, but it starts to pop up in plastic bottles and wine festivals from around September until the end of November. Warning: this easy-to-drink autumn treat packs a killer headache upon overconsumption.

When the weather turns cold, gloved hands begin to clutch glasses of *svařák,* the local take on mulled wine sold at most Christmas markets and some traditional Czech pubs in winter. *Svařák* is less sweet and more citrusy than traditional mulled wine, and often spiked with Czech rum or brandy.

To satisfy a sweet tooth at Christmas or Easter markets, try a small glass of *medovina,* a sugar-packed honey wine that can be served hot or cold.

SPIRITS

For a taste of local spirits, skip the absinthe and order a throat-burning shot of *slivovice,* a clear plum brandy. Alternatively you could try some *Becherovka,* an herbal liqueur with hints of cinnamon and pine from a distillery in Karlovy Vary, best described with the phrase "it tastes like Christmas." In warmer weather, order it with tonic and a slice of lime to create a "Beton" cocktail.

NON-ALCOHOLIC

Domácí limonády translates literally to "homemade lemonade" but means a freshly mixed, sparkling drink infused with fresh fruit, cucumber, ginger, or mint, to name a few flavors. Prague's rapidly growing **specialty coffee scene** has sparked a generation of baristas who embrace the craft as a passion beyond a profession.

Kasárna Karlín

The Karlín neighborhood is known for food, wine, and being an ideal place to live, but is also a neighborhood in transition: there is construction around the neighborhood, such as the rebuilding of a bridge of railway tracks into shops that will fill the stone arches underneath it. (At the time of writing, they were covered in scaffolding.) **Kasárna Karlín** (Prvního Pluku 2, www.kasarnakarlin.cz, 1pm-11:30pm) Kasárna Karlin, which opened in June 2017, is part of the early generation making the neighborhood an up-and-coming destination. Every corner of the outdoor space, located inside repurposed industrial barracks, is packed with entertainment, with rotating options like a volleyball court, outdoor cinema, view tower, and a metallic unicorn statue in the summer, an ice rink in winter. Open doors offering mini-art galleries, cafes, bars, and live music are tucked into the various doorways surrounding the square, making it easy to drift from one space to the next for a change of scenery. This year-round hot spot attracts an ultra-cool international crowd. Come for a drink, or to catch some unstructured live music performances. (The live music shows are more like seeing a band in a friend's basement than a concert venue—people wander into the room, listen to a song, and then wander back out to the courtyard.)

Kasárna Karlín, former army barracks turned bar and event space

speakers of questionable quality and neighborhood dogs run free in the surrounding grass while local residents sip Staropramen under beach umbrellas. This residential favorite feels endearingly stuck in a previous era and makes for a perfect stop before or after climbing Vitkov Hill to admire the view.

Letná and Holešovice
★ LETNÁ BEER GARDEN
Letenské sady 341, +420 233 378 200, 11 am-midnight daily from May-Sept (depending on weather)
You can tell that Prague summer has begun when the drinks start flowing around Letná Beer Garden, located inside the park of the same name, with arguably the best view in town over the Vltava River and Old Town. Hundreds of international visitors pack the rows of picnic tables along the edge of the hillside park, with dogs and their humans often stopping here for a break on a walk through the park. Carts and stands along the edges serve primarily beer with some

vendors offering cider, wine, and shots of liquor. Available snacks are largely meat-based dishes like grilled sausages. Feel free to bring a deck of cards or entertainment for your group, but no outside food or drink is allowed, so step into the grassy lawn of the surrounding park if you want to bring a picnic or vegetarian snacks.

COCKTAIL BARS
Old Town
(Staré Město)
L'FLEUR
V Kolkovně 5, +420 734 255 665, www.lfleur.cz, 6pm-3am, 175-250 CZK cocktails
Most of Old Town's cocktail bars center around speakeasy style, prohibition, or a bygone era of New York City, complete with suspendered staff and Manhattan prices. L'Fleur, with its stained-glass windows, exposed brick walls, and cozy banquette seating, offers a different twist. The staff are both knowledgeable and refreshingly unpretentious. The cocktail

list takes inspiration from museums and artistic eras, like Art Nouveau-named drinks served in glasses with swirling designs, and the presentation strikes the right balance of cute without falling into kitsch. Try a Thé Vert and Passiflore ("green tea and passionflower") or go for the current featured cocktail usually based around a seasonal fruit of herb. L'Fleur is praised equally for their champagne list alongside their mixology, and an unpublicized food menu is available upon request. Reservations recommended.

CLUB NOD

Dlouhá 33, +420 733 307 600, www.nod.roxy.cz, 2pm-1am Mon-Fri, 4pm-midnight Sat-Sun, 100-130 CZK cocktails

Housed inside a progressive experimental theater, Club NoD serves simple-but-good drinks in a visually stimulating environment of rotating art exhibitions, from photography and paintings to light installations, to explore with your beverage of choice in hand. This café-by-day becomes a pre-and-post-theater bar by night. The mid-sized room of white booths and wood tables is populated with an all-ages crowd discussing the latest gallery exhibit or enjoying a pre-party drink before heading next door to dance at Club Roxy.

New Town
(Nové Město)
ANONYMOUS SHRINK'S OFFICE

Jungmannova 11, +420 608 911 884, 6pm-2am Sun.-Thurs., 6pm-3am Mon.-Fri., 235 CZK cocktails

The ingredients may be a mystery, but that's half the fun of ordering "cocktail therapy" based on a Rorschach test menu at Anonymous Shrink's Office. Settle into a high-backed, brown leather chair in this candlelit, underground brick cave or, if you're looking for private table, and you ask nicely as you enter, the bar staff might show you the spot along the walls to reveal a secret hidden room behind a bookshelf. This newcomer to the Prague cocktail scene attracts young professionals and international travelers, but a doorbell required for entry ensures

that it's never overcrowded. Reservations recommended.

THE FUNKY BEE

Křemencova 8, +420 777 918 916, www.funkybee. cz, 6pm-2am Mon.-Thurs., 6pm-4am Fri-Sat, 6pm-midnight Sun, 100-150 CZK cocktails

If the Funky Bee is quiet enough to strike up a conversation with your bartender, ask them about the cocktail list. There's a good chance that the mixologist in this casually cool, family-owned establishment also helped create some of the signature drinks. Try the Hypno for an interesting blend of vanilla vodka, citrus flavor, and chili spice. The soundtrack in this dimly lit room of black furniture and soft purple lighting delivers on the funky promise of the name. Reservations recommended.

★ GLASS BAR

Jiráskovo Náměstí 6, +420 703 651 330, www. glassbar.cz, 10am-midnight, 125-200 CZK cocktails

To access the 360-degree views from the rooftop of the Dancing House you can: 1) stay at the Dancing House Hotel, 2) pay 100 CZK for terrace access, or 3) order a cocktail (125-200 CZK) or non-alcoholic drink (55-75 CZK) at the Glass Bar with entry included. The cozy, window-lined indoor space on the top floor of this architectural masterpiece offers quiet elegance in the off-season. Summer months bring a livelier vibe to the summer terrace surrounding the twisted metal orb atop the building.

Vinohrady and Vršovice
★ CAFÉ BAR PILOTŮ

Dónská 19, Prague 10, 101 00, +420 739 765 694, 5pm-midnight Mon-Thurs, 5pm-1am Sat-Sun, tram and bus stop Krymská

For craft cocktails and a casual atmosphere, head to Café Bar Pilotu near the top of bar-lined Krymská street in the trendy Vršovice neighborhood. Bookshelves and a grand piano establish a living room vibe hosted by inventive mixologists. The creative cocktail list is inspired by neighboring businesses—think fresh ingredients for a vegetarian restaurant

Local Beer Culture

As one of the oldest brewing cultures around, Czechs take pivo (beer) very seriously, and the country ranks among the highest per-capita consumption rates in the world. A few things you should know:

Pilsner is king. While local microbrews are starting to expand the national palate, don't expect to find stouts, reds, or IPAs outside of select beer pubs. Try a Pilsner Urquell for the classic experience, and if you spot a Svijany sign (my personal favorite beer) outside any neighborhood pubs, duck inside for at least one.

Foam is a sign of freshness. You haven't been shortchanged if the liquid doesn't reach the brim of your glass. A typical pour has a frothy head that leaves rings below the rim with each sip.

Choose your size. When ordering a beer, you'll be asked if you want a large (*velké*), which is a half-liter (almost 17 ounces), or small (*male*) one of 0.3 liters (just over 10 ounces), particularly if you appear to be female.

Nothing says summer in the Czech Republic like a cold beer outdoors.

Practice your toast. The Czech version of "cheers" is *"Na zdraví"* literally meaning "to health" and pronounced roughly as NAH-straw-vee. Emphasizing on the first syllable is important to differentiate it from the Russian *"na zDROvvje"* (being lumped in or confused with other Slavic-speaking countries is a pet peeve among many Czechs). Toasting in a Czech pub is common for the first round. To toast, each person at the table should make eye contact while clinking glasses. Reaching over or under another set of arms is not allowed. Yes, this takes some time for each pair to acknowledge everyone else—it's a ritual that highlights the personal connection of sharing a beverage.

Drink to your health. If you share a *pivo* with a local, you might be surprised to hear people describe it as "healthy." Many Czechs like to tout the level of vitamins in their favorite beverage and will counter any health-conscious criticisms by pointing out the amount of sugar in most non-alcoholic options.

Take your time. Prague is not a binge-drinking city, and you won't win any points for chugging in record time. In fact, many young people find it strange that the losers in American drinking games are punished with sips. In true Czech style, beer is to be enjoyed, savored, and revered all day long over lunch, dinner, and evenings with friends.

or an everything-on-the-shelves approach for the convenience shop.

Žižkov
BUKOWSKI'S BAR
Bořijovova 86, +420 773 445 280, 7pm-3am, 90-150 CZK cocktails

Bukowski's Bar is cool for all the same reasons as the Žižkov neighborhood. It's affordable, comfortable, non-judgmental, a little grungy,

and always up for a party. The friendly staff at this long-standing, all-ages, local favorite know their way around the bar. Dim lighting and a candle-lined bookshelf covering one wall set a homey atmosphere to the multi-room venue, with conversations varying from intimate whispers to slurred debates from table to table.

1 a beer garden with a view at Letná Park 2 try the Hypno martini for a cocktail with a kick at the Funky Bee 3 thirty-two microbrews on tap at Beer Geek

OBLACA BAR

Mahlerovy sady 1, +420 210 320 086, www.towerpark.cz, 7pm-3am, 250 CZK cocktails

For a more upscale experience, try a cocktail with a panoramic view at Oblaca Bar inside the Žižkov TV Tower. The unofficial dress code in this sophisticated crowd is fashion forward, and you'll need to check in with a hostess on the ground floor to be allowed access to the elevator. Reservations required, especially on weekends or during peak seasons.

Letná and Holešovice

COBRA

Milady Horákové 8, +420 778 470 515, www.barcobra.cz, 8am-2am Mon-Fri, 10am-2am Sat, 10am-midnight Sun, 50-150 CZK glass of wine

The bar staff at Cobra like to get creative so investigate the latest specialty cocktail list. This trendy, minimalist environment of exposed lightbulbs and bar stool seating includes a rotating set of DJs from Thursday-Saturday nights. Take note of the address or look for the small door sign of this otherwise unmarked and easy-to-miss venue.

CLUBS AND LIVE MUSIC

Dance clubs start to fill up around 10pm and "last call" is generally up to the venue with no legally required closing times.

Old Town

(Staré Město)

CLUB ROXY

Dlouhá 33, +420 608 060 745, www.nod.roxy.cz, 10pm-5am, 90-140 CZK cocktails

Club Roxy has been packing the dance floor since 1992 for as long as the independent Czech Republic has existed. The underground, Art Deco concert space hosts an international lineup of electronic music, hip hop and rock shows that draw a mixed crowd on any given night of the week. Tickets and cover charges vary so browse the lineup to see what's on during your stay.

New Town

(Nové Město)

NEBE

Křemencova 1, +420 608 644 784, www.nebepraha. cz, 6pm-3am Tues, 6pm-4am Wed-Thurs, 6pm-5am Fri-Sat, 100-125 CZK cocktails

For a dressed-up night of drinking and dancing, head to any of Nebe's three locations across Náměstí Republiky, Václavské náměstí, and Karlovo náměstí. The underground club near Karlovo náměstí attracts a young, lively bunch bouncing to current Top 40 hits well into the pre-dawn hours. Reservations recommended for early evening cocktails or a table to call home base.

★ LUCERNA MUSIC BAR

Vodičkova 36, +420 224 217 108, www.musicbar.cz, 100 CZK cocktails

Friday and Saturday nights at Lucerna Music Bar flash back to the tunes from the 1980s and '90s—decades that Communist Czechoslovakia only partially got to experience. The crowd at this massive dance hall spans decades, but every one of them can pull out the moves to "(I've Had the) Time of My Life" and "Greased Lightning" on cue when these crowd favorites hit the speakers. Weekdays offer an international live music lineup of slightly more current artists. Hours vary per event, but the box office is open for questions from 9am to 7pm on weekdays.

Lesser Town (Malá Strana) and Anděl

U MALÉHO GLENA

Karmelitská 23, +420 257 531 717, www.malyglen.cz, 7:30pm-2am, 200 CZK cover charge downstairs

The intimate underground jazz club at U Malého Glena draws a packed house nearly every night of the week for live music on a small stage, so reservations are recommended. The main floor restaurant above the performance area offers a menu of Tex-Mex, Czech classics, American burgers, and vegetarian

LGBTQ+ Prague

Prague's live-and-let-live attitude ranges from tolerance to celebration for the gay community, with a popular Pride parade each summer and a Mezipatra film festival each fall, but is less accepting towards the trans community. The overall landscape is generally safe for LGBTQ+ residents to enter any pub, dance in any nightclub, or hold hands while walking down the streets, but a romantic advance towards another patron outside of a designated gay club may not be well received. **Prague Pride** (www.praguepride.cz) keeps a list of recommended hotels and bars where visitors should be welcomed with open arms.

Prague's gay club scene has historically centered around the Vinohrady neighborhood but has expanded into multiple neighborhoods.

- The small, neon-lit dance floor at Vinohrady's **Termix** (Třebízského 4a, +420 222 710 462, www.club-termix.cz, 10pm-6am Wed-Sat) is generally packed with young men dancing to Top 40 hits, while the bar just a few streets away, **Termax** (Vinohradská 40, +420 222 710 462, www.club-max.cz, 10pm-7am Fri-Sat) claims the title of Prague's largest gay bar.

- **Freedom Night** parties (www.freedomnight.cz) cater to a lesbian crowd with monthly DJ dance parties around Prague every third Friday, plus additional events in Brno, Pilsen, and Bratislava, Slovakia. The Prague party is often hosted at **PM Club** (Trojická 10, +420 222 518 097, www.pmclub.net, 4pm-4am daily) near the Vltava River and the base of Vyšehrad hill.

- For a quieter vibe during daylight hours, head to **Q Cafe** (Opatovická 12, +420 776 856 361, www.q-cafe.cz, 1pm-2am daily) for a relaxing atmosphere with subtle rainbow-themed touches around the bar and bench seating. This New Town location near Karlovo náměstí welcomes a mixed crowd of the LGBTQ+ community and allies. Their website also provides an up-to-date database of "Where to Go" for LGBTQ-friendly dining, dancing, shopping, accommodation, and wellness experiences across the country.

options, also available downstairs, so come early for dinner to get a great seat for the 9pm nightly shows.

JAZZ BOAT

Přístaviště Čechův most, nástupiště č. 5, +420 731 183 180, www.jazzboat.cz, 7:30pm-2am, 700-900 CZK cover charge

For live music with a little more room to move, head to the dock under the Čechův Bridge. Jazz Boat is a floating venue that spans styles from traditional, modern, and Latin jazz to swing, blues and funk. Reserve a table for two, four, six, or eight people with dinner and drinks available on board—one welcome drink is included in the cover charge. Jazz Boat boards from 8-8:30pm and spend two-and-a-half hours cruising the Vltava River before docking at 11pm. Student tickets (400 CZK) are available for remaining spaces five minutes before departure.

Vinohrady
RADOST FX

Bělehradská 120, +420 224 254 776, www.radostfx. cz, 11pm-5am Thurs-Sat, 100-150 CZK cocktails

A late-night party at Radost FX can keep the dance floor packed until 5am on a good night. The mid-sized dance floor with partitioned areas of lounge seating around it and intricate lighting set an atmosphere of casual elegance. Rihanna's video for "Please Don't Stop the Music," shot here in 2007, will give you a stylized glimpse inside. Thursdays are a hip hop party, Fridays nights spin house or electronic beats, and Saturdays blast R&B and trap to keep the crowds energized.

Letná and Holešovice
CROSS CLUB

Plynární 23, +420 736 535 010, www.crossclub.cz, 6pm-5am Sun-Thurs, 6pm-7am Fri-Sat, around 100 CZK cocktails

The steampunk decor of mechanical sculpture

and moving gears make **Cross Club** easy to spot on the streets of Holešovice. Two stages of hip hop, dubstep, drum and bass, and electronic music draw a rowdy crowd until all hours. Weekends often come with a cover charge around 100 CZK.

Performing Arts

With glamorous interiors, affordable prices, and a rich history of classical music, there's good reason that Prague is ranked one of Europe's top cultural and creative destinations.

CLASSICAL MUSIC

MUNICIPAL HOUSE

Náměstí Republiky 5, www.obecnidum.cz, 500-1,500 CZK tickets depending on event, tram or metro stop Náměstí Republiky

Smetana Hall inside the Municipal House has the honor of opening the Prague Spring concert each year with a performance of its namesake's symphony *Má vlast* ("My Country"). Gorgeous murals encircle the domed ceiling of this home to the Prague Symphony Orchestra (FOK). More than 1,250 seats line the floor and surrounding balconies, with fantastic acoustics no matter which you choose. The smaller 300-seat **Sladkovsky Hall** and 150-seat **Gregr Hall** provide more intimate settings for chamber concerts.

RUDOLFINUM

Alšovo nábřeží 12, +420 227 059 227, www.rudolfinum.cz, Box Office Sept-June 10am-6pm Mon-Fri, July-August 10am-3pm Mon-Fri, 300-3,000 CZK tickets depending on event, tram or metro stop Staroměstská

There are two concert halls housed inside the Rudolfinum—the stately Dvořák Hall, named for the renowned composer Antonin Dvořák, who conducted the first Czech Philharmonic concert in 1896, and the smaller chandeliered ceiling of the Suk Hall, added during the 1940s renovations. This home of the Czech Philharmonic also hosts concerts by the Prague Symphony Orchestra (FOK), Prague Philharmonia (PKF), smaller chamber ensembles, and visiting musicians during the Prague Spring Festival.

THEATER, DANCE, AND OPERA

★ NATIONAL THEATER

Národní 2, +420 224 901 448, www.narodni-divadlo.cz, 100-1,500 CZK tickets depending on event, tram stop Národní divadlo or metro stop Národní třída

You can spot the golden-crowned rooftop of the National Theater from almost any point along the Vltava River. This queen of the cultural scene was built in the late 1800s, along with the National Museum, as part of the Czech National Revival—a movement that focused on reclaiming the Czech language and cultural identity from the creeping influences of the surrounding empires. Inside the columned walls of this Renaissance Revival building, the rows of plush red seats, painted ceiling, and golden detailed opera boxes create an aura of pure elegance. Get your tickets for ballet, opera, and theater performances online or at the box office next door, inside the New Stage.

NEW STAGE (Nová scéna)

Národní 4, +420 224 901 448, www.narodni-divadlo.cz, 250-700 CZK tickets depending on event, tram stop Národní divadlo or metro stop Národní třída

The beehive-like glass building beside Prague's National Theater is the New Stage. A little more experimental than its stately neighbor, this theater started as the home of circus arts troupe Laterna Magika before both were adopted by the National Theater

---

1 Cross Club's steampunk exterior 2 National Theater (Národní divadlo)

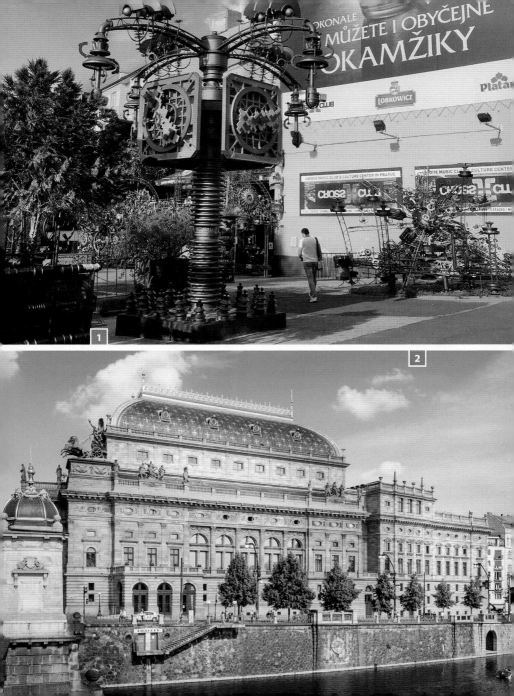

Dressing for a Night at the Theater

When it comes to fashion in the Czech Republic, a sense of appropriateness often trumps being trendy. At theaters and concert halls, tourists won't be turned away for wearing jeans or shorts, but they're definitely likely to get a few sideways glances. Instead, aim for wedding-appropriate attire when visiting the ornate halls of the national theaters and concert venues. Cocktail dresses and a suit and tie (at least a collared shirt or unwrinkled top and trousers) are a safe bet. Opening nights and premieres may even inspire floor-length gowns and tuxedos among some regular theater-goers. The more avant-garde theaters (e.g. Nova Scena or Jatka 78) can be a little more casual, but overall a night of entertainment is treated with a sense of reverence.

Now, this doesn't mean that Czech theaters are elitist environments. On the contrary, Prague is one of the most affordable European capitals to take in a show. Enjoyment and appreciation for fine arts is an ingrained element of Czech culture—this is, after all, a country that elected a playwright as their first president. Dressing up is simply a sign of respect, so throw a special occasion outfit into your suitcase to complement the beauty of your theatrical surroundings.

in 2010. Today the stage is shared between dance, drama, and circus performances in a modern, intimate setting. Young artistic types and audience members congregate at the casual (and Wi-Fi-free) Café Nona on the second floor. Stop by Václav Havel Square, the courtyard between the New Stage and National Theater, to see the glowing red heart memorial and signature of the first Czech president—appropriately surrounded by performance spaces as a former playwright himself.

ESTATES THEATER
(Stavovské divadlo)

Železná, +420 224 901 448, www.narodni-divadlo. cz, 100-2,000 CZK tickets depending on event, metro stop Můstek

Don't let anyone convince you that the cloaked statue outside of the Estates Theatre is connected to a *Harry Potter* dementor or to Emperor Palpatine from *Star Wars*. It actually represents the premiere of Mozart's opera *Don Giovanni* inside this Neoclassical 18th-century building in 1787. The Estates Theater was also the first place that the Czech national anthem, "Where is My Home?" was sung in 1843—marked by a plaque on the wall to the right of the main entrance. Today, the luxurious pale blue and gold interior hosts a full program of ballet, theater, and opera.

JATKA 78

Bubenské nábřeží 306, +420 773 217 127, www.jatka78.cz, 10am-12am Mon-Fri, 9am-12am Sat, 100-550 CZK tickets depending on event, tram stop Pražská tržnice or metro stop Vltavská

Jatka 78 takes its playful name from the building's former life as a slaughterhouse. This gritty, multi-use performance space with an emphasis on circus performances opened its doors in 2015 inside the grounds of Holešovice's Prague City Market (Pražská tržnice). The artfully curated warehouse now houses resident arts companies, plus a bar and bistro.

JÁRA CIMRMAN THEATER
(Žižkovské divadlo Járy Cimrmana)

Štítného 5, +420 222 781 860 or +420 222 783 260, www.zdjc.cz, cimrmanenglishstudio@gmail.com, 200-350 CZK tickets, tram stops Husinecká or Tachovské náměstí

Czech-language plays have traditionally been inaccessible for an English-speaking audience. Fortunately, a small group of drama lovers took on the challenge of translating the country's most beloved fictional character in 2014. The Cimrman English Theatre company performs comedic shows of the Czech's most interesting man in the world. Czech-language versions of Jara Cimrman's antics—named "the Greatest Czech" in a 2005 national poll—have been gracing this stage since 1967.

Festivals and Events

NEW YEAR'S EVE
(Silvestr)

The local name for New Year's Eve, "Silvestr," takes its name from the Czech saints' days calendar (which can be found on the lower clock face of the Astronomical Clock in Old Town Square). Fireworks are the centerpiece of the party, and not just the official kind—teenagers and young adults shoot bottle rockets at each other in the main squares, turning them into a bit of a war zone. Tons of bars and restaurants across the city, especially those lining the **Vltava River**, put on their own unofficial fireworks shows at midnight on December 31 (bundle up and head to **Letná Park** for a great view). The city of Prague postpones its official show until the early evening of January 1, making it accessible to families with young children, and also marking the anniversary of the Czech Republic's independent split from Slovakia on January 1, 1993.

ČARODEJNICE
("Witches Day")

April 30 is a family-friendly event marking the end of winter in the Czech Republic. Many of Prague's parks, particularly **Ladronka Park** just west of the Anděl neighborhood, prepare bonfires topped with a wooden figure dressed in witch's clothing. Many local children attending the celebrations also don their pointed black hats and cloaks as part of the fun. From around noon to early evening, the area around the fires entertain the crowds with beer stands, grilled sausages, and free concert stages of local Czech bands. Around sundown everyone circles around the witch to watch the pile go up in flames and bid farewell to the cold months of winter.

PRAGUE SPRING
(Pražské jaro)

The Prague Spring International Music Festival (www.festival.cz) centers around a number of significant dates. It began in 1946 to celebrate one peaceful year since the end of WWII. A performance of Bedřich Smetana's "Má vlast" (My Country) kicks things off in the **Municipal House's Smetana Hall** every year on the anniversary of the composer's May 12 passing. The following three weeks fill Prague's concert halls, from the **Rudolfinum** to the **National Theater**, with international symphony orchestras and up-and-coming young musicians competing for prizes. Tickets (200-2,000 CZK depending on the the show) for this late spring festival generally go on sale around Christmas the year before, so feel free to book early and up the anticipation factor for your trip.

PRAGUE FRINGE FESTIVAL

Fans of avant-garde theater, comedy, and cabaret should think about a trip in late May or early June to catch the Prague Fringe Festival (www.praguefringe.com). This English-language festival takes over the Malá Strana neighborhood for nine days of comedy, cabaret. music, dance, and theater. Performers come from England, America, Australia, and all across Europe to play in various spaces from traditional theaters to cafes and cave-like cellars. The shows (150-200 CZK) are roughly an hour long with family-friendly content in the afternoon and adults-only entertainment stretching into the evenings. Inspired by the Edinburgh Fringe, the Prague version is an intimate event where audiences and artists mingle until all hours at the bar of **Malostranská beseda** (Malostranské náměstí 21, +420 257 409 112, www.malostranska-beseda.cz) after the program finishes.

Czech Holiday Traditions

In addition to festive markets that pop up around the city, Christmas and Easter are commemorated with some noteworthy local traditions.

EASTER

For a largely non-religious country, Easter (Velikonoce in Czech, which comes from "velká noc" meaning "great night") is a really big deal, with festive markets popping up around town. Many of the local traditions have roots in paganism rather than Christianity so the holiday often feels more like a celebration of spring.

Easter in Prague is also accompanied by an unusual tradition. On Easter Monday (not Sunday) before noon, boys and men take braided, ribbon-covered whips made from young saplings and visit the women in their lives. They knock on their neighbors' doors and sing "Hody, hody doprovody, dejte vejce malovaný, nedáte-li malovaný, dejte aspoň bílý, slepička vám snese jiný..." which means roughly "Give me a painted egg, or at least a plain one. The hen will give you another."

The boys then (gently) whip the women to ensure beauty, health, and fertility for the next year, and are rewarded with eggs, chocolate, or a shot of liquor for teens and fathers. The rules vary slightly between regions, but some also dictate that guys visiting after noon will be greeted with a bucket of water in the face rather than a reward.

While this tradition makes my feminist blood boil a bit (along with some Czech female friends), I am assured by other locals that the intention is light-hearted and nostalgic. You're unlikely to witness the tradition in the city center, but might spot groups of young men with their decorated sticks on some of the outer neighborhood streets or day trip towns.

CHRISTMAS

Prague's Christmas season kicks off on **December 5**, which is the name day for **St. Mikuláš** (the Czech version of St. Nicholas). You might spot the costumed saint, accompanied by an angel and a devil, hanging around Prague's streets or shopping malls. In more residential neighborhoods, the trio goes door to door visiting children. Czech kids sing a song or recite a poem to show they've behaved and are rewarded with candy. The devil comes along to see if naughty children show fear (because good kids should have nothing to hide).

Another staple of Prague's street corners around Christmas, visible from about mid-December through the 24th, are fishmongers with mini-swimming pools of carp. These fish, breaded and fried, serve as the main course of a traditional Czech Christmas dinner, celebrated on the evening of December 24. Some families bring the fish home to live in the bathtub until the big day, while others have the fishmonger do the scaling and beheading right there on the corner (so watch your step in the messy sidewalks around these stands).

KARLOVY VARY INTERNATIONAL FILM FESTIVAL

The Karlovy Vary International Film Festival (www.kviff.com) has brought the international film community to this small Czech spa town since 1946. The festival runs from morning to night for eight days in late June or early July. Roughly 200 feature-length and short films from around the world grace the screens in venues around town. Tickets range from 80 CZK for a single show to passes for one day (250 CZK), three days (600 CZK), five days (850 CZK), and the whole festival (1,200 CZK). A handful of Hollywood celebrities are always in attendance, and hotels start to book up a few months in advance.

PRAGUE SIGNAL FESTIVAL

The Czech Republic's largest cultural event takes place on the streets of Prague for one long weekend (usually Thursday-Sunday) each October. Signal Festival (www.signalfestival.com) brings millions of visitors to witness the light installations and video mapping shows projected onto some of Prague's architectural beauties around the city. Vendors offering hot wine, beer, and snacks surround the most popular venues. Most of the exhibitions are free to enjoy with a mobile app leading foot traffic through the various sites across **Vinohrady, New Town, Old Town,** and **Malá Strana**. Some interactive events require a small admission price (50-100 CZK). The video mapping on the Cathedral of St. Ludmila at **Náměstí Míru** is always a crowd favorite, repeating between 7pm and midnight throughout the night.

ST. MARTIN'S DAY

The legend of St. Martin has historical roots, but the local wine and dining traditions have only developed in recent decades. According to the story, St. Martin rides into town on a white horse every **November 11** (his name day) and is meant to bring with him the first snow of the season. Winemakers and sommeliers across the country also pay close attention to the time—at 11:11am on November 11 they open and pour the first taste of that year's Svatomartinské young wine, which is on the sweet side. Almost every **Czech restaurant** in town offers a special menu of the St. Martin's meal: roast goose served with red cabbage and dumplings (usually 150-500 CZK depending on the venue).

Recreation and Activities

Being in nature is a national Czech pastime. Whenever the weather is nice (and sometimes even when it isn't), a significant portion of Prague clears out of the city to spend time amongst the trees.

PARKS
Lesser Town
(Malá Strana)
WALLENSTEIN GARDENS
(Valdštejnská zahrada)

Letenská 4, +420 257 075 707, www.senat.cz, April-May and Oct 7:30am-6pm Mon-Fri, 10am-6pm Sat-Sun; June-Sept 7:30am-7pm Mon-Fri, 10am-7pm Sat-Sun, closed Nov-Feb, free, tram or metro stop: Malostranská

Reasons to visit the manicured, Baroque-style **Wallenstein Gardens**: free-roaming peacocks, a peaceful carp-filled pond, a wall of gargoyle-like faces in a stalactite rock wall, an aviary of owls, outdoor summer evening concerts, the frescoed ceiling of Greek/ Roman gods and Trojan War scenes in the Sala Pavilion, and a quiet respite from Malá Strana's busy streets. The tall hedges lining the paths provide a labyrinth-like atmosphere between the pond and fountain at one end of this secluded garden and the open courtyard and bench seating at the other. Do be on your best behavior—the buildings surrounding these gardens also house today's government officials of the Czech Senate. The entrance is tucked back from the street on the left side when facing the Malostranská metro station.

Petřín
PETŘÍN PARK AND GARDENS
(Petřínské sady)

You could easily get lost for an afternoon among the curving pathways throughout this park that stretches across roughly 20 acres (8 hectare) of land. Start with a visit to the rose gardens surrounding the base of the Petřín Lookout Tower. Heading downhill, you'll pass a statue of Czech poet Karel Hynek Mácha, who wrote the locally famous poem "Maj" ("May"). Couples come to share a kiss in his presence (preferably under a birch or cherry tree) on the first of May, the day on which Czechs celebrate love, but with way less pressure or commercialization than Valentine's Day. The quiet Kinsky gardens cover the southern area of the park, divided by a castle fortification known as the Hunger Wall. This fortification was commissioned by Charles IV in the mid-14th century and named for the jobs providing an income to poor communities of the time.

Vinohrady
REIGROVY PARK
(Reigrovy sady)

One of the most popular places to watch the sunset is the great lawn of **Reigrovy Sady** alongside nature-loving folks and couples cuddling on blankets. The distant view of the Prague Castle over iconic red rooftops in Malá Strana sets a peaceful scene, punctuated by occasional cheers or groans from sports fans watching the projection screen at the nearby 1,400-seat Reigrovy Sady Beer Garden. The enclosed outdoor pub in the park also hosts live music and DJs. Puppies and their human companions frequent the surrounding paths, which stretch from the main train station (*hlavní nádraží*) uphill towards Jiřího z Poděbrad Square.

HAVLÍČKOVY PARK
AND VINEYARDS
(Havlíčkovy sady)

You might hear **Havlíčkovy sady**, the name of the park, and **Grébovka**, the internal vineyards, used interchangeably to describe this hilly green area on the southern edge of Vinohrady. The Stone Grotto's curved walls, arched doorways, and sculpted fountain are a photographer's dream. The summer and autumn months bring a variety of wine festivals to the grounds, and the **Viniční Altán** gazebo wine bar and **Pavilon Grébovka** restaurant (Havlíčkovy sady 2188, Prague 2, 120 00, +420 725 000 334, www.vinicni-altan.cz, 10am-10pm daily, 60-100 CZK glass wine, tram and bus stop Krymská) pours drinks all year long. This area offers a relaxing, sophisticated alternative to the rowdy Reigrovy Sady beer garden or urban square of Jiřího z Poděbrad.

Letná and Holešovice
LETNÁ PARK
(Letenské sady)

Letenské sady, www.letenskyzamecek.cz,
beer garden 11am-11pm, tram stops Čechův most,
Letenské náměstí, or Strossmayerovo náměstí

The main draw for many of Letná Park's visitors is one of the city's largest beer gardens overlooking the Vltava River and the rooftops of Old Town. Outside of those imbibing around the rows of picnic benches, local residents come to the park to walk their dogs, admire the blooming flower beds, or tie a slackline between two trees and spend an afternoon testing their balance. Entrance to the park is possible via an uphill hike from the Vltava River banks near the Čechův most tram stop, or a more leisurely walk from the opposite side of the park around tram stops Letenské náměstí or Strossmayerovo náměstí.

CYCLING

If you're okay with the bumps of some cobblestone streets, cycling can be a fun way to get around Prague.

Bike Tours and Rentals
PRAHA BIKE

Dlouha 24, +420 732 388 880, www.prahabike.cz,
Mar 15th-Oct 15th 9am-8pm, Oct 16th-Mar 14th
10am-5pm

You can get an overview of the city with Praha Bike offering tours around the Prague Castle, the Vyšehrad Complex, beer gardens, or panoramic viewpoints (650-1250 CZK) or just rent a bike (220 CZK for two hours) and explore on your own.

Bike Sharing
REKOLA

www.rekola.cz

You'll also find pink ridesharing Rekola (www.rekola.cz) bikes around the city. These are available for rent by downloading a mobile app. Don't worry if the first two screens ask for your email and password in Czech—you can set the default language to English as soon as

Cats and Dogs

The Czech Republic is a dog-loving country with one of the highest canine ownership rates in all of Europe. Don't be surprised to see these furry companions on public transport (with a muzzle), in pubs and restaurants, or with their ears flopping in the wind while racing across Prague's many parks. Czech dogs are well trained and owners are very responsible for their pets' behavior and pretty good about cleaning up their poo on the sidewalks.

But what about the cat lovers? Prague has experienced a surge in cat cafes, creating feline-friendly spaces in almost every neighborhood.

Cuddle up with some coffee and kittens.

CAT CAFES

Prague's first cat café, **Kockafe Freya** (Bořivojova 43, +420 222 722 959, www.kocicikavarnapraha.cz, 11am-8pm) opened in Žižkov in October of 2014. Seven furry friends cuddle with customers while they enjoy cakes, coffee, and wine. This cozy space fills up fast, so reservations are recommended.

Karlín's **Kavárna Kočiči** (Křižíkova 22, +420 223 008 284 www.kavarnakocici.cz, Sun-Thurs 11am-8pm, Fri-Sat 11am-9pm) spreads comfy sofas and wooden tables over two floors for their nine feline residents to roam. Coffee, quiches, soups and cakes with strong WiFi keep the crowd of digital nomads and curious visitors in their seats for hours. Payment includes a 20 CZK "cat cover charge" per person.

At **Social Point Cat Café Prague** (Gorazdova 20, +420 774 301 394, www.catcafeprague.com, 10am-8pm), just behind the Dancing House in New Town, visitors pay 120 CZK for the first hour and 1 CZK per additional hour for unlimited access to self-serve coffee, tea, light snacks, and multiple rooms of sofas, board games, video games—and the company of cats, of course.

If someone in your travel group has allergies, or you love cat-themed decor but want to eat and drink in peace, there are options for you, too. Letná's **Creperie U slepé Kočičky** (Milady Horákové 38, +420 233 371 855 www.slepakocicka.cz, 11am-11pm daily) is decked out in adorably kitschy cat style and serves sweet and savory crepes (75-175 CZK), and the Old Town pub **U Dvou Koček** (Uhelný trh 10, +420 224 229 982, www.udvoukocek.cz, 11am-11pm daily) is a beer and cat lover's paradise serving traditional Czech cuisine (100-300 CZK entrees).

you're registered. The first fifteen minutes are free and then users are charged 24 CZK per hour using a credit card.

SPECTATOR SPORTS

Many Czechs are more likely to play a sport themselves than to spend much time watching them. Lots of adults participate in organized leagues for ice hockey, floorball, soccer, and other active hobbies (with the requisite meeting in the pub afterwards). However, when it comes to national and international championships or intercity rivalries, there are a few local sports that result in locals donning jerseys and hitting the streets.

Ice Hockey

Ice hockey is a top contender for the most popular national sport. Jaromír Jágr of NHL fame is a national hero, despite leaving the Czech Republic to play across the pond. Every pub in town will have multiple screens devoted to matches during the Winter Olympics or the World Hockey Championships in May—Czechs broke IHF attendance records with more than 11,000 fans per game when they hosted these championships in 2015.

Prague's two main teams are **HC Sparta Praha** (www.hcsparta.cz) and **HC Slavia Praha** (www.hc-slavia.cz), who play in the **Tipsport Arena** (Za Elektrárnou 419/1, +420 266 727 411, http://tipsportarena-praha.cz, tickets around 100-300 CZK) in Holešovice or the **O2 Arena** (Českomoravská 2345/17, +420 266 771 351 www.o2arena.cz, tickets around 100-300 CZK) east of the city center.

Football

On the world stage where "football" means soccer, you'll know when the two biggest rivals in Prague are playing. Fans of **SK Slavia Praha** (www.slavia.cz) and **AC Sparta Prague** (www.sparta.cz) often get a police escort to march through the city, before the match. Slavia's home stadium is the **Sinobo Stadium** (U Slavie 1540/2a, +420 725 875 438, www.slavia.cz, tickets cost 200-1,000 CZK) formerly known as Eden Arena, in Vršovice while AC Sparta calls Letná's **Generali Arena** (Milady Horakove 1066/98, +420 296 111 400, https://sparta.cz/cs, tickets cost about 170-500 CZK) their home base. Rivalry games are a rowdy, beer-fueled glimpse into local fandom from an otherwise fairly subdued national character.

ESCAPE GAMES

LOST ROOMS

Opatovická 18, +420 777 434 533, www.lostrooms.cz, 10am-9pm, 850-1500 CZK per team

You might get lost just trying to find the second-floor entrance to New Town's Lost Rooms and maybe that's part of the challenge. Their nine different scenarios spread across three locations include a portal to another universe, a prison break, and a haunted school. Grab a team of 2-5 players to escape in under an hour.

GETAWAY PRAGUE

Blanická 9, +420 776 084 796, www.gtwy.cz, Mon-Fri 11am-10pm, Sat-Sun 11am-11pm, 1,000-1,200 CZK per team

Getaway Prague, near the square at Náměstí Miru, provides a historic vibe of being locked up in a historic prison or investigating a crime scene. Celebrate your escape in under an hour over craft beers at the nearby 20 PIP Gastropub.

EXIT GAME RUNAWAY

Parléřova 7, +420 602 666 668, www.runaway.cz, 9am-7pm, 1,200-1,400 CZK per team

The scenarios at Exit Game RunAway cross borders and decades, with themes from Christopher Columbus to Al Capone, Alchemy to an Escape from Guantanamo Bay. The multi-room challenges in this space near the Strahov Monastery Brewery will test the minds and imaginations of teams from 2-4 players.

Shopping

The retail landscape is not necessarily Prague's man attraction, but there are a few places worth heading if you're looking for retail therapy or a souvenir.

SHOPPING DISTRICTS

Prague's one well-known shopping destination is **Pařížská ulice** (www.parizskastreet.cz) which fittingly translates to "Parisian street," where the most famous names in luxury fashion line the storefronts. The high-end shopping lane branches off from Old Town Square between St. Nicholas Church and the Tourist Information Center and runs through the Jewish Quarter of Josefov. Pařížská is where the visiting

1 drinking wine in a vineyard at Viniční altán in Grébovka **2** ice hockey is one of the most popular sports **3** take home some Czech gingerbread from Perníčkův sen

Geek Culture in Prague

Historical Prague was all about the kings and castles, but modern day Czech life embraces technology in all its many forms. The city has a thriving startup scene and pockets of the counterculture vibe found among the crowds of its annual Comic Con. Fans of video games, innovation, or an evening of Settlers of Catan all have a place in Prague.

The unofficial **Apple Museum** (Husova 21, +420 774 414 775, www.applemuseum.com, 225 CZK, 10am-10pm daily), just off Old Town Square, is a tribute to the complicated genius of Steve Jobs. The space claims to be the largest private collection of Apple products in the world, from 1980s desktops to limited-edition iPods. A mobile app guides visitors through Jobs' career, from Macintosh to Pixar, plus a café and a pop art gallery housed in the basement.

New Town's **Joystick Bar** (Jindřišská 5, +420 732 473 788, www.joystickbar.cz) serves one of Prague's favorite microbrews, Uněticky Pivovar, in a room filled with classic arcade games and pinball machines (10 CZK). This old-school gamers bar is open from 4pm to 2am Tuesday to Saturday, closing at midnight on Sundays and Mondays.

Prague's **Bitcoin Café** (Dělnická 43, www.paralenipolis.cz, 8am-8pm Mon-Fri, noon-9pm Sat-Sun, prices vary with currency) in Holešovice provides a home for the local crypto-anarchist crew devoted to an open and decentralized internet. They don't take cash or cards, but the staff will teach you how to buy cryptocurrency using their onsite machine to pay for your specialty coffee and cake.

A Maze in Tchaiovna (Kafkova 18, +420 776 332 765, www.tchaiovna.cz, 11am-midnight daily) may appear small at first glance, but this tea house, performance space, and meetup hub has many hidden rooms where all are welcome. Find your way through the labyrinth of rooms that contain secret entrances, informal language lessons, a small stage hosting free standup comedy or improv theater, and a *Dr. Who* reference.

Bohemia Boards & Brews (Charkovská 18, +420 252 548 435, www.bohemiaboardsandbrews.com, 5pm-11pm Mon-Fri, 4pm-11pm Sat-Sun) in Vršovice has a massive collection of board games available for a 60 CZK cover charge. A menu of sandwiches, snacks, and beverages ensure that players don't have to take a hunger break in between turns.

European fashion elite, decked out in designer shades in the summer and fur coats in winter, peruse collections from Tiffany's jewelers, Prada handbags, and Louis Vuitton luggage.

A walk around the edges of **Wenceslas Square** or **Na Příkopě street,** dividing Old Town and New Town might be fun for some window shopping of Czech names interspersed with international chain stores that show Prague's identity as modern cosmopolitan city as much as historical European capital. Many of the souvenir shops around Old Town and Malá Strana fall distinctly into the tourist trap category, so stick to recommendations below for truly local gifts and memorabilia hiding in plain sight in these areas.

GIFTS AND HOME DECOR
Old Town
(Staré Město)
MANUFAKTURA-ORIGINAL CZECH TRADITION

Karlova 26, +420 601 310 605, www.manufaktura.cz, 10am-8pm daily, 100-1,000 CZK

The Manufaktura—Original Czech Tradition concept grew out of a desire to offer truly local souvenirs. The company began in 1991 by collecting handmade goods from small towns across the country. More than 25 years later, they have kept a network of independent producers of wooden toys, candles, cosmetics, and household accessories in business and accessible to Prague tourists wanting to support local craftspeople.

Lesser Town
(Malá Strana)
PRAGTIQUE
Mostecká Street 20, https://www.pragtique.cz,
10am-8pm daily, 50-500 CZK
For a gift that supports local, independent designers, try Pragtique just off the Malá Strana side of the Charles Bridge. This trendy boutique is self-described as "where love for Prague meets a sense of style." Modern designs on t-shirts, onesies, notebooks, postcards, magnets, tote bags, posters, and accessories are inspired by classic Czech symbols such as the Astronomical Clock, the Prague Castle, Golem, and the Tyn Church in Old Town. Stop into neighboring Roesel—Beer and Cake for a post-shopping snack. You can find a **second location** (Národní 37) in between Old Town Square and Wenceslas Square.

Prague Castle District
(Hradčany)
FROM PRAGUE WITH LOVE
Loretánská 13, +420 736 751 012,
www.frompraguewithlove.eu, 10am-6pm daily,
100-2,000 CZK
Want to grab a locally made t-shirt, tote bag, or kitchen accessories near the Prague Castle? Stop in From Prague with Love, just a few streets away from the main castle gates near Hradčanské náměstí. The family-owned shop of screen-printed cotton, porcelain, and wooden goods uses simple line drawings of Prague symbols, city maps, or the souvenir-appropriate name of their brand.

BEAUTY PRODUCTS
New Town
(Novy Město)
MANUFAKTURA HOME SPA
Na Příkopě 16a, +420 601 310 645,
www.manufaktura.cz, 10am-8pm daily, 150-500 CZK
In 2005, the Manufaktura team took the idea that beer and natural ingredients are good for your hair and skin and expanded it into an entire brand of shampoo, cosmetics, and home spa treatments. The Manufaktura Home Spa makes their products from natural local ingredients, including beer, wine, herbs, and minerals, and are not animal tested. You can find additional Manufaktura Home Spa shops in shopping malls such as Náměstí Republiky's Palladium mall, the Flora shopping mall in Žižkov, the Novy Smichov mall in Anděl, and inside Prague's main train station (Hlavní Nádraží).

SHOES
New Town
(Nové Město)
BAT'A SHOE STORES
Václavské náměstí 6, +420 221 088 478,
www.bata.cz, 9am-9pm Mon-Sat, 10am-9pm Sun,
1,000-5,000 CZK
One of the country's biggest names in fashion, Tomáš Baťa, came from generations of shoemakers in the South Moravian town of Zlín. Shoppers can browse his styles today in Baťa shoe stores. Baťa established the brand in 1894 and improved production processes around the turn of the century after witnessing US assembly-line production techniques. Baťa was also known for creating communities around his factories through urban planning that focused on residences and green space for his workers in the areas around the factories. Today, his mid-range styles are sold in shopping malls around the world, and the Tomáš Baťa institute in his hometown trains future generations of entrepreneurs. You can find additional locations in New Town at the Palladium mall on Náměstí Republiky and in Žižkov at the Flora shopping mall.

Žižkov
BOTAS 66
Křížkovského 18, +420 774 981 418,
www.botas66.com, 11am-7pm Mon-Fri, 11am-5pm Sat,
1,800-2,100 CZK
The casual, independent style of Botas 66 represents a more modern name in local shoe design that fits perfectly into the effortlessly cool Žižkov neighborhood. The Botas brand has deep local roots, founded

Best Souvenirs

There are some great options to bring a piece of Czech culture home with you:

- **Gingerbread:** Gingerbread has a local history dating back to at least the 16th century, with the Czech recipe originating in the Pardubice region. You won't find a household without at least a few different designs around Christmas time, often baked in huge batches and shared with friends, neighbors and coworkers in the weeks before the holiday season. Visit the family-owned **Perníčkův sen** (Haštalská 21, +420 607 773 350, www.pernickuvsen.cz, 10am-6pm daily) in Old Town for a wide selection of adorably hand-designed sweets.

- **Pilsner Beer or Becherovka:** You can find bottles from most of the bigger breweries in any local supermarket, or hold off until duty-free shopping on your trip home. Many of the Czech Republic's big name distilleries (e.g. Becherovka, Žufánek) are based in cities outside of Prague, so a supermarket or the airport is your best bet for spirits.

- **Wine:** Your best bet for wine in Prague is choosing from the wine bar scene, where most of those you taste are also available to take home. **Vinograf** (www.vinograf.cz) has locations in Anděl, Malá Strana, and New Town, while **Veltlin** (www.veltlin.cz) in the Karlín neighborhood focuses on small, independent wine producers. Gala wines are one of the most trusted names on the Czech wine landscape, available at **Vinoteka u Mourenina** (www.vinotekaumourenina.cz) in Malá Strana.

- **Cider:** For a more unusual (but delicious) alternative to beer, try some local cider or non-alcoholic juices from **F.H. Prager** (www.pragercider.cz), with a retail shop and tasting room in Žižkov. Prague's cider scene is on the rise, with cider festivals lining the Náplavka riverbanks at least once every summer.

- **No. 2 Pencils:** Czechs also had a hand in the popularity of #2 pencils. The 18th-century art supply company **Koh-i-noor** (Na Příkopě 26, +420 739 329 019, www.koh-i-noor.cz, 10am-8pm daily) patented the blend of lead inside and made the pencil yellow, which spread to copycats and became the industry standard. Their colored pencils and art supplies remain incredibly popular, particularly for fans of children's or adults' coloring books.

- **"The Little Mole":** An authentic choice for young ones is Krtek (or Krteček), the locally loved cartoon character known as "the Little Mole." In 2009, NASA astronaut Andrew Feustel, who is married to a Czech woman, took a toy version of Krtek into space in honor of a 1965 episode detailing a similar adventure. This Czech alternative to Mickey Mouse entered into a Chinese partnership in 2016, giving the character a modern reboot and new location, but the vintage look still dominates Czech toy shops. Buy the Little Mole and other toys at **Rocking Horse Toy Shop** (Loretánské náměstí 3, +420 220 512 234 or +420 603 515 745, 11am-6pm daily, 50-500 CZK).

One particular plea is to avoid purchasing the Soviet-era memorabilia that's sold in a number of shops. Czechoslovakia was forcefully occupied by the Soviet Union from 1968-1989 so any investment in Russian nesting dolls or trinkets and t-shirts with a hammer-and-sickle insignia is ultimately celebrating the oppression of Czech people. In other words, just don't do it.

in the late 1940s, and their iconic Botas Classic brand gained popularity in the 1960s. The slang word "botasky" was added to the Czech dictionary as a catch-all term for sport shoes, but the brand had more of an old-fashioned, nostalgic appeal until 2008. Two students, Jan Kloss and Jakub Korouš, gave the design a reboot with the Botas 66 line as part of a school project. The company embraced the update and the brand's popularity has grown among a new generation of sneakerheads. There is also **another location** (Skořepka 4) tucked among the busy streets of Old Town.

WINE, BEER, AND SPIRITS

Lesser Town
(Malá Strana)

VINOTÉKA U MOUŘENÍNA

Tržiště 17, +420 606 483 087, www.vinotekaumourenina.cz, 2pm-10pm daily

The wooden cabinets lining the walls of Vinotéka U Mouřenína are stocked with Czech, Italian, and French wines and cognacs in a wide range of price points (200-5,000 CZK) with a few small tables in the front and rear of the store for tasting. When in doubt, look for bottles by Gala, one of the country's most celebrated winemakers. International shipping is available in store or on their website (only in Czech, so you'll need your preferred translation tool).

Vinohrady

BEER GEEK PIVOTÉKA

Slavíkova 10, +420 775-260-871, pivoteka.beergeek. cz, 1pm-9pm Mon-Fri, 11am-9pm Sat, 3pm-9pm Sun

Beer Geek Pivoteka is the place for microbrews in Prague. This beer-lover's boutique, arranged on shelves by country of origin, stocks over 500 different bottles (60-400 CZK) from across Europe and the US. A few local Czech favorites include anything by Clock, Matuška, Raven or Zichovec. You can find many of the local bottles on tap at nearby Beer Geek Pub if you want to try before you buy. International shipping is available online (only in Czech, so you'll need your preferred translation tool).

MARKETS

The most current Czech designs don't have a permanent home, but they do have a presence. **Mint Design Market** (www.mintmarket.cz) is an independent pop-up concept of fashion, design, and food that has been bouncing around the country—from Brno to Pilsen to Prague and beyond—since 2015. The collection of young of independent designers run an e-shop and offer information on the time and location of their events on their website.

Old Town
(Staré Město)

SMETANAQ

Smetanovo nábřeží 4, www.smetenaq.cz, 10am-8pm, tram stop Národní divadlo

The SmetenaQ complex, which opened in 2016, houses a young group of independent furniture and accessories designers on its second floor, and a small Deelive Design Store selling their ideas come to life on the ground floor. The riverfront spot also includes a popular café and a gallery on the top level. Located next to Prague's prestigious FAMU school of TV and film, the crowd skews young, hip, and artsy.

Food

Traditional Czech cuisine is hearty, meaty, and often covered in sauce. Local meals (including most daily lunch specials) are divided into grilled meats (pork, beef, game, chicken, or duck) with some form of potatoes or dumplings on the side. Vegetables are scarce and seafood is uncommon (or pricey) in this landlocked country. Enjoy the indulgence of comfort foods like *svíčková* (a national favorite) or a rich roast duck, or grab some *chlebíčky* for a lighter lunch.

OLD TOWN
(Staré Město)

Czech

KRČMA

Kostečná 4, +420 725 157 262, www.krcma.cz, 11am-11pm, 175-300 CZK entrees

Krčma is an underground den of deliciousness just steps from Old Town Square. Enjoy hearty portions of grilled meats, sauces, and dumplings in a medieval setting of cave-like brick

Easter and Christmas Markets

Prague is magical all year round, but the holiday markets around Christmas and Easter turn the volume up to eleven. Wooden stands fill every square in town with the smells of warm spiced wine (*svařák*), hot honey wine (*medovina*), and street food blends of meats and potatoes. Old Town Square and Wenceslas Square Christmas markets run through most of December and into the New Year, while some of the smaller neighborhood markets may have more limited runs. The landscape is equally festive during the week before Easter in the same locations, just swapping Christmas decorations for pastel colors.

Prague's holiday markets are generally cheerful and family-friendly, with tourists dominating Old Town Square and locals often stopping by locations near metro stops (e.g. Náměstí Miru, Náměstí Republiky, or Anděl) for a festive pre-commute drink or snack. Most market visitors spend their time browsing and chatting while occasionally picking up some presents. Delicately carved ornaments of wooden scenes and Christmas symbols (around 50-300 CZK) are traditional trinkets. At the Easter markets, you'll find intricately painted wooden eggs called *kraslice* (100-500 CZK) alongside one unusual element: a braided, ribbon-covered whip made from young saplings (50-300 CZK). (Wondering how this whip is used? See page 104).

Holiday market stalls generally come to life around 10am and stay busy until 10pm, with food and drinks served in the city center until midnight. Details can change from year to year. Prague Markets (www.trhypraha.cz) and Prague Tourism (www.prage.eu) are good resources to double check the dates and times around your visit.

OLD TOWN SQUARE
(Staroměstské Náměstí)
The markets on Old Town Square are the most crowded and commercial of the bunch, with a strong focus on consumable goods like sweets, hot drinks, and street food. The layout is designed for photo ops, including a large Christmas tree in front of the towers of the Church of Our Lady Before Týn plus stairs to a festive viewing platform in the center of it all.

walls. Vegetarian options are minimal in this old-style, traditional Czech tavern.

LOD' PIVOVAR
Dvořákovo nábřeží, kotviště č. 19, +420 773 778 788, www.pivolod.cz, 11:30am-11pm Sun-Thurs, 11:30am-midnight Fri-Sat, 200-300 CZK entrees

This microbrewery is on a boat! The top-floor restaurant of Lod' Pivovar offers fresh, modern takes on Czech cuisine—think rabbit, duck, or pork knee accompanied by more vegetables than you'd find in a traditional pub. The below-deck seating area strikes a more casual pub vibe, serving beer snacks and in-house microbrews.

★ SISTERS BISTRO
Dlouhá 39, +420 775 991 975, www.chlebicky-praha. cz, 8am-7pm Mon-Fri, 9am-6pm Sat, 35-55 CZK sandwiches

When all you need is a quick bite between sightseeing, stop into Sisters Bistro for a fresh, modern take on traditional Czech *chlebíčky* (open-faced sandwiches). Instead of the old-fashioned classic of ham and potato salad on white bread, these artisan updates include beetroot with goat cheese or roast beef with sprouts, not to mention service with a smile. Mix and match to make a meal or take a selection across the river for a picnic in Letná Park.

WENCESLAS SQUARE
(Václavské náměstí)

Wenceslas Square's market is a low-key experience usually lined with more food and beverage stands than gifts or trinkets. There is room to enjoy a warm drink and a bite if you can find a spot at the few standing tables.

REPUBLIC SQUARE
(Náměstí Republiky)

Náměstí Republiky adds a light-hearted presence in front of the busy Palladium shopping mall. This medium-sized market wraps around a busy transportation corner and caters to shoppers grabbing a quick drink, bite, or small gift among their holiday errands at the mall. If you spot a Včelcovina stand, try a glass of their hot honey wine (*medovina*).

PEACE SQUARE
(Náměstí Míru)

Old Town Square Christmas market

The local favorite is usually Náměstí Míru with a mix of treats and handmade crafts, plus a small Christmas tree, in the shadow of the Church of St. Ludmila. The pace at this market is slower, made for eating, browsing, and absorbing the atmosphere.

AROUND ANDĚL METRO STATION

The streets around the Anděl metro station host a crowded market of their own. The aisles are narrow and hurried workers from the surrounding offices channel their inner Grinch when annoyed with nowhere else to walk, but a small petting zoo and street musicians still draw families here to keep young ones entertained.

★ NAŠE MASO

Dlouhá 39, +420 222 311 378, www.nasemaso.cz, 10am-8pm Mon-Fri, 10am-6pm Sat, 75-200 CZK entrees

With a staff committed to traditional butchery techniques and cooperation with Czech farmers, this carnivore's favorite is accurately named "Our Meat." Be bold and work your way to the counter to order—the tiny butcher shop is generally packed with residents doing their grocery shopping, food tours sampling Prague ham and sausages, and a lunch crowd enjoying burgers and beef tartare. Two beverages, beer and water, flow from self-service taps on the wall. Meat enthusiasts will want to reserve a seat for dinner with the butcher

Mondays to Wednesdays at 7pm. Bring your appetite and your questions—he speaks five languages (including English).

International
HOME KITCHEN

Kozí 5, +420 774 905 802, www.homekitchen.cz, 10am-8pm Mon-Fri, 10am-6pm Sat, 200-300 CZK entrees

On a cold day, the selection of soups at Home Kitchen will warm you up from the inside out. Browse the display of main courses (e.g. grilled meats and pastas), starters (e.g. hummus or soup), and salads to inspire your appetite. The trendy staff in skinny jeans and well-groomed facial hair cater to a casual clientele of leisurely lunchers alongside tourists finishing up tours of the Jewish Quarter in this mid-sized bistro. Reservations recommended.

ENGAWA
Petrském náměstí 5, +420 775 383 999, www.nasemaso.cz, 11am-11pm, 250-600 CZK entrees

As a bona fide sushi snob raised in Seattle, I had forgotten the flavor of fresh fish until my first bite of Engawa sushi. The staff at this casually elegant, multi-room Japanese restaurant take quality seafood seriously, even in a landlocked country. The extensive menu includes grilled meats and Japanese hot pots alongside sushi sets and a la carte sashimi on a quiet square near the eastern edge of Old Town.

Vegetarian
★ LEHKÁ HLAVA
Boršov 2, +420 775 383 999, www.lehkahlava.cz, 11:30am-11:30pm Mon-Fri, noon-11:30pm Sat-Sun, 225-275 CZK entrees

In a meat-heavy country, Lehká Hlava ("Clear Head") is a vegetarian oasis. The intimate dining room includes a dark blue ceiling, twinkling star lights, and calming fish tank to set the scene for a mellow meal. Browse the meat-free menu from Thai curry to quesadillas, with a glossary of potentially unfamiliar terms like tempeh or seitan. Reservations required.

Coffee, Tea, and Sweets
GRAND CAFÉ ORIENT
Ovocný trh 19, +420 224 224 240, www.grandcafeorient.cz, 9am-10pm Mon-Fri, 10am-10pm Sat-Sun, 100-200 CZK entrees

The only café in Prague with exclusively Cubist decor takes its commitment to right angles down to the details. Everything from the coat hooks to the light fixtures is on point. Enjoy a slice of homemade cake, a breakfast croissant, or a toasted baguette on the second floor of Prague's historic House of the Black Madonna (named for the identifying marker outside) to refuel before climbing the nearby Powder Tower or touring the Municipal House.

NEW TOWN
(Nové Město)
Czech
ZVONICE
Jindřišská věž, +420 224 220 009, www.restaurantzvonice.cz, 11:30am-midnight, 600-900 CZK entrees

Fine dining and traditional Czech cuisine aren't often synonymous, but this high-end establishment inside the Jindřišská bell tower offers an exception to that rule. Classic takes on Old Bohemian recipes of meat and game come with impressive views and top-notch service. Try the sauerkraut soup (trust me, it's 100 percent better than it sounds) before choosing a main course from veal cheeks, wild boar, or grilled duck breast. Reservations required.

★ CAFÉ LOUVRE
Národní 22, +420 724 054 055 or +420 224 930 949, www.cafelouvre.cz, 8am-11:30pm Mon-Fri, 9am-11:30pm Sat-Sun, 150-300 CZK entrees

Café Louvre has been satisfying local appetites since 1902 and can even claim Albert Einstein and Franz Kafka as former regulars. Enjoy Czech and Austro-Hungarian cuisine in the chandeliered elegance of the First Republic café style established in the early years of Czechoslovakia, located just down the street from the National Theater. This is a great place to try *svíčková*, a Czech favorite of sirloin beef in vegetable cream sauce with cranberries, cream and bread dumplings, reminiscent of the rich blend of flavors in a Thanksgiving dinner. Select the *kavarna* (café) or *restaurace* (restaurant) when making your online reservation for the most ornately decorated rooms—you can order food in either.

International
LEMON LEAF
Myslikova 14, +420 224 919 056, www.lemon.cz, 11am-1pm Mon-Thurs, 11am-midnight Fri,

12pm-midnight Sat, 12pm-11pm Sun, 225-275 CZK entrees

Arguably the city's best-loved Thai restaurant sits between Karlovo náměstí and the Vltava River. When your tongue is craving spice beyond the relatively mild palate of Czech cuisine, this menu of soups, spring rolls, and curries will perk up your taste buds, with a few continental options also available. Reservations recommended.

PIZZERIA KMOTRA

V Jirchářích 12, +420 224 934 100, www.kmotra.cz, 11am-midnight, 135-185 CZK entrees

The extensive, menu of pizza, pasta, and salads at Pizzeria Kmotra caters to a budget-conscious crowd of university students and casual patrons on their way to Klub Vzorkovna. Split one of their massive pizzas (ignore any recommendations that these are personal-sized) in an underground, brick-walled cavern setting with cutlery-inspired décor. Reservations recommended.

★ GRAN FIERRO

Voršilská 14, +420 773 700 377, www.granfierro.cz, 5pm-midnight, 200-500 CZK entrees

The trendy atmosphere at this Argentinian steakhouse and cocktail bar is perfect for a pre-theater meal or post-show drink around a performance at the National Theater or New Stage. Wine fans missing the flavor of rich reds will appreciate a glass of Malbec paired with an order of empanadas. Reservations recommended on weekends, which sometimes include live flamenco music.

Breakfast and Brunch
CACAO

V Celnici 4, +420 773 700 377, www.cacaoprague.cz, 8:30am-10:30pm Mon-Thurs, 9:30am-11pm Fri-Sat, 9:30am-10:30pm Sun, 100-150 CZK entrees

Health conscious travelers and restricted diets are no problem for the staff at Cacao, located right next door to the Museum of Communism. The large, two-story dining room near Náměstí Republiky serves bagels, egg breakfast, smoothies, acai bowls,

and delicious espresso to start your day. The menu transitions into fresh soups, salads, and sandwiches for lunch or dinner. Homemade ice cream and a considerable array of cakes will placate the sweet tooth of anyone in your group.

ETNOSVET

Legerova 40, Prague 2, 120 00, +420 226 203 880, www.etnosvet.cz/en, lunch 11:30am-4pm Mon-Fri, noon-4pm Sat-Sun, dinner 5pm-11pm Sun-Thurs, 5pm-11:30pm Fri-Sat, 250-400 CZK entrees, tram stops IP Pavlova or Bruselská or metro stop IP Pavlova

For a high-end vegan or vegetarian meal, head to Etnosvet, a short walk from Náměstí Míru. Sample multi-course tasting menus plus wine pairings or choose from the a la carte menu, including tempura vegetables, pesto linguini, or bulgur and cheese salad, at this gastronomic hub of international influences. Reservations recommended.

Coffee, Tea, and Sweets
STYL & INTERIER

Vodičkova 35, +420 773 700 377, www.stylainterier.cz, 10am-10:00pm Mon-Sat, 10am-8pm Sun, 100-150 CZK entrees

It's easy to miss the entrance to Styl & Interier tucked into a quiet courtyard just off the bustling streets around Wenceslas Square. This friendly café doubles as an interior design showroom of wicker home accessories and colorful accent pieces, plus a peaceful summer garden. The seasonal bistro menu of light egg breakfasts and quiches, colorful salads, and homemade desserts is popular with locals and tourists, so reservations are recommended. Try a sparkling, fruit-infused lemonade in the coveted garden seats during summer or some homemade svařák (hot spiced wine) and Christmas cookies in winter.

OLIVER'S COFFEE CUP

Václavské náměstí 58, +420 234 101 138, www.oliverscoffeecup.cz, 8:30am-8:30pm Mon-Fri, 9am-8pm Sat-Sun

For a warm drink and a cozy sofa, take the

Czech Cuisine

ENTREES

- **Svíčková:** a local favorite of thinly sliced sirloin beef in vegetable cream sauce with cranberries, cream and bread dumplings, almost like a Czech take on Thanksgiving flavors. This is what every Czech child writes under "favorite food" in school and continues to love throughout adulthood. Try a classic one at Café Louvre, while local vegetarian favorite Maitrea (Týnská ulička 6, www.restaurace-maitrea.cz) in Old Town does make a soy-based, meat-free version.

- **Pražská šunka** (Prague ham): Head to Naše Maso to try *Pražská šunka* (Prague ham), a cured, lightly smoked, boneless ham prepared with traditional butchery techniques recognized by the EU as a regional specialty. Avoid the stands in Old Town Square, known for scamming customers with prices by weight not portion.

- **Pečená kachní stehna** (roast duck leg): U Modré Kachničky serves delicious duck-based dishes, including *pečená kachní stehna*, which is usually paired with red cabbage and dumplings. This hearty, Bohemian-style classic is served on the bone often in one-quarter or one-half portions.

- **Pečené vepřové koleno** (roast pork knuckle): Try the *pečené vepřové koleno* (roast pork knee) at Lod' Pivovar, a floating brewery on a boat focused on classic Czech dishes with quality ingredients. The potent flavors of a dark beer sauce, mustard, and horseradish are perfect for refueling on a winter evening.

- **Guláš** (goulash): The Czech version of this Hungarian classic involves less (or no) paprika and acts more as a thick sauce than soup. Pork, beef, and venison versions are available in different venues. Eating Prague tour guide Jan Macuch (a food lover I trust) claims that Czech-Slovak Pub makes the best one in Prague.

- **Smažený sýr** (fried cheese): Apologies to any vegan readers, but the only traditional vegetarian "meal" is a thick slice of white cheese (often a mild, white Edam) that is breaded, fried and served with French fries and tartar sauce without a vegetable in sight. The version at Czech pub Lokal is a local favorite.

SOUPS

In the same way that many people think of a small salad as a starter to a meal, a Czech lunch always begins with soup:

- **česneková polévka** (garlic soup): Different versions of this fragrant and flavorful dish range from a creamy base to a light broth, often garnished with ham, cheese, potatoes, and croutons. *Česnečka* (the short name) is a fantastic cure for the common cold. Soup menus in Czech pubs often change daily, so keep an eye out for this classic when the weather turns cold.

- **kulajda** (dill and vegetable soup): For a more unusual flavor, watch soup of the day menus for *kulajda*, a blend of dill, mushroom, potato, and egg. You'll find this consistently on the menu at Staročeská restaurace V Ruthardce if you take a day trip to Kutna Hora.

SMALL BITES AND PASTRIES

A quick snack in Prague usually centers around bread or a sweet shop:

Chlebíčky (open-faced sandwiches) are popular at parties and weddings.

- **Chlebíčky** (open-faced sandwiches): The traditional version of *chlebíčky* would be white bread topped with potato salad and sliced ham, possibly garnished with a radish or carrot. These simple hors d'oeuvres are particularly popular at Czech weddings or New Year's Eve parties at a cabin in the countryside. **Sisters Bistro** makes incredible modern versions with fresh ingredients such as beetroot and goat cheese.

- **Klobásy** (sausage): This staple of any pub, beer garden, outdoor market, or food stand is the go-to solution for "we should probably serve some kind of food" at any Czech event. They can be pork or beef, grilled or smoked, and mild or spiced and usually served with mustard and a few sliced of brown bread.

- **Medovník** (honey cake): Czech cakes and pastries offer a wide range of flavors (e.g. gingerbread, poppy seed, forest berries and cream-filled dough) but one of my personal favorites is *Medovník* or *Medovy Dort*, which translates to "honey cake." Taste this light, flaky delight in Cubist form at Old Town's **Grand Café Orient**.

- Local note: **trdelník**, a doughy spiral pastry cooked over coals and dipped in sugar and cinnamon, is a delicious guilty pleasure sold at stands all around Old Town, but it is about as Czech as an "I ♥ NY" t-shirt—its prevalence is a pet peeve of the Honest Prague Guide on YouTube. With claimed roots in Romania, Hungary, Sweden, and Slovakia, it has become a popular tourist attraction across the former Austro-Hungarian Empire. Feel free to indulge, but to maintain your traveler's credibility and avoid dirty looks from locals, skip the Instagram-inspired, sugar-overload trend of filling it with ice cream or hashtagging #traditional.

escalator to the second floor inside one of Wenceslas Square's oldest shopping centers below the National Museum. Oliver's Coffee Cup draws a crowd of young families, friends, and local office workers with a selection of specialty coffee, tea, homemade lemonades, and cakes Snag a seat beside the picture window for prime people-watching on the square below. Strangely, the only way to exit is an elevator ride one floor down.

KAVÁRNA SLAVIA

Smetanovo nábřeží 2, +420 773 700 377, www.cafeslavia.cz, 8am-midnight Mon-Fri, 9am-midnight Sat-Sun

The First Republic style of early 20th-century Czechoslovakia is enshrined in Kavárna Slavia. This historic café has stood across from the National Theater since 1884, and is famous for its popularity with politicians and intellectuals. Stop in for coffee and share some sweet crepes accompanied by live piano soundtrack. Request a seat near the front windows when making an online reservation to enjoy a riverfront view of the Prague Castle.

LESSER TOWN
(Malá Strana)
Czech
★ U MODRÉ KACHNIČKY

Nebovidská 6, +420 602 353 559, www.umodrekachnicky.cz, 12pm-4pm and 6:30pm-11:30pm daily, 500-600 CZK entrees

The tasting menus of duck or game at U Modré Kachničky are 100 percent worth the splurge. Five or seven courses of decadent flavors can also be paired with local wines and liquors in the most fashionable, old-world living room settings that you can imagine. The staff walk a talented tightrope of friendly professionalism for largely couples sharing a romantic meal. Duck and game specials are also available a la carte, and the roast duck with apples, raisins, and honey is a standout. Reservations recommended.

ST. MARTIN

Vítězná 5, +420 731 136 144, www.stmartin.cz, 12pm-11pm, 200-250 CZK entrees

The brother and sister chef team at St. Martin blend traditional Czech recipes with French and Asian touches discovered through travels. Mix-and-match from the seasonal menu of soups, salads, grilled meat and vegetarian main courses, and continental side dishes. The mini turkey burger plus a side dish makes a great light meal, and the wild boar burger is a carnivore favorite. Both the food and white domed walls of the small dining room embody classic, modern quality. You'll find a young, trendy crowd on the outdoor patio in the summer.

★ LOKÁL U BÍLÉ KUŽELKY

Míšeňská 12, +420 257 212 014, www.lokal-ubilekuzelky.ambi.cz, 11:30am-midnight Sun-Thurs, 11:30am-1am Sat-Sun, 100-125 CZK entrees

Lokal's simple, modern take on traditional Czech recipes is an almost universally praised local favorite. This makes reservations required to join the crowd of travelers and young residents grabbing after work drinks at the lively tables of this casual beer hall just off the Charles Bridge. Try simple bar snacks like sausages or marinated cheese with a cold glass of Pilsner Urquell on draft.

Coffee, Tea, and Sweets
★ ROESEL-BEER & CAKE

Mostecká 20, +420 777 119 368, 8am-10:30pm Mon-Fri, 9am-10:30pm Sat-Sun, 75-150 CZK entrees

The quiet patio and low ceilings of this casual café offer a hidden escape from the crowds surrounding the Lesser Town entrance to the Charles Bridge. In addition to craft beer and homemade sweets, this small, friendly spot with simple wooden furniture serves specialty coffee, seasonal pâtés (try the trio of spreads with fresh bread), and a daily lunch special. The young, multilingual staff are patient with an international clientele of locals, foreigners, and families.

ANDĚL

The Anděl neighborhood, which stretches south of Lesser Town along the riverbank, is a good spot for dining.

Czech
CZECH SLOVAK RESTAURANT

Újezd 20, +420 257 312 523, www.czechslovak.cz, 11am-midnight Mon-Fri, 3pm-midnight Sat-Sun, 200-300 CZK entrees

The jury's still out, but some claim the venison goulash at Czech Slovak Restaurant to be "the best in Prague." The trendy, dimly lit atmosphere surrounds an international crowd enjoying modern twists on traditional dishes. The menu includes Bohemian baked snails, dill and mushroom soup, wild rabbit and a local-leaning wine list. Reservations recommended.

KOLKOVNA OLYMPIA

Vítězná 7, +420 251 511 080, www.kolkovna.cz, 11am-midnight, 175-300 CZK entrees

Dark wood details and copper accents set a traditional Czech pub scene in this 222-seat member of the Pilsner Urquell Original Restaurant group, where quality beer is a way of life. Freshly poured pints (or technically, half-liters) complement the menu, from bar snacks of pickled sausage and marinated cheeses to main courses like roast duck and pork knee. The building has been serving customers since 1903, and Kolkovna gave the space a restorative makeover in 2003 without losing any of its historical charm. Grab a hearty meal here after walking (or riding the funicular) down Petřín Hill.

International
MR BANH MI

Seifertova 13, +420 774 319 355, www.mrbanhmi. cz, 11am-9pm Mon-Fri, 11:30am-8pm Sat, 100-150 CZK entrees

Prague's sizable Vietnamese community deserves credit for introducing the city to banh mi sandwiches. These thick, flaky baguettes come filled with pork and lemongrass, ginger chicken, hoisin beef,

garlic-and-tomato-soaked tofu, or marinated portabella mushrooms. The casual underground dining room expands to an outdoor summer garden when the weather allows. Lunchtime reservations recommended to join the local office crowd.

Breakfast and Brunch
CAFÉ SAVOY

Vlašská 7, +420 257 219 728, www.cafesavoy.ambi. cz, 8am-10:30pm Mon-Fri, 9am-10:30pm Sat-Sun, 200-400 CZK breakfast

The conversations are quiet, chandeliers sparkle overhead, and the patrons practice their best etiquette at this ornate café in the style of the First Czechoslovak Republic. Observe the on-site bakery behind a glass window as the staff prepare the pastries and fresh bread that keeps a large, multi-level dining room smiling. Reservations required.

Coffee, Tea, and Sweets
KAVÁRNA CO HLEDÁ JMÉNO

Stroupežnického 10, +420 770 165 561, www.kavarnacohledajmeno.cz, noon-10pm Mon, 8am-10pm Tues-Sat, 9am-7pm Sun

The industrial vibe of Kavárna Co Hledá Jméno ("Café in Search of a Name") is popular with young coffee lovers and remote workers—both the coffee and WiFi are strong. This large, multi-room café is set back from the street, so if you're walking down a driveway it's likely you're in the right place. Brunch is served until noon (or 1pm on weekends) and includes an impossibly fluffy eggs benedict soufflé.

VYŠEHRAD
Czech
HOSPŮDKA NA HRADBÁCH

V Pevnosti 2, +420 734 112 214, 2pm-midnight Mon-Fri, noon-midnight Sat-Sun, 50-150 CZK entrees

The best way to enjoy a meal inside the Vyšehrad Complex is outdoors. This locally-loved beer garden offers bar snacks like grilled Hermelin cheese or pickled sausages alongside heavier meals of grilled meats, to be eaten under the umbrella-topped picnic benches lining the garden. Imagine a casual,

Prague Food Tours

One of the most enjoyable ways to discover Prague's local culture is through your taste buds. These multi-stop adventures usually include small bites at culinary hot spots, with a local guide sharing bits of history and stories about the sights you pass in between restaurants. At the table, guests can chat with each other or ask questions (when their mouths aren't full). A daytime tour often leaves travelers full for hours, so plan on a lighter evening meal if you do add this experience to your itinerary. These tours are generally run by independent teams without an office, so booking is done online.

Eating Prague Tours is the Prague branch of Eating Europe Food Tours (www.eatingeurope.com) with a wide range of daytime and evening options: A four-hour afternoon Prague Food Tour through Old Town and New Town (about 2,300 CZK, Mon-Sat), a four-hour Evening Food Tour though Malá Strana (about 2,500 CZK, Sun-Thurs), and a three-and-a-half-hour afternoon Craft Beer and Food Tour with some incredible skyline views (about 1,600 CZK, Tues-Sat). Most dietary restrictions can be accommodated, but vegan restrictions drastically limit the enjoyment of most tours.

The local Czech couple, Jan and Zuzi, behind **Taste of Prague** (+420 775-577-275, www.tasteofprague.com) are known for having one of the most meticulously updated and beautifully photographed food blogs in town. They offer a Traditional Czech Food Tour (4 hours, 2,500 CZK) beginning from 1pm-3pm that includes 5-6 stops for classic Czech cuisine and beverages. The Prague Foodie Tour (4 hours, 2,700 CZK) includes 5-7 stops beginning from 11am-5pm and including modern takes on Czech food in more local neighborhoods. Some dietary restrictions require an extra charge, and they cannot accommodate vegan diets.

family BBQ setting with the added bonus of a panoramic view from the tables lining the perimeter.

International
YAM YAM VYŠEHRAD

Vyšehrad Metro Station 1670, +420 734 112 214, www.yamyam.cz, 11am-11pm, 50-150 CZK entrees

Yam Yam Vyšehrad's convenient location just outside the Vyšehrad Metro Station make it an easy stop for simple, quality Thai food. The clean lines, stenciled vines, and splashes of red create a relaxed environment for an international clientele. The extensive, light-hearted menu includes "Ca-la-la-mari" and sections of main courses encouraging visitors to "Eat Some Meat" and "Curry On."

Coffee, Tea, and Sweets
KAVÁRNA ČEKÁRNA

Vratislavova 8, +420 601 593 741, 8am-10pm Mon-Fri, 10am-8pm Sat, 1pm-8pm Sun, 50-150 CZK entrees

The unassuming entrance to this casual café

extends into long halls of cushions and simple wooden furniture, leading to a massive backyard garden at the base of Vysehrad hill. Patio seating is tucked under brick arches and around patches of grass where the noise of the city disappears. Pair your specialty coffee with homemade cakes, quiches, or the soup of the day.

PURO GELATO

Na Hrobci 1, +420 721 438 209, May-Sept 10am-9pm Sun-Thurs, 10am-10pm Fri, 9am-10pm Sat, Oct-April 9am-8pm daily

This cozy gelato shop below Vysehrad is a perfect stop before a stroll along the nearby Náplavka embankment beside the Vltava river (where you might have to hide your treat from a few hungry swans). Choose a scoop of your favorite from the daily-made and often unusual flavors (an orange scoop might be mango or carrot) including vegan options, or try the artfully designed cakes and tarts for some warm-weather indulgence.

VINOHRADY AND VRŠOVICE

Czech

RESTAURACE U RŮŽOVÉHO SADU

Mánesova 89, Prague 2, 120 00, +420 222 725 154, www.uruzovehosadu.cz, 10:30am-midnight Mon-Thurs, 10:30am-1am Fri, 11am-1am Sat, 11:30am-10pm Sun, 115-215 CZK entrees, tram and metro stop Jiřího z Poděbrad

Restaurace U Růžového Sadu serves classic, hearty, meat-and-potato meals in a comfortable 90-seat pub with an additional outdoor patio during sunny seasons. Work up an appetite with a walk through nearby Reigrovy sady, then stop in for one of the simple daily lunch specials (think pork schnitzel or grilled chicken with potatoes) served until 3pm at less than 100 CZK for a true taste of Czech-style dining.

International

★ PHO VIETNAM TUAN & LAN

Slavíkova 1, Prague 2, 120 00, 11am-10pm daily, 100-150 CZK entrees, tram and metro stop Jiřího z Poděbrad

The best advertising for the unassuming storefront of Pho Vietnam Tuan & Lan is a regular line out the door. As one of the longest-running Vietnamese establishments in town, this grab-and-go option of pho in a Styrofoam bowl or fresh rolls in rice paper are best enjoyed on a bench across the street at Jiřího z Poděbrad Square (unless you can find space to stand at one of the few standing tables inside the tiny space). Bring cash and choose your meal before you reach the counter to keep the efficiency moving at its usual fast pace. Vegetarian options are slim to non-existent.

MARTHY'S KITCHEN

Francouzská 13, Prague 2, 120 00, +420 608 313 436, www.marthyskitchen.cz/en.html, 8am-10pm Mon-Fri, 9am-10pm Sat-Sun, 100-200 CZK breakfast, 175-250 CZK entrees, tram stop Jana Masaryka or metro to Náměstí Míru

Daytime reservations are unavailable at Marthy's Kitchen but a short wait for their eggs Benedict on brioche is always worth it for brunch served daily until 5pm. The detailed care for quality and presentation in this adorably tiny, French-inspired bistro extends into the evening menu of seasonal meat and seafood combinations. I love the grilled tarragon tuna with vegetables in a creamy sauce or savory crepes. Dinner reservations recommended.

Vegetarian

RADOST FX

Bělehradská 12, Prague 2, 120 00, +420 224 254 776, www.radostfx.cz, kitchen open 11am-midnight Tues-Sat, 11am-11pm Sun-Mon, tram stop IP Pavlova metro stops Náměstí Míru or IP Pavlova

Radost FX has been a dependable vegetarian haven in Prague since 1992. The eclectic menu jumps from nachos to gnocchi, stir-fry to salads (175-215 CZK) with salmon sneaking onto the brunch menu (100-200 CZK). The laid-back vibe extends from a small, quiet café out front to the crowds nursing hangovers and Bloody Marys in the high-backed booths of the windowless restaurant. Some hard-core diners may have not even made it home between breakfast and the all-hours dance party in the downstairs club on Thursday through Saturday nights. Brunch reservations recommended.

Coffee, Tea, and Sweets

MONOLOK

Moravská 18, Prague 2, 120 00, +420 739 018 195, www.monolok.cz, 8am-10pm Mon-Fri, 9am-7pm Sat-Sun, tram stops Šumavská or Jana Masaryka or metro Náměstí Míru

Friendly service and quality coffee, plus a peaceful courtyard away from the street and surrounded by manmade waterfalls make Monolok a refreshing place to catch your breath. This multi-room cafe on a quiet side street in the heart of Vinohrady complements their cakes and light food (think variations on avocado toast or seasonal salads) with a solid wine list and a WiFi signal strong enough to keep digital nomads satisfied.

ŽIŽKOV
Czech
★ U SLOVANSKÉ LÍPY

Tachovské náměstí 6, +420 739 003 999,
www.uslovanskelipy.cz, 11am-midnight, 175-225 CZK
entrees

This large, casual, traditional Czech pub near the Žižkov Tunnel offers hearty meals with no-nonsense service that keeps the *pivo* (beer) flowing. Slightly off the beaten path below Vitkov hill and the Žižkov Beer Garden, this local favorite caters to a mixed crowd of residents and visitors (assisted by English-friendly menus). Choose from ten rotating taps of Czech beers and a main course of flank steak or schnitzel with potato salad. Cash-only.

U SADU

Škroupovo náměstí 5, www.usadu.cz, +420 222 727
072, 8am-2am Sun-Mon, 8am-4am Tues-Sat 125-250
CZK entrees

With pub food served late every night, this neighborhood watering hole near the base of the Žižkov TV Tower is a last stop for pub-goers on their way home (if they can find a seat among the regulars who have been there since early evening). The large, multi-floor interior has an eclectic, thrift-store style décor of globes, baskets, and random items hanging from the walls and ceilings. Try a Svijany beer with some *smažený sýr* (fried cheese) and tartar sauce, potato pancakes, or a grilled steak to satisfy your late-night cravings.

International
★ MARTIN'S BISTRO

Velehradská 4, +420 774 100 378, 11am-10pm
Mon-Sat, 150-300 CZK entrees

Friendly, multilingual service and seasonal, fresh-from-the-farmers-market ingredients define the vibe at Martin's Bistro. Choose from a weekly revamped menu that might include pasta tossed with fresh veggies and herbs, roast duck or pork entrees, Asian-inspired noodles and curries, or shrimp and cheese appetizers, plus soups, quiches, and desserts. Vegetarian options almost always available. This local favorite fills up fast, so call for a reservation to ensure an available seat.

Breakfast and Brunch
ŽIŽKAVÁRNA

Kubelíkova 17, +420 606 281 546, 7:30am-9pm
Mon-Fri, 8:30am-9pm Sat-Sun, 50-75 CZK entrees

This quiet neighborhood favorite of international residents and remote workers camped out for hours serves quality coffee and light homemade meals with a friendly, patient approach. The seasonal menu often includes omelets, sandwiches, granola, and a soup of the day, with a slice of carrot or honey cake for dessert. If you can't score one of the ten tables, take your coffee to go for a short walk to the benches of Jiřího z Poděbrad square.

MY COFFEE STORY

Štítného 8, +420 776 343 008, 8:30am-8pm
Mon-Fri, 9am-3pm Sat, 50-150 CZK entrees

Stop into My Coffee Story for a breakfast of scrambled eggs and waffles or some late-afternoon coffee and homemade cake before heading to the lawn of Riegrovy sady or top of Vitkov Hill to watch the sunset. This cozy, modern café makes a nice pre-theater meeting point before catching a show at The Jára Cimrman Theatre. During the summer months, head to the back of the building to access the rooftop summer terrace.

KARLÍN
Czech
ESKA

Pernerova 49, +420 731 140 884, www.eska.ambi.
cz, 8am-11:30pm Mon-Fri, 9am-11:30pm Sat-Sun,
200-600 CZK entrees

Eska is internationally celebrated for serving great food at fair prices. The ground floor of this light, modern warehouse space is dominated by an in-house bakery. Upstairs, the dining room serves simple plates of seasonal vegetables and fresh meats in a laid-back atmosphere of structural support beams softened by hanging plants. Grab an open-faced sandwich for lunch or try the eight-course tasting menu for an indulgent dinner. Reservations recommended.

International
CAFÉ FRIDA
Karlínské náměstí 11, +420 728 042 910, www.cafefrida.cz, 9am-midnight Mon-Fri, 4:30pm-midnight Sat-Sun, 125-175 CZK entrees

This casual, colorful, Mexican-inspired restaurant is named for Frida Kahlo. Don't expect too much spice from the burritos, quesadilla, and burgers tailored to a milder local palate. Plenty of vegetarian and meat-lover's options keep this popular establishment packed with a young, international crowd. Reservations recommended.

★ MANIFESTO MARKET
Na Florenci Street, www.manifesto.city, April-Dec 8am-10pm Mon-Fri, 11am-10pm Sat-Sun, 100-200 CZK entrees

Local culinary connoisseurs rejoiced when this container-based outdoor market opened in the summer of 2018. Popular restaurant names from across the city occupy the booths, serving a wide selection of meals from poke bowls to burgers, tacos, and Czech open-faced sandwiches. The central location just a few streets from the Florenc metro station make this an easy solution for a group with differing tastes. Evening entertainment includes DJs and film screenings. There is one caveat—payment is by card only, with no cash accepted.

Breakfast and Brunch
MUJ ŠÁLEK KÁVY
Křižíkova 105, +420 222 310 361, www.mujsalekkavy.cz, 9am-10pm Mon-Sat, 10am-6pm Sun, 100-150 CZK entrees

Reservations are essential to try one of the most beloved brunches in town. Můj šálek kávy ("My Cup of Coffee") helped to establish a love of high-quality coffee and leisurely weekend meals in the Czech capital. The connoisseurs behind the bar are passionate about their products, catering to the coffee snobs of the Prague community—you may get an eye roll for requesting milk and sugar instead of taking your fair-trade filter coffee black. Choose from a seasonal menu of omelettes and English breakfasts, blueberry pancakes, or light salads and sandwiches as lunchtime hours approach.

LETNÁ AND HOLEŠOVICE
Czech
PIVOVAR MARINA
Jankovcova 12, +420 220 571 183, www.pivovarmarina.cz, 11am-midnight, 175-350 CZK entrees

This massive riverside venue on the eastern edge of Holešovice houses a brewery serving Czech culinary specialties in one half of the space, and an Italian restaurant in the other. The casual vibe and high, vaulted ceilings of the brewery area is popular with large groups and sports fans during important matches. Try the *svíčková* (roasted sirloin in a sweet vegetable sauce with dumplings) or pork ribs with a local lager.

International
MR. HOT DOG
Kamenická 24, www.mrhotdog.cz, +420 732 732 404, 11:30am-10pm, 50-125 CZK entrees

For a quick bite, grab one of the namesake hot dogs or sliders at this low-key local favorite. The menu of American classics is supplemented with limited-time specials such as lobster rolls, plus a yearly eating contest. Indoor seating is limited, making take-out service before hitting nearby Letná Park a popular option.

HILLBILLY BURGER
Pplk Sochora 21, www.hillbilly.cz, +420 774 156 735, 4pm-10pm Tues-Fri, noon-10pm Sat, noon-9pm Sun, 150-200 CZK entrees

The guiding principle behind this newcomer to the Prague landscape is simple: Just F*@¢ing Good Burgers. The below-ground dining room is decorated with chalkboard scrawls and exposed brick, with a long backyard patio where smokers congregate. The

burgers are hearty, the coleslaw is delicious and (unlike many local places) the nachos come piled with toppings—meat, beans, corn, sour cream, and guacamole—far beyond the Prague trap of using "nachos" to mean chips, cheese, and salsa.

GARUDA

Milady Horákové 12, www.garudarestaurant.cz, +420 730 890 424, 10:30am-10pm, 150-275 CZK entrees
The two-story café, restaurant, and "chill out zone" at Garuda blends relaxing elements (think water features and soft lighting) with a trendy, low-key vibe and delicious Indonesian food. This newcomer to the neighborhood is still relatively undiscovered, but an online reservation never hurt anyone. Grab an early meal at a daily happy hour discount from 2:30-5:30pm before watching the sunset at nearby Letná Beer Garden.

SASAZU

Bubenské nábřeží 306, www.sasazu.com, +420 284 097 455, noon-midnight Mon-Thurs, noon-1am Fri-Sat, noon-11pm Sun, 300-1000 CZK entrees
High-end dining in Holešovice is rare, but SaSaZu breaks that rule with Southeast Asian-inspired cuisine in a dimly lit nightclub setting inside the Holešovice Market grounds (also referred to as Pražská tržnice). Share plates are served family-style with starters such as salmon tartar and lobster soup, and flavorful meat-based dishes from a stone oven or grilled in a wok. Glowing red lanterns and sculpted figurines set a vibe that blends elegance and kitsch. Follow up your meal with a performance at nearby circus arts venue Jatka 78, or stick around SaSaZu for that night's dance party or concert in the adjoining club venue. Dinner reservations required.

Breakfast and Brunch

KAFÉ FRANCIN

Dukelských Hrdinů 35, www.francin.cz, +420 778 719 217, 7:30am-8pm Mon-Fri, 9am-6pm Sat-Sun, 125-185 CZK entrees
Breakfast at Kafe Francin can fuel a full day of sightseeing. Try the massive sweet or savory crepes, a hard-to-find bagel sandwich, or an egg and fresh bread breakfast with your morning coffee. Head to the back of the restaurant for plush sofa seating and a browsable bookshelf if space is available or squeeze into one of the smaller tables in the front of this cozy cafe.

★ THE FARM

Korunovacni 17, +420 773 626 177, 8am-10:30pm Mon-Fri, 9am-10:30pm Sat, 9am-8pm Sun, 100-175 CZK entrees
If you're willing to venture a little further for breakfast, join the local crowd of young families and friend groups brunching on fresh eggs, omelets, and avocado toast variations at The Farm. Add a Bloody Mary or mimosa to start your day in style. These fresh-from-the-farmers-market meals take full advantage of seasonal flavors in a tightly-squeezed dining room and outdoor summer patio. Reservations required.

Vegetarian

LOVING HUT

Dukelských hrdinů 18, www.lovinghut.cz, +420 222 950 768, 11am-9pm Mon-Fri, noon-9pm Sat, 100-150 CZK entrees
The safest bet to ensure you're eating vegan cuisine in Prague is to stick to entirely meat-free establishments. This international chain based around the philosophy of "Be Vegan, Make Peace" offers buffet-style salad bars of vegetable-based options. The simple, cafeteria-style atmosphere inspires a quick meal before hitting the town again.

---

1 a trio of spreads at ROESEL Beer & Cake
2 Argentinian appetizers at Gran Fierro 3 fresh from the farmer's market meals at Martin's Bistro 4 Styl & Interier's patio is a coveted lunch spot

Coffee, Tea, and Sweets
CAFÉ JEDNA

Dukelských hrdinů 47, www.cafejedna.cz, +420 778 440 877, 9:30am-10pm, 75-150 CZK entrees

The Veletržní palác ("Trade Fair Palace") branch of Prague's National Gallery also houses a large café lined with sunlit windows and high ceilings. The massive family-friendly seating area is regularly filled with freelance workers, parents with baby strollers, and art fans of all ages. The menu of fresh hummus, soups, sandwiches, and cakes provides a perfect snack or light meal before browsing the multi-story art exhibits next door.

BITCOIN CAFE

Dělnická 43, www.paralenipolis.cz, +420 777 409 056, 8am-8pm Mon-Fri, noon-9pm Sat, noon-8pm Sun

As the name would imply, the only way to pay for your coffee in this cafe is with cryptocurrency (either Bitcoin or Litecoin). Luckily, there is a machine on site and staff on hand to show you how to purchase enough to cover your bill. The gimmick will get you in the door, but the yummy cakes and espresso drinks will keep you in the large, black leather sofas inside this building founded by the Institute for Cryptoanarchy. Observe the tech-focused crowd working to make the internet a place of free information to support a decentralized economy... or just enjoy some quality coffee and a comfortable seat.

Accommodations

Prague's accommodation offerings reflect the distinctive personalities of its different neighborhood. Malá Strana and Old Town are known for historical luxury hotels within steps of major sights. New Town and Vinohrady offer more apartments and trendy, boutique hotels—the Bohemian Hotels and Hostels Group is a local favorite for mid-range, modern style. Vyšehrad, Letná, and Karlín have a more peaceful neighborhood vibe, while Vršovice, Holešovice, Žižkov tend to draw younger, budget-conscious crowds looking for nightlife and not afraid of public transport.

Some of Prague's older mid-range and budget hotels can feel quite dated, and payment in cash only is not unheard of, so read your booking details carefully when choosing a place. Renovation restrictions in public buildings and a prevalence of stairs also make it a less-accessible landscape for travelers with disabilities. Hotels that do offer specially equipped rooms are noted below when possible, but is definitely not standard in all accommodation options, so ask about barrier-free travel or accessibility needs before booking.

The Prague landscape offers many alternatives beyond traditional hotel chains. Pensions and aparthotels provide more residential living environments with access to cooking facilities and family-friendly amenities. Design hotels cater to architecture lovers and the luxury level maintains the outstanding service and modern touches that their clientele expect. If you have any concerns about specifics that might make or break your stay, contact your hosts before booking to confirm your expectations.

OLD TOWN
(Staré Město)
Under 4,000 CZK
HOSTEL HOMER

Melantrichova 11, +420 722 661 922, www.hostelhomer.com

The 16th-century building of Hostel HOMEr is just steps from Old Town Square and a lively nightlife scene. Choose from 4-bed, female-only spaces (750 CZK) to mixed, 16-bed dorms (600 CZK) plus a few private double and triple rooms (2,500-3,500 CZK), all with shared bathrooms. The domed ceilings, historical décor, friendly 24-hour reception, plus free adapters and WiFi make this a favorite for backpackers of all ages. Payment in cash only.

4,000-7,000 CZK
★ THE EMERALD
Žatecká 7, www.the-emerald-prague.com,
4,000 CZK s 5,000 CZK d
Every design detail of The Emerald tells a story inside this historic Art Nouveau building in the Josefov neighborhood. Thirteen individual rooms take inspiration from themes including the Orient Express, the Italian region of Tuscany, and Japanese principles of natural harmony. The original architecture is highlighted with copper chain shower curtains, distressed walls, and natural wood touches. Rooms include a fridge, oven, and private bathroom among the minimal, customized furnishings. There is WiFi but no elevator. These aparthotels, newly opened in the summer of 2018, cater to independent travelers looking for a familiar, photogenic alternative to hotel life.

Over 7,000 CZK
EMBLEM HOTEL
Platnéřská 19, +420 226 202 500,
www.emplemprague.com, 5,000-10,000 CZK
doubles, 10,000-20,000 CZK suites
The cozy rooms at the family-owned, boutique Emblem Hotel make up for their size with comfortable public spaces to socialize. Fifty-nine small rooms (including one accessibility equipped) are decked out in modern style and private bathrooms inside a 1908 building just one street off Old Town Square. A private, 30-minute (1,200 CZK for 2 people) or 60-minute (2,200 CZK for 2 people) reservation of the rooftop Jacuzzi and terrace includes a bottle of prosecco to toast the incredible view. Guests exchange travel tips over complimentary wine in the M Lounge from 6pm-8pm. Splurge on the Library Suite (around 20,000 CZK) with a huge copper bathtub and sliding bookshelf separating the bedroom from a reading lounge.

NEW TOWN
(Nové Město)
Under 4,000 CZK
SOPHIE'S HOSTEL
Melounova 2, +420 246 032 621,
www.sophieshostel.com, 400 CZK
Sophie's Hostel is a peaceful alternative to the rowdy, bunk bed dorm experience. With twelve light, clean, private rooms and apartments with en suite bathrooms, or seventeen shared dorm rooms of up to five people (women-only dorms available), this central location near Karlovo náměstí and Náměstí Miru provides an affordable place to lay your head and a ten-minute walk from Wenceslas Square without sacrificing a good night's sleep.

MOOO APARTMENTS
Myslikova 22, +420 608 278 422, www.
mooo-apartments.com, 2,600 CZK s, 3,200 CZK d
Treat yourself to a comfortable home-away-from-home decorated in bovine kitsch at MOOo Apartments. What's with the name? The designers wanted to combine the relaxing feel of the countryside with the urban energy of the city, and many New Town restaurants, bars, and clubs are just stumbling distance down the street. Sixteen one-bedroom apartments (2,000 CZK) and five two-bedroom apartments (3,300 CZK) are available, plus two penthouse suites (10,000 CZK) for up to eight people, all with private bathrooms.

MOSAIC HOUSE
Odborů 4, +420 277 016 880, www.mosaichouse.
com, 350 CZK dorms, 3,500 CZK d
This nearly 100-room structure includes both a 38-room hostel ranging from 4-bed to 26-bed shared dorms with bathrooms, plus a 55-room design hotel with one accessibility equipped private double room. Mosaic House uses energy-efficient appliances, renewable energy sources, and a grey water system to make it Prague's greenest accommodation

option. The décor is fun and funky including a Mediterranean-and-Middle-East-inspired restaurant by day and in-house dance party every night on the ground floor. Look for the giant mushroom statues outside the entrance to find your way home to the southern edge of New Town and Vyšehrad. Rooms book out fast so make your reservation early.

4,000-7,000 CZK
CAPITAL APARTMENTS
Václavské náměstí 36, +420 224 240 876, www.capitalapartmentsprague.com, 3,000 CZK studio, 5,000 CZK apartment
Capital Apartments cater to families, large groups, and young travelers looking for a front row seat to the action around Wenceslas Square. With 23 apartments spread across three central buildings, options range from studios to 4-bedroom suites accepting up to twelve guests. The décor is modern, minimal, and comfortable with basic kitchen amenities and private bathrooms. Request a Wenceslas Square location for balcony views or just around the corner on Vodičkova Street for a (slightly) quieter experience.

MISS SOPHIE'S
Melounova 3, +420 210 011 200, www.miss-sophies.com, 4,000 CZK s, 4,500 CZK d
The convenient location and casual chic of Miss Sophie's 16-room boutique hotel with en suite bathrooms makes this an elegant favorite just one metro stop or a ten-minute walk off of Wenceslas Square. A newly added private Jacuzzi and sauna are waiting to pamper tired travelers after a long day of crisscrossing cobblestoned streets. A simple buffet breakfast or hot brunch is served across the street at Sophie's Kitchen for an extra 150-200 CZK.

★ DANCING HOUSE HOTEL
Jiráskovo Náměstí 6, +420 720 983 172, www.dancinghousehotel.com, 5,000-8,000 CZK d
There is no comparison for sleeping inside one of the city's most famous sights, the Dancing House. Request a riverside room with floor-to-ceiling windows and wake up to a view of the Prague Castle. You set the mood inside these thirty-one spacious, modern rooms with en suite bathrooms and a choice of multi-colored LED lights. A welcome drink and buffet breakfast served under a sparkling chandelier are included from the Fred and Ginger restaurant on the top floor.

Over 7,000 CZK
HOTEL BOHO
Senovážná 4, +420 234 622 600, www.hotelbohoprague.com, 6,500 CZK s, 8,000 CZK d
While many of Prague's central hotels go for historical charm, Hotel BOHO offers fifty-seven rooms and suites of pure modern elegance in muted neutral tones, including two equipped for accessibility, and all rooms include private bathrooms. Curl up beside the library fireplace after admiring the architecture of nearby Náměstí Republiky in the winter months. Health-conscious guests will appreciate the onsite gym, small plunge pool, sauna, and spa.

LESSER TOWN
(Malá Strana)
Under 4,000 CZK
★ THE NICHOLAS HOTEL RESIDENCE
Malostranské náměstí 5, +420 210 011 500, www.thenicholashotel.com, 2,000 CZK d, 3,500-5,000 CZK suites
The charming, nine-room Nicholas Hotel Residence offers one of the most centrally located home bases in Malá Strana, just next door to the Church of St. Nicholas and the busy square of Malostranské náměstí. The expansive, comfortable furnishings include living room spaces, well-equipped kitchen facilities, washer-dryer, and free WiFi, great for families and couples of all ages. Toss on your robe for the continental breakfast buffet served in the hallways, where you can load up your plate and say "Dobré ráno" (good morning) to your neighbors before taking breakfast back to your room to enjoy. Twenty-four-hour reception is friendly and helpful, even if you've got an odd-hour arrival.

OLD CROOKED BEAMS

Malostranské náměstí, +420 604 212 613,
www.oldcrookedbeams.com, around 3,000 CZK d

For a truly personal experience, try the privately-owned apartment at Old Crooked Beams. This comfortable apartment with one queen sized bed plus a kitchen and private bathroom is perfect for couples and includes customized restaurant advice from the English owner and a convenient location beside St. Nicholas Church. Get the experience of visiting a local friend even if you don't know anyone in town.

★ ROYAL COURT APARTMENTS

Legerova 48, +420 725 702 326, www.royalcourhotel.
cz, 3,000 CZK studio, 3,500 CZK suite

The boutique selection of 17 studios and family apartments at Royal Court Apartments are decorated with brightly colored details, ranging from purple roses to American flags, that give each room a playful personality. With full kitchen amenities and private bedrooms and bathrooms, these spacious temporary residences are great for couples, small friend groups, and families traveling with teens. The lively surrounding area just off the IP Pavlova metro stop is flush with restaurants and public transport connections, with a tourist information center on the ground floor to answer any questions.

4,000-7,000 CZK
★ LOKAL INN

Malostranské náměstí 5, +420 257 014 800,
www.lokalinn.cz, 3,500-5,000 CZK d

In true tavern style, the Czech pub Lokál U Bílé kuželky also offers lodging upstairs in the boutique, fourteen-room Lokal Inn. Simple, clean lines and en suite bathrooms housed under exposed wooden beams offer modern comfort with the added ability to stumble upstairs after your last beer from the popular pub below. This is also a great location for photographers hoping for a sunrise session on the Charles Bridge, just steps away.

Over 7,000 CZK
MANDARIN ORIENTAL

Nebovidska 1, +420 233 088 888,
www.mandarinoriental.com, 10,000-20,000 CZK d,
20,000-40,000 CZK suites

Attentive service, Spices Asian Restaurant, and a spa housed inside a Renaissance chapel keep the guests of Mandarin Oriental in a state of bliss. The quiet location, with 79 en suite guest rooms (one accessibility equipped) plus twenty suites is tucked between the green lawns of Park Kampa and Petřín Hill. Guests are encouraged to relax and unplug, andWiFi comes at a premium. Start your day with morning yoga in the chapel instead of checking your email, and end with tikka masala on the terrace dining room.

AUGUSTINE HOTEL

Letenská 33, +420 266 112 233, www.augustinehotel.
com, 10,000 CZK d, 15,000-40,000 CZK suites

The luxurious Augustine Hotel spreads 101 en suite rooms of historical ambiance (with one equipped for accessibility) across seven historic buildings, including a 13th-century former monastery. The Cubist details and a subtle color palette create a sense of regal calm just off the bustling square and transport hub of Malostranské náměstí, with individual suites offering tower views, historic frescoes, or custom glass designs. A twenty-four-hour fitness center plus a wellness center of spa treatments and a Turkish hammam round out the menu of indulgent experiences.

THE ALCHYMIST GRAND HOTEL AND SPA

Tržiště 19, +420 257 286 011, www.alchymisthotel.
com, 8,000 CZK d, 9,000-25,000 CZK suites

The Alchymist Grand Hotel and Spa goes all in on the historic charm of its 16th-century Baroque surroundings. Rich hues, ornate headboards, private bathrooms and decorative details in every room and suite set a truly regal tone. The underground Ecsotica Spa includes a plunge pool, saunas, Indonesian-inspired massage and aromatherapy treatments, and a small, stone-walled fitness center. A buffet breakfast is included and can also be delivered to your room.

ARIA HOTEL

Tržiště 9, +420 225 334 111, www.ariahotel.net, 6,000 CZK d, 7,000-25,000 CZK suites

Aria Hotel's roughly 50 music-themed rooms with en suite bathrooms are dedicated to the greats of contemporary, classical, opera and jazz music ranging from Beethoven to the Beatles. Elegant touches include a rooftop terrace, fireplace lounge, small fitness center, free access to the neighboring Vrtba Gardens, and a music concierge offering personal recommendations for local concerts. Buffet breakfast and WiFi are complimentary.

PRAGUE CASTLE DISTRICT

(Hradčany)

Under 4,000 CZK

ROMANTIK HOTEL U RAKA

Černínská 10, + 420 220 511 100, www.hoteluraka.cz, around 3,500 CZK d

To mix a peaceful, residential vibe with the convenience of walking to the Prague Castle, book early for a spot in the six-room Romantik Hotel U Raka. This tiny, family owned cottage at the top of hilly Hradčany is as cute as they come. Comfortable apartments with en suite bathrooms are decorated in deep reds and exposed brick, accented with the artistic family's own paintings and sculptures. Private residences surround a quiet cobblestoned courtyard. Enjoy a light snack in the warm breakfast nook or outdoors on the terrace in summer months.

Over 7,000 CZK

★ GOLDEN WELL HOTEL

U Zlaté studně 4, +420 257 011 213, www.goldenwell.cz, 6,500-8,000 CZK d

The boutique Golden Well Hotel, known as U Zlaté Studné in Czech, is as well known for its impressive rooftop restaurant as the decadence of its 17 en suite rooms and two luxurious suites (around 15,000 CZK). This peaceful property tucked between the Prague Castle's lower gardens and Wallenstein Gardens, just slightly off the main tourist track through Malá Strana, was originally owned by Roman Emperor and Bohemian King Rudolf II and refurbished after decades of neglect to reopen in the new millennium. This splurge-worthy destination is perfect for a romantic weekend.

VYŠEHRAD

4,000-7,000 CZK

CORINTHIA HOTEL

Kongresová 1, +420 261 191 111, www.corinthia.com, around 3,500-5,000 CZK d

You don't have to stay in the tourist center to enjoy five-star elegance in Prague. The towering Corinthia Hotel offers more than 500 rooms with private bathrooms and modern amenities, five of which are equipped for accessibility, and incredible views of the city skyline. Located just off the Vyšehrad metro stop, this location is perfect for relaxing evening walks around the Vyšehrad Complex or exploring more of Prague's neighborhoods. The hotel itself houses four restaurants for breakfast, grilled meats and pizzas, Asian cuisine, and a cocktail lounge as well as a full swimming pool, top-floor spa, and gym facilities.

VINOHRADY AND VRŠOVICE

Under 4,000 CZK

CZECH INN

Francouzská 240/76, +420 210 011 100, www.czech-inn.com

For lively budget accommodation in Vršovice, steps away from trendy bistros and adult beverages of Krymská Street, check into the pun-intended Czech Inn. This massive, modern staple of the Bohemian Hostels group offers stylish rooms from private studios (1,500 CZK) to 36-bed mixed dorms and shared bathrooms (125 CZK) with free WiFi throughout the building. There is a seven-night maximum stay.

APARTHOTEL LUBLAŇKA

Lublanska 59, +420 222 539 539, www.lublanka.hotel.cz, around 2,000 CZK d

This relatively quiet side street between Náměstí Miru and Karlovo náměstí makes Aparthotel Lublaňka a comfortable home with basic furnishings to lay your head. Thirteen en suite rooms are kitchen-equipped and breakfast is included. The newly opened Berlin Bar in the courtyard serves all-day brunch and cocktails making it a livelier location in warmer months.

PURE WHITE

Koubkova 12, +420 220 990 100, www.purewhitehotelprague.com, 2,500 CZK s, 3,500 CZK d

Pure White boutique hotel offers 37 en suite rooms of modern comfort on a quiet side street. Reception is open 24 hours with a menu of pillow preferences, in-room WiFi, and breakfast included. Business travelers and sophisticated sightseers can decompress in the lobby bar.

ŽIŽKOV
Under 4,000 CZK
HOTEL THEATRINO

Borivojova 53, +420-227 031 894, www.hoteltheatrino.cz, 1,750 CZK s, 3,000 CZK d

Hotel Theatrino sits in the heart of this pub-heavy residential neighborhood popular with international students, young professionals, and long-term local residents who remember its working-class roots. Far from the crowds of the city center, this large, five-story collection of simple rooms with rich red accents and a large, ornate conference hall cater to groups and business travelers. Free WiFi, 24-hour reception, and a private sauna for rent round out the offerings.

HOTEL AMADEUS

Dalimilova 10, +420 210 011 400, https://www.hotelamadeus.cz, 1,200 CZK s, 1,500 CZK d

In the year 2019, Hotel Amadeus, is slowly transforming from an older Czech hotel to a trendy Žižkov branch of Miss Sophie's Hotel under new management by the Bohemian Hostels Group. This live-like-a-local environment of 28 en suite rooms is located on a quiet square near the Jara Cimrman Theater, far from the crowds of the city center. No matter the hotel name on the door upon your arrival, you can expect clean lines vintage design touches, and friendly service in this boutique multi-story location with a tranquil courtyard.

Over 7,000 CZK
ONE ROOM HOTEL

Mahlerovy Sady 1, +420 210 320 081, www.towerpark.cz, 15,000-20,000 CZK d

The level of exclusivity is right there in the name. One Room Hotel describes the single luxury suite available at the top of the Žižkov TV Tower. Wake up to a panoramic view, set your musical mood with the in-room computer and Bose sound system, and enjoy the complimentary L'Occitane cosmetics of the en suite bathroom. With breakfast included and Oblaca restaurant and bar occupying the floors below, you may struggle to find reasons to leave your sky-high perch over Prague.

KARLÍN
Under 4,000 CZK
PENTAHOTEL PRAGUE

Sokolovská 112, +420 222 332 800, www.pentahotels.com, 2,500 CZK s, 3,000 CZK d

The neon lighting and modern design of the seven-story, Pentahotel Prague demonstrate the growing (and grown up) nightlife scene. The 227 en suite rooms are a bit outside the center, but right on a public transportation line in this largely residential neighborhood packed with restaurants and wine bars. Free WiFi is natural for the young, trendy clientele, and the bar staff of the lobby's Penta Lounge perform double duty as the reception desk.

LETNÁ AND HOLEŠOVICE

Under 4,000 CZK

SIR TOBY'S

Dělnická 24, +420 210 011 610, www.sirtobys.com, 650-900 CZK dorms

Sir Toby's has been a favorite of the backpacking community, and those looking to escape the traditional tourist track, since its humble beginnings in 1999. Vintage-style, 4-bed or 12-bed dorm rooms with shared bathrooms are restricted to travelers ages 18-39, while the all-ages, private, en suite rooms (2,000-3,500 CZK) upstairs are impressively insulated from noise. The WiFi is strong, the staff are friendly, and your bunkmates are likely to stumble home at all hours. Buffet breakfast in the downstairs bar includes fruit, cereal, and a make-it-yourself pancake station.

RESIDENCE MILADA

Milady Horákové 12, +420 775 888 830, www.residencemilada.com, 2,500 CZK s, 3,500 d

Rich red tones and eight multi-bed, en suite apartments in the boutique Residence Milada cater to families and close friends comfortable with shared sleeping areas. Deluxe and Family Apartments (5,000-9,000 CZK) with soundproof rooms can sleep up to five guests, and include a washing machine, modern bathroom facilities, fully equipped kitchen and dining room spaces. If you don't feel like cooking, grab breakfast nearby at Café Letka, or try a film brunch at independent cinema Bio Oko.

Information and Services

TOURIST INFORMATION

If you're looking for brochures of entertainment options and day trips, answers to lingering questions about transportation, or really just anything you want to ask in English, Prague's Tourist Information Centers are there to help. You'll find offices in some of the most popular tourist areas. The **Old Town Square location** (Staroměstské Náměstí 1, 9am-7pm) is at the Old Town Hall, next to the Astronomical Clock, while **Wenceslas Square's closest base** (Rytířská 12, 9am-7pm) is on the main street connecting it to Old Town—walk past the large New Yorker store at the base of the square and keep an eye out your left-hand side. You'll also find a tourist-friendly base beside the **Charles Bridge Tower** (Mostecká 4, 9am-8pm) on the Malá Strana side of the Vltava River.

One local magazine, **The Prague Visitor,** also has an informal information office just below the Prague Castle (Nerudova 25, 8am-5pm Mon-Fri). This office is not officially run by the city, but the cheerful young staff of Prague transplants are happy to offer basic advice over a cup of coffee.

BUSINESS HOURS

While office workers may get an early start and fill public transport from 6am-9am, many independent shops don't open until 10pm (although supermarkets and shopping malls tend to open earlier at 8am or 9am). Shops start to close down between 5pm-7pm. Most weekend hours are limited, but not closed entirely.

Lunch hour is early during weekdays, and pubs may fill up as early as 11am. You can usually expect dinner service to last until at least 10pm. Many independent coffee shops don't cater to the pre-work crowd and instead open around 10 am on weekdays and possibly even later on weekends.

EMERGENCY NUMBERS

The universal emergency number across Europe is 112, and operators can direct you towards any specific emergency needs if you are unable to reach a police station. Additional numbers are available for fire (**150**) and ambulance (**155**), but these services are not guaranteed to speak English, so 112 is your safest bet to be redirected.

In case of emergency (e.g. lost or stolen possessions, criminal encounters) you'll want to file a police report for official documentation. English fluency among Prague police officers on the street is not guaranteed, but the following stations are intended to have an interpreter on site at all times for concerns in multiple languages.

- **New Town** (Jungmannovo námesti. 9, +420 974 851 750)

- **New Town** (Krakovská 11, +420 974 851 720)

- **Old Town** (Benediktská 1, +420 974 889 210)

- **Malá Strana** (Vlašská 3, +420 974 851 730)

CRIME

The Czech Republic was ranked 7th in 2018s Global Peace Index. Crime is low, water is safe to drink, threat of terror attacks is minimal, and solo travelers can walk almost all streets safely at any hour. However, travelers from some ethnic or religious backgrounds, particularly those with darker skin, may experience xenophobic attitudes and unwanted attention. Anti-immigrant or anti-Muslim marches are usually met with an equal or larger march in support of diverse societies, but this is a divisive political issue in the country.

HOSPITALS AND PHARMACIES

If you're in need of emergency medical attention, **Motol Hospital** (V Úvalu 84, www.fnmotol.cz, metro stop Nemocnice Motol) has a specific, English-speaking reception area for foreigners. Depending on the type of insurance you have, visitors may have to pay a deposit on arrival before seeing a doctor and then settle the bill after receiving treatment. **Na Homolce Hospital** (Roentgenova 2, +420 257 273 289, www.homolka.cz, bus stop Nemocnice Na Homolce) also offers an English-speaking reception and quality medical care.

You can spot pharmacies (*lékárna* in Czech*)* by looking for a green cross outside the buildings. **Lékárna U svaté Ludmily** (Belgická 37, www.lekbelgicka.cz, +420 222 513 396) is located next to Náměstí Miru and open 24 hours a day.

Mental Health Services and Emergency Support

Local expat Gail Whitmore (+420 775 248 363, www.counselinginprague.com) offers crisis support specializing in depression, sexual violence, domestic violence, and LGBTQI+ support to English-speakers in Prague. Confidentiality is ensured and help is available at any hour of day or night.

FOREIGN CONSULATES

- **Embassy of the United States** (Tržiště 15, www.cz.usembassy.gov, +420 257 022 000)

- **Canadian Embassy** (Ve Struhách 95/2, www.canadainternational.gc.ca, + 420 272 101 800)

- **British Embassy** (Thunovská 14, www.gov.uk, +420 257 402 111)

- **Irish Embassy** (Tržiště 13, www.dfa.ie, +420 257 011 280)

- **Embassy of South Africa** (Ruská 65, www.mzv.cz, +420 267 311 114)

- **Australian Consulate** (Klimentská 10, 6th Floor, www.dfat.gov.au, +420 221 729 260)

- **Consulate of New Zealand** (Václavské náměstí 9, www.mfat.govt.nz, +420 234 784 777)

CURRENCY EXCHANGE

Many of the city's currency exchange offices advertise 0 percent commission in large letters, but offer abysmal rates in small print when you actually hand over your cash. Two trusted offices to change money are **Visitor**

Change (Na Můstku 2, 9am-7pm) at the information center or eXchange (Kaprova 14) just off Old Town Square past St. Nicholas Church. ATMs generally offer a fair rate, but check with your bank about any fees for withdrawing money abroad.

Transportation

GETTING THERE
Air
International flights will most likely arrive at **Vaclav Havel International Airport** (Aviatická, www.prg.aero). There are two terminals, with Terminal 1 serving flights from outside the Schengen area (e.g. North America, the UK, Asia, Africa, and the Middle East) and Terminal 2 serving flights from within Europe's Schengen countries. The airport is small and reasonably easy to navigate with hit-or-miss public WiFi available.

From Budapest: Czech Airlines (www.csa.cz) operates flights three times a day (1.5 hours).

From Vienna: The short distance between Prague and Vienna means that buses and trains are more efficient than flying, but **Austrian Airlines** (www.austrian.com) does connect Prague and Vienna. Flights are just under an hour.

AIRPORT TRANSPORTATION
The airport is 17 kilometers (about 10.5 miles) east of the city center, and transportation from the airport to the city center is not always straightforward. There is no direct public transportation link, but you can catch **buses** from Terminal 1 or Terminal 2 (routes 100 or 119, 32 CZK transport ticket) which run frequently from about 4:45am until around 11pm. After about a 15-20-minute ride, transfer to the green metro line at the last bus stop, Nádraží Veleslavín. The trip between the airport and the city center takes roughly 35-55 minutes total.

For an easier (and usually slightly cheaper) ride into the city, try local ride-sharing providers **Liftago** (www.liftago.cz) or international operators **Taxify** (www.taxify.eu) and **Uber** (www.uber.com). These do require setting up a profile, so best to download and enter information before arrival in the airport. Rideshares pick up passengers along the strip of pavement in the short-term parking lot that sits in front of Terminal 1 and Terminal 2 (not at the sidewalk in front of arrivals). The ride into the city takes roughly 20-30 minutes and costs 350-700 CZK.

There are no taxi stands at the Prague Airport, so if you want to take a taxi, ask one of the airport information desks (Fix Taxi or Taxi Praha) to arrange one for you or negotiate your fare in advance—Prague taxis have a reputation for overcharging foreigners. The ride into the city takes roughly 20-30 minutes and costs around 500-800 CZK in a taxi.

Train
The national rail company is called **České dráhy** (www.cd.cz), with unpredictable service varying between older models with minimal amenities and newer trains with WiFi and electrical outlets. When booking a ticket in person or online, make sure to specify that you want a seat reservation unless you're okay standing in the train car halls during peak seasons. Two private carriers, **Regiojet** (www.regiojet.com) and **Leo Express** (www.leoexpress.com) also run on the same lines with more consistently modern service and guaranteed seating at varying prices. Trains arrive and depart efficiently and reliably, so be sure to find your platform with plenty of time to spare.

There are three train stations serving Prague. The Main Railway Station is called **Praha - Hlavní nádraží** (Wilsonova 8), and often written as Praha hl. n in Czech. This station is located in the center of New Town

Did You Know...?

Every city has its fun facts and local secrets that define its personality. Here are a few nuggets of knowledge you should know about Prague and the Czech Republic:

- There are more than 10 million people in the Czech Republic, and about **1.3 million** of them live in Prague. Roughly 7 million tourists join them on the streets and beds of the capital each year.

- The Czech Republic's second-largest city is **Brno,** in the southeast region of Moravia, and the third-largest is **Ostrava,** a former mining town located in the northeast near the borders of Poland and Slovakia.

- Prague has a number of **nicknames** including the Golden City, the Heart of Europe, and the City of a Hundred (or a Thousand) Spires.

- Despite all those spires, a large portion of the population identify as **atheist or agnostic,** followed by **Catholics** as the largest organized religion. There is also a sci-fi streak, with more than 15,000 Czechs identifying as **"Jedi Knights"** as their religious affiliation on the last census.

- The Czech Republic is the official name of the country, and **Czechia** was approved in 2016 as an official short version accepted on paperwork and uniforms for the national sports teams. The controversial decision is divisive among the locals, who either love it or hate it and refuse to use it.

- Decisions in Prague have had a galactical impact. The 2006 meeting of the International Astronomical Union that decided to demote **Pluto** was held in Prague.

- The US and the Czech Republic have been connected since the formation of Czechoslovakia in 1918. **Thomas Garrigue Masaryk,** the first Czechoslovak president, married an American woman and took her maiden name as his middle name—how's that for avant-garde feminism?

and connects directly to the red Metro line C. This station serves both domestic and international destinations and is filled with restaurants, shopping, and even a supermarket. This is the most common station that international tourists will arrive or depart from.

Two smaller stations also offer connections to destinations abroad and within the Czech Republic: **Praha - Masarykovo nádraží** (Havlíčkova 2) is in New Town not far from Náměstí Republiky and next to tram stop Masarykovo nádraží. Indirect trains requiring transfers to Vienna (Wien) and Budapest may depart from or arrive at this station.

Train station **Praha-Holešovice** (Partyzánská 26) is located along the red Metro line C at the metro stop with the same name. Some indirect trains to Vienna (Wien) or Budapest may stop at this local station, one stop outside of Prague's main central train station (Hlavní nádraží). This may be a more convenient place for travelers staying in Letná or Holešovice to board or depart these trains.

From Vienna: Trains to Prague (4 hours, €19-66) depart Vienna's Wien Hauptbahnhof station between 6:30am and 10:10pm every one or two hours. Most trains are operated by **ÖBB Railjet** (www.oebb.at) or **RegioJet** (www.regiojet.com). Fares vary depending on the train company. (RegioJet tends to be cheaper, but ÖBB Railjet have some discounted tickets.) There is also a night train operated by **EuroNight** (an international night train that is run by various operators, like ÖBB Railjet; you can buy tickets on the ÖBB Railjet website) that leaves Vienna around 10pm and arrives in Prague at 6am and tickets cost from €60.

From Budapest: Trains operated by EuroCity, a cross border train category running within the European intercity rail network run by more than one train company, run from Budapest Keleti every two hours between 5:40am and 3:40pm (6.5 hours, €20-30/6175-9750 HUF). You can buy tickets from the MÁV website (www.mavcsoport.hu). There is also a night train available, but you need to book this in advance if you want a sleeper (€29-39/9425-12,675 HUF).

Bus

Prague's main **Florenc Bus Station** (Křižíkova 6, www.florenc.cz) can be tricky to find. It is connected to the Florenc Metro station along the red Metro line C and yellow metro line B, but you have to follow signs for the specific exit to "Autobusové nádraží" or you may find yourself a few streets away. Multiple bus companies arrive and depart from Florenc at all hours, but the terminal building of fast food, indoor seating, carrier information counters, and luggage storage is only open between 6am and 10pm. Travelers may have to wait outside for late-night connections and overnight buses.

The **Na Knížecí Bus Station** (Na Knížecí) in the Smichov neighborhood serves domestic routes to places such as Český Krumlov or Karovy Vary. The outdoor platforms do not offer much customer service or shelter so double check your departure information and bundle up in winter if departing from this station. Na Knížecí is easily accessible on the yellow metro line, just follow the signs with a picture of a bus for the correct exit out of the large, underground Anděl metro stop. Na Knížecí is also accessible via tram 20 from Malá Strana (10-15 minutes) or tram 5 from Wenceslas Square (15-20 minutes). A taxi from Wenceslas Square takes 10-20 minutes, depending on traffic, and should cost 150-250 CZK.

The **Černý Most** bus station lies at the end of the yellow Metro line B. The bus stops are located downstairs from the subway platforms. Day trips to Liberec depart hourly from this outdoor station for most of the day, and

there are a few fast food options and a RegioJet information center on the lower level.

From Vienna: You can get the bus with **FlixBus** (www.flixbus.com) from Wien Erdberg or **RegioJet** (www.regiojet.com) from Wien Hauptbahnhof from Vienna to Prague 6am-11:30pm. Buses go every hour and a half for FlixBus, whereas for RegioJet there are services running 6 times a day. The journey takes around 4-5 hours and tickets cost €15-23.

From Budapest: FlixBus (www.flixbus.com) in collaboration with the domestic Volánbusz company (http://nemzetkozi.volanbusz.hu) has buses to Prague (7.5 hours, €15-26) several times a day, approximately every 2 hours, usually going from the Népliget bus station.

Car

An international license is required to drive in the Czech Republic. To access the highways, you'll need to purchase a sticker at a border crossing point, post office, or gas station and display it on your windshield. Prague's highways, particularly the D1 highway connecting Prague and Brno, are notorious for heavy traffic and construction delays. Satellite navigation or GPS is recommended for visitors navigating the Czech Republic by car.

From Vienna: Plan on three-and-a-half to five hours if you want to drive the roughly 250km (155 miles) from Vienna to Prague. Take the A5 north to Brno (a great place for lunch or a stopover) and then take the D1/E65 highway West to Prague. This route has roads with tolls so you will need a vignette for Austria (€9) and the Czech Republic (CZK 350).

From Budapest: Drive the M1 west from Budapest towards the Hungarian border and continue northwest towards Vienna. Follow the A5 north to Brno before heading west on the D1/E65 to Prague. The route is 525 km (325 miles) long and takes 5 hours. There are tolls in both Austria (€9) and Hungary (HUF 3000), so you will need a vignette for each country.

GETTING AROUND

Prague's public transportation system, **Dopravní podnik hlavního města Prahy** (www.dpp.cz) is one of the best in the world, with easy access to almost every part of the city via metro and tram for most neighborhoods or bus for a few of the more residential areas or the outskirts.

Transit Passes

Public transport tickets are sold in chunks of time, not single rides. They are valid from the moment they are validated, *not* when they are bought, so don't forget to stamp your ticket when you're ready to use it. Individual tickets are available for 30 minutes (24 CZK) or ninety minutes (32 CZK), as well as 24-hour passes (110 CZK) or 72-hour passes (310 CZK). There are no week passes, but a monthly unlimited pass (550 CZK) is less expensive than two three-day tickets. Prague transport tickets can be used on all metro, tram, and bus lines and also include use of the funicular on Petřín Hill and the ferries crossing the Vltava River during warmer months. Tickets are valid for unlimited rides during the allotted time, including transfers between the various modes.

Paper tickets are available to purchase from yellow automated machines inside Metro stations and near some major tram stops, or in person at limited information desks (see www.dpp.cz for locations). A few updated machines accept credit cards, but many require cash in coins (not bills), so a multi-day pass can save the hassle of finding a machine plus the right change for every individual ride, especially if searching late at night. Some corner stores around town also sell transport tickets, but availability is inconsistent. It is not possible to buy a ticket on public transport in Prague.

Tickets work on an honor system. You validate your ticket before entering and then keep the ticket with you as proof of payment. Inspectors can do random checks at any time, and anyone caught without a ticket will be removed and required to pay a hefty 1,500 CZK fine on the spot—inspectors will accompany you to an ATM if you don't have cash on hand.

Excuses, ignorance, or simply forgetting to stamp your ticket is not accepted as an excuse so be sure to validate every time and keep your ticket in a safe, accessible place.

Metro

Prague's underground subway system consists of three lines: the green **Metro line A** running from Dejvice through the Old Town and into Vinohrady and Žižkov, the yellow **Metro line B** running from Anděl across Old Town and New Town and into Karlín, and the red **Metro line C** connecting Holešovice with the city center and Vyšehrad. Most stations have a single platform with service in both directions (with Vyšehrad, Hlavní Nádraží, and Černý Most as exceptions).

The metro runs from 5am to midnight daily, with trains arriving every two-to-three minutes in peak hours and five-to-ten minutes in off-peak hours. Many stations have a digital display counting down until the arrival. Validate your ticket in yellow boxes located at the entrance to the stations, usually at the top of stairs or escalators before you reach the platform.

Not all metro stations are accessible via elevator (see www.dpp.cz for barrier-free travel) and most stations combine escalators and stairs, so be prepared to lift any luggage that you're traveling with. Many of the escalators are quite steep and faster than travelers may be used to. The deepest station at Náměstí Miru takes over two minutes to travel 53 meters (almost 175 feet) down one of the longest escalators in all of Europe.

Tram

The tram system runs 24 hours a day, switching to limited night-tram schedules at midnight. **Tram 22** is particularly popular among tourists, connecting the Prague Castle to Malá Strana, Vinohrady, and New Town. Night trams generally begin with the number nine (e.g. 92, 97). If you have a single-ride paper ticket, be sure to validate it onboard in small yellow boxes near some of the doors. Tram rides can be a bit jerky so be sure to hold on

Transit Etiquette

color-coded signs in Prague's Metro stations

- **Noise:** The atmosphere on Prague's public transport is generally quiet, and loud conversations or phone calls will be met with dirty looks from the residents.

- **Seating:** There is a line of succession when it comes to seating—riders are expected to stand up and offer their spots at any stop to elderly people, injuries with crutches or a cane, pregnant women, and young children.

- **Boarding:** Always let the departing passengers exit before attempting to board. During rush hours, passengers near the doors often step off the train and stand near the doors to let passengers off before re-entering, so maintain an awareness of anyone needing to squeeze past, especially when traveling with luggage or a backpack.

- **Escalators:** When riding the escalator in metro stations, passengers who want to walk use the left side and those who want to stand stay to the right—the locals take this seriously so don't block the path with luggage or a group of side-by-side riders.

when the train starts to move to avoid tumbling down the aisles.

Construction and maintenance on the tram lines are popular during the summer months, so many tram routes may be interrupted. Information is often posted at the stop, but not always in English, so having a map or data-enabled phone can be useful to tackle surprise route changes. The transit authority website (www.dpp.en) usually provides updates in English.

Bus

Prague's city buses connect to some of the more remote neighborhoods and trips to the Prague airport. Validate your ticket on-board in small yellow boxes near some of the doors. Like trams, buses run at all hours, and night buses also begin with the number nine (e.g. 92, 97).

Taxi and Ride-Sharing

Taxi service in Prague is notorious for taking indirect routes and overcharging foreigners, particularly if flagged down off the street near touristy areas. You may ask your hotel or restaurant to call a cab for you to be on the safe side. Smartphone travelers can also use local ride-sharing providers **Liftago** (www.liftago.cz) or international operators **Taxify** (www.taxify.eu) and **Uber** (www.uber.com) for a safe ride, tracked on a map, and that doesn't require having the local currency on hand.

Public transport can generally take you anywhere that taxis could during the day, but a taxi can be helpful if you're out on the town after midnight, when the metro stops running and trams and buses switch to limited night routes.

Car

Driving in Prague is more trouble than it's worth: lots of one-way streets, confusing parking zones, and restrictions (see www.parkujvklidu.cz for details). Cars stick to the right side of the road in the Czech capital, so look right first at any intersections.

However, a car can be useful for day trips and seeing some of the countryside. You can find many international rental car companies, including **Avis** (www.avis.cz, +420 221 851 225, 7:30am-6pm Mon-Fri, 8am-noon Sat-Sun) or **Budget** (www.budget.cz, +420 602 165 108, 8am-8pm daily), at the Prague Airport.

Day Trips from Prague

Prague is filled with incredible sights, but it can also be filled with millions of fellow travelers during peak seasons. A day trip is a great way to see another side of the country with a little more breathing room.

A visit to the protected natural landscape of the aptly named Bohemian Paradise offers a glimpse of small town Czech life and incredible views of rock formations, plus access to a nearby brewery. Kutná Hora's Sedlec Ossuary (also known as the "bone church") regularly makes travel lists of unusual sights to see in your lifetime. Liberec, just an hour outside Prague, offers a slice of local life.

Farther away are the peaceful spa town of Karlovy Vary and the whimsical 13th-century city of Český Krumlov, one of the country's most popular attractions. Finally, the youthful city of Brno, with a vibrant nightlife, and the pair of grand chateaux near Mikulov offer convenient stopping points for travelers en route to Vienna or Budapest.

Highlights

Look for ★ to find recommended sights, activities, dining, and lodging.

© MOON.COM

★ **Sedlec Ossuary:** Kutná Hora's famed "bone church" contains thousands of artfully arranged human skeletons. It's surprisingly peaceful (page 146).

★ **Hiking in Bohemian Paradise:** Trek through a small town to reach the forests, rock formations, castle ruins and impressive viewpoints of a massive protected nature reserve (page 153).

★ **Karlovy Vary's Thermal Springs:** Natural mineral waters flow from public fountains housed in ornate locations lining the river of this peaceful valley town. Fill your spa cup and drink up (page 156)!

★ **Český Krumlov Castle:** This castle and royal residence draw visitors to the whimsical 13th-century city of Český Krumlov. The Baroque

Theatre contained within is a particular highlight (page 161).

★ **Rafting the Vltava River:** Pile into rented boats and paddle down the river alongside the locals, stopping at pubs and restaurants on the shores and in the middle of the river itself (page 163)!

★ **Ossuary at St. James Church:** Brno's ossuary—the second-largest in Europe—isn't as famous as the one in Kutná Hora, but the local sculptures and classical music composed specifically for its halls make it a worthwhile sight in its own right (page 167).

★ **Valtice and Lednice Chateaux:** These aristocratic residences in the heart of Moravian wine country embody the glamour of the Austro-Hungarian empire (pages 178 and 179).

Day Trips from Prague

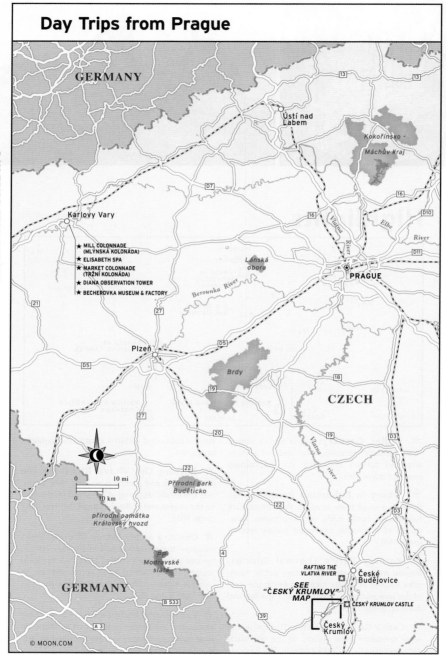

GERMANY

13

13

Ústí nad Labem

Kokořínsko - Máchův kraj

D7

16

D10

Karlovy Vary

16

Vltava River

Elbe

River

★ MILL COLONNADE (MLÝNSKÁ KOLONÁDA)
★ ELISABETH SPA
★ MARKET COLONNADE (TRŽNÍ KOLONÁDA)
★ DIANA OBSERVATION TOWER
★ BECHEROVKA MUSEUM & FACTORY

Lánská obora

D11

PRAGUE

Berounka River

21

27

D5

Plzeň

Brdy

18

D5

19

CZECH

27

20

19

D3

22

Vltava river

0   10 mi
0   10 km

Přírodní park Buděticko

22

D3

přírodní památka Královský hvozd

PP Modravské slatě

4

RAFTING THE VLATVA RIVER

České Budějovice

GERMANY

SEE "ČESKÝ KRUMLOV" MAP

ČESKÝ KRUMLOV CASTLE

B 533

39

Český Krumlov

A 3

© MOON.COM

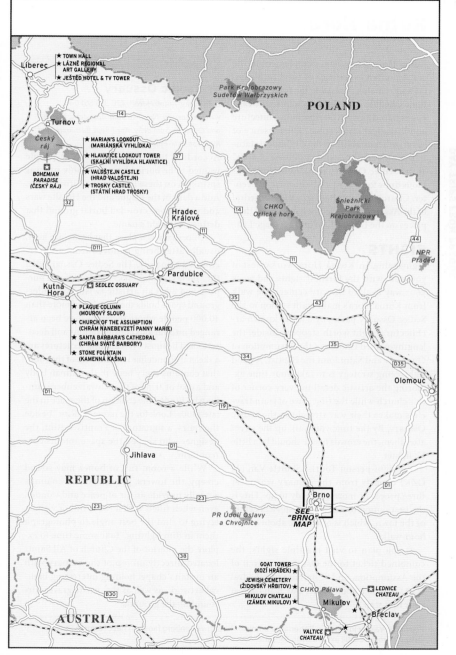

★ TOWN HALL
★ LÁZNĚ REGIONAL ART GALLERY
★ JEŠTĚD HOTEL & TV TOWER

Liberec

Park Krajobrazowy Sudetów Wałbrzyskich

POLAND

Turnov

14

Český ráj

★ MARIAN'S LOOKOUT (MARIÁNSKÁ VYHLÍDKA)
★ HLAVATICE LOOKOUT TOWER (SKALNÍ VYHLÍDKA HLAVATICE)
★ VALDŠTEJN CASTLE (HRAD VALDŠTEJN)
★ TROSKY CASTLE (STÁTNÍ HRAD TROSKY)

37

BOHEMIAN PARADISE (ČESKÝ RÁJ)

32

Hradec Králové

11

14

CHKO Orlické hory

Śnieżnicki Park Krajobrazowy

D11

11

44

NPR Praděd

Kutná Hora

Pardubice

SEDLEC OSSUARY

35

43

★ PLAGUE COLUMN (MOROVÝ SLOUP)
★ CHURCH OF THE ASSUMPTION (CHRÁM NANEBEVZETÍ PANNY MARIE)
★ SANTA BARBARA'S CATHEDRAL (CHRÁM SVATÉ BARBORY)
★ STONE FOUNTAIN (KAMENNÁ KAŠNA)

35

Morava

34

D35

D1

Olomouc

19

Jihlava

D1

REPUBLIC

23

23

Brno

SEE "BRNO" MAP

D1

PR Údolí Oslavy a Chvojnice

38

GOAT TOWER (KOZÍ HRÁDEK) ★

JEWISH CEMETERY (ŽIDOVSKÝ HŘBITOV) ★

MIKULOV CHATEAU (ZÁMEK MIKULOV) ★

CHKO Pálava

LEDNICE CHATEAU

B30

Mikulov

Břeclav

AUSTRIA

VALTICE CHATEAU

Kutná Hora

Kutná Hora is a quieter complement to the cosmopolitan experience of the Czech capital and remains accessible for travelers on a tight schedule. Less than an hour to the east, you can find a city of fascinating architecture and historical importance. The presence of silver mines established the city's royal status in the 14th century, while its "bone church" at the Sedlec Ossuary remains the most famous draw for tourists. The historic city center, Church of Saint Barbara, and Cathedral of the Assumption at Sedlec have earned their places on the UNESCO World Heritage List.

SIGHTS

Sightseeing in Kutná Hora works best if you start with the furthest sights and work your way back to the city center. The walk from Kutná Hora's main train station to the Sedlec Ossuary passes by a lesser known architectural sight worth stepping inside, the lengthy-named Church of the Assumption of Our Lady and Saint John the Baptist. A good sightseeing strategy is to take your time exploring the artistic detail in every corner of this church while the first wave of train travelers makes their way straight to the Sedlec Ossuary. By the time you walk up the street after them, the crowds inside should be a little bit lighter.

An eight-person Tourist Shuttle Van (35 CZK) departs from the ossuary whenever three people or more are ready to go. This is the best option to reach the historical center of the town, which is otherwise about a half-hour walk.

If you plan to visit multiple sights, the combined ticket to the Ossuary, Church of the Assumption, and St Barbara's Cathedral (220 CZK) is a good value. Buy it in cash at your first stop.

TOP EXPERIENCE

★ Sedlec Ossuary

U Zastávky, Kutná Hora, +420 326 551 049, www.ossuary.eu, Nov-Feb 9am-4pm daily, March and Oct 9am-5pm daily, April-Sept 8am-6pm Mon-Sat 9am-6pm Sun, 50 CZK

According to legend, hundreds of people wanted to be buried here after holy soil was sprinkled on these lands in the 13th century. Add a dash of the Plague and the Hussite wars and you get one crowded burial ground that defines this sight's name.

An ossuary is a place that bones are kept, usually after being removed from an overcrowded cemetery. The Sedlec Ossuary, aka the "bone church," takes that functional purpose and adds an artistic twist. The underground space holds the remains of more than 40,000 people whose skeletons have been arranged into various configurations and decorations. The most eye-catching structures are a skeletal chandelier in the center of the room that contains every bone in the human body and a coat of arms of the Schwarzenberg family, who funded the creation of the space in the late 1800s. Look for the name "F. Rint" beside the stairs, a signature of František Rint, the designer who shaped the space into its current form.

While a room full of bones may sound creepy, the towers, pyramids, and columns actually provide an air of peace and wonder, even when filled with a room full of visitors trying to find the best angle to photograph them in dim lighting. Take some time to explore the interior of the Church of All Saints located directly on top of the ossuary with an upstairs chapel holding interesting biblical artwork, as well as the ornate graves surrounding the grounds.

Previous: Valdštejn Castle in Bohemian Paradise; The Schwarzenberg family's coat of arms in Sedlec Ossuary; Trosky Castle in Bohemian Paradise

Church of the Assumption
(Chrám Nanebevzetí Panny Marie)
Zámecká 279, Kutná Hora, +420 326 551 049, www.ossuary.eu, 50 CZK

The excessively named and inconsistently translated Church of the Assumption of Our Lady and Saint John the Baptist is the oldest Cistercian cathedral in Bohemia, built at the end of the 12th century. Tall, pale yellow walls curve into thin white beams lining the muraled ceiling. A spiral staircase on the left-hand side leads to a behind-the-scenes tour of the wooden attic. The church opens at 9am Mon-Sat and 11am on Sundays all year long, closing at 4pm from Nov-Feb, 5pm in March and Oct, and 6pm April-Sept.

Plague Column
(Morový sloup)
Šultysova, Kutná Hora, www.destinace.kutnahora.cz, free

The early 18th-century Plague Column is a memorial to over a thousand people who lost their lives to the Plague of 1713. The Virgin Mary looks over the city from atop a base held by symbolic miners from this treasury town, which was historically known for its silver reserves. Photography fans may spend some time finding their favorite angle of this 16-meter (roughly 50-foot) decorative feature with various pastel colored buildings in the background.

Stone Fountain
(Kamenná kašna)
Husova, Kutná Hora, www.destinace.kutnahora.cz, free

The 15th-century Gothic Stone Fountain located just a few streets from the Plague Column, served as a reservoir for drinking water when the silver mining trade interfered with the natural flow of groundwater, making fresh water harder to come by. The ornate, twelve-sided design was filled by a system of wooden pipes that functioned until 1890.

Today, the ornate stone work of the exterior against an open cobblestoned square make for a particularly photogenic moment.

Santa Barbara's Cathedral
(Chrám svaté Barbory)
Barborská, Kutná Hora, +420 327 512 115, www.destinace.kutnahora.cz, 10am-4pm Jan-Feb, 10am-5pm Mar, Nov, and Dec, 9am-6pm April-Oct, 220 CZK combined ticket

The crown jewel of Kutná Hora and symbol of the city is the Gothic Santa Barbara's Cathedral. St. Barbara's is named after the patron saint of the miners who defined this town. A walk towards the cathedral along Barborska Street, a cement walkway lined with stone statues, whets the visual appetite. The tall sloping curves of the exterior combined with the frescoed ceilings inside will give your neck a workout to admire every detail. The grass courtyard around the church provide a peaceful place to relax after a day of sightseeing.

The church is about half an hour to an hour's walk from either Kutná Hora město or Kutná Hora hl.n, so you may want to take a taxi.

FOOD
★ STAROČESKÁ RESTAURACE V RUTHARDCE
Dačického náměstí 10, www.v-ruthardce.cz, +420 607 286 298, noon-11pm Sun-Thurs, noon-1am Fri-Sat, 150-300 CZK entrees

If you can manage a balcony seat at Staročeská restaurace V Ruthardce, you might catch a glimpse of St. Barbara's Cathedral across the park. No matter which chair or wooden bench you claim in this massive, multi-room Czech restaurant, you can expect hearty meals and efficient service. Try the *kulajda* soup of dill, cream, potatoes, and a poached egg as a starter, or pair it with a beet root and goat cheese salad for a lighter meal. Hungrier visitors should stick to one of the many grilled

chicken or steak dishes. Make a reservation online to request an outdoor (or indoor) seat.

RESTAURACE DAČICKÝ

Rakova 8, +420 603 434 367, www.dacicky.com, 11am-11pm Sun-Thurs, 11am-midnight Fri-Sat, 150-350 CZK entrees

Restaurace Dačický located just down the street from the Gothic Stone Fountain, sets a friendly, Old Bohemian atmosphere for traditional Czech cuisine. Choose from beef or wild boar goulash, roast duck or goose dishes, or dumplings in dill sauce for a vegetarian option. This popular choice for tour groups is often crowded so reservations are recommended.

ORGANZZA CAFÉ

Palackého náměstí 14, +420 777 635 565, 8:30am-9:30pm Mon-Thurs, 8:30am-midnight Fri, 9am-midnight Sat, noon-7pm Sun

In need of a caffeine fix or sugar rush to maintain a day trip of sightseeing? Stop by Organzza Café on your walk to St. Barbara's Cathedral for specialty coffee or some cake. The cozy interior of wooden tables is also a nice place to warm up with your hands wrapped around a mug during colder months.

GETTING THERE

Train

You can reach Kutná Hora in about an hour on the national rail service **České dráhy** (www.cd.cz, 200-250 CZK round trip) leaving from Prague's main train station (Praha hl. n.) about once an hour from 4:30am, with the last trains departing to Prague around 10:15pm. Some trains are direct while others require a transfer in Kolín. There are three stops: Kutná Hora město is closest to the center of town, Kutná Hora–Sedlec is closest to two major sights, and Kutná Hora hl. n. is the third stop requiring the fewest transfers but a short walk.

Before purchasing your ticket, you have a decision to make: 1) buy a direct ticket to Kutná Hora hl.n. and walk for 10-15 minutes to the Sedlec Ossuary or 2) purchase your ticket to Kutná Hora-Sedlec, which means going to Kutná Hora hl.n. and transferring to a small local train that drops you off steps away from the Church of the Assumption and Sedlec Ossuary. Either way, you are likely to return to Prague from the Kutná Hora město station, closest to the center of town, which is included in a return ticket to either station.

Car

Kutná Hora is just over an hour east of Prague (roughly 50 miles) on highway D11, Route 2, or D1/E65.

GETTING AROUND

Because Kutná Hora's sights and train stations are spread across town, they are more easily reached with a little help from local transport options. The **Tourist Bus** (+420 733 551 011) provides rides for 3-8 people from the Sedlec Ossuary to the city center, to the Cathedral of St. Barbara, or to the main train station when time allows (at driver's discretion). For traditional taxi service, call **Taxi Kutna Hora** (+420 800 100 512, +420 777 239 909, or +420 327 512 618).

1 the majestic beauty of St. Barbara's Cathedral **2** Vienna's Town Hall has a twin in Liberec **3** the Liberec reservoir, a local summertime favorite **4** Ještěd Tower defines the Liberec skyline

Liberec

Liberec, located an hour bus or car ride to the north of Prague, falls halfway between cosmopolitan and country life. This university town near the German border is filled with interesting architectural sights, a diverse selection of international restaurants, and a popular summertime base for sunbathing and beach volleyball. Get a peek at local life with some tourist-friendly attractions thrown in.

SIGHTS

Ještěd Hotel and TV Tower

Horní Hanychov 153, Liberec 460 08, www.jested.cz/en, Hotel: +420 485 104 291, +420 605 292 563, Restaurant: +420 731 658 045

Liberec's most distinctive building overlooks the city from a perch on top of the surrounding mountain range. The slender point of the Ještěd Hotel and TV Tower has earned international architectural acclaim for its ability to blend seamlessly into the natural silhouette.

On a clear day, visitors can see beyond the borders of Germany and Poland from the surrounding courtyard. The bronze "Little Martian" statue by sculptor Jaroslav Róna, who spends a lifetime crying at the base of the tower, plays off comparisons of the structure to a spaceship in the sky. On the opposite side of the tower, a plaque embedded in bricks marks the location of the last free radio broadcast in 1968 Czechoslovakia made by Vaclav Havel and Jan Tříska before the next few decades of Russian occupation.

The hotel and restaurant housed inside the curved walls maintain a charmingly nostalgic imagination of futuristic design from a 1970s perspective. Rounded chandelier light fixtures hang overhead the visitors staring out the floor-to-ceiling windows of the 120-seat restaurant and 50-seat café. A spontaneous snack or afternoon drink is usually available, but reservations are recommended to enjoy dinner with a panoramic view among the stars.

The easiest way to reach the tower is a cable car ride, departing from the base of the hill, a short walk from the Horní Hanychov tram stop. In winter, the ride includes a view overlooking the small Ještěd ski slope, which reverts to green grass in the warmer months.

Town Hall

Náměstí Dr. E. Beneše 1, Liberec, 460 59, +420 485 101 709, www.visitliberec.eu, 9am–3pm weekdays 9am–11am Sat from June–Sept, 9am–3pm Thurs from Oct–May, English tour 170 CZK, tower access 30 CZK, tram stop Šaldovo Náměstí

The Liberec Town Hall draws the eye of anyone setting foot on Šaldovo Square. Designed by Austrian architect Franz von Neumann, the building draws comparisons to another masterpiece you might see at another point on your trip—the Vienna Town Hall. The intricate Neo-Renaissance façade and turquoise-topped spires are a testament to the Austro-Hungarian rule of the 19th century. Balcony access is fun for a bird's-eye view of the area. Otherwise, set up shop across the square next to the statue of Neptune and his trident, which used to provide drinking water to local residents, and find the best angle to fit the entire building inside your camera lens. Around the holidays, the town hall overlooks Christmas and Easter markets on Šaldovo Square with homemade crafts, hot wine (*svařák*), and fresh pastries, while summer months bring food, beer, and music festivals. The lively, central location means easy access to lots of pubs and restaurants, including Radniční sklípek in the town hall basement.

Giant's Feast

Nám. Dr. E. Beneše 27, Liberec, free

One of Liberec's bus stops is topped with a fairy tale scene from sculptor David Černý in his signature controversial style. The bus stop entitled "Giant's Feast" is shaped like a table and topped with two beer mugs in Czech and German style on either side of a severed head on a plate. The head is rumored to symbolize Konrad Henlein, a German politician from the Sudetenland and member of the Nazi party. A menorah on its side refers to a local synagogue that was burned down in 1938. The vase and Venus flytrap are thought to symbolize the Liberec museum and botanical gardens along Masarykova street. A pair of Czech sausages sit beside a trash can on the sidewalk next to the stop. This quirky artistic statement is located just beyond F. X. Šalda Theatre and the Liberec Town Hall.

Lázně Regional Art Gallery

Masarykova 14, Liberec, 460 01, +420 485 106 325, www.ogl.cz, 10am-5pm Tues-Wed and Fri-Sun, 10am-7pm Thurs, 80 CZK, tram stop Muzeum-Výstaviště

A blend of historic roots and modern innovation are embodied in the walls of the Lázně Regional Art Gallery. This former spa and swimming pool built in the early 1900s underwent extensive interior renovations to create the clean lines and bright archways that welcome visitors since its reopening in 2013. Grab coffee in the café and a quick peek at the current art exhibit between a visit to the zoo and a walk back to the town center for dinner.

RECREATION
Liberec Reservoir
(Liberecká Přehrada)

Liberecká Přehrada, Liberec, 460 15, +420 485 101 709, www.liberecky-kraj.cz, enter near bus stops Poliklinika or Technická Univerzita

Students and young families sprawl across blankets on a grassy hill beside the Liberec Reservoir on any sunny day—fair warning that swimsuits are somewhat optional for the under six or 60+ crowds. Sausages, cold beer and soft drinks from the onsite snack bar keep the crowds in good spirits. Park bench seating is available under the shade of a wooden roof. For healthier picnic fare, stop into nearby Kavarna Bez Konceptu in advance for homemade sandwiches, pastries, and specialty coffee. The just-over-a-mile pathway around the reservoir offers a peaceful walk—particularly around sunset—surrounded by a lush ring of evergreen trees and alongside runners, a few cyclists, and parents pushing baby strollers. The footpath draws consistent traffic through all seasons, circling around ice skaters and hockey players if the reservoir freezes over in winter. The stone dam flanked with turrets on the west adds the requisite fairy tale backdrop to the photogenic scene. Bílý Mlýn bed and breakfast with a luxury restaurant is hidden behind a wall of greenery on the quiet eastern end of the reservoir.

NIGHTLIFE AND ENTERTAINMENT
FX ŠALDY THEATER

Náměstí Dr. E. Beneše 22, Liberec, 460 01, +420 485 101 523, www.saldovo-divadlo.cz/en, tram stop Muzeum-Výstaviště

The sculpture-topped, Neo-Renaissance F. X. Šalda Theater hosts opera, ballet, and theater—largely in Czech but sometimes with subtitles—directly behind the Liberec Town Hall. The elegant interior décor includes a main curtain by Austrian painter Gustav Klimt.

THE PUB

Pražská 13, Liberec, 460 06, +420 485 108 889, www.thepub.cz/liberec, 11am-midnight Mon-Thurs, 11am-1am Fri-Sat, 125-400 CZK entrees, tram stop Šaldovo Náměstí or Fugnerova

If you prefer competitive drinking to an evening of culture, reserve a table at The Pub. This Czech chain is known for its self-service taps of free-flowing Pilsner at every table, with push-button service keeping track of individual consumption. Leaderboards on multiple walls show how your table stacks up to the rest of the room, plus how your pub compares to locations across the Czech Republic and Central Europe.

FOOD
Czech
RADNIČNÍ SKLÍPEK

Náměstí Dr. E. Beneše 1, Liberec, 460 59, +420 602 602 260, www.sklipekliberec.cz/en, 11am–11pm Mon-Thurs, 11am-midnight Fri-Sat, 125-300 CZK entrees, tram stop Šaldovo Náměstí

The translation of Town Hall Cellar—Radniční Sklípek—tells you exactly where to find this 250-seat, traditional Czech beer hall. Try the pork schnitzel (known locally as *řízek*) with a foam-topped glass of locally brewed Svijany beer, and glance up between bites to admire the stained glass windows and dark wooden details. Despite the massive dining room size, reservations are recommended, particularly on weekends.

BALADA

Moskevská 13, Liberec, 460 01, +420 485 110 109, www.balada-liberec.cz, 10:30am-midnight Mon-Sat, 12pm-10pm Sun, 125-300 CZK entrees, tram stop Šaldovo Náměstí

For a cozier setting, head down Moskevská Street to Balada. Exposed-brick walls and eclectic wooden furniture set a warm, comfortable vibe across three small rooms. The garlic soup (*česneková*) is a perfect starter before a hearty Czech meal on a cold day.

International
MASA BUKA

Sokolská 168, Liberec, 460 01, +420 723 153 523, www.masabuka.cz, 11am-10:30pm Tues-Thurs, 11am-midnight Fri, 11:30am-midnight Sat, 125-300 CZK entrees, tram stop Šaldovo Náměstí

Fans of Greek cuisine encircle the dining room floor and indoor balcony of family-owned Masa Buka. The bright, blue-and-white design and fresh ingredients set the Mediterranean scene at this popular restaurant, just a two-minute walk from the Liberec Town Hall. Make a reservation, and note that the kitchen closes roughly two hours before the restaurant, to ensure a leisurely meal.

Coffee, Tea, and Sweets

A growing interest in specialty coffee has created a turbulent landscape of aspiring cafés opening (and closing) around Liberec. That said, there are two established favorites serving delicious lattes and lemonade alongside homemade cakes and open-faced sandwiches:

KAVARNA BEZ KONCEPTU

Husova 87, Liberec, 460 01, +420 485 111 947, www.bezkonceptu.cz, 8am-10pm Mon-Fri, 9am-10pm Sat-Sun, bus stop Technická Univerzita

Kavarna Bez Konceptu offers a bright, relaxed atmosphere with outdoor seating near the Liberec Reservoir.

MYKINA

5. května 62, Liberec, 460 01, +420 482 710 746, www.mikynapoint.cz/en, 9am-9pm Mon-Sat, 10am-6pm Sun, tram stops Průmyslová Škola or Ulice 5. Května

Between the Lázně Regional Art Gallery and Town Hall Mykina's friendly baristas keep the brunch crowds satisfied.

GETTING THERE
Bus

Regiojet (www.regiojet.com) offers hourly service to Liberec from Černy Most bus station located at the end of Prague's Yellow metro line B, for about 100 CZK. Download the Regiojet app for impressive flexibility—cancelling and rebooking is available online up to 30 minutes before departure for most tickets. Ride in comfortable style with reasonably reliable WIFI, leather seats, and a complimentary choice of coffee, tea, or hot chocolate. Take note that buses run from Prague-Liberec from 7am-11pm, but the last Liberec-Prague bus departs at 9pm. Book your trip to Liberec-Fugnerova (instead of Liberec—AN) to be dropped off at the first stop in the center of town instead of the main bus terminal—the Fugnerova bus stop is smack in the middle of town.

Car

Liberec is located about 70 miles (110 kilometers) north east of Prague on Route D10/E65.

GETTING AROUND

You can walk about 1 km to the city center or get a tram No 3. From there almost every sight can be reached on foot. The city transport consists of buses and a tram line. The central terminal is Fügnerova stop (see www.dpmlj. cz). You could also try **City Taxi Liberec Ltd** (+420 800 501 501).

Bohemian Paradise (Český ráj)

For Czechs, spending time outdoors (or "in the nature" as Czechs like to say) is a national pastime. One of the most accessible places to explore on a day trip from Prague is the protected landscape area of Český ráj (+420 481 540 253, www.cesky-raj.info/en) known as either "Bohemian Paradise" or "Czech Paradise." The main draw to this UNESCO-protected, 181 km.[2] (roughly 70 mi.[2]) area is the vast landscape of geographic beauty. A walk from the train station through small town life in Turnov leads to the vast forest, dirt paths, and sandstone rock formations—not to mention a few castle ruins for ambitious hikers.

★ HIKING

You could return to Bohemian Paradise multiple times, taking multiple paths (over multiple days, even), and stumble upon something new on every visit. The route below is a good place to start.

A day in Bohemian Paradise will most likely begin at the Turnov train station. Dress for the journey and pack light so that you can set off as soon as your train pulls into the station. Hiking boots aren't required for the route below, but comfortable shoes that you don't mind getting a little dirty are definitely recommended. Keep an eye out for brown street signs in Turnov pointing towards popular tourist sights along with color-coded stripes along the streets and hiking paths to ensure that you're going the right way.

Train Station to Valdštejn Castle

This moderate, ten-kilometer (six-mile) round trip outline focuses on an accessible route along the green and red lines. It includes the

Bohemian Paradise is known for its sandstone rocks.

rock formations that the area is known for, multiple viewpoints of both civilization and natural landscapes, and one historic chateau, with no guide or overnight camping required. This route is not terribly well signed, so a paper map or phone with GPS can be handy, or keep your eyes out for green stripes on light posts and gates along the way for reassurance.

If you're on a tight schedule, Janova vyhlídka (or "Jan's Viewpoint") roughly five kilometers or three miles from the train station, is a good place to turn back, while more adventurous travelers may prefer to explore more of this fascinating nature preserve. Also take note that while this area draws many hikers, the level of signage and the amount of English spoken in shops and restaurants in Turnov is far more limited than the capital city, so consider navigating the language barrier a part of your adventure.

HLAVATICE LOOKOUT TOWER
(Skalní vyhlídka Hlavatice)
www.cesky-raj.info/en, free

After about a 30-minute stroll heading south through the streets of Turnov from the main train station you'll finally hit the edge of what feels like a forest. Follow the green or red paths uphill into the forest (they largely run along the same route), past the wooden sculptures marking the Gate to Bohemian Paradise and up to Hlavatice Lookout Tower. A 36 step, iron staircase spirals around the outside of this small sandstone rock serving as a viewpoint over the surrounding towns. A plaque at the top points out the skyline highlights, including the Jizera River and the Ještěd Tower over the city of Liberec.

VALDŠTEJN CASTLE
(Hrad Valdštejn)
+420 739 014 104 or +420 733 565 254,
www.hrad-valdstejn.cz, 10am-5pm weekends only in
April and Oct, 9:30am-5pm Tues-Sun in May
and Sept, 9am-6pm daily from June-Aug

Follow the red path on an easy incline from Hlavatice Lookout Tower to Valdštejn Castle.

The royal residence was established in the 13th century and—when it wasn't under attack—was owned by the Valdštejn (or Wallenstein) family, whose name you may recognize from the peaceful senate gardens below the Prague Castle. All visitors are free to admire the expressive stone sculptures of patron saints that line the cement bridge leading to the entrance.

If you like, you can buy a ticket (70 CZK, cash only) to head inside. The interior of the castle showcases its centuries of renovations and additions with variety of architectural styles. Exhibits range from a Classicist Palace decorated in simple elegance and family portraits to the more historic feel of the mid-1800s Romantic Palace, now devoted to local plant life and former hunting lifestyles. A chapel to St. Jan of Nepomuk, who you can see on the cement bridge with his golden crown of five stars, helped to establish this site as a pilgrimage from the surrounding areas. Guided tours in English (40 CZK per person, cash only) must be arranged in advance.

JAN'S VIEWPOINT
(Janova vyhlídka)
www.cesky-raj.info/en, free

Follow the red path for about 15-minutes beyond Valdštejn Castle, keeping an eye out for a blue trail on the left-hand side and a small sign marked with the name Janova vyhlídka in Czech, which means "Jan's Viewpoint." Turning left onto this blue path leads to a railing-lined corner of the forest overlooking sandstone rock formations. If you look closely, you might spot a few climbers ascending or descending. This is also a good point to evaluate how much farther you want to continue—it's another hour to the Marian Lookout (Mariánská vyhlídka), and at least another two hours to the twin peaks of Trosky Castle.

MARIAN'S LOOKOUT
(Mariánská vyhlídka)
www.cesky-raj.info/en, free

Continuing south from Janova vyhlídka, the

blue trail will run into the yellow trail, where you'll want to turn right to reach Mariánská vyhlídka or "Marian's Lookout." While Janova vyhlídka (Jan's viewpoint) focuses on the natural beauty of the sandstone rocks, Mariánská vyhlídka adds the pointed towers of the Renaissance Hrubá Skála Chateau to the panoramic skyline alongside the distant silhouette of the Trosky Castle ruins.

TROSKY CASTLE
(Státní hrad Trosky)

www.hrad-trosky.eu, 9am-4pm weekends only in April and Oct, 9am-4pm Tues-Sun in May and Sept, 9am-5:30pm Tues-Sun from May to June, and 9am-5:30pm daily from June-Aug, 90 CZK cash only

Before you venture any further from Mariánská vyhlídka, consider that going on to Trosky Castle will leave you more than 13km (over 8 miles) from the Turnov train station, and there are no public transport options from Trosky back to Prague. That said, if you've got the daylight hours and the energy to spare, continue along the yellow trail until it intersects with the red trail. This will lead you to the twin towers of the Trosky Castle Ruins which each have their own names: the old woman or crone (*Baba*) tower is shorter and wider, while the young lady, maiden, or virgin (*Panna*) is the taller and thinner of the two. This 14th-century fortress on top of volcanic rocks stood strong throughout the Hussite Wars but was eventually abandoned leaving the remains with an air of mystery—plus some modern touch ups—that you can visit today. The two-towered silhouette is a defining symbol of Bohemian Paradise and regular source of inspiration for Czech poets and painters.

FOOD

Many hikers prefer to pack a bag with snacks to eat along the hike. The walk through Turnov also offers plenty of small shops to grab a pre-made sandwich, pretzels, or a cold drink to toss into your backpack for a picnic later on.

HOSPŮDKA U HRADU

Turnov 24, +420 773 686 064, www.hrad-valdstejn. cz, 10am-5pm weekends only in April and Oct, 10am-5pm daily from May-Sept, 100-200 CZK entrees

If you prefer to pack light and don't mind a slightly touristy vibe, try the Hospůdka U Hradu or "Pub at the Castle" outside Valdštejn Castle. The hearty menu of traditional Czech cuisine, from fried cheese to grilled sausages, is best enjoyed outdoors on the surrounding picnic benches.

PIZZERIE RESTAURANT PLAUDIT

Bezručova 698, +420 481 311 288, www.plaudit.eu, 11am-11pm Sun-Thurs, 11am-midnight Fri-Sat, 150-200 CZK pizzas

For a slightly more formal bite in town (but no need to change out of your hiking clothes before catching the train back to Prague), head to Pizzerie Restaurant Plaudit. This North Bohemian chain offers a wide selection of thin-crust pizzas with interesting toppings (think corn or a fried egg) alongside a full menu of chicken, steak, and pasta dishes. The ten-minute walk from the station allows for a leisurely meal to refuel after a day on your feet.

PIVOVAR SVIJANY

Svijany 25, +420 481 770 770, www.pivovarsvijany.cz, 11am-8pm Sun-Mon, 11am-10pm Thurs-Sat, 135-175 CZK entrees

The surrounding towns are fairly quiet when it comes to entertainment, so a trip back to Prague is generally better than searching for any signs of nightlife. Beer fans might want to add a side trip to Pivovar Svijany, a local brewery that recently celebrated its 450th birthday. The one-hour brewery tour is only available to groups of 10 or more, but they can arrange an English guide with advance notice. The onsite pub and restaurant is also the place to get a fresh taste of my personal favorite Czech lager with easy drinkability. The brewery is about a 10-minute drive for about 350 CZK in a taxi (or about 90-minute walk) from the center of Turnov.

ACCOMMODATIONS
SKÁLA CHATEAU AND WELLNESS CENTER

Hrubá Skála 1, +420 271 090 832,
www.hrubaskala.cz, 1,800-2,500 CZK d

To add a touch of luxury to a hiking trip, consider spending the night inside the protected area of Český ráj at the Hrubá Skála Chateau and Wellness Center. The Renaissance-style chateau includes 6 simple, dorm-style rooms sleeping 3, 4, 5, or 6 guests (1,250-1,700 CZK) plus double, triple, and family rooms with en suite bathrooms. Revitalizing massages, full body wraps, and Turkish baths at the onsite spa are available to pamper your body after hours on your feet.

GETTING THERE
Train

The easiest way to explore Český Ráj without a car is by train to the small town of Turnov. Trains depart from Prague's main train station (Praha hl. n.) roughly every two hours via the national rail service **České dráhy** (www.cd.cz, 250-300 CZK round trip). Service to Turnov begins just before 6am with the last train from Turnov back to Prague departing shortly after 9pm. The journey takes just under two hours and arrives in Turnov, which is about a 30-minute walk to the edge of Bohemian Paradise.

Car

Český Ráj is roughly 55 miles northeast of Prague on highway E65. The drive takes about an hour. Parking lots are available near some popular areas (e.g. Turnov or Trosky Castle), usually for a fee around 50-100 CZK.

Karlovy Vary

An aura of relaxation surrounds this peaceful valley town of pastel buildings and natural springs beside the Ohře River. The main attractions of Karlovy Vary (also known as Carlsbad in English) are the fifteen thermal springs of drinking water, tapped and free-flowing for all pedestrians to taste. Tiny, decorative "spa cups" with a helpful spout are sold every few steps in shops and stands. The various temperatures and mineral contents give each spring a distinctive flavor and are believed by many to have healing powers. Join the ranks of King Charles IV, who founded the town in the 14th century, along with Russia's Peter the Great, Mozart and Beethoven, Franz Kafka, and many modern Hollywood stars who have come to "take the waters" over the centuries.

Once you get indoors, spa towns in the Czech Republic focus less on indulgence in white fluffy robes and more on natural treatments to improve your health. It's not unusual for local physicians to prescribe an extended stay for locals suffering from various illnesses and conditions. Services like mineral baths, salt caves, aromatherapy, and massages are usually accessible to travelers with a reservation in advance, but other services may require a physician's consultation, so read the fine print when booking online. The overall environment of these spas may also have a more clinical vibe than travelers are used to, but don't let that deter you from indulging in the local approach to wellness.

★ THERMAL SPRINGS

To experience the most popular activity in Karlovy Vary, all you have to do is take a walk. The mineral springs that flow underground have been organized into a system of fountains housed inside gazebos and stone temples alongside the river. Many of these open-air structures are named "colonnade" for the rows of columns making up their architectural style.

The Karlovy Vary International Film Festival

Cannes, Venice and…Karlovy Vary, Czech Republic? That's right: since 1946, Karlovy Vary has hosted the **Karlovy Vary International Film Festival** (www.kviff.com), an annual gathering of the international cinematic community. The film festival (one of the oldest in the world, even operating for forty years under Communist occupation) screens around 200 feature-length and short films from around the world in venues across town over eight days in late June or early July. Awards are given for the Official Selection (a Best Picture equivalent), "East of the West" (for films from Central and Eastern Europe, the Balkans, Greece, the former Soviet Union, and the Middle East), and Best Documentary.

The Crystal Globe for Outstanding Artistic Contribution to World Cinema is known to bring Hollywood actors and filmmakers to the festival. Past recipients include Morgan Freeman, Judi Dench, and Susan Sarandon.

The **Grand Hotel Pupp** serves as both a screening location and popular accommodation choice among the celeb set. The etched names in the brick courtyard of the hotel act as a mini-Walk of Fame or a guestbook of the hotel's esteemed visitors from centuries before the film festival began. These famous names range from Empress Maria Theresa in 1732 to Leonardo DiCaprio in 1994. Daniel Craig's brick (2006) is a testament to the hotel's starring role in the James Bond film *Casino Royale*.

If you want to join the film-loving fun of the festival, book your lodging (and your spa treatments) well in advance as this quiet town comes alive.

Visitors are free to walk the city streets and sample most of the waters at all hours of the day. You can fill any container you like, although plastic bottles are not the best choice for the hottest of the springs. For the best experience, grab a porcelain spa cup (prices vary wildly depending on size and decoration, but expect between 100-1,000 CZK) from any of the vendors along the colonnades.

Mill Colonnade
(Mlýnská kolonáda)
Mlýnské nábř., www.karlovyvary.cz

The 19th-century stone design of the Mill Colonnade embodies the royal atmosphere of Karlovy Vary's history. This temple of health is the largest and most popular in town, housing five separate springs between its symmetrical, arched halls. Some of the waters flow from taps emerging from the floor or walls, while others pool into shallow basins around the fountains. The triangle-topped entrances to this open-air structure are embellished with twelve sandstone statues representing the calendar months.

Market Colonnade
(Tržní kolonáda)
Tržiště, www.karlovyvary.cz

The white latticed exterior of the Market Colonnade sets a more natural, delicate tone around the spring named for Charles IV as well the Market Spring and Lower Castle Spring. The building was designed in the late 1800s in a Swiss-inspired style, and sits near the Moser glassware store of equally delicate souvenirs.

As you continue along the river, keep an eye out for a musical patch of sidewalk, where stepping on the metal plates creates different tones, about halfway between the Market Colonnade and the Grand Hotel Pupp.

SPA
Elisabeth Spa
Mírové náměstí 2, +420 353 109 111, www.spa5.cz, 8am-7pm Mon-Fri, 9am-7pm Sat, 10am-6pm Sun, 120-800 CZK treatments

The manicured courtyard of the Elisabeth Spa, named for Austro-Hungarian Empress Sisi, sets a decadent atmosphere as you enter the massive, early-1900s building. Inside, the

individual treatment rooms feel more like doctor's offices that offer mineral baths, aromatherapy and hot stone massages, heat-, hydro- and electro-therapy treatments, and a swimming pool. Splurge on a relaxation package or spend an affordable 45 minutes wrapped in a blanket and breathing deeply in the salt caves to feel your stress melt away. This long-running local favorite combines relaxation with the historic ambiance that defines this town for a memorable wellness experience. Most spa treatments require advance booking.

OTHER SIGHTS
Diana Observation Tower

Vrch přátelství 1, +420 353 109 111, www.dianakv.cz,
9am-4:45pm Nov-Mar, 9am-5:45pm April and Oct,
9am-6:45pm May-Sept; free entry

Avid hikers can climb the hill to the Diana Observation Tower but many travelers opt for an easy three-minute ride from the funicular beside the Grand Hotel Pupp (90 CZK return), saving their strength for the 150-step climb to the top of the tower, although elevator access is also available. The roughly 130-foot (40-meter) structure offers sweeping views of the city center and the surrounding forests in a remote area on the edge of town.

To hike to the tower, follow a path winding off Pod Jelením skokem street through the forest for about one-and-a-half miles (2.2km) to the west.

Becherovka Museum & Factory

T. G. Masaryka 57, +420 359 578 142,
www.becherovka.com, 9am-5pm Tues-Sun, 150 CZK

Legends has it that the only two people in possession of the herbal recipe to make the Czech digestif Becherovka refuse to fly together in order to ensure its safety. The Jan Becher Museum holds more fun facts about the eventful history of this local cure-all liquor,

created in 1807 and best described as "tasting like Christmas." Reserve a place online in advance to ensure a tour in English.

SHOPPING
MOSER GLASSWARE

Tržiště 7, + 420 353 235 303, www.moser-glass.com,
9am-6pm daily, 775-50,000 CZK glass items

For a splurge-worthy souvenir or just some high-end window shopping, peek inside Moser Glassware near the Market Colonnade. This luxury Czech line of hand-crafted glass objects was founded in 1857 and boasts Emperor Franz Josef and King Edward VII of England as some of its earliest fans.

FOOD
International
CHARLESTON

Bulharská 1, +420 353 230 797, www.charleston-kv.
cz, 2pm-11pm, 200-500 CZK entrees

Refuel after a day of walking with a hearty meal of steak, poultry or seafood at Charleston. This English-style pub tucked below street level is decorated in dark wood and warm reds, serving a late-night crowd of international diners and drinkers.

Vegetarian
DOBRÁ ČAJOVNA

Bulharská 1, 2pm-11pm, 100-130 CZK entrees

The Dobrá čajovna teahouse and hookah bar offers a number of cozy nooks inside its underground layout of dimly lit, pillow-lined rooms to kick back and relax. Choose from a simple menu of Indian and Middle Eastern-inspired dishes and an extensive selection of loose-leaf teas.

Breakfast and Brunch
REPUBLICA COFFEE

T.G.Masaryka 28, +420 720 347 166, 7am-7pm
Mon-Fri, 8am-7pm Sat-Sun, 100-150 CZK entrees

Karlovy Vary's coffee snobs congregate at Republica Coffee for flat whites and breakfast pastries. The efficient baristas don't skimp on quality to increase efficiency, so there may be a short wait at peak times. Grab a table in

---

1 Karlovy Vary, a town of peaceful relaxation
2 bridge to Valdštejn Castle, Bohemian Paradise
3 Mineral springs housed in elegance at the Mill
Clonnade 4 Elisabeth Spa: elegance outside,
health inside

the pop-art balcony area or one of the candy-colored chairs on the outdoor terraces.

ACCOMMODATIONS

APARTMANY VICTORIA

Jugoslávská 10, +420 222 532 547,
www.apartments-victoria.penzion.cz, 1,500 CZK d

Apartmany Victoria provides a comfortable home base and a helpful staff full of personal recommendations. These kitchen-equipped apartments with one-, two-, or three-bedroom options are decked out in clean, light-wood details. The convenient location is just around the corner from the Tržnice bus terminal and a fifteen-minute walk from the Mill Colonnade, surrounded by casual dining options. The one quirk of this quiet, mid-sized option with on-site massage services is the cash-only payment upon arrival.

★ GRAND HOTEL PUPP

Mírové náměstí 2, +420 353 109 111,
www.pupp.cz, 8,000 CZK s, 10,000-20,000 CZK d

There is no comparison to the luxury of sleeping in a landmark at the Grand Hotel Pupp. The 228-room selection ranges from basic singles to premier suites and apartments with balcony views stretching over the river. Décor goes from simple, modern design in forest-facing rooms to the jewel-toned, 18th-century elegance of the riverside suites. Facilities include an on-site spa and wellness center, relaxation pool and sauna, a salt cave and a fitness center. Breakfast and room service tack on additional costs, and accessible rooms are available. This special occasion splurge ups the aristocratic feel of a royal spa weekend.

Don't miss the names etched in brick in the outer courtyard, offering a mini-Walk of Fame of the celebrities who have stayed here. For a taste of the interior elegance without the hefty luxury hotel price tag, try an afternoon drink at the **Malá Dvorana** just off the lobby, where a portrait of Morgan Freeman keeps watch over the white tablecloths and French doors, or splurge on dinner at **Becher's Bar** decorated in deep red, green, and bronze tones.

GETTING THERE

Buses are a better option than the train for getting to Karlovy Vary. Trains take longer, cost twice as much, and drop you off at a less convenient station.

Train

State-run **České dráhy** (www.cd.cz,) trains depart from Prague's main train station (Praha hlavní nádraží) roughly every two hours from about 5am to 7pm (3 hours, 300-350 CZK round trip). The train station is across the Ohře River from the center of town, requiring a 15-minute walk to hotels on the northern side of town and about half an hour's walk from the Grand Hotel Pupp at the opposite end.

Bus

Comfortable coach service from **Regiojet** (www.regiojet.com, 300-350 CZK round trip) or **Flixbus** (www.flixbus.com, 250-315 CZK) depart from Prague's Florenc bus station almost every hour between 6am and 10pm. The journey takes just over two hours, finishing at two stops both on the northern end of town. The first bus stop, Karlovy Vary's Tržnice will be more convenient for the majority of visitors walking ten minutes into town, while the main bus station just five minutes further down the river can be an easier place to find a taxi if you have large luggage or would like a ride to accommodation near the Grand Hotel Pupp at the opposite end of town.

Car

Karlovy Vary is located about two hours (roughly 80 miles) west of Prague on Route 6. www.karlovyvary.cz offers updated information and pricing on parking garages around town.

GETTING AROUND

With a compact city center lining the river, most of Karlovy Vary is designed to be walkable. If you need a taxi, try **KV Taxi** (+420 777 141 413, www.kv-taxi.cz).

Český Krumlov

Pastel colors and a preserved medieval atmosphere have earned Český Krumlov its UNESCO-protected status. The main draw to this whimsical 13th-century city is the Český Krumlov Castle encircled by the curves of the Vltava River, and the chance for summer river rafting fun.

Expect heavy tourist traffic during summer months. (A local artist even hired people to live "normal" lives in the summer of 2018 to draw attention to tourism pushing the locals out of town.) However, this popular city is equally beautiful and half as crowded in late spring and early autumn while the castle sights are still open, or even a peaceful day in winter when fewer sights are open but the city streets are dusted in snow. Many tour groups also treat the city as a day trip, so an overnight stay allows you to explore in a more peaceful evening setting.

SIGHTS
★ Český Krumlov Castle
(Zámek Český Krumlov)

Zámek 59, Český Krumlov, +420 380 704 721,
www.zamek-ceskykrumlov.cz

This castle and chateau served as a royal residence to a variety of aristocratic families—the Lords of Krumlov, the Rosenbergs, the Eggenbergs, and the Schwarzenbergs—between the 13th and 19th century, and was privately owned up until the 1940s before becoming state property. The collection of 41 buildings includes private residences, theaters, wine cellars, and gorgeously manicured gardens. Entrance to the castle courtyards and bridges is free of charge, while tickets to individual attractions and tours are arranged onsite.

How much time you spend at the castle depends entirely on your interests. For a simple, budget-friendly overview of the atmosphere, go for the iconic view from the Castle Tower,

a free walk through the open courtyards, and a stroll through the massive manicured gardens. The Baroque Theater (my personal favorite part of the castle) is a worthwhile addition for performing arts fans, and the Royal Residences add a glimpse of historical glamour, but guided tours are the only way to gain access to these areas. Scoring a ticket often requires early arrival at the counter to buy an in-person ticket for that day, and then planning your afternoon around whichever hour was available.

CASTLE TOWER
The tower opens at 9am daily closing at 3:15pm from Nov-March, 4:15pm from April-May and Sept-Oct, and 5:15pm from June-August. 100 CZK

The Castle Tower dominates the silhouette of the hilltop fortress and symbolizes the city itself. A climb up 162 stairs rewards visitors with impossibly wide panoramic views of the city. Arrive early or towards the end of the day to avoid the maximum limit of 50 people on the snug balcony.

BEAR MOAT
(Medvědí Příkop)

Zámek 59, Český Krumlov,
www.castle.krumlov.cz, free

The Bear Moat surrounding the castle serves as home to these adorable-from-a-distance creatures, introduced to the area as a form of defense as early as the 16th or 17th centuries. Their enclosure sits in the dug out area below the castle grounds (hence the name "moat"). Renovations in the 1990s gave the space an upgrade to keep these lovable creatures safe and comfortable. To catch a glimpse of the bears, you may need to hang around the bridge leading into the castle, or time your visit around the Bear Festival on Christmas Eve, when the animals enjoy a lavish feast prepared by local children.

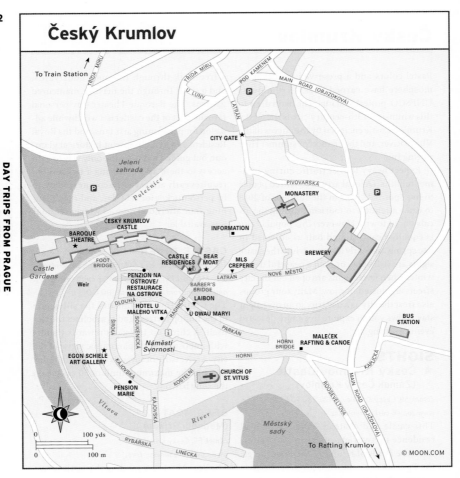

Český Krumlov

Map labels:

To Train Station

TŘÍDA MÍRU · U LUNY · TŘÍDA MÍRU · POD KAMENEM · MAIN ROAD (OBJIZDKOVÁ) · LATRÁN

CITY GATE

Jelení zahrada

Poleňnice

PIVOVARSKÁ

MONASTERY

ČESKÝ KRUMLOV CASTLE

INFORMATION

BAROQUE THEATRE

Castle Gardens

FOOT BRIDGE

CASTLE RESIDENCES

BEAR MOAT

MLS CREPERIE

BREWERY

Weir

PENZION NA OSTROVE/ RESTAURACE NA OSTROVE

BARBER'S BRIDGE

LATRÁN · NOVÉ MĚSTO

DLOUHÁ

LAIBON

HOTEL U MALEHO VITKA

U DWAU MARYI

RADNIČNÍ

SIROKÁ

SOUKENICKÁ

PARKÁN

BUS STATION

Náměstí Svornosti

HORNÍ BRIDGE

MALEČEK RAFTING & CANOE

EGON SCHIELE ART GALLERY

KÁJOVSKÁ

HORNÍ

KAPLICKÁ

KOSTELNÍ

CHURCH OF ST. VITUS

PENSION MARIE

Vltava

KÁJOVSKÁ

River

Městský sady

ROOSEVELTOVA

MAIN ROAD (OBJÍZDKOVÁ)

0   100 yds
0   100 m

RYBÁŘSKÁ · LINECKÁ

To Rafting Krumlov

© MOON.COM

CASTLE RESIDENCES
(Prohlídková Trasa)

*Zámek 59, Český Krumlov, +420 380 704 721,
www.zamek-ceskykrumlov.cz*

Guided tours of the Castle Residences are the only way to get access into the personal lives of some of the famous families that called this castle home.

Tour Route I (320 CZK in English) lasts one hour and is available from April through October. This route covers older sections of the castle decorated in elegant Renaissance and Baroque styles from the 16th-18th centuries. Highlights include the golden alter of St. George's chapel, paneled ceilings over the bedrooms and dining areas used by the Rosenberg family, and the cartoon-like paintings lining the Masquerade Hall.

Tour Route II (240 CZK in English) concentrates on the 19th and 20th century influence of the Schwarzenberg family and is available from June through August and weekends in September. One-hour tours run from 9am until 4pm or 5pm except Mondays. Highlights include an extensive collection of large-scale portraits, multiple bedroom suites used by both the aristocratic residents and chambermaids, and leisure areas like the Smoking Salon, Music Room, and Reference Library.

Arrive early at the castle box office on the day you want to visit in order to book your space in person. Tours fill up quickly and reservations are only available for large groups.

BAROQUE THEATRE
(Zámecké barokní divadlo)
Zámek 59, Český Krumlov, +420 380 704 721, www.zamek-ceskykrumlov.cz
The meticulously restored Baroque Theater inside the castle is renowned across Europe for its attention to historic detail. Dramatic performances were a part of castle life as early as the 1500s, but a 17th-century remodel created the appearance that has been maintained to this day. This theater and the Drottningholms Slottsteater in Sweden are the only two preserved Baroque theaters in existence in the world. The guided, forty-five-minute tour (350 CZK) is the only way to see the hand-painted scenery, stark audience divisions between the aristocracy and the commoners, wood-and-rope mechanics used to change sets, and the inventive machines used to create sound effects like wind and rain—raise your hand fast when the guide asks for volunteers to demonstrate the sounds. Tours run in multiple languages from Tues-Sun between 10am-3pm from May through October. Hit the box office early in the morning to reserve a space in person on the day you want to see it.

CASTLE GARDENS
(Zámecká zahrada)
Zámecká zahrada, Český Krumlov, +420 380 704 721, www.zamek-ceskykrumlov.cz, 8am-5pm April-Oct, 8am-7pm May-Sept
One place to experience free, peaceful entertainment at the Český Krumlov Castle is a leisurely stroll through the colorful Castle Gardens at the back of the complex. The upper garden of rectangular edges was formerly used for horseback riding while the lower area has a more ornate, decorative feel. The 17th-century landscape of geometric hedges, swirling flowers, and stair-lined fountains stretches far enough to feel secluded even in the busiest months.

REVOLVING THEATER
(Otáčivé hlediště)
Zámecká zahrada, Český Krumlov, +420 386 711 222, www.revolvingtheatre.com
In addition to the Baroque Theater inside the castle walls, a modern, metallic Revolving Auditorium and Open-Air Theater sits at the back of the Castle Gardens. Performances range from ballet and opera to drama and puppet theater, and generally run June-September with ticket prices ranging 500-1,500 CZK depending on the show. An afternoon walk around this theater can even be fun to admire the lighting arrangements and imagine the scenes that could pop up in several open plots of grass around the rotating seats. These de facto garden stages are just waiting for the audience to swing in their direction.

Egon Schiele Gallery
Široká 71, Český Krumlov, +420 380 704 011, www.schieleartcentrum.cz, 10am-6pm daily, 180 CZK
One of the most interesting sights outside the castle grounds is the three-story Egon Schiele Gallery. Schiele was an Austrian contemporary of Gustav Klimt in the early 1900s known for his nude figures and provocative approach. A permanent exhibit chronicles his life, including his adopted home of Český Krumlov and his success in Vienna, while the gallery rotates contemporary modern artists through the space.

RECREATION
★ Rafting the Vltava River
The winding curves of the Vltava River through Český Krumlov can be as much a draw as the man-made attractions on dry land. During the summer, groups of Czechs and international travelers pile into rented boats (sometimes decked out in themed costumes) to spend the day floating and paddling

downstream. This is one of the few times that the informal version of "ahoj" (meaning "hi") gets tossed at everyone you see.

Multiple boat rental companies cater to this summertime hobby, with trips ranging from a short cruise through town (about 300-350 CZK per person) to an all-day journey from neighboring towns like Rožmberk or Vyšší Brod (about 600-750 CZK per person) on a large inflatable raft or canoe. The river is lined with pubs and restaurants for breaks and the occasional cocktail stand popping up in the middle of the water. Conditions are generally mild, but the slopes along the sides at various points can provide some excitement.

Storage is usually available at the rental office, where drivers shuttle groups to their starting points, and dry bags are provided— but to be on the safe side, leave electronics and sentimental valuables behind. You can spot the true pros with plastic bottles of beer attached with rope to the back of the boats and dragging along the water to stay cool.

MALEČEK RAFTING & CANOE
Kaplická 27, +420 380 712 508; www.malecek.cz
The laid-back staff at Maleček offer short boat trips through the city center or longer day trips from the surrounding areas. Rental prices include boat rental of inflatable rafts or canoes, paddles, life-jackets, and a sealable bag for valuables. The staff will drive you to your starting point and collect the equipment at the end point of your trip.

RAFTING KRUMLOV
Pod Svatým Duchem 135, +420 777 066 999; www.rafting-krumlov.cz
Rafting Krumlov offers similar services to Maleček of inflatable rafts and canoes with equipment and transport included for one-day excursions, plus the option to rent innertubes and paddleboards.

FOOD
Czech
★ U DWAU MARYI
Parkán 104, Český Krumlov, +420 380 717 228, www.2marie.cz, 11am-10pm daily, 125-200 CZK entrees
The riverside location of U Dwau Maryi is as much a draw as the fantastic Old Bohemian meals. On a warm day, the wooden tables along the grass-and-stone patio are filled with families and friends discussing the day's events. During cooler months, the stone walls and cozy nooks indoors keep diners warm and dry. Try the Old Bohemian Feast of smoked meat and vegetables alongside your choice of chicken, rabbit, or pheasant.

RESTAURACE NA OSTROVE
Na Ostrově 171, Český Krumlov, www.naostroveck.cz, 10am-10pm daily, 100-150 CZK entrees
Restaurace na Ostrove is tucked onto a small pseudo-island just across the river from the Castle Tower. This casual, friendly pub setting can hold thirty guests inside and another 60 outdoors. Mixed salads, soups, baguettes, and bar snacks offer lighter alternatives with full meals of mostly grilled meats also available. The laid back staff may take some time to get to each table, but they generally do so with a smile.

Vegetarian
LAIBON
Parkán 105, Český Krumlov, +420 728 676 654, www.laibon.cz, 11am-midnight daily, 125-200 CZK entrees
Laibon offers an extensive vegetarian menu ranging from guacamole and hummus to Indian-style dishes and soy or tempeh-based meals. The earthy tones and stone walls set a calm vibe inside with popular riverside picnic benches during warmer months.

1 Český Krumlov town and Castle 2 Cathedral of Sts. Peter & Paul in Brno

Breakfast and Brunch

MLS CREPERIE

*Latrán 12, Český Krumlov, +420 608 982 665, www.
mls-bistros.cz, 10am-6pm daily, 150-250 CZK entrees*

Start your morning with sweet or savory crepes at MLS Creperie, or go for an egg breakfast and see if you can resist the smell of *trdelník*, a sweet doughy treat and popular guilty pleasure in touristy areas, on your way out the door. Of the multiple locations around town, the Latrán street dining room of white walls and colorful chairs is reasonably spacious.

ACCOMMODATIONS

★ PENSION MARIE

*Kájovská 67, Český Krumlov, +420 222 539 539,
www.pension-marie.hotel.cz, 2,000-2,500 d*

Pension Marie is a cozy, home-like setting for small groups and families. The 15th-century town house setting is decorated with simple, modern furnishings and brightly colored walls in a relatively quiet area just down the street from the Egon Schiele Gallery. Free WIFI and breakfast in the on-site Italian restaurant are included.

PENZION NA OSTROVE

Na Ostrově 171, 2,000-2,500 CZK d

The small guest house at Penzion na Ostrove, a former mill, comes with the natural white noise of the Vltava River and a potential view of the Castle Tower. This small, five-room guest house on three stories provides a comfortable home base with simple, neutral décor and free WIFI, but be advised that there is no elevator. One quirk—while you can make a reservation online, payment is accepted in cash on arrival.

HOTEL U MALEHO VITKA

*Radniční 27, +420 380 711 925, www.hotelvitek.cz,
1,100-1,350 CZK s, 1,700-2,040 CZK d*

If you prefer a slightly livelier environment, Hotel U Maleho Vitka attracts a younger crowd to their twenty rooms of simple wood furnishings and exposed beams. The historic atmosphere comes with free WIFI and a central location just off the town square. Each room of these three former residences combined into one large location has a slightly different character that you can browse online before booking.

GETTING THERE

Train

The national rail service **České dráhy** (www. cd.cz, 200-350 CZK) runs one direct, three-hour train service from Prague daily around 8am. The main train station of Český Krumlov is a 30-minute downhill walk from the center of town, with local taxi service available.

Bus

Locally-owned **Regiojet** (www.regiojet.com, 125-200 CZK) coaches depart from Prague's Na Knížecí station in the Smichov neighborhood to Český Krumlov roughly every hour from 6am to 9pm. The three-hour journey includes complimentary hot drinks and seat-back screens with English movies. WIFI is solid near major cities, but less reliable in the countryside.

Flixbus (www.flixbus.com, 200-385 CZK) also runs direct buses from multiple locations in Prague, so check your departure station carefully.

The main **bus station** (Český Krumlov, AN) is about a 10-15 minute walk from the center of town.

Car

Český Krumlov is a two-to-three-hour drive, about 160 kilometers (just over 100 miles) south of Prague on highway D3 and Route 3 or taking Route 4 and Route 20/E49. The historic center is a pedestrian area, but www. ckrumlov.info details some of the parking options surrounding the town that are available to visitors.

GETTING AROUND

The historic center of Český Krumlov is a compact, walkable area and a car-free zone. If you need a taxi to transport luggage from the bus or train stations or to get close to your accommodation, try **Green Taxi** (+420 800 712 712, www.green-taxi.cz).

Brno

Prague's second-largest city and the capital of Moravia is a noteworthy hub of international and vegetarian dining, a lively cocktail and bar scene, and a diverse architectural destination in its own right. Brno's 400,000 residents skew towards a young, university-aged crowd alongside an innovative startup scene. The active streets and underground sights of Brno make for an ideal stopping point between Prague and either Vienna or Budapest.

SIGHTS

★ Ossuary at St. James Church
(Kostnice u sv. Jakuba)

Jakubské náměstí, Brno, +420 515 919 793, www.ticbrno.cz, 9:30am-6pm Tues-Sun, 140 CZK, tram stops Náměstí Svobody or Česká

Kutna Hora is probably the most well-known Czech town for skeletal sightseeing, but a discovery beneath Jakubské náměstí may be changing that status. Overcrowded cemeteries in the 18th century often led to remains being excavated every 10 to 12 years and skeletal remains moved to underground ossuaries. The Ossuary at the Church of St. James, discovered in 2001, is estimated to hold around 50,000 skeletal remains from residents lost to cholera, plague, the Thirty Years' War and the Swedish siege of 1645. This makes it Europe's second-largest ossuary behind the catacombs in Paris.

The underground space is organized into columns and pyramids built from bones with paths for visitors to observe and pay their respects. A curated selection of contemporary sculptures add to the display and a soundtrack composed specifically for the experience completes the serene scene, which has been open to the public since 2012. No more than twenty visitors are allowed to enter at one time, so reservations are recommended.

Church of St. James
(Kostel sv. Jakuba)

Jakubské náměstí 2, Brno, +420 542 212 039, www.svatyjakubbrno.wz.cz, 9am-6:30pm daily, free, tram stops Náměstí Svobody or Česká

One of Brno's (literally) cheeky monuments adorns the exterior walls of the Church of St. James. A small stone man called Nehaňba (meaning "Unashamed" or "Shameless") can be seen gripping the top of one of the exterior windows and exposing his bottom in the direction of Petrov Hill. One theory is that architect Anton Pilgram, (mentioned again in an Old Town Hall legend) was poking fun at the slow construction work on the Cathedral of Sts. Peter & Paul.

The interior of this bright 13th century church, renovated from Romanesque to Gothic to Baroque and to Gothic again over the centuries, is unusual for its three aisles of the same height. The décor is simpler than Brno's Cathedral of Sts. Peter & Paul, with tall arched windows and intricate patterns of wooden beams lining the vaulted ceilings creating an aesthetic more serene than ostentatious.

Old Town Hall
(Stará radnice)

Radnická 2, Brno, +420 542 427 150, www.ticbrno. cz, May 10am-8pm daily, June-Aug 10am-10pm daily, Sept-Oct 10am-6pm daily, Nov 10am-6pm Fri-Sun, 70 CZK, tram stop Zelný trh

The Old Town Hall holds more of the city's fantastical tales. The Brno Dragon (okay, so it's actually a taxidermied crocodile) hangs from the ceiling just inside the entrance. One theory on the longstanding legend posits that the exotic beast was imported by a wealthy resident in the city's early days, meaning the creature could easily have been mistaken for a monster by locals who had never seen one. Anyway, the crocodile terrorized the town

Brno

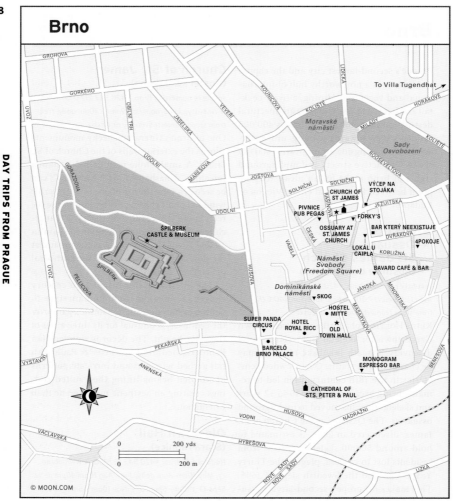

until a visiting butcher came up with a plan. He wrapped limes in an ox fur (or squeezed them onto it, depending on who tells the tale) and left it for the dragon to eat. The crocodile then drank from the river, and his stomach expanded and burst, slaying the dragon that now decorates the municipal building.

The wagon wheel on the wall beside him has a less incredible origin story. Georg Birck from the town of Lednice bet a group of his friends (likely over many beers) that he could

cut down a tree, carve it into a wagon wheel, and roll it to Brno in less than a day. His skeptical friends accepted, and were shocked when he pulled off the task. Spoiler alert: this wheel on the wall didn't actually come from a single tree, but the legend did inspire an annual event of rolling wooden wheels between the two towns each October.

The final fantastical tale of the Old Town Hall explains the front of the building. If you look closely at the sculpted turrets over the entrance, you'll find that one appears to twist off track. This is supposedly because architect Anton Pilgram was unhappy about not being paid. Of course, the other side counters that it was actually a result of the architect drinking too much. Either way, don't let structural concerns stop you from climbing the tower for a panoramic view from the city center.

These days, the Town Hall functions largely as a draw for visitors with an information center and a panoramic view of the city center rewarding visitors climbing the stairs of its 200-foot (63-meter) tower (70 CZK).

Cathedral of Sts. Peter & Paul
(Katedrála sv. Petra a Pavla)
Petrov 9, Brno, +420 543 235 031, 8:15am-6:30pm Mon-Sat, 7am-6:30pm Sun, free, tram stop Zelný trh

The towering shape of the Cathedral of Sts. Peter & Paul, also called Petrov for the hill it sits on, might look familiar to any visitors who have looked at their Czech currency. The neo-Gothic cathedral graces the face of the 10 CZK coin and is an icon of the Brno skyline. Renovations expanded the 13th-century Romanesque Basilica that previously stood on this sight. The unusual central location of the towers, crowdfunded and added to the building in the early 1900s, are the result of limited space on the top of Petrov Hill. Highlights of the ornate Baroque interior include stained glass windows that depict the life of Jesus, and climbing 30 steps to the top of the tower gives you an incredible vantage point to admire the city.

When you leave the cathedral, keep your eyes peeled for another pair of saints, Cyril and Methodius, carved in minimalist, postmodern style of two faceless bodies marked with crosses. This statue on a small platform just downhill from the entrance of the cathedral was unveiled in 2013 marking the 1,150th anniversary of the pair's arrival in Moravia. Cyril and Methodius are credited with bringing Christianity to the region in a Slavic language.

Don't be confused if you hear the cathedral's clock chime 12 times on the 11:00 hour.

Legend has it that in 1645, during the Thirty Years' War, the Swedish army was frustrated after months of unsuccessful attacks. The general declared that if they didn't take the city by noon, they would turn around and go home. An enterprising local decided to reset the bells to one hour earlier and the Swedish army stuck to their word and retreated.

Špilberk Castle & Museum
(Hrad Špilberk a Muzeum města Brna)
Špilberk 1, Brno, +420 515 919 793, www.spilberk.cz, April-Sept 10am-6pm, Oct-Mar 9am-5pm, 90 CZK, tram stop Komenského náměstí

Just outside the city center on a hill beside Petrov sits the Špilberk Castle & Museum of the City of Brno. Czech King Přemysl Otakar II established the fortified castle in the 13th century to give Moravian rulers a residence that commanded respect. The building changed hands throughout the centuries, owned by the city of Brno in the 16th century, confiscated by the Habsburg empire in the 17th century, and converted to a prison in the 17th and 18th centuries to be used later by the Nazis. Today the building is back in the hands of the city and houses the Museum of the City of Brno with the surrounding grounds offering yet another perspective to view the city from above. The permanent exhibits of the former prison grounds and historical photographs charting the city's architectural development make the castle interior a worthy draw alongside the hilltop views.

Vila Tugendhat
Černopolní 45, Brno, +420 515 511 015, www.tugendhat.eu, Mar-Dec 10am-6pm Tues-Sun, Jan-Feb 9am-5pm Wed-Sun, tram stops Tomanova or Dětská nemocnice

The Functionalist style of Vila Tugendhat was overseen by German-American architect Ludwig Mies van der Rohe around 1930 at the request of Greta and Fritz Tugendhat, a wealthy Jewish family. The modern family home included rooms for their children and nannies as well as areas to entertain. The Tugenhadt family was forced to flee in

1938, and the carefully restored furniture and grounds maintain the historical appearance designed by its innovative creator.

A tour of Vila Tugendhat requires three to four months of advance notice to experience Brno's UNESCO-protected jewel of modern architecture. The early-20th-century geometric design is unique in a country famous for spire-filled skylines. Entrance is possible only in the presence of a licensed guide. The 60-minute tour (300 CZK) points out decorative details and the history of the architect's and residents' families, while a 90-minute tour (350 CZK) tacks on technical elements like engine rooms, laundry, and storage spaces. Access to the garden (50 CZK), included in the guided tours, is available on its own for those who just want to admire the building's exterior and hillside view of the city.

Vila Tugendhat sits on the outskirts of the city and is accessible via tram number 9 from the city center or by taxi. Walking from the city center takes roughly 30-minutes uphill.

NIGHTLIFE

Thanks to its population of university students and young residents who stick around after graduation, Brno's landscape of laid-back pubs and craft cocktail bars is rarely short of customers. The streets around Jakubské náměstí in particular are lined in almost every direction (and continuously expanding) with restaurants and bars to choose from.

BAR KTERÝ NEEXISTUJE

Dvořákova 1, +420 734 878 602, www.
barkteryneexistuje.cz, 5pm-2am Sun-Tues, 5pm-3am
Wed-Thurs, 5pm-4am Fri-Sat, 100-150 CZK cocktails
Despite its name, Bar který neexistuje or "The Bar That Doesn't Exist" is absolutely real. Passionate mixologists serve craft cocktails on two floors. Choose from a specialty cocktail list, an extensive-is-an-understatement list of spirits, or just describe your mood to the staff for a custom-made order. Reservations recommended to snag a seat in this busy sophisticated space where brightly lit liquor bottles serve as the backdrop.

SUPER PANDA CIRCUS

Šilingrovo náměstí 3, +420 734 878 603,
www.superpandacircus.cz, 6pm-2am Mon-Sat,
125-150 CZK cocktails
In the words of Super Panda Circus this is "a completely different world where nothing makes sense." The cocktail experience involves surprise flavors and unusual containers in a speakeasy-style environment where patrons have to ring a doorbell and wait for an available seat. Join an upbeat, international crowd, preferably at the bar where you can watch the staff show off their flair for flipping bottles and passion for the craft.

VÝČEP NA STOJÁKA

Běhounská 16, +420 702 202 048,
www.vycepnastojaka.cz, noon-midnight Mon-Fri,
2pm-midnight Sat-Sun, 45-65 CZK beer
The local beer-drinking crowd spills out of Výčep Na Stojáka and onto the surrounding streets of Jakubské náměstí. The name roughly translates to "A Place for Standing" with the minimally decorated interior of tall tables and no stools in sight. The selection of rotating microbrews brings a steady stream of the local university student crowds and young professionals meeting after work.

FESTIVALS AND EVENTS

The **Ignis Brunensis fireworks festival** (www.ignisbrunensis.cz) lights up the sky in late May and June each summer, the **Marathon of Music festival** (www.maratonhudby.cz) brightens August with multi-genre concerts and buskers performing across the city, and **Christmas markets** twinkle in city squares in December.

FOOD

This cosmopolitan dining destination caters to a variety of tastes, including an exceptional array of vegetarian-friendly options and a specialty coffee scene so good that it inspired the creation of the **European Coffee Trip** blog (www.europeancoffeetrip.com).

Czech
PIVNICE PUB PEGAS
Jakubská 4, +420 542 210 104 or +420 542 211 232,
www.brnopivovar.hotelpagas.com, 10am-midnight
Mon-Thurs and Sat, 10am-1am, Fri, 11am-11pm Sun,
175-350 CZK entrees

Pivnice Pub Pegas located inside the hotel of the same name, is a tourist-friendly environment with the accessibility of English menus and vegetarian options (try the risotto). The staff are friendly and multi-lingual, and the décor of dark wooden tables and arched doorways sets a traditional Czech pub vibe. Try a Pegas beer from the first on-site microbrewery to open in Moravia in 1989.

LOKÁL U CAIPLA
Kozí 3, +420 731 594 671, www.lokal-ucaipla.ambi.
cz, 11am-midnight Mon-Thurs, 11am-1am, Fri-Sat,
11am-10pm Sun, 115-400 CZK entrees

If you're looking for a modern Czech pub experience, the trusted Ambiente Restaurant Group has a presence in Brno as well. Lokál U Caipla serves high-quality meat-and-cheese-based meals alongside light Pilsner and dark Kozel beers at long wooden tables wrapped around the restaurant. Bright silver tanks keeping the *pivo* cold add a modern, industrial element to the décor.

International
★ 4POKOJE
Vachova 6, +420 770 122 102, 7am-3am Sun-Tues,
7am-4am Wed-Thurs, 7am-5am Fri-Sat, 150-250 CZK
entrees

The atmosphere, menu, soundtrack, and prices at 4pokoje change nine times throughout the day. In other words, every visit in the 22 hours the venue is open is a different experience. The name, meaning "four rooms" describes the café, bistro, bar, and nightclub spread across multiple floors, each with distinct, brightly colored and neon-lit personalities. The rotating menu has plenty of international and vegetarian options like pancakes and breakfast sandwiches, hot dogs, and specialty cocktails. You'll get hearty comfort food in winter and refreshing fare on a hot day.

Vegetarian
FORKY'S
Jakubské Náměstí 1, +420 515 908 665, www.forkys.
eu, 11am-9pm Mon-Fri, noon-9pm, Sat, noon-6pm
Sun, 75-150 CZK entrees

Forky's is an entirely plant-based, vegan concept. Their 2018 move into a large, multi-story space on Jakubské náměstí pays tribute to the growing demand for ethical, health-conscious cuisine among a younger generation of Czechs and international residents, including no plastic packaging. Try one of the Asian-inspired noodle dishes, veggie burgers for a hearty meal, or build your own Superbowl of fresh vegetables.

Breakfast and Brunch
BAVARD CAFÉ & BAR
Poštovská 4, +420 734 142 108, 7am-8pm Mon-Tues,
7am-9pm Wed-Fri, 9am-9pm Sat, 9am-5pm Sun,
125-175 CZK entrees

You'll spot Bavard Café & Bar's unassuming location from the glowing coffee pot over the entrance. Young couples and crowds of friends at outdoor tables devour benedicts with various toppings over fluffy bread soaked in hollandaise sauce during the warmer months. This popular brunch spot may require a short wait, but the friendly staff will keep you in coffee when the kitchen gets backed up.

Coffee, Tea, and Sweets
SKOG
Dominikánské náměstí 5, +420 607 098 557,
www.skog.cz, 8am-1am Mon-Thurs, 8am-2am Fri,
10am-2am Sat, 12pm-10pm Sun

SKOG is the embodiment of modern coffee culture: pallet-based furniture and wooden spool tables, minimalist touches of fresh flowers and exposed lightbulbs, solid WIFI for the freelance crowd, and a purist approach to specialty coffee. The two-story space just around the corner from the Town Hall offers plenty of seating spread across creaky wood floors.

Seasonal food options are strictly vegan and vegetarian.

MONOGRAM ESPRESSO BAR

Kapucínské náměstí 12, +420 603 282 866, www. skog.cz, 8:30am-6:30pm Mon-Fri

Monogram Espresso Bar earns a discerning stamp of approval from the European Coffee Trip blog, run by two Brno-based caffeine connoisseurs. The intimate space draws an informed crowd able to discuss the quality of beans, preferred preparation method, and favorite flavors from around the globe. The passionate staff are equally happy to share their expertise in English.

ACCOMMODATIONS

BARCELÓ BRNO PALACE

CL Šilingrovo námestí 2, +420 532 156 777, www.barcelo.com, 2,000-3,500 CZK d

The tall arched windows and skylight-lit lobby of Barceló Brno Palace may solicit an involuntary "wow" muttered under your breath. This five-star, 119-room stunner offers a quiet, modern, luxury-level home base between the hills of Špilberk Castle and the Cathedral of Sts. Peter & Paul. The onsite fitness center and sauna are free for guests, with a variety of massage services for extra pampering.

HOTEL ROYAL RICC

Starobrněnská 10, +420 542 219 262, www.royalricc.cz, 2,000-2,500 CZK d

The family-run Hotel Royal Ricc combines old-world charm and a convenient location just off Brno's cabbage market square. Exposed beams, rich dark wood furnishing, and muraled staircases add an air of elegance to a comfortable atmosphere with 24-hour reception happy to answer questions. Don't skip the beautifully presented breakfast buffet before heading uphill to the Cathedral of Sts. Peter & Paul or a few streets down to the town hall.

★ HOSTEL MITTE

Panská 11, +420 734 622 340, www.hostelmitte.com

Both the ground floor cafe and the individual rooms of Hostel Mitte manage to squeeze quality and personality into every bit of available space. The hostel rooms (450-1,000 CZK) are decorated around historic trivia connected to the city (The Battle of Austerlitz or Vila Tugenhadt) while private apartments (1,350-2,000 CZK) focus on famous names like Alfons Mucha or Mozart. Details in each room give travelers information on where to explore their namesakes. Cozy rooms and curtains around the bunks provide an air of peace and privacy.

GETTING THERE

A train ride from Prague to Brno offers the most comfortable ride for a reasonable price.

From Prague

TRAIN

The national rail service České dráhy (www. cd.cz, 125-350 CZK) takes about two-and-a-half hours from Prague's main train station (Praha hl. n.) to Brno's main train station (Brno hl. n.) leaving roughly twice an hour from 4:45am until almost midnight.

Local providers Regiojet (www.regiojet. com) run direct two-and-a-half hour trains (100-175 CZK) roughly every two hours from around 5:30am until roughly 8:30pm. Splurge on business class (250-450 CZK) for a reserved leather seat in a four-seat compartment, free sparkling wine and coffee on departure, food available for purchase, and solid WIFI.

The main Brno train station is located just off the center of town, with an easy walk to most accommodation options.

BUS

Czech company Regiojet (www.regiojet. com) runs three-and-a-half-hour coach service (150-200 CZK) from Prague's Florenc Bus Station to Brno's Grand Hotel, located directly in front of the main train station. Service includes an attendant offering complimentary hot drinks and in-ride entertainment with English movies on seat-back TV screens. WIFI is solid near major cities, but less reliable in the countryside.

Leo Express (www.leoexpress.com) and **Flixbus** (www.flixbus.com) also offer regular bus connections (150-375 CZK) from Florenc.

Brno's main bus stops are both located in the city center offering an easy walk to most accommodation options.

CAR
Brno is located about 130 miles and between two and three hours (depending on traffic) southeast of Prague on highway D1/E65. As of 2018, parking rules in Brno were in the process of changing, with the latest information available at www.parkovanivbrne.cz.

From Vienna
TRAIN
Trains from Vienna to Brno (wwww.cd.cz, 350-650 CZK) run almost hourly around 7am-10pm from Wien Hbf to Brno's main train station, with some routes transferring at Břeclav for the 90-minute journey. **Regiojet** (www.regiojet.com) train service also runs from Wien Hbf to Břeclav (150-375 CZK) about four times a day from 6:30am-6:30pm, but requires a transfer to České dráhy to reach Brno.

BUS
Regiojet (www.regiojet.com) coach service also runs from Wien Hbf to Brno's AN u hotelu Grand stop (175-350 CZK) about 7-8 times a day from 4:30am-11:45pm. This centrally located bus station is within easy walking distance to most accommodation options

Leo Express coaches (www.leoexpress. com, 200-400 CZK) run from the Wien, Flughafen Schwechat bus stop once a day around 6:30pm to Brno's ÚAN Zvonařka stop just south of the main train station (a little over a two-hour journey). Another Leo Express coach route departs from Wien Hbf to Brno's ÚAN Zvonařka stop once a day around 7pm (just under a two-hour journey).

CAR
Brno is located about 80 miles north of Vienna, between two and three hours (depending on traffic) on highway D1/E65 and A5.

From Mikulov
Regional bus 105 run by the **South Moravian Integrated Public Transport System** locally known as Integrovaný Dopravní Systém Jihomoravského Kraje (www.idsjmk.cz, 60 CZK, just over an hour's journey) departs from the main train station around once an hour and stops at Mikulov's u parku bus stop in the south and the Brněnská stop on the northwestern side of town before continuing to Brno.

Leo Express coaches (www.leoexpress. com, 200-250 CZK, about 45 minutes) also run from Mikulov's u parku bus stop once a day around 8:15pm.

GETTING AROUND
Brno's city center is fairly flat and walkable with easy public transport options (www. dpmb.cz, 16 CZK) that include a tram line running through the center of town. Local rideshare app Liftago offers local service around Brno or you can use the **City Taxi** service (+420 777 014 004, www.citytaxibrno.cz).

Lednice and Valtice Chateaux

Think of Mikulov, Lednice, and Valtice as a sort of tri-city area, often referred to as the Lednice-Valtice Area or Complex. The strategic location of this trio on the southern border of the Czech Republic and Austria, roughly halfway between Vienna and Brno, made it an important historic center of trade routes and observation. Today the area is best known for the majestic chateaux that once housed the aristocracy of the Austro-Hungarian Empire.

These chateaux served as royal residences and summer homes, particularly for the Liechtenstein family. Although this family name is now associated with a smaller European country far to the west, the family was particularly prominent in acquiring and renovating many of the properties across this area. Each of these distinctive chateaux grounds and gardens are open to visitors, with interior access provided by guided tours of individual areas.

In addition to grand chateaux, South Moravia is also prime location for some of the country's best vineyards. The Wine Salon of the Czech Republic in the cellar of Valtice Chateau ranks the country's 100 best local wines every year, while smaller wine bars in Mikulov offer a more intimate environment for a taste.

MIKULOV

Czech poet Jan Skácel famously compared the town of Mikulov to a piece of Italy that God moved to Moravia, making it a beautiful home base for day trips to the surrounding area. The center of this small town is easily walkable with regular public transport connections to the neighboring chateaux.

Sights
MIKULOV CHATEAU
(Zámek Mikulov)
Zámek 1, Mikulov, +420 519 309 014, www.rmm.cz, May-June and Sept 9am-5pm Tues-Sun, July-Aug 9am-6pm daily, April and Oct-Nov 9am-4pm Fri-Sun

When approaching the town from the train station, the red rooftops and single tower of the Mikulov Chateau may not exactly stun observers. However, this gift from Otakar II of the royal Přemysl dynasty to the Liechtenstein family in the 13th century was an influential move. The Liechtensteins completed construction and used Mikulov as a home base to spread their influence across South Moravia, including the area's other more famous (and arguably more impressive) chateaux.

Entering through the main gate from the center of town opens up views of manicured gardens, curved archways, detailed sculptures, and a lookout point from the edge of the gardens over the city that will take your breath away. The interior is semi-accessible through a mix-and-match package of guided tours through various exhibits located inside the chateau. The indoor exhibitions, including an 18th-century library (60 CZK), octagonal chapel (30 CZK) and an enormous barrel from 1643 in the wine cellar (60 CZK) are more appropriate for curious history buffs than the general public, and a stroll through the courtyard may be enough for visitors on a tight schedule or saving their chateau enthusiasm for Lednice and Valtice.

JEWISH CEMETERY
(Židovský hřbitov)
Kozí hrádek 11, +420 519 512 368 or +420 731 484 500, www.zidovskyhrbitovmikulov.cz, May-June 10am-5pm daily, July-Sept 10am-6pm daily, April-Oct 10am-4pm Tues-Sun, 30 CZK

Mikulov's Jewish Cemetery, the largest in the Czech Republic, stands in sharp contrast to the cramped headstones of Prague's Old Jewish Cemetery. This quiet hillside resting place has easy paths that wind between more than 4,000 graves.

In previous centuries, Mikulov provided

sanctuary to Jews who were fleeing from religious persecution in Austria. Rabbi Loew, the infamous creator of the Golem hiding in Prague's Old-New Synagogue, served the area in the mid-16th century, bringing even more importance to the town. The Jewish population grew to nearly half of the town in the 1800s, with Jews and Christians co-existing in peace and tolerance. Tragically, a combination of emigration and the horrors or WWII left no Jewish residents in the area today.

GOAT TOWER
(Kozí Hrádek)

Na Jámě, +420 608 002 976, www.mikulov.cz, free

The easy incline of a ten-minute walk from the town center or five-minute journey from the Jewish Cemetery to the "Goat Tower" of Kozí hrádek makes a hilltop vantage point accessible to even the most novice hikers. This 15th-century structure served as strategic defensive surveillance of the surrounding trade routes leading to Vienna, Brno, and Prague. The inconsistent opening hours are signaled manually when the flag is flying, but entrance to the small building is secondary to the panoramic views of the city from its base.

Wine
VINOTÉKA VOLAŘÍK

Kostelní náměstí 9, +420 353 230 797,
www.mhmikulov.cz, noon-midnight Mon-Sat,
10am-10pm Sun, 45-75 CZK glass

The lantern-lit, covered terrace of Vinotéka Volařík along with a few indoor tables seat wine connoisseurs comfortably, even during the occasional summer storm. This intimate wine shop next door to Hotel Piano also serves as a tasting room with a mid-sized wine list of local varietals available by the glass. The relaxed, award-winning wine bar is a great place to enjoy an evening al fresco. Smoking is permitted on the outdoor terrace.

Food

Mikulov's city center is quite compact, with dining options lining Náměstí (which in

Miklov is more of a street than a "square") along the center of town, plus a few outlying favorites worth a five-minute walk.

RESTAURACE TEMPL

Husova 50, +420 721 095 111, www.templ.cz,
11am-11pm Monn-Thurs, 11am-midnight Fri-Sat,
11am-11:30pm Sun, 150-300 CZK

Restaurace Templ inside the hotel of the same name, blends regional Czech flavors with modern style in a variety of indoor and outdoor spaces—a 20-seat, Renaissance-style restaurant, a bright 22-person bistro, and a relaxing outdoor patio in the summer. The menu skews towards meats like grilled pork loin, bacon-wrapped rabbit, and beef tartare with more adventurous vegetarian options (cauliflower burgers and mushroom ragout) than you'll find elsewhere. Reservations recommended.

★ RESTAURACE MARCELA IHNAČÁKA

Husova 8, +420 608 822 348, www.hotel-tanzberg.
cz, 11am-11pm, 150-350 CZK entrees

No matter where you stay in Mikulov, stop into Boutique Hotel Tanzberg for a meal at the 45-seat Restaurace Marcela Ihnačáka. If the weather allows, request one of the additional 25 coveted spots on the quiet outdoor terrace. Named for the famed local chef, this upscale yet casual choice serves fresh, seasonal salads, pastas, and meat dishes alongside a full menu of Jewish specialties (not guaranteed to be kosher) in tribute to the restaurant's location in the historical Jewish Quarter. Reservations are essential, but the same menu is also available in the casual pub setting of **Pivnice Golem,** also on the ground floor of the hotel.

AMICI MIEI

Alfonse Muchy 10, +420 608 822 348,
www.amicimiei.eu, 9am-11pm Sun-Thurs,
9am-midnight Fri-Sat, 150-200 CZK entrees

Italian flags and red and green décor set the bright, kitschy scene at Amici Miei, which is Italian for "my friends." This small restaurant and wine bar just downhill from the

main restaurant row of Náměstí street draws Czechs as well as international travelers. Choose from a small selection of pasta dishes and bruschetta with seasonal toppings. In the summer, grab an outdoor table in front of the restaurant or across the street on the covered patio. This is a great place to pair your meal with a local glass of sweet white Palava wine indigenous to this region. Cash only payments. Some staff speak English.

BISTRO KUK

Kostelní náměstí 4, +420 728 332 485, 8am-10pm Sun-Thurs

The bright, geometric design and upbeat soundtrack at Bistro KUK sets a modern vibe for the young crowd of coffee lovers and fans of fresh-baked goods. This is one of the few places in town that you'll find any non-dairy milk options. Menus are available in Czech and English.

(NE)VINNÁ KAVÁRNA

Náměstí 18, +420 776 257 829, www.nevinnakavarna. cz, 8am-6pm Sun-Thurs, 8am-10pm Fri-Sat

Despite its name, (Ne)Vinná Kavárna meaning "(No) Wine Café" actually has plenty of *vino* to offer alongside specialty coffee and sweet homemade treats. The walls are lined with wooden china cabinets, typewriters, a piano, and other home-style touches to create a comfortable, casual vibe.

Accommodations
HOTEL GALANT MIKULOV

Mlýnská 2, +420 519 510 692, www.mikulov.galant.cz, 2,500-3,000 CZK d

If you're all about the amenities, go for one of the modern, brightly colored rooms (one of which is accessibility equipped) at Hotel Galant Mikulov. Families take advantage of the complimentary rooftop pool and hot tub from 8am-noon, with a surcharge in the afternoon setting a quieter scene. A long list of spa services are available by appointment. A multi-floor family suite (3,500 CZK), on-site winery and microbrewery, free WIFI, and 24-hour reception cater to guests' every remaining whim. This eco-friendly hotel is also committed to energy-efficient design and sustainable practices.

BOUTIQUE HOTEL TANZBERG

Husova 8, +420 519 510 692, www.hotel-tanzberg.cz, 1,700 CZK s, 2,500 CZK d

A plaque near the entrance commemorates the year that Art Nouveau painter Alfons Mucha spent living in the ivy-covered building of Boutique Hotel Tanzberg. These seventeen rooms are decked out in basic, neutral furnishing on a quiet street near the Jewish Quarter of Mikulov. The hotel also runs the lively Pivnice Golem pub and one of the best restaurants in town. Summer weekends book out months in advance at this award-winning hotel, but weekdays remain accessible.

★ HOTEL PIANO

Česká 2, +420 519 512 076, www.mhmikulov.cz, 1,300 CZK d

Whoever trains the staff at Hotel Piano should teach a worldwide master class on cultivating friendly service. This smack-in-the-center boutique hotel of 13 double rooms plus family suites (1,800 CZK) makes full use of the available space. Super comfy beds, free WIFI and hints of subtle elegance, like mini-chandeliers or framed fine art prints, enhance the modest appeal along with bonus views of the small chapels sitting on top of the grass-covered Holy Hill to the east or the Mikulov Chateau to the southwest. The impressive breakfast buffet includes eggs, sausage, and bacon alongside cereal, fresh bread, fruit, tea, and coffee to be enjoyed in the jazz-themed dining room or quiet terrace. Stays beyond two nights are treated to a complimentary bottle from neighboring wine bar Vinotéka Volařík.

1 the palace Lednice in the Lednice-Valtice complex 2 the aristocratic beauty of Valtice Chateau 3 Moravian Wine Country 4 historic town of Mikulov in Moravia

Getting There

FROM PRAGUE

The easiest way to get from Prague to Mikulov is by train. The national rail service **České dráhy** (www.cd.cz, 450-500 CZK) runs hourly, transferring at Břeclav for the four-hour journey. Trains depart from just before 6am until around 6pm, with a few late night options requiring multiple transfers. **Regiojet** (www.regiojet.com, 150-550 CZK) also runs between Prague and Břeclav every two hours from about 5:30am-5:30pm, but this requires a transfer to České dráhy to reach Mikulov. The main train station of Mikulov na Moravě is a 15-20 minute walk from the center of town, with local taxi service available.

There is no direct bus connection from Prague to Mikulov.

If you're driving, Mikulov is roughly three or four hours (about 150 miles) southeast of Prague on highway D1/E65.

FROM BRNO

Regional bus 105 run by the **South Moravian Integrated Public Transport System** locally known as Integrovaný Dopravní Systém Jihomoravského Kraje (www.idsjmk.cz, 60 CZK, just over an hour's journey) departs from Brno's ÚAN Zvonařka stop just south of the main train station around once an hour. Local service in Mikulov stops at the Brněnská bus stop on the northwestern side of town before continuing to the u parku bus stop to the south.

Leo Express coaches (www.leoexpress.com, 200-250 CZK, about 45 minutes) also run from Brno's ÚAN Zvonařka bus stop once a day just before 7am.

If you're driving, Mikulov is located about 35 miles (roughly 55 km) south of Brno, which takes about an hour on Routs 52/E65.

FROM VIENNA

Trains from Vienna to Mikulov (www.cd.cz, 350-550 CZK) run almost hourly from around 8am-7pm from Wien Hbf, transferring at Břeclav for the 2-to-3 hour journey (depending on connections). **Regiojet** (www.regiojet.com) train service also runs from Wien Hbf to Břeclav (150-375 CZK) about four times a day from 6:30am-6:30pm, but requires a transfer to České dráhy to reach Mikulov.

Leo Express coaches (www.leoexpress.com, 200-400 CZK) run from the Wien, Flughafen Schwechat bus stop to Mikulov's u parku bus stop once a day around 6:30pm (about a 90-minute journey). Another Leo Express coach route departs from Wien Hbf to Mikulov's u parku bus stop once a day around 7pm (just over an hour's journey).

If you're driving, Mikulov is located about 50 miles (roughly 85 km) north of Vienna, which takes about 60 to 90 minutes on highway A5.

Getting Around

The compact center of Mikulov is entirely walkable, with multiple bus stops connecting Mikulov to the surrounding chateaux in Lednice and Valtice. For taxi service, try **Nejlevnější Taxi Mikulov** (+420 607 856 205, www.nejlevnejsi-taxi-mikulov.cz) or **Taxi Mikulov** (+420 606 707 770, www.taxi-mikulov.cz).

★ VALTICE CHATEAU

Zámek 1, Valtice, +420 778 743 754,
www.zamek-valtice.cz

The Liechtenstein family helped to establish the splendid, 100-room Valtice Chateau in the 14th century. In 1945, it was confiscated to be used for various labor camps under Communist rule. Ongoing renovations since the 1970s have maintained the beauty of the building, which is only available through a one-hour basic guided tour (320 CZK) running every 1-2 hours either in English or with printed English text provided. Small groups don slippers over their shoes to protect the floors and swish through around 25 staged rooms and halls of royal portraits, mura-led ceilings, and canopy beds. The chateau opens at 9am from late March until the end of October, closing at 3pm in October, 4pm in March and April, and 5pm from May to September. Monday entry is only available during the months of July and August.

Beyond the basic chateau, theater fans will enjoy a behind-the-scenes tour of the newly reconstructed Baroque Theater (90 CZK), modeled after the historically preserved Baroque Theater in Český Krumlov. The 45-minute theater tour runs every 1-2 hours based on demand, either in English or with English text provided. Be sure to save time to visit the National Wine Cellar in the basement of the chateau, pouring tastes of the country's 100 most prized wines.

Wine
★ NATIONAL WINE CELLAR
Zamek 1 - Valtice Chateau, +420 519 352 744, www.vinarskecentrum.cz, Feb-Dec 9:30am-5pm Tues-Thurs, 10:30am-6pm Fri-Sat, Sundays only from June-Sept 10:30am-5pm, 100-500 CZK tastings

For an overview of the best Czech wines available, add a trip to the National Wine Cellar, located in the basement of Valtice chateau. Every August, a professional panel selects the hundred best wines in the country. The winners are available to taste in this cellar, arranged by varietal along the long brick halls. Tasting packages are based on time: Taste as many wines as you like in 90 minutes (399 CZK) or 150 minutes (499 CZK) or chose 16 pre-paid pours on a shorter time limit (a hearty lunch before visiting is a good idea to avoid getting overly tipsy). Descriptive charts in multiple languages offer detailed information including the varietal, winemaker, region, alcohol and sugar contents, and the number of bottles produced. Grab a bottle for purchase from below these posters.

Food
AVALON KELTIC RESTAURANT
Příční 46, +420 721 095 111, www.avalonvaltice.com, 11am-11pm Tues-Sun, 125-250 CZK

Budget time for a quick lunch at Avalon Keltic Restaurant as part of your day trip to the Valtice Chateau. The light-hearted, medieval hunting lodge decor indoors is accented by patches of exposed brick and swords fastened to the walls. The summer garden is cloaked in ivy around a serene waterfall and a fish pond dotted with water lilies, with Celtic music keeping the mood light and fun. This is a popular stop for cyclists in spandex crisscrossing the Moravian wine trails. The menu items resemble Czech specialties but with a lighter twist—grilled chicken and cranberry sauce or duck confit with beet root and potato dumplings, and vegetarian options available. Try a cold Svijany (my personal favorite Czech beer) with your meal before walking around the corner to the chateau gates.

Getting There
Bus route 585 (20 CZK) on the **South Moravian Integrated Public Transport System** locally known as Integrovaný Dopravní Systém Jihomoravského Kraje (www.idsjmk.cz) departs at least once every hour between 5:30am-3pm from Mikulov to Valtice. The ride takes about 20 minutes with multiple stops in Mikulov, terminating at bus stop Valtice, Aut.St. just a few streets away from the chateau entrance. Return service on Route 585 to Mikulov from the Valtice, Aut. St stop runs about once an hour until around 7pm. Bus route x58 runs more often, but with fewer stops in Mikulov, so it may require a longer walk.

★ LEDNICE CHATEAU
Zámek 1, Lednice, +420 519 340 128, www.zamek-lednice.com

Lednice Chateau provides the most striking exterior silhouette of the three stately homes in this region. The Lichtenstein family, who dominated the area from the 13th century onwards, renovated the existing structure into a bright, Neo-Gothic summer palace in the mid-1800s, smaller in size than Valtice but with much more expansive gardens and equally ornate interiors. A stroll through the swirling floral patterns takes visitors to the Minaret (80 CZK), also called the Turkish Tower, which gives you an aerial viewpoint of the entire grounds.

Different guided tours are the only opportunity for visitors to explore the chateau's interior and surrounding buildings. Highlights worth the price include the one-hour Representative Rooms tour (330 CZK), which explores the ground floor's distinctively color-coded décor, including the Blue Room, Turquoise Hall, and Red Smoking Hall. Gardening fans will want unlimited, non-guided access to the greenhouse (80 CZK), to see the plantlife housed in steel, iron, and glass design that was ahead of its time in 1842. Additional tour options focus on Princely apartments (300 CZK) and marionettes (300 CZK). The Lednice Chateau opens at 9am from late March until the end of October, closing at 4pm from October to April, and 5pm from May to September. Monday entry is only available during the months of July and August.

Getting There

Bus number 570 (25 CZK) on the **South Moravian Integrated Public Transport System** locally known as Integrovaný Dopravní Systém Jihomoravského Kraje (www.idsjmk.cz) takes just under an hour to get to from multiple stops around Mikulov (see www.idsjmk.idos.cz for route details) to the Lednice náměstí bus stop just outside the chateau. Route 570 runs every 1-2 hours from around 6:30am-7:30pm.

Vienna

Once the imperial capital of the Austro-

Hungarian Empire, Vienna doesn't skimp on opulence. Beneath gilded
and damask-upholstered interiors, Vienna is a city that has music in
its soul and psychoanalysis in its blood. Beyond the Habsburg grandeur, the waltzes composed by the Strauss family, the nostalgic coffeehouses, and gold-clad Klimt paintings adorning Vienna's galleries and
museums, it's a city that bursts with history and stories. Vienna invites
you to look closer at the details, to glance up at the painted façades of
Otto Wagner's buildings, and admire the colorful geometric fantasies
by architect Friedensreich Hundertwasser. You can wander over the
cobbles that once led to a 14th-century synagogue, ride a 100-year-old
Ferris wheel that still turns above the city, or take a tram up into the

Highlights

Look for ★ to find recommended sights, activities, dining, and lodging.

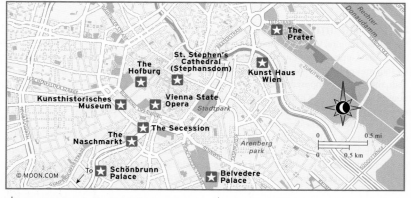

★ **St. Stephen's Cathedral (Stephansdom):** Vienna's Gothic masterpiece towers over the historic center. Climb up the top for the great views, or head below ground to its macabre skull-clad catacombs (page 194).

★ **The Hofburg:** The resplendent base for the Habsburg rulers is worth exploring for its exquisite architecture alone. It also houses a diverse set of museums (page 201).

★ **Kunsthistorisches Museum:** One of the world's most important art museums, with a vast selection of Bruegel pieces and works by Raphael, Velazquez, Rubens, Rembrandt, and more (page 204).

★ **The Naschmarkt:** This cluster of stalls and gourmet bistros peppers a long stretch along the Weinzeile. Come on Saturday when the flea market is also trading (page 211).

★ **The Secession:** The world's oldest exhibition space dedicated to contemporary art was once the stomping ground of Vienna's avant-garde artists. Klimt's *Beethoven Frieze* is its most popular piece (page 212).

★ **Vienna State Opera:** One of the most esteemed opera houses in the world is also a recognizable landmark, thanks to its neo-Renaissance architecture (page 214).

★ **Belvedere Palace:** The former Habsburg residence. Enclosed within its frescoed halls is one of Vienna's best art museums, which features Klimt's *The Kiss* as well as an excellent collection of work by Schiele and Kokoschka (page 217).

★ **Kunst Haus Wien:** This Hundertwasser-designed building with undulating floors and colorful ceramic columns contains the largest permanent collection of Hundertwasser's paintings (page 222).

★ **The Prater:** Vienna's biggest park encompasses woodlands, meadows, and boulevards, hemmed in by chestnut trees. You'll also find the giant Ferris wheel that was immortalized in Orson Welles' *The Third Man* (page 222).

★ **Schönbrunn Palace:** The former summer residence of the Habsburg dynasty is now a museum where the opulent grandeur from the former Austrian Empire is on full display (page 231).

hills for an afternoon of wine and song in one of the many taverns near the city's vineyards.

If you're a music lover, you won't tire of things to do in Vienna. Take a tour of the Staatsoper (the Vienna Opera House) or see a concert at the Musikverein (Vienna's best-known concert hall). You can even make a pilgrimage to the Vienna Central Cemetery to see where some of the city's most famous musical residents are buried.

Setting aside some time to sit in Vienna's smoky cafés and sip a *Melange* (a local foamy coffee) or tuck into a succulent pastry is a must. You may find yourself lost in people-watching as locals come to read the paper and meet up with old friends. Then, you may feel the urge to relax in the city's lush green parks under the shadow of baroque palaces. The more you uncover Vienna, it seems, the deeper the rabbit hole goes.

HISTORY

The area surrounding the Danube just outside today's Austrian capital once housed a thriving prehistoric civilization before the city became a Celtic trading post. In the first century A.D., the **Romans** arrived and named their camp Vindobona. The town flourished, and around this time, the Romans introduced vineyards to the surrounding hills; Emperor Marcus Aurelius died in Vindobona in 180 A.D.

In the ninth century, Wenia surfaced as a city from the ruins of Vindobona, and from that time Vienna as a city changed hands frequently. First, the Babenbergs ruled before the territory passed into Habsburg control. Times were turbulent in Vienna until the 18th century: The city was besieged by the Turks in the 16th century (and again in the 17th century), and it dealt with the backlash from the Reformation and Counter-Reformation—and then the devastation of the Plague at the end of the 17th century.

The 18th century became Vienna's golden age, when civil reform, architecture, and classical music rose to its zenith in the era of Maria Theresa and her son Joseph II. Classical music exploded from the capital of the Habsburg Empire, leaving Vienna with a musical legacy that pervades to this day.

Vienna saw another wave of art and culture after Napoleon occupied the city twice. The fin de siècle became another golden era for Vienna, with the rise of Austria's own brand of art nouveau and the foundation of **the Secession,** which included noted figures such as Klimt, Moser, and Schiele. This period also brought Otto Wagner's *Stadtbahn* (today's U-Bahn, the subway, line 4) and buildings, along with the newly constructed **Ringstraße** (also known as the Ring) defining the cityscape. Emperor Franz Joseph I ruled the Austro-Hungarian Empire and encouraged the city's development. This era also ushered in the birth of psychoanalysis from Sigmund Freud's apartment in Alsergrund.

The 20th century also saw considerable shifts in Vienna. First, the assassination of Archduke Franz Ferdinand ushered in World War I—and signaled the end of Habsburg rule and the breakup of the Austro-Hungarian Empire. In 1938, the Anschluss (the occupation and annexation of Austria by Nazi Germany) took place, locking Vienna into Axis hands until the end of World War II.

A few days following the war, the Allied Forces occupied Austria, and Britain, France, Russia, and the U.S. partitioned Vienna into quadrants (except for the 1st district, which was equally controlled by all four countries) until 1955. Austria then grew as an independent republic that lay on the western border of the Iron Curtain. More recently, Vienna has gained attention as one of the world's most livable cities, and it is a fascinating European capital patched together by its history and culture.

VIENNA

Vienna

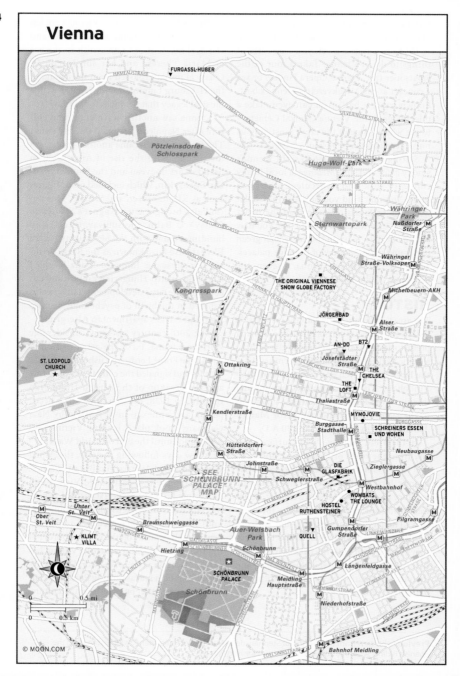

FURGASSL-HUBER

Pötzleinsdorfer Schlosspark

Hugo-Wolf-Park

Währinger Park

Sternwartepark

Nußdorfer Straße

Währinger Straße-Volksoper

THE ORIGINAL VIENNESE SNOW GLOBE FACTORY

Michelbeuern-AKH

Kongresspark

JÖRGERBAD

Alser Straße

AN-DO

B72

ST. LEOPOLD CHURCH

Ottakring

Josefstädter Straße

THE CHELSEA

THE LOFT

Thaliastraße

Kendlerstraße

MYMOJOVIE

Burggasse-Stadthalle

SCHREINERS ESSEN UND WOHEN

Hütteldorfert Straße

Neubaugasse

Johnstraße

DIE GLASFABRIK

Zieglergasse

SEE SCHÖNBRUNN PALACE MAP

Schweglerstraße

Westbahnhof

WOMBATS THE LOUNGE

Unter St. Veit

HOSTEL RUTHENSTEINER

Pilgramgasse

Ober St. Veit

Braunschweiggasse

Auer-Welsbach Park

QUELL

Gumpendorfer Straße

KLIMT VILLA

Hietzing

Schönbrunn

Längenfeldgasse

SCHÖNBRUNN PALACE

Meidling Hauptstraße

Schönbrunn

Niederhofstraße

0   0.5 mi

0   0.5 km

Bahnhof Meidling

© MOON.COM

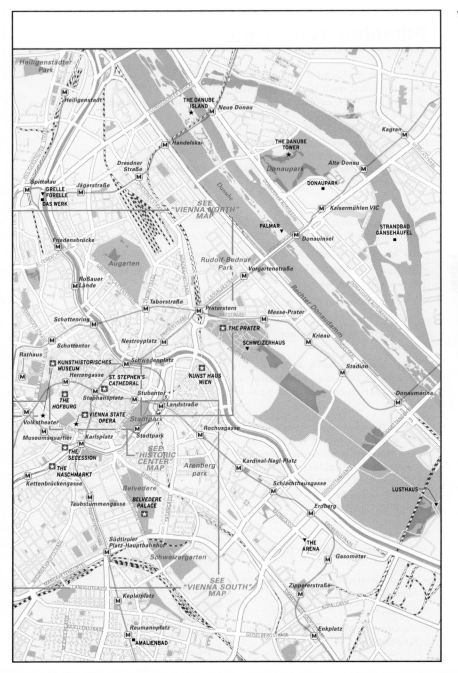

Heiligenstädter Park

Heiligenstadt

THE DANUBE ISLAND

Neue Donau

Kagran

Handelskai

THE DANUBE TOWER

Alte Donau

Dresdner Straße

Donaupark

DONAUPARK

Spittelau

GRELLE FORELLE

DAS WERK

Jägerstraße

Kaisermühlen VIC

SEE "VIENNA NORTH" MAP

PALMAR

STRANDBAD GÄNSEHÄUFEL

Friedensbrücke

Donauinsel

Augarten

Rudolf-Bednar Park

Vorgartenstraße

Roßauer Lände

Taborstraße

Schottenring

Praterstern

Messe-Prater

Krieau

Nestroyplatz

THE PRATER

Schottentor

SCHWEIZERHAUS

Rathaus

KUNSTHISTORISCHES MUSEUM

Schwedenplatz

Stadion

Herrengasse

ST. STEPHEN'S CATHEDRAL

KUNST HAUS WIEN

Donaumarina

THE HOFBURG

Stephansplatz

Stubentor

Landstraße

Volkstheater

VIENNA STATE OPERA

Stadtpark

Museumsquartier

Karlsplatz

Stadtpark

Rochusgasse

THE SECESSION

SEE "HISTORIC CENTER" MAP

Arenberg park

Kardinal-Nagl-Platz

THE NASCHMARKT

Kettenbrückengasse

Belvedere

Schlachthausgasse

LUSTHAUS

Taubstummengasse

BELVEDERE PALACE

Erdberg

Südtiroler Platz-Hauptbahnhof

THE ARENA

Gasometer

Schweizergarten

SEE "VIENNA SOUTH" MAP

Zippererstraße

Keplerplatz

Reumannplatz

AMALIENBAD

Enkplatz

Planning Your Time

You can see the highlights of Vienna in **three days,** but you'll really need to prioritize based on your interests (don't be surprised to leave with a yearning to come back for more). If your schedule is tight, home in on the Habsburgs, go on a pilgrimage to the great artistic haunts of the 1900s Vienna of Klimt and Otto Wagner, or follow in the footsteps of Hollywood stars.

Daily Reminders

Some of Vienna's most popular museums and attractions are not open daily.

- The **Secession** is closed on Monday.
- The **Kunsthistorisches** is closed Monday between September and May.
- The **Leopold Museum** is closed on Tuesdays.
- The **Naschmarkt** does not open on Sundays.
- Some museums (such as the Kunst-historisches, Belvedere, or the Museum of Applied Arts stay open as late as 9 p.m. or 10 p.m.

Some of the more niche attractions only open a few days out of the week, such as the **Narrenturm** (Weds, Thurs, Sat) **Josephinum** Medical Museum (Wed, Fri, Sat) **St. Leopold Church** (Sat and Sun only, but worth seeing for the exterior) and the **Klimt Villa** (Thurs-Sun).

MONDAY
Many museums, including the following, are closed:

- Kunsthistorisches Museum (but open Monday June-Aug)
- The Secession
- The Literature Museum (but open Monday June-Sept)

- The Viennese Clock Museum
- Chapel of St. Virgil
- Austrian National Library (but open Mon. June-Sept)
- ZOOM Children's Museum
- Imperial Furniture Collection
- Wien Museum
- Haydn House
- Museum of Applied Arts
- Johann Strauss Residence
- Criminal Museum
- Beethoven Pasqualatihaus
- Museum of the Johann Strauss Dynasty

TUESDAY
The following are closed:

- Leopold Museum
- Imperial Treasury
- Austrian National Library
- Natural History Museum
- Museum of the Johann Strauss Dynasty

SATURDAY
The following are closed:

- The Jewish Museum Vienna Judenplatz
- The Jewish Museum Vienna Dorotheergasse

The following attractions are open only on Saturday:

- Third Man Museum
- Flohmarkt flea market

SUNDAY
Many shops close on Sundays, as do the following sights:

- Naschmarkt
- Funeral Museum

- Augarten Porcelain Manufactory and Museum
- Museum of the Johann Strauss Dynasty

CLOSED ON HOLIDAYS

- Hofburg Chapel at the Imperial Palace
- Haydn House is closed Jan 1, May 1, and Dec 25

Advanced Bookings and Time-Saving Tips

It's a good idea to book tickets in advance for tours of the **Spanish Riding School** or the **Third Man Tour of the Vienna Sewers** as they often sell out. Many museums will have queues during the high season, but they move pretty quickly. If you have large bags (approximately 12 inches or larger) most museums require you to use a storage locker during your visit. Keep a euro or 50 cent coin on you as you may need a deposit.

Sightseeing Passes

There are two cards to choose from. First, the **Vienna City Card** (www.viennacitycard.at) from the Vienna Tourism Board. The Vienna City Card gives you free transport and discounts for over 200 sights, shops, bars, and restaurants.

Current pricing is:

- 24 hours: €17
- 48 hours: €25
- 72 hours: €29

The Vienna City Card gives you free transport and discounts for over 200 sights, shops, bars, and restaurants.

The **Vienna Pass** (www.viennapass.com) costs more but includes free entrance to 60 sites as well as use of the Hop-On Hop-Off Bus (www.viennasightseeing.at/hop-on-hop-off) and city boat cruises (www.viennasightseeing. at/hop-on-hop-off/boat-ride). The Vienna Pass also grants you fast-track access to some of the most popular sites, like the Belvedere and Schönbrunn Palace, so you can skip the lines. Pricing is as follows:

- 1 day: €59
- 2 day: €89
- 3 day: €119

If you're literarily inclined, you can purchase a **Universal Weekly Ticket** (€15) that gets you into the National Library, the Literature Museum, and also the Esperanto, Globe and Papyrus Museums over the course of a week. You can buy a ticket online at https://eticket.onb.ac.at/eticket_files/onb/index_en.html or at one of the museum service desks.

The **MQ Kombi Ticket** (€32, valid for one year) will get you into all the museums in the MuseumsQuartier, with a discount on the ZOOM Children's Museum and the Tanzquartier Wien and Halle G Studios.

The **MQ Art Ticket** (€26, valid for one year) covers the most popular museums in the quarter—the Leopold Museum, Kunsthalle Wien, and mumok—with the same discounts that are offered with the MQ Kombi ticket.

Orientation

Vienna's "downtown" area is very compact, but many historical sites are spread out, so you will likely need to use public transport. Vienna has a great public transport network run by **Wiener Linien** (www.wienerlinien.at) that includes six U-Bahn (subway) lines (the local subway/metro, which sometimes runs above ground on bridges), the *straßenbahn* (trams), and buses.

Today's U-Bahn line 4 was designed at the turn of the 20th century as one of the city's *Stadtbahns,* and has some beautiful art nouveau details.

Budapest and Prague are centered around their rivers, but in Vienna, the Danube flows through the suburbs toward the east of the city; you can easily spend a few days seeing the main sites without ever spotting it. (In fact, the Danube splits in Vienna, partly making its way towards the center in a small canal, which divides the 1st District from the 2nd.) Downtown Vienna is mostly situated within the **Ringstraße,** a circular road that traces the city walls which formerly enclosed the Old Town—today's 1st District. There are 23

districts, and they can be referred to by the district name (for example, the 2nd District is Leopoldstadt). You can tell which district you're in from the street signs, which usually have a number before the street name (for example, 2. Praterstraße is in District 2).

Street names usually end with -straße or -gasse (usually a narrower street). You'll also see platz (or square), and -ring, which is part of the Ringstraße.

HISTORIC CENTER AND HOFBURG AREA
(1st District)

The **oldest part of Vienna** lies inside the 1st District, clustered around the Gothic **St. Stephen's Cathedral and the Hofburg,** the former residence of the Habsburg Emperors. Despite its compact size, you could spend days in the Historic Center and only uncover a fraction of the stories of the baroque houses, 15th century frescoes, medieval courtyards, and streets that were once part of the Jewish Quarter. The U-Bahn to Stephansplatz will take you right to the heart

Vienna's trams rattling through Neubau.

of this district, but the best way to get around is to walk. The area is bordered by the Danube Canal, the Ringstraße and the Hofburg. **The Graben,** one of Vienna's most famous pedestrianized streets, is lined with shops, cafés and restaurants that run from the Kohlmarkt to Stephansplatz, cutting through the center of the district.

VIENNA SOUTH

The following areas lie in the area south of the historic center and the Hofburg and can be seen on the Vienna South map.

Neubau and the MuseumsQuartier
(7th District)

Art lovers will love the MuseumsQuartier, an area set in the former Imperial Stables that's densely packed with Vienna's **top museums, restaurants, theaters** and **cafés.** Just on the other side of Museumsplatz (which, despite the name, is a busy road), you'll find the **Kunsthistorisches (Art History) Museum** and the **Naturhistorisches (Natural History) Museum.**

Southwest of the MuseumsQuartier, the vibrant Neubau district is populated with quirky **design shops, trendy restaurants,** and **cobbled alleyways.** In the evenings, young people spill out of tiny exhibitions or sit in small bars and café terraces with a spritzer (wine with carbonated water), on warm summer evenings. **Mariahilferstraße** is the main shopping artery, along with lively **Neubaugasse** (with smaller shops) that runs adjacent to it.

Around Naschmarkt and Karlsplatz
(1st, 6th, and 4th Districts)

Three different districts convene around **Karlsplatz,** a transport hub in the inner city where three metro lines meet. This large square is covered with pockets of parkland. Just southwest of the golden-domed Secession, the Naschmarkt begins, a **large open-air market** that runs for 1,800 ft (approx. 0.5

km), ending at Kettenbrückengasse, where the famous flea market sets up shop on Saturdays. The neighborhood north of the market is marked by **winding hilly streets** interconnected with beautiful staircases, while the area south is home to **quirky cafés** and **student hangouts.**

Belvedere Palace Area
(3rd District)

Beginning around Belvedere Palace and stretching down the Danube Canal to the southern edge of the city, this area is characterized by **eclectic architecture**—the highlight being the grandeur of the **Belvedere Palace** with its landscaped gardens and baroque and rococo details. Near the palace, you'll find lively street art and intimate cafés.

VIENNA NORTH

The area around the Danube in Vienna, as well as the districts of Alsergrund and Josefstadt, lie around the historic center to the north and can be seen on the Vienna North map.

Prater and Around the Danube
(2nd and 22nd Districts)

Across the Danube Canal from the Historic Center, the 2nd District (also known as **Leopoldstadt**) lies on an island in the Danube. Most come to this part of Vienna for the **Prater,** a large green area famous for its historic amusement park, the **Würstelprater.** The 2nd district is also home to the **Augarten,** a 129-acre public park with a variety of French baroque-inspired public buildings.

Northeast of Leopoldstadt, **Danube Island** features parkland and riverside bars. Even farther east, the ultra-modern **Donaustadt,** located on another island, features the Danube Tower, the tallest building in the city. Meanwhile, on the southern banks of the Danube Canal, a vibrant residential area with surreal, colorful architecture by Friedensreich Hundertwasser (like the **Hundertwasserhaus** and **Kunst Haus Wien**) is worth exploring.

Alsergrund and Josefstadt
(9th and 8th Districts)

Alsergrund and Josefstadt lie just northwest of the Ringstraße. Josefstadt is a small district, where **independent shops and cafés** dot the upward-angled streets. Neighboring Alsergrund, just north of Josefstadt, was once the former stomping ground of Sigmund Freud (whose apartment you can still visit today).

If you visit this district, you'll discover a **student area** with three universities, and you'll also find many large old hospitals—including the grounds of the former **Vienna General Hospital** (now a university) where Freud began his medical career. It's a youthful area, with plenty of cheap eateries and **student bars.**

Running parallel to the Ringstraße is the **Gürtel,** an important main road that divides the inner and outer districts. The outer borders of Josefstadt and Alsergrund feature viaducts built for the *Stadtbahn* (now used for the U6 line). You'll also find some of the city's **hottest nightlife** under the railway arches.

SCHÖNBRUNN PALACE AND GROUNDS
(13th and 14th Districts)

The imperial summer palace of Schönbrunn is dominated by **parkland.** You could spend a day lounging in the beautiful landscaped park, visiting the oldest **zoo** in Europe, or strolling through the **Palm House** for a botanical fix. Outside the park, the area is filled with **luxurious villas,** including the villa built around Klimt's old garden house and studio. Head further up into the hills to see **Kirche am Steinhof (St. Leopold Church),** a stunning art nouveau church by Wagner, and beautiful high-level views of Vienna.

Itinerary Ideas

You really need more than three days to appreciate Vienna fully—you could easily spend an entire day at either the **Kunsthistorisches Museum** (not included in the below itineraries) or the **MuseumsQuartier** alone. However, if you just want a taste of the city, these three days will show you a few popular highlights as well as a few hidden local secrets to whet your appetite to return to Vienna for more.

DAY 1

Before heading out, reserve a table for lunch at Figlmüller around 1pm.

1 Before you get ready to walk around the kernel of the old city, grab a coffee at one of Vienna's classic downtown coffee houses, like **Café Hawelka.**

2 Wander down the cobbled streets 5 minutes away to the **Hofburg.** You can get a Sisi ticket for the museums in the Hofburg—hold onto the ticket if you plan to go to Schönbrunn Palace—to see how the Habsburg-half lived.

3 Walk 10 minutes down Kohlmarkt and the Graben to **St. Stephen's Cathedral.** Look inside Vienna's most famous landmark or take the elevator or the stairs up to one of the towers for panoramic views over the historic center and the colorful tiled roof.

4 Try a Schnitzel or some other Austrian special at **Figlmüller** in the historic center—just make sure you reserve a table first.

5 Heading over to the **Stadtpark** on a 10-minute walk southeast down Bäckerstraße—see if you can find the golden Strauss statue in the park.

6 Get on the tram D just 10 minutes away and get off at the Schloss Belvedere for the **Belvedere Museum** to see Klimt's famous *The Kiss.*

7 From the Belvedere Museum, take the S-Bahn S1 or S2 from the Quartier Belvedere station at the southern entrance to the palace to the Praterstern station for an evening at the **Prater.** Ride the iconic Riesenrad for vistas over the Danube, Old Vienna and sometimes even the mountains beyond. The best time to come is at sunset.

8 Head back on the U1, or walk it, to Schwedenplatz for the riverside bars at the Danube Canal, like the **Strandbar Herrmann,** which is open till 2am.

DAY 2

1 Start off in Karlsplatz and wander over to the **Secession.** Stop and admire the golden dome before popping inside to admire Klimt's stunning Beethoven Frieze. You only need about an hour to explore this small museum.

2 Walk over to the **Naschmarkt,** right next to the Secession. Head into one of the trendy market restaurants for a hearty brunch, then take some time to wander through this vibrant market, but don't forget to look up at the flower and gold covered art nouveau apartment blocks on the Wienzeile by Otto Wagner. If it's a Saturday, check out the flea market nearby.

3 Get on the metro at Kettenbrückengasse to Schönbrunn. Explore **Schönbrunn Palace,** the famous Habsburg summer residence.

4 After you've explored the palace, head out into the park beyond, and hike up the hill to the **Gloriette** for magnificent vistas of the Schönbrunn. Exploring the palace and park together will take a total of a couple hours.

5 Take the U-Bahn from Heitzing—see if you can spot the exclusive train station built for Emperor Franz Joseph I by Otto Wagner—to Schottenring. It's only a short walk from here to the **Sigmund Freud Museum,** the former residence of the famous psychoanalyst.

6 Walk over or take the U-Bahn to the Rathaus and explore the Josefstadt area for its culinary scene. For a recommended dish, try the *Backhendl* (fried chicken) at **Café Hummel.**

7 In the evening, check out the live music scene around the **Gürtel,** like the Chelsea and B72.

VIENNA LIKE A LOCAL

Although it's easy to lose yourself in Vienna's grand downtown sites, there is more to the city than the area enclosed by the Ringstraße. You can still fit some spectacular sights in while slipping into some of the outer districts away from the crowds for a taste of local Viennese life.

1 Head down to the Danube Canal in the morning. You'll find plenty of breakfast options here, like **KYLO** in the old Urania observatory.

2 Saunter 10 minutes due east over to the **Kunst Haus Wien** to explore the art and architecture of one of Vienna's most experimental architects, Friedensreich Hundertwasser.

3 After you've done the museum, have your camera ready to see Hundertwasser's most spectacular building in Vienna—the **Hundertwasserhaus**—which is a five-minute walk away.

4 Take the bus 4A to Karlsplatz and walk 5 minutes to Albertinaplatz to the **Bitzinger Würstelstand** for a light lunch. Try the *Käsekrainer,* a sausage filled with cheese. Don't forget to order a couple of slices of bread and some pickles to go with it.

Vienna Itinerary

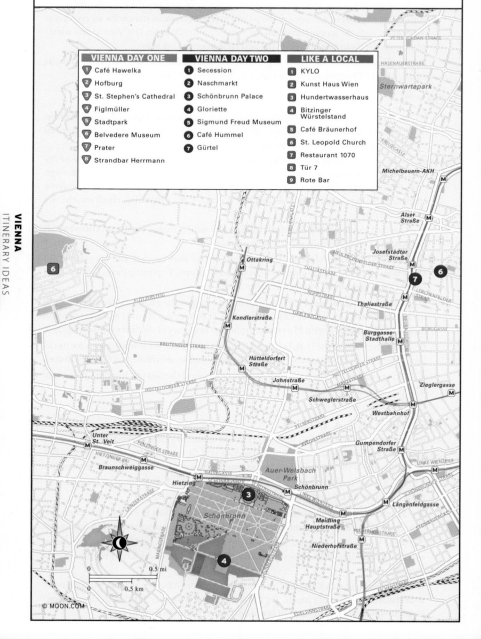

VIENNA DAY ONE

1. Café Hawelka
2. Hofburg
3. St. Stephen's Cathedral
4. Figlmüller
5. Stadtpark
6. Belvedere Museum
7. Prater
8. Strandbar Herrmann

VIENNA DAY TWO

1. Secession
2. Naschmarkt
3. Schönbrunn Palace
4. Gloriette
5. Sigmund Freud Museum
6. Café Hummel
7. Gürtel

LIKE A LOCAL

1. KYLO
2. Kunst Haus Wien
3. Hundertwasserhaus
4. Bitzinger Würstelstand
5. Café Bräunerhof
6. St. Leopold Church
7. Restaurant 1070
8. Tür 7
9. Rote Bar

© MOON.COM

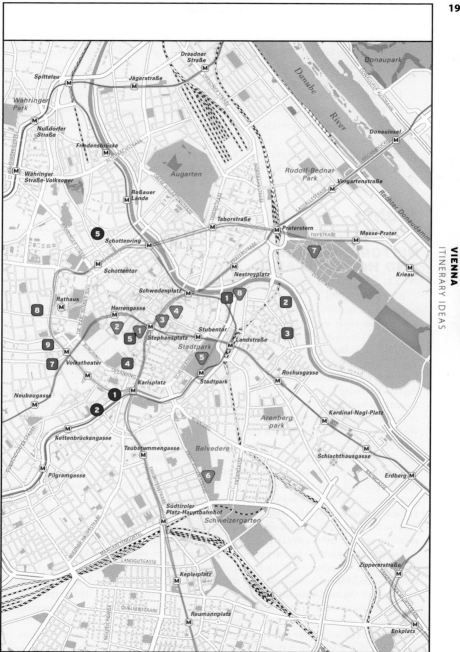

5 Follow up with a coffee at **Café Bräunerhof** just 5 minutes away to fuel up at this traditional Viennese café without the crowds. Try their strudel!

6 Take the U3 U-Bahn to Ottakring and then transfer onto the bus 48A and get off at the Spital Otto Wagner. Wander uphill following the signs to the stunning art nouveau **St. Leopold Church** by Otto Wagner.

7 To get back to the center, come the way you came and jump back to the 48A bus to St. Ulrichs Platz for dinner at **Restaurant 1070,** tucked away on the narrow cobbled streets in the Neubau neighborhood. There are only eight tables, so be sure to book ahead!

8 Ring the doorbell to get into **Tür 7,** a hidden bar only 10 minutes away on foot and try one of their cocktails.

9 If it's after 10pm, head over to the Volkteater to the **Rote Bar** for late night festivities. You never know if you'll walk into a cabaret, a theater after party or a swing night!

Sights

HISTORIC CENTER AND HOFBURG AREA

★ St. Stephen's Cathedral (Stephansdom)

Stephansplatz 3, tel. 01/51552-3054, www.stephanskirche.at, Mon-Sat 6am-10pm, Sun 7am-10pm, €6 entry to North Tower or catacombs, 5€ South Tower, U: Stephansplatz

You can spot the Gothic spires of St. Stephen's Cathedral from as far as the hills surrounding the city, rising high above all of Vienna's downtown buildings. Construction began in the 12th century, but most of what you'll see today dates back to the 14th century, after Rudolf IV, the Duke of Austria, built the cathedral on the foundations of the older Romanesque church. It's become a symbol of the city, not only as its most important religious monument, but also as the site of imperial weddings and royal funerals. (Its crypt became the resting place for the organs from members of the Habsburg dynasty.)

The cathedral itself is a tapestry of Gothic architecture superimposed by baroque style. You could spend hours inside and still not catch all the quirky details, such as the stone basilisks, snakes, dragons, eagles and lions, toads, and salamanders carved into royal tombs and on display throughout the cathedral. (See if you can spot the cheeky self-portrait of the sculptor staring out of the window beneath the stairs.)

Real beasts once wandered Vienna. The **Giant's Gate,** the main entrance, gets its name not just from its grand size, but also from the mastodon thigh bone unearthed when the foundations for the North Tower were built in 1443. At the time, people believed the bone belonged to a giant that perished in Noah's great flood.

You'll appreciate the cathedral's colorful tiled rooftop and the view of the old town—which is why it's worth the hike up the 343 steps to the **South Tower** after a few too many decadent cakes. Alternatively, save your energy by taking the lift in the **North Tower,** which provides a view just as spectacular.

To truly appreciate St. Stephen's Cathedral, you don't just need the view from above—you need to go deep below. Tours of the **catacombs** run every 15 or 30 minutes, depending on demand, and last around half an hour. At first, you may think you're just in a musty chapel with whitewashed walls. You'll see the final resting places of the bishops who once served the cathedral. But as the guide leads you into the crypts, things get interesting. First, you'll come upon the 70 copper urns that house the Habsburgs' internal organs, "preserved" in alcohol. (Their bodies rest in the Kaisergruft, while their hearts lie in the crypt of the Augustiner Church, a few streets away.) Passing the lapidarium of broken stone sculptures, the temperature drops as the tunnel swerves into the unrenovated part of the crypt where the bones of thousands of Plague victims from the 18th century lie stacked up behind iron bars.

The cathedral can get crowded during the high season, but you can escape the hordes if you head out early in the morning.

Once you've had your fill of the cathedral, head next door to the **Dommuseum** (Stephansplatz 6, tel. 01/51552-5300, www.dommuseum.at, Wed-Sun 10am-6pm, Thu 10am-8pm, €8) for a treasure trove of religious art.

Mozarthaus

Domgasse 5, tel 01/512-1791, www.mozarthausvienna.at, daily 10am-7pm, €11, U: Stephansplatz

Mozart moved frequently during his stay in Vienna, but the first floor of this three-story home (now a museum) is one of the few surviving apartments where the famous composer lived. He resided in the space for two and a half years, and it is where he penned his most famous opera, *The Marriage of Figaro*. Today, the entire house is dedicated to Mozart, and is a must for music lovers interested in the life of the child prodigy who rose to fame, then crashed into debt and sickness. He passed away at the age of 35.

Once you get your ticket, the museum will give you a worthwhile audio guide, and you can either climb the stairs or take the lift to the top floor, where the exhibit illustrates Mozart's life in Vienna. You can see original music scores, instruments and other collections in the museum, but the museum also explores Mozart's involvement with the Freemasons, as well as his vices, such as his escapades with women and gambling. Before you head down to the residential part of the flat, make sure you check out the mesmerizing holographic presentation with a scene from the *Magic Flute*, the last opera Mozart ever composed.

The Literature Museum (Grillparzerhaus)

Johannesgasse 6, www.onb.ac.at/literaturmuseum, Tue-Wed and Fri-Sun 10am-6pm, Thu 10am-9pm Oct-May, also Mon 10am-6pm June-Sept, €7, U: Stephansplatz

Book lovers will love this interactive museum dedicated to Austrian literature, whether or not they've read Joseph Roth's *Radetzky March* or Robert Musil's *A Man Without Qualities*. Although the exhibition is in German, you'll get a tablet computer at the ticket office that will let you scan the barcodes around the exhibit for English translations. You can get to know the literary life of the city from the 18th century to the present, with an interesting collection of books, letters, artifacts, photographs, and multimedia installations. Compare Rilke's elegant handwriting to Kafka's scrawl, or learn about how Alma Mahler's salons influenced the literary scene of Fin de Siècle in *Vienna*. The permanent collection of the museum is fairly extensive; expect to spend two hours here, especially if you want to read all the notes provided via the tablet.

The Jewish Museum Vienna Judenplatz

Judenplatz 8, tel. 01/535-0431, www.jmw.at, Judenplatz Sun-Thu 10am-6pm, Fri 10am-5pm, Closed Jewish Holidays, €12 combined ticket with Dorotheergasse Museum, U: Herrengasse or U: Stephansplatz

The area surrounding Judenplatz was once the center of medieval Jewish life. Today, the only traces of the historic community are in the ruins of the synagogue lying under the poignant Holocaust memorial by Rachel Whiteread. It's a concrete block formed in the shape of an inverted library, where the spines of the books are invisible—a metaphor for Jews as the "People of the Book"; each book symbolizes a Holocaust victim. Next to the memorial on the square lies the entrance to this branch of the Jewish Museum (the other branch is on Dorotheergasse). It focuses on Jewish life in the neighborhood in the 14th century up to the Wiener Gesera in the early

Historic Center

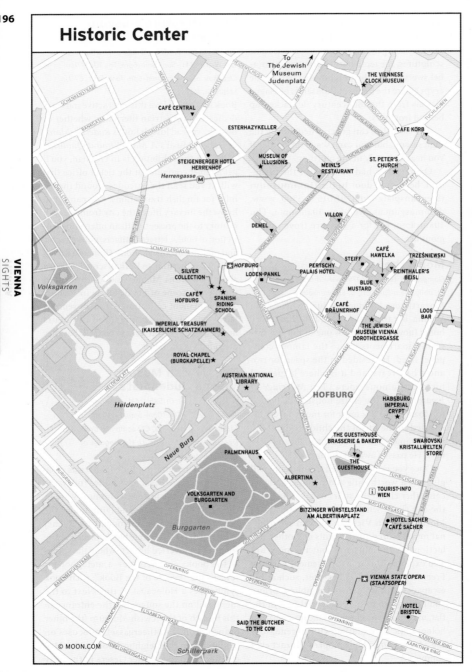

To
The Jewish
Museum
Judenplatz

THE VIENNESE
CLOCK MUSEUM

CAFÉ CENTRAL

ESTERHAZYKELLER

CAFE KORB

STEIGENBERGER HOTEL
HERRENHOF

MUSEUM OF
ILLUSIONS

MEINL'S
RESTAURANT

ST. PETER'S
CHURCH

Herrengasse M

VILLON

DEMEL

CAFÉ
HAWELKA

TRZEŚNIEWSKI

Volksgarten

HOFBURG

STEIFF

PERTSCHY
PALAIS HOTEL

REINTHALER'S
BEISL

SILVER
COLLECTION

LODEN-PANKL

BLUE
MUSTARD

CAFÉ
HOFBURG

SPANISH
RIDING
SCHOOL

CAFÉ
BRÄUNERHOF

LOOS
BAR

IMPERIAL TREASURY
(KAISERLICHE SCHATZKAMMER)

THE JEWISH
MUSEUM VIENNA
DOROTHEERGASSE

ROYAL CHAPEL
(BURGKAPELLE)

AUSTRIAN NATIONAL
LIBRARY

HOFBURG

Heldenplatz

HABSBURG
IMPERIAL
CRYPT

Neue Burg

THE GUESTHOUSE
BRASSERIE & BAKERY

SWAROVSKI
KRISTALLWELTEN
STORE

PALMENHAUS

THE
GUESTHOUSE

ALBERTINA

BURGRING

VOLKSGARTEN AND
BURGGARTEN

TOURIST-INFO
WIEN

Burggarten

BITZINGER WÜRSTELSTAND
AM ALBERTINAPLATZ

HOTEL SACHER
CAFÉ SACHER

OPERNRING

OPERNRING

VIENNA STATE OPERA
(STAATSOPER)

ELISABETHSTRASSE

HOTEL
BRISTOL

© MOON.COM

SAID THE BUTCHER
TO THE COW

OPERNRING

KÄRNTNER RING

NIBELUNGENGASSE

Schillerpark

KÄRNTNER RING

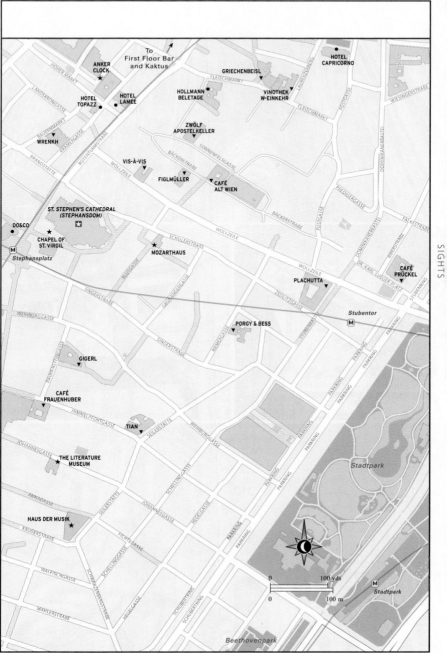

To
First Floor Bar
and Kaktus

ANKER
CLOCK

HOTEL
CAPRICORNO

HÖHER MARKT

GRIECHENBEISL

FLEISCHMARKT

HOLLMANN
BELETAGE

VINOTHEK
W-EINKEHR

LAURENZERBERG

POSTGASSE

LANDSKRONGASSE

HOTEL
TOPAZZ

HOTEL
LAMÉE

FLEISCHMARKT

WIESINGERSTRASSE

BAUERNMARKT

KRAMERGASSE

ZWÖLF
APOSTELKELLER

WRENKH

SONNENFELSGASSE

ROTENTURMSTRASSE

BRANDSTÄTTE

VIS-À-VIS

WOLLZEILE

BÄCKERSTRASSE

DOMINIKANERBASTEI

PILGRAMGASSE

FIGLMÜLLER

CAFÉ
ALT WIEN

BÄCKERSTRASSE

POSTGASSE

FALKESTRASSE

ST. STEPHEN'S CATHEDRAL
(STEPHANSDOM)

WOLLZEILE

DO&CO

CHAPEL OF
ST. VIRGIL

SCHULERSTRASSE

WOLLZEILE

DR. KARL-LUEGER-PLATZ

DOMINIKANERBASTEI

BIBERSTRASSE

M

Stephansplatz

MOZARTHAUS

BLUTGASSE

WOLLZEILE

CAFÉ
PRÜCKEL

PLACHUTTA

SINGERSTRASSE

GRÜNANGERGASSE

RIEMERGASSE

WEIHBURGGASSE

ZEDLITZGASSE

STUBENBASTEI

Stubentor

M

PORGY & BESS

SINGERSTRASSE

STUBENRING

PARKRING

GIGERL

RAUHENSTEINGASSE

PARKRING

CAFÉ
FRAUENHUBER

HIMMELPFORTGASSE

TIAN

SEILERSTÄTTE

WEIHBURGGASSE

PARKRING

JOHANNESGASSE

THE LITERATURE
MUSEUM

SCHELLINGGASSE

JOHANNESGASSE

PARKRING

Stadtpark

ANNAGASSE

SEILERSTÄTTE

HEGELGASSE

HAUS DER MUSIK

KRUGERSTRASSE

FICHTEGASSE

SCHUBERTRING

PARKING

WALFISCHGASSE

SCHELLINGGASSE

SCHWARZENBERGSTRASSE

M

Stadtpark

MAHLERSTRASSE

HEGELGASSE

SCHUBERTRING

0 ____ 100 yds

0 ____ 100 m

Beethovenpark

15th century, when the Jews were expelled, and the quarter destroyed. The permanent exhibition, depicting relics and excavations dating back to the 14th century, is underground. One of the most poignant things you'll see are the ruins of the synagogue, accessible by a subterranean passage running under the square that takes you up inside the memorial.

A ticket to the museum, which can be used within four days of issue, includes both branches of the Jewish Museum. Although the Jewish Museum in Judenplatz is quite small, most travelers visit it in conjunction with the Jewish Museum on Dorotheergasse, which is a 10-minute walk away.

The Jewish Museum Vienna Dorotheergasse

Dorotheergasse 11, Sun-Fri 10am-6pm, €12 combined ticket with Dorotheergasse Museum, U: Herrengasse or U: Stephansplatz

This museum, renovated within the last few years, is set in a former palace that once belonged to a Jewish family, and it charts the history of Jewish Vienna where the Judenplatz museum leaves off. The permanent "Our City!" exhibition traces Jewish life through Vienna under the Habsburgs, at the Fin de Siécle, and through the dark times of the Holocaust and World War II through to the present day. The museum also offers a mix of artifacts interspersed with contemporary art installations and personal stories. On the top floor, you'll find relics and ceremonial art rescued from Vienna's destroyed synagogues. Expect to spend a couple hours exploring this museum.

The Viennese Clock Museum (Uhrenmuseum)

Schulhof 2, tel. 01/533-2265, www.wienmuseum.at/ en/locations/uhrenmuseum.html, Tue-Sun and Public Holidays 10am-6pm, €7, U: Herrengasse

The Vienna Clock Museum occupies one of

Vienna's oldest buildings, on a quiet square where horse carriages move along the cobbled street. This tower-like building contains over 20,000 curious timepieces, including 15th-century painted Gothic clocks, the world's smallest pendulum clock (the size of a thimble), musical clocks, computer clocks, and intricate astronomical clocks. The museum allows visitors to see how measuring time has evolved over the centuries, from the 700-kg (approx. 1.5-ton) clock movement taken from St. Stephen's Tower, as well as grandfather clocks, and on to tiny pocket watches and digital wristwatches. Try to be there on the hour, when every clock strikes on the hour in choral unison.

Anker Clock

Hoher Markt 10-11, free, U: Schwedenplatz, Stephansplatz

A few streets down from St. Stephen's Cathedral, the Anker Clock is an art nouveau masterpiece that's worth a look if you're passing by. Franz von Matsch created this copper green and gold clock, constructed 1911-1914. It adorns the bridge between two buildings currently owned by the Anker Insurance Company. At noon, with music playing, its figurines move across the clock face. Each character represents a historical figure from Austrian history, like Roman Emperor Marcus Aurelius, and Maria Theresa. The precession of 12 figures lasts around 10 minutes, and the organ music you'll hear is made up of excerpts representative of the time periods in which the famous figures lived.

St. Peter's Church

Petersplatz, Mon-Fri 7am-8pm, Sat-Sun 9am-9pm, U: Stephansplatz

As you walk down the Graben, a pedestrianized street lined with shops and restaurants, you will pass St. Peter's Church. Its imposing turreted green dome and baroque façade are inspired by St. Peter's Cathedral in Rome. This Catholic church has been in the hands of the Opus Dei since the 1970s, and it's worth stepping inside just to see the rich, bright frescoes

1 Interior of St. Stephen's Cathedral 2 Detail of the St. Stephen cathedral roof 3 The Art Nouveau Ankeruhr is one of the quirkier landmarks in Vienna's historic center. 4 The Hofburg was the permanent powerhouse of the Habsburg emperors.

Jews in Vienna

Judenplatz was once part of the Medieval Jewish Quarter; today a memorial covers the historic synagogue, which can be visited via the Jewish Museum.

The first written record of Jews in Vienna dates back to the 12th century, with a mint master named Schlom—but there was little to no evidence of an established community till 1230. In a compact area in today's 1st District, 70 two-story houses were once home to around 800 Jews in the Middle Ages; the community congregated around the synagogue (whose ruins you can see in the Jewish Museum in Judenplatz). Jewish life thrived here until the Wiener Gesera, when King Albert V ordered the annihilation of the city's Jews in the 1420s. And after being allowed to settle again two centuries later, they were expelled by Leopold I (circa 1670).

Under Emperor Joseph II, Jews acquired more rights, although forming a religious community was still forbidden. It was only in the mid-19th century that the community was allowed to flourish; by 1900 it became the largest German-speaking Jewish community in the world (around 185,000). Prominent figures like Sigmund Freud, Gustav Mahler, Stefan Zweig, Arnold Schoenberg, and Theodor Herzl made significant contributions to that community and to the world. Until 1938, Jews in Vienna were an integral part of society. Following the Holocaust, only 9,000 Jews were part of that community—and out of the 94 temples that once stood, only one survived the war.

of cherub-like figures and toga-clad saints painted by JM Rottmayer which decorate the ceiling and dome. Try to get there on Monday at 3pm for one of their free organ concerts.

Chapel of St. Virgil

Stephansplatz, tel. 01/664-882-93930,
www.wienmuseum.at/en/locations/virgilkapelle.html,
Tue-Sun 10am-6pm, €5, U: Stephansplatz

As you leave the U-Bahn at Stephansplatz, make sure you look to the right before going

up the escalator to the square for a glimpse of one of Vienna's most fascinating places: the Chapel of St. Virgil. This medieval chapel was built in the early 13th century, and now exists where the Chapel of St. Mary Magdalene (built in the late 14th century), once stood. The Chapel of St. Mary Magdalene was destroyed completely in a fire in 1781.

Upon entering the chapel, you can use one of the tablet computers there which works as an interactive audio guide. When you descend the iron staircase into the heart of the chapel, it's easy to lose yourself in the dimly lit chamber, accented with crusade-like crosses (which have faded over the centuries into a light pink) painted into the alcoves of the chapel. A small museum in the back of the chapel covers Vienna's medieval history.

★ The Hofburg

Michaelerkuppel, http://hofburg-wien.at,
U: Herrengasse

This palatial complex, home to the Habsburgs from 1273 to 1918, was the epicenter of life for the European royals. It now offers numerous museums, Café Hofburg, libraries, and more—and it serves as the residence of the Austrian president. It is a historical tapestry, where renaissance details mingle with baroque grandeur. The oldest section is the 13th century Swiss Courtyard. (Various additions to the building were created by monarchs trying to outdo previous rulers.)

Some of Vienna's best museums are located on-site, like the Albertina. The Hofburg also features the Imperial Apartments and the Spanish Riding School. Take some time to walk through the grand courtyards, which are open for free to the public, and take in the architectural splendor.

SILVER COLLECTION, IMPERIAL APARTMENTS & SISI MUSEUM

Michaelerkuppel, tel. 01/533-7570, http://
hofburg-wien.at, daily 9am-5.30pm Sep-June,
9am-6pm July-Aug, €13.90, U: Herrengasse

The best way to experience the Hofburg in its imperial glory is to head to the three-in-one museum at this location—comprising the Silver Collection, Imperial Apartments, and the Sisi Museum. One ticket will get you into all three. Expect to spend a few hours immersed in Habsburg opulence. You can also take a guided tour (€17), which runs daily in the Sisi Museum and the Imperial Apartments at 2 p.m.

You'll begin at the **Silver Collection** (which despite the name is more than just silverware). It offers fascinating insight into daily life in the Hofburg. You'll see imperial kitchen items ranging from copper jelly molds to linen and tableware—some used on a daily basis, others only for special occasions. You'll also see rococo-style golden candles and orientalist porcelain and ceramics. An audio guide (included with your ticket) accompanies you on your journey.

The next stop is the **Sisi Museum,** located one floor above the Silver Collection. The Sisi Museum is dedicated to the legendary Empress Elizabeth, more affectionately known as Sisi, who was the wife of Emperor Franz Joseph I and ruled alongside her husband in the second half of the 19th century. She was renowned for her looks, and is still famed for her legacy in popular culture. You'll get insights into her life as a young girl through to her more independent jaunts across Europe. The museum offers an interesting peek into the woman behind the chocolate boxes and postcards—a woman who used raw meat facials to maintain her beauty, and lived with an insatiable curiosity. (She once begged a ship's captain to tie her to a chair during a storm so she could experience it like Odysseus from Greek mythology.)

The Sisi Museum leads into the **Imperial Apartments,** where Sisi lived with her husband, the Emperor Franz Joseph. The imperial couple lived separately, and their apartments reflect their character and express their personalities. Franz Joseph's rooms are traditional, with deep-red damask walls and furniture accented with gold; Franz Joseph's study holds several intimate portraits of Sisi.

Sisi's apartments are airy and light, decorated with frescoes, and include a personal gym with small weights and workout areas that were not in vogue for women of her time.

IMPERIAL TREASURY (Kaiserliche Schatzkammer)

Schweizerhof, tel. 01/525-244031, www.kaiserliche-
schatzkamer.at, Wed-Mon 9am-5:30pm, €12

The Imperial Treasury takes you on a journey

through 1,000 years of royal and ecclesiastical history. Items on display include robes, scepters, and royal jewels, but the highlight of the collection is a golden crown encrusted with rubies, emeralds and other precious gems. If you're fascinated by religious treasures, you won't want to miss the piece of the cross on which Jesus was allegedly crucified, a tooth of St. John the Baptist, and another from St. Peter, as well as a scrap from the tablecloth used at the Last Supper.

You can easily spend one to two hours here in this literal treasure trove. The audio guide (€5) is a worthwhile tool for understanding the historical context of the precious objects.

ROYAL CHAPEL
(Burgkapelle)

Schweizerhof, tel. 01/533-9927,
www.hofmusikkapelle.gv.at, Mon-Tue 10am-2pm,
Fri 11am-1pm, free entry to visit

Originally built in the 13th century, this chapel is the oldest part of the Hofburg. Over the centuries, it has undergone numerous makeovers and additions, particularly in the 15th century and then later in the Baroque period. The Royal Chapel is perhaps most famous for the Vienna Boys' Choir performances at Sunday Holy Mass.

ALBERTINA

Albertinaplatz 1, tel. 01/534-83540,
www.albertina.at, Mon, Tue, Thu, Sat-Sun 10am-6pm,
Wed and Fri 10am-9pm, €12.90, U: Karlsplatz

Today, the Albertina is home to one of the greatest art collections in the world, so vast that rotating exhibitions are required. The permanent exhibition covering avant-garde art is impressive, and goes from Monet to Picasso. You'll also be able to view pieces from Pointillism, Expressionism, Fauvism, Surrealism, and Cubism.

You can get a standard audio guide (€4) when you buy your ticket. You can install the Artvive app on your smartphone (make sure you bring headphones!) and hold your phone up to designated paintings for augmented reality views and more information.

HOFBURG COURTYARDS

The Hofburg is a labyrinth of courtyards and gates. If you start at Augustinerstraße, then you'll come to Josepfsplatz.

Movie lovers may recognize the entrance of the Austrian National Library, which was part of the scene of Harry Lime's accident in the film *The Third Man*, starring Orson Welles. Continue down Reitschulgasse, past the Spanish Riding School stables to Michaelerplatz, and take the path under the arches of the main gate to the first grand courtyard, **In der Berg,** a large enclosed square with a statue of Emperor Franz I, the last Holy Roman Emperor, and the founder of the Austrian Empire. The ornate red and black 16th-century Swiss Gate leads into the oldest part of the Hofburg, the 13th century **Swiss Courtyard** (Schweitzerhof), named for the Swiss guards who once protected the palace.

Continuing towards the gate from In der Berg brings you out to **Heldenplatz** (Hero's Square), which connects with the Ringsraße.

SPANISH RIDING SCHOOL

Michaelerplatz 1, tel. 01/533-9031, www.srs.at,
daily 9am-4pm, tours €18, U: Herrengasse

The Spanish Riding School, inside the Hofburg, maintains a 16th-century tradition, with equestrian shows twice a week featuring the stable's 70 Lipizzaner stallions, a baroque breed of horse descended from the Andalusians mixed in with other horse breeds. Although shows are a little pricey (starting from €50, or from €25 for standing room tickets), you can get a sneak peek at the morning exercises on most weekdays from 10 am to midday (check the calendar on the website as this varies by season). You can't explore the riding school or the stables without a guide, but you can catch a glimpse of the horses through the stable windows as you walk down Reitschulgasse.

Ringstraße Tram Tour

The Naturhistorisches and the Kunsthistoriches Museums are both fixtures on the Ringstraße.

The Ringstraße, a 5.3 km (approx. 3.3 mi) boulevard that ranks as one of the most beautiful streets in the world, is now a fixture in Vienna's cityscape.

A tram tour of the Ringstraße is a good way to see most of Vienna's best sites. Get on the **number 1 tram at Schwedenplatz** and change to **the number 2 at the Wien Opera** stop for a full tour around the Ringstraße. The journey takes around 30-40 minutes, depending on the change time.

If you begin with tram 1 from Schwedenplatz, you'll pass the following, in this order: the Town Hall, the Parliament (both on the right), the Hofburg (on the left), the Kunsthistorisches, the Naturhistorisches (both on the right), and the State Opera House (on the left). Also keep a look out for beautiful theaters, palaces, cafés and luxury hotels along the way, noticing the melting pot of architectural influences drawn from classical Greece, Gothic Flanders, Renaissance Italy and baroque Central Europe, as well as some art nouveau styles, mixing up into an eclectic style that is unique to the boulevard.

Trams 1 and 2 don't have commentary on board, so if you want to know what you're seeing you can take the non-stop 25-minute **Ring Tram Tour** (€9) which has explanations in English. This runs every 30 minutes from Schwedenplatz between 10 am and 5:30 pm (www.viennasightseeing.at).

It's also possible to pay a visit to the horses in the Stable Castles (the stables where the horses live and sleep) across the road (€15). Inside the Stable Castles, you may catch sight of a few white stallions peering out of their boxes into the colonnaded courtyard. Stallions stand inside their own spacious pen. The stallions come in varying shades of grey (most Lipizzaners turn white as they age) and come with first and last names—the first from the stud father, the second from the brood mare.

Tricks the horses perform actually have origins in the military, with roots in Ancient Greece. Each horse specializes in a particular exercise. During the tour, you'll likely see a rare black Lipizzaner. (It's said that while there is a black Lipizzaner in the stables, the Spanish Riding School will keep going.)

AUSTRIAN NATIONAL LIBRARY
(Österreichische Nationalbibliothek)

Joseph Platz 1, tel. 01/534-10, www.onb.ac.at,
Fri-Mon 10am-6pm, Thu 10am-9pm June-Sep,
closed Mondays Oct-May, €8, combined ticket with
Literature Museum, Esperanto, Globe and Papyrus
Museums €15, U: Herrengasse

Between the Albertina and the museums in the Hofburg is the Austrian National Library, in the palace building. It was once the Imperial Library. The Ceremonial Hall is a work of art, with frescoes by court painter Daniel Gran. Over 200,000 grand tomes line the dark wooden bookshelves, punctuated by Venetian baroque globes, Corinthian marble columns, and glass cabinets full of rare texts opened up at colorful pages. The library was built in the early 1700s, after Emperor Karl VI ordered its construction. It was built as a private wing of the Hofburg, but today it belongs to the Austrian National Library.

Museum of Illusions

Wallnerstraße 4, tel. 01/532-2255, www.
museumderillusionen.at, daily 10am-9pm, €12, U:
Herrengasse

This small museum in the heart of the city opened in the summer of 2017, and has quickly become popular with locals and tourists of all ages. The museum specializes in visual illusions, from classic trippy posters that spin before your eyes to inverted faces of Albert Einstein that change expression, depending on your vantage point. The best illusions are the larger installations, like a room with a bridge above a spinning display that tricks you into thinking you're inside a spaceship zipping through outer space. There are also plenty of photo opportunities. To get the best out of the museum, book an hour-long guided tour with one of the illusionists (€80 for groups up to 10 people, plus €8 for an entrance ticket, per person) in advance.

Habsburg Imperial Crypt
(Kaisergruft)

Tegetthoffstraße 2, tel. 01/512-685-316,
www.kaisergruft.at, daily 10am-6pm, €7.50, U:

Stephansplatz

Set underneath the triangle-shaped Capuchin Church in the city center, the Habsburg Imperial Crypt is the resting place for the members of the Habsburg family. The crypt spreads out over 10 subterranean vaulted rooms; 149 Habsburgs have been buried here, from the 17th century up until the death of Otto Habsburg in 2011. This building holds pieces of 400 years of Austria's imperial history, and the sarcophagi for 12 emperors and 19 empresses and queens. Most impressive of the tombs is the double sarcophagus for Maria Theresa and her husband Emperor Franz I, a theatrical piece by Balthasar Ferdinand Moll, with the imperial couple represented on the top gazing into each other's eyes. The tombs of Franz Joseph and Elizabeth in the next room are simpler. Tours in English (€3) run Wednesday to Saturday at 3:30 p.m.

NEUBAU AND THE MUSEUMSQUARTIER

Vienna's MuseumsQuartier combines 60 cultural institutions in over 100,000 square yards of territory. This ambitious cultural hub is one of the city's biggest tourist draws, and you can easily spend days exploring these world-class museums. If you need a little orientation, head to the **MQ Point**, the quarter's information center located by the main entrance. You can get an **MQ Kombi ticket** here (which includes entry into all the museums, except Zoom—you'll get a discount), or you can purchase an **MQ Art Ticket**, which includes the Leopold Museum (covering art from the late 19th century and the early 20th century), the mumok, and the Kunsthalle Wien.

TOP EXPERIENCE

★ Kunsthistorisches Museum

Maria-Theresien-Platz, tel. 01/525-240,
www.khm.at, daily 10am-6pm except Thu 10am-9pm
June-Aug, closed Mondays Sep-May, €15, U:
Museumsquartier, Volkstheater

If you only visit one museum in Vienna on your trip, make it the Kunsthistorisches

Museum, the largest art history museum in the country—with pieces spanning chronologically from the Ancient Egyptians to the masters of the Renaissance and Baroque periods.

The idea for the museum originated with Emperor Franz Joseph I, who wanted to create a home for the extensive imperial art collection. Plans to construct the Ringstraße began in 1857. A competition to design the new museum was held a decade later, in 1867. The winner, architect Gottfried Semper, worked on two museums (the Kunsthistorisches and the Naturhistorisches) whose semi-circular façades mirror each other. The two museums opened to the public in 1891 and 1889, respectively.

Expect to spend five hours here unless you prioritize the section you're interested in. Crowds can get heavy at the museum in the early afternoon. It's best to head out in the morning when the museum opens at 10 a.m. to get the most out of your visit. You can also skip the lines by buying your tickets online via the museum website, but do factor in some extra time for security checks as you enter the museum.

If you need refueling from all the art, the café and restaurant in the Kunsthistorisches Museum Cupola Hall (www.genussimmuseum.at, Tue-Sun 10:00 a.m.-5:30 p.m.) offers plush red seating. The museum also runs gourmet evenings (Thu 6:30-10 p.m., €44).

Museum highlights include:

MEZZANINE FLOOR
Kunstkammer Collections: What you see here may seem like a mishmash of objects at first glance, but it's a fascinating collection of curiosities that never quite found a definitive functional place in history. The more than 2,200 items include odd wind-up figurines, ball-operated gilded clocks, secret boxes, and much, much more. The items span the fields of natural history, geology, ethnography, archaeology, religious or historical relics, and arts and antiquity.

Egyptian, Near Eastern, Greek, and

Roman Collection: You can easily spend a couple of hours in the Egyptian, Near-Eastern, Greek and Roman Collection, appreciating the exhibits as well as the exquisite decor that complements the art on display. In the Egyptian wing, Egyptian-style frescoes adorn the walls and the ceiling, which is propped up with authentic Egyptian columns. In the rooms featuring Roman and Greek sculpture, you feel like you're in a villa Nero himself would have been proud to call home.

FIRST FLOOR
Picture Gallery: The vast picture gallery looks like something out of a Wes Anderson movie, probably why the director decided to curate his own exhibition here in 2018-19—with classic paintings piled up upon each other in quirky symmetry against a backdrop of pastel-colored walls. Classics from the Renaissance, ranging from Raphael to Titian, plus Baroque painting from Italy, Flanders, and the Netherlands, and an exquisite collection of Pieter Bruegel the Elder occupy the walls of the labyrinthine Picture Gallery.

GRAND STAIRCASE
The Grand Staircase connects the ground floor and the mezzanine floor with the first floor. No matter which section you prioritize, do not miss the **"Stairway to Klimt,"** the authentic frescoes painted in Egyptian style by the artist that hang above the Grand Staircase.

Natural History Museum
(Naturhistorisches Museum)
Naturhistorisches Museum, Maria-Theresien Platz, tel. 01/521-770, www.nhm-wien.ac.at, Thu-Mon 9am-6:30pm, Wed 9am-9pm, €10, U: Museumsquartier, Volkstheater

The Natural History Museum features near-identical façades and a similar interior layout to the Kunsthistorisches. The museum decor features impressive art and sculpture that capture the themes of the rooms, from maidens representing various crystals to scenes from prehistory and under the sea.

You could spend days examining all the mineral samples and kaleidoscopic crystals before you even get to the fossils in the connecting wing. The highlight is a huge room with giant dinosaur skeletons—and there is even a realistic-looking robot of a T-Rex that moves and growls. Three rooms exhibit items from prehistory, like flint arrowheads and Iron Age torques, but the real treasure is the voluptuous stone figure of the 11.1 cm (4 3/8 in) Venus of Willendorf, an over 25,000-year-old masterpiece that became one of the most famous archaeological discoveries in the world.

If you're only planning on spending a couple of hours in the museum, you may want to skim the first floor (unless you're passionate about taxidermy). The second floor is home to temporary exhibitions.

Leopold Museum

Museumsplatz 1, tel. 01/525-700, www.leopoldmuseum.org, Fri-Mon and Wed 10am-6pm, Thu 10am-9pm Sep-May, €13, U: Museumsquartier, Volkstheater

Don't be surprised if you need to queue at the ticket office or the cloakroom—this is one of Vienna's most popular museums. The Leopold collection is one of the most important collections of modern Austrian art, amassed by Rudolf and Elisabeth Leopold over a period of five decades. It features the Viennese avant-garde, with works from Klimt, Schiele, Moser and other great artists.

You can expect to immerse yourself in art for a few hours in this extensive museum. Varying exhibitions shift around, but you'll find the largest collection of Egon Schiele's work on display, from distorted landscapes to poignant portraits of mothers with children, and expressive nudes. (Of course, don't miss Klimt's allegorical **Death and Life**.)

The museum contains a café (don't lose your museum ticket as you will need it to get in and out of the café).

---

1 The Kunsthistorisches Museum is one of the highlights in Vienna's museum scene. 2 Vienna is famous for its cafes and museums - drink a *Melange* at the iconic cafe in the Kunsthistorisches Museum.

Thursday nights see a lot of traffic. Afternoons are also often busy. Try to come in the morning, and if you want to save extra time, buy a ticket online.

MUMOK

Museumsplatz 1, tel. 01/525-000, www.mumok.at, Mon 2pm-7pm, Tue-Wed and Fri-Sun 10am-7pm, Thurs 10am-9pm, €12, U: Museumsquartier, Volkstheater

From the inside out, mumok—the world's largest museum dedicated to Central European modern art—pushes the boundaries. It's an imposing structure in the MuseumsQuartier. There is no permanent exhibition here; instead, there's a rotating exhibition from its extensive 9,000-piece collection that consistently looks ahead—whether the pieces are a throwback to the Actionist avant-gardes of 1960s Vienna, like Günter Brus, Hermann Nitsch, and Otto Mühl, or the works represent early 20th-century modernism, with more global names like Pablo Picasso and René Magritte, or today's media and art. Sometimes, mumok offers space for other temporary exhibits, so check the website to see the current program.

In the basement, two floors below the entry level, you'll find the mumok cinema. The films are sometimes grotesque, shocking and explicit. Most films are silent, or in German with subtitles. They are sometimes in English, depending on the work being shown. Expect to spend at least two hours here.

(You may want to skip this museum if you're with kids—a good portion of the content is intended for mature audiences.)

ZOOM Children's Museum

Museumsplatz 1, tel. 01/524-7908, www.kindermuseum.at, Tue-Sun 12:45pm-5pm Jul-Aug, Tue-Fri 8:30am-4pm, Sat-Sun 9:45am-4pm Sep-Jun, programs €5-6, U: Museumsquartier, Volkstheater

ZOOM children's museum is not a museum in the classic sense of the word. Instead of paintings or installations, children can participate in activities that range from an hour to 90 minutes in length. Activities target different age groups and sometimes tackle weighty

Vienna South

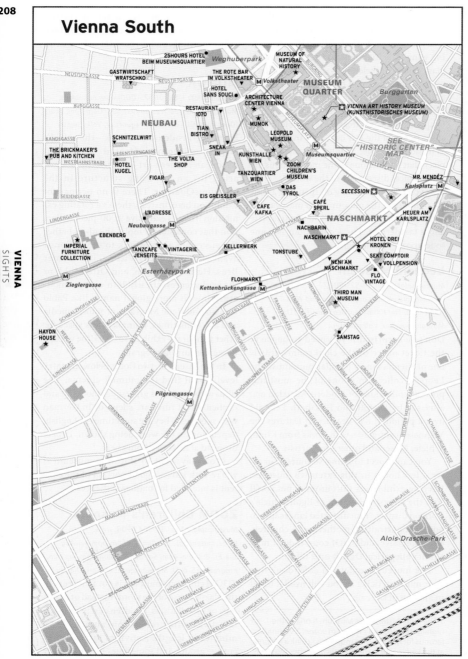

25HOURS HOTEL
BEIM MUSEUMSQUARTIER
Weghuberpark

MUSEUM OF
NATURAL
HISTORY

GASTWIRTSCHAFT
WRATSCHKO

THE ROTE BAR
IM VOLKSTHEATER

Volkstheater

MUSEUM
QUARTER

Burggarten

NEUSTIFTGASSE

NEUSTIFTGASSE

HOTEL
SANS SOUCI

ARCHITECTURE
CENTER VIENNA

VIENNA ART HISTORY MUSEUM
(KUNSTHISTORISCHES MUSEUM)

BURGGASSE

RESTAURANT
1070

NEUBAU

TIAN
BISTRO

MUMOK

LEOPOLD
MUSEUM

SEE
"HISTORIC CENTER"
MAP

KANDLGASSE

SCHNITZELWIRT

SNEAK
IN

KUNSTHALLE
WIEN

Museumsquartier

THE BRICKMAKER'S
PUB AND KITCHEN

SIEBENSTERNGASSE

WESTBAHNSTRASSE

HOTEL
KUGEL

THE VOLTA
SHOP

ZOOM
CHILDREN'S
MUSEUM

MR. MENDÉZ

FIGAR

TANZQUARTIER
WIEN

Karlsplatz

SEIDENGASSE

DAS
TYROL

SECESSION

EIS GREISSLER

CAFÉ
SPERL

HEUER AM
KARLSPLATZ

LINDENGASSE

CAFE
KAFKA

NASCHMARKT

L'ADRESSE

Neubaugasse

NACHBARIN

EBENBERG

NASCHMARKT

HOTEL DREI
KRONEN

IMPERIAL
FURNITURE
COLLECTION

TANZCAFE
JENSEITS

VINTAGERIE

KELLERWERK

TONSTUBE

SEKT COMPTOIR
VOLLPENSION

Esterházypark

NENI AM
NASCHMARKT

FLO
VINTAGE

Zieglergasse

FLOHMARKT
Kettenbrückengasse

THIRD MAN
MUSEUM

HAYDN
HOUSE

SAMSTAG

Pilgramgasse

Alois-Drasche-Park

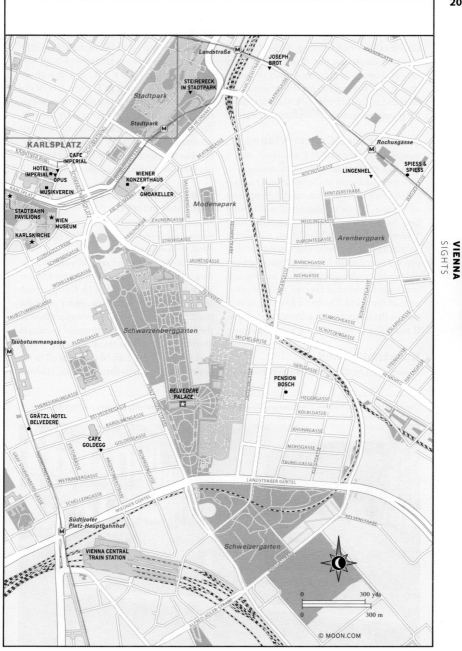

Landstraße

JOSEPH
BROT

STEIRERECK
IM STADTPARK

Stadtpark

Stadtpark

KARLSPLATZ

Rochusgasse

CAFE
IMPERIAL

HOTEL
IMPERIAL   WIENER
OPUS   KONZERTHAUS

SPIESS &
SPIESS

LINGENHEL

MUSIKVEREIN   GMOAKELLER

Modenapark

STADTBAHN
PAVILIONS   WIEN
MUSEUM

Arenbergpark

KARLSKIRCHE

Schwarzenberggarten

Taubstummengasse

PENSION
BOSCH

BELVEDERE
PALACE

GRÄTZL HOTEL
BELVEDERE

CAFE
GOLDEGG

Südtiroler
Platz-Hauptbahnhof

LANDSTRABER GÜRTEL

Schweizergarten

VIENNA CENTRAL
TRAIN STATION

0   300 yds

0   300 m

VIENNA
SIGHTS

© MOON.COM

subject matter: In 2018, one exhibition dealt with forced displacement of young refugees, showing the lives of Syrian children through activities like rug weaving. Other themes focus on creativity, like filmmaking. They may also be academic, like a study of the alphabet. See the website for the programs on offer and make sure you book in advance over the phone. Programs are available in English.

Architecture Center Vienna

Museumsplatz 1, tel. 01/522-3115, www.azw.at, daily 10am-7pm, €12, U: Museumsquartier, Volkstheater

This niche museum in the MuseumsQuartier is dedicated to the architectural development of Vienna. If you're interested in learning how the city has evolved, Architecture Center Vienna delivers with blueprints, old photographs and documents, and interactive displays. The museum follows the development of Vienna's architectural history in comparison with famous landmarks built in other parts of the world. This museum is an immersion in the nuances of Austrian architecture. If you'd like to visit, plan for at least an hour.

Kunsthalle Wien

Museumsplatz 1, tel. 01/521-890, www.kunsthallewien.at,

Fri-Wed 11am-7pm, Thu 11am-9pm, €12, U: Museumsquartier, Volkstheater

The Kunsthalle is a series of exhibition halls for contemporary and international art. The industrial, windowless setting with high ceilings is a perfect black box, and one of the best exhibition spaces in Europe. Check the website before visiting to determine whether the current exhibition sparks your interest. Programs usually rely on video, film, installations, and photography. If you're only interested in the space, head up to the café on the top floor for a coffee or a light meal.

Imperial Furniture Collection (Hofmobiliendepot)

Andreasgasse 7, tel. 01/524-3357, www.hofmobiliendepot.at, Tue-Sun 10am-6pm, €9.50, U: Neubaugasse

The Habsburgs owned several palatial residences around the Austro-Hungarian Empire. With the exception of the Hofburg, which was permanently furnished, every piece for the other imperial residences was stashed in the *Hofmobiliendepot*, the Imperial Furniture Storehouse. Once the royals came up with a wishlist, the depot shipped the items off to the desired location: Schönbrunn Palace, Gödöllő

Once the Habsburg stables, the MuseumsQuartier is a triumph in modern city planning, as this exciting arts hub draws in the crowds each day.

Biedermeier Vienna

The term *Biedermeier* is used often around Vienna and Austria. It refers to the period in Central Europe between 1815 to 1848, when there was a boom in the region's middle class, and it describes art, design, music, and literature from this time.

Growing urbanization and industrialization, along with political stability following the end of the Napoleonic Wars led to a thriving middle class hungry for the arts. Interior and furniture design blossomed with the market demand for a comfortable home life. Biedermeier style was simple, utilitarian, and drew subtle influences from Roman Empire styles. It would go on to influence other styles like Bauhaus. Locally-used materials like oak, cherry and ash wood were favored in place of imported timbers. Art during the Biedermeier period reinforced the feeling of security through everyday realism and eschewed political commentary. Portraits became increasingly popular, as well as landscapes and contemporary scenes from daily life. The Biedermeier period ended in 1848 with the wave of political unrest sweeping Europe.

You can see examples of Biedermeier art in the **Upper Belvedere,** and furniture and design in the **Museum of Applied Arts** or the **Imperial Furniture Collection.**

chateaux in Hungary, the Castello Miramare in Italy in the summer, or hunting lodges within Austria for the hunting season, usually in autumn.

The storehouse (now museum) holds the Imperial Furniture Collection, made up of 165,000 objects (some carefully arranged, others behind locked-up cages), offering time-travel through regal furniture history, from the baroque furniture used during Maria Theresa's reign to Biedermeier pieces from well-to-do Viennese households. At the end of the tour, you'll find furniture from post-Habsburg days, such as curved art nouveau chairs and a 1960s café setup and apartments.

It's easy to spend an hour or two wandering the rooms and pondering the evolution of Austrian life, from Habsburg grandeur to daily life in late 20th century Vienna. If you're a fan of the old Sissi films with Romy Schneider, look for some of the authentic furniture used in the films, like a baroque writing desk, or the imperial bed. Until the 1970s, furniture from the collection was loaned out for film productions; but after damage and losses, the museum cut its ties with the film industry. However, when Queen Elizabeth II was in town in 1969, the hotel where she stayed brought in a bed from the collection just for the British monarch.

AROUND NASCHMARKT AND KARLSPLATZ
★ Naschmarkt
Wienzeile, www.wienernaschmarkt.eu, Mon-Fri 6am-7:30pm, Sat 6am-6pm, U: Kettenbrückengasse

More than a market for shopping or dining, Naschmarkt is a sight in its own right, and it's worth spending a morning or an afternoon negotiating crowds of local shoppers and tourists to grab some great food and soak in the atmosphere at this large, open-air market. It starts just across the road from the golden-domed Secession and goes on for just under a mile alongside the Wienzeile main road. There are no less than 120 market stalls, where you'll find fresh vegetables, dried fruit, cheese, cold cuts and much more. The best time to come is in the morning in the middle of the week if you want to skip the crowds and get your hands on the best produce and enjoy a good breakfast.

The market is split into two lanes. The north side lane is made up of trendy global restaurants. You'll find what you're craving, whether it's Turkish home cooking, an Indian thali, pad thai, sushi, or Wiener Schnitzel. The lane on the southern side is lined with stalls selling fresh seasonal vegetables, cured meats, olives, vats of hummus, freshly cooked falafel balls, dried fruit, and artisanal cheeses.

VIENNA
SIGHTS

The Golden Age of the Secession

In 1897, a group of artists, including Gustav Klimt and Koloman Moser, broke away from Vienna's mainstream art scene and founded the Secession in a bid to escape the conservatism that they felt was suffocating mainstream art. This new movement, which was philosophical as well as aesthetic, is embodied in the motto that's still inscribed above the entrance to the Secession: *Der Zeit ihre Kunst. Der Kunst ihre Freiheit* (To every age its art. To every art its freedom.)

The work of various Secession artists ranges from Klimt's seductive golden portraits of femme fatales to Schiele's disjointed lines and organic color palette. Aesthetically, these works, some of which are graphically sexual in nature, may not have much in common. But what united these artists was a manifesto of artistic freedom, a hunger for modernity and new ideas—like the psychoanalytic writings of Sigmund Freud, who was a contemporary of the artists. Otto Wagner's thirst for modernity and modern application of architecture fit into the philosophy of the Secession as well.

Here's a summary of some of the best work that captures the spirit of the Secession in Vienna:

The Secession Building: Joseph Maria Olbrich's daring building, nicknamed the "Golden Cabbage" when it was built, became an architectural manifesto for the movement, and a space for artists who chose to break away from the status quo to exhibit.

The Beethoven Frieze: Located in the Secession, Klimt's *Beethoven Frieze* captures the spirit of the Secession by embodying the idea of the *Gesamtkunstwerk*, a total artistic environment. For the Secessionists, it was not only the visual arts that were reflected in the movement, but also music. For example, at the launch of the exhibition where the piece was presented, Gustav Mahler adapted Beethoven's *Ninth Symphony*. You may not hear Mahler play in the background when you visit the work, but you can still see the *Gesamtkunstwerk*, like the real gems incorporated into the fresco details.

The Stadtbahn Pavilions: Otto Wagner's Stadtbahn Pavilions embrace the modern spirit of the Secession by incorporating technology with aesthetics. Wagner did not only break from classical art in form, but also sought functionality in his art with his metro line and its gilded pavilions. The pavilions rely on three colors—green, gold, and white—in a similar style to the

In the 16th century, the market specialized in selling milk bottles made from ash wood. (It gets most of its name from the word Aschenmarkt.) It became closer to the market we know today in the 18th century when a law decreeing that produce brought in by cart rather than boat had to be sold on-site. (More recent urban legends tell of stall vendors who hid cocaine in vats of sauerkraut.)

The market gets its look from the Fin de Siècle, in true art nouveau style. If you're a fan of Vienna's art nouveau, you'll definitely want to hike up to the end by Kettenbrückengasse and look up at Otto Wagner's Majolica Wienzeile—beautiful apartments painted with roses and floral motifs.

If you come the market on Saturday, keep walking and you'll find a fascinating antique flea market, the **Flohmarkt** (see page 256).

★ The Secession

Friedrichstraße 12, tel. 01/587-5307, www.secession. at, Tue-Sun 10am-6pm, €9.50, U: Karlsplatz

The Secession building, by Joseph Maria Olbrich, after the movement of the same name, is the Secession's architectural manifesto. It may be a symbol of the city today, but the exhibition hall caused a scandal when it was built in 1897. Its austere block-like shape topped with a dome of gold leaves was dubbed the "Golden Cabbage," and pushed the boundaries of the traditional art scene—which is exactly what its founders and members wanted. Artists such as Klimt, Kolo Moser, Joseph M. Olbrich, and Josef Hoffman wanted to break away from the mainstream and create a space where art broke the shackles of convention.

The building has suffered over the years. It functioned as a hospital in World War I. It

When the Secession was built, it's avant-garde design and golden dome caused a scandal.

lithographs by Kolo Moser and other contemporaries, showing a continued exchange between the artists.

Egon Schiele's Self Portrait: If any artist broke away from the respected forms of classical art, it was Egon Schiele, whose jagged lines and intense colors captured the Expressionist form of art that rose up after the Secessionist movement. Schiele was a contemporary of Klimt, Moser, and Wagner, and his intense, eroticized self-portrait on display at the Leopold Museum captures the movement's rebellious spirit.

was later torched by the Germans in retreat in World War II. But today, it once again functions as an exhibition hall. The ground floor and top floor host temporary, contemporary art exhibitions, but the biggest draw is Klimt's *Beethoven Frieze*. The fragmented frieze is one of Klimt's most recognized works. The top left corner of the frieze is an artistic symphony based on Richard Wagner's interpretation of Beethoven's *Ninth Symphony*, with allegories and personification of three sins: lust, gluttony, and unchastity. It was only meant to be a temporary exhibit back in 1902, but since the 1980s, it's become a fixture in the Secession.

Compared to other museums, the Secession is small, and you can see it in roughly an hour. There are one-hour guided tours in English (€3) at 11 a.m. on Saturdays. The Secession doesn't get as crowded as other Vienna museums, but the best time to visit is later in the afternoon or first thing in the morning.

Stadtbahn Pavilions

Karlsplatz, U: Karlsplatz

Otto Wagner left his mark on Vienna. The *Jugendstil* (the German word for Art Nouveau) artist fused modern function and architecture to create buildings for a new age—among them his metro stations. The twin Stadtbahn Pavilions on Karlsplatz are his most beautiful, with floral designs enhanced by gold trim on white marble that complements the apple green of the *stadtbahn* (the tram or metro railway). One pavilion has reopened as a small museum, the **Otto Wagner Pavilion Karlsplatz** (Karlsplatz, www.wienmuseum. at, Mar-Oct Tues-Sun 10 a.m.-6 p.m., €5) devoted to Wagner's principle works, like the gold-domed *Kirche am Steinhof* in the hills above Vienna. The building opposite is a café and a club, the **Café Restaurant Karl-Otto im Otto Wagner Pavilion** (tel. 01/505-9904, 9 a.m.-2 a.m.) and **Club U** (tel. 01/505-9904, 10 p.m.-4 a.m.).

Karlskirche

Karlsplatz, www.karlskirche.at, Mon-Sat 9am-6pm
Sun midday-7pm, €8, U: Karlsplatz

Rising above Karlsplatz, this baroque church, built between 1716 and 1736, is one of Vienna's most beautiful churches and one of the most famous landmarks in the city. You can take an elevator up to the dome ceiling, which towers at over 230 feet. Inside, you'll get a close-up of the beautiful frescoes of the Glory of St. Charles Borromeo (the leading figure of the counter-reformation against the Protestant Reformation), along with an abundant collection of fleshy cherubs by Johann Michael Rottmayr. The lift to the dome is included in the admission price, but expect to queue for as long as an hour. To avoid lines, come as soon as the church opens its doors.

Even if you don't go inside, make sure you stop and admire Karlskirche from the outside (including the enormous twin columns that were modeled on Trajan's Column in Rome). Look closely at these columns to see scenes from the life of Charles Borromeo, from whom the church gets its name, and whom helped plague victims in Italy.

Haus der Musik

Seilerstätte 30, tel. 01/513-4850, www.hdm.at, daily
10am-10pm, €13, U: Karlsplatz

The Haus der Musik (which means House of Music in German) is a unique museum that combines Vienna's music history with the science of sound. The museum is located in a tall townhouse in the heart of the city.

The first floor is accessible by a set of stairs that doubles as piano keys (there is also a lift if needed). The first floor covers the history of the Vienna Philharmonic. This floor is a classic museum, with personal relics like conductors' letters, old watches, photographs, and scribbled sheets of music. There are also interactive listening stations.

On the second floor, devoted to the science of sound, is the Sonisphere, which is like an interactive art installation—with screens that demonstrate how your ear works, and exhibitions like an indented globe you can duck your head inside and hear music and sounds from around the world. Another feature allows you to perform specific experiments with your voice.

The third floor is a walkthrough, tactile installation on Vienna's most famous composers, beginning with Mozart and moving up to 20th century composers like Schönberg, Berg, and Webern. Each room has a theme that ties in with the spirit of the composer.

On the fourth floor, you can experience what it's like to be a conductor. Virtual conductor rooms let you see if you've got what it takes to take over the Vienna Philharmonic.

★ Vienna State Opera (Staatsoper)

Opernring 2, tel. 01/514-442-250,
www.wiener-staatsoper.at, English language tours
usually on the hour. See website for times. Tours €9,
U: Karlsplatz

The Vienna State Opera is a cathedral to classical music. The best way to experience one of the world's most prestigious opera houses is to get a ticket for a production. But if you can't, it's worth taking the 45-minute guided tour for a behind-the-scenes peek into a world hidden away from regular opera goers.

Only a third of the original opera house built in 1869 remains (after bombs in World War II devastated the iconic building), but the building has been beautifully restored. One of the few intact rooms is the tea room, where Emperor Franz Joseph sipped tea near golden silk wall panels and marble cladding. The tea room is only open during tours of the opera

---

1 staircase in Vienna State Opera House
2 Karlskirche, perched on Karlsplatz, is a stunning piece of Baroque architecture. 3 The area around the Naschmarkt is a vibrant neighborhood, with its famous market and stunning Otto Wagner houses.

house, and not during productions—unless you want to hire it for 20 minutes in a break during a show for €500.

The tours also take you through the maze-like passages beyond the gilded Grand Staircase to the main auditorium or the stage area, where you can see the set designers getting ready for the latest production.

The Vienna State Opera runs shows virtually every night. Each night brings a different opera or ballet production. Sets are mounted on the six platforms on the revolving stage. The tour gives insight into just how much work goes into each production. Approximately 120 stage hands work day and night to ensure flawless shows.

The Third Man Tour of the Vienna Sewers

Karlsplatz/Girardi Park, tel. 01/4000-3033,
www.thirdmantour.at, May-Oct English tours at
3pm daily, €10, U: Karlsplatz

If you're a fan of *The Third Man* or you love exploring weird and wonderful places, then sign up for one of the one-hour tours that run from May to October. Although the film is the main theme of the tour, you'll also see the sewers. The sewers themselves are spectacular, especially the banks of the covered Vienna River.

The Vienna sewers are a subterranean labyrinth that run below the city in a complex network of tunnels. As sewers go, it doesn't smell that bad, and you also get to see part of the Vienna River (Wien River) which was forced underground during the time of Franz Joseph, when the sewer system was built. Since then, the sewers have served as a backdrop for movies and music videos, the most famous of which is the finale of Orson Welles' *The Third Man.*

First, you'll don your provided hard hat with flashlight, then follow the sewer workers down into the Viennese underworld. You'll learn what it's like to work in the sewers—from the 13-pound steel-cap boots worn by sewer workers to pranks played

on newcomers. You'll also watch a surreal screening of *The Third Man* projected on the wall right where the memorable scene was shot. You'll also get a chance to see the underground river before resurfacing. Wear sensible shoes, and don't panic if you see a sewer rat on your subterranean journey. Disinfectant is provided when you return to the surface. (You won't really get dirty, but I wouldn't dress for the opera before going on this tour.)

Third Man Museum

Preßgasse 25, tel. 01/586-4872, www.3mpc.net,
Sat 2-6pm €8.90, U: Kettenbrückegasse

Even if you're not a movie buff, it's worth visiting this eccentric and special museum to learn more about the strange and turbulent time in Vienna in which *The Third Man* with Orson Welles was set, when the black market was thriving and people lived in a city with borders.

The museum's collection is a passion project by married couple Gerhard and Karin, who put the museum together without outside help. The museum's collection started in 1997 and keeps growing. Today, it spans three separate buildings.

In the first building, you're submerged in an eccentric collection of movie memorabilia, photographs and newspaper cutouts and stories of both the famous and local actors in the film. You'll get a glimpse of rare items like pages of the original script.

In the second building, you can watch two minutes of the film, via a projector from 1936. The iconic zither theme by Anton Karas gets its own dedication in a small room with pictures from the tavern the musician played in.

The third building is a museum of Vienna just before and after World War II, with rare photos of the devastation the city endured, as well as memorabilia, including soldiers' uniforms and newspaper clippings from the time Vienna was partitioned into American, British, French, and Russian zones.

Haydn House

Haydngasse 19, tel. 01/596-1307, www.wienmuseum. at/index.php/standorte/haydnhaus.html, Tue-Sun 10am-1pm, 2pm-6pm, €5, U: Zieglergasse

This garden house set on a quiet side street just moments away from one of Vienna's busiest shopping hubs was composer Joseph Haydn's last home, and where he died at age 77 in 1809. Here he wrote some of his most important pieces, including "The Creation" and "The Seasons."

Today, the home is a two-floor museum. The ground floor provides a narrative of the story of Haydn's arrival to the neighborhood (known as Gumpendorf) after returning from London. The rooms where he lived and composed are on the top floor—and you'll get a glimpse into Haydn's life. You'll find a wall of music scores, info describing the composer's daily routine, along with rooms dedicated to his most important later compositions, with handwritten notes and old programs. If you're a Haydn fan or you're passionate about classical music, it's worth going out of your way to get up close and learn more about the composer.

Wien Museum

Karlsplatz 8, tel. 01/505-8747, www.wienmuseum.at, Tue-Sun 10am-6pm, €10, U: Karlsplatz

Take a journey through Vienna's history at the Wien Museum, featuring ceramics, furniture, fine arts, and paintings dating back to 1400 and tell the city's personal story. See the city's history told through various paintings and maps covering the 17th century, when the Ottomans besieged Vienna, a collection of Biedermeier furniture, and post-1900 art. Highlights include Klimt's purple-dappled portrait of Emilie Flöge, Schiele's intense portraits, and the 14th century statues that were once part of St. Stephen's Cathedral.

You can easily spend two hours or more here if you take in the details. If you want to grasp the context of the history of the Austrian capital without reading a textbook, the Wien Museum can help.

BELVEDERE PALACE AREA
★ Belvedere Palace

Prinz Eugen-straße 27, tel. 01/795-570, www.belvedere.at/de, daily 9am-6pm, Fri until 9pm, €20 for a combined ticket to the Unteres and Oberes Belvedere

The Belvedere Palace was designed by Johann Lukas von Hildebrandt as the summer residence for Prince Eugene of Savoy, the general of the Imperial Army, who beat back the Turks at the beginning of the 18th century. It is one of the most spectacular examples of baroque architecture you can explore.

The Belvedere offers the main palace building, and state and ceremonial rooms that serve as spaces for fine art, including Klimt's famous piece *The Kiss*. You need at least half a day to really get the most out of both. The museum is always busy, but if you arrive when it opens or after 4pm in the afternoon (especially on weekdays), the crowds thin out slightly. Buying tickets online also can help cut down time spent in line.

You can rent audio guides (€6) for both parts of the museums, but if you want the VIP treatment, sign up to a bespoke tour for €90 (not including admission price), or for €110 after 6pm on Fridays. Note that the ticket office is not in the palace, but in an outbuilding to the west, just after the gate from Prinz Eugen Straße (it is signposted, so just follow the arrows). There is also a ticket office in the Lower Belvedere from Rennweg (the entrance here is also marked).

LOWER BELVEDERE
(Unteres Belvedere)

Lower Belvedere was built in the early 1700s and lies at the northern end of the garden, at the bottom of the slope. The u-shaped palace's grand ceremonial salons and state apartments, along with the adjoining buildings, the former horse stables, and the Orangerie (a building once used to store citrus and other exotic plants in the winter), are home to the museum's temporary collections and a permanent collection of Gothic art.

As you approach the museum from Upper Belvedere, you'll find the entrance on the western side of the palace, which leads into the Hall of Grotesques, an entrance hall decorated with allegorical figures from Greco-Roman mythology. Turn right, and this will take you into the main wings of the former residential palace, now home to temporary exhibitions across its 14 rooms, with the Marble Hall, a grand hall clad in marble friezes and frescoes, at the center of the palace. However, if you go straight ahead in the Hall of Grotesques, this takes you through the lavish ceremonial rooms, first into the Marble Gallery, an ornamental hall lined with marble statues, mirrors, and carved stuccos, and then into the spectacular Golden Cabinet, originally a conversation room later clad out all in gold and mirrors. Beyond the Golden Cabinet a covered walkway will lead you to the Orangerie and the stables, the latter of which now hold an exquisite collection of 150 medieval paintings, sculptures, and triptychs. If you want to visit the stables, make sure arrive between 10am and midday when it is open. The Orangerie, on the other hand, also hosts temporary exhibitions in a large hall.

Although the Lower Belvedere is worth visiting for the spectacular Marble Hall, Marble Gallery, and Golden Cabinet, check the program for the exhibitions that are on to see if these would be of interest to you. If you plan to visit the Lower Belvedere, you could easily spend one to two hours.

UPPER BELVEDERE
(Oberes Belvedere)

Whereas the Lower Belvedere was meant as a residence, Prince Eugene of Savoy built the impressive Upper Belvedere largely for show and ceremonial purposes. This is where you'll find the palace's permanent art collection chronicling the history of art from medieval times to the early 20th century.

The museum's exhibitions spread out over the three palatial floors. The entrance on the ground floor opens into the Sala Terrena, a brilliant white lobby decorated with stucco and columns sculpted into muscular Atlas figures that appear to be holding up the ceiling. Turn right at the entrance and you enter Carlone Hall in the west wing, covered entirely with extravagant baroque frescoes. It was originally used in the hot summer months for guests to stay cool. From the Carlone Hall, there are four halls filled with medieval art. And on the other side of the Sala Terrena, in the east wing, you'll find rooms for temporary exhibitions and two rooms devoted to the history of the palace.

Take the Grand Staircase to the first floor (there are also lifts available on both sides of the staircase), which leads into the Marble Hall at the top. This magnificent antechamber occupies two stories, resplendent in reddish marble, gold leaf accents, dangling crystal chandeliers, and elaborate frescoes depicting the glorious Prince Eugene as the Greek god Apollo. In the west wing, the rooms are filled with excellent baroque paintings and sculptures that glorify the Habsburg legend. The east wing on the first floor offers an impressive collection of Viennese art from the 1900s.

The star of the show is Klimt's *The Kiss*. You'll also find Klimt's *Judith*, a seductive golden portrait rich with detail. Works by contemporaries like Schiele, Kokoschka, and Moser also line the grand walls, and explore themes like psychoanalysis and mortality.

On the second floor, the four rooms open in the west wing have some nice Biedermeier landscapes, impressionist works from Monet and Degas, and in the four rooms in the east wing there is also a great collection of post-World War I art, with works from the expressionist movement.

A good time to visit the Upper Belvedere is first thing in the morning before the midday crowds hit, or towards the end of the day.

1 Gardens of the Belvedere Palace 2 Klimt's *The Kiss* is the highlight of the Belvedere Palace. 3 Belvedere Palace

GARDENS

If you find you're oversaturated with art, take a break in the beautiful gardens.

The name Belvedere means "beautiful view." When you take a stroll through the landscaped Baroque gardens, you'll see statues inspired by Greek mythology, along with winged, voluptuous Sphynxes, sculpted hedges, ornate parterres (flat stretches of garden populated with ornate flower beds), and cascading fountains. The garden links the Upper and Lower Belvedere palaces.

Entry to the garden is free. On the southern end, you can walk into the neighboring **Botanical Garden** (Rennweg 14, www.botanik.univie.ac.at, daily from 10am-1 hour before dusk; free admission) and the **Alpine Garden** (Prinz Eugen Straße 27, www.bundesgaerten.at, Mar-Aug 10am-6pm; €3.50) to the east of the garden walls.

Museum of Applied Arts

Stubenring 5, tel. 01/711-360, www.mak.at, Tue 10am-10pm, Wed-Sun 10am-6pm, €12, U: Stubentor

It's worth stepping inside the Museum of Applied Arts for the architecture alone—the huge central courtyard looks like a Roman palace. You'll want to stay for the exhibits delving into Vienna's history with arts and crafts. This museum is more than just a collection of pretty objects; it will leave you thinking about how you perceive design and its function.

The museum spreads over three floors. The ground floor displays Rococo style furniture, with the porcelain room originally in the Palais Dubsky as the highlight. In the 1700s, it became fashionable to decorate rooms as "porcelain cabinets," such as this room, with cups and vases set into the wall as decoration. This porcelain room, once located in Brno during the 1740s, has been reconstructed inside a block in the middle of the museum hall with golden damask upholstery, Rococo furniture and porcelain accents. There is also an exquisite collection of art from East Asia, porcelain from China, Korea, and Japan, as well as carpets from the Middle East. On the other side of the hall you'll find furniture from the Biedermeier era, as well as wooden art nouveau chairs and benches. The Jugendstil creations are backlit behind a white screen, which really brings out their curved forms.

For more art nouveau, head up to the first floor, where you'll see examples of Viennese pieces along with contemporary pieces from France, Belgium, Hungary, as well as ceramics influenced by motifs drawn from Japanese art, which was fashionable at the turn of the 20th century.

The basement charts the history of design across time and cultures. Many displays are tactile, allowing you to touch and feel, like the replica of the world's first fitted kitchen—the Frankfurter Küche—designed by Austria's first female student of architecture, Margarete Schütte-Lihotzky. There are also documentaries playing on a loop with English subtitles, and creative installations about the future of design and how it will affect how we eat, cook, and sit as we progress into the digital age.

Vienna Central Cemetery (Wiener Zentralfriedhof)

Simmeringer Hauptstraße 234, tel. 01/534-692-8405, www.friedhoefewien.at, free

Vienna's main cemetery captures the essence of Vienna and its former residents. It's one of Europe's largest cemeteries, with over 330,000 graves within its grounds that spread out over 620 acres. The resting places represent all religious denominations.

If you take tram 6 or 71 to Zentralfriedhof tor. 2 from the Simmering U-Bahn, you will arrive right at the main gate—the most impressive entrance. Since Austrians value their cakes as much as their respect for the dead, you'll find an **Oberlaa** café and patisserie just inside, so you can grab a Melange and a Sacher cake before heading out to discover the graves (Simmeringer Hauptstraße 232, tel. 01/767-1768-0, www.oberlaa-wien.at daily 8am-4:30pm Jan-Feb and Nov-Dec, 8am-5:30pm Mar and Oct, 8am-6:30pm Apr-Sep).

As you take the main pathway to the **St. Charles Borromeo Church**

Death in Vienna

The Viennese have a unique fascination with death, and the idea of the "beautiful corpse", or *Schöne Leich,* celebrates the idea that death is a part of life. The concept of the *Schöne Leich* became immortalized in songs, poetry and in the funerary arts of Vienna in the mid-19th century. When the Austro-Hungarian Empire was at its height, Vienna experienced a large influx of wealth, and extravagant funerals became a status symbol and a festive occasion. Viennese funerals were a form of art and theater, with each funeral trying to surpass the next.

Some odd traditions also tie in with a fear of being buried alive, like attaching a bell-like device to the corpse inside the coffin so should the worst case happen, someone would be alerted.

The tradition of death lies all around Vienna, whether it's in the grand cemeteries of the city or the Habsburg resting places. Within literature, art, music, death is very much on the forefront of Viennese minds.

The Cemetery of the Nameless is a small cemetery dedicated to anonymous bodies pulled from the Danube.

VIENNA
SIGHTS

(Karl-Borromäus-Kirche) at the heart of the cemetery, to the left there is an area dedicated to composers and musicians. This is where you'll find the graves of Beethoven, Johann Strauss (father and son), Brahms, Schubert, and a memorial grave to Mozart.

Don't skip the church. From the outside, it seems simple (white and square with a green dome), but inside, it's an art nouveau masterpiece. The cupola strikes you with its intense turquoise blue and painted gold stars. The white-walled interior of the church also has colorful stained glass and mosaic work.

Before leaving the cemetery, head over to the old part of the Jewish Cemetery in the northwest corner. This is the most atmospheric part of the cemetery, with romantic neoclassical mausoleums and overgrown tombstones inscribed in Hebrew.

Funeral Museum

Simmeringer Hauptstraße 234, tel. 01/76-067, www.bestattungsmuseum.at, Mon-Fri 9am-4:30pm, Sat (Mar-Nov) 10am-5:30pm, €6

This quirky museum set just next to the main entrance inside the cemetery offers insight into Vienna's decadent traditions surrounding death. From the role of the undertaker to funerary haute couture for elegant widows, this interactive museum with touchscreen displays and audio collections of popular funeral songs spreads out in a 3,200 square foot basement underneath a chapel. There are all kinds morbid curiosities on display, from death masks to Joseph II's "foldaway coffin" (an unpopular idea proposed by the Emperor to recycle coffins) as well as photographic material depicting grand funerals for Vienna's bourgeoisie. All aspects of Viennese funerary life can be traced in this near blacked-out basement, showing an evolution of funerals and how they became a status symbol. You can expect to spend around 40 minutes to an hour in this museum.

Cemetery of the Nameless

Alberner Hafenzufahrtsstraße, tel. 06/60-600-3023, http://friedhof-der-namenlosen.at, Nov-Feb daily 7am-5pm, Mar and Oct 7am-6pm, Apr and Sep 7am-7pm, May-Aug 7am-8pm, free

It feels like a pilgrimage to get to this cemetery just off the Danube shore. The 76A bus puts you down next to industrial buildings and silos—and you may feel you're in the middle

of nowhere. But take the path next to the bus stop and turn left at the train tracks and you'll see a sign post to the cemetery. There are around 100 graves here, marked by black iron crosses, some adorned with flowers, others with children's toys. Few have names, but most bear *Namenlos*, or nameless.

Even though the last burial here was in the 1940s, all the graves are lovingly tended with fresh flowers. Film buffs may recognize this moving cemetery from the movie *Before Sunrise*, when Julie Delpy and Ethan Hawke's characters find themselves at the graveyard. (The movie is a bit misleading—don't expect it to be a short stroll to the Riesenrad of the Prater afterwards.)

If you love cemeteries, it's worth combining a trip with the Vienna Central Cemetery and taking a taxi or public transport over.

PRATER AND AROUND THE DANUBE
Hundertwasserhaus
Kegelgasse 37-39, U: Landstraße
Architect Hundertwasser built this house in the 1980s, drawing inspiration from his love of color, curved lines and incorporating nature. A private residence, the building is not open to the public, but you could spend hours looking at the façade, snapping photos, or simply admiring the details from the bench opposite. This building is a kaleidoscope of colors, lines and some 200 trees and shrubs sprouting from the roof, terraces, alcoves, and anywhere else plants can grow.

You can drop by the **Kunst und Cafe coffee house** (daily 10am-6pm) on the ground floor for a free short film about the architect shown continuously on a loop or head to **Hundertwasser Village** (a former tire workshop turned into a shopping quarter that Hundertwasser also designed) which now houses a shopping center with bars and souvenir shops. If you need a public toilet, the "Public Toilet of Modern Art" is on display with its colorful mosaics and ceramics, and is a good way to spend any loose change.

★ Kunst Haus Wien
Untere Weissgerberstraße 13, tel. 01/712-049512, www.kunsthauswien.com, daily 10am-6pm €11, U: Landstraße
If you're hungry for more Hundertwasser, take the five-minute walk from the Hundertwasserhaus to the Kunst Haus Wien, a museum set in one of his apartment blocks which scales three floors. Not only do you get a peek inside one of his buildings, with undulating floors and rooms propped up by colorful columns in glazed ceramics, but you can see the largest permanent collection of Hundertwasser's paintings. His style emulates his architecture, with irregular, organic forms playing with color and texture (you'll see his use of silver and gold foil). Hundertwasser established the museum in a 19th-century building he reconstructed in the 1990s. It's one of the top places to visit in Vienna, particularly if you love modern art and architecture. There are also temporary photography exhibitions held on the top floor. Expect to spend between an hour to two hours here.

★ The Prater
Prater, tel. 01/728-0516, www.prater.at, open all the time, free, U: Praterstern
The Prater is Vienna's largest park, stretching 60 square kilometers. The Prater is all about fun, whether that means being thrown about like laundry in a centrifuge on one of the rides at the Würstelprater or having a beer at Schweizerhaus, a breezy *biergarten*. Joggers run along the tree-lined Hauptallee, the main promenade that cuts through the Prater, and locals regularly relax in the meadows and grassy patches away from the mayhem of the city.

The Prater has been a place of pleasure for more than 200 years, declared as a place for public enjoyment in 1766—first as a retreat, but in true Viennese fashion, it has turned into a place populated by taverns, cafés, swings, carousels, and the huge Ferris wheel (the iconic Riesenrad) that dominated the skyline in the 19th century.

WÜRSTELPRATER

Free, open 24 hours

At the northern end of Prater lies this retro amusement park, the Würstelprater, which is one of the city's most iconic spots. There are some 250 attractions here, including roller coasters, ghost trains, and bumper cars. Buy your ticket for rides (usually €1.50-10) at the ride booth. You can also invest in a **Prater Highlights Card** for €45 that will get you access to the 20 most famous attractions, you can buy it online (www.praterhighlights.at, note the site is only in German) or at the information office at the entrance (open Mar-Oct 10:30am-10pm).

Access to the Würstelprater grounds is free and the park itself is open 24 hours, but most attractions operate from 10am-midnight or 1am.

As you walk around, notice the architecture, which has an old-world carnival feel, with painted statues, cardboard cutouts, and Jugendstil buildings. You may also want to ride on the nostalgic pastel-hued **Luftikus Carousel** that has exhausted riders for decades (don't worry, it's been restored with state-of-the-art technology). Or you may want to ride on the 380-foot tall **Praterturm** that will whisk you around at 38 miles per hour for a huge adrenaline rush (don't eat before riding).

RIESENRAD

Prater 90, tel. 01/729-5430, www.wienerriesenrad. com, daily 10am-11:45pm (winter has shorter hours and can be closed in January), €10, U: Praterstern

Rising above the Prater over 200 feet, the Riesenrad, or Giant Ferris Wheel, is a symbol of the city. (You may have seen it in movies like Orson Welles' *The Third Man* or in *Before Sunrise*). It's absolutely worth taking a ride on this 110-year-old Ferris wheel (unless you have a fear or heights or enclosed spaces!).

Once you've bought your ticket, you enter a circular room enclosed by a wall of mirrors and filled with vintage carriages. Each carriage features insights into Vienna's history, including a model of the Prater. From here,

exit through a door (which may take you a moment to find) and get in line to board the red carriage, which fits around 15 people. Although the Riesenrad is the gentlest of the rides in the Prater, its height can induce vertigo (you can always sit down on the wooden bench inside the carriage if it gets too much.) The wheel moves incredibly slowly and is stable, and you are secure inside. The ride takes approximately 20 minutes. The view from the top is worth it: You'll see most of the city's most prominent landmarks from above, like St. Stephen's Cathedral, and also beyond to the Danube and the hills surrounding Vienna.

The Riesenrad has been part of the cityscape since 1897 (marking the 50th year of Emperor Franz Joseph's rule). It can also be booked for special events, like dinners, weddings or breakfasts. Weekday mornings and evenings after 9pm are generally quiet, but if you come during the weekend, especially in the afternoon, expect queues.

PRATER PLANETARIUM

Oswald-Thomas-Platz 1, tel. 01/891-7415-0000, www.planetarium-wien.at, show times vary, €9, U: Praterstern

The Prater Planetarium takes you on an hour-long journey into outer space. The shows are in German. If you're tired and want to sit and take a break, the exploration through the solar system and asteroid belt to the outer galaxy is a great respite. If you know basic astronomy, then you can follow most of the program.

PRATER MUSEUM

Oswald-Thomas-Platz 1 (inside the Planetarium), tel. 01/726-7683, www.wienmuseum.at, Fri-Sun 10am-1pm and 2pm-6pm, €5, U: Praterstern

Theater and circus beat at the heart of the Prater, and this museum, set in the same building as the planetarium, depicts the evolution into the amusement park we see today. Highlights include the dragon from the grotto railway from the 1950s, the tall centerpiece from a 19th century merry-go-round, coin-operated machines from the early 1900s, and a somewhat creepy collection of ventriloquist

VIENNA
SIGHTS

Vienna North

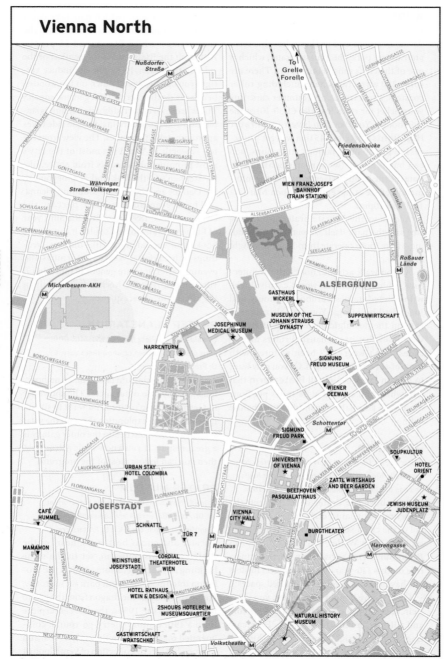

Nußdorfer Straße

To Grelle Forelle

Friedensbrücke

WIEN FRANZ-JOSEFS-BAHNHOF (TRAIN STATION)

Roßauer Lände

Währinger Straße-Volksoper

Michelbeuern-AKH

ALSERGRUND

GASTHAUS WICKERL

MUSEUM OF THE JOHANN STRAUSS DYNASTY

SUPPENWIRTSCHAFT

JOSEPHINUM MEDICAL MUSEUM

NARRENTURM

SIGMUND FREUD MUSEUM

WIENER DEEWAN

Schottentor

SIGMUND FREUD PARK

UNIVERSITY OF VIENNA

SOUPKULTUR

HOTEL ORIENT

URBAN STAY HOTEL COLOMBIA

ZATTL WIRTSHAUS AND BEER GARDEN

BEETHOVEN PASQUALATIHAUS

JEWISH MUSEUM JUDENPLATZ

CAFÉ HUMMEL

JOSEFSTADT

VIENNA CITY HALL

SCHNATTL

TÜR 7

Rathaus

BURGTHEATER

Herrengasse

MAMAMON

WEINSTUBE JOSEFSTADT

CORDIAL THEATERHOTEL WIEN

HOTEL RATHAUS WEIN & DESIGN

25HOURS HOTELBEIM MUSEUMSQUARTIER

NATURAL HISTORY MUSEUM

GASTWIRTSCHAFT WRATSCHKO

Volkstheater

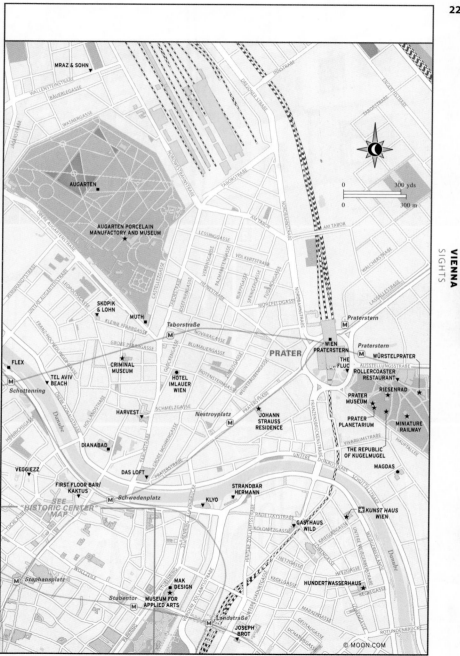

© MOON.COM

dummies and puppets. The park's dark history is on display as well, with former human zoos depicted in black and white photographs from the early 1900s, along with pictures and objects, such as tiny shoes, from little people who once resided in the "Lilliputian cities" within the Prater and held theater performances. It's worth the visit to this one-room museum for context and the evolution of change.

UNTERER PRATER

Away from the bright lights of the amusement park, the Unterer Prater relaxes into grassy meadows, and woodlands filled with slender poplar and chestnut trees and lakes. You'll spot families and groups of friends picnicking away from the chaos of the city in the summer, along with joggers, cyclists, and in-line skaters along the Hauptallee, which begins up by the Praterstern and ends at the Lusthaus, a 16th century hunting lodge that's now a restaurant set next to a golf course and a riding school. Nature lovers hike towards the water meadow at Freudenau at the southern end of the Prater, or relax and stroll by the water at the Heustadlwasser, a channel-like lake that once linked up with the Danube at the middle of the Hauptallee.

MINIATURE RAILWAY

Prater 99, tel. 01/726-8236, www.liliputbahn.com, daily 10am-5pm Oct and March, 10am-6pm Apr and Sep, 10am-7pm May and June, 10am-8pm Jul and Aug, €4, U: Praterstern

This tiny railway trundles through the Prater for 4km, taking you on a 20-minute roundtrip from the foot of the Riesenrad to the edge of the Prater, and to the Hauptallee—a tree-lined boulevard that is the closest the Prater has to a main road. The train even plunges into woodland before making its turn and bringing you

back to the amusement park. The railway is great fun for the kids, and a vertigo-free alternative to the Giant Ferris Wheel. Get your tickets from the kiosk by the train platform before getting on.

THE REPUBLIC OF KUGELMUGEL

Antifaschismus Platz, www.kugelmugel.at, U: Praterstern

While you're in the Prater, you'll want to stop by the world's smallest micronation, the Republic of Kugelmugel, a tiny 35-square-yard republic created by Edwin Lipburger following a dispute with the Austrian government in 1984 after he built his house without a permit. (He almost went to jail for refusing to pay taxes and for printing his own stamps.) The republic is essentially a spherical house that looks like something from a 1960s UFO film. It's surrounded by a barbed border, so unless there is an exhibition on, you won't be able to cross.

The Republic of Kugelmugel wasn't always in the Prater, making it one of the few mobile nations. Stop by while you're in the Prater and see if you can get a glimpse inside this surreal nation (which is mostly made up of artists working inside the spherical house). The republic now holds 650 non-resident Kugelmugel citizens.

Johann Strauss Residence

Praterstraße 54, tel. 01/214-0121, www.wienmuseum. at, Tue-Sun 10am-1pm and 2pm-6pm, €5 U: Taborstraße

Johann Strauss immortalized the Danube River (a notable natural feature in the neighborhood of Leopoldstadt, where this residence is located) in his waltz *The Blue Danube*. The compact museum occupies the seven rooms once part of the original apartment (a section of the Strauss apartment lies in a private residence). The museum holds some of the composer's original scores, with handwritten notes like, "Please forgive the bad and untidy handwriting, I had to finish this off in a few minutes," scribbled in the margins. Make sure you look over the caricatures, not only those

1 Don't miss the Hundertwasserhaus in Vienna. 2 The Danube Canal is a relaxing spot in Vienna and best visited by boat. 3 The Narrentum was once an asylum that is now a museum of pathology in the Alsergrund district. 4 Riesenrad, the giant Ferris wheel in the Prater.

of the composer but by the composer himself, who drew them as a way to relax.

Criminal Museum

Große Sperlgasse 24, tel: 06/64-300-6577, http://wien.kriminalmuseum.at, Tue-Sun 10am-5pm €8 including the short guide in English, U: Taborstraße

(Note: This museum is not appropriate for children.)

This morbid collection of criminal documents, skeletons, and torture equipment resides in a 17th century town house with a labyrinth-like interior winding through 15 rooms and corridors. The museum details the evolution of Vienna's justice system from the 17th century, when a dismembered corpse was found close to today's museum, up to post-war Vienna. The museum covers forensics in the 19th century, attempted assassinations on the Emperor Franz Joseph I, and photographic documentation of gruesome crimes. There are plenty of skulls, a mummified head, and uncensored photographic evidence. Anyone fascinated with the history of crime could easily spend hours perusing old newspaper cuttings, murder weapons and vintage forensic tools.

Augarten Porcelain Manufactory and Museum

Obere Augartenstraße 1, www.augarten.com, Mon-Sat 10am-6pm, €7, €11 for the guided tour, U: Taborstraße

Porcelain production began in the Augarten in 1718, making this factory (located in an 18th century former imperial pleasure palace) the second oldest of its kind in Europe. The museum takes you through the history of porcelain and its various uses—in excessively ornamented rococo pieces up through modern times, as designers draw inspiration from the simple lines of the 1920s. The exhibition includes the original kilns (no longer in use) used to make porcelain. If you're interested to learn more about how quartz, white kaolin, feldspar can be molded, cast and luted into the creations you'll see in the exhibition and the shop, you can take an hour-long tour at 2pm or 3pm on Saturdays.

Tours are in German and English. Make sure you check out the shop if you want to take some unique porcelain pieces, such dishes, cups, dining sets, and figurines home with you.

The Danube Island (Donauinsel)

www.wien.gv.at, open all times, free, U: Donauinsel

This slender island cleaves Vienna's Danube landscape in two and runs about 13 miles. The Danube Island is a place of leisure, with cycling paths, not-so-sandy patches of Danube beaches, stretches of parkland hugging the waterfront, and also watersports, like boating. (Note that parts of the island marked FKK are nudist areas.)

Close to the U-Bahn stop, bars and restaurants cluster together in an area known as the **Sunken City,** with some bars set on little islands in the river accessible by jetties. Grab a cocktail and recline in a hammock or a deck chair among the palm trees or under the fairy lights once the sun goes down, and you'll feel like you're on holiday in a tropical resort. There is also a huge 6,000 square yard water playground that's free, and if you head towards Reichsbrücke, the main bridge that stretches to the island from the city center, you can find **Danube Jumping** (www.danubejumping.at, Mar and Oct 1pm-7pm, Apr 1pm-8pm, Sep 1pm-9pm, May-Aug 1pm-11pm, €3 per 10 minutes) a huge trampoline center that's fun for adults and kids alike. And in June, Donauinselfest takes over the island.

The Danube Tower (Donauturm)

Donauturmstraße 4, www.donauturm.at, daily 10am-midnight €14.50, U: Neue Donau

Rising out of Donaupark, the 825-foot Danube Tower, *Donauturm*, is the tallest building in the city. Ride the lift up to the viewing platform for 360-degree views look over the Danube and towards the old part of the city and the hills beyond. There is a revolving restaurant at the top serving Viennese food, and there's also a café.

ALSERGRUND AND JOSEFSTADT

Vienna City Hall (Rathaus)

Rathausplatz 1, www.wien.gv.at, guided tours take place Mon, Wed, Fri 1pm, U: Volkstheater

The Rathaus rises up above the Ringstraße in a dramatic architectural symphony of spires and Gothic arches. This City Hall was built in 1883 by Friedrich von Schmidt in the neo-Gothic style and is one of the Ringstraße's finest buildings. It still functions as an official seat of the mayor and houses the provincial government. You can take tours inside on Mondays, Wednesdays and Fridays, but you're better off saving the time and just appreciating the building from the outside when you're strolling past.

Sigmund Freud Museum

Berggasse 19, tel. 01/319-1596, www.freud-museum. at, daily 10am-6pm, €12, U: Schottentor

Whether or not you agree with his theories in psychoanalysis, Sigmund Freud's theories on symbols, dreams and sexuality are deeply woven into the cultural fabric of Vienna—and the world, so if you're in Vienna, it's worth paying a visit to his former home, the epicenter of his most famous theories, and of course, that infamous couch (which, sadly, doesn't exist anymore, except for a golden statuette as an homage). The museum occupies the former apartment where the "Father of Psychoanalysis" lived and practiced most of his life till he was forcefully exiled to Britain by the Nazis in 1938. Today, the museum spreads out across the first-floor apartment. Some of the rooms capture Freud's daily life, such as the cramped entrance hall where one of his iconic bronze ashtrays is on display, and his furnished waiting room, which contains a cabinet of antique curiosities in the corner, stacked with Greek and Egyptian statuettes, along with other archaeological relics. Freud's study and the rooms where Freud held consultations are presented more as an exhibition to his life and his work, with letters, notes and photographs along with first editions of his most famous books. Freud's youngest daughter, Anna Freud—also a noted psychoanalyst in her own right—helped put the museum together in the 1970s, and there is even a room dedicated to her.

You can spend as little as an hour in this small museum, with the audio guide included in the entry fee. If you opt for a real guide, you could easily spend hours learning all about Freud's life. **Context Travel** (www.contexttravel.com/cities/vienna) does a great walking tour on Sigmund Freud that includes the museum as well as the surrounding neighborhood.

Narrenturm

Uni Campus, Spitalgasse 2, tel. 01/521-77606, www.nhm-wien.ac.at/narrenturm, Wed 10am-6pm, Thu 10am-1pm, Sat 10am-1pm, €4 entrance, an extra €4 for the tour, U: Schottentor

Looming above the former grounds of the Vienna General Hospital where Freud began his career, the *Narrenturm*, which translates as "the Fools Tower," is an imposing structure. It was built in 1784 and was Continental Europe's oldest insane asylum. Neither the Narrenturm nor the grounds surrounding it currently function as a hospital (in fact, the surrounding hospital buildings now make up the campus grounds for the University of Vienna). Today you'll find a pathological museum in the claustrophobic rooms and tight circular corridor of the infamous tower. The ground floor gives you an overview of the collection, a few musty apothecary cabinets, deformed baby skeletons, and some waxworks of skin diseases, but to get the gruesome details, make sure you register for the one hour-long tour in English (which runs depending on demand on the hour, so contact the museum to arrange a tour before).

The tour takes you to the normally closed first floor, where one of the medical students from the university guides you through the collection of waxworks graphically depicting diseases, skeletons of conjoined twins, and organs preserved in formaldehyde. This graphic collection was once intended to teach medical students about diseases in a time before color photography, with some pieces dating back to the 18th century. It's informative for anyone fascinated with pathology and medical history, but it is graphic, and may be upsetting for some.

Josephinum Medical Museum

Währinger straße 25, tel. 01/401-602-6001, www.josephinum.ac.at, Wed 4pm-8pm, Sat 10am-6pm, €8, U: Schottentor

Dreamt up by Emperor Joseph II, the Josephinum became a medical academy with the ambition to modernize medicine. The building itself is a stunning example of neoclassical architecture, but more interestingly, it's worth visiting for the medical museum with a fascinating collection of 18th century wax models realistically depicting all facets of human anatomy in its three grand rooms. Some pieces are morbidly beautiful, like the Medici Venus, a golden-haired dissected maiden whose skin is stripped away to show all the vital organs. She is naked except for her pearls and she reclines on a satin bed in a rosewood casket enclosed with hand-blown Murano glass. In the next case, a man wearing only muscles and veins is displayed. The figures in the room have glass for eyes, but the hair is real. Details and close-ups of anatomy are featured in the room, which are sculpted out of wax made from Ukrainian wild bees.

Unlike the Narrenturm, the waxworks here depict healthy bodies, some even posed in statuesque forms. There is something oddly beautiful and eerie about the collection (think the "Body Worlds" exhibition but with baroque aesthetics). If you want to learn more about these historic waxworks, you can take an hour-long English language tour (€4) at 11am on Saturdays.

Beethoven Pasqualatihaus

Mölker Bastei 8, tel. 01/535-8905, www.wienmuseum.at, Tue-Sun 10am-1pm and 2pm-6pm, €5, U: Schottentor

The Beethoven Pasqualatihaus was once the composer's favorite residence. Its transformation into a museum began in the 1930s, when the Nazis expelled the Jewish family living in this residence and turned the apartment into a memorial to the composer in 1941. (Some members of that family, the Ecksteins, died in Auschwitz, while the children escaped to England in in 1938.)

The museum you see today was redesigned in the 1990s. The museum occupies an apartment on the fourth floor of the old townhouse perched on the former city wall that resembles a bastion. Beethoven loved living here and composed his only opera, *Fidelio*, in this house. You'll find a collection of scores handwritten by Beethoven, as well as his piano, and portraits of Beethoven and his family scattered around the six-room apartment. You can also sit down at one of the desks and put a pair of headphones on to listen to the composer's most famous work.

Museum of the Johann Strauss Dynasty

Mülnergasse 3, tel. 01/310-3106, www.strauss-museum.at, Wed-Sat 2pm-6pm, €7, Roßauer Lände

This museum, tucked away in a townhouse, commemorates the dynasty of the Strausses, Vienna's iconic composing family. Rather than charting the life of the family, the documents, photos, and old program leaflets on display intend to express the spirit of the family and their times through the Strauss family's music. You can sit down at a music station with a pair of headphones to listen to the some of the more famous as well as lesser-known pieces by the family, and works from their contemporaries, like Carl Michael Ziehrer. Posters and memorabilia help lend context to the music. The text is in German, but you can find booklets scattered around the museum with translations of captions over the six rooms. The museum is a passion project of its knowledgeable owner and collector, Helmut Reichenauer. This is the kind of museum in which you need to take your time when viewing its exhibitions.

SCHÖNBRUNN PALACE AND GROUNDS

★ Schönbrunn Palace

Schönbrunner Schloßstraße, tel. 01/811-13-239, www.schonbrunn.at, daily 8am-4:30pm Nov-Mar, 8am-5pm Sep-Oct and Apr-Jun, 8am-6pm Jul-Aug, €14.20-17.50, U: Schönbrunn

The Hofburg may have been the permanent home of the Habsburgs, but the imperial family preferred to summer further out in the leafy suburbs in the brilliant yellow Schönbrunn Palace, with 1,441 rooms—only 40 of which can be visited.

This palace is the centerpiece of Habsburg grandeur. Most of the rooms are Rococo. Some are clad with porcelain, others are inspired by ancient Chinese art, and still others feature original Indian and

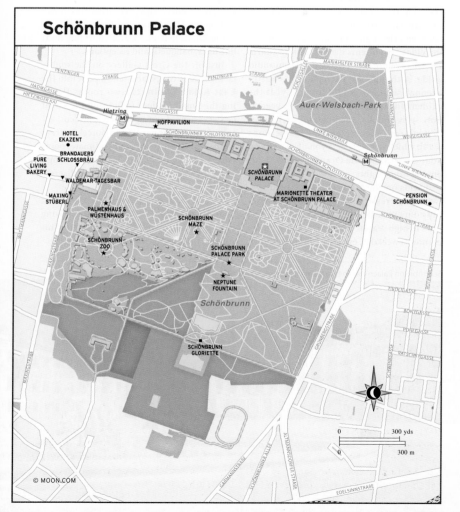

Schönbrunn Palace

embedded Persian miniatures. Most of the palace dates back to the 18th century, and it became the heart of court life during Maria Theresa's reign. The stylistic influences of the different eras of the Habsburg monarchy are clear as you wander through its maze of rooms.

There are two ways to visit the palace. The self-guided **Imperial Tour** (€14.20, 30-40 minutes) will guide you through 22 rooms, which include the state rooms and Sisi and Franz Joseph's apartments. The **Grand Tour** (€17.50, 50-60 minutes) takes you through 40 rooms, with some of the older apartments dating back to Maria Theresa's reign, is self-guided with an audio guide. Although the Palace itself is one of Vienna's wonders, you'll want to visit the gardens that surround it with lush vegetation, secret nooks, and amazing views over the palace. I recommend a **Classic Pass** (€24), which not only gets you on the Grand Tour but includes the Orangerie and Maze, among other sights.

This is one of Austria's most visited sites (with good reason) so plan your visit carefully. Buy your ticket online to skip the long lines in high season. A good tip is to get there early on a weekday, especially in the summer.

Your ticket will come with an allocated time of entry, so get in immediately and explore the park afterwards. Even with a ticket, you may need to wait a long time to enter the palace.

PALACE HIGHLIGHTS

Each room will leave you gawking at something, especially the **Great Gallery** occupying the center of the palace between the two wings, with its hall of mirrors, chandeliers, and gold underneath a colorful fresco depicting the Habsburgs and their lands. The 131-foot-long hall once served court functions like balls, banquets, and receptions.

Just off the Great Gallery on the south-facing side of the palace, take a peek into the **East Asian Cabinets**, two rooms flanking the Small Gallery (adjoining the Great Gallery) decked out in rococo grandeur, accented by lacquer panels and porcelain from China and Japan; these small, intimate rooms once served Maria Theresa's small gatherings, either for a game of cards or more discrete conferences.

Both of these can be visited on the Imperial Tour, but the **Millions Room** in the east wing can only be seen with the Grand Tour. This room is fitted with rich rosewood paneling.

Schönbrunn Palace was the summer palace for the Habsburgs and one of the top attractions in Vienna.

An Imperial Metro Stop

Otto Wagner built his Stadtbahn for everyone, including the Emperor Franz Joseph I, whose imperial station can be found at Schönbrunn.

When you go to Schönbrunn Palace Park or the zoo and get off the metro at Hietzing, you can also check out Otto Wagner's **Hofpavilion** (Schönbrunner Schloßstraße, tel. 01/877-1571, www.wienmuseum.at, Mar-Oct Sat-Sun 10am-1pm and 2pm-6pm, €5, also run by the Wien Museum), which he made for the Emperor so he could use the innovative metro like everyone else. (Despite the plush carpets, wood paneling, and private entrance, Franz Joseph only attended the opening.) You can visit the pavilion from street level and take a look inside the lush waiting room and cloak rooms. The entrance down to the U-Bahn is, however, closed.

Schönbrunn Palace Park
(Schlosspark)

Schönbrunner Schlossstraße, tel. 01/811-130, www.schonbrunn.at, daily 6:30am-5:30pm Nov-Feb, 6:30am-7pm Feb-Mar and Sep-Oct, 6:30am-8pm Mar-May and Mid Aug-Mid Sep, 6:30am-9pm May-Mid Aug, Free, U: Schönbrunn, Heitzing

Even if you're on a budget, you should still pay a visit to Schönbrunn, if only for the

magnificent park grounds surrounding the palace. Most of the park is free, but with the Classic Pass, you can also enter the Maze—a labyrinth of shrubs, fountains, statues and woodland paths that extend for almost a mile east to west, and just over half a mile north to south. The best time to come is in the morning, when you'll generally only see joggers on the winding graveled pathways.

There's more than one way to enter the park. The Hietzinger *Tor* (Gate), the gateway on the western end of the park, is perhaps closest to the U-Bahn and tram networks, and brings you into the park around the Palm House and the zoo. The gate on the southeastern end of the park on the hill brings you out to the Gloriette, a triumphal arch flanked by arcaded wings facing the palace from the hill opposite. There are also a couple of gateways around the palace itself.

The best way to visit the park is simply to explore and let it surprise you, but if you want some orientation, head over to the **Great Parterre,** a large open stretch that lies between Schönbrunn Palace and the Gloriette, surrounded by statues, high hedges and patches of flower-covered lawns that sometimes draw their designs from embroidery patterns. This is the backbone of the garden and one of the best places to get your bearings. Facing the Gloriette, you'll find the Columbary (a gorgeous aviary full of pigeons—which you can see from the outside for free—that looks like a gigantic lantern) and the Roman Ruins (fake, but beautiful). To the right are the maze, Palm House and the zoo. Straight ahead, you'll find the Neptune Fountain, one of the highlights of the garden, commissioned by Maria Theresa in the 1770s.

GLORIETTE

Facing Schönbrunn Palace, this elaborate pavilion crowns Schönbrunn Park. Built in 1775 during the reign of Emperor Joseph II and Maria Theresa, the Gloriette, with its triumphal arch flanked by arcaded wings, is renowned for its impressive views over the Habsburg summer palace and the surrounding grounds, and is a major focal point in the garden. It functioned as a dining and festival hall for the Habsburg monarchy, but today its café, **Cafe Gloriette** (tel. 01/879-1311, www.gloriette-café.at, 9am until sunset) is not only recommended, but reservations must be made four weeks in advance). You can traipse up the spiral staircase to the **viewing platform** (daily, 9am-6pm Apr-Jun and Sep, 9am-7pm Jul-Aug, 9am-5pm Oct, €3.80).

SCHÖNBRUNN ZOO

Maxingstraße 13b, tel. 01/877-93940, www.zoovienna.at, daily 9am-4:30pm Nov-Jan, 9am-5pm Feb, 9am-5:30pm March and Oct (until end of daylight savings time), 9am-6:30pm Apr-Sep, €20, U: Hietzing

Schönbrunn Zoo (*Tiergarten* in German), is the oldest zoo in the world. It's also large, so expect to spend a few hours here.

The best way to enter is from the Hietzing Entrance, which will bring you right into the heart of the action. You'll have the koala house to your left and the giraffes to the right, and straight ahead is the Kaiser Pavilion, a café set inside a pavilion, which is a lunch stop fit for a Habsburg with its frescoed interior and gold leaf accents on dark wooden panels.

The animals here have plenty of room to roam. The Vienna Zoo celebrated the first panda babies born in a zoo in 2007, and celebrated twin baby pandas again in 2016. Don't miss the tropical house, with tropical birds and bats. Head into the cave on the lower level if you're brave: The tiny bats there fly around your head so closely you can almost feel the flap of their wings.

Head into Franz Josef Land to catch a glimpse of the polar bears in the 18,000-square-foot enclosure, or the playful penguins nearby. You can catch a little dotto train at the Kaiser Pavilion from 10am to 6pm; the journey takes around 20 minutes and runs every 45 minutes, taking you from the pavilion to the Elephant House and the Tirolerhof, the exit gate on the southern end of the zoo near the Gloriette.

PALM HOUSE
(Palmenhaus)

Schlosspark, tel. 01/877-5087, www.bmnt.gv.at, daily 9:30am-5pm Oct-Apr, 9:30am-6pm May-Sep, €6 palm house, daily 9:30am-4:30 pm Oct-Apr, 9:30am-5:30pm May-Sep, U: Hietzing

The Palm House, the largest in continental Europe, built from elegant green iron beams and 45,000 panes of glass, is split into three pavilions to accommodate different climate zones that are connected by glass corridors: one representing Mediterranean climate, another with plants from Asia and New Zealand, and one dedicated to tropical and subtropical flora. The largest palm stands 75 feet high. You can also visit a jungle populated with blooming flowers, carnivorous plants, various smaller palms, and the world's largest water lily. Opposite, **Wüstenhaus** (the desert house, €6, daily 9am-5pm Oct-Apr, 9am-5pm May-Sep) resides in a less impressive building, but contains a broad range of arid specimens like cacti and other water-retentive plants.

SCHÖNBRUNN MAZE

Schlosspark, daily 9am-5pm October, 9am-6pm Mid-March-June and Sep, 9am-7pm Jul-Aug, €5.50, U: Schönbrunn, Hietzing

This maze (two mazes, actually) of tall hedges sits on the site of an old maze from the 18th century. One of the two mazes is smaller and easier to navigate. The other takes you round dead ends and repetitive turns until you finally reach the middle where you can clamber up to the viewing platform to watch others fumbling their way through the labyrinth. When it's time to leave, you're given the option for the short way out (easier) or the long way, which will plunge you back into the heart of the maze. Depending on how good you are at getting in and out of mazes, you can expect to spend 30 to 40 minutes here.

NEPTUNE FOUNTAIN

At the heart of Schönbrunn Park between the palace and the Gloriette, the Neptune Fountain, carved out of white marble, rises up in all its Greco-Roman glory. The sea god

Otto Wagner

If there is one architect who captures the spirit of Fin de Siècle, Vienna's journey into modernity, it's Otto Wagner. Otto Wagner blended modernity with an art nouveau aesthetic that is at once beautifully simple. His work is visible in his golden-domed Kirche am Steinhof up in the hills, the flower-inscribed apartment block close to the Naschmarkt, infrastructure like the U-Bahn stations and bridges.

Wagner also was the designer behind the first *Stadtbahn*, the city train which became part of today's U-Bahn. The most famous monuments as part of his legacy include the Stadtbahn Pavilions in Karlsplatz and the Hofpavilion. He believed in advancing the city for the better. When he built his U-Bahn stations, his vision was inclusive of all classes, including the Emperor—which is why he opened the royal Stadtbahn Pavilion in Hietzing near Schönbrunn Palace. (Emperor Franz Joseph I used it once during the grand opening, but never again.)

Otto Wagner's Kirche am Steinhof is a masterpiece in modernist architecture.

Neptune with his trademark trident in hand towers over a cascade of water, with the sea goddess Thetis kneeling beside him, and a nymph reclining opposite, against the rocks. Below the main figures, Tritons, mythological creatures who are half fish and half men, frolic on the level below on backs of "sea horses" that pull Neptune's chariot across the sea. This impressive folly makes for great photo opportunities.

St. Leopold Church
(Kirche am Steinhof)

Kirche am Steinhof, Baumgartner Höhe 1, tel. 01/910-601-1007, Sat 4-5pm, Sun Midday-4pm, €8

If you're an architecture lover, visit this art nouveau church built by Otto Wagner, up in the hills above Vienna. The church is perhaps Otto Wagner's masterpiece, built between 1904 and 1907. It's one of the first churches in Europe to embrace this bold modern style, echoing the design of the Secession with its cube-like structure and golden dome. You'll find art nouveau angels with gold wings guarding the entrance, and glass mosaics on the windows by Koloman Moser.

The inside of the church is only open Saturdays from 4-5pm or Sunday midday-4pm. Guided tours are in German. The interior is strikingly simple compared to the drama you'll feel when you see it first from the outside. Consider enjoying a picnic in the park behind the church, where you'll have flawless views over the hills surrounding Vienna.

You can get to the church in two ways. One option is to go to the Otto Wagner Spital, either by taxi or by bus 47A from U-Bahn stop Unter-St.-Weit (two stops from Heitzing), or by bus 48A from Ottakring (if coming from Stephansplatz). Both routes take around 30 minutes. Once you reach the psychiatric institute, it's a 10-minute climb up to the church along the path that's signposted from the entrance.

Alternatively, you can take bus 46A from Ottakring to Feuerwache Am Steinhof, lasting 15 minutes, and cross the meadows and the Park Steinhofgründe to get to the golden-domed church.

If you arrive via the hospital route and leave through the park, you get to meet the church at the most dramatic vantage point, towering above the hospital in architectural splendor.

If you have a pass for public transport, the journey should be free on all modes of transport, otherwise a single ticket of €2.40 should cover you for the journey.

Klimt Villa

Feldmühlgasse 11, tel. 01/876-1125, www.klimtvilla.at, Thu-Sun 10am-6pm Apr-Dec, €10

Take the tram 10 a few stops from Schönbrunn Park to Verbindungsbahn and you'll find yourself in an area populated with residential villas, one of which has a prominent connection to one of Vienna's most iconic artists. Klimt lived and worked in this single-story garden house. The wealthy family who bought the property after his passing built a whole new villa surrounding it. Fortunately,

the original rooms Klimt resided in are still present.

Today, the villa is privately owned, and functions as a museum that mixes permanent installations with temporary exhibits. The most interesting parts are the two rooms where Klimt lived and worked, which the curators reconstructed by studying old photos. One is filled with Japanese art loved by the artist, while the other (Klimt's bedroom) is filled with copies of Klimt's original paintings. You can wander through his model room, leading into the bedroom, or through the garden that inspired his rose garden paintings—which the museum's owners replanted using the paintings for inspiration. If you're a Klimt fan, it's worth the trek out to this small, special museum dedicated to the final years of Klimt's life.

Bars and Nightlife

Vienna may not have the same lively reputation as Budapest and Prague when it comes to bars and nightlife, but there's plenty of nocturnal activity to keep you dancing or drinking until dawn. Vienna's nightlife comes with its own unique flavor, with repurposed venues underneath railway arches, old factories, or former bordellos. For a truly Viennese experience, you can also while away the hours in the city's *Heurigen*, rustic wine taverns serving local wine from vineyards within the Austrian capital's limits.

A domestic beer will set you back around €4 (perhaps more for a craft beer), and a cocktail is around €11-15. In the summer, try the Spritzer, a drink made by mixing white wine or rosé with soda water (carbonated water). Most venues won't have a cover charge unless there is a special event or a concert.

Many venues only take cash, so it's a good idea to have some euros with you.

Despite Vienna's less-wild reputation, drinking laws set the drinking age at 16 (18 in

some other parts of Austria). Drunk and disorderly behavior, however, can result in heavy fines. Some bars and clubs do permit smoking or have indoor smoking areas.

NIGHTLIFE DISTRICTS
Bermudadreieck

Nicknamed the "Bermuda Triangle" in German, this small area in the historic center, close to Schwedenplatz, earned its title for the countless forgotten nights enjoyed by locals and tourists in the area. This party district rose in the 1980s, but its overpriced downtown bars draw in the tourists more than the locals looking for a night out, but there are a few bars worth visiting.

Gürtel

If you're in the mood for live music, make a beeline to the arches under the elevated U-Bahn rails at the Gürtel ring road between Thaliastraße and Nussdorferstraße, where classic bars and new music venues jostle together under the rumbling metro. The vibe around Gürtel is gritty—it's a red light district with sex shops—but over the past few years, it's become a happening night spot, particularly for live music.

Naschmarkt to Mariahilferstrasse

By day, the Naschmarkt bustles with foodies, but when the day is over, it's great for a night out. Whether you pick the trendy bistros for an evening cocktail or you head into the side streets, you'll find stretches of bars, cafés and clubs on the cobbled roads between Mariahilferstrasse. The clubs and bars here appeal to students and young creatives, like Café Kafka or Tanzcafé Jenseits.

Around the Danube Canal

When summer comes around, the Danube Canal is the place to be. Beach bars line the grassy embankments, and if you take a stroll along here, make sure you stop to admire the street art at Vienna's largest legal graffiti zone. Afternoons are lazy; by night the clubs start to kick off and energy buzzes in venues like Flex.

BARS AND PUBS
Historic Center and Hofburg Area
FIRST FLOOR BAR

Seitenstettengasse 5, tel. 01/532-1163,
http://firstfloorbar.at daily 8pm-4am

In the heart of the infamous "Bermuda Triangle," there's the First Floor Bar, a mainstay for 20 years. As its name suggests, you need to head up to the first floor to reach this cocktail bar. A fishless aquarium filled with swaying plants sits behind the bar, and the cocktail menu contains more than 200 drinks. Try the champagne cocktails or the more robust Whiskey Business, made with bourbon, rye, cocoa syrup and port. Jazz music floats in the background—it's sometimes live, too, usually on Thursdays. In the winter, you'll need to check your coats into the cloakroom.

KAKTUS

Seitenstettengasse 5, tel. 06/76-670-4405,
www.kaktusbar.at, daily 7pm-4am

Kaktus is another venue to lose yourself in within Vienna's *Bermudadreieck*, with a solid reputation as one of the city's most exciting night spots. You won't find a quiet night here—parties rock late into the night with a young and energetic crowd dancing to local and guest DJs. With flashing neon and primary colors, bare bricks, spiral metal staircases and robust tables that have a history of being danced on, the décor adds to this bar's club atmosphere.

PALMENHAUS

Burggarten 1, tel. 01/533-1033, www.palmenhaus.at,
Mon-Fri 10am-midnight, Sat 9am-midnight,
Sun 9am-11pm

Not many bars are housed in an art nouveau palm house, so when it comes to location, the Palmenhaus (not to be confused with the Palmenhaus at Schönbrunn) is pretty special. The interior, with high arched ceilings, abundant palm trees, and glass-paneled walls, is stunning. In the summer, people gather on its terrace overlooking the Burggarten that once belonged to the Hofburg. This chilled-out bar serves food throughout the day, and on Friday nights or weekends, DJs sometimes spin until midnight. For something unique, try the Palmenhaus Pimm's No. 1, which is Pimm's with lime juice, basil, cucumber, and ginger beer. If you want a table, it's a good idea to reserve in advance.

★ LOOS BAR

Kärntner Durchgang 10, tel. 01/512-3283,
www.loosbar.at, daily midday-4am

Sip on a classic dry martini in this tiny 32-square-yard American-style cocktail bar that opened in 1908. What it lacks in size, it makes up for in style with onyx panels, brass details and mirrored walls. The bar was designed by and named for modernist architect Adolf Loos, whose architectural mission was to break down Vienna's obsessive love for ornamentation. This bar is a piece in Vienna's architectural history. The vibe is both classy and classic, so you may want to dress up.

Neubau and the MuseumsQuartier
★ ROTE BAR IM VOLKSTHEATER

Neustiftgasse 1, www.volkstheater.at/spielstaette/rote-bar/, Mon-Fri 10pm-2am Sat 10pm-4am, Sun 10pm-1am

When the curtain falls in the Volkstheater, head to the Rote Bar around 10pm for one of Vienna's most unique watering holes. This opulent 125-year-old bar decked out in plush red velvet and theatrical grandeur also has a small stage that often hosts burlesque and cabaret shows, poetry nights, live music and improv shows. It's an elegant place to grab a late-night drink, but expect the unexpected to happen, like tipsy actors getting up to dance on the tables.

Around Naschmarkt and Karlsplatz
MR. MENDÉZ

Karlsplatz 2, tel. 06/76-511-3099, www.mendez.at, Thu-Sat 8pm-3am

From the front, it looks like a café, but cross the Cafe Mendéz and there is a "secret" room in the back of the café decorated with Mexican-inspired murals depicting colorful flowers and *calavera* and luchador masks, where you'll find a hidden craft cocktail bar: Mr. Mendéz. The staff are friendly, and the cocktail menu is creative—many of the cocktail ingredients here are homemade. Try their tequila-based cocktails, or ask the bartenders to prepare your favorite concoction. You can get nachos and other spicy snacks with your beverages of choice.

TONSTUBE

Laimgrubengasse 5, tel. 06/99-107-378883, http://tonstube.at, Wed-Sat 7pm-2am

In the late hours, this simple bar with dark walls and interconnecting rooms is packed with young locals, and the vibe is always friendly. They have local beer on tap, but try their Kaluko, a handmade drink created by the bar owners (who come from the Bregenzerwald in the Alps), made with Alpine spring water, black tea and hibiscus, mint and rosehip teas, plus citrus, raspberry, ginger, and mint. The bar is usually packed, especially if they have a DJ playing.

★ TANZCAFÉ JENSEITS

Nelkengasse 3, tel. 01/587-1233, www.tanzcafé-jenseits.com, Tue-Sat 8pm-4am

Cozy, with red damask-upholstered walls and low lighting, this bar was once the site of a brothel. It still keeps its old-world seedy charm—just without the prostitution. The name translates as the "Afterlife Dance Café," and the place comes to life around 11pm and stays lively until the early hours. DJs start to play after midnight, and people crowd onto the tiny dance floor. There is usually a special cocktail menu written up on the chalkboard above the bar, and you can ask for a cigar menu, too, if you're feeling fancy. The main bar area is still smoker-friendly, but there is a non-smoking room to the side.

CAFÉ KAFKA

Capistrangasse 8, tel. 01/586-1317, Mon-Sat 8am-midnight

Café Kafka is a popular student hangout, with worn-looking walls plastered with film festival posters, exhibition openings and other art. Seating is in the form of welcoming vintage furniture. It's one of the few cafés that still allows smokers. During the day, young creatives gather to collaborate on projects, but in the evening, it turns into a trendy bar packed with 20-something hip Viennese. The vibe is laid-back, and a good place to start the evening with a few drinks.

HEUER AM KARLSPLATZ

Treitl straße 2, tel. 01/890-0590 www.heuer-amkarlsplatz.com, Mon-Fri 11am-2am, Sat-Sun 10am-2am

This trendy bar shares the building with the Kunsthalle Wien in downtown Vienna. It blends old and new with Thonet chairs and green leather benches. The shelves are lined with apothecary-like jars filled with cocktail ingredients like homemade pickles, preserves and syrups, some of which are used to make "shrubs," surprisingly refreshing vinegar-based drinks. Cocktails here are made from a selection of 350 spirits from the world over. Try an original creation like Bob Dill'n, made with dill-infused vodka, lemongrass syrup and cucumber.

Prater and Around the Danube
DAS LOFT
Praterstraße 1, tel. 01/90-616-8110,
www.dasloftwien.at, daily 10am-2am
You can't beat the view at Das Loft, set on the 18th floor of the Sofitel Hotel. You'll need to take the lift to get to this swanky, backlit bar. Das Loft serves a variety of cocktails that cater to more serious drinkers. (For example, the "Last Word" is made with Tanqueray no. 10 gin, chartreuse, maraschino, absinthe and lime. The dress code is to impress, so put on your fanciest dress or suit when in town. The city seems tiny from the 18th floor.

Alsergrund and Josefstadt
TÜR 7
Buchfeldgasse 7, tel. 06/64-54-63-717 http://tuer7.at,
daily 9pm-4am
It takes a little sleuthing to find, but this little speakeasy-type bar is worth the hunt. It fits no more than 35 people. (Because it's hidden away and not advertised, there aren't queues out the door, but you may want to book a table, just in case.) You need to ring the doorbell to get in. There are seven cocktails on the menu, and the bar is non-smoking. Look for the door marked with a seven—at 7 Buchfeldgasse.

WINE BARS
Wine is a big part of Viennese culture, with vineyards sprawling within the city limits and being cultivated nearby. Try some of the classics, like the Grüner Veltliner, a white wine with hints of fruit like citrus and pear, or the Blauburgunder, the local, complex pinot noir red. There's also the Riesling, a bold fruity white with plenty of acidity, or the Zweigelt, a bold red with aromas recalling cherries.

Historic Center and Hofburg Area
VIS-À-VIS
Wollzeile 5, tel. 01/512-9350, www.weibel.at,
Tue-Fri 4pm-10:30pm and Sat 3pm-10:30pm
Set in a tiny venue that fits around 10 people tucked inside a tiny passage connecting Wollzeile and Bäckerstraße, this wine bar may be small, but it offers a massive collection of 350 wines. The focus is on Austrian wine, but you can also try international varieties. Order some antipasti to help the tasting go more smoothly.

VINOTHEK W-EINKEHR
Laurenzerberg 1, tel. 06/764-082854, www.w-einkehr. at, Tue-Fri 3pm-10pm and Sat 4pm-10pm
This small wine bar has only 15 seats indoors, with eight more on the terrace, so get here early to snag a seat. Austrian wines from around the country dominate the menu. Reserve a table if you want to make an afternoon of your visit or drop in for a taste if you're downtown. Come for the unpretentious atmosphere and dedication to serving the best Austrian wines available.

VILLON
Habsburgergasse 4, www.villon.at,
Tue-Fri 6pm-midnight Sat 7pm-midnight
Right below the city center, plunging 52 feet below ground, this cellar dating back to 1701 is a place to forget the outside world. The wine bar is elegant and modern. You can order wine by the glass or by the bottle, and also order snacks for pairing. Keep your appetite at bay with goose liver pâté or truffle crostini.

Around Naschmarkt and Karlsplatz
SEKT COMPTOIR
Schleifmühlgasse 19, www.sektcomptoir.at,
Mon-Thu 5pm-11pm, Fri-Sat noon-11pm
Sparkling wine lovers should head down to this bar by the Naschmarkt to try a glass of the

Heurige

Head out towards the Vienna Woods, and you'll see row upon row of vines being cultivated within the city limits, taking up around 700 hectares of land. Where there is a vineyard, there will be a Viennese *Heuriger* nearby. These rustic wine taverns fill with locals and visitors who come to drink the local tipple, eat heavy portions of rich Austrian food, and have a good time. Only local wines are served in *Heurige* (plural for *Heuriger*), and the experience is as Viennese as riding the Riesenrad in the Prater or looking at portraits of Sisi hanging in the Hofburg. Songs have immortalized these wine taverns, which are legendary for their homey feel, and—unlike the grumpy charm of Viennese coffee house—have a welcoming atmosphere.

Usually drinking and dining in the *Heuriger* is al fresco, in the breezy courtyards and gardens, making it perfect on a hot summer or fall day—but most will have a cozy parlor, so the elements won't get in the way of your drinking. The wine served in the *Heuriger* is made by the owner (each *Heuriger* has its own vineyard) and the wine will also be just around a year old—in fact the word *Heuriger* actually means "this year's wine." If you prefer your wine more mature, you can ask for a *bouteille,* higher-quality wines that are bottled in 0.75 liter bottles. Sometimes, things can get a little festive and you may even be treated to live violin or accordion music.

FURGASSL-HUBER

Neustift am Walde 68, Vienna, tel. 01/440-1405, www.fuhrgassl-huber.at, Mon-Sat 2pm-midnight, Sun midday-midnight, glass of wine €2-3.20

This *Heuriger* on the outskirts of Vienna has been running for forty years. When the weather is good, grab a glass or two of the *Heuriger*'s own wine and sit down to one of the green wooden benches on the terrace overlooking the vineyards and the Vienna Woods behind the garden. If the weather goes off, you can while away the cold and the rain inside this old, rustic house dating back to the 17th century with a glass of Wiener Gemischter Satz—a white cuvee that is slightly sweet and fruity—and a few traditional *Heurigen* dishes, such as *Kümmelbraten,* a pork roast with crispy skin, vegetable strudel, grilled chicken, and vinegary potato salad.

You can reach this *Heuriger* by taking the 35A bus from the Nussdorferstrasse or the Spittelau U-Bahn stations.

Burgenland Sekt, a local Austrian, award-winning bubbly from the bar's vineyard, Szigeti. This cozy bar is popular with locals.

STADTHEURIGEN

Keep an eye out for sign that read *Stadtheuriger,* meaning a city wine tavern. These taverns are the urban form of *Heurige,* traditional taverns located near vineyards on the outskirts of the city, where visitors can sip wine in a large yard with bench seating. *Stadtheuriger* are located in the city center and lack the atmospheric proximity to vineyards, but the wine is excellent.

Historice Center and Hofburg Area
GIGERL

Rauhensteingasse 3, tel. 01/513-4431, www.gigerl.at, Sun-Thu 3pm-1am, Fri 3pm-2am

Tucked into a cobbled side street in the inner city, Gigerl has a rustic feel, with low, arched ceilings and wooden tables, and waitresses outfitted in traditional dirndl dresses. Despite being in the heart of the city, it still has that *Heuriger* feel, with local wines from surrounding vineyards in Vienna and Austria. You can also order substantial Austrian food like Schnitzel and Heurigenplatten to share, with cold cuts, pickles, and salads. This downtown spot is popular with locals and tourists alike.

MAYER AM PFARRPLATZ

Pfarrplatz 2, Vienna, tel. 01/370-1287, www.pfarrplatz.at, Mon-Sat 4pm-midnight,
Sun midday-midnight, glass of wine €2.20-4.90
This *Heuriger* is famous for two things: Beethoven and wine. In 1817 Ludwig van Beethoven resided on the first floor of this charming house, which today is home to one of Vienna's most famous *Heurige*. In the summer, its vine-clad inner courtyard fills up with locals and tourists who come here to sample the wine from the nearby Mayer winery. Try the *Heuriger* wine, a young wine like the Mayer's Grüner Veltliner, a crisp dry white, or one of their more mature wines. You can even try a red like their fruity Pinot Noir. When it comes to food, order the crispy and succulent *Backhendl*, golden fried chicken – and accompany it with the traditional potato salad.

From the Heiligenstadt U-Bahn station, take the 38A bus to Fernsprechamt Heiligenstadt stop, which puts you three minutes away from the *Heuriger*.

HEURIGER SIRBU

Kahlenberger straße 210, Vienna, tel. 01/320-5928, www.sirbu.at, Mon-Sat 4pm-11pm,
glass of wine €3-4
Grab a bench on the wooden picnic-style tables on the slopes of the vineyards overlooking the Danube. Sirbu is perhaps Vienna's most beautiful *Heuriger* and worth the journey for a glass of wine on its panoramic terrace. Pair your wine with a cheese plate or an assortment of meat cuts, and just make your way through the wine list trying this year's specials. You'll find the usual Viennese wines such as Grüner Veltliner and the Gemischter Satz cuvee, but try some of the winery's special wines, such as their Gemischter Satz Rot, a red cuvee, or the Frizzante Schweizerberg, a sparkling wine. It's a good idea to book a table here in the summer!

From the Heiligenstadt station, take the 38A bus to the end of the line at Kahlenberg and then walk down hill, first down Höhenstraße and then down Kahlenberger straße till you reach the *Heuriger*.

ESTERHAZYKELLER

Haarhof 1, tel. 01/533-3482, www.esterhazykeller.at,
Mon-Fri 6pm-11pm, Sat-Sun 4pm-11pm, cellar closed
July-September, summer in the courtyard above

This wine cellar has a unique history that dates back to 1683. As soldiers defended the city from the Turkish siege, they were supplied with wine before the fight to give them courage—and that was the first wine tasting in the Esterhazy Cellar. Its handmade bricks date back to the 15th century. The wine offered here bears the Esterhazy name—the name of a Hungarian aristocratic family who resided in Vienna. You can try wines from the Weingut Esterhazy winery, with classic Austrian wines like Grüner Veltliner and Blaufränkisch.

Mains and snacks are also available with the usual suspects like Schnitzel, but there are also spicy sausages on offer.

Alsergrund and Josefstadt

WEINSTUBE JOSEFSTADT

Piaristengasse 27, tel. 01/406-4628 daily
4pm-midnight Apr-Dec

You can easily lose an afternoon in this secluded sanctuary in the city center. At the Weinstube Josefstadt, local wine flows liberally, and at good prices too. You can also get good food to go. Finding this *Stadtheuriger* is a little challenging; look for the green wreath on the doorway to uncover the entrance.

BEER

Beer is just as popular in Austria as wine. In fact, if you head away from the vine-clad hills around Vienna towards the Alps, you'll notice beer becomes more popular. Typical Austrian beers include Dunkel, dark beer with an intense flavor; Helles, light and hoppy; Pils, a crisp, strong beer inspired by Pilsner; Zwickel, unfiltered beer with a cloudy complexion (which also tastes good in non-alcoholic varieties); and finally, Märzen, a red beer with a malty taste.

If you're looking for something Viennese, beer from the Ottakringer brewery, the largest brewery still working in Vienna, is available all over the city. Beyond the traditional beers, craft beers are slowly gaining popularity, so if you really want a good IPA or Porter, you can find some great local concoctions made in local microbreweries.

Neubau and the MuseumsQuartier

THE BRICKMAKER'S PUB AND KITCHEN

Zieglergasse 42, tel. 01/997-4414, www.brickmakers.at, Mon-Fri 4pm-1am, Sat midday-1am, Sun 10am-1am

With 150 bottled beers and 29 beers on tap, it's easy to see why the Brickmaker's Pub, known by locals as Briskies, is one of Vienna's most-loved craft beer joints. It's home to one of the largest beer collections in Austria. The prices are somewhat steep, but this bar has hand-picked some of the best beers in the world for your consumption. The unpasteurized, gasless Cask Ale, a golden, creamy beer, is perhaps the bar's most loved brew.

BEACH BARS

Austria is a landlocked country, but like Budapest, there's plenty of activity going on alongside the river. Around the Danube Canal and the Danube, Vienna heats up in the summer with beaches—some even complete with their own sand—that pop up for the season along the waterfront.

Prater and Around the Danube

TEL AVIV BEACH

Obere Donaustraße 65, https://neni.at/restaurants/tel-aviv-beach-bar, midday-midnight Apr-Oct

Head down to the Danube Canal when the sun comes out for summery drinks and great Middle Eastern food and staple burgers. Tel Aviv Beach (a seasonal bar complete with sand and shirtless men) popped up along the canal banks with plans to stay around for just a year, but it has decided to stay and has become a summer fixture in the city. Grab a TLV Beach Teller with generous amounts of hummus, falafel, tahini, pickled vegetables and pita bread, and try their cocktails, like the TLV Beach Mule, with vodka infused with lemongrass, fresh ginger, cucumber, ginger beer and lime juice.

★ STRANDBAR HERRMANN

Herrmannpark, tel. 07/20-229-996, www.strandbarherrmann.at, daily (in good weather) 10am-2am

Facing the Urania Observatory where the Vienna River meets the Danube Canal, this bar is kaleidoscope of color with deckchairs, hammocks and an abundance of sand. It also offers amazing views of the Canal while sunbathing. Once the sun goes down, the DJs supply dance music until the early hours of the morning. Cocktails and beer are the most popular drinks, and if you're hungry you can always grab a burger or one of the daily specials. If you come between 10am-2pm on weekends, you can get a great brunch (€16.90) with a wide range of favorites to choose from like scrambled eggs, jams, cereal, granola, salad, and more.

PALMAR

Sunken City, Donauinsel Mon-Fri 3pm-midnight, Sat-Sun 2pm-midnight

With hammocks and palms, Palmar has holiday beach vibe right on the Danube Island. Grab a cocktail from the wooden beach bar and relax, away from the busy pace of the city. It's a great place to stay after dark. It can get crowded on the weekends, so make sure you keep an eye on any belongings you have with you.

CLUBS

When it comes to electronic music, Vienna has venues reaching cult status. The area down by the Danube Canal is a hot nightlife spot, featuring clubs that pair well with the beach bars (some seasonal, some more temporary) along the embankment or up by the Gürtel. To get you started, here are a few clubs to check out.

Historic Center and Hofburg Area
FLEX
Donaukanal - Augartenbrücke, tel. 01/533-7525, www.flex.at, Thu-Sat 11pm-6am, cover charge depends on the event, but in the range of €8-10

Since Flex relocated to a former metro tunnel by the Danube Canal in 1995, it's become one of Europe's hottest clubs. Its state-of-the-art sound system and atmosphere mixes dance culture and alternative music, including rock, drum and bass, and dub. Clubbers spill out onto the bank of the Danube Canal to cool down on balmy summer nights. Music genres are mixed, and it's worth checking the program out on the website.

Alsergrund and Josefstadt
THE LOFT
Lerchenfelder Gürtel 37, www.theloft.at, Wed-Thu 7pm-2am, Fri-Sat 8pm-4am; cover fee varies depending on the event, ranging from no cover to €10

This club occupies three levels of a former wooden floor factory, with a café on the ground floor (where you'll probably stumble into an exhibition or a concert), a dance floor in the basement, and a bar with plenty of seating on the first floor. The action happens in the basement, with techno and house beats going until late night. The atmosphere here is chill—so if you love your electronic dance music without going somewhere too fancy, this is the spot for you.

DAS WERK
Spittelauer Lände 12, Stadtbahnbogen 331, www.daswerk.org, daily 8pm-6am, cover charge usually between €7-10 depending on the event

Go here for heavy electronic music and industrial ambience. This club has roots in a cultural association and can now be found under the arches of a former railway. It has a raw, work-in-progress look. Locals come here on the weekends for legendary parties with the best DJs from Vienna's underground electronic scene. Apart from epic club nights, this is also a place for theater productions, concerts, readings and screenings, so expect an alternative artistic crowd.

GRELLE FORELLE
Spittelauer Lände 12, www.grelleforelle.com, Fri-Sat 11pm-6am, cover around €12

Located next door to Werk, this club on the Danube Canal focuses on house, techno and other electronic music categories. Famous international DJs from the underground scene play here and take advantage of the fantastic sound system. Finding the club is almost like a rite of passage: Follow the fish symbols that resemble arrows on the Danube Canal.

Note: admission here is 21 and above, and photography is forbidden.

LIVE MUSIC
THE CHELSEA
Lerchenfelder Gürtel, Stadtbahnbögen 29-30, tel. 01/407-9309, www.chelsea.co.at, daily 6pm-4am, concert tickets fall in the range of €12-25

This club, owned by a former professional soccer player, hosts both live soccer broadcasts and rock music shows. It's an institution on Vienna's Gürtel, occupying three interconnected railway arches, and hosting rock, indie and alternative concerts, but they also hold club nights. You can see the full list of entertainment on The Chelsea's website. The club has a soccer-themed interior and a great selection of British beers and ales. The venue can fit around 250 people (standing) for concerts.

B72

Hernalser Gürtel, Stadtbahnbögen 72,
tel. 01/409-2128, www.b72.at, Sun-Thu 8pm-4am,
Fri-Sat 8pm-6am, depends on the event as some
are free, others €8-15

Not far from The Chelsea, you'll also find B72 also under two U-Bahn arches—it's a club with a focus on rock and alternative performances. Gigs here are from up-and-coming and better-known Austrian and international bands. Unlike other bars on the Gürtel, B72 occupies two stories. The ground floor is home to the bar, stage and dance floor, and the mezzanine is a chillout area with tables, chairs and a good view of the stage. This hip venue draws young, passionate music lovers and is a great place if you want to catch a good live music.

THE FLUC

Praterstern 5, www.fluc.at, daily 6pm-4am,
entry free to €15

When you're done with the adrenaline-fueled rides at the Prater, head over to the Fluc, a unique fixture in Leopoldstadt's nightlife and music scene by the entrance of the Prater at Praterstern. There is something going on every day here. Entrance to parties and concerts is free upstairs, and admission to club nights and concerts downstairs depends on the act, but generally ranges from €5-15. Rock concerts and electronic club nights make some noise, but among the live music there are usually readings and art exhibitions as well. Regulars are mostly young and bohemian.

Performing Arts

TOP EXPERIENCE

CLASSICAL MUSIC AND OPERA

More famous composers have lived and worked in Vienna than anywhere else in the world, with names like Mozart, Beethoven, Strauss, Schubert, and more. Still today, Vienna is world-renowned for the Vienna Philharmonic Opera (*Staatsoper*) and its flawless productions.

★ VIENNA STATE OPERA (Staatsoper)

Opernring 2, tel. 01/514-442-250,
www.wiener-staatsoper.at

This grand opera house never rests. There are different productions on each night—over 60 shows and performances take place at this legendary opera house, 350 days of the year. The members of the orchestra are also musicians in the famous Vienna Philharmonic Orchestra.

The opera has capacity for 1,700 viewers, and there are 567 standing tickets available. Although getting a seat at the *Staatsoper* can cost over €40 (or even over €100 for seats in the mid-price range), you can actually buy tickets for as little as €3 or €4 if you get a last-minute standing room space.

To get these tickets, you need to be in line at the standing room ticket office *at least* 80 minutes before the curtain goes up. (You will find the office under the arcades at Operngasse.) Tickets are first come, first served. (It's a good idea to bring a scarf or something you can tie on the railing at your standing position to reserve your spot.)

If you want to delve deeper into the lives of Vienna's composers, the **Staatsoper shop** (Arcadia Opera Shop, Kärntnerstraße 40, Mon-Sat 9:30am-7pm, Sun 10am-7pm) sells plenty of interesting reading material and music.

★ MUSIKVEREIN

Musikvereinsplatz 1, tel. 01/505-8190,
www.musikverein.at

Famed for its New Year's Day Concert, the *Musikverein* is one of Vienna's best-known classical music halls. The Vienna Philharmonic Orchestra is often found in this

Vienna Boys' Choir

Emperor Maximilian I founded the imperial Vienna Boys' Choir in the 15th century, and it has since become one of the most famous choirs in the world. The young male singers in the choir range in age from 10-14. If you want to see the choir perform, you have some options:
On Friday afternoons, the choir performs 5:00pm to 6:45pm in **MuTH,** a Baroque concert hall. Tickets range from €69- €89. Between September and June, the choir also performs at Sunday Holy Mass in the **Royal Chapel** (9:15am, tickets €11- €37, box office open Fri 11:00am-1:00pm and 3:00-5:00pm, Sun 8:00-8:45am. Tickets can also be bought online at www.culturall.com/ticket/hmk) in the Hofburg. Booking in advance is required.

elegant building constructed and decorated with neoclassical columns, statues of Apollo and the Muses, and liberal quantities of gold leaf. This is also one of the best places in the world for spatial acoustics. There are shows 364 days of the year in its five halls. Away from the famous Golden Hall, there is the Glass Hall, Metal Hall, Stone Hall, and Wood Hall—each of these smaller halls focuses on young artists, jazz and literary performances.

WIENER KONZERTHAUS
Lotheringerstraße 20, tel. 01/242-002,
www.konzerthaus.at
The Wiener Konzerthaus caters to a wide range of musical tastes, going beyond Classical. It also taps into baroque and medieval through to jazz and world music performances. It's set in an art nouveau building that opened in 1913. Emperor Franz Joseph I attended the first gala concert, and the concert house has played a varied repertoire ever since. There are three concert halls on one level, which fill up over the season, running from September to June. On average, Wiener Konzerthaus houses 750 events, 2,500 compositions, and around 600,000 visitors over a season. Check the website for the program.

MUTH
Obere Augartenstraße 1e, tel. 01/347-8080,
www.muth.at, ticket range for Boys' Choir
performance €69-89
MuTH (which stands for music and theater) is the home of the world-famous Vienna Boys' Choir (Wiener Sängerknaben), who once

only performed at the Hofburg. You can see the choir during Friday afternoon choral sessions from 5:00pm to 6:45pm in this 400-seat auditorium.

MuTH also stages theater and dance productions, as well as various classical music and jazz performances.

THEATER AND DANCE
BURGTHEATER
Universitätsring 2, tel. 01/514-444-140,
www.burgtheater.at, tickets €7.50-61
The grandiose Burgtheater is not only Vienna's most popular theater, but one of the most pivotal in the German-speaking world. There are over 530 people working at the theater producing some 20 premiers each year, from Shakespeare and Goethe to contemporary work. Architecturally, this over 1,000-seat theater is a work of art, from the Historicist-style exterior to the Klimt frescos inside. Selected performances are subtitled in English. See the website for the program.

MARIONETTE THEATER AT SCHÖNBRUNN PALACE
Schloss Schönbrunn, Hofratstrakt, tel. 01/817-3247,
www.marionettentheater.at, tickets €11-39
Take the kids to see a production of Mozart's *The Magic Flute* performed by wooden marionette puppets. Even adults will love these delightful productions with ornately dressed puppets in this small theater. All the marionettes, costumes, stage technology and scenery are produced with prominent directors and top designers. (There is a reason this little

theater has won awards.) The performances are in German, but English-speaking guests can get a program with the synopsis in English.

TANZQUARTIER WIEN

MuseumsQuartier, Museumsplatz 1, tel. 01/581-3591, www.tqw.at, tickets €15-25

The Tanzquartier Wien is Austria's hub for contemporary dance. Part of the MuseumsQuartier, this theater stages around 120 performances a year, with productions from local and international artists. Some of the performances are performed in the large Halle G and Halle E in the MuseumsQuartier. Check the website for the program.

CONCERT VENUES

Vienna is more than just waltzes and Mozart. Get a great feel for live music at these unique and much-loved venues, whether you're up for jazz or something heavier.

PORGY & BESS

Riemergasse 11, tel. 01/512-8811, www.porgy.at, performances from 9pm; €8-50 depending on the show

Named after George Gershwin's iconic jazz opera of the same name, Porgy & Bess captures the best in Vienna's jazz scene, while retaining that feel of the music it hosted as part of the "underworld" of the city in the 1940s. The area was replete with bars, clubs and cabarets for more than a 100 years. This dimly lit Jazz club, which fits 350, captures that original spirit; today, it's a non-profit club that serves as a musical hub for local arts. Top jazz acts perform here alongside up-and-coming young performers from the area. Booking ahead is recommended.

THE ARENA

Baumgasse 80, tel. 01/798-8595, www.arena.co.at, events ranging from free entry to €30

Set in a former slaughterhouse under the shadow of the old Gasometer towers, the Arena has become one of Vienna's hottest venues, with 450 events per year. Local and international punk bands, pop groups, rock bands, and drum and bass DJs play here. The history of the Arena goes back to the 1970s, when a neighboring slaughterhouse was occupied by activists, kickstarting a countercultural movement in the city. Though the original site was destroyed with wrecking balls, the neighboring slaughterhouse became today's Arena. Leonard Cohen once described it as "the best place in Vienna."

Festivals and Events

DONAUINSELFEST

https://donauinselfest.at

The Donauinselfest is one of the largest open-air music festivals in the world, with three million visitors flocking to the three-mile stretch of the Danube Island at end of June each year. There are usually 11 open-air stages and 16 tented areas, featuring local bands, international acts like Billy Idol and Simple Minds, and DJs. This festival has been active since 1984 and is still a summer highlight. Book your accommodation as early as possible.

Bringing your own alcohol is a huge no-no (there are plenty of bars at the festival), and security may also stop you from entering with a large backpack or bag.

JAZZ FEST WIEN

www.jazzfest.wien

This annual festival, dedicated mostly to jazz, is held in various venues across the city from the middle of June to July, and features top international acts in funk, soul, jazz and pop. Recent acts have included Caro Emerald, Kris Kristofferson, and CeeLo Green.

VIENNA OPERA BALL

www.wiener-staatsoper.at

Vienna hosts around 450 balls every year.

The most famous is the Vienna Opera Ball at the end of February. The entire opera house is transformed into a spectacular ballroom, with over 5,000 guests. The crème de la crème of Viennese society attends this illustrious occasion. Tickets go on sale as early as two years prior, and usually sell out fast. Tickets begin at €315, but only really get you in through the door. The tickets don't include a seat (reserving a box will set you back €11,000—at least). However, you'll find numerous bars, a casino and a spectacular dance floor.

REGENBOGEN PARADE

www.hosiwien.at/regenbogenparade

Vienna's Regenbogen Parade paints the Ringstraße rainbow as one of the headlining events of the year on the LGBTQ calendar. Although the parade is the highlight, the weeks surrounding the event also get the city in the mood with parties, events, performances and a Pride Beach set up along the Danube Canal. The parade is usually held in mid-June. Check the website for details.

IDENTITIES

www.identities.at

Held during odd-numbered years in June,

Identities is Vienna's International Queer Film Festival that takes place across the city in various venues, like the Filmcasino on Margeritenstraße and Top Kino on Rahlgasse near the Museumsquartier. The Vienna Tourism board lists it as going ahead as of June 2019—www.wien.info/en/vienna-for/gay-lesbian/events.

CHRISTMAS

From mid-November into the new year, Vienna turns festive with Christmas markets that pop up on pretty much any free town square. The most spectacular are the Christmas markets by the Rathaus (from mid-November to 26 December, www.wienerweihnachtstraum.at, Sun-Thu 10am-9:30pm, Fri-Sat 10am-10pm) and Schönbrunn Palace (from end of November-26 December, www.weihnachtsmarkt.at, daily 10am-9pm).

EASTER MARKETS

Schönbrunn Palace is home again to the city's most romantic Easter market, with some 60-plus exhibitors offering decorative Easter decorations and Austrian Handicrafts (www.oestermarkt.co.at, daily 10am-6pm, dates vary each year so see the website).

VIENNA
FESTIVALS AND EVENTS

Christmas Market in front of the Vienna Rathaus

Recreation and Activities

PARKS

Vienna is a green city: You can escape to a vineyard, a water forest, or the woods without having to leave the city limits. But if you're looking to pick up some snacks from the Naschmarkt and want to find a wonderful picnic spot close to the city center, you have plenty of parks and gardens to choose from. The obvious are Schönbrunn Park, or the parkland around the Prater, or the Danube Island, but if you need more inspiration, the following parks are worth spending a lazy afternoon in.

AUGARTEN

U Taborstraße

Out of all the parks in Vienna, there is something really special about the Augarten—129 acres enclosed inside an old wall just northwest of the Prater. The Augarten began as a pleasure garden in the 18th century and was loved so much by Emperor Joseph II that he released a flock of nightingales on the grounds every year. In 1775, the gardens opened to the public, and Mozart conducted the first Augarten concert here.

The Augarten, accessible through five gates open from dawn till dusk, mixes French landscaped gardens with elegant rows of chestnut trees and trimmed hedges, and meadow-like lawns where locals sunbathe or practice yoga under the shadow of the imposing and sinister Flak Towers (air defense towers built by the Nazis) that still haunt the grounds. In the summer, the Augarten comes to life with picnicking Viennese carrying bottles of Grüner Veltliner in coolers, old men playing boules, or youths lounging in hammocks they bring to the park. If you prefer to sit at a proper table and admire the park, head to the **Café Augarten Restaurant** (Apr-Oct 9:00am-10:00pm, Nov-Mar 9:00am-6:00pm, free entry from the park) on the terrace of the Augarten Porcelain Factory and the Augarten.

STADTPARK

U Stadtpark

Stadtpark, Vienna's first public park, opened in 1862 and lies just to the south of the Museum of Applied Arts. It's a popular spot for picnics and evening strolls as the sun sets in the summer. It's one of Vienna's most elegant parks, flanked with art nouveau architecture at the U-Bahn pavilions, the bridge across the Vienna River as it emerges from being forced underground before Karlsplatz, and of course, the famous golden statue of Johann Strauss on his fiddle (which is one of the most photographed memorials in Vienna). Coffee and ice cream trucks are conveniently parked around this gorgeous park, but the best way to experience it is to head to Naschmarkt, gather ingredients for a picnic, and hop on U-Bahn line 4, then get off at the Stadtpark station. There are plenty of benches for seating if you need them.

VOLKSGARTEN AND BURGGARTEN

U Volksteater, Karlsplatz

These large parks on the grounds of the Hofburg lie next to each other, but they have their own histories. The Volksgarten (meaning "the people's garden") was built over the 16th century fortifications destroyed by Napoleon in 1809 and opened to the public in the 1820s. It's a stunning landscaped garden with monuments like the neoclassical Theseus Temple, a small-scale replica based on the Temple of Hephaestus in Athens. You'll also see sculpture clad fountains and rose gardens.

Nearby, the Burggarten was once the private grounds of the Emperor Franz Joseph I. It opened to the public in 1919. You'll find the art nouveau Palm House here, which is now a

Lobau: Vienna's Water Forest

Inside Vienna, you can still visit an ancient waterforest that branches off the Danube.

Vienna is an unusual city when it comes to its abundance of green spaces, but the Lobau is particularly special. This water forest and wetlands in the eastern suburbs of the city cover 2,300 hectares and make up a rich ecosystem with diverse species of plants, mammals, birds, reptiles, fish and amphibians. Taking a walk through the Lobau, you'll be accompanied by an active, noisy chorus of birdsong echoing among the trees. Other signs of life include chewed pieces of wood (the work of the local beavers). The Lobau is not only loved as Vienna's "jungle"—locals also come here to canoe, hike, ride their bikes and swim (some areas are particularly loved by nudist bathers).

If you want a taste of the Lobau, take the daily boat tour in the summer. Booking is a must as the boat is pretty tiny. It can be reserved online (www.donauauen.at/experience/trips/mit-dem-nationalparkboot-von-der-city-in-die-au/491). Tours (€12) last 4 hours, leaving at 9am from the banks of the river next to the bridge called the Salztorbrücke, near Schwedenplatz. Tours are in German, but it's a convenient and cheap way to get out to this unique nature reserve from the city center. You'll get a ride up the Danube Canal for an hour before taking an hour-long walking tour in the Lobau with a guide, and hopping back on the boat. Plus, you get a boat ride down the Danube Canal at a fraction of the price of most boat tours (usually around €20) as a bonus!

trendy bar and a butterfly house (tel. 01/533-8570, www.schmetterlinghaus.at, Mon-Fri 10am-4:45pm, Sat-Sun 10am-6:15pm Apr-Oct, daily 10am-3:45pm Nov-Mar, €7).

SIGMUND FREUD PARK

U Schottentor

Reachable just across from Vienna's main university, lounging students are a common sight at this park named after the famous psychoanalyst. The towers of the Votive Church dominate the sky, but the church's presence doesn't deter sunbathers who camp out on the grass. In the summer, around 100 sun loungers are delivered each morning and collected around 9pm. You can visit free of charge. Free WiFi is also available here.

DONAUPARK

U Kaisermühlen VIC

There is 99 hectares of parkland here in this new part of the city in the 22nd district.

Set between the Danube Island and the Old Danube—a crescent shaped arm of the Danube populated with boats, canoes, and waterside promenades, this park rose out of a 1960s garbage dump to become an oasis filled with flowers, paths, playgrounds and an aviary. The main landmark is the 830ft (250 m) high Danube Tower (Donauturm), and there are thousands of roses that bloom in the summer months in the **Rosarium** (free, open all hours, in the southeastern corner of the park). You can explore the park on foot or hop on the **Donauparkbahn,** a small train that will take you around the park every half an hour for €4. You can board at numerous locations, including the Donauturm or the Rosarium.

HIKING

CITY HIKING TRAIL 9

Best known for its retro amusement park, the Prater is also a popular hiking destination. Just get off at the Praterstern U-Bahn stop and follow the signs for the City Hiking Trail 9, an 8-mile (13km) long round-trip deep into the water meadows and wooded areas of a former imperial hunting ground. The trail loops back to where you started.

CYCLING

Vienna is a bike-friendly city with 800 miles (1300 km) of cycle paths and a bike sharing program known as Vienna Citybike.

Bike-Sharing

CITYBIKES

www.citybikewien.at

Vienna's bike-sharing program can be used at over 120 stations around the city. Register online, or just use your credit card (Visa or MasterCard) at any of the Citybike terminals across the city. You pay a one-time fee of one euro; then, the charges go up depending on how long you rent the bike. The first hour is free—after that, it's €1 per started hour, €2 in the third hour, and so on. If you go over 120 hours, there is a flat fee of €600.

When you're done using the bike and you're ready to return it, you'll see a green light come on when the bike is placed in the rack correctly.

Bike Paths

SIGHTSEEING BICYCLE PATH RINGSTRAβE

Head down to Urania (an old observatory on the Danube Canal where the Vienna River flows into the canal) and you can cycle along the paved, traffic free Sightseeing Bicycle Path Ringstraße (Ring-Rund-Radweg) that will take you along the old city and past some of the most famous landmarks, like the Staatsoper (Opera House) and the Parliament along a three-mile route. You can begin by the Urania Kino—either take tram 1 to Julius-Raab Platz, or from Schwedenplatz by U-Bahn, or just take your bike.

HAUPTALLEE TO LOBAU WATER FOREST

Nature lovers can cross the Aspern Bridge and take the bike route down the Praterstraße and Prater Hauptallee (the main promenade that cuts through the Prater) and cycle all the way down to the Lobau water forest. Cycle five miles down the Hauptallee into the Unterer Prater and turn left. Take the road to the Donaustadtbrücke (the bridge crossing Danube Island and over the river), then turn right when you get off the bridge. The route along the Hauptallee is paved, flat, and lined with trees, taking you past woods and meadows. The bridge runs along the A23 road so it is a little busier, but on the other side, you'll be treated to a Danube-side cycle.

DANUBE ISLAND

There are also cycle paths running along the length of the 13-mile long Danube Island. Cycle across Leopoldstadt and just take any of the bridges, like Brigittenauerbrücke, to reach the island.

---

1 the Vienna Woods lie in the hilly suburbs of the city 2 Augarten Park with picnic goers, yoga lovers, and also the surreal Flak towers left behind by the Nazis 3 Vienna Citybikes 4 statue of Johann Strauss in the Stadtpark

BEACHES

STRANDBAD GÄNSEHÄUFEL

Sommerbad Moissigasse 21, Gänsehäufel,
tel. 01/269-9016, www.gaensehaeufel.at, May and
Sep Mon-Fri 9am-7pm, Sat-Sun 8am-7pm, May-Aug
Mon-Fri 9am-8pm, Sat-Sun 8am-8pm, €5.90

Gänsehäufel Island is in an arm of the Old Danube, northwest of the city center, and east of Danube Island. It becomes crowded in the summer, when locals come to splash around and bake in the sun. This 30-hectare island has 4,000 trees and sandy beaches that back onto grassy lawns. The bathing areas are split into family areas, but there are also nudist zones, designated by signs marked as FKK, meaning *Freikörperkulture*, or free body culture. (When you arrive at the entrance, these areas are also marked on the map.) You can easily spend most of the day here swimming, bathing, or playing tennis (bring your own racket).

To get here, you can take free shuttle service from the U-Bahn station Kaisermühlen to the beach.

SIGHTSEEING CRUISES

DDSG BLUE DANUBE

www.ddsg-blue-danube.at

You can book Danube cruises directly with DDSG Blue Danube. There are three routes you can choose: Route A (duration 2 hours, 4 times a day, €23) sails down the green part of Vienna, from Schwedenplatz past the Urania Observatory on the Danube Canal to the south, and then up the Danube to Reichsbrücke; Route B (duration 1.5 hours, 4 times a day, €23) begins at Reichsbrücke, heads north on the Danube, and turns into the Danube Canal from the northern end, passing the new part of Vienna (like the Donaustadt and Donuturm) before returning to Schwedenplatz. You can stay on the boat for a round-trip for a total of €29. If you're tired of sightseeing on foot, it's a good way to relax and see a different side of the city from the water.

SWIMMING POOLS

JÖRGERBAD

Jörgerstraße 42-44, tel. 01/406-4305, Tue 9am-6pm,
Wed and Fri 9am-9:30pm, Thu and Sun 8am-7pm, Sat
8am-8pm, €5.90

Among one of Vienna's oldest indoor swimming pools, Jörgerbad was built before World War I and is an art nouveau-style pool with tiles in shades of rusty orange and sky blue. If you love architecture and want to grab a swim before or after sightseeing, then check out this stunning pool.

AMALIENBAD

Reumannplatz 23, Mon 12:30pm-3pm (senior
citizens only), Tue 9am-6pm, Wed 9am-9:30pm, Thu
7am-9:30pm, Sat 7am-8pm, Sun 7am-6pm, €5.90

For a local experience, head over to the Amalienbad. Inside, the Amalienbad looks like something out of a Wes Anderson movie. You'll find the pool under a tiled glass ceiling with accents of art nouveau and art deco styles.

Get your ticket at the cash desk, then hand it in at the desk by the entrance to the baths to get your wristband. Chances are you have a locker and not a private cabin (cabins have to be requested), so instead of slipping into one of the elegant changing cabins surrounding the pool, look for the women's and men's lockers and changing rooms sign. When you're ready to swim, just hold the wristband to the lock and press, and it's locked.

The Amalienbad also offers saunas, a restaurant, and more for a day of elegant relaxation.

DIANABAD

Lilienbrunngasse 7-9, tel. 01/219-81810,
www.dianabad.at, Mon-Tue, Fri-Sat 10am-10pm,
Wed-Thu 13:30-10pm, Sun 10am-8pm, €17.10-26.50
bath and sauna depending on the day and duration

The Dianabad lies just off the Danube Canal in Leopoldstadt, and is home to the city's largest adventure pool, themed water slides (from wild stream to dinosaurs), a wave pool and a pirate boat, and also a sauna area for adults to detox while the kids (or adults with adventurous hearts) splash around. Palm trees and a controlled balmy temperature keeps things feeling tropical, so if you're in Vienna in the winter or it happens to rain, you can escape to the tropics for a bit in the city center.

SPA
THERME WIEN
Kurbadstraße 14, tel. 01/680-09, www.thermewien. at, Mon-Sat 9am-10pm, Sun 8am-10pm, €19 for a three-hour ticket

If you take U-Bahn line 1 to the end of the line to Oberlaa, in just 20 minutes, you'll make it out to one of the largest and most modern city spas in Europe. Unlike pools in the inner city, Therme Wien uses sulfur springs once loved by the Romans for their healing properties. With multiple areas in the complex featuring pools, sauna and steam rooms, aquatic gymnastics, lounge areas, health and fitness, meals, rehabilitation programs, and much more, you may never want to leave.

TOURS
GOOD VIENNA TOURS
www.goodviennatours.eu/

Get your bearings in Vienna with a free walking tour of the city center hosted by Good Vienna Tours. These tours last just under three hours and take you around the 1st District. You'll see details of the city you might otherwise miss, like the curious medieval mural on the façade of the Hare House of a cow wearing glasses playing backgammon with a wolf, or the story behind the name of the Albertina (which is where the tour starts). If you like their free tour, they have other tours (paid) like the 2 hour and 30 minute walking tour of Hitler's Vienna (€21).

CONTEXT TRAVEL
www.contexttravel.com/cities/vienna, prices range €94-117 per person for group tour

Context Travel tours offer you the unique opportunity to see the city with a docent who has an academic background in the topic of your choice, whether you're interested in Sigmund Freud or Vienna's culinary history.

CLASSES
WALTZ IN VIENNA
www.waltzvienna.com

While you're in the city of Strauss, why not learn how to dance the Viennese Waltz? Waltz in Vienna (www.waltzvienna.com) offers daily private classes (45 minutes, €75 per couple) for couples looking to learn more about this side of Vienna's heritage. Classes are available in English covering dance steps and etiquette.

Shopping

When it comes to shopping for souvenirs in Vienna, there's plenty to choose from. If you want to take home a Sachertorte (whether large or small), there is no need to worry about transporting this decadent cake as it stays fresh (the hotel even ships the cake abroad by mail). The same goes for the Imperial Torte.

If you or your loved ones would rather not return home with a stack of cakes and pastries, then you might choose a bottle of pumpkin seed oil, a dark green, cold-pressed oil that is nutty and uniquely Austrian, which you can pick up from one of the stalls in the Naschmarkt, supermarkets, or certain souvenir shops.

On a different note, did you know that Austria invented the snow globe? If you or someone you know is a fan, you're in the right pace to pick up one or two (or more). If you have the opportunity to spend, you may want to consider some Swarovski crystal or a beautiful piece of porcelain from the Augarten Porcelain Factory. For something different, explore Vienna's design scene and discover original and contemporary art pieces or décor that are uniquely Viennese.

Note: If shopping is on your itinerary, please be aware that many shops are closed on Sundays.

SHOPPING DISTRICTS

Downtown Vienna is threaded with pedestrianized zones, shopping streets, design shops and quirky markets. Some, like the flea market, happen only on specific days. Popular souvenirs like a Klimt handbag or boxes of chocolates with Sisi's or Mozart's portrait usually pop up in the typical souvenir shops around the Hofburg and Schönbrunn.

If you want to shop where the locals go, head to the following neighborhoods.

Kärntnerstraße (U Stephansplatz, Karlsplatz) lies right in the heart of the 1st district. This half-mile shopping artery (which stretches between St. Stephen's Cathedral and the Staatsoper) is one of Vienna's longest shopping streets, and this pedestrianized zone is always busy with locals heading into popular European mainstream fashion stores like H&M, Zara, or Mango. There are also few designer shops thrown into the mix, like Austria's flagship Swarovski store, and labels like Hugo Boss and Karl Lagerfeld.

Just like Paris' Champs Elyseés and London's Bond Street, Vienna also has its quarter of luxury boutiques and stores set in the in the heart of the old city, only a short distance from St. Stephen's Cathedral. The **Goldenes Quartier** (U Stephansplatz) offers luxury blended with the historical character of the neighborhood. It lies between the streets of Tuchlauben, Am Hof, and Bognergasse. You can shop designer labels here like Prada, Armani, Louis Vuitton, Chanel, and other big names.

A few streets down towards the Hofburg, the **Kohlmarkt** (U Herrengasse, Stephansplatz) is Empress Elizabeth's favorite confectionary, Demel. This pedestrianized zone of shops is where you come if you're looking to buy jewelry and gems from the likes of Tiffany and Cartier. High fashion houses you may have missed in the Goldenes

Quartier set up shop with a more imperial view here, like Gucci and Dior.

The 1st District may bring in the rich hitting up the luxury boutiques and tourists shopping for souvenirs, but young locals prefer to cross the Ringstraße to the trendy 6th District to **Mariahilferstraße** (U Museumsquartier, Neubaugasse, Zieglergasse), a lively shopping street running for over two miles (3 kilometers) between the MuseumsQuartier and Schönbrunn Palace. It's one of Vienna's longest streets, and much of the shopping action takes place between the Ringstraße and the Westbahnhof. Browse the department stores, malls and small boutiques in and around this shopping metropolis, and don't be afraid of stumbling into side streets, like Neubaugasse or Zollergasse.

Naschmarkt (U Karlsplatz, Kettenbrückengasse) has such an iconic status in Vienna it's become a sight in its own right. Naschmarkt is more of an experience than a place to buy souvenirs, but if you want to grab some cheese, freshly cooked falafels, and slices of smoked sausage and head to the Stadtpark for a picnic, this is the place to come. The customers here are a mix of tourists and local foodies, but on Saturdays, the crowd is more eclectic when the Flohmarkt (flea market) is on.

DESIGN SHOPS AND MARKETS
Neubau and the MuseumsQuartier
THE VOLTA SHOP

Siebensterngasse 28, www.thevoltashop.com, Mon-Fri 10am-6:30pm, Sat 11am-5pm

Volta bills itself as the "palace of minimalism" for interior design, arts and crafts, and accessories, such as copper mugs, natural linens, and amber glass bulbs. Volta's minimalist design with stark white walls, meticulously lined with dark wooden shelves stacked with textiles and ceramics keeps the focus on product. If you love light bulbs, you'll find an amazing selection of filters, settings and filaments.

Around Naschmarkt and Karlsplatz
KELLERWERK
Gumpendorferstraße, www.kellerwerk.at,
Wed midday-6pm, Thu-Fri 11am-6pm
Kellerwerk is home to old furniture discarded because it is deemed too old or unusable—and furniture doctors Sascha and Romana give old pieces new life. Apart from beautiful, revived antiques, random objects make their way into upcycling designs. You can get coffee tables with suitcases as legs, hair drying hood lampshades, and other original pieces, including jewelry and accessories from other designers. Each piece tells a story, and the shop is worth visiting.

Belvedere Palace Area
MAK DESIGN
Stubenring 5, www.makdesignshop.at,
Tue 10am-10pm, Wed-Sun 10am-6pm
This shop, set inside Vienna's Museum of Applied Arts, has been around since 1991, and it was the very first design shop in the city. You won't need a museum ticket to get into the shop—there is a separate entrance from the outside via the Österreicher Restaurant. MAK is packed with great gifts for any design lover, from notebooks and crockery to more left-field souvenirs that make for great conversation pieces, like designer eye patches made by a local goldsmith and sculptor, or a breadbasket made with a stainless steel mesh that you can form into any shape you want.

CLOTHING AND ACCESSORIES
Historic Center and Hofburg Area
LODEN-PANKL
Michaelerplatz 6, www.loden-pankl.at, Mon-Sat
10am-6pm Mar-Jun and Sep-Dec, Mon-Sat
10am-5pm Jan-Feb and Jul-Aug
For something authentically Austrian, you can don traditional clothing at this 180-year-old tailoring and clothing shop. You'll find handmade Dirndls (traditional Austrian dresses for women), along with loden (fabric made of wool that's been combed and boiled), as well as blouses and coats. This quality clothing shop also offers contemporary designs.

Around Naschmarkt and Karlsplatz
NACHBARIN
Gumpendorferstraße 17, www.nachbarin.co.at, Mon midday-6:30pm, Tue-Fri 11am-6:30pm, Sat 11am-4pm
Nachbarin is a local favorite with Viennese fashionistas. The inventory of women's designer fashion and shoes is made up of hot names from the European design scene, like Veronique Leroy and Anita Moser. Whether you're shopping for clothes, accessories, bags or jewelry, you can be sure of the quality and cult status of each item stacked up in the wood-paneled shop.

SAMSTAG
Margaretenstraße 46, www.samstag-shop.com,
Wed-Fri midday-7pm, Sat 10am-6pm
Close to the Naschmarkt, this high-fashion store for men and women, run by designers Peter and Christian, focuses on young Austrian designers, but you'll also find international labels. Everything about this shop is a collaboration, including the fun black and white graffiti that animates the facade. The entire boutique lives and breathes the Vienna design scene and is worth dropping by if you want to find something truly local and contemporary.

FLO VINTAGE
Schleifmühlgasse 15a, www.vintageflo.com, Mon-Fri 10am-6:30pm, Sat 10am-3:30pm
Love vintage? Then check out Flo Vintage, with an excellent collection of women's clothing, dating from 1880 and up to 1980. This store been running since the 1970s. The stock here is substantial, and most of it is meticulously preserved and seldom worn. If you want a pearl-studded dress from the Fin de Siecle, an authentic Flapper dress, or

something from the 1950s, you'll find it in this boutique.

EBENBERG

Neubaugasse 4, tel. 06/99-1528-7226, Mon-Fri 11am-7pm, Sat 11am-5pm

This tiny ethical fashion concept store on Neubaugasse is the passion project of designer Laura Ebenberg, who is dedicated to sustainable and ethical fashion. She handpicks items from the European sustainable fashion scene, like Austrian organic brand anzüglich and Berlin-based fair trade fashion company SlowMo—but Ebenberg also presents her own creations in this intimate boutique. Here, you can pick up shoes made from organic ingredients and bags made from recycled sails.

L'ADRESSE

Zollergasse 4, tel. 06/76-653-7911, www.ladresse.at, Mon-Wed and Fri 11am-7pm, Thu 11am-8pm, Sat 10am-6pm

Founded by French mother-daughter duo Anne and Hanae, these two ladies decided to open this boutique in the trendy Neubau district. The concept? That each item has a story to tell. The bright, airy boutique sells both women's and men's fashion, with items ranging from bags to pajamas and lingerie.

ANTIQUE SHOPS AND MARKETS
Around Naschmarkt and Karlsplatz
FLOHMARKT

Linke Wienzeile 48-52, Sat 6:30am-6pm

If you're in Vienna on a Saturday, make sure you venture one block west of the Naschmarkt for the weekly flea market with some 400 sellers. The chaos of stalls selling everything from antique chandeliers to old vinyl records and clothing takes place in the vicinity of Otto Wagner's residential Linke Wienzeile building. Even if you don't plan on buying, it's worth heading down to the market just to immerse yourself in this Viennese experience. Brush up on your German numbers if

you're the kind of person who likes to negotiate the price.

VINTAGERIE

Nelkengasse 4, www.vintagerie.at, Mon-Fri midday-7pm, Sat 11am-6pm

This unique shop occupies a former hair salon on a side street close to Mariahilferstraße. It's a junket of rare furniture and once-loved items from yesterday. If you're a collector, you'll love the design pieces that make their way into the collection as well as vintage items from the 1930s to the 1980s. You may be able to squeeze a 1960s lamp or a designer clock in your suitcase; if not, you may be tempted to ship something home. It's worth it for the experience alone to stop by. There are no price tags, meaning you can negotiate within reason.

Schönbrunn Palace and Grounds
DIE GLASFABRIK

Lorenz Mandl Gasse 25, www.glasfabrik.at, Tue-Fri 2pm-7pm, Sat 10am-2pm

This former glass factory consists of two warehouses packed with antiques. No replicas here—this industrial setting is home to unique treasures for sale dating from the 1670s to the 1970s. You'll find furniture, sculpture, chandeliers and a variety of home decor, including lamps, candle holders, and ceramics. Cash only.

GIFTS
Historic Center and Hofburg Area
STEIFF

Bräunerstraße 3, www.steiff-gallerie-wien.at, Mon-Fri 10am-12:30pm and 1:30-6pm, Sat 10am-12:30pm and 1:30-5pm

Steiff—founded by the inventor of the teddy bear, Richard Steiff—has its origins in 19th century Germany. Its main Austrian shop

---

1 The Saturday flea market just next to the Naschmarkt brings the crowds in droves. 2 Vienna's cafes and bars are the life of the city, and there is no institution quite like Cafe Sperl.

is worth the visit. When you step inside this nostalgic shop, you'll and find yourself surrounded by rows upon rows of cute cuddly toys, from the classic teddy bear to other members of the animal kingdom, like pandas and puppies, and some of them may be waiting for you to take them home.

Greater Vienna
THE ORIGINAL VIENNESE
SNOW GLOBE FACTORY
Schumanngasse 87, tel. 01/486-4341, www.viennasnowglobe.at, Mon-Thu 9am-3pm

At the end of the 19th century, Erwin Perzy, a producer of surgical instruments, received the first patent for his invention of the *Schneekugel* (snow globe). You can head out to the original Viennese snow globe factory in a suburban house in Hernals, the neighborhood just outside the Gürtel near the Alsergrund. Today the factory is run by the grandson of the inventor, Erwin Perzy III. You can peruse rows upon rows of snow globes with miniature, snowy landscapes of the Riesenrad, Schönbrunn Palace, and Stephansdom inside. There is also a small

museum (free entry) that illustrates how they're made, along with the workshop where the snow globe was invented. If you have a special gift in mind, you can request custom snow globes to order. Snow globes cost from €7-25, depending on the size.

SWAROVSKI CRYSTAL
Hofburg and Surroundings
SWAROVSKI
KRISTALLWELTEN STORE
Kärtner Straße 24, tel. 01/324-0000, www.swarovski.com, Mon-Fri 9am-9pm, Sat 9am-6pm

If you're strolling down Kärtner Straße in the evening, you may see the Swarovski Kristallwelten store's façade lit up by LED crystal light modules and art installations. Go inside and immerse yourself in the dazzling world of cut and polished crystal from the iconic Austrian crystal manufacturer. It's more than just a place to take home crystal jewelry, watches, and Christmas ornaments—it also features crystal installations by different designers and artists. You can find everything crystal here in all colors, styles, and shapes.

Viennese Coffeehouses

TOP EXPERIENCE

Even more essential than a visit to the Hofburg is a trip to an authentic *Kaffeehaus*. Although some have morphed into "museums," you can still find classic coffee houses that capture the Viennese spirit. Each café has its own character and style, and some are more opulent than others, but they will usually have cozy booths and marble tables where you could comfortably sip coffee all day, newspapers, coat stands by the door, and elegantly dressed waiters. Some have quirky features as a nod back to their late 19th century/early 20th century heritage, like old telephone boxes in the back.

Some of the traditional coffee houses also serve classic Austrian dishes like Schnitzel and

have strudels and cakes. These cafés are all have waiter service, but don't expect a service with a smile—the waiters' grumpy demeanor (or perhaps grumpy by American standards) is part of the coffee house experience.

The best thing about Vienna's cafés is the people watching. Put down your phone and watch some of the eccentric characters come and go, from elegantly dressed old men to art students sketching in the corner.

HISTORIC CENTER
AND HOFBURG AREA
CAFÉ ALT WIEN
Bäckerstraße 9, tel 01/512-5222, www.kaffeealtwien.at, Sun-Thu 10am-3am, Fri-Sat 10am-3am

The Alt Wien is plastered wall-to-wall with

What to Order in a Kaffeehaus

When you arrive at a coffeehouse, slip into one of the cushioned booths and choose the coffee of your choice from the menu (which may include more than 30 choices). The classics are:

- *Kleiner/Großer Schwarzer.* Single or double espresso, depending on whether you order small (kleiner) or large (großer).

- *Kleiner/Großer Brauner.* Similar to the *Schwarzer*, except you get a little cream on the side, so you can tailor your coffee as you like it.

- *Verlängerter.* Close to the classic Americano: a small cup of espresso served in a large cup with hot water added. Sometimes you'll get cream or milk on the side.

- *Melange.* The ultimate Viennese coffee drink—a small espresso topped half with steamed milk and milk froth.

- *Franziskaner.* Like a Melange, but with whipped cream on the top in place of milk foam.

- *Einspänner.* Double espresso topped with a dollop of fresh whipped cream. The name in English is hansom (a one-horse carriage typical for 19th century Vienna). Legend has it that the drink was once a favorite with the carriage drivers who used the cream to stop the coffee from getting cold.

movie, exhibition and event posters, and it's an institution locals love. It's a cozy place to forget the world, with a *Melange* at hand as you recline in your chair and observe the regulars who frequent the café like their second home.

CAFÉ PRÜCKEL

Stubenring 24, tel. 01/512-6115, http://prueckel.at, daily 8am-10pm

Some cafés take pride in their historic literary legacy, and the Prückel is still a hangout for writers in Vienna's contemporary literary scene. The café dates back to 1904—you'll see the odd art nouveau detail here and there, but most of it bears a pink and tan look from the 1950s. You should come to Prückel for the sumptuous cakes, apple strudel, colorful fruit-based cakes or rich chocolate.

CAFÉ FRAUENHUBER

Himmelpfortgasse 6, tel. 01/512-5353, www.caféfrauenhuber.at, Mon-Sat 8am-11pm, Sun 10am-10pm

Vienna's oldest *kaffeehaus* dates back to the 18th century, and it carries a classical cache since Mozart and Beethoven performed here.

This café is cozy and refined, with low, arched ceilings and red damask armchairs. Grab one of their house strudels with a coffee and bask in the ambience.

★ CAFÉ HAWELKA

Dorotheergasse 6, tel. 01/512-8230, www.hawelka.at, Mon-Thu 8am-midnight, Fri-Sat 8am-1am, Sun 8am-midnight

Hawelka is perhaps the most iconic of the Viennese cafés. It's dark and a bit moody, with faded upholstered booths, wooden coat stands and local art on the wall. It was opened in 1939 by Leopold and Josephine Hawelka (who formerly ran the Alt Wien). It has catered to an artistic clientele, counting Hundertwasser, Andy Warhol and Arthur Miller among its former regulars. Go after 8pm when freshly made *Buchteln,* baked dumplings filled with jam (Josephine's family recipe) are available, fresh out of the oven.

★ CAFÉ BRÄUNERHOF

Stallburggasse 2, tel. 01/512-3893, Mon-Fri 8am-8pm, Sat 8am-6pm, Sun 10am-6pm

A street away from the Hofburg, Bräunerhof still retains its timeless local charm. It was once the haunt of Thomas Bernhard (author of *Wittgenstein's Nephew*). You won't see Bernhard today, but if you're lucky, you may see actor Christoph Waltz sitting in one of the booths. Otherwise just enjoy the old-world charm of this café with a classic Viennese coffee like an *Einspänner*, a black coffee topped with cream.

AROUND NASCHMARKT AND KARLSPLATZ

★ CAFÉ SPERL

Gumpendorfer straße 11, tel. 01/586-4158, www.cafésperl.at, Mon-Sat 7am-10pm, Sun 10am-8pm

Sperl, which opened in 1880, has hardly changed—and without turning into a caricature of itself. It's a cozy café you could easily lose an afternoon inside, just sitting in one of the upholstered booths reading the paper, playing a game of billiards, or drinking from the menu of 34 coffees. You may want to try the house cake, the Sperl Schnitte, a rich chocolate wafer.

BELVEDERE PALACE AREA

CAFE GOLDEGG

Argentinierstraße 49, tel. 01/505-9162, www.cafégoldegg.at, Mon-Fri 8am-8pm, Sat 9am-8pm, Sun 9am-7pm

You won't find crowds of tourists in this café (opened in 1910, close to Belvedere). Instead, you'll find a coterie of locals who come here for their ritualistic coffee. It's quiet at times—the only noise you might hear are cooking sounds from kitchen. If you're looking for a moment of peace and quiet, head to this demure café painted in tones of burgundy, green and gold. (Note: Smokers have their own section here).

Food

Austrian food is rich and hearty, and meat and cakes dominate menus around the city. Unless you're vegetarian, it would be a crime to miss out on the famous Wiener Schnitzel in its many varieties here—most traditionally veal. If you're hungry for Wiener Schnitzel, look for the word *Beisl*, which is the word for a typical Viennese tavern that cooks up good Austrian comfort food. These cozy pubs tend to be old fashioned, with dark wood paneling and plain, undecorated wooden tables, and low lighting.

Breakfasts in Austria are a feast. A traditional breakfast usually features *Semmeln*, white bread rolls that are crusty on the outside and soft and spongy on the inside (the singular noun is *Semmel*), along with butter and coffee. You may also find cold cuts, boiled eggs, cakes and pastries, jams and orange juice. Most hotels in Vienna will offer a luxurious buffet you can fill up on in the morning. If you choose to go into a café, many will offer a breakfast menus. You may notice something called a Viennese Breakfast in a café—this is a portion for a single person, with a *Semmel*, jam, coffee, butter, and a glass of orange juice. You can also get a savory breakfast with slices of cheese and ham, or a boiled egg. Breakfast is usually served until noon and sometimes to 2pm. Cafes mostly buzz with crowds around 9-10am.

In general, portions are generous, and unless you're in a fine dining place it's OK to ask for a container for leftovers.

Viennese Eateries

BEISL

These unique Viennese bistros serve hearty local cuisine and have their origins in the 18th-century inns. The word "Beisl" perhaps originates from the Yiddish word for house, "Bajiss." Most Beisln, the plural in German for Beisl, are simple on the inside, with dark painted wood paneling and plain tables that sometimes sprawl out onto the cobbled streets on the outside or into a courtyard. Food is hearty, dense, and focuses on local specials, think Schnitzel, goulash, pastries, and clear consumes served with strips of pancakes. Although most Beisln root themselves in tradition, a new wave of Beisl has taken over the city known as neo-Beisln, where old recipes get a modern twist.

HEURIGE

For something genuinely Viennese, visit a *Heurige*, one of the rustic wine taverns you'll usually find on the outskirts of the city, like Grinzing or Oberlaa. Legends and songs have sprung up in honor of these taverns, it would be a crime to miss one on your trip. They are the perfect place to try local, Viennese wines with the ideal food to go with them. Look out for the signs with the pine branches on them and the word "Ausgsteckt," with the time the tavern opens. The most important feature of any *Heurige* is the Heuriger Wine, usually made by the owner of the inn and often a very young wine, around a year old. In the *Heurige*, food is sold by the decagram, with a mix of warm and cold food. You can usually get roast pork, blood sausage, cured meats and other dishes that go well with the local wine.

WÜRSTELSTAND

Try some Viennese street food for something local and on a budget—or for a late-night snack—at one of the many sausage stands scattered around the city. Give the *Käsekrainer*, sausage stuffed with cheese, a taste for something unique, but you can also go for the usual Frankfurters, Bratwurst, and other sausage specials. Order a slice of bread, pickles, fries, and even a beer. These quirky kiosks where all walks of life come to snack—from taxi drivers to the drunken elite in their opera gowns—are meant to be dined at standing. Have some mustard (strong or sweet) with your meat, but don't ask for mayonnaise unless you're having fries.

KAFFEEHAUS AND KONDITOREI

It would be a crime to leave Vienna without visiting an iconic Kaffeehaus. You could spend a day in Vienna's coffeehouses sipping *melanges* and people watching. Another establishment to look out for is the *Konditorei*, confectionary shops with beautiful cakes with generous layers of marzipan or jellied fruit toppings, or lashings of cream. Vienna is famous for its pastries so make sure you order a strudel or a Sacher cake while you're here.

HISTORIC CENTER AND HOFBURG AREA
Austrian
★ FIGLMÜLLER

Wollzeile 5, tel. 01/512-6177, www.figlmueller.at, daily 11am-9:30pm, mains €10-20.50

Figlmüller is a Viennese institution—a traditional *Beisl* that serves some of the biggest schnitzels in the city. (At 12 inches in diameter, you won't leave hungry.) The owner has his own vineyard, so try local varieties like the Grüner Veltliner if you like whites, or the Blaufränkischer if you prefer spicy reds. This atmospheric old wine tavern is hidden in an alleyway just off the Wollzeile. It's a popular place (reservations are a must!), but you can also try your luck at Bäckerstraße, Figlmüller's second location.

PLACHUTTA

Wollzeile 38, tel. 01/512-1577, www.plachutta.at, daily 11:30am-11:15pm, mains €16.50-30

This restaurant is the place to try Franz Joseph's favorite dish: *Tafelspitz*, boiled cuts of beef served over three courses: beef broth, beef marrow, on toast, and finally the meat itself. An international crowd dines here. There are other items on the menu, but with 13 varieties of Austrian-reared beef cuts to choose from for inclusion in your *Tafelspitz*, ordering anything else would be waste of a visit. Waiters bring out the *Tafelspitz* in copper pots that are kept warm throughout your meal, along with accompaniments like cream of spinach, roasted grated potatoes, plus horseradish and applesauce. Plachutta gets pretty packed around lunchtime, so book ahead.

Austrian Specialties

Viennese specials often revolve around two things: meat and sweets. Expect food to be heavy, hearty and filling. You may feel the urge to resist the cakes and chocolates, but I highly discourage this—The Austrians make some of the best cakes and pastries in the world. (Did you know the croissant is actually Austrian?)

RESTAURANT ENTREES

- **Tafelspitz:** A classic dish featuring boiled beef with horseradish, potatoes, and apples.

- **Schnitzel:** A slice of pork or veal (a true Wiener Schnitzel is made with veal) that's been hammered into a thin disc, then coated with breadcrumbs and fried, and usually drizzled with lemon.

- **Backhendl:** Made from the succulent Austrian Styrian chicken, this half or whole chicken is coated in bread crumbs and fried until golden. The chicken is best eaten with a vinegary potato salad drizzled with pumpkin seed oil, and served with a side of lingonberry jam.

STREET FOOD

- **Bratwurst:** Fried sausage, available from *Würstelstand*—sausage stands you'll see around the city. Slice it up and eat it with a side of mustard, or ask for an extra slice of bread.

- **Käsekrainer:** Another hit at the *Würstelstand*, these fried and grilled sausages are filled with cheese. Eat these with a white bread roll or a slice of dark bread with a dash of mustard.

DESSERT AND CAKES

- **Sachertorte:** This iconic cake is a dense, rich chocolate sponge with a thin spread of apricot jam in the middle layer. The whole cake is covered in a layer of chocolate icing and served with whipped cream.

GRIECHENBEISL

Fleischmarkt 11, tel. 01/533-1977, www.griechenbeisl.
at, daily 11:30am-11:30pm, mains €15-30

Beethoven, Brahms, Strauss, and even Mark Twain once frequented this traditional Viennese restaurant (one of the city's oldest, dating back to the 15th century). You can enjoy all the classic meat-heavy Viennese favorites, like Schnitzel, *Tafelspitz* and Goulash. (There are options for vegetarians as well.) Take a seat in the garden if you can, but if the weather is not on your side, try to get a table in the oldest section, like the Zither Stüberl rooms, where you can view famous autographs displayed on the walls.

ZWÖLF APOSTELKELLER

Sonnenfelsgasse 3, tel. 01/512-6777,
www.zwoelf-apostelkeller.at, daily 11am-midnight,

mains €8-20

Zwölf Apostelkeller (12 Apostles Cellar) lies deep in a gorgeous vaulted 14th century cellar below the old city; it can seat over 300 people. Time seems to stop here as you dine on traditional Austrian cuisine made with local ingredients. Try their *Fiakergulasch*, a beef goulash stew with sausage and fried egg, along with one of their beers on tap, or local Viennese white wines, like the Gemischter Satz, a special Viennese blend. You may get lucky and be treated to a concert of *Heurigen Musik*, Austrian tavern music.

CAFÉ HOFBURG

Innerer Burghof 1, tel. 01/241-00400,
www.café-hofburg.at, daily 10am-6pm, mains €13-16

Set inside the Hofburg, this café and bistro serves classic Austrian cuisine like Viennese

Vienna's sausage stands are serve up the ultimate local street food catering to both budget travelers and locals.

- **Imperial torte:** the Sacher is not the only hotel with a signature cake. The nearby Imperial also has a legendary cake: The Imperial Torte. The cake is made with layers of whipped chocolate cream, sliced almonds, covered with marzipan and topped with a chocolate glaze.

- **Apfelstrudel:** this hearty Austrian classic is a rich, flaky pastry filled with a stewed apple filling. It comes with a serving of cream on the side.

beef consommé, Schnitzel, Goulash, and sausages. A classic Viennese coffeehouse environment, with plush velvet seating and decadent cakes on display behind a glass cabinet adds to the cozy atmosphere, making it a good place to stop in for lunch after a long tour.

REINTHALER'S BEISL

Dorotheergasse 2-4, tel. 01/513-1249,
www.reinthalersbeisl.com, daily 11am-11pm,
mains €9.80-16.20

If you're looking for the traditional *Beisl* experience, Reinthaler's has it. Complete with dusky wood paneling, low-hanging lights and packed with locals tucking into a plate of *Tafelspitz* or smoked pork, you should find the Viennese atmosphere you're looking for here. Food is good, hearty, inexpensive, and the service is prompt and friendly.

International
★ BLUE MUSTARD

Dorotheergasse 6-8, tel. 01/934-6705,
http://bluemustard.at, Tue-Sat 5pm-11pm,
mains €22-36, 4-5 course menu €42-58

This creative restaurant serves light bites, mains, and desserts inspired by from cuisine from around the world, with artfully presented ingredients and creative dishes celebrating molecular gastronomy. The menu changes seasonally, but creations might include items like lamb tartar with braised eggplant, half-desiccated figs and a creamy parsley cream, or Swedish chocolate cake with a sorbet of spruce shots and beetroot (a surprisingly delicious combination). The atmosphere is modern, just a bit whimsical, and inviting. The cocktail pairing is highly recommended.

MEINL'S RESTAURANT

Graben 19, tel. 01/532-33-34-6000,
www.meinlamgraben.at, Mon-Sat noon-midnight,
mains €16-40, 4-5 course menu €67-85

Offering impeccable wine coupled with haute cuisine, Meinl's is popular with foodies looking to savor dishes like oyster ostra regal with gin and lemon, and served with a cucumber granité or an roasted seabass on a shellfish-jus with avocado ravioli. The dishes mix flavors inspired by cuisines from over the world. You can also drop in for lunch during the week—head down to the cellar wine bar for a lunch menu that will set you back around €10-15.

Fine Dining
★ TIAN

Himmelpfortgasse 23, tel. 01/890-46652,
www.tian-restaurant.com, Tue-Sat 5:45pm-9pm,
also midday-2pm Thu-Sat, 8-10 courses €127-137

Tian is unique in the Michelin-starred restaurant world for its exclusively vegetarian culinary creations. Set aside two hours to pace yourself through 8-10 creative courses that will make you see cauliflower, cabbage and kohlrabi in a new light. Christian Halper and chef Paul Ivić use organic, locally sourced and seasonal produce—some from Tian's own garden. When you arrive, you'll be led down into the low-lit basement and welcomed on their culinary journey. Each course resembles a piece of modern art. Your server will not only deconstruct the ingredients but explain how to taste each dish, whether it's composed of a single vegetable or designed with creative pairings like dark chocolate and beetroot. (Don't skip the raw cheese plate.)

The menu is a great experience even if you aren't vegetarian, and it can be tailored for vegans upon request. If you don't have the budget to dine here, you can head over to Tian's sister restaurant, **Tian Bistro**, in Neubau.

Brunch
KLYO

Uraniastraße 1, tel. 01/710-5946, www.klyo.at, daily
9am-1am, breakfasts €6.50-10.50, mains €10-35

KLYO serves up delicious breakfasts until 10:30pm, like poached eggs with saffron hollandaise and avocado mash, or various muesli and porridge, as well as vegan options. You'll also find mains and tempting desserts. For something non-alcoholic, try their turmeric and ginger water.

This café and restaurant is located in the Urania building, an observatory built at the beginning of the 20th century in the art nouveau style. There's also a cinema there, a puppet theater and lecture halls. The café has amazing views of the Danube Canal.

THE GUESTHOUSE BRASSERIE & BAKERY

Führichgasse 10, tel. 01/512-1320,
www.theguesthouse.at/breakfast.html, daily
6:30am-11:30pm, breakfasts €9-21

You don't have to be a hotel guest to enjoy the breakfasts at The Guesthouse: This bistro occupying the ground floor of the boutique hotel overlooking the Albertina is popular with locals and tourists alike. Many come for the all-day breakfasts, served with homemade bread and pastries. The Eggs Benedict and Eggs Florentine are house favorites, but for a more indulgent spread, opt for the Guesthouse Breakfast, which comes with delicacies like smoked salmon, dry cured ham, soft and hard cheeses, and more. The coffee served here is the hotel's special roast. Book a table if you plan to come in the morning.

Street Food
★ TRZEŚNIEWSKI

Dorotheergasse 1, www.trzesniewski.at,
Mon-Fri 8:30am-7:30pm, Sat 9am-6pm, Sun
9am-5pm, sandwiches €1.30

With windows of opaque glass, Trześniewski may look like a clandestine establishment from the outside—but inside, it's a popular sandwich bar where you can get small open-faced sandwiches topped with local produce, paprika-laced cream cheese or pates—for just over a euro each. Just point to the sandwiches you want to order. Ask for a beer when you pay and you'll get a poker chip to hand to the person pulling Hobbit-sized "pints." There are a few tables, but it's mostly standing room only. Other branches of Trześniewski can be found around Vienna, but the atmosphere here is special.

★ BITZINGER WÜRSTELSTAND AM ALBERTINAPLATZ

Albertinaplatz, www.bitzinger-wien.at,
daily 8am-4am, sausages €3.40-5

Sausage stands are iconic in Vienna, and you'll see them all across the city, but this *Würstelstand* sandwiched between the Albertina and the Opera House has cult status. Don't be surprised if you see people dressed for the opera standing around drinking champagne and eating inexpensive sausages late after a show. Go for the *Bratwurst* (fried sausage) or the *Käsekrainer* (sausage infused with cheese), with a slice of bread and some sweet (*süß*) or spicy (*scharf*) mustard. You can also grab some beer or wine for a few euros, of if you're feeling fancy, a 0.2 liter bottle of champagne (around €20).

Cafés and Cakes
CAFE KORB

Brandstätte 9, tel. 01/533-1526, www.cafékorb.at,
Mon-Sat 8am-midnight, Sun 10am-midnight, mains
€6-10

This café has a couple of claims to fame. The first: It was one of Sigmund Freud's many hangouts. The second: it's *Apfelstrudel* (apple strudel). This café has a retro 1960s look, with faded photographs and cozy booths. This coffee house also serves Schnitzel and sausages, but most come here for the strudel and to relax with a coffee. The crowd here is eclectic and artistic; literary and other creative events are held in the basement from time to time.

DEMEL

Kohlmarkt 14, www.demel.at, daily 9am-7pm,
coffees €6, cakes €4-6

This legendary café and cake shop just a short stroll from the Hofburg was once a favorite hangout of Empress Sisi. (One story tells of a tunnel that ran from the palace to the patisserie so the Empress could have her cake incognito. It's also said that the waitresses wear black to mourn their beloved patron, who was stabbed on Lake Geneva.) Grab an indulgent cake or a coffee in the café's elegant mirror lined salon. Favorites include the decadent chocolate-nougat house cake, the Anna Demel Torte. You can also try the Demel's Sachertorte—the cake that launched a lawsuit between the Sacher Hotel and the café. (Sacher was once a pastry chef at Demel, and there was a decade long dispute as to who had the rights to the cake.) If you want to take something special home, buy a box of candied violets from the shop on the way out. (They were one of Sisi's favorite sweets!)

★ CAFÉ CENTRAL

Herrengasse 14, tel. 01/533-3763-24,
www.cafécentral.wien, Mon-Sat 7:30am-10pm,
Sun and Public Holidays 10am-10pm, coffees
€3.50-7.30, cakes €4.20-6

With arched ceilings, marble columns, decadent cakes and literary history, Café Central (set in a former stock exchange) draws in the tourists by the mile. Locals prefer less-touristy venues, but if you're in Vienna, you may as well have a coffee where Trotsky played chess and Freud smoked cigars. Order a *Melange*, pick out one of the colorful cakes behind the glass casing, and let your waiter do the rest. Expect queues out the doors in the afternoon, especially weekends. You can book a table on weekdays, or just come early for breakfast (€6.70-18.90).

Vegetarian, Vegan, and Gluten-Free
WRENKH

Bauernmarkt 10, tel. 01/533-1526, www.wrenkh-wien.
at, Mon-Sat 11am-11pm, mains €8-25

This friendly downtown bistro specializes in seasonal vegetable-based dishes, like pumpkin seed oil "Spätzle," an Austrian pasta dish served with ewe cheese and roasted pumpkin seeds in the fall, or creative soups like saffron-fruit consommé in the summer. The menu changes weekly.

Wrenkh also offers cooking courses.

The best time to drop in is at lunchtime on weekdays, when you can get a two or three-course lunch for around €10. The service here comes with a smile. Reservations are a must.

VEGGIEZZ

Salzgries 9, tel. 01/532-2650, https://veggiezz.at,
Mon-Fri 11am-11pm, Sat-Sun midday- 10pm, mains
€10-15

Veggies, vegans, and those on a gluten-free or carb-free diet will love this casual dining restaurant. The menu offers a range of healthy dishes, including "superfood" soups and vegan gourmet burgers (with or without the bun). This is a good bet if you have special dietary needs (or if you've overdone the Schnitzel and Sachertorte).

NEUBAU AND THE MUSEUMSQUARTIER
Austrian
SCHNITZELWIRT

Neubaugasse 52, tel. 01/523-3771, www.schnitzelwirt.
co.at, Mon-Sat 11am-9:30pm, mains €11-20

This restaurant is huge. It's popular with the locals for its traditional food—especially the Schnitzels (which no one finishes, apparently, but the good news is the waiters will wrap it up in wax paper and a bag so you can take it home and have it later). The Schnitzels don't come with sides; you need to ask for fries, sauerkraut, salad, or potato salad as an extra. There are other options on the menu, but this place is about the Schnitzel.

GASTWIRTSCHAFT WRATSCHKO

Neustiftgasse 51, tel. 01/523-7161, www.wratschko.
wien, Mon-Sat 5pm-1am, mains €7-20

Satisfying Austrian cuisine made with organic produce awaits here. You can try some interesting Austrian dishes, like *Gröstl*, meat and potatoes cooked together in a pan, or creative takes on classics like their peach strudel. (Note: This pub is smoker-friendly, with only one non-smoking section in the back of the restaurant.)

If you plan on visiting here on the weekend, make sure you book ahead.

Bistro
RESTAURANT 1070

Gutenberggasse 28, tel. 01/676-566-1774,
www.restaurant-1070.com, Tue-Sun 5:30pm-1am,
3 courses €30

Restaurant 1070 (named after its postal code) is tucked away on a cobbled backstreet in the 7th District. This bistro, set in a quaint, cozy old townhouse, serves Mediterranean and Austrian recipes with a modern twist. All the dishes are prepared fresh daily from seasonal ingredients. Don't expect a menu: the default is three courses, but the food is so good most people ask for a fourth. The experience is slightly theatrical without being pretentious. There are only around eight tables inside, with limited outdoor seating, so make sure you book ahead (the online form on the website makes this easy). Let the server know if you have any dietary requirements, and they'll take care of the rest.

Brunch
FIGAR

Kirchengasse 18, www.figar.net, Mon-Fri
8am-10:30pm, Sat-Sun 9am-4pm, mains €10-15

This hot little brunch spot decorated with street art is popular with young 20-somethings. You can get filling breakfasts of sausages, eggs, vegetables and cold cuts, as well as lighter options like muesli and yogurt until 2pm. You can also grab lunch items like burgers and salads, and even lamb fillets or grilled salmon. Come in the evening for a different vibe, when it goes from being a breakfast bar to a craft cocktail bar (or come back in the morning to cure your hangover with the Working Class Hero Breakfast, with baked beans, mushrooms, mini *Käsekrainer*—sausages filled with cheese—spinach, and roasted cherry tomatoes).

SNEAK IN

Siebensterngasse 12, www.sneakin.at, Tue-Thu 10am-midnight, Fri-Sat 10am-6pm, brunch €18

If you want an Instagrammable brunch, Sneak In offers spectacular brunches in building that serves as a bar, café and sneaker store with a gallery. It's popular with trendy young locals living in the area who come for the ambience. The food is served up on wooden boards. Brunch menus include a hot beverage and a buffet, where you'll find salads, cold cuts, cheeses, various breads and tasty dips. If you plan on coming on a weekend, make sure you reserve your spot!

Vegetarian, Vegan, and Gluten-Free
TIAN BISTRO

Schrankgasse 4, tel. 01/890-466-532, www.tian-bistro.com, Mon-Fri 11:30am-10pm, Sat and Sun 9am-10pm courses €10-18

Tian Bistro (the less expensive sister restaurant of fine dining spot Tian) serves delicious vegan and vegetarian dishes, both indoors and on a spacious patio (weather permitting). Breakfast is served until 2pm on the weekends. Try the savory TIAN Raphaello, a creative dish made from white polenta, or their vegan tarte flambée.

AROUND NASCHTMARKT AND KARLSPLATZ
Austrian
CAFE IMPERIAL

Kärntner Ring 16, tel. 01/501-10389, www. café-imperial.at, daily 7am-11pm, mains €18-30

Cafe Imperial, first opened in 1873, can be found on the ground floor of the grand hotel of the same name, boasts a guestbook of illustrious guests like Sigmund Freud, Gustav Mahler, and Stefan Zweig. It's elegant and modern with contemporary chandeliers and plush velvet booths. Despite being set inside a hotel, its sumptuous buffet champagne breakfasts (€41), and other meals are open to non-hotel guests. The chefs here cook up Austrian classics like Wiener Schnitzel (some argue it's the best in the city). And don't miss the house cake (the Imperial Torte), made with layers of marzipan and chocolate. If you're a fan of dark chocolate, they also have a wonderful chocolate orange version.

International
NENI AM NASCHMARKT

Naschmarkt 510, tel. 01/585-2020, https://neni.at, Mon-Sat 8am-11pm, mains €12.50-18

You'll find NENI by the cheese mongers and the baklava stand in the heart of the Naschmarkt. This industrial-looking restaurant dishes out delicious and nutritious breakfasts, tasty Middle Eastern specials like shakshuka and hummus, along with creative dishes like spicy caramelized eggplant or the Israeli dessert Knafeh, a sweet pastry filled with cheese. Afternoons and evenings are packed, especially if there's a DJ—so it's smart to book in advance. It's also worth coming in the morning when things are quiet: Order the avocado breakfast toast served on sourdough bread, topped with pickled carrots and served with hard-boiled organic eggs.

SAID THE BUTCHER TO THE COW

Opernring 11, tel. 01/535-69696, http://butcher-cow. at, Tue-Sat 5pm-11pm mains €11-32

If you're craving a burger, head over to this joint, where the burgers live up to the hype. Served with brioche buns, you'll find innovative options such as grilled octopus tentacles, or chicken teriyaki with mango chutney. Vegetarians should try the marinated halloumi burger or the black bean burger. You can also get great steaks, and there is a gin bar with over 30 varieties, plus a selection of tonics. For something different, try the saffron gin.

VIENNA FOOD

Fine Dining
OPUS
Kärntner Ring 16, tel. 01/501-10389,
www.restaurant-opus.at, daily 6pm-11pm,
4 to 6 course tasting menus €69-120
This cozy Michelin-starred restaurant is hidden inside the Hotel Imperial behind the Cafe Imperial. The decor dates back to the 1930s and is decorated with restored furniture and elaborately paneled walls—and with a wide choice of tasting menus and main courses it's an experience. All dishes are inspired by Austrian cuisine and have a modern and playful take. (There is a vegetarian tasting menu available.) Dishes vary by season, but can include razor clam with fennel, sirloin of dry-aged beef with polenta and porcini mushrooms, or zucchini blossoms with artichoke and red pepper.

Cafés and Cakes
CAFÉ SACHER
Philharmoniker-straße 4, tel. 01/514-561-053,
www.sacher.com, daily 8am-midnight, original
Sachertorte €7
Try Vienna's most famous cake in its namesake café—but you may have to queue to get in at peak times or book a table on certain day for breakfast via the website. The café has an imperial feel, with red damask fabrics on the walls and white wood paneling, marble tables, and plush burgundy carpets.

The Sacher cake is a dark chocolate, layered cake with a glazing of apricot in the middle, topped with chocolate fondant icing. It is best served with a *Melange* to cut the sweetness.

The café may not be the least expensive place to try the Sacher cake, but considering the recipe is tightly guarded by the hotel (having been passed down through the Sacher family), it's worth it. If you can't get into the original café, head to the other side of the hotel to the Sacher Eck, another café located within the hotel, where you'll find a shop selling the cakes and a more modern café.

★ VOLLPENSION
Schleifmühlgasse 16, tel. 01/585-0464,
www.vollpension.wien/, Mon-Sat 9am-10pm,
Sun 9am-8pm, mains €6.20-8.90
This cozy café is welcoming, with bare brick walls adorned with family portraits, and old, mismatched armchairs. The coffee shop is open to everyone. And here, young people and senior citizens working side-by-side. Vollpension serves home cooking and cakes made with love. The menu changes regularly. (Soups, stews and sandwiches are among the staples.)

Head up to the counter to place your order, and the food will be delivered to your table. Try the cakes of the day (there are over 200 in this establishment's repertoire). Your options include everything from classic carrot cakes to strudels. You can also get a great breakfast here with cold cuts, cheese and rolls.

EIS GREISSLER
Mariahilferstraße 33, www.eis-greissler.at,
daily 11am-10pm, scoop €1.50
Just look for the queue to find this ice cream parlor. When the sun comes out, locals line up to try Els Greissler's ice cream, made from organic milk, cream and yogurt from its very own farm in nearby Lower Austria. (You can also get vegan friendly scoops made from oat or soy milk.) The flavors come and go seasonally, and it's worth popping in and seeing what's on offer the day you decide to go—chocolate, butter caramel, strawberry, raspberry, or pear.

BELVEDERE PALACE AREA
Austrian
GASTHAUS WILD
Radetzkyplatz 1, tel. 01/920-9477,
http://gasthaus-wild.at, Mon-Fri 9am-1am Sun
9am-midnight, mains €11-27.50
Hundred-year-old Gasthaus Wild rebranded itself in 2002 as a modern *Beisl*, offering a new take of the classic Viennese inn. It still looks like a traditional *Beisl*, with the trademark

dark wood interior you'll find in inns across the city, but Viennese dishes are served with Mediterranean touches and updated recipes. You'll find the usual suspects, like Schnitzel and *Tafelspitz*, but also a range of vegetarian dishes, like mushroom paprikash with dumplings or a couscous vegetable cheese bake with lemongrass sauce.

GMOAKELLER
Am Heumarkt 25, tel. 01/712-5310, www.gmoakeller. at, Mon-Sat 11am-midnight, mains €9-18

If you want a taste of authentic local cuisine Gmoakeller is a good choice. Brick vaults, parquet floors, and wooden panels lining the walls give it a cozy, feel, but it's the food that's worth the visit. They've been cooking up Austrian specials since 1858. Try the *Zwiebelrostbraten*, a Viennese dish made with roast beef, topped with onions, and served with potatoes, or the roasted or baked veal with parsley potatoes or mayonnaise salad. Above all, make sure you try the crisp and aromatic Austrian wines on the menu, like the red Zweigelt or the white Viennese cuvee, the Gemischter Satz.

Bistros
LINGENHEL
Landstraßer Hauptstraße 74, tel. 01/710-1566, www. lingenhel.com, Mon-Sat 8am-10pm, mains €20-25

This deli-bar-restaurant that also houses a shop has taken over a manor house dating back to 1795 and brings in the crowd for the cheeses produced in their own dairy, along with fine wines and salami cold cuts. Asides from picks of deli cuts, this restaurant with whitewashed walls also serves gourmet dishes, like gazpacho with avocado cream or burrata with passionfruit. You can also simply pop in before dinner for an aperitif with a glass of the house vermouth. But if you love cheese, this establishment worth the detour. Sample the buffalo mozzarella if you can, or try to get into one of their cheese-making workshops.

JOSEPH BROT
Landstraßer Hauptstraße 4, www.joseph.co.at/d, Mon-Fri 8am-9pm, Sat-Sun 8am-6pm, mains €13-18

Joseph Brot is one of the best bakers in Vienna, baking creative loaves (like rye-honey-lavender or olive and tomato ciabatta). This bistro is ideal for a hearty breakfast, but you can also get smoothies, tea and coffee, and pastries to die for. The breakfast menu is diverse, with items like eggs benedict, and options like whole grain bread with avocado cream and chia pudding. Later in the day, you can get seasonal bistro dishes, including soups, salads, quinoa bowls or a classic burger.

Fine Dining
STEIRERECK IM STADTPARK
Am Heumarkt 2a, tel. 01/713-3168, http://steirerek. at, Mon-Fri 11:30am-2:30pm and 6:30pm-midnight, mains €50-55, 6 or 7 course menus, €142/152

Set in a former 20th century dairy in the elegant Stadtpark, Steirereck im Stadtpark has two Michelin stars. You really need to try the tasting menus here to get the full experience. Menus vary with the season, and they also get creative with international flavors. For example, you can try reinanke with coconut, fennel pollen and sorrel, or pigs trotter with wild chervil, woodruff and black carraway. Do save space for the cheese plate and tempting desserts. You can opt to add in wine pairing for €79-89. Reservations are a must.

Cafés and Cakes
★ KONDITOREI OBERLAA AT THE ZENTRALFRIEDHOF
Wiener Zentralfriedhof, Simmeringer Hauptstraße 234, tel. 01/767-1768, www.oberlaa-wien.at, daily 8am-6:30pm, cakes €3.80-4.10

Oberlaa is one of the best-known confectionery and cake shops in Vienna, and is now a chain with multiple locations across the city.

This branch is perhaps the most surreal and Viennese—it's located inside the gates of Vienna's Central Cemetery. Once you're done with the Funeral Museum or wandering the graves, you can come back to this large, grand café (whose terrace is packed in the summer with visitors to the cemetery) and savor one of their many cakes. You can try the house cake, the Oberlaa Kurbad Torte—made with layers of spongy nut-based dough and chocolate mousse, covered with a nougat glaze. (For those with gluten allergies, Oberlaa carries plenty of gluten-free alternatives.)

PRATER AND AROUND THE DANUBE

Austrian

SCHWEIZERHAUS

Prater 116, tel. 01/728-01520, www.schweizerhaus.at, Mar-Oct daily 11am-11pm, mains €3.80-4.10

This huge beer garden at the heart of the Prater is the perfect place to fuel up after the carnival rides. The specialty here is the pork knuckle, but there are other great local delicacies, such as the fried cheese with lingonberry jam.

The beer here is also great, with a selection of draft and bottled beers from Austria and Bavaria, as well as a gluten-free option from Salzburg. With over 2,100 seats, Schweizerhaus is vast. Take a seat and let your server take care of the rest.

LUSTHAUS

Freudenau 254, tel. 01/728-9565, Mon-Fri midday-10pm, Sat-Sun midday-6pm, shortened hours in the winter, mains €11-20

Head deep into the more rural part of the Prater to find this 16th century hunting lodge, which hosted Habsburg imperial festivities in the 18th century and now houses an Austrian restaurant that captures the old-world feel of the Prater. Try the Schnitzel or other Viennese classics such as the apricot dumplings. The Lusthaus is far southwest, deep in the Unterer Prater, and you can either get here by bus, take the 77A from the Donaumarina U-Bahn stop, or stop by if you find yourself cycling or hiking down this part of the Prater.

International

SKOPIK & LOHN

Leopoldsgasse 17, tel. 01/219-8977, www. skopikundlohn.at, Tue-Sat 6pm-1am, mains €13-27

The culinary focus here is to blend French dishes with a Mediterranean accent. The menu stars creations like pasta leaves with monkish ragout and truffle, or corn-fed chicken served with pickled grapes, cranberry jus, and black salsify. Apart from the experimental cuisine, in the main indoor dining area, globe lights hang from the ceiling—which is decorated with abstract ink-like markings. You'll also find a space with red walls covered with sculptures of flying geese, making this an adventurous and modern dining experience.

ROLLERCOASTER RESTAURANT

Riesenradplatz 6/1, tel. 06/60-244-3823, www.rollercoaster.rest, Mon-Thu 5pm-10pm, Fri-Sat 11:30am-10pm, mains €10-15

Continue the amusement park festivities at the Rollercoaster Restaurant in the heart of the Prater. (The restaurant has its own small-scale rattling rollercoaster to go with the flashing lights and the techno soundtrack!) Order your food from a menu on a touchpad tablet, and it will come sealed, sliding down (on rails) to your table. Cocktails are mixed by robots, then delivered by rollercoaster (drink containers are strapped down, so they won't go flying). The food here is typical burgers, pasta, or salad, but this is more a place for a fun experience.

Fine Dining

MRAZ & SOHN

Wallensteinstraße 59, tel. 01/330-4594, www.mraz-sohn.at, Mon-Fri 7pm-midnight, 12 course menus €140

A restaurant with two Michelin stars, Mraz & Sohn stays true to its family-owned roots. Chef Markus Mraz is the creative brains behind the kitchen, with innovative combinations, like razor clams with elderflower sauerkraut, wild asparagus with umeboshi, or venison with shiso. The food here is inspired by fusion, with exotic ingredients thrown into the mix. The wine here is excellent, and comes from small-scale wineries where the wines are handmade. You can add a wine pairing for €85.

Vegetarian, Vegan, and Gluten-Free

HARVEST
Karmeliterplatz 1, tel. 06/76-492-7790, www.harvest-bistrot.at, Wed-Sun 10am-midnight, mains €10-15

Offering vegan and vegetarian dishes, Harvest is a cozy place with a quirky living-room feel. Mismatched furniture and soft lighting contribute to the ambience, and in the summer you can sit out on the terrace. The menu changes on a daily basis and keeps up with the season, but you can expect creations such as vegetable curries, and homemade vegan cakes, along with freshly roasted coffee. On the weekend, there is an all vegan brunch served until 4pm.

ALSERGRUND AND JOSEFSTADT

Austrian
★ CAFÉ HUMMEL
Josefstädter straße 66, tel. 01/405-5314, http://caféhummel.at, Mon-Fri 7am-midnight, Sat-Sun 8am-midnight, mains €10-20

This Viennese café-restaurant has classic café ambience without the tourist crowd. Their fried chicken (*Backhendl*) comes with a vinegary potato salad (don't forget to ask for a side of lingonberry (*Preiselbeeren*) jam as an accompaniment). You can also get other Austrian dishes, like schnitzel and Austrian goulash. Give their homemade cakes a try if you can. This is also a great place to pop in for breakfast, which is served until 2pm.

SCHNATTL
Lange Gasse 40, tel. 01/405-3400, www.schnattl. com, Mon-Thu 11:30am-5pm, Fri 11:30am-midnight, mains €25-30

Open only on weekdays, this restaurant pulls in the local artists living in Josefstadt, and

you can expect to see them hanging out in the warm, inviting space full of tables with white tablecloths, or in the courtyard. Dishes are cooked on a seasonal basis. You can see specials like pumpkin and black chanterelle risotto in the fall, or brown trout fillet with lemon cucumber gnocchi in the summer.

GASTHAUS WICKERL
Porzellangasse 24a, tel. 01/317-7489, www.wickerl. at, Mon-Sat 10:30am-11:30pm, Sun 11am-11pm, mains €10-20

This *Beisl* captures the Viennese tavern tradition without the kitsch. This traditional small tavern welcomes guests with a seasonal menu of Austrian specials, like *Spargel* (white asparagus) in the spring and pumpkin goulash in the fall, as well as the universal favorites like *Tafelspitz* and Schnitzel. This *Beisl* is popular—it gets packed with locals around mealtimes. Pack your phrasebook to make communicating with the staff easier.

ZATTL WIRTSHAUS AND BEER GARDEN
Freyung 6, tel. 01/533-7262, www.zattl.at, Mon-Thu 10am-1am, Fri-Sat 10am-2am, Sun 10am-10pm mains €11-18

This Austrian restaurant and beer garden is best enjoyed in the summer, when you can sit out in the leafy courtyard with one of the traditional Czech or Bavarian beers they have on tap and try some good Austrian food. The Schnitzels here are massive! But you can also try the *Tafelspitz* (boiled beef), the fried chicken, or the meatless *käsespätzle*, dumplings cooked with cheese. In the winter or if it's raining, there is a huge indoor section with wooden benches and a nice cellar. The space is huge, so you really don't need a booking.

International
MAMAMON
Albertgasse 15, tel. 01/942-3155, www. mamamonthaikitchen.com, Mon-Fri 11:30am-9:30pm, Sat midday-9:30pm, mains €7-10

Locals love Mamamon for its authentic Southeast Asian street food, like fish cakes with chili peanut sauce, crisp, fresh papaya salad, and of course, sticky rice. This friendly venue is often extremely busy, especially in the summer when the courtyard opens. The menu is seasonal and packed with stir fries, curries and snacks. On Friday, the focus is on fish— arrive early if you want to try it.

WIENER DEEWAN

Liechtensteinstraße 11, tel. 01/925-1185, www.deewan. at, Mon-Sat 11am-11pm, pay what you can

Wiener Deewan is popular with students, and with good reason. This Pakistani restaurant cooks up three vegetarian and three meat dishes per day, plus one dessert, and is set up like an "eat as much as you like" buffet. There is a great spirit of generosity here: there are no fixed prices, instead you pay what you feel the meal is worth. Please be aware that the proprietors don't like food being wasted, so try to only take what you feel you can actually eat. Please note that this restaurant is cash only.

Brunch
AN-DO

Brunnenmarkt Stand 169, tel. 01/308-7575, www. caféando.at, Mon-Sat 8am-midnight, mains €7-15

You can find all kinds of trendy restaurants around the Brunnenmarkt, a lively open-air market with 170 stalls, just outside the Josefstadt in the 16th district, but AN-DO stands out for its breakfasts, which are served until 4pm. You can get traditional Austrian breakfasts with rolls, boiled egg, coffee and jam, but there are more adventurous dishes like halloumi cheese served with runny eggs and guacamole or more Mediterranean-inspired choices with feta, olives and hummus.

Street Food
SOUPKULTUR

Wipplingerstraße 32, www.soupkultur.at, Mon-Thu 11:30am-3:30pm, Fri 11:30am-3pm soups €2.50-5

Get some soup to take away from this small, chic, hole-in-the-wall venue, like Hungarian goulash or spicy red lentil soup. You can also

pick up salads and other snacks, and if you're lucky, you can grab one of the few seats at the counter. Soupkultur uses organic produce and spices to create a unique and different menu each week. If you want something tasty on the go, this is a good place to stop.

SUPPENWIRTSCHAFT

Servitengasse 6, www.suppenwirtschaft.at, Mon-Fri 11:30am-6pm, soups and snacks €5-7

This dine-in and takeaway venue focuses on soups, salads, and a few curries that alternate on a weekly menu. All the ingredients are carefully picked out from the Naschmarkt, so you can eat good food on a budget—especially if you go between 5 and 6pm when prices are slashed in half. This is a great option if you're traveling on a budget.

SCHÖNBRUNN PALACE AND GROUNDS
Austrian
QUELL

Raindorfgasse 19, tel. 01/893-2407, www. gasthausquell.at, Mon-Fri 11am-midnight, mains €7-15

Quell captures the feel of a traditional *Beisl,* an Austrian tavern with ceramic stoves and wooden chandeliers. Regulars pack the place around lunch, and the Viennese menu comes with all the usual suspects like Schnitzel and Goulash soup; however, there are also meat-free alternatives and fish dishes.

MAXING STÜBERL

Maxingstraße 7, www.maxingstueberl.business. site, Mon-Thu 5pm-10pm, Fri 11am-midnight, Sat 11am-2am, Sun 11am-midnight, mains €10-20

You can't get more Viennese than a former haunt of Johann Strauss. Maxing Stüberl prepares Austrian dishes with a gourmet twist, using local produce from the owner's home region. In the evening, you can dine by candlelight, and if there's live music, you may be serenaded. Try some local specials like the fried blood sausage with sauerkraut, or curd dumplings accompanied by stewed berries. However, do note that service is slow and not a place to head to if you're in a hurry.

BRANDAUERS SCHLOSSBRÄU

Am Platz 5, tel. 01/879-5970, www.bierig.at,
daily 10am-1am, mains €10-20

This microbrewery not only sells great house brews and specialty beers—it also serves a menu of tasty Austrian food. Expect heavy meat dishes like spare ribs with potatoes on the side, goulash stews, Schnitzel, and also vegetarian dishes. Come for lunch, when you can get a buffet on a budget for €10 between 11:30am-3pm on weekdays. When the sun comes out, head to the courtyard.

Cafés and Cakes
WALDEMAR-TAGESBAR

Altgasse 6, tel. 06/643-616127, www.
waldemar-tagesbar.at, Mon-Fri 7:30am-8pm,
Sat-Sun 9am-8pm, mains €5-10

Drop in to Waldemar-Tagesbar to grab breakfast, a light lunch or a sandwich to go. Breakfast lasts until 3pm, and there are daily lunch specials with a seasonal slant, like curries or quinoa bowls for dine-in or takeout. The space is modern and clean, the coffee is good.

PURE LIVING BAKERY

Altgasse 12, www.purelivingbakery.com,
daily 9am-9pm, snacks €5-11

Offering a laid-back atmosphere, especially in the summer when you can camp out in the colorful deckchairs in the garden, this little café was inspired by the owner's time in the States. Inside, wicker chairs and surf boards rest against coffee sacks, inviting you to come and relax over a cup of coffee or a toasted bagel topped with avocado and salmon. Grab a smoothie, or even better, try one of the fresh, home-baked pies, cookies and cakes. You can also find veggie-friendly and gluten-free options on the menu.

Accommodations

When it comes to picking a neighborhood to stay in Vienna, if you want to be within walking distance from the main sights and classic Viennese cafés, you can't go wrong with the Historic Center or the Hofburg area—but staying in this area does come at a price. Budget-conscious travelers can do better by booking a hotel or a hostel in the outer neighborhoods, like Alsergrund, or around the Prater. Nightlife lovers may prefer to stay in Josefstadt close to the Gürtel (although this area may feel a little seedy once the sun goes down).

Foodies may want to book something close to the Naschmarkt to pick up fresh produce, or dine out in one of the many restaurants near or along the market. And art lovers may want to camp out in Neubau, within easy reach of the MuseumsQuartier and the Kunsthistorisches Museum. Each neighborhood in Vienna has its own character and price tag, so where to book ultimately depends on your budget and needs.

HISTORIC CENTER AND HOFBURG AREA
€150-250
HOLLMANN BELETAGE

Köllnerhofgasse 6, tel. 01/961-1960,
www.hollmann-beletage.at, €160-250 d

There are only 25 rooms in this downtown design boutique hotel, but staying here means only a two-minute walk from St. Stephen's Cathedral. The decor with classic yet comfortable furniture manages to be modern yet cozy at the same time. Guests can use the terrace and the lounge, and free snacks are offered around 2pm. A delicious buffet breakfast is included in the price, which goes on until 11:30am. As a great bonus, there is a small cinema in the hotel, and you can also request a free iPad to use for the duration of your stay.

HOTEL CAPRICORNO

Schwedenplatz 3-4, tel. 01/533-31040, www.
schick-hotels.com/hotel-capricorno/, €150-200 d

The Hotel Capricorno stands by the Danube

Canal in the old inner city. Inside, it's a burst of color and modern design. There are 42 rooms, with some overlooking the canal, others the quiet courtyard (some room have balconies) and there's a delicious buffet breakfast included in the price. If you're arriving or leaving by air, an airport shuttle is available upon request for €45-50.

PERTSCHY PALAIS HOTEL

Habsburgergasse 5, tel. 01/534-49,
www.pertschy.com, €145-210 d

Get the Hofburg experience by staying in an 18th century palace just minutes away from the Habsburg imperial monuments. The hotel's 55 rooms maintain an old world feel with white silk wallpaper, red damask curtains, and baroque-style furniture, while still sporting a modern look. The price includes a lavish Viennese buffet breakfast with a substantial selection of organic produce.

Over €250

★ HOTEL LAMÉE

Rotenturmstraße 15, tel. 01/532-2240,
www.hotellamee.com, €170-280 d

Located between St. Stephen's Cathedral and the Danube Canal, the Lamée is centrally located. This boutique hotel with 32 rooms and suites evokes the feel of old Hollywood with dark paneling, and delicate gold and plush hot pink fabrics. Some rooms include spacious marble bathtubs. The buffet breakfast is extra (€21), with a wide selection of cold cuts, cheeses, smoked salmon, rolls and muesli. (It's possible to get a deal that includes breakfast when you book online, or directly through the hotel website.) The best part is the colorful rooftop bar with stunning views over the city. The hotel has its own vineyard, so make sure you try a bottle of house wine.

HOTEL TOPAZZ

Lichtensteig 3, tel. 01/532-2250,
www.hoteltopazz.com, €170-380 d

Opposite the Lamée, the Hotel Topazz blends early 20th century Jugendstil design with a modern look. There are 32 rooms in this luxury boutique hotel. The rooms have oval-shaped windows. Some rooms come with a small balcony. Breakfast is extra (€21) and is available at the sister Hotel Lamée across the street; however, the Topazz has its own salon, with coffee and tea available for guests.

DO&CO

Stephansplatz 12, tel. 01/241-88,
www.docohotel.com, €240-300 d

A five-star hotel in modern steel and glass, DO&CO stands just opposite St. Stephen's Cathedral in a building. The interior is luxuriously modern and clean, and the 43 rooms designed in warm, earthy colors. Some rooms have Jacuzzis, but all have a seating area with a mini bar and a state-of-the-art entertainment system with large flat-screen TVs and DVD players. Some views let you see the cathedral, others overlook the surrounding streets. Head up to the rooftop bar for drinks. Breakfast is extra at €35.

★ HOTEL SACHER

Philharmonikerstraße 4 tel. 01/514-560,
www.sacher.com, €400-600 d

The Hotel Sacher is a Viennese institution that is as much part of the city's history as the Staatsoper and the Hofburg. The iconic hotel lies just across the road from the opera house (request a room looking over the Staatsoper if you like). Stepping into the lobby is like being transported to another era. The hotel's 149 rooms and suites, however, are an eclectic mix of traditional Viennese and modern design—particularly the rooms on the top floors. There is a wonderful boutique spa on-site with saunas, steam and aroma rooms, and massages are available. The in-house Blue Bar, Red Bar, and Green Bar serve food and cocktails, and the famous Café Sacher is located here as well (guests get to skip the line). Breakfast (€41 extra) is a decadent spread that includes champagne, the famous Sachertorte, wonderful cheeses, and freshly prepared egg dishes.

★ THE GUESTHOUSE

Führichgasse 10, tel. 01/512-1320,
www.theguesthouse.at, €250-325 d

This boutique hotel has 39 rooms overlooking the Albertina. Most of the rooms offer window seats that give you both a view of the city square and a great place to catch up on some reading. The Guesthouse also provides a free wine bar in each room. Breakfast is a la carte, so it's not included in the price, but their breakfast is one of the most popular in the city, known for its bakery items and eggs benedict.

STEIGENBERGER HOTEL HERRENHOF

Herrengasse 10, tel. 01/534-4040, www.
steigenberger.com/en/hotels/all-hotels/austria/
vienna/steigenberger-hotel-herrenhof, €175-300 d

Only footsteps away from the Hofburg, the Steigenberger Hotel Herrenhof has a spacious 196 rooms decorated in a modern palette of white, eggplant and lime green. There is a wellness area in the hotel with a sauna and a steam room, as well as a fitness center. Buffet breakfast is extra at €30.

NEUBAU AND THE MUSEUMSQUARTIER

Under €150

HOTEL KUGEL

Siebensterngasse 43, tel. 01/523-3355,
www.hotelkugel.at, €110-130 d

Cozy, romantic and feminine, the Hotel Kugel is a family-owned hotel in the trendy Neubau district just 10 minutes' walking distance from the MuseumsQuartier. This boutique hotel has 25 rooms, each individually designed with different colors. Most of the rooms have a large canopy bed decked out in floral motifs, comfy pillows and cute vintage teddy bears. A buffet breakfast is included in the price, and offers the usual cheese, ham, bread, yogurt, and cereal selection, but what makes Kugel stand out is its selection of local produce, delicious jams, and local honey.

MYMOJOVIE

Kaiserstraße 77, tel. 06/765-511155,
www.mymojovie.at, €60-80 d

MyMOjOvie is not a conventional hotel, but rather a cluster of apartments, rooms and dorms, centered around self-catering kitchen units and lounges that allow you to immerse yourself in local life. It occupies an old, residential building that may seem a little shifty when you get in the cage-like lift to reach the top —But inside, it's a cute, design centric residence decorated with fairy lights and thoughtful accents. A simple breakfast of bread, jam and muesli is included. You can rent apartments for groups of up to six people or an en suite room for five, making it a good option for groups or families traveling together.

€150-250

25HOURS HOTEL BEIM MUSEUMSQUARTIER

Lerchenfelder straße 1-3, tel. 01/521-510,
www.25hours-hotels.com/hotels/wien/
museumsquartier, €105-190 d

Minutes from the trendy MuseumsQuartier, this hotel makes a great base to explore Vienna's museums, but you don't have to wait to go out the door for art. Stepping inside this 183-room and 34-suite hotel, you're treated to bold colors, murals and playful design mixed in with vintage finds. The hotel's highlight the rooftop terrace with views over the MuseumsQuartier, where you can order cocktails or Italian food. There is also a spa area, the Mermaid's Cave, with a sauna and relaxation area. The hotel also organizes bike tours and electric bike rentals.

Over €250

HOTEL SANS SOUCI

Burggasse 2, tel. 01/522-2520,
www.sanssouci-wien.com, €370-420 d

Hotel Sans Souci combines luxury with a central location near the city's museums. There is a spa as well as indoor pool. The 63 rooms are airy with large windows letting in a lot of

Hotel Orient

Discretion is the key at the Hotel Orient, a rent-by-the-hour hotel with a complex history.

The **Hotel Orient** (Tiefer Graben 30, tel. 01/533-7307, www.hotel-orient.at) has been a secret sanctuary for lovers since it opened in the 17th century, the street it's located on was not a street at all, but a side branch of the Danube Canal. This channel became a place where contraband—like spices, fabrics, and jewels—sailed up the Danube from the East and made its way into the heart of Vienna—which is how the hotel (which began life as a boatman's tavern) came to be called "The Orient." The hotel grew up into its current form in 1896, when discrete "rent by the hour" hotels, *Stundenhotels,* became popular with bourgeoisie looking for privacy. Most *Stundenhotels* became seedy places associated with prostitution from the 1960s, however, The Orient kept a classy touch.

There's usually a line of Mercedes and Porches parked outside The Hotel Orient, which still rents rooms on a three-hourly, or occasionally nightly, basis. This opulent hotel clad in crimson drapes, accented with hints of gold, gilded mirrors and baroque splendor has its regulars, but each visitor is a first timer the moment they step through the door.

Part of the Orient's charm is its discretion, but that doesn't mean that illustrious figures aren't known to have visited here, like the Emperor Franz Joseph I (without his wife Sisi) or more artistic figures like Orson Welles and Graham Greene. The hotel is walk-in. Aliases are not only acceptable, but encouraged. Stays are normally three hours (but you can extend your hours upon request). Breakfast is served all day. There are six suites, and each room has its own theme, from Habsburgesque opulence to 1,001 Nights.

Prices range €63 to €95 for three hours.

light. Purple accents dominate, and modern design is mixed with antique furniture and fine art. A sumptuous breakfast (included in the price) is served on the veranda with eggs benedict, freshly squeezed juices, and a buffet.

★ SCHREINERS ESSEN UND WOHNEN

Westbahnstraße 42, tel. 01/676-4754060, www.schreiners.cc/index_full.php, €240-360 d

Schreiners Essen und Wohnen is the ultimate urban sanctuary. The setting is reminiscent of a Biedermeier-era garden house, each spacious room in this hotel has its own balcony or terrace overlooking the lush, vine-covered grounds. The rooms have oak flooring, wood furniture and white walls, and comfy king-size beds. There is a Viennese restaurant on-site, but breakfast is included in the price, and served in the garden or in the breakfast room. It includes locally sourced produce, freshly baked bread, free-range eggs, natural fruit juices, and more.

AROUND NASCHMARKT AND KARLSPLATZ

€150-250

HOTEL DREI KRONEN

Schleifmühlgasse 25, tel. 01/587-3289, www.hotel3kronen.at, €125-200 d

Art nouveau lovers should book the Hotel Drei Kronen, set in a building constructed in 1897 in the Jugendstil style, right next to the Naschmarkt and the Secession. The building's highlights include the beautiful golden spiral staircase and art nouveau details, like the murals in the entrance. The historic hotel and its 41 rooms were renovated in 2008 and given a modern, comfortable style with pale hues splashed with accents of colors. An excellent Austrian buffet breakfast is included in the price.

Over €250

★ HOTEL IMPERIAL

Kärntner Ring 16, tel. 01/501-1100, www.imperialvienna.com, €300-500 d

Hotel Imperial towers over the Ringstraße. Inside, the hotel is opulent, with marble colonnades and staircases and silk-upholstered rooms. The guest book at this legendary five-star hotel is inscribed with the names of royalty and politicians. The Imperial was originally built as a palace in 1863 for the Prince of Württemberg, but became a hotel 10 years later. Some of the rooms overlook the Musikverein classical music hall; top floor rooms and suites look out onto the dome of the Karlskirche. If you want an extra dash of luxury, the Imperial also offers butler service. Breakfast is sometimes included in the price (depending on the package you book when reserving a hotel room online). See the website for current pricing.

HOTEL BRISTOL

Kärntner Ring 1, tel. 01/515-5160, www.bristolvienna.com, €350-550 d

The Hotel Bristol stands next to the Vienna State Opera and within walking distance of the main sites of the city. This luxury hotel opened in 1892 and has 126 rooms and 24

Deluxe room, Hotel Imperial, a Luxury Collection Hotel

suites. The styles of the rooms range from Biedermeier to Art Deco. Guests can use the business center and the in-house gym 24 hours a day. If you love food, this hotel offers plenty of local and international dishes to enjoy. The Bristol Bar is in the heart of the hotel, and is the oldest American-style bar in Vienna.

DAS TYROL

Mariahilferstraße 15, tel. 01/587-54150, www.das-tyrol.at, €230-300 d

Within Vienna's shopping artery, Das Tyrol is at the center of the action, and gives you convenient walking distance from the Naschmarkt and the MuseumsQuartier, as well as downtown happenings in Neubau. Renovated in 2018, this is a modern art hotel with 25 rooms and five studios, featuring original artwork and classic furniture from noted Viennese manufacturers like Thonet. Despite being a boutique hotel, Das Tyrol has a spa in on the premises, with a Finnish sauna and steam bath, plus a light therapy shower and relaxation areas. You can even rent out a private spa for yourself if you like. Luxurious breakfast spreads are extra and cost €20.

BELVEDERE PALACE AREA
Under €150
PENSION BOSCH

Keilgasse 13, tel. 01/798-6179, http:// hotelpensionbosch.com, €85-95 d

Pension Bosch occupies the first floor of a residential apartment block in a Jugendstil building. The interior is like a time capsule of art nouveau furniture and porcelain figurines. If you're looking for old, creaky charm, this hotel is for you. It's simple and comfortable.

Do note when booking that some of the rooms may have a shared bathroom in the lower price category.

A good buffet breakfast is included in the price, with fresh rolls, cheese and ham slices, jam, and of course, freshly brewed coffee and tea.

GRÄTZL HOTEL BELVEDERE

Central office at Favoritenstraße, tel. 01/208-3904, www.graetzlhotel.com/home/graetzl/belvedere, €105-130d

The Grätzl Hotel is actually a set of ground-floor suites throughout Vienna, occupying former shops which have been renovated by a group of young architects. There is a central office where you can leave luggage and have questions answered; there's also a help number 24/7 and daily room cleaning service. Breakfast is not included, but the staff is happy to give local recommendations. There are five suites around the Belvedere Palace, plus more in other neighborhoods, including Leopoldstadt, and close to Schönbrunn. Check-in is easy: Punch the code (provided in your booking email) into the key box outside your apartment to get your key.

€150-250
SPIESS & SPIESS

Hainburger straße, tel. 01/714-8505, www.spiess-vienna.at, €205-220 d

Travelers with allergies can be sure of a good night's sleep at Hotel Spiess & Spiess, which has been certified by the European Center for Allergy Research Foundation. This family-owned hotel close to the Danube Canal on a quiet backstreet offers guests elegant and crisp white rooms—some with balconies and fireplaces. Breakfast is included, and is a feast of high-quality, regionally produced organic products. Expect freshly squeezed orange juice, fresh bread and rolls, cold cuts, cheese spreads, jams, fresh fruit and yogurt, and more.

PRATER AND AROUND THE DANUBE
Under €150
★ MAGDAS

Laufbergergasse 12, tel. 01/720-0288, www.magdas-hotel.at, €80-122 d

Magdas is a hotel with a mission—begun by architect Johanna Aufner and the charity Caritas. This is Austria's first hotel operated by refugees (in conjunction with local tourism professionals). It opened in 2015 in a former Leopoldstadt retirement home. This boutique hotel is colorful and modern. Rooms are fitted with upcycled furniture, and some look out onto the famous Riesenrad in the nearby Prater. There is also a beautiful garden with rainbow-colored benches. There is also an open-air cinema, where movies are occasionally screened on summer nights. You can request a tablet for use for the duration of your stay, or you can rent a bicycle. Breakfast (an extra €14), is served in the Green Salon, and it includes fair trade organic coffee. If the weather is nice, you can take your breakfast in the garden.

Over €250
HOTEL IMLAUER WIEN
Rotensterngasse 10, tel. 01/211-400, https://imlauer.com, €315-330 d
Hotel Imlauer lies in a peaceful part of Leopoldstadt, close to the U-Bahn and 10 minutes away from the Riesenrad. This 4-star hotel has 117 en suite rooms decorated with earthy tones. Each room has a minibar, safe and a flat-screen satellite TV. A highlight of the hotel is the glass-covered conservatory, where you'll find a cocktail bar and a fitness center with a sauna. This is a good hotel if you want the comforts of a 4-star in a peaceful, yet central part of town. Breakfast is extra at €18.

ALSERGRUND AND JOSEFSTADT
Under €150
CORDIAL THEATERHOTEL WIEN
Josephstädter straße 22, tel. 01/405-3648, www.theaterhotel-wien.at/, €110-140 d
This hotel next to the famous German-language Theater in Josefstadt lies within walking distance from the Ringstraße. There are 54 comfortable and simply furnished rooms and suites, each with a flat-screen TV, radio, and minibar (some rooms come with a kitchenette). There is even a sauna, and massages are available on request. Underground

parking is available. It's great for the location, but without the premium prices you'd find across the Ringstraße.

€150-250
HOTEL RATHAUS WEIN & DESIGN
Lange Gasse 13, tel. 01/400-1122, www.hotel-rathaus-wien.at, €170-220 d
Wine lovers will love this hotel. Each of the 39 rooms in this old former residential building is dedicated to an Austrian winemaker. The bar here has over 450 Austrian wines, and some of which are available in the minibar in each room. The buffet breakfast, including regional specials like local cheeses, egg dishes and antipasti is an extra €18.

URBAN STAY HOTEL COLOMBIA
Kochgasse 9, tel. 01/405-6757, www.urban-stay.at/de/wien, €120-160 d
This family-run guest house occupies the ground and first floors in a 120-year-old residential building just behind the Town Hall. Its 10 rooms feature bright colors, cutting-edge design and a clean, modern feel. You won't have a minibar in your room, but there is a communal fridge in the public area with drinks for sale. Some prices include breakfast; otherwise the buffet breakfast from local producers and suppliers, like locally baked bread or homemade cakes and jams, costs €11.

SCHÖNBRUNN PALACE AND GROUNDS
Under €150
HOSTEL RUTHENSTEINER
Robert-Hamerlinggasse 24, tel. 01/893-4202, www.hostelruthensteiner.com, €62-80 d, €20-30 for dorms
The Hostel Ruthensteiner has been open since 1968, offering travelers a refuge in the city with art-covered common areas, garden spaces with large homemade wooden chess sets on the patio and even musical instruments for the impromptu jam. There is also a fully equipped kitchen for guests, and there are always friendly staff on hand to help with any inquiries you may have. Backpackers and

travelers love coming here for the community spirit. Minimum stay is two nights.

WOMBATS THE LOUNGE

Mariahilferstraße 137, tel. 01/897-2336, www. wombats-hostels.com/vienna/the-lounge/, €68-75 d, €25-30 for dorms

This popular hostel lies close to the Westbahnhof Train station on the trendy Mariahilferstraße. Dorms here are four to eight-person rooms, but private and double rooms are also available. Savvy backpackers, both younger and older, come to this rainbow-colored hostel for a sense of community and to do Vienna on a budget. The hostel offers a pool table and a bar on site to help you make some new friends. The company also has another hostel in the Naschmarkt area.

PENSION SCHÖNBRUNN

Schönbrunner Schloßstraße 30, tel. 01/815-50270, www.pension-schoenbrunn.at, €59-79 d

For something simple away from the hustle and bustle of the city center, this family-run 3-star bed and breakfast in an art nouveau building just next to Schönbrunn Palace is great for those looking for a break in Vienna and want to be close to green, lush parkland. Most rooms in this B&B face a quiet courtyard garden. Buffet breakfast is extra at €8. The rooms are minimalist, but comfortable, and the building is charming with art nouveau details, like the green wrought iron staircase.

HOTEL EKAZENT

Hietzinger Hauptstraße 22, tel. 01/877-7401, www. birghotels.com/hotel_ekazent, €80 d

For a hotel that meets your needs as a traveler and that's close to the Schönbrunn Palace and Palace Gardens, Hotel Ekazent does the job on a budget. You'll find this hotel on the top floors of a shopping center, but the views from the terrace over the hills and the Vienna Woods make you forget you're staying in a shopping center. In minutes from the hotel, you're in the park or at the Hietzing U-Bahn station with connections to the city center. There are 40 en suite bedrooms and they are simple, classic rooms. Buffet breakfast is extra at €8.

Information and Services

TOURIST INFORMATION

Vienna's main tourist information office can be found in Albertinaplatz. **Tourist Info Wien** (Albertinaplatz 1, tel. 01/245-55, www. wien.info, daily 9am-7pm) can help you get oriented and organize tickets for sites and shows, get your plan set up with maps, and they can also help with hotel booking. Their website has every single piece of information you need on Vienna—what to see, where to eat and stay, and you'll find topical articles about events in the city.

Other information offices around Vienna include the **Airport Information Center** (7am - 10pm) located within the airport, with full tourist information services. This is also a place where you can get hotel booking and a Vienna City Card. Just look for the information center when you get to the arrival hall.

You can also find help at the City Hall, via the **Rathaus Information Office** (Rathaus, Friedrich-Schmidt-Platz 1, tel. 01/525-50, www.wien.gv.at, Mon-Fri 8am-6pm). You can get information on events around the city here, like cultural events, and information that's both useful for tourists and locals.

BUSINESS HOURS

Count on the shops being closed on a Sunday or public holidays in Vienna. However, if you urgently need supplies, the main railway stations, the airport and museum shops are usually open.

EMERGENCY NUMBERS

The emergency number in Austria is **112**, and it's also possible to call this number without a SIM card. Operators speak English. If you need an ambulance, called **144;** the fire brigade, **122;** or the police, **133**. There is also a 24-hour English speaking medical hotline, **ViennaMed**: 01/513-9595, and an emergency drugstore—dial **1455**.

CRIME

Vienna has been ranked as one of the world's safest cities, but as with any unfamiliar city, it's best to exercise caution. Take care of valuables in large, busy public spaces or on public transport.

HOSPITALS AND PHARMACIES

Vienna has a range of hospitals all across the city, the largest being the **Vienna General Hospital** (Währinger Gürtel 18-20, tel. 01/404-000, www.akhwien.at), with more than 1,900 beds. There are also a number of English-speaking clinics, like the **Ambulatorium Augarten** (Untere Augartenstraße 1-3, tel. 01/330-3468, www.ambulatorium.com).

There are pharmacies all over Vienna. In German, the word you're looking for is *apotheke*. Be careful not to confuse this with *drogerie*, which may sound like drugstore but actually stocks shampoos and toiletries. Most pharmacies are open during shop hours, but Vienna's pharmacies take turns opening at night or on the weekends. You can find a list posted outside each pharmacy for the week, marking the closest one open.

FOREIGN CONSULATES

If you have an emergency, like losing your passport, or if you need consular help, you can head over to the **United States Embassy** (Boltzmanngasse 16 tel. 01/313-390) which is located in Alsergrund (9th District). The **Canadian Embassy** (Laurenzerberg 2, tel.01/531-383-000) can be found in the Inner City; the **British Embassy** (Jauresgasse 12, tel. 01/716-130) is next to the Belvedere Palace; and the South African Embassy (Sandgasse 33, tel. 01/320-6493) is outside the center in the 19th district. You can find the **Australian** (Mattiellistraße 2-4, Vienna, tel. +43-1-506-740) and **New Zealand Embassy** (Mattiellistraße 2-4, Vienna, tel. +43-1-505-3021) in Vienna as well.

Transportation

GETTING THERE
Air

Vienna International Airport (VIE, tel. 01/700-722-233, www.viennaairport.com) is 10 miles southwest of the city center. There are four terminal buildings, 1, 1A, 2, and 3, and two runways.

Flights between Budapest and Vienna take 45 minutes and between Prague and Vienna 1 hour (but once you factor in the time to check in, getting to the airport and so on, you're better off taking the train). **Austrian Airlines** (www.austrian.com) does connect Vienna with both cities.

AIRPORT TRANSPORTATION

From the airport, it's easy to get to Vienna on public transit. The most direct option is the **City Airport Train** (CAT, www.cityairporttrain.com, €11 one way, €19 return valid for 6 months). This brings you into the Wien Mitte train station. It takes 16 minutes, and runs every half hour from 6am to 11:30pm daily (from the airport to Wien Mitte) and from 5:30am to 11pm (from Wien Mitte to the airport). Select airlines allow you to check in your luggage at the train station, so you don't have to worry about getting the suitcases on and off the train.

Another option is to take the ÖBB Raijet (www.oebb.at) from the Flughafen Wien Bahnhof (the airport train station) to Wien Hauptbahnhof (the city's main train station). From Wien Hauptbahnhof, it takes 15 minutes and costs €4.10 to get to the city center. You can get tickets from the ticket counter or from the ÖBB (Austrian Federal Railways) ticket terminals in the train stations. If you're using this option to get back to the airport, make sure you get on the right train at Hauptbahnhof—often the airport train splits here with one side going onto Budapest or another city.

Vienna Airport Lines (www. viennaairportlines.at/en/) runs direct buses from the airport to various spots in Vienna (€8, 20 minutes to the city center). Buy tickets from the driver, from the ticket machines near the stop, or online (if buying online, show your ticket on your phone via the app).

Taxis to and from the airport cost €25-50 and take 20-30 minutes to reach the city center. As you come out of Arrivals, the yellow **Taxi 40100** (tel. 01/401-00, www.taxi40100. at) offers a fixed rate of €36, or you can go with the **C&K Airport Service** (tel. 01/444-44, www.cundk.at); you can find their desk at arrivals.

Train

Vienna has four train stations. **Wien Hauptbahnhof** (Main Train Station) the **Wien Meidling, Westbahnhof,** and **Wien Mitte.** All four train stations are close to the city center and are connected via the U-Bahn, tram and bus lines. Most international departures go from Wien Hauptbahnhof (some pass through Meidling as well).

From Prague: Trains run by **Ceske Drahy** (www.cd.cz), **Regiojet** (www.regiojet. com) or **Leo Express** (www.leoexpress.com/ en) depart for Vienna (Wien) from Hlavní nádraží every 1-2 hours from about 6am to 7pm with a few late night options until midnight. The journey takes about 4 hours during the day and about 8-10 hours for an overnight

train. Prices range roughly 650-1,200 CZK on different carriers and direct trains or transfers.

From Budapest: Trains run from Budapest Keleti to Vienna every one to two hours (2.5-3 hours, €13-30/4225-9750 HUF). Trains are operated by multiple companies, like **ÖBB Railjet** (www.oebb.at), but you can buy tickets on both the ÖBB Railjet website, or the **MÁV website** (www.mavcsoport.hu— but note that international tickets bought here must be printed out at one of the ticket machines and you will only find in one of the main Hungarian train stations, such as Budapest Keleti or Nyugati).

One thing to note is that not all trains going to Vienna are going to be the same. ÖBB Railjet trains begin in Budapest Keleti and usually depart on time, and will go onto further destinations like Munich or Zurich, but there are also trains coming from Romania, Záhony (which begins in Hungary just across the Ukrainian border but connects with passengers coming on the train from Kiev), and Serbia. A word of caution about the train coming from Belgrade (Serbia) is it can be up to an hour late as it is coming from outside the EU and gets held up at customs.

Bus

If you're coming to Vienna by bus from another country, you'll arrive at the **Vienna International Bus Terminal** (Erdbergstraße 200A, www.vib-wien.at, U Erdberg). You can reach the city center by U-Bahn (U3 to Stephansplatz) in under 10 minutes. **Eurolines** (tel. 09/001-28712, www.eurolines. at) has routes to Vienna from all over Europe, including Budapest and Prague.

From Prague: Buses from Prague Florenc to Vienna (Wien) depart almost every hour between 5am-8pm with a few late-night options closer to midnight. The journey takes about 5 to 6 hours and ranges from 350-550 CZK with different carriers, like **Eurolines** (www.eurolines.eu) and **FlixBus** (www. flixbus.com).

From Budapest: FlixBus in collaboration with the domestic **Volánbusz** company (http://nemzetkozi.volanbusz.hu/en/) has several buses per day, once an hour or more, (3 hours, €9-14/2925-4550 HUF).

Car

Driving to Austria is easy, as there are well-maintained highways in the country and the surrounding region. There are over 20 highways in Austria alone.

Note that all highways, *Autobahn*, require a vignette or a toll. Display your highway vignette (toll sticker, www.asfinag.at/toll/vignette/, €9 for 10 days) as you enter Austria—or if you have a digital sticker, this is tied to your number plate. You can either buy these online or at borders, gas stations, or post offices. Rental agencies may also be able organize a sticker for you.

From Budapest: Drive 150 miles northwest on the M1 and A4 highways to reach Vienna (tolls apply, in addition for the Hungarian motorway vignette, which is HUF 3000, you'll also need the Austrian one, which costs €9 for a 10-day sticker). The drive takes around 2.5 hours.

From Prague: If you're driving from Prague, you'll drive 200 miles for 3.5 hours. You need to head south on the E50 towards Brno, and then take the E461 towards the Austrian border and then the A5 to Vienna. There are tolls on parts of the route (CZK 350 in the Czech Republic for 10-day stickers).

GETTING AROUND

Vienna is quite spread out, but it has impeccable public transport which makes it easy and quick to get around. The public transport network, run by **Wiener Linien** (www.wienerlinien.at), includes the U-Bahn (subway), trams, S-bahn (suburban railway), and buses. Buses take you more into the suburban parts of the city, which is useful if you're going off the beaten track a bit, but in general you're more likely to use the U-Bahn or the tram to get around. The S-Bahn is useful to get between stations like the Hauptbahnhof, Praterstern, Wien Mitte, and Wien Meidling. You can also take it for daytrip destinations, like Mödling.

Transit Passes

Buy transit passes at the red kiosks in the metro, from ticket offices in the main metro stations, or any of the city's tobacconists. You can even buy tickets online (shop.wienerlinien.at) or via an app. Passes can come in 24 hours (€8), 48 hours (€14.10), or 72 hours (€17.10) and are valid on all forms of public transport. Single tickets cost €2.40—valid on all forms of transport, including changes, but only for uninterrupted journeys. Make sure you validate your tickets and passes when you enter the U-Bahn (these are boxes as you enter the subway), or on the tram or bus on your first journey.

U-Bahn

Vienna has five subway lines, known as the U-Bahn (short for *Untergrundbahn*—underground train) and lines are denoted by numbers and colors. Although these mostly run underground, sometimes they cross bridges, raised platforms, or just run along open "ditches" below the city. The **red U1 line** runs from Orberlaa to Leopoldau, crossing the city center before heading out to Leopoldstadt, the Danube Island and the Old Danube. The **purple U2 line** begins in Karlsplatz, goes under the MuseumsQuartier and under the Ringstraße before crossing the Danube Canal and the Danube. The **orange U3 line** runs from Simmering in the south of the city to the Ottakering, also going under the inner city. The **green U4 line** is one of the most beautiful (it's one of the famous train lines built by Otto Wagner). It goes from Heiligenstadt in the north down to Karlsplatz and Schönbrunn, all the way to Hütteldorf. The **brown U6** from Floridsdorf near the New Danube skims the city center over the arches of the Gürtel to Siebenhirten. And what about U5? This missing subway was planned in the 1960s, but never actually got built.

You can change between U-Bahn lines at various locations, the busiest being **Karlsplatz** (U1, U2, U4). The U-Bahn runs between 5am and midnight on weekdays, but goes all night on Fridays, Saturdays and days before national holidays.

Tram and Bus

There are 29 tram lines and 127 bus lines. Between 12:30am and 5am, 24 of these routes become night lines. The tram is an easy way of getting around the city, and you can even ride around the Ringstraße by combining tram lines 1 and 2, changing at the Oper, Burgring or Volkstheater stops. You can buy tickets from the bus or tram driver.

Taxi

Vienna has a few taxi companies you can call on, like **Taxi 60160** (tel. 01/60-160), **Taxi 40100** (tel. 01/40-100), **Taxi 31300** (tel. 01/31-300), or you can use an app like **mytaxi**.

Car

Vienna is an easy city to get around on foot or on public transport, but should you want to head out into the countryside, it may be worth renting a car. Your best bet is to rent cars from international rental companies such as **Hertz** (tel. 01/795-32; for local reservations, www.hertz.at). There are other options with Sixt (tel. 01/505-264000, www.sixt.at) and **Avis** (tel. 01/402-5592, www.avis.com/en/locations/at/vienna). Avis also has a rental office at the airport.

Day Trips from Vienna

Austria is not a big country, which makes it easy to explore in a few day trips from Vienna, whether you take a quick jaunt into the Vienna Woods or a longer trip out to Salzburg.

Day trips near Vienna include hiking trails through the Vienna Woods and vineyards, or a slightly longer excursion to the Wachau Valley. The Danube cuts through this valley, and on a boat trip you'll be surrounded by vine-clad hills topped with ruined castles and baroque monasteries.

Some travelers want to throw in another country into their travels, which is why the day trip to Bratislava is so popular. The small Slovak capital is only an hour away, which is why many just hop on the train and cross the border for the day—or take scenic route by catamaran.

Despite being on the other side of Austria, Salzburg is still one of

Highlights

Look for ★ to find recommended sights, activities, dining, and lodging.

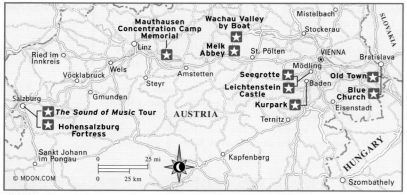

© MOON.COM

★ **Liechtenstein Castle:** This spectacular Medieval bastion perched up in the hills is outside Vienna. The castle is packed with historic details and offers sweeping views over the Vienna Woods (page 290).

★ **Seegrotte:** Tour this former gypsum mine along with a boat ride across the largest subterranean lake in Europe (page 290).

★ **Kurpark:** Monuments to composers decorate this charming park in the Vienna Woods town of Baden bei Wien (page 295).

★ **Melk Abbey:** Look out over the Danube from the impressive terrace of this tangerine-colored abbey (page 297).

★ **Wachau Valley by Boat:** The banks of the Danube in the Wachau Valley are lined with vineyards and castles that are best viewed by boat (page 298).

★ **Mauthausen Concentration Camp Memorial:** This former concentration camp is a moving and poignant reminder of the horrors of the Holocaust (page 304).

★ **Hohensalzburg Fortress:** This 11th century fortress in Salzburg, one of Europe's largest fortifications, offers impressive views from its free viewing terrace. There is also a cluster of museums within the fortress (page 306).

★ *The Sound of Music* **Tour:** Ride a bus to famous locations from the movie, including locations in the stunning countryside surrounding Salzburg (page 309).

★ **Old Town Bratislava:** The historic center of Slovakia's capital includes historic buildings as well as tempting cafes and quirky design shops (page 311).

★ **Blue Church:** Hungarian architect Ödön Lechner designed this stunning art nouveau church in Bratislava in no less than fifty shades of blue (page 312).

Austria's most popular destinations outside Vienna, with its dramatic Alpine landscape, striking castles, connections to Mozart, and, of course, being the home of *The Sound of Music.*

PLANNING YOUR TIME

When it comes to choosing a day trip, think about the time you're prepared to travel, the time of year, and what you're interested in. Most destinations can be visited year-round, but if you want to take a boat down the Wachau Valley, this only runs from April to October, so take seasonality into account.

If you don't want to spend a whole day away from Vienna, exploring the countryside around Mödling or Baden bei Wien, towns set in the hills of the Vienna Woods, is a good option, and can be reached in 20-30 minutes by train.

One of the most popular trips is nearby Wachau Valley, where boat rides down the Danube are popular. Melk is a good starting place along the River Danube, and reachable on a one-hour train ride from Vienna. From Melk, you can cruise down to Krems on a boat or bike, then take the train back to Vienna from Krems in the evening.

Bratislava, the capital of Slovakia is just an hour away by train—or take scenic route by catamaran. A more somber day trip option that's just over an hour away by train is the poignant Mauthausen Concentration Camp. Mauthausen is best experienced as part of a tour, but it can also be done solo.

Salzburg, known for Mozart and *The Sound of Music,* is 2.5 hours from Vienna by train. Salzburg can be done in a day, but you may want take an overnight trip to get the most out of it.

Vienna Woods

The Vienna Woods (*Wienerwald* in German) lie on the western edge the Austrian capital, stretching beyond the city limits into Lower Austria, covering an area of about 1350 square kilometers (520 square miles). The northern part of the Vienna Woods skirting the suburbs of the Austrian Capital is densely packed with stretches of oak and beech trees punctuated by grassy meadows and vineyards, whereas evergreens and pine trees dominate the southern part around Mödling and Baden bei Wien. This branch of the woods making up the foothills of the Alps is not only popular for hiking, but is also designated as a Biosphere Reserve by UNESCO and home to 2,000 plant species and 150 bird species—including the nearly extinct Ural Owl.

Getting to the Vienna Woods is easy by public transport. You can go as part of a day trip to areas in Lower Austria, such as Mödling, around the Castle Liechtenstein. Or another memorable option is to take one of the many hiking trails in the city.

AROUND MÖDLING

Mödling (pop. 20,500) is a charming historic town with tight streets among its thick-stoned medieval buildings. Mödling backs on to the hills of the Vienna Woods, packed with castle ruins and hidden caves. Most come to visit Liechtenstein Castle, a spectacular medieval bastion perched up in the hills, or the Hinterbrühl Seegrotte, the largest subterranean lake in Europe.

Sights

Mödling is pleasant enough, but many come here to visit the sights that surround it. Of the sights below, Thonetschössl is located in

---

Previous: Bratislava Castle; Hauptplatz in Baden bei Wien, Schönbühel Castle seen from Wachau Valley river cruise.

Day Trips from Vienna

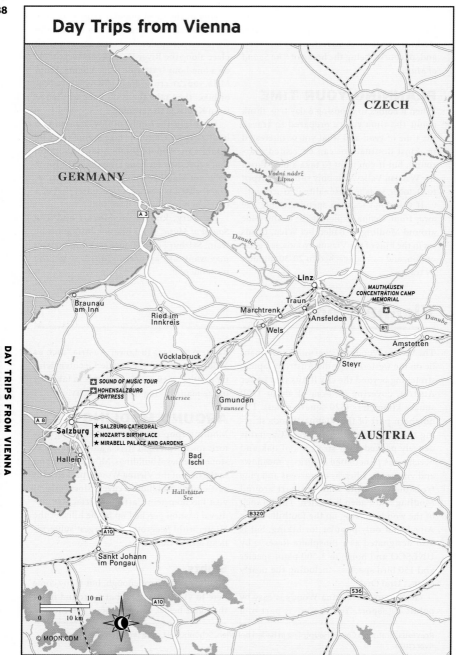

CZECH

GERMANY

Vodní nádrž
Lipno

A 3

Danube

Linz

MAUTHAUSEN
CONCENTRATION CAMP
MEMORIAL

Braunau
am Inn

Ried im
Innkreis

Marchtrenk

Traun

Ansfelden

Danube

Wels

B1

Amstetten

Vöcklabruck

Steyr

⊞ SOUND OF MUSIC TOUR
⊞ HOHENSALZBURG
   FORTRESS

Attersee

Gmunden
Traunsee

A 8

AUSTRIA

Salzburg

★ SALZBURG CATHEDRAL
★ MOZART'S BIRTHPLACE
★ MIRABELL PALACE AND GARDENS

Hallein

Bad
Ischl

Hallstätter
See

B320

A10

S36

0   10 mi

0   10 km

A10

© MOON.COM

Sankt Johann
im Pongau

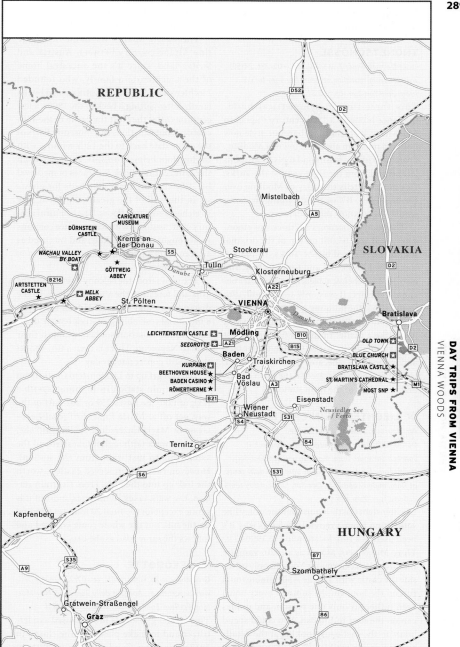

Mödling; the other sights are located outside the historic town.

THONETSCHÖSSL

Josef Deutsch-Platz 2, Mödling, tel. +02/236-24159,
www.museum-moedling.at, Mon-Thu 9am-1pm, Sat
10am-2pm Sun 2pm-6pm, € 3

This three-floored symmetrical building, once home to a 17th-century Capuchin Monastery, influenced by baroque style now houses a museum about the town of Mödling. From prehistoric fossils and tools to weapons left behind from the fight against the Turks, this museum tells the story of Mödling over the centuries. It's worth dropping in if you would like to know the town more.

The building occupies a 17th-century monastery that was rebuilt on top of the original building destroyed by the Turks. In 1686, it was turned into a silk and towel factory, and also used for chemical bleaching, and later became a theater. It was only in the mid-19th century that the building got its current look, when Countess Eise von Salm rebuilt it to look more like a castle. In the 1880s, the Thonet family bought the castle (hence the name), and in the 1930s it became the town museum.

The museum is located in the town center, and very close to the train station.

★ LIECHTENSTEIN CASTLE

Am Hausberg 2, Maria Enzersdorf tel.
06/50-680-3901, www.burgliechtenstein.eu/,
Jan-Feb Sat tours 11am, Mar-Jun and Sep-Oct daily
10am-4pm, Jul-Aug daily 10am-5pm, Nov daily tours
at 11am, midday and 2pm, Dec Sat, Sun, holiday tours
midday, 1pm, 2pm, € 9

Liechtenstein Castle looms over the valley like something from a movie—which is why it's been used as a film location in the 1990s *The Three Musketeers,* as well as a 1970s vampire film from West Germany. You can go inside the castle with a guide—50-minute tours run on the hour (in the summer every hour) even if there is only one person, and guides can do the tour in English. You could spend hours in the castle just looking at the details and soaking in the history, so your guide has

quite the job to keep within the one hour time limit on this fascinating journey back in time.

The castle shares its name with the tiny Alpine country between Austria and Switzerland, since it's the ancestral home of the Liechtenstein family, who founded Liechtenstein. The castle is still owned by the family (after getting it back in the 1800s, a few centuries after they lost the castle in the 13th century), but functions as a museum. Parts of the castle date back to the 12th century, with the top floor being a romantic extension from the 19th century. Look for traces of medieval life, like the tiny niche-like beds for guests set in the wall of the great hall, which now stretches across two floors. The beautiful century staircase lined with Renaissance columns was brought over from Italy, and was used as a green-screen backing in one of the *Lord of the Rings* movies.

The views from the balcony stretch over the hills and forests of the Vienna Woods. In the distance you may spot the Hussar's Temple, a memorial resembling a Greek temple dedicated to the Austrian soldiers who lost their lives to Napoleon. There is even a tiny chapel that is still consecrated today.

You can get up to Lichtenstein Castle from Mödling train station in 10 minutes with a taxi, or take the buses 259 or 262 part of the way, get off at Maria Enzerdorf Josef-Leeb-Gasse or Maria Enzersdorf Siedlungsstraße, and then walk (although it takes around the same time to just walk from the station). However, the well-preserved castle is worth the trek up into the hills. From the train station, the walk takes 50 minutes, most of it is gentle except for the final 20 minutes winding up the hill, but the whole route is paved and follows the same road as the cars.

★ SEEGROTTE

Grutschgasse 2a, Hinterbrühl, tel. 02/236 26364,
www.seegrotte.at, Apr-Oct daily 9am-5pm, Nov-Mar
Mon-Fri 9am-3pm, Sat-Sun 9am-3:30pm, € 11

This former gypsum (a mineral used as a fertilizer and to make plaster) mine closed in 1912 after water flooded the mine with 20 million liters of water. Since the 1930s the underground lake has become a tourist attraction, and offers regular bilingual tours in German and English, which takes approximately an hour.

The tour takes you deep into the hill, around 550 meters (1,640 feet) down a brick clad tunnel past waxwork figures replicating daily scenes for the miners and horses that worked the gypsum mine 100 years ago. But the highlight is the lower chamber, which contains a lake lying around 60 meters (200 feet) underground. Beside the platform, an overwrought golden barge used in the 1990s film *The Three Musketeers* adds to the cave backdrop. You'll get in a boat with your guide and sail around the illuminated lake. Look down, you can see blocks of eroded gypsum beneath the clear water. After the tour, you have time to explore the rest of the mine and cave at your own pace, or if you've had enough of the cold you can just leave through the tunnel you came down.

Seegrotte is located in the village of Hinterbrühl, about a 20-minute walk from Lichtenstein Castle. As the temperature of the cave is 9°C (48 Fahrenheit) all year round, you will want to dress up warm, especially in the summer, but if you forget to pack a jacket in June, you can rent a blanket for a euro.

MÖDLING CASTLE RUINS

Jägerhausgasse 11, open all the time, free
The ruins of this 11th-century castle are worth the hike up into the hills—in fact, it's a popular hiking destination for locals. Much of the castle was damaged during the Turkish siege in 1529, and it was completely destroyed when it burned down after being struck by lightning 27 years later. The walls of the old castle still stand, but the whole sight is open to the elements. The best thing about the castle here is the romantic view through the ruins over to the woods and the hills surrounding the site.

From the train station in Mödling to the castle, it'll take you around 40 minutes to walk it, or 20 minutes walking if you come from the Seegrotte in Hinterbrühl.

Food

MAUT WIRTSHAUS

Kaiserin Elisabeth-Strasse 22, Mödling, tel.
02/236-24481, www.mauts.at, daily 10am-midnight
€8-16
Come for the good, home cooked Austrian food in this single story townhouse that opens onto a terrace in the summer. The menu is in German, but you can't go wrong with Schnitzel. For something different try the Tyrolean liver with bacon and apple (*Tiroler Leber mit Speck und Apfel*)! Note that some of the rooms indoors are smoking, so you may want to book for the non-smoking section. This restaurant is close to the station, which makes it a good pitstop before visiting Liechtenstein Castle or the Seegrotte.

PINO

Brühler Strasse 6, Mödling, tel 02/236-860187,
http://pino-ristorante.at, Mon-Sat 11:30am-2:30pm,
6pm-10:30pm €15-25
This restaurant follows the "Slow Food" movement with local, fresh, and seasonal ingredients used to make Italian classics. You'll find incredible pizzas and freshly made pastas as well as daily specials, fish, and meat dishes. Booking is highly recommended (in the summer try to get a seat on the leafy terrace). Take your time to dine here, as the food is slow cooked to perfection and you need time to savor. You will find this restaurant 15 minutes walking from the main train station.

EIS PETER

Hauptstrasse 17, Mödling tel. 02/236-865151, www.
eispeter.at, Mar-Sep daily 10am-10pm, €2 per scoop
This small ice cream parlor specializes in traditional gelato, you can try them served up in scoops to take on the go, but if you sit down try their creative sundaes named after Habsburg royals with imperial lashings of cream. In the summer, there is often a queue out the door made up of both visitors and locals eagerly waiting for a cone on the go—or a much coveted table. Being just a five-minute walk from the train station, you may want

1

2

to fuel up if you're planning to hike up to Liechtenstein Castle.

Getting There

From Vienna, train is the easiest way to get to Mödling. Bus tickets cost €4.60 one way—the same as the train—so unless you are near the bus station, it's easier and more comfortable to take the train.

TRAIN

There are frequent train connections from Vienna to Mödling, with local trains and suburban trains, both operated by **ÖBB Railjet** (www.oebb.at), running every 10 minutes from Wien Hauptbahnhof. You can take the regional trains, which take 20 minutes, or the S2 or S3 suburban trains (S-bahn) which take 25 minutes. These also stop in other parts of the city, like the Praterstern (30 minutes) or Wien Mitte (26 minutes). Tickets cost €4.60 one way.

Mödling's train station is located in the center of town.

BUS

From Vienna, a few buses also run to the train station in Mödling. Take the U6 to Siebenhirten, then take the bus 269 or 270 from there. The bus ride takes around half an hour.

Getting Around

You can get around Mödling easily on foot, but most of its famous attractions lie beyond walking distance outside the town, such as Liechtenstein Castle or the Seegrotte. You'll usually find a taxi just next to the train station, but you can also call **City Taxi Mödling** (tel. 02/236-29000) if there are no cabs parked outside. Fares to Liechtenstein Castle are around €12.50 and to the Seegrotte €13.50. Uber also works as far out as Mödling.

---

1 Lichtenstein Schloss, the ancestral home of the Lichtenstein family in Mödling **2** Baden bei Wien was loved by composer Beethoven, and in the Kurpark you can find a temple dedicated to him.

BADEN BEI WIEN

Set in the foothills around the Vienna Woods, Baden bei Wien (pop. 25,000) with its temple-dotted parkland, Biedermeier-era houses, repurposed neo-classical bathhouses, rose gardens, and of course, the thermal water, has been a popular place to escape for centuries. This classic Central European spa town captures a bygone era, and makes a pleasant day trip from Vienna for wellness lovers, or for anyone wanting to walk in the footsteps of Beethoven, who visited the town often for his health.

Baden bei Wien is half an hour by train from Vienna, but there is also an S-Bahn running from the Staatsoper taking an hour to get to town. However, if you want to get the full spa town experience, it's best to spend the night in one of the town's luxury hotels.

Sights
RÖMERTHERME

Brusattiplatz 4, Baden bei Wien, tel. 02/252-45030, www.roemertherme.at, daily 10am-10pm, 3-hour ticket weekdays €14.10, weekends €16.10

The alleged curative properties of its sulfur-rich water have made Baden bei Wien popular for centuries. If you stroll the town you'll spot various colonnaded buildings with the word "bad" in it, meaning bath, but only the Römertherme ("Roman Bath")—along with a smaller, more luxurious Turkish bath—operate today.

Although the original 19th century facade of this bath house still exists, most of the Römertherme lies inside a huge, modern glass covered complex where you can swim or relax in 900 square meters (9700 square feet) of pools. One of the small pools accessible through a water channel leading outside is filled with the thermal water, whereas the rest are Jacuzzis, whirlpools, pools with massage jets, and classic swimming pools. There is a separate section (€7.60 extra) for the saunas and steam baths, but note, you must go naked in this section and it's coed, so it may not be for everyone. You can rent towels and bath sheets at the cash desk, but you'd probably

Hiking in the Vienna Woods

Vienna has hiking trails going for more than 240 kilometers (150 miles), called the *Stadtwander-wege* (City Hiking Paths), most of which you can reach easily by public transport. Some of these trails wind through the **Vienna Woods,** which, despite the name, are not just stretches of wooded hills, but open meadows and vineyards add a little diversity to the landscape.

CITY HIKING PATH 1

One of the most famous trails, City Hiking Path 1, begins at the end of tram line D, at Nussdorf, which is a moderate 7-mile-long hike going through the Vienna Woods, trailing vineyards, past Danube beaches, and loops back to Nussdorf. This hike will take you around three to four hours. Restaurants and wineries—like the Heuriger Sirbu and the sister winery of **Mayer am Pfarrplatz** (Mayer am Nussberg, Kahlenberger straße 210 www.mayermnussberg.at)—dot the trail, so you can take this route at your leisure. At the top of Kahlenberg, you also have lunch options at the self-service **Café Kahlenberg** (Am Kahlenberg 3, www.kahlenberg.wien/cafekahlenberg/) and the more upscale **Skyline Restaurant Kahlenberg** (Am Kahlenberg 2-3, www.kahlenberg.wien), which you'll reach approximately half way along the trail.

COBENZL TO GRINZING

For a gentler walk through the vines, take the 38A bus from Wien Heiligenstadt to the end of the U4 line in Vienna and get off at Cobenzl Parkplatz, and wander down hill taking the Oberer Reisenbergweg—a paved road taking you right past the vineyards—for beautiful vine-clad views over the city, which will take you back to the picturesque suburb of Grinzing, with single-story baroque houses. From here you can take the 38A back to Heiligenstadt or the 38 tram which will take you back to Schottentor in the city center. This downhill walk is approximately 2.5 kilometers (1.5 miles).

want to bring your own bathers and shower slippers.

BADEN CASINO

Kaiser Franz-Ring 1, Baden bei Wien,

tel. 02/252-44496, www.casinos.at,

daily 3pm-3am, free entrance

Gambling and taking the waters often went hand in hand all across Central Europe's spa towns, and Baden bei Wien is no exception. This beautiful casino, built in the 1880s, on the site of an old bath house, is one of the big draws to the town, offering all the classic games from blackjack and roulette to slots and poker. There is a smart dress code, but if you pop in spontaneously you can rent a jacket from the casino. Admission is strictly from the age of 18, so make sure you bring ID with you. When you arrive, buy your chips at reception and hit the tables or the slots. There

is a fine dining restaurant on site, so you can dine before hitting the casino games.

BEETHOVEN HOUSE

Rathausgasse 10, Baden bei Wien,

tel. 02/252-868-00630, www.beethovenhaus-baden.

at, Tue-Sun 10am-6pm, €6

Beethoven came to Baden bei Wien frequently for his health and spent most of his time at this two-story town house in Rathausgasse at the center of the town. The composer even wrote part of the famous *9th Symphony* here. This small museum commemorates Beethoven's life and his compositions through eccentric curiosities, like his death mask, a wax or plaster cast made of a person's face just after they die, and a lock of hair behind a glass cabinet. Sit down at the listening stations to hear recordings of his most famous pieces upstairs in the museum. There is also a sound lab in the basement that explores Beethoven's deafness and how he composed using bone conduction. You can even try bone conduction for yourself by placing the specially made headphones against your temple, wrist, and other parts of your body to experience the *9th Symphony* and Beethoven's other works through vibration in place of sound.

Parks and Gardens
★ KURPARK

Kaiser Franz-Ring, Baden bei Wien, tel. 01/234-56789, always open, free

This charming park scaling up the hill is one of my favorite parts of Baden bei Wien. The garden was created in the 18th century to honor the Empress Maria Theresa, but its monuments are instead dedicated to composers, like the temple to Mozart and Beethoven. The best view point is from the Beethoven Temple, a neoclassical structure overlooking the town from the side of the hill. Make sure you look up at the allegorical frescoes under the dome. The scent of pines and flowers perfume the tree-clad gravel paths winding up the hillside. At the base of the Kurpark, close to the casino, there are plenty of benches for sunbathing, along with a small kiosk selling coffees and cakes. Deckchairs are nearby, too, that you can simply recline in to enjoy the sun. Make sure you also check out the beautiful art nouveau theater between the casino and the park. If you're lucky, you may even catch a concert on the bandstand.

DOBLHOFF PARK AND ROSARIUM

Doblhoffpark, Baden bei Wien, always open, free

Baden bei Wien is full of parkland, and if you head over to the other side of the town to the Doblhoff Park in June, prepare for a sensory overload when the 75,000-square-meter (90,000-square-yard) park is filled with 30,000 roses in bloom—and over 600 types. The centerpiece of the park is the baroque orangery, a house used to store citrus trees and other exotic plants in the winter built in the 18th century, making the perfect photo backdrop against the rose carpet. Even when the roses are not in bloom, the Doblhoff Park and the Rosarium are charming enough for a stroll. If you have time only for one, go for the Kurpark, especially if you come off season.

Food
BADENER ECK

Heiligenkreuzer Gasse 2, Baden bei Wien, tel. 02/252-86695, www.badener-eck.at, daily 10am-11pm, €9.50-20

This tavern just behind the Römertherme serves up all the Austrian specials, such as Schnitzel, Tafelspitz, and sausages at a good price. It's a simple restaurant with a retro look, as seen in its brown wooden panels and slightly yellowed walls. Locals pack the place at lunchtime, and dining here feels authentically Austrian. Just note that smoking is allowed indoors, which can inhibit your dining enjoyment.

EL GRECO

Theresiengasse 1, Baden bei Wien, tel. +02/252-253071, www.restaurantelgreco.at, daily 11am-3pm and 6pm-midnight, mains €9.50-20

You can spot this Greek restaurant from the outside easily by the classical-style statues in the doorway leading to the courtyard. The main restaurant lies in a basement decorated with Cretan paintings, Greek painted plates and small statues, and the menu has all the classics, including Meze plates with an assortment of stuffed vine leaves, Tzatziki and other cold starters, as well as cooked dishes like Moussaka, and Souvlaki. You can wash down all the freshly prepared Greek food with Ouzo, Retsina, or other Hellenic wines.

EL GAUCHO

Josefsplatz 2, Baden bei Wien, tel. 02/252-80399, www.elgaucho.at, Mon-Sat 11:30am-midnight, Sun 11:30am-11pm, mains €16-40

Housed in a former bath house that looks like a neoclassical temple, El Gaucho is a premium steak house inspired by Argentinian cuisine. The interior is modern and cozy, with leatherette booths and an open kitchen. Aside from delicious cuts of steak—including dry aged beef—you can find a mix of international fusion dishes such as grilled lamb chops, scallops, fish, and even burgers. The desserts are creative, especially the coconut cream sorbet with marinated pineapple, and if you're really feeling fancy go for the amazing cheese plate with a glass of tawny port. El Gaucho also has an excellent wine selection, and the Austrian wines served here are especially good.

CAFE CENTRAL

Hauptplatz 19, Baden bei Wien, tel. 06/80-2004508, http://cafe-central.at, daily 8am-8pm, cakes €3.70-5

Even when you're not in Vienna you can find a classic Viennese cafe. Cafe Central in Baden bei Wien is the ultimate people-watching spot, whether you grab a table on the plaza overlooking the town hall or sit inside besides one of the large windows or mirrored walls. This is a place where you can spend a good hour or two with a coffee or a cake—try the house cake the Cafe Central Torte made with white chocolate mousse and passion fruit.

CAFE KONDITOREI ULLMANN

Schlossergässchen 16, Baden bei Wien, tel. 02/252-48665, Thu-Tue 8am-6pm, cakes €3-5

Hidden at the end of a picturesque alley lined with shops and alternative therapy clinics close to the Rosarium, Cafe Konditorei Ullmann is like stepping back in time a century. This cafe with its white wood-paneled interior, portraits of Sisi, and dainty chandeliers has an old-world charm that adds to the flavor of the cakes. Try the cream cake with a *Melange* and just savor the experience. It's a little on the edge of town, but on the way to the Rosarium and the park if you find yourself heading this direction.

Accommodations

HOTEL ADMIRAL AM KURPARK

Renngasse 8, Baden bei Wien, tel. 02/252-86799, www.hotel-admiral.at, €125-150

Hotel Admiral has the best views in town, overlooking the casino and the Kurpark. Ideal for anyone wanting to spend the day strolling among the trees and hitting the roulette wheel at night. And if you don't want to trek out to the thermal bath, you can get some wellness treatments at the in-house sauna, steam bath, and sun bed. The rooms are modern and simple, with a palette of beiges, browns, and gold, with allergy tested bedding. A buffet breakfast spread is included in the price of the room. There are 22 rooms stretching over 3 floors.

HOTEL SCHLOSS WEIKERSDORF

Schloßgasse 9-11, Baden bei Wien, tel. +43 02/252-48301, www.hotelschlossweikersdorf.at, dd €95-150

This 4-star hotel in a restored Renaissance Castle overlooks the Rosarium. The hotel has 99 rooms and spreads out through the old part of the buildings and parts of the former converted stables, backing onto the ground of the Doblhoff Park. A buffet breakfast—included in the price—is served in the old part of the castle, and if the weather is good you can even sit out with a coffee and a croissant on the colonnaded terrace and watch the roses (whether in bloom or not). There is also a spa on site with a swimming pool and sauna, which offers massages and other treatments.

Getting There

All public transit options from Vienna to Baden bei Wien cost €5.80 one way. The train is the fastest option. The Badner Bahn long-distance tram takes longer but is convenient, as it drops you in the center of Baden bei Wien.

TRAIN

The fastest way to get to Baden bei Wien from Vienna is to take the local train (30 minutes) operated by **ÖBB Railjet** (www.oebb.at) from Wien Hauptbahnhof, which run at least every half an hour. There are also S-Bahn services that take longer (50 minutes), also running from Wien Hauptbahnhof once an hour from 5am to 1am, and will also drop you off at the Baden bei Wien Bahnhof. The train station in Baden is 10-15 minutes walking from town center. You can also get a taxi, which you will usually find parked outside the train station, or call **Funktaxi Baden** (tel. 02/252-88500). Taxis will cost around €7.50 for the 5-minute drive into town.

However, if you simply want to hop on a train from the city center, grab the Badner Bahn (WLB) a long-distance tram run by the Wiener Lokalbahnen (www.wlb.at) from next to the Staatsoper which will take you into the center of Baden bei Wien. These trains run every 15 minutes to half an hour from around 5:30am to 11:40pm. This takes just over an hour, but is more convenient when you add the time it takes to get to and from the main stations at each end.

BUS

Bus 360 goes from the Wien Oper stop next to the Staatsoper Baden bei Wien (40 minutes, €5.80 one way). These buses operated by **Wiener Lokalbahnen** (www.wlb.at) run once to twice an hour from 7am to 3am, and will take you into the city center to Josefplatz and the Bahnhof.

CAR

Baden bei Wien is a 40-minute drive from Vienna, and the best way to reach the town is to take the Süd Autobahn E59 southwards. Note that this road has tolls, so make sure your car has the correct vignette for Austria. If you rent a car in Austria, this should come with a vignette, but if you're bringing a rental car from abroad, like Hungary or Czech Republic, you may not have the appropriate vignette. Make sure to confirm with your rental company.

The Wachau Valley

The Danube River runs through the Wachau Valley and is lined with ruined castles, vineyards, and rolling hills, making it the perfect day trip from Vienna—especially if you choose to experience it by boat. The valley has been settled since prehistoric times and is immersed in ancient history. It's even the home of the Venus of Willendorf, a small statue dating back to 30,000 BC, which you can visit in the Naturhistorisches Museums—so plenty of stories and historic sites await, including the castle that imprisoned Richard the Lionheart and one of the most beautiful baroque abbeys in Europe.

The easiest way to reach the Wachau Valley from Vienna is by train to Melk or Krems, where you get on a boat to cruise down the Danube. If you're going from Melk to Krems, you'll pass the castle of Schönbühel perched on a rock recognizable from the single tower with the onion shaped dome in the top on the southern shore. Shortly after, you'll reach the town of Spitz, famed for its Gothic church and vineyards on the northern shore, and then you pass by Dürnstein, a spectacular small town with its pastel-blue abbey and ruined medieval castle, and then finally you will arrive at Krems an der Donau.

MELK AND VICINITY

Melk (pop. 5,300) is a pretty town with wood-beamed old houses lining cobbled streets looking like something you'd find on a confectionary box, but towering over the valley, it's the tangerine-colored abbey that dominates the town. You can spend a good three hours or more in Melk just exploring the abbey and the grounds with some time for lunch as well, so bear that in mind if you're planning on starting in Melk and then take the boat down the river.

Sights
★ MELK ABBEY

Abt-Berthold-Dietmayr-Straße 1, Melk, tel. 02/752 5550, www.stiftmelk.at, Apr-Oct 9am-5:30pm, Nov-Mar only with tours running 11am and 2pm, €11, €13 with the tour

Crowning the town of Melk in hues of oranges and yellow, Melk Abbey is one of the

Cruising Through the Wachau Valley

The best way to take in the Wachau Valley is by boat between the towns of Krems and Melk, but you can also take a bicycle and cycle along the river, or go by car and stop on the way.

There is also a bus running between Melk and Krems. **ÖBB Postbus** (www.oebb.at) goes once to twice an hour and takes just over an hour. Tickets cost €9.20.

★ BY BOAT

Brandner (www.brandner.at, Apr-Oct 10:10am and 15:40 Krems-Melk, 13:45 Melk-Krems, €25.50 one way) runs boats down the Danube daily from mid-April to the end of October. You can start from Krems or Melk (or any of the stops in between). The boat is very comfortable, with an indoor area plus an outdoor terrace that's nice and breezy on warm days. There is a restaurant and a bar on board, so all you just need to do is sit back and relax and watch the river go by. It's best to go out on the terrace rather than choosing a seat inside as you won't know which side to look as you sail past Schönbühel Castle, Spitz and Dürnstein on the way down the valley. A return ticket is only 4 euros more, and if you choose to return that way, just make sure you're on the other side of the boat for the trip back. It takes around an hour and a half downstream (from Melk to Krems), upstream (Krems to Melk) takes around 3 hours, stopping at Spitz, Weißenkirchen, Dürnstein en route. Ships have around 290 seats inside spread over two decks and 200 seats on the sun deck.

BY BIKE

Cycling down the Wachau Valley between Melk and Krems is one of the most popular activities in the region. The route runs for 24 miles and follows a relatively flat bike path, which even goes downhill if you're cycling in the direction of Melk to Krems.

First take the train to Melk, and pick up a bike to rent at the Nextbike (www.nextbike.at). Once you've got your bike, follow the signs marked "Donauradweg." (You can also find a map with bike trails here at www.donau-oesterreich.at). There are two bike paths, one on the north side of the river and another on the south. For the most scenic route, ride along the south for around one and a half hours until you reach the cable ferry going across to Spitz (costs €1.80 per person and another €1.20 per bike and ferries go regularly upon request between 6.15am-6pm April to October). You can also take another cable ferry further along at Rossatz to Dürnstein (costs €2.70 per person and another €1.20 per bike, also goes on request, 9:30am-6pm daily May to September,

most spectacular sites along the Danube. Although the abbey was founded in the 11th century, it gets its current look from the 18th century and is a huge complex that's still in use as an abbey today. One part still houses a group of monks, another courtyard encloses a school, and another wing is the museum – which along with the church is the only part of the abbey open to the public. The museum presents the history of the abbey with an immersive mix of art installations and historic objects, such as an 11th century portable altar, books from the 16th century, and plenty of jewel-clad crosses, from the abbey's past. But the main highlight is the stunning terrace

overlooking the Danube, which leads into the equally beautiful library with 16,000 ancient books and its brightly colored ceiling frescoes. At midday, you can also see the monks perform the midday prayer in the golden baroque church—which usually coincides with the end of the morning guided tour. You can also visit the abbey gardens just behind the complex.

The Benedictine Abbey is a short hike from the train station and the boat dock, and worth the climb. In the summer, you can visit the museum on your own, but for only a couple of euros extra it's worth taking the guided tour running at 10:55am and 2:55pm.

Danube river boat

and on Friday-Sun 10am-5pm April and October). From the north side continue cycling down to Krems. Riding without stopping will take you 3-4 hours, but if you want to sightsee and have lunch, budget around 7-8 hours. You can just deposit the bike at the Nextbike station next to the train station in Krems. You can take the train directly back to Vienna from Krems.

BY CAR

The drive from Melk to Krems takes around 35-40 minutes and will take you along the northern banks of the Danube through the picturesque towns of Spitz and Dürnstein. From Melk take the Donaubrücke Melk across the river to Emmersdorf and turn onto the Donau Bundesstraße and continue northeast towards Krems following the river. This route will take you through Spitz and Dürnstein before you finally reach Krems.

ARTSTETTEN CASTLE

Schlossplatz 1, tel. 07/413-8006, www.schloss-artstetten.at, museum and family crypt Apr-Nov Tue-Sun 9am-5:30pm, castle nature park Apr-Nov Tue-Sun 9am-1:30pm, €8.30 for the museum, €3.50 castle nature park

If you're interested in the legacy of the crown prince Franz Ferdinand, who was assassinated in Sarajevo—the event that kick-started World War I—then you may find this castle, his former home, of interest. Set in an enchanting verdant parkland high up in the hills above the Danube, this seven-turreted castle that wouldn't be out of place in a fairytale is the resting place for Franz Ferdinand

and his wife. If you're interested in history, check out the museum in the castle about the crown prince and his family or simply just get a ticket to the lush gardens surrounding the historic castle.

If you're traveling the Wachau Valley by public transport, it may not be worth the trip to this castle, unless you have a fascination with the Habsburg family. Should you want to visit, the best way is to take the train from Melk to Pöchlarn Bahnhof (trains run once an hour and take 5 minutes, costs €2.30) and then take the bus NG1A to Artstetten Ortsmitte (going 8:40am, 11:40pm, 3:40pm on weekday, and there is also a bus at 5:40pm on weekends, taking 15 minutes and costs €2.30). However, if you are driving, it takes 20 minutes from Melk and is worth the detour then.

Bike Rentals
NEXTBIKE
www.nextbike.at

If you want to cycle down the Danube from Melk to Krems, the NextBike bike rental station right next to the railway station is the place get a bike. You just need to download the Nextbike app, register online, or call the hotline. Once you're registered via the app you will either get a bike number to enter on the back of the bike, or a QR code to scan on the bike, after which you will get a code via SMS to unlock it. To avoid using the app, call the hotline (02/742-229-901) to rent the bike, and receive the code via SMS. You can just deposit the bike at the Nextbike station next to the train station in Krems. The app and website will also show you other locations where you can rent bikes (there are other locations in Melk if you can't find any free bikes at the station). Hourly rental rates are €1, or you can rent a bike for 24 hours at €10.

Food
RATHAUSKELLER MELK
Rathausplatz 13, tel. 02/752 20460, www. rathauskeller-melk.at, daily 10am-11pm, mains €11-30

In the summer, this vaulted cellar in the center of Melk makes the perfect refuge from the heat—it's also quite cozy and warm in the winter. The menu serves all the usual Austrian favorites, from different types of Schnitzel to goulash stews with dumplings, but you can also get some vegetarian and vegan dishes. Central location, large portions and reasonable prices. You can also sit out in the streetside terrace if you prefer dining in the sun.

MADAR CAFE RESTAURANT ZUM FURSTEN
Rathausplatz 3, tel. 02/752-52343, www. kaffeehaustradition.at, daily 7am-11pm, mains €7-10

Despite its setting in a beautiful historic building on Rathausplatz, the prices at Madar cafe are budget friendly. You can spot this restaurant—which is more like a traditional inn with a few hotel rooms on hand too—as it presents the perfect photo op being set in a cute, 16th-century town house with a frescoed facade. It's not a place for fine dining, but the food here is cheap and cheerful, featuring pizzas and breaded meat dishes, but do stay for a coffee and a cake. Cakes are homemade and the coffee comes from the cafe's own roastery.

BACKEREI KONDITOREI MISTLBACHER
Hauptstrasse 1, tel. 02/752-52350, www.mistlbacher. com, Mon-Sat 7am-6pm, Sun 1pm-6pm, cakes €2.90-4

Grab a coffee and a cake at this traditional cafe at the foot of the Melk Abbey. This huge cafe complex occupies a townhouse, with an 80-seater garden, and also has two indoor areas split into smoking and non-smoking that can seat 50 guests each. Come for the homemade pastries and ice cream and try some of the local specials. Taste a slice of the Melker Torte, a rich cake made with almonds, dark chocolate, and a filling of apricot jam.

Getting There

The easiest way to reach the Wachau Valley from Vienna is by train served by **ÖBB Railjet** (www.oebb.at). The best option is to take a train to Melk from the Wien Westbahnhof (1 hour, €18.40). Trains are direct and run once an hour from 6:20am-1am.

To reach Melk by car from Vienna, take the A1 due west for approximately an hour.

DÜRNSTEIN CASTLE
Dürnstein, tel. 02/711-200, www.duernstein.at, open all the time, free

If you take the Danube boat cruise, you'll surely be tempted to disembark when you float by the picturesque town of Dürnstein, with its pastel blue abbey and ruined castle. If you do decide to take a detour in this beautiful river-side town, then take the steep but short 20-minute hike from the town center up to the 12th century ruined castle. The castle became famous because of Richard the Lionheart, the legendary English King who even gets a mention in the Robin Hood folklore. Local legend says the king was imprisoned in this very castle after he tore up the Austrian flag and refused to share his spoils of war. The castle is entirely ruined and exposed to the elements, so you won't find any museums here, but the ruins are romantic, and you can clamber around the walls to get a sense of the old castle that occupies 6.5 square miles. Although the castle is lit up at night, if you're planning to head there after dark take a flashlight as the paths are not well lit. It's worth the hike if you love history or simply want amazing views over the Danube from above.

Getting There

The **ÖBB Postbus** (www.oebb.at) that runs between Melk and Krems will also take you to Dürnstein (45 minutes, €8).

If you're driving from Melk, drive over the Danube taking the Donaubrücke Melk and take the road northeast in the direction of Krems. The drive will take around 30 minutes. Coming from Krems, it's only a 10-minute drive on the B3 road southwest to Dürnstein.

KREMS AN DER DONAU

Connected to Melk by boat, Krems (also known by its longer name Krems an der Donau) lies at the eastern stretch of the Wachau Valley. It's a large, historic town dotted with winding cobbled streets, modern art galleries, historic churches and wine bars, but is a little bit of a come down after Melk and Dürnstein. In the summer, it draws in crowds of tourists from the riverboats, along with and trendy arts crowds who come for avant-garde events. The best thing to do is when you get off the train or the boat in Krems is just wander around aimlessly (along the Danube, if you like), or grab a coffee in the historic streets. However, I would recommend spending time in Dürnstein or Melk more and just use Krems as a base to get the train back to Vienna.

Sights

KUNSTHALLE KREMS

Franz-Zeller-Platz 3, tel. 02/732-908-010,
www.kunsthalle.at, Tue-Sun 10am-6pm, €10

If you're interested in the contemporary art scene outside Vienna, then check out the Kunsthalle Krems. This art hall resides in a former tobacco factory built in the mid-19th century and functions as an exhibition space stretching over 1,400 square meters (15,000 square feet). Exhibitions here are temporary and feature art created after 1945 and showcase work from young Austrian artists as well as international ones. The Kunsthalle Krems curates exhibitions usually centered around a theme, like sculptures made out of paper or work by an artist in residence, covering all forms of artistic media, whether it's more traditional forms like painting or sculpture through to video, photography, performance arts and installations. Each April and May it is one of the hosts of the Donaufestival (www.donaufestival.at), a large contemporary art festival that lasts a couple of weeks.

FORUM FROHNER

Minoritenplatz 4, tel. 02/32-908-010,
www.forum-frohner.at, Tue-Sun 11am-5pm, €5

You'll find art lovers congregating at this art space housed inside a former Minorite Monastery. The Forum Frohner, named after artist Adolf Frohner, holds regular exhibitions and events, and you'll usually find hip young Austrians hanging around the cool stone corridors or in the white, cube-like exhibition space inside. Sometimes when there is an event on, or the Donaufestival is in full swing, you may find street food carts in the square outside selling craft beer and snacks, or a pop-up coffee bar inside. Exhibitions and events continually change, so you can either look at the program on the website (in German) or just pass by and see what's happening.

CARICATURE MUSEUM

Steiner Landstraße 3a, tel. 02/32-908-010,
www.karikaturmuseum.at, daily 10am-6pm €10

Krems is home to Austria's only museum

dedicated to Caricatures. The museum stretches over 780 square meters (8,400 square feet) over the three-story building (only the ground floor and the upper floor are open to the public) and is loyally dedicated to satirical art, comics, cartoons, and caricatures. The museum is split up into sections, mostly covering temporary exhibitions, with permanent collections including the IRONIMUS Cabinet on the ground floor with its collection of political caricatures and the upper floor with work by cartoonist Manfred Deix.

Food
2STEIN
Dr.-Karl-Dorrek-Straße 23, Krems an der Donau, tel. 02/732-71615, www.2stein.at, Mon 11am-midnight, Tue-Wed 8am-midnight, Thu-Sat 8am-1am, Sun 9am-10pm, mains €8-30

2STEIN is a restaurant with a modern edge and a varied menu, offering everything from dry aged steak to gourmet burgers and vegan dishes. Design lovers will adore 2STEIN with its glass conservatory, contemporary chandeliers and randomly placed bicycle parts that accent the walls. Many come for the gourmet burgers, which include those made with dry-aged beef, Wagyu beef, and also the veggie and vegan version, such as the Vegan Hero made with a brown rice, butternut squash, green bean and malazini pattie. Pastas, curries, and other international fusion favorites all make the menu. Reservations highly recommended.

MOYOME
Obere Landstrasse 10, Krems an der Donau, tel. 06/64-5144686, www.moyome.com, Mon-Fri 8am-7pm, Sat 8:30am-5pm, Sun 9am-5pm, dishes €5-9

This popular and cozy cafe spills out onto the street-side terrace in the summer. You'll find an extensive selection of all-day vegetarian and vegan breakfasts and dishes inspired by Middle Eastern and Asian cuisine.

---

1 Dürnstein Abbey in Wachau Valley **2** the historic town Krems an der Donau **3** town of Melk with the Melk Abbey above

Try one of their curries or their breakfast dishes. Most of the dishes on the menu are vegetarian or vegan—which are marked respectively—but there is the odd meat dish as well. Don't be shy about checking out their daily menu, which is very reasonably priced, so good for the budget traveler. Do order the coffee here, which comes from a local roastery in a nearby town.

Getting There
From Wien Franz-Josefs-Bahnhof, a train station in Alsergrund in the 9th District, you can take a train with **ÖBB Railjet** (www.oebb.at) to Krems an der Donau once an hour from 4:50am-10:50pm, which takes just over an hour, costing €18.40.

If you want to drive to Krems an der Donau from Vienna take the A22 north and then onto the S5 in the west direction. The drive will take around an hour.

GÖTTWEIG ABBEY
Stift Göttweig 1, Furth bei Göttweig, tel. 02/732-85581, www.stiftgoettweig.at, Mar-Nov 10am-6pm, €8

Rising above the river in the hills with maroon turrets, the Göttweig Abbey sits on a mountain side overlooking the surrounding vineyards of the Wachau Valley. It was founded in the 11th century, but like Melk, this Benedictine Abbey gets its look from the 18th century. It's worth the trip for the view across the surrounding valleys and the Imperial Staircase crowned with a ceiling fresco painted by Paul Troger with intense colors, Rococo drama, and cherub dotted blue skies. You can also shop for fruit brandy and other fruit products made by the monks from produce grown on the surrounding grounds.

Getting There
The easiest way to get to this working abbey is to take the bus WL4 to Göttweig from Krems, running every 3 hours from 7:20am to 4:20pm, taking 15 minutes and costs €2.30. This will take you up to the abbey. You can

also take a train to Furth bei Göttweig, which takes 6 minutes and goes once an hour (tickets €2.30), but you will need to hike up to the abbey a good 40 minutes.

Mauthausen

Just outside the city of Linz lies a small, sleepy village (pop 4,800) set up in the undulating hills overlooking the Danube with a dark history. Even as you take the wooded paths up the hill on the way to the Mauthausen Concentration Camp memorial, it's hard to imagine that thousands met their death here and in the neighboring village of Gusen under the Nazi regime. Many make the journey to Mauthausen alone or on a tour from Vienna, to remember those who were sent here.

★ MAUTHAUSEN CONCENTRATION CAMP MEMORIAL

Erinnerungsstraße 1, Mauthausen, tel. 07/238-22690, www.mauthausen-memorial.org, Mar-Oct daily 9am-5:30pm, Nov-Feb 9am-3:45pm, free

Mauthausen may not have an instantly recognizable name like Auschwitz, but a few hours at this former concentration camp will leave an impact. On first impression, it's a peaceful place with wonderful views stretching as far as the Alps on a clear day and bird song coming from the surrounding trees, but it's a haunting place where Jews, Roma, homosexuals, and political prisoners were imprisoned, worked to death, and following the 1940s, gassed.

Initially, Mauthausen was used as a labor camp for the nearby quarry, and only German and Austrian men were imprisoned here. The complex resembles a barracks when you walk through the towering brick gates with green-painted containers once crammed with prisoners living in squalor under unhygienic conditions. To get some context, head over to the Infirmary where a well-curated museum with personal artifacts, uniforms, documents, photographs, and footage narrates the story of the camp from 1938 to 1945. Afterwards,

The Mauthausen concentration camp is a poignant reminder of the horrors of the 20th century.

descend into the basement and head towards the Room of Names, a moving installation where the names of those sent to their death are inscribed on huge backlit blocks. There are a couple of tomes recording names and personal details—date of birth, hometown, date of death—in the room. The crematorium and the killing facilities in the adjacent room may distress you, as it did me, although nothing graphic is shown.

In July and August, English language tours run at 2pm lasting 2 hours for €5, no booking required. You can also get an audio guide for €3 from the information center at the entrance.

FOOD
MOSTSTUBE FRELLERHOF
Frellerhofweg 13, Mauthausen, tel. 07/238 2789, www.frellerhof.at, Tue-Fri 10am-3pm, Sat-Sun 11am-10pm, mains €10-20
Up on the hill, just a five-minute walk from the Mauthausen Memorial, Moststube Frellerhof has a wonderful garden and terrace in the summer, but also has a rustic indoor section if the weather is a bit off. Try their cold plates, with a selection of cheese, cured meats, and pickles, and if you're drinking, you'll want to try their homemade spirits!

GETTING THERE
Train and Bus
To get to Mauthausen, you first need to take the train with **ÖBB Railjet** (www.oebb.at) to Linz from Vienna (a little over an hour, €36.20 one way). Trains run 3 times an hour.

In Linz, change to the bus 361 run by **OÖVV** (www.ooevv.at) to Mauthausen Linzerstraße/Neue Mittelschule (40 minutes, €5.40 one way). These buses run from 10am from Linz Hauptbahnhof hourly on weekdays, and on even numbered hours on weekends.

From here, just follow the signposts up the hill to the Mauthausen Memorial, which takes an additional 20 minutes on foot.

Another option is to take another train from Linz to Mauthausen OÖ, costing €5.40 one way but note that direct trains are less frequent than the bus, with sometimes as much as a four-hour gap between trains, but you can also take the train and change at St. Valentin which go more frequently and costs the same. From the train station take a taxi the 4 kilometers (2.5 miles) to reach the memorial. There are three taxi firms in Mauthausen: **Taxi Brixner** (07/238-2439), **EasyCab** (06/64-57-12100), **4 You Taxi St. Georgen** (06/60-63-64-657).

Car
It's a two-hour drive from Vienna to Mauthausen. Take the A1 westwards in the direction of Linz. Once you reach St. Valentin take the B123, which will lead you over the Donaubrücke Mauthausen, and follow the signs to the town. You will need a vignette for Austria as the highways have tolls. There is a parking place at the memorial, which is free for four hours and then €2 per additional hour.

Tours
Vienna à la Carte (www.vienna-alacarte.com, duration of 8.5 hours, costing €148 per person) run group tour to Mauthausen three times a week from Vienna.

Salzburg

The hills are alive with the sound of music may sound cliché, but it rings true in Salzburg (pop. 150,000). Mozart's hometown as well as the setting for *The Sound of Music*, Salzburg carries plenty of musical cachet, and with its fortress perched up on the top of a rocky outcrop and the Alpine views surrounding the town, it's easy to see why it's one of the most visited places in Austria.

You can hop on a train in Vienna and be in Salzburg two and a half hours later, making it possible to do it as a day trip. However, to really appreciate everything Salzburg has to offer, it's ideal to spend a night or two.

SIGHTS
Salzburg Old Town

Salzburg Old Town spreads out on both sides of the River Salzach, over an area of 236 hectares (close to a square mile), and is a cocktail of Medieval and Baroque buildings. You could find your way to the Old Town just by looking out for the Hohensalzburg Fortress, which towers over the city at an altitude of 506 meters (1660 feet).

The whole Old Town is a UNESCO World Heritage Site, and when you stroll through the cobbled alleys and wander past its domed churches, through its open squares, it's easy to see why. The Old Town covers a large area on both sides of the river. On the south bank, it includes winding streets around the Cathedral, the Hohensalzburg fortress, and the hill running northward from the fortress. On the northern side of the river, the Old Town also stretches to the Capuchin Monastery and the Mirabell Palace and Gardens. But don't let all that history fool you into thinking this is a living museum—there are 2,500 stores and 300 restaurants perched inside the old town, not to mention the concerts, street festivals, and markets that add some color to the cobbled streets and open squares. The best thing to do is just wander,

whether it's exploring a church and the surrounding cemetery, exploring some of the shops set into narrow alleyways, or taking a stroll besides the river.

★ Hohensalzburg Fortress

Mönchsberg 34, Salzburg, www.salzburg-burgen.at, Jan-Apr and Oct-Dec daily 9:30am-5pm, May-Sep 9am-7pm, all-inclusive ticket €15.50

Crowning Salzburg from above, the 11th century Hohensalzburg Fortress is one of Europe's largest fortifications—and one of the most photogenic places in Central Europe. Hohensalzburg Fortress is striking from any view in the city, especially from afar on the pedestrianized love lock-covered Makartsteg Bridge or from Kapitalplatz, the square besides Salzburg Cathedral. But to experience it best you'll want to make it up to the top of the hill that it sits on, to visit the museums and wander the ramparts for a stunning panorama over the Alps and the city.

You can walk most of the castle grounds including the viewing terrace for free, but to go into the museums you'll need your ticket. There are also two restaurants and two souvenir shops within the complex. Expect to spend a good couple of hours up here going through the museums and enjoying the view.

GETTING TO THE FORTRESS

You have a couple options for getting there: You can hike up the 400-meter (1,300-feet) steep rocky outcrop from Kapitalplatz, which will take around 15 minutes. Take the cobbled streets up Festungsgasse until you reach Oskar-Kokoschka Weg and follow the sign posts to the top. Alternatively, if you get an all-inclusive ticket—just buy this at the entrance to the funicular on Festungsgasse—you can

---

1 Mozart's birthhouse is a big draw to Salzburg
2 old part of Bratislava with towers of the castle
3 The Hohensalzburg is the highlight of Salzburg.

hop on the funicular railway, which goes at the speed of a roller coaster up and down the steep 45-degree rail tracks, dropping you off right at the fortress entrance.

VIEWING TERRACE

Once you arrive at the viewing terrace, take in the amazing panoramas over the Alps in both Austria and across the border in Germany, as well as over rooftops and church domes down in the old city itself.

MUSEUMS

To head into the museums, follow the signs within the fortress. Most of the museums – the Castle Museum and the Rainer Regiment museum—occupy the Hoher Stock, the top floor of the Prince-Bishop's apartments in the inner courtyard.

The **Castle Museum** covers 1,000 years of the castle's history, leading you from its archaeological finds discovered in the area (a Roman fort stood here centuries before the current fortress) to the more than 900 years of history of the current castle. Highlights here are the brightly colored Gothic state rooms once belonging to the prince archbishop, which link to the Castle Museum.

The **Rainer Regiment Museum** on the military history of the imperial and royal infantry regiment also occupies nine rooms in the Hoher Stock, next to the Castle Museum.

The **Puppet Museum** (you'll find this on the northwest side of the fortress on the ground floor of the Hoher Stock building) and the observation tower (the west side of the castle), which will take you through the old torture chambers and includes an audio guide in the tour.

You can also visit the **Medieval Prince's Chambers** and the **Golden Hall**, which is worth the entrance fee, with its gold-speckled ceiling resembling a starry sky.

Mozart's Birthplace

Getreidegasse 9, tel. 06/62-844313,
www.mozarteum.at, daily 9am-5:30pm, €11
This canary-yellow five-story house where

Mozart was born is home to a museum dedicated to Mozart's life and the life of his family. Rooms are filled with portraits, personal artifacts—such as a lock of the composer's hair—and music scores. The museum, which spans across the three floors of the building, offers fascinating insight into the composer's early life in Salzburg before he went to Vienna to find glory. If you visit the Mozart House in Vienna, this is an interesting contrast. There is a strict no photography policy and the museum can get crowded. Expect to spend around an hour to an hour and a half here.

Mirabell Palace and Gardens

Mirabellplatz, Salzburg, tel. 06/62-80720,
daily 8am-6pm, free
Across the river from the Hohensalzburg Fortress, the flamboyant Mirabell Palace, built in 1606 by the reigning prince-archbishop Wolf Dietrich, is one of Salzburg's most popular sites. Aside from stunning views up to the castle from afar, the gardens are filled with roses, playful classical statues and atmospheric fountains. If you've seen *The Sound of Music,* these gardens will look familiar, especially the "Dwarf Garden" and the Pegasus fountain—all of which are featured in the "do-re-mi" song sequence. You can also go inside the palace for free to climb the cherub clad "Angel Staircase" and take a peek inside the Marble Hall, where Leopold Mozart and his children, including Wolfgang once played.

Salzburg Cathedral

Domplatz 1a, Salzburg, tel. 06/62-80477950,
www.salzburger-dom.at, Jan-Sat Mon-Sat 8am-5pm,
Sun 1pm-5pm, Mar-Apr and Oct Mon-Sat 8am-6pm,
Sun 1pm-6pm, May-Sep Mon-Sat 8pm-7pm, Sun
1pm-6pm, free
Salzburg Cathedral with its cupola and twin spires is as much part of Salzburg's cityscape as the fortress. Although today's cathedral dates back to the 16th century, you can find traces of its predecessors in the crypt, with the oldest parts being from the 8th century. It's worth going inside to look at the ceiling frescoes depicting the Passion of Christ, then

head down into the crypt for the resting places of the Salzburg bishops, subterranean chapels, and parts of the Romanesque cathedral.

★ Sound of Music Tour

www.panoramatours.com/en/salzburg/tour/original-sound-of-music-tour-tour-1a-28/ daily 9.15am and 2pm, €45

Many come to Salzburg to walk in the steps of Julie Andrews, Christopher Plummer, and the von Trapp children and take *The Sound of Music* Tour, one of the most popular excursions in Austria. The four-hour tour takes you to the most famous locations, such as the gazebo, the lake where the kids and Maria fall from the boat, and then up into the hills to the stunning lake district in the company of a guide who will give you the backstory of each location (both its role in the movie and in real life). Salzburg is a stunning town; however, one of the best things about following in the footsteps of the movie is getting out into the countryside surrounding the town. You head up the hills alive with the sound of music, and if they're not, you can be sure people on the bus will start to sing along to the soundtrack playing on the 40-minute scenic bus tour between Salzburg and Mondsee in the nearby lake district.

FOOD
Austrian
GASTHOF GOLDGASSE

Goldgasse 10, tel. 06/62-848-200, www.gasthofgoldgasse.at, daily 7am-11pm, €15.90-24.90

Tucked on the ground floor of a 700-year-old house, in a narrow street in the Old Town, Gasthof Goldgasse is a cozy inn serving excellent Austrian dishes made with fresh, seasonal, and locally sourced ingredients from regional farmers. Gasthof Goldgasse updates the traditional look with clean, cream-colored walls and light wood paneling accompanied by modern purple lampshades and chandeliers along with artfully presented cuisine. You can't go wrong with their Veal Wiener Schnitzel and Bratwurst, which always get rave reviews.

GASTHAUS SCHACHLWIRT

Moosstrasse 133, Salzburg, tel. 06/62-830728, www.schachlwirt.at, Mon-Tue and Thu-Fri 11:30am-2pm and 5:30pm-10pm, Sat-Sun 10am-10pm, mains €10-15

Just because this large guest house lies outside the old town, doesn't mean it's not worth the trip. Locals and visitors crowd into the three 20-30 person rooms, and a huge 50-seater garden, for Austrian and Hungarian home cooked specials. You can get classics such as Schnitzel and Goulash, and vegetarians should try the crispy-creamy cheese noodles. Don't skip dessert, especially one of the house specials: Salzburger Nockerl, a baked dessert made with egg whites and dusted with powdered sugar.

AUGUSTINER BRAUSTUBL

Lindhofstrasse 7, Salzburg, tel. 06/62-431246, www.augustinerbier.at, Mon-Fri 3pm-11pm, Sat-Sun 2:30pm-11pm, dishes €5-10

You won't want to miss this brewery in an Augustinian Monastery that's been making potent beers since 1621. It's a little outside the city center, but worth the detour. In the summer, you can sit out in the huge 1,400 seat beer garden, one of the largest in Austria. There are various little snack stands scattered around the courtyard to choose from once you've grabbed your beer at the foyer pump. You also buy pretzels, fried fish, ham hocks, fries, and other local snacks served in carton trays that go perfectly with the local brew. It's worth the visit to this beer garden if only for the vibrant atmosphere in the summer, but the good news is in the winter there is a 5,000-square-meter (54,000-square-feet) hall, so you can keep drinking beer even when the weather goes off.

International
ORGANIC PIZZA SALZBURG

Franz-Josef-Strasse 24A, Salzburg, tel. 06/64-5974470, www.organicpizza-salzburg.com Tue-Wed 5pm-10pm, Thu-Sat midday-10pm, pizzas €10-18

For delicious, organic pizzas, head straight to Organic Pizza Salzburg. Vegan pizzas are available, but meat eaters, have no fear: You can still get prosciutto-topped specials. This tiny, cozy place, with friendly staff, makes all their pizzas with organic, fresh and seasonal ingredients. And if you're not drinking, they also have the best non-alcoholic beer ready to serve by the bottle! You can also ask for a pizza crust made out of spelt flour or gluten free. Even the cola here is organic!

Cafés and Cakes

CAFE AM KAI

Müllner Hauptstraße 4, Salzburg, tel. 06/64-1707899, www.cafeamkai.eu Mon-Wed 9am-6pm, cakes €3.90-4.20

A favorite with locals, especially in the summer, this cafe on the riverside is the perfect spot for cake, coffee, or breakfast. Try to grab a table on the terrace overlooking the river and the Hohensalzburg Fortress in the distance. And it's not just the view that makes it worth the riverside stroll to this café, but the fact that everything is made with organic, locally sourced products, including eggs from the cafe's own farm. Don't miss the homemade strudel.

ACCOMMODATIONS

HOTEL GOLDENER HIRSCH

Getreidegasse 37, Salzburg, tel. 06/62-80840, www.goldenhirsch.com, dd €329-435

Only minutes away from Mozart's birthplace in Salzburg, Hotel Goldener Hirsch is one of the oldest hotels in Vienna, with 600 years of hospitality in its history, making it as much of Salzburg's legacy as Mozart. Set in a stone town house dating back to the 1400s, and, later, functioning as an inn in 1564, today this is a luxury hotel with hunting trophies and old prints lining the whitewashed walls of the hotel. There are 70 rustic-style rooms in the house, with hand-painted antiques rescued from the nearby farms following World War II. You still have the comforts of the 21st century, like the modern bathroom and the flat screen television. There are gourmet restaurants serving Austrian food inside the hotel, and for an extra €50 you can indulge in a luxury breakfast buffet spread including artisanal cheeses, breads, and egg dishes made

to order, such as eggs Benedict, or try some *Palatschinken*, which is Austrian pancakes.

★ VILLA TRAPP

Traunstraße 34, Salzburg, tel. 06/62-630860, www.villa-trapp.com, dd €75-275

If you're a *Sound of Music* fan, you may want to stay in the house once belonging to the real von Trapp family. Although the movie used various mansions in the area, this 19th century villa has now opened as a low-key bed and breakfast. Set behind a walled garden in the city suburbs, its location may not be central, but it's a fascinating place to stay, especially with all the family memorabilia decorating the walls and rooms. There are 15 rooms in this small bed and breakfast, and breakfast is an extra €12 including a copious buffet with fresh fruit, bread, jam, cheese, and cold cuts.

ARTHOTEL BLAUE GANS

Herbert-von-Karajan-Platz 3, Salzburg, tel. 06/62-8424910 www.blaue-gans.com, dd €175-400

Even though the artHOTEL occupies a 14th century house that's been an inn for centuries, it blends the old and new world flawlessly with more than 100 pieces of contemporary art, sculptures, and photographs dotting the individually decorated 35 rooms in the hotel. It lies at the foot of the Hohensalzburg Fortress, making it the ideal location to explore the old town. Breakfast is usually included in the price, but there is also a traditional Austrian restaurant on the premises and a bar filled with plush armchairs. Check out the herb garden on the first floor, or see if you can grab a jazz gig in the cellar during the Fall.

GETTING THERE

The best way to get from Vienna to Salzburg is to take the train, as the bus trip takes around 8-10 hours.

Train

ÖBB Railjet (www.oebb.at) operates regular train services to Salzburg from Wien Hauptbahnhof or Wien Westbahnhof (2.5 hours). Trains run every half hour from Wien

Hauptbahnhof, whereas the trains to Salzburg going from Wien Westbahnhof go every hour. One way tickets usually cost €54, but check out the ÖBB Railjet website and buy a ticket in advance for special offers, which can cost as low as €34 a ticket if bought in advance.

From the train station, it takes 10 minutes to reach the Old Town in Salzburg on foot, 25 minutes to Salzburg Cathedral. There are also regular bus services operated by **Salzburg Verkehrsbund** (salzburg-verkehr.at) running outside the station (single tickets cost €2) that will take you into the city center. **Salzburg Taxi** (06/76-3347-141) is one of the taxi firms to use from the station.

Car

Going to Salzburg by car won't save you time compared to the train, as the journey will take around three hours. Take the A1 running west from Vienna for the fastest route, but make sure your car has a vignette as this route has tolls.

GETTING AROUND

Salzburg has a good public transport system, but the city center is compact enough to get around on foot. It's best to get a taxi from the front of the train station if you're not familiar with the city.

Bratislava, Slovakia

If you fancy including another country and capital to your Central European itinerary, you can easily add Bratislava (pop. 420,000) as a day trip from Vienna. It's rare that you have two capital cities only an hour's ride from each other, so you can just hop on a train or bus and visit Slovakia and be back in Vienna by the evening.

Although Bratislava is not as spectacular as Prague and Budapest, nor as interesting and complex as Vienna, it's still a city that has plenty of charm, with medieval streets winding up to the whitewashed castle overlooking the Danube, or wide boulevards taking you just streets away to Ödön Lechner's Blue Church. Bratislava also has a very chilled-out, new wave cafe culture filled with hip and young creatives and you could easily spend the day just hopping between coffee shops.

Slovakia is also in the EU and in the Schengen Zone, so there won't be border checks on the way but still bring your passport or ID card with you, just in case. Like Austria, Slovakia uses the Euro. Slovak is the official language spoken in Slovakia, a Slavic language similar to Czech, but you will find that many speak English in the capital.

You can use Bratislava as a base to break

the journey between Budapest and Prague (it's located on the same train route), but if you choose to visit Bratislava when traveling between the two cities, it's best to spend the night. If you're looking to add Bratislava in your Budapest-Vienna itinerary, I would advise doing Bratislava as a day trip from Vienna rather than taking the detour with all that luggage.

SIGHTS
★ Old Town

Bratislava's compact historic nucleus is the old heart of the city. It's also the site of the festivals and vibrant cafes that keep the Slovak capital's blood pumping. The area in the Old Town around Hlavné námestie, the Main Square, is worth visiting for the Old Town Hall, whose stone tower dates as far back as the 14th century, and for the 16th century Roland Fountain featuring the Habsburg king Maximilian II depicted as a knight on the column towering above the fountain. From the Main Square, head up Michalská to the St. Michael's Tower, one of the only preserved gate towers dotted around the original city wall. Or turn down to the intersection of Panská and Rybárska Brána and see if you can catch sight of the bronze sculpture: a man peeking out from under a manhole cover. Keep your eyes peeled as you wander through the district for little architectural details, quirky design shops, and tempting little cafes.

Bratislava Castle

Bratislava Hrad, tel. 02/544-114-44, www.bratislava-hrad.sk Tue-Sun 10am-6pm, €8

Bratislava Castle is a symbol of the city. A huge cube-like structure with four stocky turreted towers topped with terracotta tiles sits on top of a hill overlooking the whole town. The original castle dates back to the 9th century, but the building you see today is actually a 1960s reconstruction based on a Renaissance style, as the original castle burned down in 1811.

You can climb up to the castle grounds for wonderful views over Bratislava, and there is also a museum inside the castle that will take you back in time through history of the castle. Climb up the Crown Tower for amazing views, and make sure you stop to look at the *Assumption of the Virgin Mary* painting by Anton Schmidt in the Music Hall, which is a wonderful example of local baroque art. It's a good idea to hit the castle first thing in the morning if you want to avoid the crowds

coming with the Danube cruises and the tour buses.

★ Blue Church

Bezručova 2534/2, tel. 02/527-335-72, www.modrykostol.fara.sk, Mon-Sat 7am-7:30am, 5:30pm-7pm, free

This stunning art nouveau church in various shades of blue by Hungarian architect Ödön Lechner is worth the short detour out of the Old Town. Its official name is the Church of St. Elizabeth of Hungary—named after Empress Elizabeth, "Sisi", Franz Joseph I's wife—but its blue hues earned it the more common "Blue Church" title. Although the opening hours are sporadic, and only really open for services, you can admire the marzipan-like building from the outside where even the roof is lined with blue-glazed ceramics. If you can make it inside, then you'll notice even the interior is entirely blue, with pews painted in baby blue tones decorated with gold accents.

Most SNP

Viedenská cesta, tel. 02/6252-0300, www.u-f-o.sk, daily 11am-11pm, €7.40

Towering nearly 95 meters (104 yards), the UFO Bridge (as it's known in English) offers

evening in Old Town Bratislava

amazing views over Bratislava. From afar the viewing platform looks like a flying saucer, and is a rather an odd sight in the capital. Built in 1972, the bridge and the highway running over it has left a bittersweet taste in locals' mouths after its construction took many historic buildings as casualties. Today, it's become integrated into Bratislava's cityscape and there is a pedestrian walkway across the river from the Old Town. Take the elevator—which takes 45 seconds to rocket up—to the observation deck, from which on a clear day you can see as far as 100km (62 miles) into the distance. On good days, makes sure you check out the beach just below the bridge where you can grab street food and drinks, or later in the evening catch some DJs spinning on hot summer nights.

St. Martin's Cathedral

Rudnayovo námestie 1, tel. 02/30 544334, http://dom.fara.sk, May-Sep Mon-Sat 9am-11:30am and 1pm-6pm, Sun 1:30pm-4pm, Oct-Apr 9am-11:30am and 1pm-4pm, Sun 1:30pm-4pm, free

Like many Central European churches, St. Martin's Cathedral is a tapestry of architectural styles from different time periods. It was built on the site of an earlier Romanesque church. The Gothic tower juts up 85 meters (280 feet), which once functioned as a lookout point and is topped by 660 pounds of real gold. Much of the cathedral dates back to the 14th century and despite the humble interior has held 19 coronations over the centuries. On the outside, it's worth taking a look at the walls of the house next to the cathedral that's filled with colorful artwork in the stone niches. Make sure you bring a scarf or a cardigan to cover bare shoulders before entering.

FOOD

Slovak food is influenced by its Czech, Austrian, and Hungarian neighbors. Local ingredients that could withstand the hot Slovakian summers and cold winters dominate the dishes, like potatoes, wheat, dairy products, sauerkraut, onion, and pork. Dumplings made from bread, wheat, or potato are popular, as are pork products like sausages, smoked bacon, and lard.

When you're in Slovakia you must try the Bryndzové halušky, potato dumplings with a tangy local sheep's cheese called bryndza, or the Bryndzové pirohy, cheese-filled boiled dumplings. Another local special is the Segedin goulash, which, despite the name, is actually nothing like the Hungarian gulyás or Viennese goulash, but a pork stew made with sauerkraut and cream, and served with dumplings.

Slovak
MODRÁ HVIEZDA

Beblavého 292/14, tel. 0948 703 070, http://modrahviezda.sk/, daily 11am-11pm, mains €10-20

Try some Slovak specials at Modrá Hviezda, which means "Blue Star." You'll find this brick-lined restaurant in a cellar in the back streets winding up towards Bratislava Castle, where you can sample Slovak specials like rabbit in red wine or locally caught baked trout. The menu changes with the seasons, but this cozy restaurant with antique wooden farming equipment on the wall and brick-lined cellar is inviting all year round.

BRATISLAVSKÝ MEŠTIANSKY PIVOVAR

Drevená 8, tel. 09/44-512-265, www.mestianskypivovar.sk/, Mon-Sat 11am-midnight, Sun 11am-10pm, mains €7-30

This vaulted microbrewery is worth the visit for the in-house beers and hearty Slovak food. The beer here is unfiltered, unpasteurized, and served fresh from the tap, with a mix of lagers, dark beer, and German style Weissbier. If you're thirsty, you can get beers by the liter as well. Food includes cold cut and cheese plates if you just want something to go with the beer, but you can also try their special beef goulash made with beer, roasted pork knuckle, Schnitzel, and other Central European specials.

HOUDINI RESTAURANT

Tobrucká 6953/4, tel. 02/577 846 00,
www.restauranthoudini.sk/, daily noon-3pm
and 6pm-10:30pm mains €15-35

Set in the ground floor of the Marrol Hotel, Houdini Restaurant offers fine dining at affordable prices. You can order a la carte, but a four-course tasting menu with wine pairings won't break the bank at €40, with beautifully presented dishes such as rabbit leg confit and cheese risotto. The setting strikes a balance between elegant and cozy, with library-like shelves stocked with bottles of wine and wood paneling. The dishes here are Slovak with an international twist and a Mediterranean accent.

International

U KUBISTU

Grösslingová 2524/26, tel. 09/48-077-845,
www.ukubistu.sk, Mon-Fri 8am-10pm, Sat-Sun
10am-10pm, mains €12-15

If you're looking for great fusion food made with local, organic ingredients and freshly cooked dishes, then this trendy modern bistro just streets away from the Blue Church is a hit. You can get hearty soups, seasonal dishes like daily game specials, braised chicken in white wine, as well as vegetarian friendly soups and bites. The design is clean and modern with white walls, large windows and Edison bulbs, and in the summer there are outdoor tables too.

Cafés and Cakes

ŠTÚR

Štúrova 8, tel. 09/44 960 352, www.sturcafe.sk,
Mon-Fri 8:30am-10pm, Sat 9am-10pm,
Sun 9am-9pm, snacks €4-7

Štúr is a trendy cafe named after the Slovak literary poet and linguist Ľudovít Štúr, whose face you'll find all over the walls of the modern-looking cafe. It pulls in a young crowd in the evening, but people of all ages come during the day for its freshly baked range of cakes. If you want to grab a snack or a light lunch, it's a relaxed place to have lunch.

CAFE VERNE

Hviezdoslavovo námestie 175/18, tel. 02/544-305-14,
Mon-Fri 8am-midnight, Sat-Sun 10am-midnight,
mains €4-11

In the summer, Cafe Verne spills out onto the square at Hviezdoslavovo námestie in the Old Town, and in the winter you can escape into this colorful basement with red velvet booths, lace curtains and old books. It's a great place to hop in for a coffee—especially if the terrace is out—and despite its central location it's a place where even the locals come here to catch up with friends or read the morning paper. If you're hungry, grab something from the daily menu for some simple, yet hearty home cooking. Try the pancake filled with sweet cottage cheese!

ACCOMMODATIONS

ARCADIA BOUTIQUE HOTEL

Františkánska 3, Bratislava tel. 02/594-905-00,
www.arcadiahotel.sk, dd €98-135

Set in a 13th century building in the heart of Bratislava's Old Town, this charming 4-star boutique hotel makes the perfect base to explore the Slovak's capital's historic heart. There are 34 rooms and suites decked out in fabrics and plush carpets in rich reds or bold emerald greens. At the heart of the hotel, the lobby lies within a colonnaded courtyard enclosed by a stained glass ceiling. There is a small wellness area set up in a former medieval prison with a plunge pool, saunas and gym. Guests are treated to a full breakfast buffet included in the price.

LOFT HOTEL BRATISLAVA

Štefánikova 4, Bratislava tel. 02/575-110-00, www.
lofthotel.sk, dd €89-146

The 4-star LOFT Hotel overlooks the Presidential Palace in the center of the city. There are 111 modern rooms with an LCD TV and a daily refilled minibar. If you love industrial chic go for one of the premium rooms with its exposed brick and brass lamps. Beer lovers will want to check out the Fabrika Beer Pub where you can get beer brewed on site.

You can also get a rich buffet breakfast (included in most room packages, otherwise it's an additional €14) with full view of the brewery behind the Plexiglass.

GETTING THERE
From Vienna
TRAIN
You can catch trains every half an hour from Wien Hauptbahnhof to Bratislava main station with **ÖBB Railjet** (www.oebb.at). The train journey takes approximately an hour, with tickets costing €10.50-17 one way, depending on the train.

From the main train station, get tram number 1 to the Old Town, which will take around 10 minutes to reach the city center, departing every 10-15 minutes. Single tickets cost 70 cents.

BUS
For €5-10 one way, you can also grab the bus from Wien Erdberg to Bratislava, which also takes around an hour. Tickets can be bought on the Flixbus website (www.flixbus.com) which has regular bus services between the two cities.

Bratislava Central Bus Station is a 20-minute walk out of town, but you can take a local bus 202, 208, 212 every 10 minutes and it takes 10 minutes to reach the center. Single tickets cost 70 cents. You can also get off the bus at Most SNP, which will leave you close to the center.

BOAT
Take the scenic route between Vienna and Bratislava with the catamaran run by **Twin City Liner** (www.twincityliner.com). It takes 75 minutes and you get a Danube cruise thrown in. You also have the added advantage of being dropped off right in Bratislava's Old Town.

Boat services run five times a day and start from the Vienna City ship station on the Danube Canal between Marienbrücke and Schedenbrücke. Tickets cost €30 one way. You

can see more information about boat services, timetables and buy tickets online at the Twin City Liner website.

CAR
Take the A4 southeast from Vienna and then turn onto the A6 towards the Slovak border. The drive takes around an hour, but note that the highways have tolls within Austria and partial tolls in Slovakia.

From Budapest
TRAIN
You can catch trains hourly or every two hours from Budapest's Nyugati Train Station to Bratislava main station with **EuroCity** (www.bahn.de). The train journey takes approximately two and a half hours, with tickets costing €9-12 one way, depending on the train.

From the main train station, get tram number 1 to the Old Town, which will take around 10 minutes to reach the city center, departing every 10-15 minutes. Single tickets cost 70 cents.

BUS
For €12-17 one way, you can grab the bus from Budapest Népliget to Bratislava, which also takes around two and a half hours. Tickets can be bought on the Flixbus website (www.flixbus.com) which has regular bus services between the two cities.

Bratislava Central Bus Station is a 20-minute walk out of town, but you can take a local bus 202, 208, 212 every 10 minutes and it takes 10 minutes to reach the center. Single tickets cost 70 cents. You can also get off the bus at Most SNP, which will leave you close to the center.

CAR
Take the M1 northwest from Budapest following signs for Ausztria/Slovákia/Bécs-Wien-Győr, until you take the exit 166 to take the M15 towards Pozsony-Bratislava to the Slovak border. Once you cross the border take the E75 and follow the signs for Bratislava. The

drive takes around two hours, but note that the highways have tolls within Hungary and partial tolls in Slovakia.

From Prague

TRAIN

The fastest and most comfortable way to travel is by taking the **EuroCity train** (www.goeuro.com). The train journey takes approximately 4 hours, with tickets costing €12-25 one way, depending on the train.

BUS

If you do choose to travel by bus, the **RegioJet** (www.regiojet.com) is another convenient and popular choice. This bus is comfortable and is set up with WiFi, and coffee and tea are included in price. The ticket is cheaper as a train ticket.

CAR

Take 5. května to Brněnská in Praha 11. Follow D1/E65 to Lamačská cesta/Route 2 in Bratislava, Slovensko. Take the exit toward Centrum Patrónka from E65. Continue on Lamačská cesta/Route 2. Take Route 572 to Hodžovo námestie in Staré Mesto. The drive takes around three hours and twenty minutes, but note that the highways have tolls.

GETTING AROUND

Dopravný podnik Bratislava (DPB, www.dpb.sk—Slovak only, but you can check out the time tables and information in public transport on imhd.sk in English) runs the public transport in Bratislava, which is well connected with a network of trams, buses and trolley buses. Like Vienna, Prague and Budapest, public transport operates on a trust system, so make sure you validate your tickets (70 cents for a single ticket, no transfers allowed) otherwise you could get fined by plain clothes inspectors who check the trams and buses at random. You cannot buy tickets from the drivers, so your best bet is to buy from the yellow ticket machines at most tram or bus stops.

The good news once you're in the Old Town, you can get around Bratislava on foot pretty easily.

Budapest

Divided by the Danube River, Budapest is a city

with two personalities. On the Buda side, hills curve up from the river, topped with palaces and citadels. Game-filled forests and ivy-covered villas stand above an underworld of caves. The Pest side spreads out on a plane built up with wide boulevards and grand monuments.

Budapest began as three separate towns: Buda, Pest, and Óbuda. Built on the Roman ruins of the city of Aquincum, Modern Budapest is punctuated by medieval relics, Ottoman monuments, Habsburg grandeur, ceramic-clad art nouveau buildings, and communist brutalism. It's this architectural diversity, along with an attractive tax incentive, that draws Hollywood producers to Budapest to shoot on location.

But you don't need to go to the movies for compelling

Highlights

Look for ★ to find recommended sights, activities, dining, and lodging.

★ **Buda Castle:** This Habsburg palace houses the Hungarian National Gallery and Budapest History Museum. It stands on the ruins of castles that have been razed and rebuilt over time (page 330).

★ **Fisherman's Bastion:** This neo-Gothic lookout platform offers spectacular views over the Danube (page 333).

★ **Hungarian Parliament:** Whether you view it from the Danube or take a tour, the country's political powerhouse dominates the cityscape with its towering spires and claret-hued rooftop (page 335).

★ **St. Stephen's Basilica:** Climb the dome for 360-degree views over Budapest. Then, stop to see the mummified hand of St. Stephen in a jewel-encrusted box (page 340).

★ **Dohány Street Synagogue:** The second-largest synagogue in the world is the heart of the historic Jewish Quarter (page 343).

★ **Hungarian State Opera:** A bastion of Hungary's excellent classical music scene, and one of the most important buildings on the UNESCO-protected Andrássy Avenue (page 345).

★ **Gellért Hill:** Take a hike up this hill beside the Danube for the best views over Budapest (page 353).

★ **Memento Park:** This graveyard for Communist statues turned open-air museum is the best place to visit to glimpse Hungary's Communist past (page 355).

★ **Hungarian National Museum:** The largest museum in the country, with an eclectic collection of artifacts from Roman times to the 19th century (page 358).

★ **Széchenyi Thermal Bath:** Budapest's most famous thermal bath with its canary-yellow

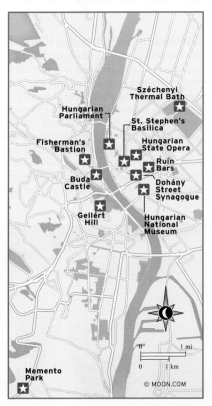

pools, is one of Central Europe's largest thermal bath complexes. It's also notorious for its "sparties," raucous parties held on summer weekends (page 365).

★ **Ruin Bars:** These watering holes have sprung up in condemned buildings in the city. Head to Szimpla Kert, the ruin bar that started the craze, for a beer in its labyrinth of graffiti-covered crumbling rooms (page 370).

stories—Budapest's complex and diverse history is written on its bullet-scarred walls and within the memories of its residents.

Hungarians are renowned for their creativity and innovation, boasting 13 Nobel Prize winners, and inventions like the Rubik's Cube and the ballpoint pen. This innovation spills out into the city's showrooms, eccentric bars, art galleries, and into the basement that birthed the world's first room escape game.

While rougher around the edges than Prague and Vienna, dilapidation has become part of Budapest's attraction. Flaking buildings now house vibrant ruin bars—unique watering holes that marry eccentric junk with art. These bars serve as alternative culture hubs. Today, revelers flock to former apartment blocks and factories for shots of *pálinka* or local craft beer and party until the late hours of the morning. Get to know Budapest by wandering the winding streets of the Castle District. Stop for views over the Danube, or ride a boat on the river. Explore the Jewish District's synagogues and the bars that spice up the quarter at night. Revel in the paprika-laden aromas of Hungarian cuisine and enjoy a spicy *Bikavér*, a red wine from Eger. Budapest is a city to be experienced, not just seen. Dare to venture beyond the ruin bars and discover where the locals go to enjoy life, celebrate, and give a toast to each other's health with *egészségedre* ("cheers" in Hungarian).

HISTORY

A tale of three cities, Budapest's history is long and complicated. It only unified into the capital we know today when the towns of Buda, Pest, and Óbuda merged in 1873. History is on the walls of Budapest, in the scars left behind by shots fired during World War II and the 1956 uprising. There's also much to learn in the Roman ruins and Ottoman baths scattered around the city.

The region of the **Carpathian Basin** (the area between the Carpathian Mountains and the Alps) has been populated for hundreds of thousands of years by **Celtic** tribes (who arrived around today's Budapest in the third century BC). The **Romans** set up camp on the Danube in the first century BC. Eventually, the town of **Aquincum** grew into one of the largest Roman settlements—but it came crashing down when Attila and the Huns razed the city in the fifth century AD. (Despite the English name for the country, the Huns only played a short part in Hungary's history.) Following Attila's death, Germanic tribes occupied the region for a century. The Avars (Eurasian nomads) controlled the Carpathian Basin in the sixth century. Charlemagne later conquered the area around today's Budapest and incorporated it into the Frankish Empire.

The Magyars, a nomadic people, arrived in the Carpathian Basin around the ninth century, conquering and settling the land under the leadership of Árpád, a chief military commander. In 1000, King Stephen I founded the Hungarian State and embraced Christianity as the new country's religion. The cities of Buda and Pest were villages at the time; they only became a principal seat of the nation following the Mongol invasion in the 13th century. King Béla IV rebuilt the devastated country and founded a fortress in the Buda Hills, but Buda saw most of its development during the Renaissance under the rule of King Matthias, who transformed Hungary into one of the leading powers in Europe at the time.

In the sixteenth century, the **Turks** invaded Hungary and defeated the Hungarian army in the southern town of Mohács in 1526. Large parts of Hungary, including Buda (occupied in 1541), existed under Ottoman rule for 150 years.

After the Ottomans came the **Habsburgs,** who liberated Buda and Pest in 1686, and Austria absorbed Hungary into the Habsburg Empire. Buda and Pest were rebuilt in the baroque style, shaping the Castle District's

---

Budapest

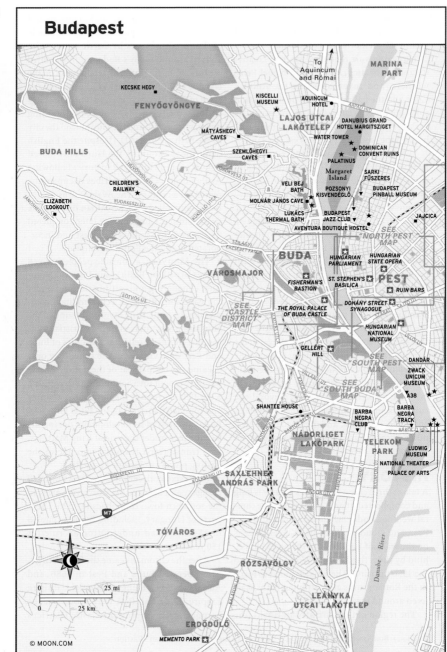

To Aquincum and Római

MARINA PART

KECSKE HEGY

FENYŐGYÖNGYE

KISCELLI MUSEUM

AQUINCUM HOTEL

LAJOS UTCAI LAKÓTELEP

DANUBIUS GRAND HOTEL MARGITSZIGET

MÁTYÁSHEGY CAVES

WATER TOWER

DOMINICAN CONVENT RUINS

BUDA HILLS

SZEMLŐHEGYI CAVES

PALATINUS

Margaret Island

SARKI FŰSZERES

CHILDREN'S RAILWAY

VELI BEJ BATH

POZSONYI KISVENDÉGLŐ

BUDAPEST PINBALL MUSEUM

ELIZABETH LOOKOUT

MOLNÁR JÁNOS CAVE

LUKÁCS THERMAL BATH

BUDAPEST JAZZ CLUB

JAJCICA

AVENTURA BOUTIQUE HOSTEL

SEE "NORTH PEST" MAP

BUDA

HUNGARIAN PARLIAMENT

HUNGARIAN STATE OPERA

VÁROSMAJOR

FISHERMAN'S BASTION

ST. STEPHEN'S BASILICA

PEST

RUIN BARS

SEE "CASTLE DISTRICT" MAP

THE ROYAL PALACE OF BUDA CASTLE

DOHÁNY STREET SYNAGOGUE

HUNGARIAN NATIONAL MUSEUM

GELLÉRT HILL

SEE "SOUTH PEST" MAP

DANDÁR

ZWACK UNICUM MUSEUM

SEE "SOUTH BUDA" MAP

A38

SHANTEE HOUSE

BARBA NEGRA CLUB

BARBA NEGRA TRACK

NÁDORLIGET LAKÓPARK

TELEKOM PARK

LUDWIG MUSEUM

NATIONAL THEATER

PALACE OF ARTS

SAXLEHNER ANDRÁS PARK

M7

TÓVÁROS

Danube River

RÓZSAVÖLGY

0   25 mi

0   25 km

LEÁNYKA UTCAI LAKÓTELEP

ERDŐDŰLŐ

© MOON.COM

MEMENTO PARK

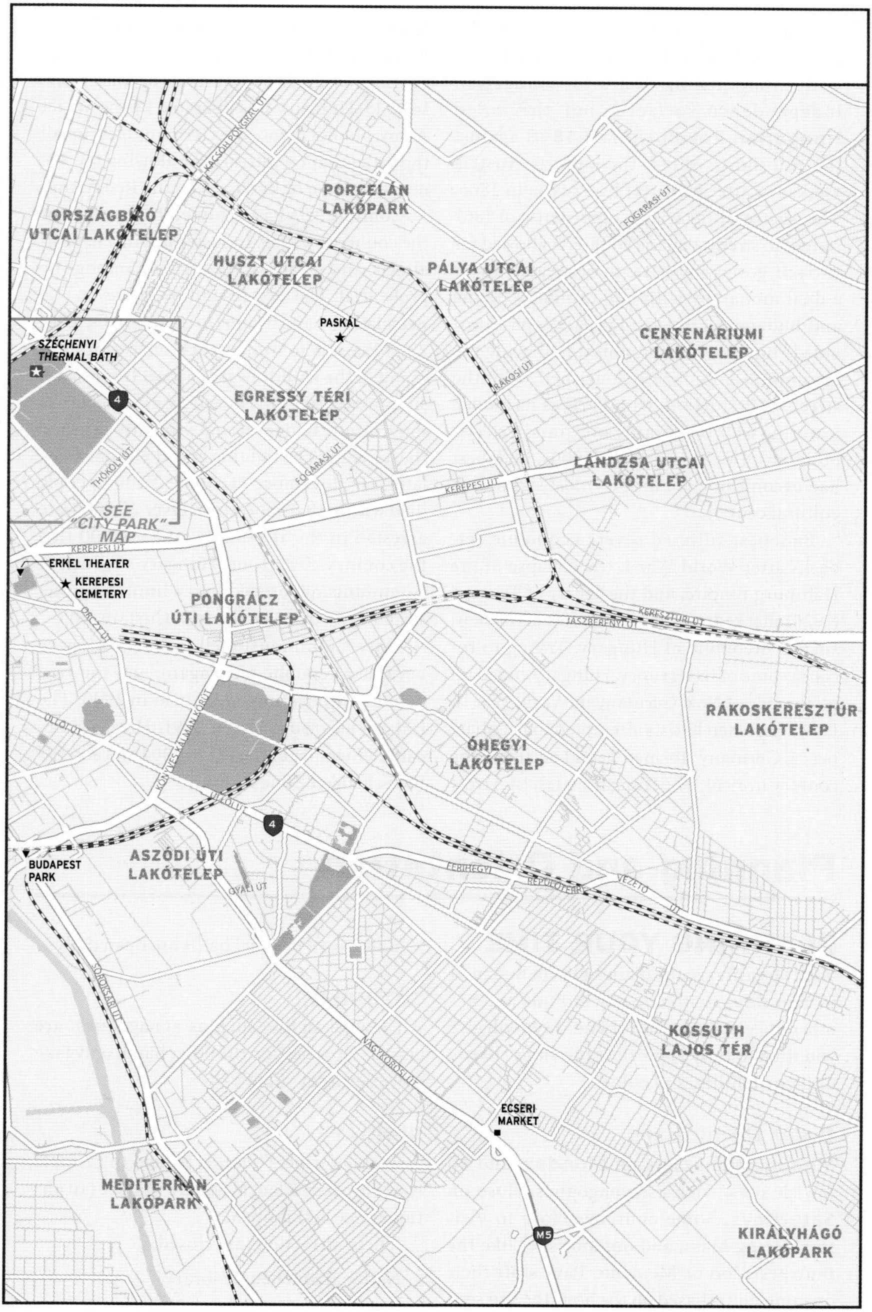

PORCELÁN
LAKÓPARK

ORSZÁGBÍRÓ
UTCAI LAKÓTELEP

HUSZT UTCAI
LAKÓTELEP

PÁLYA UTCAI
LAKÓTELEP

PASKÁL
★

CENTENÁRIUMI
LAKÓTELEP

SZÉCHENYI
THERMAL BATH

4

EGRESSY TÉRI
LAKÓTELEP

LÁNDZSA UTCAI
LAKÓTELEP

SEE
"CITY PARK"
MAP

ERKEL THEATER

KEREPESI
CEMETERY

PONGRÁCZ
ÚTI LAKÓTELEP

RÁKOSKERESZTÚR
LAKÓTELEP

ÓHEGYI
LAKÓTELEP

BUDAPEST
PARK

ASZÓDI ÚTI
LAKÓTELEP

4

KOSSUTH
LAJOS TÉR

ECSERI
MARKET

MEDITERRÁN
LAKÓPARK

M5

KIRÁLYHÁGÓ
LAKÓPARK

current look today. Pest also grew rapidly around the Inner City in today's V District.

A strengthening desire for Hungarian independence surfaced, but the failed **Hungarian Revolution of 1848** against the Habsburgs shook the empire. Austria weakened after its defeat by Prussia in 1866. The Austro-Hungarian Compromise of 1867 sought to strengthen the empire. It allowed for two self-governing states to be created under a dual monarchy with two capitals, Vienna and Budapest. Emperor Franz Joseph I provided Hungary full autonomy. Following the compromise, Budapest flourished, with the streets of Pest rebuilt with Paris as its model, featuring wide boulevards and grand, eclectic buildings. By the end of the 1900s, Budapest had become one of Europe's most significant cultural centers.

Budapest suffered severe economic setbacks after World War I, the collapse of the Habsburg Empire, and the Treaty of Trianon (1920) that redrew the boundaries of the new, smaller Republic of Hungary. Trying to reclaim some of its territory, Hungary ended up on the side of Nazi Germany in World War II. However, when leftists attempted to negotiate peace, Germany stormed in and occupied the country in 1944. The Hungarian fascist Arrow Cross Party rose to power and rounded up Budapest's Jews—and immediately began deporting hundreds of thousands to Auschwitz. In 1945, Hungary was liberated by the Soviet Army, but not before the Germans blew up all the bridges upon retreating following the 50-day long Siege of Budapest by the Red Army.

Communists had assumed full control of the country by 1949. Industry became nationalized, and estates were divided among the proletariat. The next revolution, however, was percolating—and it came to a head on October 23, 1956 when student demonstrators demanded the withdrawal of Soviet troops, and shots were fired. On November 4, Soviet tanks moved into Budapest and violently crushed the uprising. The fighting ended just one week later, on November 11. Some 25,000 people died within that short time. Over 20,000 were arrested in the aftermath, and 250,000 fled the country. Over time, Hungary's branch of Communism loosened into a limited market system, and by 1989, the Iron Curtain fell.

Once Communism fell in 1989, Hungary became a republic once again, and the first democratic elections were held in 1990. The last Soviet troops left in 1991. Hungary became a member of the EU in 2004 and entered the Schengen Zone in 2007.

Planning and Orientation

PLANNING YOUR TIME

You can easily see the main sights in Budapest in **two days,** with one day in Buda and another in Pest. But at least **three days** will give you time to fully appreciate the city's charm, unique nightlife, and culture.

Daily Reminders

Most museums close on **Monday,** and all Jewish sites, such as synagogues, close on **Saturdays.** Some churches close to visitors during Mass, and outdoor sites like the Budapest Zoo or Memento Park shift their opening hours based on the hour the sun sets.

Budapest's thermal baths are open daily.

SATURDAY

All Jewish sights, such as synagogues, are closed. "Sparties" on the other hand, only take place Saturday nights.

SUNDAY

A weekly farmers' market is held in Szimpla Kert ruin bar; Klauzál Square Market (an antiques market) is open.

These attractions are closed:

- National Széchényi Library

- Hungarian House of Art Nouveau (Bedő House)
- Cave Church
- Central Market Hall
- Zwack Unicum Museum

MONDAY

Most museums are closed, including:

- Hungarian National Gallery
- Budapest History Museum
- National Széchényi Library
- House of Terror
- Vajdahunyad Castle
- Miksa Róth Memorial House
- Budapest Pinball Museum
- Hungarian National Museum
- Holocaust Memorial Center
- Ludwig Museum
- Aquincum
- Kiscelli Museum

Advanced Bookings and Time-Saving Tips

You can buy tickets online for popular sites like the Hungarian National Gallery or the Hungarian Parliament Building. Buying online will help you skip the queues, but at most of the sites, you can just buy tickets when you arrive without any issues. Some places (like the Parliament or the synagogues and Jewish museums) may want you to put your bags through a security check, so account for a little extra time for that as well.

If you want to go to a "Sparty" (a rowdy party in a thermal bath (https://spartybooking.com, €50, over 18 only), make sure you buy a ticket in advance from the website, as these sell out fast.

Sightseeing Passes

The **Budapest Card** (www.budapest-card.com, 24-hour card/19€; 48-hour card/29€; 72-hour card/37€) includes public transport, free entrance to 13 museums (including the museums in Buda Castle, the Hungarian National Museum, and Memento Park), two walking tours, free entrance to the Lukács Baths, and discounts. The Budapest Card is available at Budapestinfo Points, and you can also buy it online. If you're planning to pack a number of museums into your trip and use the public transport often it's worth investing in a card.

Exploring the City

Budapest is easy to explore on foot, but the public transport run by the BKK (Budapest's public transport network) is also very efficient. There are four metro lines and several bus and tram links, such as the 4/6 running along the entire stretch of the Grand Boulevard and the 2 tram that gives you front-row seats for the banks of the Danube.

ORIENTATION

The Danube River divides the city into Buda (western side) and Pest (eastern side). Budapest is also split up into 23 numbered municipal districts (*kerület*) that spiral out almost clockwise from the Castle District. White placards on street corners are labeled with the Roman numeral district number, the neighborhood name (*Erzsébetváros*), followed by the street name and the numbering of the houses on the block. If you're asking for directions, you can refer to the district number (for example, ask where "the seventh district" is if you're trying to get to VII District).

With street names, it's important to know your *utca* (street) from your *út* (boulevard or avenue), so you don't, for example, confuse Váci utca (a shopping artery in the Inner City) with Váci út (a long road leading to industrial suburbs). Other names are tér (square), körút (ring road or boulevard), sor (row) and rak-part (embankment). In some locations, you may notice street signs crossed out in red, which denote former place names that have been changed following the communist regime; these have been replaced with the new name on the placard below.

Castle District (I District)

Budapest's I District (on the Buda side of the river) centers on Castle Hill, which rises sharply above the Danube, and is crowned by **Buda Castle.** The Castle District packs history into a dense space. Traces of the old medieval city can be seen in the excavated ruins near Buda Castle, but much of the original Buda lies in rubble or is hidden away. Much of the district is dominated by **cobbled, narrow streets, pastel-hued baroque houses,** and romantic stone staircases that lead up the hill.

Inner City and Around Parliament (V District)

The V District, located right on the riverbank in Pest, exudes elegance, from its promenades dotted with **riverside cafés** to **grand buildings** with elaborate friezes, columns, and wrought iron façades. Pedestrianized **Váci utca** is the main road for shopping and dining. Where Váci utca ends (at Vörösmarty tér) is where the neighborhood of Lipótváros begins. This is where you'll find the most famous landmarks, like the **Hungarian Parliament** and **St. Stephen's Basilica.** Around the Parliament Building and Liberty Square,

keep your eyes peeled for incredible specimens of **art nouveau architecture.**

Jewish Quarter (VII District)

Though the neighborhood itself is older, the Jewish Quarter lies inside the former 1944 ghetto. **Memorials** on both Dohány and Király utca mark the location of the former wall. You can still find signs of Jewish life scattered about the streets of the inner VII District, from the grand **Dohány Street Synagogue** to kosher restaurants, bakeries, butchers, and Hebrew lettering on building doors. Most tourists flock to this part of the VII District after dark, when the Jewish Quarter energizes with its vibrant **nightlife,** including Budapest's most famous ruin pub, **Szimpla Kert.** This neighborhood is located east of the Inner City.

Around Andrássy Avenue (VI District)

Some consider **Andrássy Avenue** (Andrássy út), which stretches northeast from the Inner City, to be Budapest's answer to the Champs-Élysées. This **elegant, wide boulevard,** lined with eclectic palatial apartment blocks and slender trees, stretches just under than two miles. The avenue itself falls under UNESCO World Heritage protection. The

Ride on Continental Europe's oldest metro line, beginning at Vörösmarty Tér in the old inner city.

first half is dominated by luxury boutiques; it shifts to palatial villas enclosing embassies up in the vicinity of City Park.

City Park and Around (XIV District)

City Park, northeast of the Jewish Quarter, is one of Pest's main green lungs, a place of recreation with **thermal baths**, picnic spots, and a popular **ice-skating rink** in the winter. City Park lies in the residential XIV District, but there's plenty to see and do in and around the park, from the **Budapest Zoo** to the sites at **Vajdahunyad Castle**. There are also plans to turn this area into a museum quarter by 2020.

Margaret Island and Around (II and XIII Districts)

When the sun comes out, locals head to Margaret Island (Margitsziget), in the Danube. It's accessible by Margaret Bridge and Árpád Bridge for picnics, strolls and sunbathing. The island is mostly **car-free** (local bus service and taxis do operate). The island is over 1.5 miles long, and 550 yards wide. You'll find **medieval ruins, thermal baths,** and abundant **green parkland here.** (This is also allegedly where German composer Richard Wagner almost drowned after falling from a boat.) Flanking the island on the mainland, the northern parts of Buda and Pest have a few points of interest, from Turkish remains to quirky museums.

South Buda (XI District)

The area stretching south of the Castle District spills into the XI District, and it's mostly **off the tourist track.** There's plenty to do, from **hiking up Gellért Hill** to sipping a coffee in a trendy café on lively **Bartók Béla Avenue.** Although you may need to use public transport to get to some of the area's sites, you can be sure to escape the crowds and see a bit more of less touristy Budapest. Head further down along the river to **Kopaszi dam** (Kopaszi gát) for a **Danube beach** area with riverside cafés and water sports.

South Pest (VIII and IX Districts)

Stretching south of the Jewish Quarter and the Inner City, the VIII and IX Districts lie slightly **off the beaten track** for most tourists. However, you can take a walk past the grand, palatial apartments of the **Palace District** or head down to the Danube banks around the formerly industrial IX District, where old factories have been converted into **cultural centers** or **craft beer bars,** and you'll find a different, more laid-back side of Budapest.

The **Millennium Quarter** along Soroksári út, up by Rákóczi híd, is a new cultural hub for the city, with the **Palace of Art,** the **Ludwig Gallery** and the **National Theater.**

Óbuda (III District)

Óbuda (meaning Old Buda) was once a city in its own right, and it's outside the boundaries of historic Buda and Pest. Today, **Roman ruins** lie beneath **Communist-era apartment blocks,** and two-story baroque townhouses back onto industrial complexes. It has a different character from the rest of Budapest. While far flung from the center, it has plenty to offer, from dining around **Kolosy tér** to **beaches** and **riverside bars at Római Part.** Meanwhile, **Óbuda Island** hosts one of Europe's largest music festivals— **Sziget**—in August.

Buda Hills (II, III and XII Districts)

What distinguishes Buda from mostly flat Pest is its hills. Gellért Hill and Castle Hill are the most prominent in the city center; the hills out in the II, III and XII Districts feel like they belong somewhere in the countryside and not in a capital city. You'll find **lookout points** offering views over the city, **hiking trails,** and even networks of **caves** running below the city for miles on end. The **Children's Railway,** a small railway run by children as a relic left over from Communist times, is located here.

Itinerary Ideas

Budapest is more compact than Vienna—although still a bit more spread out than Prague—and you can divide the main sites between the Buda and Pest. To get away from the crowds, explore the Buda Hills to see a different side of the city.

And you will want to save one of Budapest's iconic experiences—soaking in a thermal bath—for the last day. It'll be a relaxing end to your trip.

DAY 1

Spend Day 1 in Budapest's Castle District.

1 Start the day at one of Budapest's most spectacular bridges, the **Chain Bridge,** with amazing views over the river.

2 From the bridge and Clark Ádám Square take Hunyadi János út heading uphill north of the Chain Bridge and keep walking till you reach the stairs leading up to **Fisherman's Bastion.** Usually, this is one of Budapest's most crowded sites, but early in the morning there are only a few people here, and it's the perfect spot for snapping a few photos of the river.

3 There are plenty of breakfast options up in the Castle District. **Baltazár,** which is a 5-minute walk down Országút, will keep you fueled up for the morning.

4 Return to **Matthias Church** next to Fisherman's Bastion for its incredible frescoes. If you make it on the hour, get a ticket and go up the church tower.

5 For something off-beat, head over to the **Hospital in the Rock** just 5 minutes away for a subterranean journey back in time to World War II, the 1956 revolution and the Cold War.

6 Stop at **Ruszwurm,** the oldest café and confectionary in Budapest, which you will have passed on the way to the museum.

7 In the afternoon, you'll want to spend a couple of hours at the **Hungarian National Gallery** in the Royal Palace, just a 10-minute walk away.

8 Once you're done learning about the history of Hungarian art, take the elevator in the Castle Garden down to the **Castle Garden Bazaar** for the scenic route down the castle and get on the 41 or 19 tram to Gárdonyi tér.

9 Have dinner and drinks at **Hadik,** a former literary hangout in the early 1900s that's now a trendy bistro.

DAY 2

On your second day, explore around the Parliament and Inner City.

1 Kickstart your morning with breakfast in a classic café, like **Café Central** in the old part of the Inner City.

2 Walk 5 minutes towards the Danube and get on the number 2 tram. Get off at the **Széchenyi István tér** and turn around and take some pictures of the Royal Palace, the river and Chain Bridge from the Pest side of the city.

3 Turn into Zrínyi street and pay a visit to **St. Stephen's Basilica.** Make sure you head up to the top inside to the dome, where amazing 360 degree views await.

4 It's a good time for a lunch break, and restaurants and cafes spill out onto the squares and streets surrounding the Basilica. **Zeller Bisztró** on Hercegprímás utca is a good option.

5 Once you've eaten, stroll over to Hold utca for the **Royal Postal Savings Bank** by Ödön Lechner two blocks away. If you want to see the rooftop from above, head into the Hotel President across the street to the rooftop café—it's worth it for the view.

6 Stroll over to Freedom Square and head over to the **Hungarian Parliament.** Get on one of the English language tours of the Hungarian Parliament—it's easier to get on a tour if you buy a ticket online—to see inside this amazing building.

7 Get yourself on a **Danube cruise.** You take the tram number 2 to Vígadó and get on a boat organized by Legenda.

8 Once the boat docks, walk up to Vörösmarty tér and take the metro to Opera. Turn into Székely Mihály utca and then Kazinczy utca, passing the art nouveau **Kazinczy Street Synagogue.**

9 Grab a bite to eat at the **Karavan Street Food Court** at the end of Kazinczy utca.

10 End the night at Budapest's most famous ruin bar, **Szimpla Kert,** located just next door.

BUDAPEST LIKE A LOCAL

Today, head outside Budapest's center and into the Buda Hills.

1 Start with a decadent breakfast at the beautiful **Villa Bagatelle** at the base of the Buda Hills.

2 Walk down the hill 5 minutes and get on the 61 tram and go to the end of the line to Hűvösvölgy. Take the carved wooden staircase leading up the hill pointing you in the direction of the **Children's Railway** and hop on this retro locomotive operated by children under 14 (drivers and engineers excepted) that will take you through the wilderness of the Buda Hills.

3 Get off the train at János Hegy and hike around 20-30 minutes from the train station up to the **Elizabeth Lookout Tower** following the sign posts up to Budapest's highest point.

4 At the base of the tower, take the chairlift down to Zugliget, where you can connect with the bus 291 and get off at the Margit híd, Budai hídfő stop and cross the road and head due north through Elvis Presley Park to the **Lukács Thermal Baths** for a soak and swim.

5 After relaxing a little at the baths, take the number 9 bus to Jászai Mari tér and walk 10 minutes north to the **Pozsonyi Kisvendéglő** for a hearty Hungarian dinner.

Budapest Itinerary Ideas

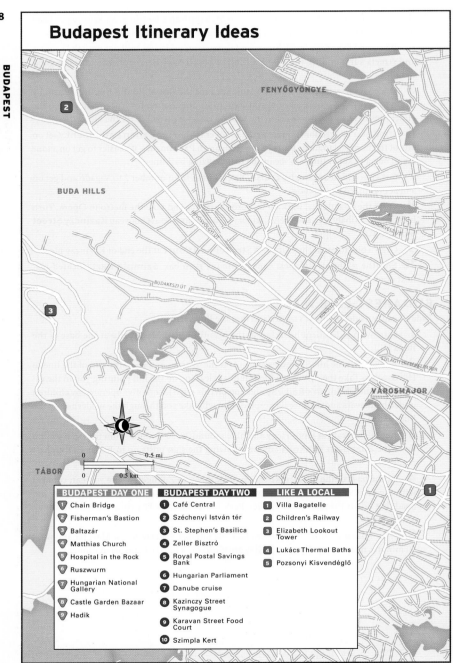

BUDAPEST DAY ONE
1. Chain Bridge
2. Fisherman's Bastion
3. Baltazár
4. Matthias Church
5. Hospital in the Rock
6. Ruszwurm
7. Hungarian National Gallery
8. Castle Garden Bazaar
9. Hadik

BUDAPEST DAY TWO
1. Café Central
2. Széchenyi István tér
3. St. Stephen's Basilica
4. Zeller Bisztró
5. Royal Postal Savings Bank
6. Hungarian Parliament
7. Danube cruise
8. Kazinczy Street Synagogue
9. Karavan Street Food Court
10. Szimpla Kert

LIKE A LOCAL
1. Villa Bagatelle
2. Children's Railway
3. Elizabeth Lookout Tower
4. Lukács Thermal Baths
5. Pozsonyi Kisvendéglő

FENYŐGYÖNGYE

BUDA HILLS

VÁROSMAJOR

TÁBOR

0   0.5 mi

0   0.5 km

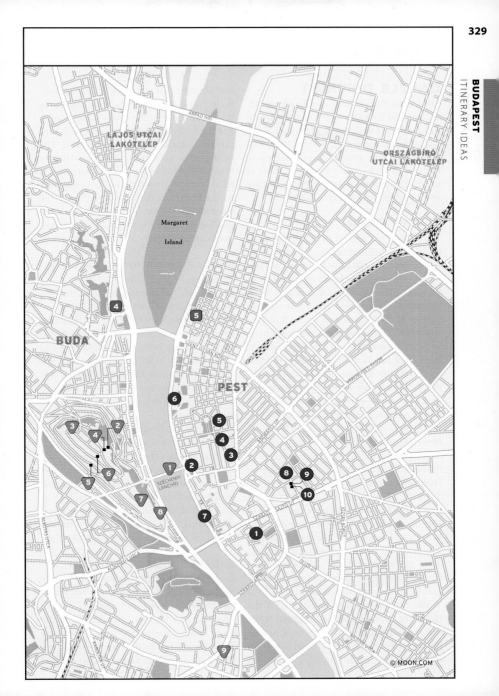

Sights

CASTLE DISTRICT

The Castle District was razed and rebuilt, occupied by Turks for over a century, left in ruins following the Habsburg liberation in the 17th century, besieged again in the 1849 revolution, and then damaged during the Siege of Budapest in 1945. When exploring, think of the district as a patchwork of history, where you'll find stories within the details.

★ Buda Castle

Buda Castle is a symbol of the city, perched on top of the hill overlooking the Danube. Its neo-baroque façade spreads out in columns under a copper-green dome, and is worth the hike up for the views from the terrace.

Despite centuries of history, the palace you see today is fairly new in the Budapest cityscape. The original gothic and renaissance palace was destroyed during the liberation from the Turkish occupation in 1686, then rebuilt from scratch in a baroque style. Much of the façade you see today, including its iconic dome, comes from a post-World War II reconstruction after much of the castle was damaged during the Siege of Budapest. However, you can still find traces of the old castle around the reconstructed turrets or in the foundations in the on-site Budapest History Museum.

Inside, the Spartan walls offer a stark contrast to the Habsburg opulence you'd find in Vienna, as the interior was severely damaged in the war. Later, the interior was gutted and "modernized" under the communist regime of the 1950s. Today, Buda Castle is an important cultural center, home to two museums and the National Széchenyi Library.

You can easily access the castle via the Habsburg steps next to the funicular, at the end of the flagpole-lined promenade, or take the back way via the lift and escalators from the Castle Garden Bazaar, which leads out into the older part of the castle. This is my favorite part of the castle, where you can see the layers of history in the stones lying around, and the reconstructed turrets and walls capture the historic essence of the building. The herb garden next to the Budapest History Museum is a hidden, quiet spot that can be a relief from the crowds packed onto the main terrace. If you take the steps down through the old tower and out the old gate towards Tabán, you'll even find a cluster of Ottoman tombstones under the tree.

HUNGARIAN NATIONAL GALLERY

Szent György tér 2, tel. 06/20-439-7331, http://mng.hu, Tues-Sun 10am-6pm, HUF 1,800 permanent exhibition, audio guides HUF 800

The Hungarian National Gallery occupies the river-facing wings of Buda Castle, and chronicles Hungarian art from the Middle Ages to the avant-garde in the period following 1945. Highlights include late-Gothic winged altarpieces, the realism of Mihály Munkácsy, and the explosive colors from Hungarian expressionists.

Don't miss the dreamlike paintings by Tivadar Csontváry Kosztka on the staircase landing between the first and second floor. Climb up into the cupola and its terrace (open between April and October) for views across the city, or lie on beanbags and look up at hanging wire sculptures. You can easily spend two to three hours here, especially if you decide to see one of the temporary exhibitions.

BUDAPEST HISTORY MUSEUM

Szent György tér 2, tel. 06/1-487-8800, www.btm.hu, Tue-Sun 10am-6pm Mar-Oct, 10am-4pm Nov-Feb, HUF 2000 entrance, HUF 1200 audio guide

The Budapest History Museum sits in the south wing of Buda Castle and is split into three floors. In the basement, you'll find traces of renaissance and medieval relics of

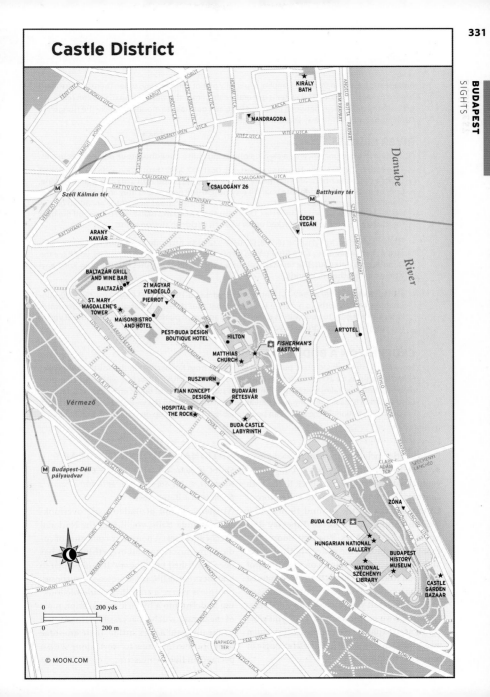

Castle District

Budapest by Boat

Budapest is best seen from the Danube, especially on hot summer days when there's a refreshing breeze to keep you cool. The water is generally calm. From the view of a boat, you can really appreciate the differences between Buda and Pest, and get close to monuments like the Hungarian Parliament Building in a way you can't on land.

RIVER CRUISES

Options in this category include a classic sightseeing cruise, speedboat tour, or amphibious bus:

- **Legenda** (Dock 7 Jane Haining rakpart, tel. 06/1-317-2203, https://legenda.hu, HUF 3900) offers a classic one-hour and 10-minute long sightseeing cruise with a glass of sparkling wine, beer or soft drink included. The boats fit around 150-180 people and they are adaptable to the weather. If you're interested in knowing more about the various sites, there are audio guides available. Otherwise, just sit and relax. Once you get to Margaret Island, you can get off the boat for 90 minutes before being picked up, or you can decide to stay on board.

- **RiverRide** (Széchenyi István tér 7-8, tel. 06/1-332-2555, http://riverride.com, HUF 9000) operates an amphibious bus tour. After taking an on-road tour through the Inner City, you'll see the Danube on a water bus. The tour takes around an hour and 35 minutes and starts on Széchenyi István tér near the Chain Bridge.

- **Dunarama** (tel. 06/70-942-2613, https://dunarama.hu, HUF 36,000-66,000 for 25- or 50-minute long cruises without a guide) is a speedboat tour down the Danube. This luxury water limousine fits only 10 people in its closed cabins and open platform, so this is an option if you're traveling with a small group or you're really feeling fancy.

CRUISING ON A BUDGET

From March through October, public BKK boats run from Kopaszi gát in the south to Margaret Island, or even as far as Rómaifürdő in the north. The route (HUF 750, or free with a city transport pass on weekdays) takes two hours. These boats stop at a variety of docks en route, including the Castle Garden Bazaar, the Hungarian Parliament Building, and on the weekends, Margaret Island.

A word of caution: These boats can be unreliable (i.e. not turn up on schedule), and if the boat

Buda Castle, including parts of the older palace like the 14th century tower chapel and vaulted palace rooms dating back to the 15th century. There is an exquisite collection of Gothic statues on the ground floor, and a unique Hungarian-Angevin Tapestry dating to the Middle Ages. The first floor offers further insight into the history of the palace, and an interactive exhibition on the history of Budapest from the Romans to the Communist era. The top floor is dedicated to the Romans and prehistory. If you're passionate about history, you love gothic sculpture, or you simply want to explore a part of the castle hidden away, the history museum is worth a couple of hours of your time.

NATIONAL SZÉCHÉNYI LIBRARY
Szent György tér 4-6, tel. 06/1-224-3700, www.oszk.hu, Tue-Sat 9am-8pm, HUF 400 for museum and exhibitions

At the back end of Buda Castle overlooking the Buda Hills, you'll find the National Széchényi Library, home to a collection of codices, manuscripts, and everything that has been published in Hungary. It's only open to members of the library for research purposes. So unless you're a traveling academic looking to delve into a historic manuscript, most of the library will be inaccessible. However, if you really want a peek inside, there are some temporary exhibitions to view, along with a permanent library museum.

The view of Buda Castle from a boat on the Danube.

is already full, it won't dock. Your best bet is to embark at one of the first ports of call, like Kopaszi gát, the National Theater, or Rómaifürdő if you want a good seat and a guarantee to board.

Boats are packed on weekends, but weekday mornings are quiet (for locals, it's not the fastest commute). The boats are a little rustier than the touring boats, but the view is still the same. If you're lucky, there is a working bar or toilet on board.

One thing that public boats have over the sightseeing cruises (other than the price tag) is that they go further than the central part of the river, taking you down into the Millennium Quarter and the Kopaszi Dam to the south, and up past Margaret Island and Óbuda Island to the north. Beyond the usual sites, like Buda Castle, the Parliament and the Chain Bridge, The boat north passes offbeat sites like the Óbuda Gas Works, which looks more like a turreted castle than an old factory.

TOP EXPERIENCE

★ Fisherman's Bastion

Halászbástya, Szentháromság tér, March-April 9am-7pm, May-October 9am-8pm, HUF 800

Glimmering white above the Danube, the romantic Fisherman's Bastion overlooks the Hungarian Parliament Building and the rooftops of Pest. Built as a spectacular viewing platform by Frigyes Schulek between 1890 and 1905, it's still one of Budapest's most beautiful structures. Its seven turrets represent the seven tribes that came to the Carpathian Basin back in the ninth century. With winding staircases and arched colonnades, it may look medieval, but it's a 19th century folly.

Why the odd-sounding name? In the Middle Ages, it was very close to a fish market. The Guild of Fisherman defended that portion of the castle wall.

In the summer, the colonnade below turns into a café. It certainly has one of the best views in the city, but let's say it's not necessarily a place locals would go to hang out.

If you want to skip the crowds and the price tag that comes with getting to the top of the viewing platform, then head to the main staircase in the middle—you'll see medieval-style carvings in the arches. The view through those arches is one of the most beautiful over the bastion.

Matthias Church

Mátyás Templom, Szentháromság ter 2,
tel. 06/1-488-7716, www.matyas-templom.hu,
Mon-Fri 9am-5pm, Sat 9am-midday, Sun 1pm-5pm,
HUF 1500 church admission, HUF 1500 tower visit

The Church of Our Lady of Buda Castle (more colloquially known as Matthias Church after the Renaissance monarch was married twice in this church), presents an eclectic architectural tapestry, beginning as early as the 1200s. The colorful interior, painted with frescoes of angels, saints, floral and leaf motifs, can be traced back to the 19th century. Like the rest of the historic district, Matthias Church has seen significant damage (at one point, the Turks turned it into a mosque, stripped it bare and painted its walls). For a different perspective, climb the intricately carved neo-Gothic stairway to the gallery for views across the church and to see exquisite stained-glass windows illuminating the nave from above.

Hospital in the Rock

Lovas út 4/C, tel. 06/70-701-0101, www.sziklakorhaz.
eu, daily 7am-10pm, English language tours depart on
the hour, HUF 4000

Hospital in the Rock is a curiosity built into the caves under Castle Hill. After beginning life as a wine cellar, it was reinforced with concrete in the 1930s and was used as an underground military hospital during World War II (and again in the 1956 Uprising). Later, it was used as a prison for revolutionaries, and then as a secret nuclear bunker during the Cold War. Declassified in 2002, it now houses one of Budapest's most fascinating museums. All the medical equipment on display is original, and the eerie waxwork figures give a lifelike depiction to the hospital. You can only visit the hospital with a guide, but tours run on the hour for English speakers. The tour ends in the decontamination chambers of the shelter (reinforced to withstand nuclear and chemical attack).

Buda Castle Labyrinth

Labirintus, Úri utca 9, tel. 06/70-312-9097,
www.labirintus.eu, daily 10am-7pm, HUF 2500

The entire Castle District sits on top of hollow marl and limestone caves, and underneath each street is a tunnel of similar length. Initially, these natural subterranean pockets were used only as cellars, storage rooms and wells. The Turks later connected many of these underground chambers for strategic reasons, digging almost a mile of tunnels.

Today, you can visit a section of this labyrinth at Buda Castle. The labyrinth winds past a surreal waxwork exhibition with figures dressed in costumes once belonging to the Hungarian State Opera House. You'll then wander into smoky chambers illuminated with eerie blue light where Vlad the Impaler was allegedly imprisoned.

You'll also see marble and limestone relics from Buda's medieval past, along with Turkish tombstones. For an adrenaline-pumping experience, head to the ticket office at 6pm and pick up an oil lantern to guide you through the tunnels when the lights go out. (This is something I do not recommend doing alone—unless stumbling around a dark labyrinth alone sounds like an enjoyable experience).

St. Mary Magdalene's Tower

Kapisztran tér 6, www.budatower.hu, daily 10am-4pm
Mar-Dec, Sat 10am-4pm Jan-Feb, 1500 HUF

Take a stroll around the Castle District, and you may notice a lone church tower hovering above the two-story houses at the corner between Kapisztrán tér and Országház utca. The original church was built in the 13th century as a Franciscan Church for Hungarian-speaking worshippers. Under the Ottoman occupation, it was the only place of worship for Christians in Buda, as the rest of the churches had been converted into mosques. Catholics were confined to the chancel, and the Protestants to the nave, both of which were destroyed in World War II. Only the 15th-century bell tower and a reconstructed window survived the bombing. You can go up the tower if you want a view over Castle Hill; otherwise, it's enough to see the grounds from below.

Castle Garden Bazaar

Várkert Bazár, Ybl Miklós tér 6, tel. 06/1-225-0554, www.varkertbazar.hu, tram 41, 19

Originally built in the 19th century as a pleasure park along the Danube, the Castle Garden Bazaar fell into decay over the decades—but it was renovated in 2014. Today, this neo-Renaissance stretch of sloping promenades featuring statues, fountains, and elegant pavilions has reopened as a cultural center with exhibition halls, film screening space, and restaurants and shops. Head up the walkway and you'll come to the neo-Renaissance gardens. You'll find an escalator and a lift (if needed) that can carry you up to Buda Castle without having to hike up or take the bus or the funicular railway.

INNER CITY AND AROUND PARLIAMENT

★ Hungarian Parliament Building

Kossúth tér 1-3, tel. 06/1-441-4904, http:// latogatokozpont.parlament.hu/en/, daily 8am-6pm Apr-Oct, daily 8am-4pm Nov-Mar, tours run daily from 10am to 4pm, HUF 6000 non-EU citizens including guide, Metro 2

Facing the Danube, in carved blocks of white Hungarian marble, and topped with neo-Gothic spires on a wine-hued rooftop crowned with a dome, the Hungarian Parliament Building is a symbol of the city. An architectural wonder built by Imre Steindl and completed in 1902, its 691 rooms exist in a labyrinth of gold-gilded corridors and grand staircases. It's still in use today, which is why you'll only see part of the building on the tour (and only with a guide).

You can head to the Visitor's Center underground to join a 45-minute tour—but first, you'll want to guarantee your place by buying a ticket online (www.jegymester.hu) because

openings will fill quickly. You'll have a time allocated for your English language tour and you'll have to go through a security checkpoint (similar to an airport check) before you're handed a headset.

The tour takes you up a golden staircase (there is a lift as an alternative to the 100-plus stairs of that staircase). The staircase leads to a corridor lined with stained-glass windows and accents of real gold. (More than 40kg of gold was used to create the gold leaf that covers the Parliament building.)

In the hall under the dome, you'll see the Hungarian Crown Jewels, which once belonged to the canonized King Stephen, the first monarch of Hungary. The crown has led an adventurous life over the past 1,000 years—it has been lost, stolen, and was locked up in Fort Knox at one point until its return to Hungary in 1978. It resided in the Hungarian National Museum until 2000, and then found a new home under the iconic dome.

The tour will take you into the Lobby Room, where you'll spot statues dedicated to Hungarian shepherds, doctors and theologians. You'll then enter the Session Hall and the north gallery overlooking the Danube. Make sure you take some time in the final exhibition room, where you'll find interactive screens and curious information about Budapest and the Parliament building. (For example, there are no chimneys on the structure, and the central heating actually comes from a boiler room in a nearby building—hot air is funneled through a series of shafts and tunnels. And cold air from ice wells under the square was once used as an early form of air conditioning.) You can also see the original red star that was on top of the building in the Communist era.

Chain Bridge

A symbol of a unified city, the Chain Bridge (Lánc híd) is Budapest's oldest permanent stone bridge. This suspension bridge features two vaulted, classical style-pillars connected by large iron chains. Count István Széchenyi

North Pest

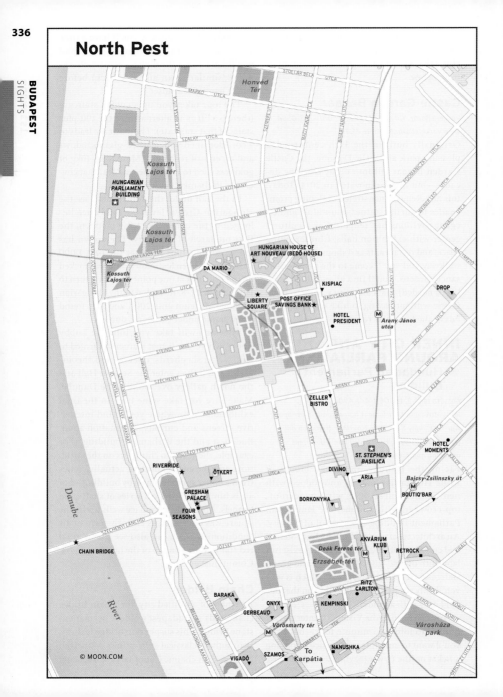

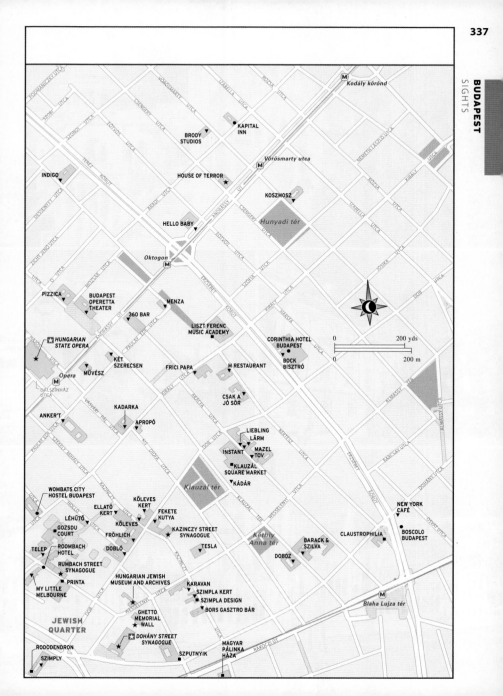

Kodály körönd

KAPITAL INN

BRODY STUDIOS

Vörösmarty utca

INDIGO

HOUSE OF TERROR

KOSZMOSZ

HELLO BABY

Hunyadi tér

Oktogon

PIZZICA

BUDAPEST OPERETTA THEATER

MENZA

360 BAR

LISZT FERENC MUSIC ACADEMY

CORINTHIA HOTEL BUDAPEST

HUNGARIAN STATE OPERA

KÉT SZERECSEN

FRICI PAPA

M RESTAURANT

BOCK BISZTRÓ

Opera

MŰVÉSZ

BÁLSZÍNHÁZ UTCA

CSAK A JÓ SÖR

KADARKA

ANKER'T

APROPÓ

LIEBLING

LÄRM

INSTANT

MAZEL TOV

KLAUZÁL SQUARE MARKET

KÁDÁR

Klauzál tér

WOMBATS CITY HOSTEL BUDAPEST

KŐLEVES KERT

ELLATÓ KERT

FEKETE KUTYA

NEW YORK CAFÉ

LÉHÜTŐ

KŐLEVES

GOZSDU COURT

FRÖHLICH

KAZINCZY STREET SYNAGOGUE

Kéthly Anna tér

CLAUSTROPHILIA

BOSCOLO BUDAPEST

TELEP

ROOMBACH HOTEL

DOBLÓ

TESLA

BARACK & SZILVA

RUMBACH STREET SYNAGOGUE

DOBOZ

PRINTA

HUNGARIAN JEWISH MUSEUM AND ARCHIVES

KARAVAN

MY LITTLE MELBOURNE

SZIMPLA KERT

SZIMPLA DESIGN

BORS GASZTRO BÁR

JEWISH QUARTER

GHETTO MEMORIAL WALL

Blaha Lujza tér

RODODENDRON

DOHÁNY STREET SYNAGOGUE

MAGYAR PÁLINKA HÁZA

SZIMPLY

SZPUTNYIK

0   200 yds
0   200 m

Sightseeing on the Number 2 Tram

Budapest's yellow trams make it easy to navigate the city, and some lines even offer the perfect sightseeing vantage point. Hop on the number 2 tram, beginning at Jászai Mari tér near **Margaret Bridge.** The tram will take you past the Hungarian Parliament Building, down the Danube Banks past the Chain Bridge, past the Vigadó (a gorgeous concert hall) and the city's most famous bridges. Get off at Fővám tér by the **Central Market Hall,** or continue to the **Bálna cultural center** or the Müpa-Nemzeti Színház stop for the **Millennium cultural complex.** Around Christmas, the tram may be dressed up with thousands of festive fairy lights.

financed its construction, and it took almost 50 years to build.

The Germans blew up the bridge in 1945 following the Siege of Budapest, and it was rebuilt in the late 40s. Today, it's one of the most romantic spots to cross the Danube, especially at night when thousands of light bulbs come on. Make sure you stop to look at the stone lions created by sculptor János Marschalkó that flank the entrances to the bridge. Local legend says the sculptor forgot to carve the tongues and jumped into the Danube after being mocked for it. However, it's just hearsay, as the sculptor lived for decades after the bridge was built, and the lions have tongues—they can be seen from above and not from the sidewalk.

At the time of writing, the Chain Bridge was scheduled for renovations from 2019 for 24 months. But you can still get great views from the promenade on both sides of the river, or from above at the top of Castle Hill.

Shoes on the Danube

Set on the embankment just in front of the

1 Fisherman's Bastion, a scenic lookout point on Castle Hill 2 courtyards of Buda Castle 3 Chain bridge 4 Hungarian Parliament Building

Hungarian Parliament, the Shoes on the Danube memorial, envisioned by sculptor Gyula Pauer and filmmaker and poet Can Toga is a poignant reminder of the horrors of the Holocaust. Sixty pairs of iron shoes face the river bank to commemorate the Jews shot into the river by the fascist Arrow Cross party in the 1940s. Sadly, this was not the only location in Budapest where executions like these happened. The shoes—men's, women's, and small children's—were modeled after 1940s designs, with the iron creased and folded like leather.

To get here, follow the stairs down the side of the Parliament, take the crossing over, and walk back towards the Chain Bridge.

Liberty Square
(Szabadság tér)

This green patch in the heart of the city, enclosed by grand buildings housing banks, embassies and offices, was once the location of an 18th century Austrian barracks. Today, statues and memorials can be found all around the square. The **Soviet War Memorial,** an obelisk topped with a gold star, was erected in 1946 by the Soviet army. It stands directly over the resting place of the Russian soldiers who fell during the city's liberation from the Germans. Considering Hungary's communist history, it's controversial, but Hungary signed an agreement to protect the monument. On the other side of the square, a newer memorial to the **"Victims of German Occupation"** appeared in 2014. The memorial has been criticized by some for whitewashing Hungary's collaboration with the Nazis. A moving **protest memorial** made up of candles, personal memorabilia and letters by those whose family died in the Holocaust can be visited just a few feet away.

Postal Savings Bank

Postatakarék, Hold utca

Just behind Liberty Square is the former Postal Savings Bank. It is not open to the public, but is worth passing by. Completed by Ödön Lechner in 1901, this striking example of Hungarian art nouveau is an architectural symphony of Hungarian folk ornamentation, with sprouting flowers and ceramic bees "flying" up to a ceramic beehive. The design culminates with a tapestry-like rooftop made from glazed green and yellow octagonal tiles, topped with serpents, angel wings, and dragon tails.

For an excellent view of the Postal Savings Bank, head across the street to the rooftop terrace of the Hotel President. In the summer, you can sip a coffee on the terrace café, but if you're around in the winter, come up for the rooftop ice rink and a cup of mulled wine.

Hungarian House of Art Nouveau
(Bedő House)

Honvéd utca 3, tel. 06/1-269-4622,
www.magyarszecessziohaza.hu, Mon-Sat 10am-5pm,
HUF 2000 for the museum

From the outside, the Hungarian House of Art Nouveau (also known as Bedő House) looks like it was piped out of a bag full of icing. Built by Hungarian art nouveau architect Emil Viador the style is more in line with French, Belgian, or German Jugendstil than Lechner's orientalist creations. Although residential apartments and offices occupy most of the building, the rest is a shrine to all things art nouveau. You'll find a café and museum filled with antique art nouveau furniture, ceramics, and artwork. The space is more like a curious antique shop than a curated museum. It offers a fascinating collection for anyone wanting a glance into a past world and the way the Hungarian upper middle class lived in the early 1900s.

Gresham Palace

Széchenyi István tér 5

The building that is now the **Four Seasons Hotel** was once a block of luxury apartments and offices, built between 1905-1907 by the London Gresham Insurance Company, which used the building as its headquarters. The gently undulating façade is typical art nouveau style, with ceramic accents, intricate wrought ironwork, friezes, and floral motifs. It's worth taking a peek into the lobby at the intricate curved arcade made with tiles of lead glass, and the beautiful mosaic flooring.

★ St. Stephen's Basilica

Szent István tér, www.bazilika.biz, Mon-Fri
9am-5pm, Sat 9am-1pm, Sun 1pm-5pm, HUF 200
recommended donation. Viewing Platform daily
10am-4:30pm Nov-March, 10am-5:30pm Apr, May,
Oct, 10am-6:30pm Jun-Sept, HUF 600. Treasury
10am-6:30pm Jul-Sept, 10am-4:30pm Oct-Jun,
HUF 400.

It took half a century to build this basilica, partly because its iconic dome collapsed halfway through construction, and the work began again almost from scratch. Today, this impressive neoclassical cathedral stands at the same height as the Hungarian Parliament. (Both are the tallest buildings in downtown Budapest.) You can scale over 300 stairs (or take a lift) to the viewing platform outside the dome for 360° views of Budapest's most famous sites.

The interior of the cathedral—laid out in a Greek cross—is intricate, with frescoes adorning the gold-accented walls. In the chapel on the right-hand side from the entrance, head over to see a mummified relic: the holy right hand of St. Stephen, which is kept inside a gilded box. It gets taken for a yearly "walk" on August 20th, during the St. Stephen's Day procession. Throw a coin in the slot, and the gilded box will light up so you can see the relic in its full glory.

Why is there a mummified limb in the basilica? Legend has it that when the Hungarian king was canonized in 1083, part of making him a saint involved exhuming his body; his right arm was found as fresh as the day he was buried (although apparently not the rest of him). His right arm was chopped off and preserved as a Catholic relic. The hand has traveled to Bosnia, Dubrovnik, Vienna, and

1 The Shoes on the Danube Memorial to the Jews shot into the river by the facist Arrow Cross party.
2 St. Stephen's Basilica

Ödön Lechner: the Hungarian Gaudí

The rooftop of the Royal Postal Savings Bank by Lechner.

Ödön Lechner may be known as the Hungarian Gaudí, but the architect who defined **Hungarian Secession** (or art nouveau) created his most extravagant buildings a couple of years before Gaudí built his most colorful creations. Searching for a style that he could call uniquely Hungarian, and rebelling against the architectural norms of the Habsburg styles, Lechner turned to Hungarian folk art expressed through embroidery and wood painting. He also turned towards the East—following the anthropological theory popular at the time that the Hungarians were an Asiatic race. His architecture blended Indian or Persian influence, Hungarian folk art, and modern technological innovations like iron, steel, fortified concrete, and colorful glazed ceramics and tiles from the Zsolnay factory in Pécs. (Zsolnay were one of the first porcelain, ceramics, and tile manufacturers to develop pyrogranite, a durable type of ornamental ceramic fired under high temperature that could withstand the elements, like frost, making them perfect for architectural details and roof tiles.)

Ödön Lechner is regarded as the master of the Secession and the father of modern Hungarian architecture. His work was a departure from the traditional Habsburg style visible all across Central Europe (which draws its inspiration from Rococo, Baroque and Western Historicism). Hungarian Secessionism followed the art nouveau trends popping up in Europe, but it applied its own Eastern accent, whether in floral motifs inspired by embroidery or in the intricate details from Islamic architecture. His work, which can look like it's been made from gingerbread, is characterized by glazed ceramics and tiles in greens, blues and yellows. His most beautiful buildings can be found in Budapest, including the former **Postal Savings Bank, the Museum of Applied Arts** and the **Geological Institute of Hungary.**

Salzburg. (A priest from the American army returned it to Budapest in 1945.)

Outside the entrance, opposite the stairs heading up to the dome, you can take the lift to the treasury to see some of the fine silver, gold and textiles that are the property of this opulent cathedral.

If you want to get to know the basilica more, you can take a guided tour between 10am and 3pm, but you need to book in advance on the phone (06/1-338-2151). Guided tours in English cost HUF 2,000 and will also take you up to the cupola.

If you're fascinated with the huge pipe

organ inside, you can hear it in action (http://organconcert.hu) on Monday nights (HUF 3,500) and Friday nights (HUF 4,500-7,000).

JEWISH QUARTER
★ Dohány Street Synagogue

Dohány utca 2, tel. 06/1-462-0477, www. greatsynagogue.hu, Sun-Thu 10am-6pm, Fri 10am-4pm Mar-Oct, Sun-Thu 10am-4pm, Fri 10am-2pm Nov-Feb, HUF 3,000, Metro 2, tram 47, 49 Above Károly körút at the intersection with Dohány utca is the Grand Synagogue, more colloquially known as the Dohány Street Synagogue. Its twin towers, topped with onion-shaped domes (covered in intricate gold leaf) rise over 140 feet (approx. 42.67 m).

The Grand Synagogue is Europe's largest. The architecture deviates from traditional synagogues—the architects were not Jewish, and the inspiration for the building came from Christian basilicas. It includes a stunning rose window, a cluster of stars made out of stained glass; an orientalist Moorish twist symbolizes both the Jews' Eastern origins and the Neolog interest in integrating into the local community.

German-Austrian architect Ludwig Förster, along with Hungarian architect Frigyes Feszl, built this 3,000-seat synagogue

in the 1850s. Inside, the seating is divided in two, with the men taking the ground floor (gilded with golden columns) and the women meant to sit in the gallery above, beneath dripping chandeliers.

The arcaded garden outside was a make-shift cemetery during the Holocaust. The 2,000 bodies buried here are commemorated with graves and memorials. Beyond, the Heroes' Temple, also known as the Winter Synagogue, is used for weekday services. In the courtyard before the exit, you'll find the **Raoul Wallenberg Holocaust Memorial Park,** dedicated to the Swedish diplomat who saved tens of thousands of Jews during World War II. You'll see the profound metallic sculpture of a weeping willow by Imre Varga, which was placed directly above a mass grave; victims' names and tattoo numbers glint on the sculpture's dangling metal leaves. You'll also find the **Hungarian Jewish Museum and Archives** (Dohány utca 2, tel. 06/1-462-0477, www.milev.hu, Sun-Thu 10am-6pm, Fri 10am-4pm Mar-Apr and Oct, Sun-Thu 10am-8pm, Fri 10am-4pm Apr-Sep, Sun-Thu 10am-4pm, Fri 10am-2pm Nov-Feb, HUF 4,000). It includes a collection of objects from religious and daily Hungarian Jewish life.

ceiling in the Grand Synagogue

Budapest's Jews of the VII District

The Star of David on the fencing at the Dohány Street Synagogue.

Unlike Prague, Venice, or Krakow, Budapest has never had an exclusively Jewish neighborhood. Jews have lived side by side in Hungary with non-Jews. (The most famous Jewish area in the VII District received the name "Jewish Quarter" after becoming a ghetto in the 1940s.)

The story behind the Jews of the VII District ties in with the segregation rules of the 18th century—Jews could not even spend the night in the Inner City at that time. So the community grew outside the city walls. Many Jews worked as merchants, typically trading grain, cattle, leather goods, and textiles on the market just outside in today's **Deák Ferenc tér** (a large downtown central square bordering on the Inner City where three metro lines meet).

As the community prospered in the 19th century, Budapest's Jews split into two factions: **Neolog Jews,** a socially liberal group inclined towards integrating into Hungary who preferred to speak Hungarian over Yiddish, and the **Orthodox** Community, a conservative community that resisted the modern and secular leanings of the Neolog community.

Budapest's Jewish population peaked following World War I. At that time, there were 125 synagogues and over 200,000 Jews in Budapest alone. Tragically, nearly 50 percent of the city's Jews died in the Holocaust, and the community never fully recovered.

Today, a walk around this district reveals signs of Jewish heritage. But you won't only find signs of Jewish life in this district. In the **VIII District, XIII District** and in **Buda** today, you'll find active synagogues and prayer houses with tightly knit Jewish communities. Some synagogues are visible from the outside, like the **Grand Synagogue** on Dohány utca, or they may be tucked away in a private apartment, like the prayer house on Teleki tér in the VIII District.

Kazinczy Street Synagogue

Kazinczy utca 29-31, tel. 06/1-351-0524, Sun-Thu 10am-6pm, Mar-Oct Fri 10am-1pm March, Fri 10am-4pm Apr-Oct, Sun-Thu 10am-4pm, Fri 10am-1pm Nov-Feb, HUF 1,000

The Kazinczy Street Synagogue, also known as the Orthodox Synagogue, stands in the corner of the cobbled portion of Kazinczy utca. You need to look up to see the Hebrew lettering on the ashlar above the exposed brick façade. The Secessionist-style interior, drawing influences from Hungarian folk art (such as the Transylvanian wood carvings and Hungarian floral motifs) is surprising—it is the heart of Orthodox Jewry in Budapest. The complex, designed by Béla and Sándor Löffler in 1912-13, expands into a courtyard, where there is a kosher restaurant and a shop.

Rumbach Street Synagogue

Rumbach Sebestyén utca 11-13, Metro 1, 2, 3, tram 47, 49

A few blocks away from the Kazinczy and Dohány utca synagogue, the minaret-like towers of the Rumbach Street Synagogue tower over the design shops, vibrant street art, and avant-garde underground theaters that characterize the Jewish Quarter today. This Moorish-style synagogue, designed by Viennese architect Otto Wagner in 1872, is a museum and cultural hall.

Inside the synagogue, seven striking rose windows in a kaleidoscope of colors can be seen in its domed ceiling, and the walls are covered in ornate lavender-, fuchsia-, and lapis-toned friezes. The synagogue fell into disuse following the war, and then stood as a semi-derelict, pigeon-infested ruin after a partial reconstruction in the late 1980s and early 1990s. (The work had to be aborted when the private corporation that bought the building went bankrupt.) But at the time of this writing, it's now back in Jewish hands and is being restored to its former glory.

Ghetto Memorial Wall

15 Király utca

In the winter of 1944, over 50,000 Jews were moved into the ghetto, an area fortified with wooden fencing and stone walls topped with barbed wire. A local conservation group working to protect the Jewish Quarter's cultural heritage has reconstructed the original ghetto wall as a memorial. Take a walk down Király utca and peek through the bars of the gate at number 15 to see it—it's at the back of a courtyard of residential houses. The memorial was constructed from stones from the original ghetto wall and is topped with barbed wire.

AROUND ANDRÁSSY AVENUE
★ Hungarian State Opera

Andrássy út 22, tel. 06/1-814-7100, www.opera.hu, Metro 1

As you're strolling down Andrássy Avenue, stop to admire the Hungarian State Opera House, one of the world's most beautiful opera houses. This neo-renaissance structure was built in 1884 by Miklós Ybl, with the financial support of Emperor Franz Joseph I. Its exterior is decorated with stone sphinxes, muses between the columns, and images of famous opera composers on the roof terrace. Marble columns, vaulted ceilings, and chandeliers adorn the interior. The gold-covered auditorium seats over 1,200, and at the time of this writing, the building is undergoing a major renovation to improve its acoustics and staging, allowing it to compete with other great European opera houses. (It's expected to re-open in early 2019.) If you can't catch a show, you can still join one of the daily tours (HUF 2,990) at 2pm, 3pm, or 4pm. The tours include a mini concert at the end.

House of Terror

Andrássy út 60, tel. 06/1-374-2600, www.terrorhaza. hu, Tue-Sun 10am-6pm, HUF 3,000, Metro 1

This infamous four-story apartment block on the corner of Andrássy Avenue was once the headquarters of the secret police, and a place where many were tortured, killed and held captive. Today, its imposing roof with the word "TERROR" punched out in the metal overhang dominates this part of the avenue. Inside is a unique museum—a monument to the victims of Hungary's fascist and communist regimes—that opened in 2002. The interactive museum contains chilling reconstructed prison cells in the basement, rooms lined with propaganda posters, and installations from the darkest moments in Hungarian history. The museum spreads from the basement to the second floor, and it's worth taking two to three hours to go through, especially if you watch the poignant interactive video

displays, where you can listen to firsthand recorded stories of victims and survivors.

How did the infamous number 60 turn into a tourist attraction? In late 2000, the Public Foundation for the Research of Central and East European History and Society bought the building and spent a year reconstructing the interior to create a memorial and museum to the victims of the regimes.

CITY PARK AND AROUND
Vajdahunyad Castle
Városliget, tel. 06/1-422-0765, Tue-Fri 10am-4pm, Sat-Sun 10am-5pm, HUF 1,700 combined ticket for museum and towers, Metro 1

The spires of Vajdahunyad Castle may look like something out of Dracula (it has been a film location in a Dracula adaptation). But look closely, and you'll notice that this castle, built at the end of the 19th century, is an eclectic mixture of architectural styles. Medieval towers share space with baroque statues. You can get the best views from the gate tower (which you can enter through the door on the left as you go through the gate) or the Apostle's Tower, which is accessible from inside the Museum of Agriculture with a guide. The interior of the castle is just as spectacular, with ornate rococo ballrooms, crystal chandeliers, Renaissance-inspired frescoes in hues of blue and maroon, and stained-glass windows.

The interior of the castle houses the **Museum of Agriculture** (www. mezogazdasagimuzeum.hu), which showcases the history of Hungarian agriculture with reconstructed yurts and dwellings, antique plows, farming equipment, and an impressive collection of taxidermy and antlers. Upstairs, next to the intricate staircase is an interesting photographic exhibition displaying the architectural inspirations for the castle.

1 the Hungarian State Opera on Andrássy Avenue 2 the Hungarian Institute of Geology and Geophysics close to City Park by Ödön Lechner 3 Vajdahunyad Castle in City Park 4 Heroes' Square

The castle grounds are free of charge to roam. You can even go up to the hooded statue of Anonymous, the unknown chronicler who penned the history of the early Magyars in the court of King Béla III, and rub the bronze pen for literary inspiration.

Budapest Zoo
Állatkerti körút 6-12, tel. 06/1-273-4900, www.zoobudapest.com, daily 9am-sunset, HUF 2,800, Metro 1

Founded in 1872, Budapest Zoo is one of Europe's oldest zoos. Located near City Park, the zoo is a vast complex with two artificial mountains, 500 species of animals and 4,000 plant species. You can explore greenhouses dedicated to Madagascar and an Australia section where kangaroos hop right past you. Pay a visit to the turn-of-the-century palm houses built by the Eiffel Company in Paris; they feature a replica rainforest complete with sprinkler-generated "rain." The neighboring butterfly house is also worth a stop.

The main highlights of the zoo are the "Magic Mountain" set inside a hollow, artificial rocky outcrop where you'll find a life-school made up of an aquarium, games, educational experiments, 3D documentary screenings, and the art nouveau elephant house. The elephant house is a spectacular piece of architecture, with mosque-like domes covered in scaly turquoise Zsolnay tiles.

On the way in and out, notice the gate of the zoo, designed by the architect who designed the elephant house. It's flanked by elephants, topped with polar bears, and decorated with intricate botanical murals. (The zoo's art nouveau buildings have been listed as national landmarks.)

The Museum of Fine Arts
(Szépművészeti Múzeum)
Dózsa György út 41, tel. 01/469-7100, www.szepmuveszeti.hu, Tue-Sun 10am-6pm, 1,400 HUF, metro line 1

The Museum of Fine Arts, which resembles a Greek temple, lies on the northern side of

City Park

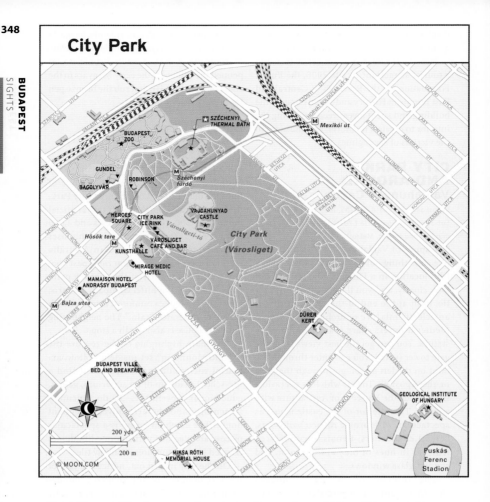

Heroes' Square. After three years of construction work, it reopened to the public in the fall of 2018. The permanent collection spans five floors, so expect to spend over 3 hours if you want to explore the whole museum—and that's without the temporary exhibitions thrown in.

Start in the basement for the museum's exquisite collection of Egyptian art and Classical antiquities. The collection features bronze statuettes of Egyptian gods, painted pottery, colorful sarcophagi, Hellenic sculpture and Roman glass, which could keep any history lover occupied for a couple of hours.

The ground floor is exciting even as this is where you will find the Romanesque Hall—which was closed to the public for 70 years after a bomb damaged the museum in 1945—a stunning hall designed to showcase Hungarian Romanesque art. The Romanesque Hall is covered wall-to-wall with colorful frescoes inspired by the art from medieval churches with a vibrant cast of characters like kings and angels, and mythological figures such as dragons, painted in hues of royal reds, lapis blues, wood green, and accents of gold leaf. This had been built to house medieval plaster casts, but now the hall itself is an exhibition in its own right.

The first floor is now home to European Art from 1250-1600, with work from Europe's greatest Renaissance and baroque masters like Raphael, Titian, Tintoretto, Van Dyck, Holbein, El Greco, and Goya. However, if you're passionate about sculpture, head to the second floor to the display of European Sculpture 1350-1800, including a statue of a horse attributed to Leonardo Da Vinci.

Level three is dedicated to Hungarian Baroque art from the 1600 to the 1800. This collection was originally housed in the Hungarian National Gallery, in the Royal Palace in Buda, which now gets a new home here in the museum.

Kunsthalle

Műcsarnok, Dózsa György út 37, tel. 06/1-460-7000,
www.mucsarnok.hu, Tue-Wed, Fri-Sun 10am-6pm,
Thu noon-8pm, HUF 2,200

Since the 19th century, the Kunsthalle has been the main hub of contemporary art in Hungary. Flanking Heroes' Square, opposite the Museum of Fine Arts, the Kunsthalle looks more like a Greek temple than an exhibition hall, with gold-gilded Corinthian columns. Kunsthalle is one of Budapest's largest exhibition spaces focusing on visual and contemporary art. Top international exhibitions change with the seasons—examples include photography from Steve McCurry and Sandro Miller.

Heroes' Square

Heroes' Square, marked by the towering pillar topped by the Angel Gabriel holding the holy crown, can be seen all the way down Andrássy Avenue. The square itself was erected in 1896 to celebrate the millennium of the conquest of the Carpathian Basin. (The rest of the work on the square was completed in 1929.) The features of the square are packed with Hungarian symbolism, from the chieftains of the seven Magyar tribes at the base of the pillar to the two semi-circular colonnades featuring bronze statues of Hungarian kings and leaders. You'll find statues of Hungarian heroes like Lajos Kossuth, a revolutionary who struggled for independence from Austrian rule during the 1848 uprising against the Habsburgs.

You can get up close to the monuments, including the tomb of the unknown soldier, a cenotaph remembering the soldiers from multiple wars. Next to the tomb is a cast-iron manhole covering for the first thermal water well used for a former thermal bath (originally made out of wood), that once stood on the square.

Today, you'll only find locals on Heroes' Square during protests and marches, like Budapest Pride, or for public events like the National Gallop, a large Hungarian cultural festival centered on horse racing. Otherwise, the square is filled with tourists.

Miksa Róth Memorial House

Nefelejcs utca 26, 06/1-341-6789,
www.rothmuzeum.hu, 2pm-6pm Tue-Sun, 750 HUF

Tucked inside a courtyard in the outer VII District, the Miksa Róth Memorial House is a fascinating and underrated museum dedicated to the life and work of stained-glass artist Miksa Róth. The entrance from the street will bring you into the courtyard. You'll need to take the door on the left to get into the museum.

The former Róth residence occupies part of the museum here, so you'll get a glimpse into the way the Roth family lived. The top floor of the building contains an exhibition of Róth's work, with beautiful panels of stained glass and stunning art nouveau mosaics.

Miksa Róth's Stained Glass

The Miksa Róth museum showcases the work of the famous stained glass artist.

Miksa Róth (1865-1944) was one of Hungary's most prolific and famous applied artists. Working for half a century, he became a master of stained glass and mosaic art. Róth's style evolved through the Secession and beyond with the renaissance of stained-glass art at the end of the 19th century. Following World War I, his art declined while Hungary suffered social and economic challenges.

Róth was Jewish, and his work suffered again during World War II. Although baptized as a Roman Catholic in 1897, Róth still struggled under the anti-Semitic law passed in 1939 that limited Jewish public and economic life. Eventually, he closed his workshop and transferred his house and possessions to his Roman Catholic wife. He died of natural causes in Budapest in 1944 at 89.

His stained-glass art can be found as far away as Oslo and Mexico City, but only in Budapest is his craft embedded into the architectural landscape of the city. Look for his work in the stained-glass windows of the **Hungarian Parliament Building** and inside the stairwell of the **Gresham Palace** building housing the Four Seasons Hotel. Beyond stained glass, Róth also created architectural mosaics, like those in the **Liszt Ferenc Music Academy** and adorning the dome inside the intricate entrance of the **Széchenyi Baths**.

Geological Institute of Hungary

Stefánia út 14, email one week in advance to visit the geological museum and the interior: muzeum@mbfsz.gov.hu, free entrance, buses 5, 7, 110, 112

It's worth going off the beaten track to see the Geological Institute of Hungary, arguably one of Ödön Lechner's most spectacular buildings. Its two-toned tiled blue roof is topped with four Atlas figures holding up a terrestrial globe. Fittingly, the building incorporates geological elements: The roof represents the Thetis Sea, and the building is embedded with

fossil-shaped ceramics. Emperor Franz Josef I approved the founding of the institute, but Lechner, who won a competition for the commission, began work on the building in 1896, finishing in 1899. The institute features the typical Lechner qualities, including folk motifs in the architectural ceramics, and flowers carved into the windows. The institute also

---

1 A cemetery for old communist statues can be found in the Memento Park. 2 The Margaret Island Water Tower has become a symbol of the island. 3 The top of Gellért Hill has some of the best views over Budapest.

houses a geology museum, which can be visited by appointment.

MARGARET ISLAND AND AROUND

Water Tower

Margitsziget, tel. 06/20-383-6352, lookout gallery open daily 11:30am-7pm May-Oct, HUF 600, bus 26

Towering above trees and grassy lawns, the Water Tower on Margaret Island is visible from both Buda and Pest. A beautiful piece of architecture embodying the Hungarian Secessionist style, the tower was also one of the first structures of its kind in Europe that employed innovative ferro-concrete engineering. Designed by Dr. Szilárd Zielinski and built by architect Rezső Vilmos Ray in 1911, it reaches over 180 feet (approx. 55 m) into the air.

The tower can be admired from most spots on the island, whether you relax with a book or ride a quadracycle. To get into the tower you must buy a ticket at the ticket office (which is also the box office for the open-air theater in the area). Then you can hike up 153 steps to the lookout platform for 360-degree views across the island, the river and the city.

Dominican Convent Ruins

Margitsziget

King Béla IV is responsible for this convent's construction. He promised God he would build a convent on the island and send his daughter Margaret there if Hungary survived the Mongol invasion in 1241. The Mongols withdrew, and his daughter, then nine years old, became a nun. She was later canonized.

The ruins of the Dominican Convent still stand on Margaret Island, and they consist mostly of excavated stone walls with a few gothic features. The ruins are available for public view for free, so anyone can stroll among them. Margaret's remains were taken off the island when the nuns fled the Turkish invasion in the 16th century, but you can still see her sepulcher marked by a slab of red marble. Nearby, a memorial enclosed in red bricks contains pictures of the saint,

and you'll likely see candles left behind by devout Catholic locals. There are metal lookout points positioned among the ruins that allow a better overview of the former convent's layout.

If you're interested in medieval history, there are more ruins scattered on the island. Just north of the convent, there is the reconstructed **Romanesque Premonstratensian Church,** dating back to the 12th century.

Budapest Pinball Museum

Radnóti Miklós utca 18, www.flippermuzeum.hu, Wed-Fri 4pm-midnight, Sat 2pm-midnight, Sun 10am-10pm, HUF 3000

Over on mainland Pest, the Budapest Pinball Museum (officially Europe's largest ongoing interactive museum dedicated to pinball machines) draws visitors from the world over. Tucked away in a 400-square-meter basement, the museum's 130 vintage pinball machines are available for play (they are not just for show). There is no need to bring any coins—a fee for playing on the machines is included in the museum's admission price. The oldest pieces in the collection are bagatelles from the 1880s, a 1920s table hockey game, and a Humpty Dumpty game from the 1940s (one of the first pinball machines to include flipper bumpers).

Margaret Bridge

Margaret Bridge is Budapest's second permanent bridge, built in 1876 by French engineer Ernest Gouin. The iron structure painted in pale yellow is suspended on seven stone pillars with statues of winged, bare-breasted women (created by French sculptor Adolphe Thabard). This bridge doesn't stretch across the river in a completely straight line running from A to B; it stands at right angles to converge with Margaret Island's southern tip. It begins from the edge of the Grand Boulevard and goes over to Buda, where the middle prong (which was added later in 1901) also runs down to the island. You can take tram 4 or 6 to the middle of the bridge and stroll down to the island.

Ottomans in Budapest

The Turks ruled over the city of Buda for 150 years (1541-1686), and you'll find plenty of Ottoman relics in Budapest today. The Turkish baths are the most famous Ottoman contribution to the city—but look closely and you'll find turban topped tombstones around **Buda Castle,** or Islamic elements left behind in Christian churches, like the mihrab (a niche in the mosque wall indicating the direction to Mecca), in the **Inner City Church** next to the Danube in Pest. On the hill overlooking the Danube in north Buda, there is also the octagonal tomb (closed at the time of writing for renovations) of the dervish, **Gül Baba,** who legend has it bought roses to Hungary.

Turkish influences still linger in the Hungarian language, with words like *dohány* (smoke) and *kávé* (coffee) in the Hungarian lexicon. **Paprika,** an ingredient synonymous with Hungarian cooking, arrived in the country during the Ottoman era and became part of peasant cooking after the Turks were seen spicing their stews with the red powder.

Only traces of the occupation can be found in Budapest, like the baths.

SOUTH BUDA
★ Gellért Hill

Gellért Hill, a green, rocky outcrop on the banks of the Danube, is named for martyred Venetian bishop St. Gellért who, according to legend, was thrown down the hill in a barrel full of nails during the Great Pagan Rebellion of the 11th century. His statue still towers above a man-made waterfall, surrounded by columns (with stone pagan Magyars by his feet) opposite Elizabeth Bridge.

You can take the stairs going past the waterfall and the statue of the saint, and then follow a labyrinth of paths to the top of the hill and the Citadel, or you can hike up alternative routes, like the path up by the Danubius Hotel Gellért and the Thermal Baths. Winding trails thread through the woodland covering the hillside, with incredible views through the trees over the river and the castle. Both routes take around 15-20 minutes to walk.

If you want the view without the hike, take the number 27 bus from Móricz Zsigmond körtér to the Búsuló Juhász (Citadella) stop for a gentle stroll to the Citadella. Stop at the lookout point on the left for amazing views of the city.

PHILOSOPHER'S GARDEN

Halfway up Gellért Hill—if you turn right at the statue rather than take the path to the Citadel—you'll find the Philosopher's Garden, named for sculptures representing figures like Gandhi, Jesus, and Lao-Tsu, among others. It's a peaceful patch of green with views over Buda Castle and the river. On the weekends, you'll find people on picnics and maybe practicing yoga here.

THE CITADEL

The Citadel fortress crowns the top of the hill. This dramatic structure was built by the Habsburgs after the 1848-49 War of Independence and became obsolete by the time it was built. Although the museum in the Citadel has closed indefinitely, it's worth the hike up for the views over the Inner City. This is the highest point in downtown Budapest,

South Buda

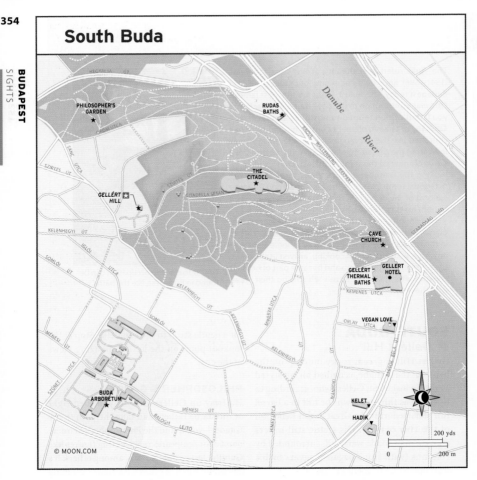

© MOON.COM

and you're rewarded with panoramas over the Danube, Buda Castle, and the bridges.

Then you can wander over to the **Liberty Monument,** which dominates the skyline with its bronze female figure clasping a palm leaf above her head. The monument, a tribute to the Soviet soldiers who died liberating the city in the wall, is one of the few Soviet relics in the city center.

Cave Church

Szent Gellért rakpart 1/a, tel. 06/20-775-2472, Mon-Sat 9:30am-7:30pm, HUF 600
Facing the entrance to the Gellért Baths on a

rocky outcrop is the cavernous entrance to the Cave Church. There's evidence that the cave was inhabited as far back as 4,000 years ago, but the earliest known inhabitant was a hermit named Iván, who resided in the Middle Ages and helped cure the sick with the bubbling thermal waters that now fill the pools of the Gellért Baths. The church's rocky interior became a home to Paulite Monks, Hungary's only homegrown monastic order, in 1926. The monks expanded the cave to make way for further chapels and attached a neo-Gothic monastery to the side of the hill looking over the Danube in 1934. The Cave Church led an active life in the 20th century: It sheltered Polish refugees in World War II, and in the 1950s, it was seized by the Communists, who briefly walled up the entrance with concrete.

Today, the church is functioning again. Outside Mass hours (daily, 8:30am, 5pm, and 8pm; Sunday, 11am), the church is open to visitors. You can explore the caverns, which lead into the turreted monastery on the outside.

Buda Arboretum

Villányi út 29-43, tel. 06/1-305-7270,
http://budaiarboretum.szie.hu, Daily 8am-4pm
Nov-Feb, 8am-6pm Mar-Oct, tram 17, 61, bus 27

The Buda Arboretum is open to the public for free. It's a quiet spot in the city with trees and plants from all corners of the world. It is beautiful in fall when the leaves change color and carpet the pathways.

★ Memento Park

Balatoni út-Szabadkai utca sarok,
tel. 06/1-424-7500, www.mementopark.hu,
daily 10am-dusk, HUF 1,500

Memento Park is a cross between an open-air museum and a graveyard to communist statues and street propaganda. Following the fall of the regime, all the communist statues and propaganda were removed from the city and relocated to this plot of land, which was transformed into a public outdoor museum in the early 1990s. It's a trek to reach—You can take the daily shuttle bus at 11am from Déak Square, which returns at 1pm (running only on Mondays and Saturdays Nov-March, HUF 4,900 return journey, including entry), or take the 150 bus from Újbuda or the Kelenföld Train Station, but the excursion up into the XII District's Buda Hills is worth it.

It's impossible to miss the imposing gate marking the entrance—a monumental red-brick structure that looks like a socialist caricature of a Greek temple. As you approach the ticket office, socialist songs and communist hymns blast out from the small kiosk. Beyond the kiosk, the walled park contains bronze statues and placards of propaganda. Statues of Hungarian communist leaders stand side by side with the likes of Lenin and Soviet soldiers. István Kiss's "Republic of Councils Monument," is a behemoth of a sculpture inspired by an avant-garde propaganda poster meant to encourage military recruitment. (The figure looks as if he is sprinting.) On your way out of the park, stop by the time-traveling phone booth, where you can dial in the year and listen to the voices of communist leaders like Stalin and Béla Kun.

Opposite the park, a replica of the gigantic boots once belonging to a statue of Stalin hold a place on a giant grandstand. Inside, there is a bunker with a few statues and busts of Lenin. Between the statue park and Stalin's boots, there is a barracks-style building with a museum inside, dedicated to the history and the fall of communism in Hungary. To the right of the entrance, you can sit down to watch a subtitled movie screening of secret police training films from Hungary's Communist era, with interesting insights like how to equip a handbag with a secret camera.

SOUTH PEST
Central Market Hall

Nagyvásárcsarnok, Vámház körút 1-4, tel.
06/1-366-3300, Mon 6am-5pm, Tue-Fri 6am-6pm,
Sat 6am-3pm, Metro 4, trams 2, 47, 48, 49

As the biggest market in the city, Central Market Hall may attract its fair share of tourists snapping shots of dried paprika and cured sausages, but it's still one of the best markets for locals. This vast, cathedral-like hall with steel beams, iron girders, exposed red brick, and large windows opened in 1897. Goods were once delivered by barges that sailed into the market thanks to special docks. That capability has disappeared from the structure, but you can still stroll past the baked goods, meat, cheeses, vegetables, and stalls specializing in Hungarian delicacies. Head up to the top floor to find stands selling folk art, such as embroidery and painted woodwork, and to sample Hungarian dishes like *lángos*. Even if you have no intention to buy, it's worth visiting the market for its grand architecture and the energy you'll experience there.

South Pest

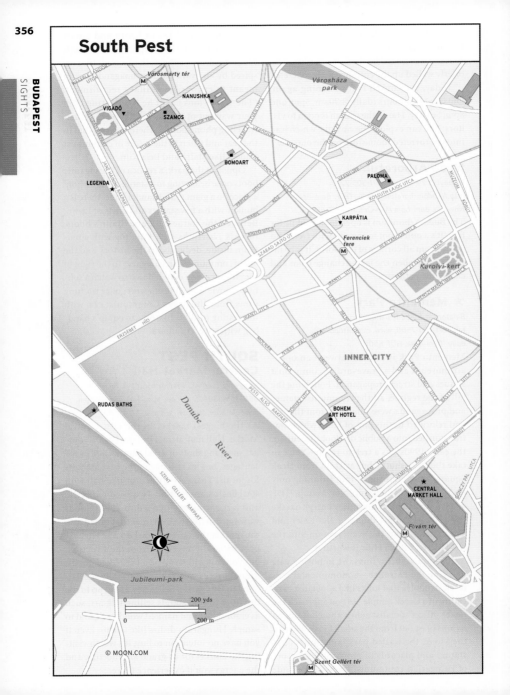

Vörösmarty tér

NANUSHKA

VIGADÓ

SZAMOS

Városháza park

BOMOART

PALOMA

LEGENDA

KARPÁTIA

Ferenciek tere

Károlyi-kert

INNER CITY

RUDAS BATHS

Danube River

BOHEM ART HOTEL

CENTRAL MARKET HALL

Fővám tér

Jubileumi-park

| 0 | | 200 yds |
| 0 | | 200 m |

© MOON.COM

Szent Gellért tér

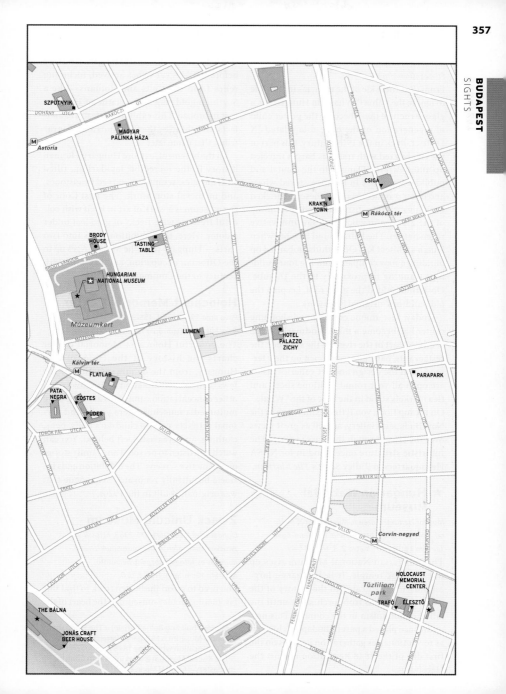

The Bálna

Fővám tér 11-12, 06/30-619-2052,
www.balnabudapest.hu, Sun-Thur 10am-8pm,
Fri-Sat 10am-10pm

From the other side of the river, it's impossible to ignore the Bálna ("Whale" in Hungarian), a glass structure that's become the poster child of regeneration of the once-dilapidated IX District. Back in the 19th century, this part of the city buzzed with trade, as barges traveled up and down the Danube to the capital and public warehouses in the area stored wheat and other produce. Many of these red bricked buildings fell into disrepair at the beginning of the 21st century but soon saw innovative regeneration. The Bálna found new life when Dutch architect Kas Oosterhuis embarked on building a new complex from the four buildings standing in proximity to the Danube. Oosterhuis added the glass roof, keeping the old buildings' original brickwork.

Today, this unique cultural and shopping center has become a main landmark on the southern part of the river. In the summer, the restaurants, bars, and cafés open up their terraces, and the design and art galleries inside are open all year round. Antique shops and flea markets stand in the base of the "Whale." On the top floor, you'll find exhibitions in the New Budapest Gallery, as well as great views over the river through the glass rooftop. The futuristic structure once stood in for NASA Headquarters in Ridley Scott's *The Martian*.

★ Hungarian National Museum

Magyar Nemzeti Múzeum, Múzeum körút 14-16,
tel. 06/1-338-2122, https://mnm.hu, 10am-6pm
Tue-Sun 1,600 HUF, Metro 2, 3, tram 47, 49

The Hungarian National Museum rises up like a Greek temple. It is Hungary's largest museum, dedicated to the history of the Carpathian Basin from prehistory until the fall of communism in the country. This museum once played a part in Budapest's history, as revolutionaries gathered on its steps on the first day of the 1848 Revolution against the Habsburgs.

An extensive archaeology exhibition can be found on the ground floor; it features excavated artifacts that chart Hungarian history before the Magyar tribes arrived, including relics from the Celts and Romans—like a Scythian gold stag and a statue of Heracles cast in bronze. This exhibit also features artifacts left behind by the first Huns and Magyar tribes that came later.

In the basement, explore Hungary's Roman history in the incredible lapidarium, filled with mosaics, sculptures, carved headstones, and medieval stonework. The first floor of the museum is a work of art in itself with colorful frescoes with flecks of gold leaf under a dome. Here, the exhibition splits into two parts — Hungary from the Middle Ages up to the Ottoman occupation, and from the 18th century to the Communist era.

Holocaust Memorial Center

Páva utca 39, tel. 06/1-455-3333,
www.hdke.hu, 10am-6pm Tue-Sun, 1,400 HUF

The powerful Holocaust Memorial Center charts the history of the Holocaust in Hungary, from the dehumanization of the Jews to their extermination at Auschwitz and other concentration camps. It's an interactive multimedia museum where you'll find personal artifacts such as children's dolls, pens, clothing, and eyeglasses left behind. You can watch and listen to personal and family stories on interactive screens. The exhibition ends inside a beautifully renovated synagogue that was originally built in the 1920s.

Zwack Unicum Museum

Dandár utca 1, tel. 06/1-476-2383, https://
zwackunicum.hu/en/zwack-muzeumok/zwack-
muzeum-es-latogatokozpont/bemutato,
Mon-Sat 10am-5pm, HUF 2,200

You need to go off the beaten track to find this fascinating factory museum in the heart of the

---

1 Modern building Balna (Whale) 2 The Hungarian National Museum is Hungary's largest museum and the location where the 1848 Revolution began 3 The Kiscelli Museum is a set in an 18th Century monastery 4 Central Market Hall

All about Unicum

Go into any Hungarian bar, and you'll see a dark-green glass bottle with a gold cross on a red background. The concoction inside, called Unicum, is made from over 40 herbs and spices from all over the world. Its recipe is a tightly guarded secret, passed down through the Zwack Family. Dr. Zwack, an imperial physician to the Habsburg court, invented the drink that helped soothe the digestion of Emperor Joseph II, who (legend has it) christened the drink by exclaiming "Das ist ein unikum!"—*This is unique!*" The Zwacks decided to bottle and sell the drink on a commercial scale in 1840.

The Zwack family was Jewish, but converted to Catholicism in 1917. Despite becoming devout Catholics, they had to hide out in cellars protected by the Swedish Embassy when members of the fascist Arrow Cross party came looking for them. Their factory, now the location of the **Zwack Unicum Museum,** suffered bombing damage in the war; in 1948, the government confiscated and nationalized the factory, and the family fled to the US, taking their recipe with them. For decades, the Unicum produced in Hungary was inferior, until Peter Zwack returned to Hungary in the 1980s and got the business back.

Discover the Hungarian spirit, Unicum, at the factory where it all started.

For many, Unicum is an acquired taste. The almost-black liquor is served as an aperitif and digestive. If you find it too bitter, try the fruity-tasting Unicum Szilva, which is aged on a bed of dried plums.

IX District, just one street off the Danube. You'll need a guide to visit the distillery, but once you reach the museum, you can explore on your own. The order of the tour can vary, but the first part is usually a guided tour around the distillery, where you'll learn a few of the secret ingredients in Hungary's iconic drink. You'll begin in a room filled with vats of cardamom pods, chamomile, ginger root, liquorice, and peppercorns you can touch and smell. Then, you'll descend into the cellar to see the distillation process before trying a shot of Unicum straight from the red and black barrels. Back in the visitors' center, you can watch a documentary about the Zwack family. The museum is filled with Unicum memorabilia, including the largest collection of miniature bottles in the world. (There are about 17,000 behind glass cabinets.)

Kerepesi Cemetery

Fiúmei út 16-18, tel. 06/1-896-3889, http://fiumeiutisirkert.nori.gov.hu, daily 7am or 7:30am - 5pm Jan, Feb, Oct-Dec, 7am-5:30pm Mar, 7am-6pm Sep, 7am-7pm Apr and Aug, 7am-8pm May-Jul, Free

Located near the Keleti Train Station, this walled cemetery, established in 1874, contains roughly 3,000 graves and mausoleums amid lush parkland. The most impressive sepulchers belong to key Hungarian figures—revolutionary heroes, politicians, and prime ministers, including János Kádár, Hungary's socialist leader for three decades, and József Antall, who was the first democratically elected prime minister following the Communist era. Beyond the statesmen, you'll also find the graves of Hungary's most beloved poets, writers, scientists, artists, architects, and music hall performers. Notable figures in this cemetery include: Attila József, Ödön Lechner, and Mihály

Munkácsy. The graveled paths lead past columned arcades to angel-guarded tombstones and memorials and grand, neoclassical mausoleums. Most spectacular is the resting place of Lajos Kossúth, a revolutionary and the governor-president during the 1848 revolution against the Habsburgs. If you wander over to plot 21, you'll find graves belonging to those who died in the 1956 Uprising.

Pick up a free map at the entrance to the cemetery to locate the noteworthy graves. There is also a small museum offering insight into the Hungarian approach to death and burials. If you want to see tradition in action, come on November 1st when the graves are lit up with tea lights and candles.

The Millennium Quarter

Take tram line 2 to the penultimate stop, Müpa-Nemzeti Színház, on the southern part of the Danube banks in Pest, and you'll come to a cultural corner built between 2001 and 2006 as part of an urban regeneration project. The Millennium Quarter is not only a cultural power hub, where you'll find the National Theater, the Palace of Arts and the Ludwig Museum in one spot—It's probably Budapest's most adventurous location for experimental modern architecture. You'll find a statue of a submerged "Greek" temple in the lake, and a riverside ziggurat overlooking the river.

PALACE OF ARTS

Müpa, Komor Marcell utca 1, tel. 06/1-555-3000, www.mupa.hu

The Palace of Arts complex is the most important building in the Millennium Cultural complex, award-winning for its cutting-edge design and simplicity. It kind of looks like a windswept box on the outside, and the interior blends a Herculean sense of space with lots of glass. It's like a cultural shopping mall home to some of the city's most important cultural venues, like the cavernous Béla Bartók National Concert Hall, the Festival Theater and the Ludwig Museum. The Palace of Arts has some of the best acoustics and sound

technology in Europe, and its consistently impressive musical lineup is booked far in advance.

LUDWIG MUSEUM

Komor Marcell utca 1, tel. 06/1-555-3444, www. ludwigmuseum.hu, Tue-Sun 8am-10pm, 1,600 HUF

The Ludwig Museum is inside the Palace of Arts. This contemporary art museum showcases Hungarian and international works. You'll find an impressive pop art collection here, including pieces by Andy Warhol, but most of the focus is on Central and Eastern European art. If you're passionate about modern art, it's worth the tram ride to this museum.

NATIONAL THEATRE

Nemzeti Színház, Bajor Gizi Park 1, tel. 06/1-476-6800, https://nemzetiszinhaz.hu

The National Theatre exudes architectural drama before you even step inside. There is a small ziggurat between the main building and the Palace of Arts; you can wander up its spirals for views over the river. When viewed outside from the front, you'll notice the theater sits on the bow of a ship, which rises above a man-made moat—look for the submerged Grecian temple. You'll also see statues of Hungarian actors on the park grounds. Inside, the setting is a bit more humble compared to the dramatic exterior (but it's probably better not to get distracted while you're watching a play).

ÓBUDA

Aquincum

Szentendrei út 133-135, tel. 06/1-250-1650, www.aquincum.hu, Tue-Sun 9am-6pm Apr-Oct, open otherwise in dry conditions, HUF 1,600

Although Roman ruins are scattered around Óbuda, the main ruins are enclosed in the main archaeological site of Aquincum, a Roman city built around 100 AD, whose citizens numbered between 30,000 and 40,000 by the end of the second century. Allegedly, Roman Emperor Marcus Aurelius penned part of his famous philosophical "Meditations" here in this Roman settlement.

You can follow in the footsteps of Roman society, winding through the excavated ruins, including a reconstruction of a painter's house, the hypocaust systems that once warmed bathhouses, and the worn-down stones once paving the marketplace and the forum. Stroll into the lapidary (with walls lined with stone carvings and tablets). Close to the entrance is a modern museum hall set in a former electrical transformer house, which contains excavated mosaic flooring, frescoes, statues, and dolphin-adorned fountains. The museum's most famous piece is the Aquincum organ, dating back to the third century, on display 75 years after its excavation.

Kiscelli Museum

Kiscelli utca 108, tel. 06/1-250-0304,
www.kiscellimuzeum.hu, Tue-Sun 10am-6pm
Apr-Oct, Tue-Sun 10am-4pm Nov-Mar, 1,600 HUF

It's a significant hike to get to the Kiscelli Museum, which is located in a former 18th-century monastery. This canary-yellow building functioned as a barracks and a military hospital before being bought up by an antiques dealer whose final wishes were for the property to become a museum. The eclectic collection includes 19th century trade signs, and the contents of an entire apothecary that was once located in Pest. Life in 18th to early 20th century Budapest is depicted through antique furniture, sketches of the city, and art nouveau stained glass. Attached to the building is the shell of an old church, used for contemporary exhibitions.

BUDA HILLS
Children's Railway

Gyermekvasút, tel. 06/1-397-5394,
www.gyermekvasut.hu, Tue-Fri 9am-4pm in winter,
daily 8:45am-5:45pm in summer, HUF 800

This small railway line chugs along for just under seven miles from Széchenyi-Hegy to Hűvösvölgy with stops in between. With the exception of the drivers and engineers, all the jobs on the railway line are staffed by school children aged 10 to 14, who sell and check tickets, signal, and salute passengers as the train pulls in and out of the station. The railway is a relic from the Communist era, built in 1951 to encourage a good work ethic. Today, the tradition continues but without the propaganda. The schools work together with the railway, permitting students with a good academic

The Children's Railway is one of the top sites up in the Buda Hills.

Roman Budapest

The name Óbuda means "Old Buda," which is fitting, since this part of the city has its roots in antiquity. The Roman settlement of Aquincum is the most famous reminder of pre-Magyar Budapest, and you'll find Roman ruins scattered around Óbuda. Close to Flórián tér, hidden under unsightly flyovers, you can visit the monumental ruins of the Roman baths (Flórián téri aluljáró, Tue-Sun 9am-6pm, Apr-Oct—open otherwise in dry conditions, free entrance) once belonging to the Roman military camp, accessible from the underpass. Travelers can also head over to the Hercules Villa (Meggyfa utca 21, Sun 11am-1pm Apr-Oct), named for the imported mosaic featuring the villa's namesake hero. The villa was discovered in the 1950s when workmen were digging foundations to build a school. There are seven rooms in the villa, accessible via a raised platform so you can get a good look at the mosaics, and there is also a museum and a garden where you'll find ancient ruins. Other ruins in Budapest include the amphitheater close to Kolosy tér that once had the capacity for an audience of 15,000. There are also a few stones of Contra-Aquincum, the former Roman military camp in Pest, just below Elizabeth Bridge. Roman Hungary came to an end with Attila the Hun in the 5th century, five centuries before the Magyar tribes led by Árpád conquered the Carpathian Basin.

record to miss the odd day of school to work here. Riding from one end to the other takes about 45 to 50 minutes; the trip goes through the woods and around the Buda Hills.

To reach each end of the railway, you can either take the 56 or 61 tram up to the end of the line to Hűvösvölgy and take the steps up to the station, or you can opt for the scenic route by taking the cogwheel railway (tramline 60) up into the hills to Széchenyi-Hegy from Városmajor, which runs on the public transportation line. You can either buy a ticket and go from one end to the other, enjoying the view, or get off on the way and hike a bit.

Elizabeth Lookout

Daily 8am-8pm, free

Hike up the highest point in Budapest, János Hill (János-hegy), which rises about 1,700 ft above sea level. At the top of the hill you'll reach the Elizabeth Lookout point, a neo-Romanesque tower with 134 steps leading to incredible views across Budapest and surroundings. If it's a clear day, you might even spot the Tatra Mountains in Slovakia in the distance. Should the tower look familiar, that's because it was designed by the same architect who constructed Fisherman's Bastion in the Castle District.

To get here, you can get off from the children's railway at the János-Hegy stop, or if you're feeling adventurous, take the 291 bus from Nyugati train station to the final stop, Zugliget-Libegő, and take the chairlift (HUF 1,000 one way, HUF 1,600 return) to the base of the tower. The climb takes around 15 minutes, and you can use the chairlift year-round from 10am until dusk (3:30pm in the winter to 7pm in the high summer).

Note that on Mondays on even-numbered weeks, it's closed for maintenance (with the exception of public holidays).

Thermal Baths

Budapest's thermal baths are a perfect anti-dote for its wild nightlife. They are a must-do item on any visit to Budapest.

At least one section of a bath complex must be filled with natural thermal water to qualify as a thermal bath. Each bath has thermal pools at different temperatures, ranging from cool plunge pools to hot pools (placards recommend staying in for less than 10 minutes), and then a main pool that's usually around body temperature (the recommended bathing time is usually 30-40 minutes). Some thermal baths will also have a swimming pool, saunas and a wellness area. Massages are offered for an extra charge.

You'll find two categories of baths in Budapest—the baths built by Turks when Hungary was occupied by the Ottoman Empire, and the grand baths built in the late 19th and early 20th centuries. The **Turkish baths** (also called Ottoman Baths) are similar to those you'd find in Turkey, with pin-pricked cupola domes and octagonal pools; but unlike the *hamams* you'd find in Istanbul, the Budapest baths have a plunge pool rather than a marble slab where you're scrubbed down, soaped and massaged. These baths date back as far as the 16th century. The later **19th-20th century baths** followed hot on the heels of Central Europe's bathing cure craze; consider Baden-Baden in Germany, or Carlsbad (Karlovy Vary) in the Czech Republic. Their grandiose baths have complexes indoors and outdoors, often ornamented with neoclassical statues or art nouveau tiling, and you'll find large swimming pools, sauna complexes and bathing terraces.

THE BATH EXPERIENCE

A few things are smart to bring with you to the baths:

- Bring your own **bathers** to Budapest. If you forget your swimsuit, some complexes allow you to rent them, along with towels and bathrobes.

- It's a good idea to pack a pair of **shower slippers** for hygienic reasons, but if you forget them, most baths rent them out as well.

- If you plan to use the swimming pools attached to the baths, make sure you wear a **swimming cap,** which you can usually buy at reception, or bring your own (even a shower cap will do).

You'll get a wristband when you buy your ticket, which will let you into the bath complex, and can be used to open and close your locker or cabin (so you can change and lock up your things in the same place). Some baths may offer different ticket packages, like a basic ticket that's only for the thermal section or the swimming pool, while others may charge a surplus for the sauna. Massages, on the other hand, require an appointment, so if you want one, ask when you're buying your ticket.

Make sure you shower before dipping into the pools and relax in the steam, whether you're indoors or outdoors.

Apart from the Rudas baths on weekdays (which is women only on Tuesdays, and men the rest of the week), the baths are open for both men and women. And although there is no hard and fast rule, they are not recommended for anyone under the age of 14.

Unless you're at one of the infamous spa parties (also known as "Sparties," which are usually ticketed and take place Saturday night at the Széchenyi Baths), Budapest's thermal baths are a place of healing, so try not to be too noisy or splash about, unless you're in one of the outdoor swimming pools.

The best time to go is first thing in the morning before breakfast, as the baths are the cleanest at this point, and you'll miss out

Choosing a Bath

It's no accident Budapest has earned the nickname "City of Spas." Below the city are over 100 geothermal springs, each with its own mineral profile. There is a bath in Budapest for everyone's taste, whether you want to bathe in a historic monument or go where the locals go.

MOST FAMOUS

The **Széchenyi Baths** is Budapest's largest and most famous thermal bath complex. Go for the stunning columned outdoor pools. Stay because you find out there are even more pools indoors (page 365).

LOCAL FAVORITE

Laid-back **Lukács** is popular with locals for its understated turn-of-the-century elegance, pump room, and the healing properties of the water (page 368).

BEST FOR FAMILIES

Open-air and seasonal, the **Római Open-Air Baths** are popular with kids thanks to the jungle of water slides there (page 369).

MOST OPULENT

The **Gellért Baths** are an art nouveau architectural treasure (page 367).

BEST BATHING IN THE BUFF

If you go to the **Rudas** on weekdays, the bath is single-sex, and bathing in the nude is permitted. Women's days are Tuesdays, and Men's are Mondays and Wednesdays-Fridays (page 367).

QUIETEST TURKISH BATH

You can easily miss the entrance to the **Veli Bej** because you have to enter a hospital to get to this hidden Turkish bath, newly renovated for the 21st century (page 368).

BEST BUDGET OPTION

If you want a simple thermal bath experience, the **Dandár** is a great choice if you're pinching pennies (page 368).

on most of the crowds. Some of the quieter baths, like the Veli Bej, are cozy on a winter's evening.

If you have any health concerns, like a heart condition, it's best to consult your healthcare provider about taking the waters in Budapest.

★ SZÉCHENYI BATHS

Állatkerti körút 11, tel. 06/1-363-3210,
www.szechenyibath.hu, daily 6am-7pm,
HUF 5,900 weekends, Metro 1

Canary-yellow walls accented by Ionian columns and sculptures of bathing nymphs and youths riding dolphins surround the large turquoise pools of the Széchenyi Baths. Built between 1909 and 1913, it's one of the largest bath complexes of its kind. Once you've explored the 13 indoor pools and the labyrinthine changing rooms above and below the three outdoor pools, it's easy to see why this elegant and relaxing place is so popular.

There are three public entrances to the baths. One main entrance faces the zoo and the circus, and has a Rococo-inspired entrance hall; the other faces the park and shows off even more opulence, with gold-tipped frescoes and Secessionist ceramics. The third entrance is hidden on the side by the metro. All three entrances are part of the same ticket, but the type of cabin varies, as the baths were

initially built with the interior side and its entrance for the aristocracy and upper classes, and the exterior part for the masses.

The complex also includes luxury massage facilities. The all-inclusive Palm House spa (HUF 32,490) can be found in the rooftop greenhouse. There is even a beer spa (HUF 14,600 combined ticket for a beer spa for one and entry to the baths) where you can lie in a wooden tub filled with hops, malt, yeast and aromas, and pull your own pints from a separate keg as you soak.

KIRÁLY BATH

Fő u. 84, tel. 06-1-202-3688, http://en.kiralyfurdo. hu, Mon.-Sun. 9am-9pm, 2,400-2,700 HUF, tram 41, 19, bus 9, 109

Built by the Turks over 450 years ago, Király Bath is Budapest's oldest still operational thermal bath. Its cupola covers an octagonal pool surrounded by crumbling plaster and exposed brickwork. While the Király Bath is in desperate need of a renovation (the last time one was completed in the 1950s to fix up the damage from World War II), it is still worth a visit. Steam hovers above its three thermal pools and its icy immersion pool. A coating of mineral deposits covers the rim of the main bath from the decades (perhaps centuries), of mineral water, which pours out of a vintage iron tap in the central pool. Rich in calcium, magnesium, hydrogen-carbonate and sulfate, with a dash of sodium and the odd fluoride ion, the water is said to soothe conditions such as degenerative joint disease and chronic arthritis.

Following the reoccupation of Buda from the Ottomans, the König family acquired the bath at the end of the 18th century. It's smaller and grittier than the other baths, but many love it for its authenticity. It's the cheapest of the historic baths, so it draws in a more local crowd, mixed in with a few tourists. The Király Bath is open to both men and women,

and it's a good alternative to the Rudas Baths, which are single-sex on weekdays.

(At the time of writing, there were plans to close the Király Baths for renovation, so they may not be open during your visit.)

RUDAS BATHS

Döbrentei tér 9, tel. 06/1-356-1322, http:// en.rudasfurdo.hu, daily 6am-10pm Turkish bath, daily 8am-10pm wellness, HUF 6,200 combined ticket for Turkish bath, wellness and swimming pool on weekends, HUF 4,000 Turkish bath only on weekends

Out of all the Turkish Baths, the Rudas Thermal Bath is indisputably the most popular. The complex is composed of three parts: the 16th-century bath built by the Ottoman Turks, the 19th-century colonnaded swimming pool, and the 21st century wellness center. The old Turkish part of the bath is nudist and single-sex bathing only on weekdays (Tuesdays for women, others for men), but on the weekend when the bath is mixed, bathers are compulsory. Expect long queues if you go on the weekends. Bathing under the cupola, with light shining through its stained-glass, it's easy to see why this bath has become so popular.

On the other side, a beautiful swimming pool (filled partly with thermal water) looks more like a Roman bath than a place to take a few laps. The wellness center uses the same water as the Turkish part, from the slightly radioactive Juventus spring, which is said to have anti-aging properties. The pools downstairs are clean, modern, and can be less crowded than the Turkish baths. (And they are open to both sexes throughout the week.) The main draw is the rooftop jacuzzi that overlooks the Danube.

GELLÉRT THERMAL BATHS

Kelenhegyi út 4, tel. 06/1-466-6166, www.gellertbath. hu, daily 6am-8pm, HUF 5,800 weekends

Behind the Danubius Hotel Gellért, the Gellért Thermal Baths capture the grandeur of Budapest's golden age at the turn of the 20th century. The bath complex may be

---

1 the Gellért Baths are famed for their art nouveau baths and 1930s wave pool 2 The famous Széchenyi Baths are beautiful, and are also one of the largest in Central Europe.

smaller than the vast Széchenyi, but there's plenty on offer both inside and outside.

The main pool lies enclosed inside an atrium with Roman-style columns and a glass rooftop. Inside the hotel, steam drips off the aquamarine Zsolnay tiles that ornament the indoor thermal pools. Of the outdoor pools, the highlight is the main pool, which still uses a wave machine on the hour (it dates back to 1927) and was one of the very first of its kind. In total there are eight thermal pools ranging from 66°F to 100°F, as well as cool plunge pools and swimming pools.

Gellért draws its water from beneath Gellért Hill—there is a hidden tunnel (not open to the public) running under the hotel and the hill going all the way to the Rudas Baths.

Aside from the medicinal waters and art nouveau splendor, the baths also offer a range of treatments for those with a medical prescription—like mud baths and carbon dioxide baths, a range of massages, and more.

LUKÁCS THERMAL BATH

Frankel Leó út 25-29, tel. 06/1-326-1695, http:// en.lukacsfurdo.hu, daily 6am-10pm, HUF 3,900 entry on the weekend, HUF 800 sauna world supplement

Although it may lack the grandeur of the Széchenyi and Gellért Baths or the history of the Turkish Baths, this tranquil 19th-century thermal bath is the place locals come to relax with a dose of old-world nostalgia.

To enter the complex, take a stroll through the garden that's next door to the Orfi hospital, past the placards on the walls from grateful patients whose ailments were cured by the mineral rich water.

Once past the turnstiles, a tiled labyrinth links to the changing rooms and down to a courtyard where you can plunge into two frigid swimming pools. In another courtyard, a warm activity pool bubbles from massaging jets and a circular current.

Indoors, the thermal baths are compact, with dark marble columns and neoclassical statues. Each pool is heated at a different temperature. The water is piped in from one of the

world's largest thermal water caves, located just across and under the road, and the pools give off a slight sulfurous whiff. For HUF 600 on weekdays and 800 HUF on weekends, you can access "Sauna World," which includes several types of saunas, a salt cabin, a steam room, and cooling pools where fresh ice is dropped in periodically thanks to a handy automated slide.

VELI BEJ BATH

Árpád Fejedelem útja 7, tel. 06/1-438-8587, daily 6am-midday, 3pm-9pm, HUF 2,800

From the street, it's easy to miss this Turkish bath, as it's hidden behind the glass windows of a rheumatological hospital. The entrance to the bath is through the hospital. Once inside, you'll see a sign that looks like a number counter, which is used when the bath is full (usually on weekend afternoons). If you have the patience to wait around 15-20 minutes, pick a number and wait in the café by the ticket counter. The waiting list system ensures that the bath will never be overcrowded.

Once you're through the ticket office and the changing room, the hospital corridors will lead you into the historic bath complex, built in the 16th century by the Turks. What's different about the Veli Bej Bath is that it's been recently renovated, so in place of crumbling stone walls, you'll find this bath painted in clean white and salmon tones. The main octagonal pool is flanked by four chambers, each with a single pool at different temperatures. Pop outdoors between the bath and the hospital to the sauna cabins, where you'll see the original Turkish bath structure in its glory, or head to the corridor on the side to view remains of Ottoman excavations.

OTHER THERMAL BATHS

Sometimes the more popular baths can get a little crowded. If you want to escape the tourist crowds, try these alternatives.

Dandár

Dandár utca 5-7, tel. 06/1-215-7084,

http://en.dandarfurdo.hu, Mon-Fri 6am-9pm,
Sat-Sun 8am-9pm, 1,900 HUF thermal bath only,
2,500 HUF wellness and thermal bath, tram 2

Just behind the Unicum Factory in South Pest, you'll notice a brick building on the side street. The Dandár Thermal Bath is a small, no-frills thermal bath with two thermal pools indoors. It's popular with locals for medicinal purposes. (There are two outdoor heated pools in the garden, but they don't use thermal water.)

Palatinus

Margitsziget, tel. 06/1-340-4500, http://
en.palatinusstrand.hu, daily 8am-8pm, 2,800 HUF
on weekends, bus 26

The Palatinus Bath, an open-air thermal complex surrounded by trees, was once the go-to spot during the summers on Margaret Island. Since its renovation in 2017, this art deco bath has extended the invitation year-round to visitors. The thermal water here comes from below the island.

Paskál

Egressy út 178, tel. 06/1-252-6944,
http://en.paskalfurdo.hu, daily 6am-8pm, 2,600

The Paskál Thermal and Open-Air Bath lies far out in residential Zugló and is popular with the locals for its blend of indoor spa with thermal water and outdoor swimming pool. The most attractive feature is the bubbling activity pool that spans both the inside and outside, with the exterior part leading right to a swim-up bar.

Római

Rozgonyi Piroska utca 2, tel. 06/1-388-9740, http://
en.romaistrand.hu, daily 9am-8pm Jun-Sep, 2,700
HUF on the weekends

Római Open-Air Baths get their name from the Romans, who used the thermal water in the area to supply the baths in Aquincum. Today, this modern outdoor swimming pool also uses the lukewarm water rich in minerals, but unlike other thermal baths, this open-air seasonal bath is popular with kids, thanks to its jungle of water slides.

Bars and Nightlife

Budapest really comes to life at night. It can be impossible to avoid costumed groups of bachelor and bachelorette parties in the Jewish Quarter, but you can escape rowdy crowds after sundown if you know where to look. Ruin bars tend to rule, but in the summer, rooftop bars, gritty "kerts," and glam Danube-side terraces become main attractions.

You'll find most of the nightlife clustered around the Jewish Quarter, which also has the nickname the *bulinegyed* ("party district") for its density of bars. Kazinczy utca is the main nightlife hub, home to Szimpla Kert and other popular bars, along with Király utca. Gozsdu Court (Gozsdu udvar), a series of interconnected courtyards filled with restaurants and bars, is another of the neighborhood's main hubs.

When planning a night on the town, it's a good idea to bring plenty of cash as some of the grittier ruin bars won't take cards. (Some of the larger ruin bars like Szimpla Kert or Fogas Ház will have ATM machines.) You'll only come across cover fees for club nights, concerts, or special events. But expect to have your bag searched by bouncers at the door on busy nights. (They want to make sure you're not smuggling alcohol in.)

A glass of beer will cost around HUF 400-700 depending on the bar, beer, size (you can get a *pohár,* a 300ml glass, or a *korsó,* a large 500ml beer glass). Cocktails tend to range around HUF 2,000-3,000. Some bars serve bar snacks, like *pogácsa,* a savory cheese or herb scone that helps soak up the booze. Aside from beer, wine, and cocktails, popular spirits include *pálinka*, a fiery fruit brandy served as a shot, and a bitter herbal liquor called Unicum.

★ RUIN BARS

Set inside crumbling, semi-abandoned buildings filled with eclectic furniture and local art, ruin bars are unique to Budapest. You'll find most of these bars concentrated around the heart of the Jewish Quarter, but some extend beyond. Many bear the name "kert" ("garden" in Hungarian), as some ruin bars pop up in empty plots in the city, serving as urban sanctuaries during the day, and party hubs at night. Ruin bars also host cultural events, like farmers' markets, movie screenings, refugee meetups, interactive art events, or charitable cooking drives.

You'll find most of the ruin bars inside or just around the Jewish Quarter.

Jewish Quarter
★ SZIMPLA KERT
Kazinczy utca 14, tel. 06/20-261-8669, https://szimpla.hu, Mon-Sat midday-4am, Sun 9am-5am
Szimpla Kert is the original and most famous ruin bar in Budapest, and over the year, it probably draws as many visitors as Buda Castle. It spans an entire gutted apartment block. It's like a nocturnal wonderland with fairy lights, old computer monitors, and creaking furniture painted in a kaleidoscope of colors. You can even sit in a Trabant car in the courtyard.

INSTANT
Akácfa utca 49-51, tel. 06/70-638-5040, http://instant.co.hu, daily 4pm-6am
Instant once resided in the VI District, but since then, the super-ruin pub has moved, with Fogas Ház taking over much of the indoor space. There are four dance floors and eight bars from the basement to the top, with music catering to different tastes. The main dance hall features pixel cloud hangings and surreal wall art, and the party goes on all night.

FOGAS HÁZ & KERT
Akácfa utca 51, tel. 06/70-638-5040, http://fogashaz.hu, daily 4pm-6pm
Fogas Ház and Kert got its name ("House of Teeth") from its residence in a former dental lab. Trees wrapped with fairy lights brighten the courtyard next to the main bar area, which is tucked beneath a circus tent. Since it

Szimpla Kert is one of the most popular ruin bars in Budapest.

Sparties

Spend a Saturday night doing something you can only do in Budapest: Go to a **Sparty** (https://spartybooking.com, €50, over 18s only). These watery nights of hedonism take place in Budapest's famous spas every Saturday, usually in the outdoor pools at the Széchenyi or the Lukács Baths. It's a mix of thermal water with DJs, atmospheric lighting and poolside bars. The demographic usually skews towards travelers in their 20s and the parties can get pretty wild, with plenty of poolside drinking, and some nudity (against the rules) or a condom floating in the water in the late hours. Make sure you buy a ticket in advance from the website—these parties sell out fast.

became housemates with Instant, partygoers flock to this ruin bar complex for hedonism until dawn.

ELLATÓ KERT
Kazinczy utca 48, tel. 06/20-527-3018,
Mon-Sat 5pm-4am, Sun 5pm-midnight
Just off Kazinczy utca, Ellátó Kert is hidden behind a plastic tent flap that brings you into an open courtyard with covered rooms to the side. The murals draw influence from Aztec art, which goes well with the taco booth at the back of the bar. Out of Budapest's ruin bars, Ellátó Kert is probably the most popular with locals.

KŐLEVES KERT
Kazinczy utca 37-39, tel. 06/20-213-5999,
www.koleves.com, weekdays 1pm-midnight,
weekends 1pm-1am, summer only
In the summer, this garden comes to life with hammocks, fairy lights, and laughter. Kőleves Kert ("Stone Soup") occupies a plot where a house once stood. There is a bar at the front in a small wooden pavilion where you'll have to get your own beer and stroll over the gravel back to your brightly painted bench or table.

Around Andrássy Avenue
ANKER'T
Paulay Ede utca 33, tel. 06/30-360-3389, Wed 6pm-1am, Thu-Sat 6pm-2am
From the outside, Anker't is just another dilapidated apartment block. But inside, this large complex has been stripped back to its foundations, and its courtyard regularly fills with crowds drinking under hanging lanterns and an open sky. At the back of this minimalist complex, you'll also find a covered bar and a dance area.

BARS AND PUBS
There's more to Budapest bar life than ruin bars, whether they're set on rooftops or cozy corners.

Jewish Quarter
TELEP
Madács Imre út 8, tel. 06/30-633-3608,
Mon-Thu midday-midnight, Fri-Sat midday-2am
You can spot Telep by the stickers plastered all over the windows, and the hip crowd spilling into the street outside. Part art gallery, part bar, Telep has become one of Budapest's core urban meeting points. It's your chance to hang out with the cool crowd in Budapest.

LIEBLING
Akácfa utca 51, tel. 06/1-783-8820,
Mon-Sat 6pm-4am
Liebling is a cozy bar in the Fogas Ház-Instant ruin bar complex. Below the huge lips on the rooftop, Liebling is decked out in brick and wood. The spiral staircase takes you up to a hidden terrace that's popular in the summer. This bar is a good alternative for a drink if you're not in the mood for the hedonism of its ruin bar neighbors.

FEKETE KUTYA

Dob utca 31, tel. 06/30-951-6095, Mon-Wed
5pm-1am, Thu-Sat 5pm-2am, Sun 5pm-midnight

A cozy pub loved by the locals, you need to go under the arches on Dob utca to find Fekete Kutya. The bar is a little on the shabby side but has a welcoming atmosphere and a great beer collection on tap. Make sure you try their chive *pogácsa*!

Around Andrássy Avenue
★ BOUTIQ'BAR

Paulay Ede utca 5, tel. 06/30-554-2323, www.
boutiqbar.hu, Tue-Thu 6pm-1am, Fri-Sat 6pm-2am

One for the cocktail lovers—Boutiq'bar can mix up any drink you desire. Try one of their creative concoctions like Bombay Nights (gin with mango masala and yogurt), or Hello Tourist, made with aged apple pálinka, wine, and a hint of pastis with cinnamon and apple. You can ask the award-winning bartenders to prepare you something unique with seasonal ingredients.

★ BRODY STUDIOS
(THE STUDIOS)

Vörösmarty utca 38, tel. 06/1-266-3707, see events
for opening hours: www.brody.land/brody.studios

The Studios, formerly known as Brody Studios, embraces the ruin bar aesthetic and frequently hosts parties and cultural events. This members' club may require you to ring a doorbell, but not all nights are members-only (see their website or Facebook page to check the program). It's best to check out the events online before going. It's worth visiting for its bohemian look and atmosphere.

360 BAR

Andrássy út 39, tel. 06/30-356-3047, www.360bar.
hu, Mon-Wed 2pm-midnight, Thu-Sat 2pm-2am, Sun
midday-midnight

360 Bar lives up to its name with panoramic views over Budapest's famous landmarks. You can reach the rooftop terrace with the lift at the side entrance of the Párizsi Department Store. In the summer, enjoy drinks al fresco; in winter, the bar sets up transparent igloos so you can still enjoy views over the Hungarian Parliament Building and St. Stephen Basilica.

WINE BARS

Wine is a big part of Hungarian culture, and at Budapest's wine bars, you can find a wide range of grape varieties from different regions across the country.

Inner City and Around Parliament
DIVINO

Szent István tér 3, tel. 06/70-935-3980,
http://divinoborbar.hu, Sun-Wed 4pm-midnight,
Thu-Sat 4pm-2am

DiVino exclusively serves Hungarian wines from its downtown location right next to the Basilica. If you want to try the best wines from upcoming Hungarian wine makers, look no further. Recommended by Michelin, this wine bar is always a hotspot of activity. DiVino has another branch in Gozsdu Udvar (Király utca 13).

Jewish Quarter
★ DOBLÓ

Dob utca 20, tel. 06/20-398-8863,
www.budapestwine.com, Sun-Wed 2pm-2am,
Thu-Sat 2pm-4am

Dobló specializes in Hungarian wine and *pálinka*. You can either take a table or sit up at the mahogany bar in the brick-walled, chandeliered tasting room. There are various tasting packages available, including packages based on terroir or grape type.

Around Andrássy Avenue
KADARKA

Király utca 42, tel. 06/1-266-5094,
http://kadarkawinebar.com, daily 4pm-midnight

This sleek wine bar on Király utca embodies a character different from the surrounding ruin bars. Their impressive wine list features wines not only from Hungary, but from surrounding countries like Romania as well. You'll get a small plate of *pogácsa* (savory scones) before tasting begins. Kadarka gets full on the weekends and evenings, so you'd be wise to make a booking.

APROPÓ

Király utca 39, tel. 06/30-193-3000, Mon-Wed
8am-midnight, Thu-Fri 8am-2am, Sat 10am-2am
This stylish wine bar embodies an industrial chic aesthetic, complete with exposed brick and Edison bulbs dangling from the ceiling. It serves a range of wines from Hungary, France and Italy. They also serve Hungarian food.

CRAFT BEER

Hungary's reputation for wine has grown significantly in recent years, and Budapest's beer scene is not far behind. The recent surge in microbreweries and craft beer bars have made it easier than ever for beer lovers to try great Hungarian beer. Try some locally brewed beers like Keserű Méz, a bitter, un-strained lager from the Fóti Brewery, or a really good IPA called Távoli Galaxis. If you like sour beers, try Rafa from the Fehér Nyúl brewery.

Jewish Quarter
CSAK A JÓ SÖR

Kertész utca 42-44, tel. 06/30-251-4737,
www.csakajosor.hu, Mon-Sat 2pm-9pm
Csak a Jó Sör (literally meaning "good beer"), lives up to its name. Although it looks like a small shop, you can choose from a wide range of rare and specialty beers, such as smoky stouts, or brews accented with coriander. There are four types of draught beer on tap if you want to drink some great beer while you're out in the Jewish District, but you can also pick up some great bottled beer to go.

LÉHŰTŐ

Holló utca 12-14, tel. 06/30-731-0430, Tue-Thu
4pm-2am, Fri-Sat 4pm-4am, Sun-Mon 4pm-midnight
You'll find Léhűtő in a brick-walled basement. This location is popular with local beer connoisseurs. The bar carries a top selection of craft beers. Six taps change regularly to showcase the best Hungarian craft beers. In addition, they carry 30 local and international beers, including IPAs, stouts, and wheat beers from the best Hungarian breweries.

South Pest
★ ÉLESZTŐ

Tűzoltó utca 22, tel. 06/70-336-1279, www.elesztohaz.
hu, Mon-Sat 3pm-3am, Sun 3pm-midnight
Élesztő was one of the first craft beer places to open in Budapest. It occupies a former glass-works factory and sports a ruin bar aesthetic, but it's unique in that it focuses on craft beer. The main bar has 21 Hungarian beers on tap, and across the courtyard you'll find imported beers.

★ JONÁS CRAFT BEER HOUSE

Fővám tér 11-12, tel. 06/70-930-1392, Mon-Thu
11am-midnight, Fri-Sat 11am-2am, Sun 11am-11pm
Jonás Craft Beer House is aptly named for its location in the Bálna (Whale). It not only serves wonderful beers, but also pálinkas and other drinks, and you can't beat the view over the river from its Danube-side terrace. Jonás regularly changes its Hungarian beers on tap, and there is always an interesting range to try.

KRAK'N TOWN

József körút 31a, tel. 06/30-364-5658,
www.krakntown.com, Mon-Fri 4pm-midnight,
Sat-Sun midday-midnight
With ship portholes, hot air balloons hanging from the ceiling, and plenty of brass accents, Krak'n Town may make you feel like you've wandered into a steampunk fantasy. The Hungarian beers on tap change regularly. The food here is a British-Hungarian fusion and worth trying as well.

LIVE MUSIC
DÜRER KERT

Ajtósi Dürer Sor 19-21, tel. 06/1-789-4444,
www.durerkert.com, Mon-Sat 5pm-5am,
Sun 5pm-midnight
Part ruin bar, part concert venue, Dürer Kert by City Park is worth the visit if you're into rock, metal, or alternative music. Relax outdoors in the pebbled garden for a few pre-gig beers, or to talk about music till dawn. There are concerts almost daily. The cover fee for concerts depends on the event. It can be as

low as HUF 500 or up to HUF 6,500 for better-known international acts.

BARBA NEGRA

There are two venues here: Barba Negra Music Club (Prielle Kornélia utca 4, tel. 06/20-563-2254, www.barbanegra.hu) and **Barba Negra Track** (Neumann János utca 2) which lies around the corner to its sister-club. The former is a large indoor club that hosts rock gigs and all-night parties; the outdoor Track is only open in the summer, with loud music, enthusiastic crowds and plenty of beer on tap.

BUDAPEST JAZZ CLUB

Hollán Ernő utca 7, tel. 06/1-798-7289, www.bjc.hu, Mon-Thu 10am-midnight, Fri-Sat 10am-2am

Budapest Jazz Club is in a converted art deco cinema and features a bar in the lobby. The music offered here is a diverse range of local and international jazz acts. This elegant jazz club is known for its high-quality sound and state-of-the-art equipment.

CLUBS
Inner City and Around Parliament
ÖTKERT

Zrínyi utca 4, tel. 06/70-330-8652, Thu-Sat 11am-5am, Sun-Wed 11am-11pm

Like many venues in Budapest, Ötkert has many facets: It's a restaurant and cultural space early in the evenings, and a party venue with live music and top DJs at night. The building has a capacity of up to 1,000 people. You may even spot the occasional movie star in the crowd.

They have a strict dress code—no metal, punk looks, or neck tattoos.

Jewish Quarter
DOBOZ

Klauzál utca 10, tel. 06/20-449-4801, http://doboz.co.hu, Wed-Sat 10pm-6am, Sun 10pm-5am

Doboz fits in with the Jewish District ruin bar look. It occupies an old apartment block. A giant metallic gorilla climbs the 300-year-old tree in the courtyard. Here, DJs work by genre in different rooms, with hip-hop in one and house in another.

LÄRM

Akácfa utca 51, tel. 06/1-783-8820, http://larm.hu, Sun-Wed 10pm-4am, Thu 10pm-5am, Fri-Sat 11pm-6am

LÄRM is a club that looks like a black box. It's dedicated to techno lovers, hidden inside the Instant-Fogas Ház complex. Despite being surrounded by the city's most popular bars, it keeps its underground feel. It's simple and all in black, with top audio equipment to keep even the most die-hard techno lovers content in these gut-shaking surroundings.

TESLA

Kazinczy utca 21/c, tel.:06/30-519-5922, www.teslabudapest.hu, Fri-Sat 11pm-5am

Sharing the former electrical transformer building with the Museum of Electrical Engineering, Tesla keeps up with the electric atmosphere with its unique Sound Ceiling and top sound system. It's one of the biggest clubs in Budapest. Its beat is intelligent electronic music.

Around Andrássy Avenue
HELLO BABY

Andrássy út 52, tel. 06/20-776-0767, www.hellobabybar.hu, Fri-Sat 10pm-5am

This palatial building is home to a library by day, but after dark on Fridays and Saturdays, its courtyard, tiers of arcades, stone balustrades and rooms are transformed into a spectacular club. Light shows play on the crumbling walls and arches as the DJ gets the crowd in the mood with urban electronic music.

South Buda
★ A38

Petőfi híd, tel. 06/1-464-3940, www.a38.hu, Mon-Sat 7:30am-11pm, Sun 12:30pm-11pm

A38 is certainly one of Budapest's most unusual venues. This former Ukrainian stone-carrying ship is permanently moored on the banks of the Danube. The bar and restaurant reside upstairs in the boat section. The stairs descend into a subterranean chamber beneath the Danube. A38 usually hosts indie and alternative concerts and club nights. The cover fee depends on the event (some are free), so check the program.

Performing Arts

CONCERT VENUES

BUDAPEST PARK
Soroksári út 60, tel. 06/1-434-7800,
www.budapestpark.hu, event days 6pm-dawn
Budapest Park is one of Budapest's largest open-air venues that has a music festival feel. It stretches over 118,000 square feet, making it ideal for large concerts and parties. It may seem like a bit of a trek to get to (especially as you have to take the number 2 tram to the end of the line beyond Rákóczi Bridge), but it's worth coming out for the buzzing atmosphere. Check the website for up-to-date listings so you know what's on.

AKVÁRIUM KLUB
Erzsébet tér 12, tel. 06/30-860-3368,
http://akvariumklub.hu, Wed-Sat midday-4:30am,
Sun-Tue midday-1am
Akvárium Klub lies beneath an artificial lake at the heart of the city. The glass roof reflects the water into the venue, so it feels as if you are inside an aquarium. There is one large concert hall (1,300 capacity) and a smaller one (fits 700). In the evenings, you'll find gigs from local and international bands here. The music is pretty eclectic, ranging from rock and metal to jazz, pop, and electronica. Although events tend to run in the evenings, the bar—especially the terrace in the summer—are open during the day.

PERFORMING ARTS AND CONCERT HALLS
Hungary, and Budapest in particular, has a solid foundation in classical music, opera and musical theater. Famous Hungarian composers and musicians are known the world over, and within Budapest alone, you can find top classical music venues and theaters dedicated to the performing arts.

Inner City and Around Parliament
VIGADÓ
Vigadó tér 2, tel. 06/1-328-3340, http://vigado.hu,
tickets range from HUF 1,000-3,500
Budapest's second-largest concert hall takes up impressive residence on the Danube. It's in a beautiful Romantic-style building with huge arched windows. The Vigadó also houses exhibitions on the upper floors, but it's most popular for classical concerts. It may not have the best acoustics in the city, but it's worth visiting for the architecture alone.

Around Andrássy Avenue
HUNGARIAN STATE OPERA
Andrássy út 22, tel. 06/1-814-7100, www.opera.hu
This is one of the most beautiful opera houses in Europe, and it's budget-friendly, too. If you can make it to an opera, try to get a ticket. With recent (and ongoing) renovations, you can expect acoustics to go with the stunning architecture. You can see the current program of shows on the website. Offerings range from well-known operas by Puccini, Verdi, and Mozart to more obscure work by Hungarian or contemporary composers. There are ballet productions as well. You can get cheap tickets for the top tier (if you do, you'll need to go through the entrance on the left-hand side to go up. Note: There's no lift.) Some seats have limited visibility. Make sure you dress up for the occasion.

The less impressive **Erkel Theater** (II

Budapest's Broadway

Budapest Operetta and musical theatre

Intersecting Andrássy Avenue, **Nagymező utca** is a lively street lined with cafés with streetside terraces, museums, and above all, theaters. Footprints belonging to Hungarian stage and screen stars line the sidewalk outside the Budapest Operetta Theater, a candy-pink building with echoes of belle epoque grandeur.

In its heyday in the early 1900s, Budapest, along with Paris and Vienna, was considered one of the most important cities for operetta theater, and even today the Operetta is one of the most popular theaters in the city, staging around 500 shows a year, from traditional Hungarian operettas to international musicals. An operetta is a light opera, characterized by fun melodies and comedic storylines, and you'll find shows here from the most famous Hungarian composers like Ferenc Lehár or Imre Kálmán.

Even if the ambience is more lighthearted than the Hungarian State Opera around the corner, people still like to dress up for a show, so it's best not to turn up in sneakers and jeans. Head across the road to the Komédiás Kávéház for a pre- or post-show drink or dinner; you'll pass a bronze statue of Imre Kálmán (one of Hungary's most loved operetta composers), sitting with a cigar in hand. The entire street is densely packed with theatrical history. Even the cafés on Nagymező utca capture the grandeur, and it's easy to picture an era when divas would come to dine or sip coffee between shows.

János Pál pápa tér 30, tel. 06/1-332-6150, www. opera.hu) steps in for productions when the Hungarian State Opera House needs to close for renovations.

BUDAPEST OPERETTA THEATER

Nagymező utca 17, tel. 06/1-312-4866, www.operett.hu, tickets HUF 1,100-8,000

Alongside Vienna and Paris, Budapest is famed for its operetta, and the Budapest Operetta Theater is one of the best places to sample this unique aspect of Hungarian culture. From the outside, the Operetta looks like a pink-frosted cake; inside, it's gilded with stained glass, chandeliers and plenty of gold. Shows are in Hungarian but come subtitled in English.

LISZT FERENC MUSIC ACADEMY

Liszt Ferenc tér 8, tel. 06/1-462-4600, http:///lfze.hu/home

The Liszt Ferenc Music Academy stands in a stunning art nouveau building on a square between Andrássy Avenue and Király utca, and it's worth a visit for the 50-minute guided tour (starting at 1:30pm, HUF 3,500) even if you can't make a concert. Some of Hungary's best composers and musicians have played at this ornate concert hall, and today you can still attend regular classical concerts from local and international orchestras.

South Pest

TRAFÓ

Liliom utca 41, tel. 06/1-215-1600, http://trafo.hu

You'd expect a theater housed inside a former electrical transformer building to be different, and Trafó delivers. If you're looking for avant-garde theater and dance, this is the place for you. (Just prepare yourself for nudity and other surprises.)

Festivals and Events

Budapest often has something on, whether it's food or wine festivals or art fairs. It also plays host to one of the most important music festivals in Europe.

SZIGET FESTIVAL

Május 9 Park, Óbudai-sziget, www.szigetfetival.com, €325 7-day pass, €79 day ticket

For one week in the middle of August, thousands of festival-goers (mostly 18- to 40-year-olds) flood the city for the Sziget Festival (https://szigetfestival.com), which takes place all the way out on Óbuda Island. Sziget features an eclectic lineup with international pop and rock acts as well as world and classical music, along with non-musical attractions in the comedy tent and circus tent. Past acts have included Muse, Lana del Rey, and Rihanna. Visitors come to the festival from over 100 countries.

Sometimes called a European Burning Man, Sziget is about more than music. Over the course of the week, Sziget becomes an "Island of Freedom," which can mean getting creative at one of the art camps, doing some yoga by the Danube, or partying late into the night after the concerts are over.

You can buy tickets months in advance (the price is also lower then—a day ticket costs €65 if you buy them before the end of December), but tickets do sell out quickly, so it's best to buy them by June at the latest.

ART MARKET BUDAPEST

Millenáris Cultural Center, tel. 06/1-239-0007 http://artmarketbudapest.hu, free entry

Central and Eastern Europe's leading art fair, Art Market Budapest (http://artmarketbudapest.hu), takes place every October, showcasing art from the Central and Eastern European regions as well as an invited guest country, like Israel or Brazil. Paintings, installations, sculpture, and photography are on display in the Millenáris Cultural Center, where art lovers can talk to the gallery owners and purchase high-end fine art.

BUDAPEST DESIGN WEEK

Various venues, www.designweek.hu

Come and see why Budapest has earned UNESCO's Creative Cities "City of Design" title. For a week in the first half of October, the Hungarian capital transforms into an open showroom for Hungarian contemporary fashion, art, and design, with exhibitions, workshops and events during Budapest Design Week (www.designweek.hu), which takes place all across the city. You can check out

Christmas Markets

Christmas market in front of St. Stephen's Basilica

Markets pop up across Central Europe as Christmas draws near, usually running from mid or end of November to January 1. Budapest's entire downtown area, as well as the squares in smaller neighborhoods will fill up with stands selling trinkets and mulled wine. The most famous is the one down at **Vörösmarty tér** (www.budapestchristmas.com, open 10am-8pm Sun-Thu, 10am-10pm Fr-Sat), which has 28 cottage-style wooden stalls where you'll find over 100 vendors focusing exclusively on local Hungarian designers. You can pick up all kinds of things like hand-bound notebooks, lavender cosmetics, bags, leatherwork, artisanal jams, chocolate and cheeses. Make sure you get a steaming hot cup of mulled wine to keep you warm as you wander around in sub-zero temperatures. At the heart, there is a large gastro terrace where you can sample some seasonal delights like roast goose thigh with braised red cabbage or roast pork knuckle. It can get crowded, especially on the weekends, so do keep an eye on your belongings at all times.

the program online (or download the booklet) for events to choose from, like parties, fashion shows, brunches, movie screenings, and open studios. You can download a design map (which you may find useful even if you don't make it to the events). Most events are free, but they may require registration in advance as places are limited.

BUDA CASTLE WINE FESTIVAL

Buda Castle, tel. 06/1-203-8507, www.aborfesztival. hu, day tickets on the door HUF 3,400

Go on a tasting trip around Hungary with the Budapest Wine Festival (www.aborfesztival. hu). This wine festival takes place around the first week of September on the terrace of Buda Castle, which provides perfect views over the city.

Make sure you buy tickets in advance. Not only does this work out cheaper (tickets bought before mid-August are HUF 2,500), but they also tend to sell out around the weekend dates. The festival lasts four days. With entry, you'll get a glass and free entry to the Budapest History Museum. Entry does not include the wine, which you pay for as you drink (and with around 200 wineries, you have plenty to choose from). Aside from wine, there are concerts and cultural programs, but the best thing is sipping a glass of wine on the Buda Castle terrace with the view over the Danube.

BUDAPEST 100
Various venues, http://budapest100.hu, free

Go behind the scenes in May at Budapest 100 (http://budapest100.hu) when certain buildings, such as private residential buildings (that are usually out of bounds) are opened to the public. The event is free, and it gives you a different way to see Budapest—from hidden courtyards and staircases. This is a must for any architecture lover who's looking for something different. You can download a map on the website (or pick up a booklet from one of the venues) and just wander to the buildings that are interesting for you. There are some tours on offer, but they are in Hungarian, so it's best to create your own itinerary and just get out to explore.

FALK ART FORUM
Falk Miksa utca, tel. 06/20-944-9155, www.falkart.hu, free

Falk Miksa utca already has a reputation for its antique shops and art galleries, but for one day around May 5th, more than 50 galleries in the area open up for exhibitions showcasing art deco furniture or Japanese kimonos, or for stage performances. There's everything from music and theater to roundtable discussions and culinary delicacies. If you prefer to go antiquing later, the shops extend their hours, so you won't run out of time to visit.

Recreation and Activities

PARKS

Budapest has a lot of green spaces, from the woods in the Buda Hills to more mainstream spots like Margaret Island and City Park.

CITY PARK
(Városliget)

City Park branches out from the end of Andrássy Avenue and Heroes' Square and extends for about a mile to Ajtósi Dürer sor on the other end. The park itself has evolved over history, along with its name, and is still transforming today with the city's plans to install a new museum quarter (scheduled to open in 2020). It's a popular place for recreation, with the Széchenyi Baths, the zoo, a circus, a lake that's open for boating in the summer and ice skating in the winter, and its own castle, **Vajdahunyad Castle**. The surrounding area is residential—you'll find romantic turreted villas and art nouveau wonders around Stefánia út.

MARGARET ISLAND

The 1.5-mile long island is mostly made up of parkland. Apart from a couple of hotels, ruins, thermal baths, and swimming pools, the stretch is populated with green lawns, wooded areas and spots that are perfect for a small tennis or soccer match with friends. There is a small Japanese garden to the north and a rose garden in the middle. If you want to find a good picnic spot, you can take the 4/6 tram to Margit Sziget and walk the bridge to the musical fountain and set your rug down there. The great thing about the island is that any spot is wonderful for lounging in the grass with friends.

BEACHES

Hungary might be a landlocked country, but it makes the most of its water. The Danube is no exception. Although the Danube is dangerous to swim in due to the powerful undercurrents (and it's illegal in most parts as well), you can still relax by the water and spend an afternoon at the beach. If you take a boat up the Danube, further up the Danube Bend, you'll see small, private beaches with one or two people who got there by canoe or bicycle. But you don't need to seek out isolated spots to enjoy Danube beaches. You can check out the venues below.

1

2

3

4

RÓMAI PART

Head out to the north part of Buda in the summer to Római Part, a stretch of embankment with pebbly beaches leading gently into the river. Locals bring beach towels and have picnics. There are cordoned-off paddling areas to enjoy (the net will stop you from going further into the river). You'll find bars, street food and riverside cafés along this leafy stretch of the Danube. You can take the 34 or 106 bus over from Lehel tér (you can reach this by Metro 3). In the summer, take the BKK boat service from any of the downtown docks, like Battyány tér, Várkert Bazár or Kossúth Lajos tér (or head to the beginning of the line like Kopaszi gát or the National Theater) for HUF 750.

KOPASZI DAM

On the other end of Buda, far south from Római Part, Kopászi Gát (dam, tram 1) is a small stretch of land that juts out, dotted with parkland and cafés and bistros. There is a sandy beach in the bay area of the dam, and while it's protected from the main flow of the Danube, it can be risky to still swim here. It's closer to the city center than Római Part, so it's more convenient if you don't want to head far into the Óbuda suburbs. I personally like this beach area for its unique setting—the walk down the dam is beautiful, with trees, trendy modern bistros and a view overlooking the enclosed "bay" where you can see little boats sailing under the shadow of the old power station. Kopaszi Gát looks its best at the golden hour just before sunset.

LUPA TÓ

Lupa Tó (lake) lies outside Budapest toward the town of Szentendre. In the past couple of years, it's been the go-to beach for Budapest denizens. This lake has crystal-clear water and has been revamped with sandy beaches and palm trees. In the VIP section you can also rent a waterside curtain-draped double sunbed with pillow for HUF 4,000 for the day, where you can sit back and sip a cocktail. On the weekends entrance to the main part of the beach is HUF 1,500 (weekdays HUF 1,000); for the VIP area, HUF 3,500 (HUF 2,500 weekdays).

HIKING

Get out of the chaos of the city and explore a side of Budapest that's a world away from the ruin bars.

KECSKE HEGY

Take the 11 Bus to the end of the line (the ride lasts 25 minutes) for hikes up around Kecske Hegy (Goat Hill). Get off at the final stop, Nagybányai út, and you should have trails marked on the trees—take the one that looks like a green arrow in a circle, which indicates a roundtrip. One of the most popular sites on this trail is the Lion's Rock (Oroszlánszikla), which resembles a lion. Nearby is the rock-covered Goat Hill (Kecskehegy), which makes for some great active hiking with some boulder climbing thrown in. Make sure you stop and look back, because the panorama is spectacular. This moderate hike takes approximately 4 kilometers and can last 2-3 hours.

ELIZABETH LOOKOUT

Take the 21 or 21A bus for approximately half an hour from Széll Kálmán to Normafa for hikes up to Elizabeth Lookout Tower, the highest point in the city, which is an easy 2.5 kilometer hike and takes approximately half an hour to reach. Around the lookout, you'll find another trail that leads you down to Tündér Szikla (Fairy Rock). Or you can continue along the ridge past the lookout tower to the neighboring hill following the trail. If you feel a little lazy after climbing up to the lookout tower, you can either go back to town by taking the chairlift down (HUF 1,000, free with the Budapest Card) or take the **Children's Railway**.

1 Margaret Island 2 In the winter, the lake in City Park becomes a popular ice rink. 3 Budapest bike share is called BUBI 4 Kopaszi Dam is a popular summer spot for water sports and Danube Beaches

SAS HEGY

Nature lovers should head south to Sas Hegy (tel. 06/30-408-4370, www.sas-hegy.hu), which is also a nature reserve complete with a visitor's center and gentle and wheelchair-accessible hiking trails. It's the closest spot to the city center, as you can get bus 8 from Keleti train station to Korompai utca and head up the hill (following the street with the same name as the bus stop). The route from the bus stop to the lookout point is around 750 meters. The visitor's center will be signposted on the way up on wooden arrows with a green dot—and you can learn about the species of plants that have survived on the hill since the Ice Age. While you're here, make sure you head up to the lookout point for one of the best spots to overlook the city.

CYCLING

For the best cycle-side views, head over to the 17-mile bike trail running along the Danube to the picturesque town of Szentendre (page 414). Margaret Island is also a good spot to take a bike—cars are banned from most of the island. You can pick up a MOL BuBi bike in the Buda or Pest side and ride the island. There are numerous paved paths on the island you can use for cycling.

Bike Sharing and Rentals
MOL BUBI
https://molbubi.bkk.hu
Budapest is popular with cyclists. Anywhere in the center, you may notice lime green MOL BuBi bike stations. You can operate the MOL BuBi system by simply using your cell phone. At select MOL BuBi stations, you will need to follow the instructions to buy a ticket. Your credit card will be charged the rental fee, along with a 25,000 HUF deposit (released at the end of the ticket period when you return your bike). Once you've bought your ticket, you will get a PIN code on your phone (see the website for complete instructions). You can return the bike at any of the docking stations in the city. You have the option of buying a ticket for 24 hours (HUF 500), 72 hours (HUF 1,000), or one week (HUF 2,000), which gets you 30 minutes free cycling time. Beyond that there are usage fees that go up the longer you use the bike (60 minutes HUF 500, 2 hours HUF 1,500, see the website for full fares).

BRINGOHINTÓ
Hajós Alfréd sétany 1, http://bringohinto.hu
If you're in a group, renting a quadracycle is a fun way to explore Margaret Island. Bringohintó can rent them on a half-hour (HUF 2,680) or hourly basis (HUF 3,980).

CAVE TOURS AND SPELUNKING

Because of an abundance of underground water, Budapest has a secret subterranean world, making the Hungarian capital the world's only city with numerous natural caves running beneath it. There are around 200 caves under Budapest. You can pay a visit to the show caves in the Buda Hills, or go underneath Buda Castle to the labyrinth below—but if you want to get down and dirty, you can also slide through honeycomb-like holes and tunnels on a spelunking expedition. If you plan on visiting the caves, it's a good idea to wear layers (it's around 54°F in the caves) and closed-toed shoes with a grip.

Cave Tours
The Pálvögyi Caves and Szemlőhegyi Caves are located relatively close to one another and can be visited on a combined ticket (2,000 HUF). **Caving Under Budapest** (http://caving.hu) provides private English-language walking tours (6,000 HUF) of these two caves as well.

PÁLVÖGYI CAVES
Szépvölgyi út 162, tel. 06/1-325-9505, www.dunaipoly.hu/hu/helyek/bemutatohelyek/ pal-volgyi-barlang, Tue-Sun 10am-4pm, tours at quarter past the hour, 1400 HUF
Located in the Buda Hills, the Pálvögyi cave system takes you through a labyrinth of chambers filled with stalactites and stalagmites,

going as deep as 98 feet underground. You can only visit the caves on the 45-minute walking tour, which is given in Hungarian, but it's possible to request a sheet with information in English, and guides can answer questions in English. While much of the showcave is paved, there are times when it will be necessary to scale up a ladder. (But you won't need to get on your hands and knees and get dirty.)

SZEMLŐHEGYI CAVES

Pusztaszeri út 35, tel. 06/1-325-6001, www.dunaipoly. hu/hu/helyek/bemutatohelyek/szemlo-hegyi-barlang, Wed-Mon 10am-4pm, tours on the hour, 1,400 HUF

Floret-like mineral and crystalline deposits coat the cave walls here (created by thermal water coming in from below), which has earned this cave system the nickname "Underwater Flower Garden." It is the most accessible out of Budapest's caves. The lower level is sometimes used as a respiratory sanitorium due to its pure air. It needs to be visited on a guided 35- to 45-minute walking tour in Hungarian, but most guides speak English and can answer questions. No climbing or tight spots with this one.

Spelunking and Cave Diving

For subterranean diving, you can head out to the submerged part of the former Kőbánya stone mine and beer factory and go on a 40-minute dive with **Paprika Divers** (www. paprikadivers.com/en/, €50 not including gear rental).

MÁTYÁSHEGY CAVES

162 Szépvölgyi út, http://caving.hu

Opposite the Pálvölgy Cave system, just on the other side of Szépvögyi út is the Mátyáshegy cave network. You'll need a guide to explore these caves, and you'll also need to change into a caving suit and wear a hard hat with a built-in lamp. **Caving Under Budapest** (http://caving.hu) will take you on a three-hour subterranean adventure (HUF 7,700 per person), where you can expect tight squeezes and rock climbing, as well as lots of wriggling on the cave floor. Make sure you book

in advance. Although tours run daily, they can fill up quickly, and there is an age limit of 10 to 55.

MOLNÁR JÁNOS CAVE

www.mjcave.hu/en

Just a few feet away from the Lukács Baths and the Danube, you have the Molnár János Cave, which is the largest known active thermal water cave, stretching over four miles; it's filled with water that reaches 80°F in places. If you want to take it to another level and you're a qualified cave diver or you have an open water diving certificate, you can dive here from €60 (for the 50- minute cave intro dive, not including dive gear rental). It's only possible to visit these caves on the diving tour.

BOATING

CITY PARK ICE RINK

Olof Palme sétány 5, tel. 06/1-261-5209, www.mujegpalya.hu, daily 10am-9pm

In the summer, the lake in City Park turns into a pleasure lake where you can rent a row boat (HUF 1,500 for 30 minutes), a canoe (HUF 1,500 for 30 minutes), or a water bicycle (HUF 2,500 for 30 minutes) for up to four people, and you can gaze at the turrets of Vajdahunyad Castle. Bear in mind that opening hours depend on the weather, and if you're coming between seasons, check the website or give them a call. You'll find a mix of families, friends and couples boating on the lake on hot sunny days. (Note that the water is unfit for bathing and life jackets are not provided.)

ICE SKATING

CITY PARK ICE RINK

Olof Palme sétány 5, tel. 06/1-363-2673, www.mujegpalya.hu

In the winter, the lake in City Park freezes over and becomes one of Europe's largest open-air ice rinks. With the romantic Vajdahunyad Castle as the backdrop, it's probably one of the most beautiful ice rinks, too. If you're visiting Budapest between December and February, it's a fun place to spend an hour or two. You can buy tickets (HUF 1,500 weekdays, HUF

2,000 weekends) online to skip the queue, and you can also rent skates (HUF 1,800) on-site.

HOTEL PRESIDENT ICE RINK

From the ice rink on top of the Hotel President, you can see the Postal Savings Bank and the Hungarian Parliament Building in the distance. Entrance to the terrace costs HUF 900 (free for hotel guests), and you can rent skates (HUF 490) on the rooftop. The 1,200 square foot ice rink is made of synthetic ice— good if you're a novice skater. You'll find a mix of locals with kids skating alongside hotel guests. Between skating sessions, grab some mulled wine and a *beigli* (a rolled Hungarian pastry filled with walnuts or poppy seeds) from the wooden hut besides the ice rink and just take in the view from one of the tables at the terrace.

ROOM ESCAPE GAMES

Room Escape Games (live action games where you have an hour to get out of a locked room using teamwork and logic) have exploded in popularity across the globe, and they were created in Budapest. Since ParaPark set up the first live room escape game, dozens of game rooms have opened in basements and apartments, sometimes even under ruin bars. They're great for groups who are up for the challenge of solving logical puzzles as the clock ticks down. You will usually have to book the room in advance, which can typically be done via the game website.

PARAPARK

Vajdahunyad utca 4, http://parapark.hu,
HUF 9,900 per 2-6 person group
ParaPark is a place of pilgrimage for Room Escape lovers. There is a selection of rooms in the basement of an VIII District ruin bar, like the Community Cube Factory game inspired by the Hungarian Rubik's Cube, or a crime scene scenario. The damaged walls and creaking doors of the basement add atmosphere to the game, but once you're locked in, you won't have time to look at the décor—you'll be on

your hands and knees looking for clues, turning dials and opening hidden doors trying to get the key.

CLAUSTROPHILIA

Erzsébet körút 8, www.claustrophilia.hu,
HUF 8,000 2 people, HUF 12,000 5 people
Claustrophilia is part role-play, part mystery and part escape game. This room escape combines intricate puzzle rooms with a story as players embark on a quest to hunt through adventurer Lord Wicklewood's treasures to find the key that unlocks the final door. Claustrophilia combines classic room escape challenges with a storyline and an old-world aesthetic, with rusted bird cages, faded stamps from around the world and worn leather suitcases that will take you back to the world of explorers and treasure hunters. (Note: you can only pay in cash.)

TOURS

BUDAPEST FREE WALKING TOURS

www.triptobudapest.hu
Familiarize yourself with the city with a free walking tour with Budapest Free Walking Tours. **The tours** have a number of interesting themes, like Communist Budapest, and there's one of the Jewish Quarter.

TASTE HUNGARY

http://tastehungary.com
Tours with Taste Hungary whet the appetite by exploring the culinary side of Budapest through food and culture walks. There's plenty to choose from, whether you want a market tour, dinner walk, or something more niche, like their coffeehouse walk or Jewish culinary tour.

CONTEXT TRAVEL

www.contexttravel.com, $57-212 to join a group tour
Context Travel caters to the intellectual traveler. The company offers tours of Budapest given by historians and academics, providing alternative insight into the city and covering specific topics like architecture and politics, conflict and culture. They also provide

more general orientation tours of the Jewish Quarter and the Castle District.

BUDAPEST FLOW
https://budapestflow.com, €35 pp per tour
If you want to explore an alternative side of the city, Budapest Flow takes you around the ruin bars or through the more interesting, non-touristy parts of the city, like the heart of the gentrifying VIII District.

CLASSES
CHEFPARADE COOKING BUDAPEST
www.cookingbudapest.com
Learn all about Hungarian cooking hands-on with ChefParade Cooking Budapest. First, you'll visit the Central Market Hall to buy the best produce. Then, you'll learn how to cook three Hungarian dishes. Courses (including the market tour), last around 4.5 hours and cost €115 per person.

Shopping

UNESCO awarded Budapest the Creative Cities title of City of Design. To get a taste for Budapest's artistic innovation, start by visiting the city's shops and showrooms. Within basements, on side streets and hidden in tea room mezzanines, you can find vintage stores selling clothes and accessories from bygone days, and often at a bargain.

SHOPPING DISTRICTS
Váci utca or **Andrássy út** both offer great high-end shopping. In some of the more exciting neighborhoods, like the Jewish Quarter or the VIII, IX, or XI Districts, you'll find independent boutiques and designers around the downtown streets. Antique lovers flock to **Falk Miksa Street** for its row of galleries and antique stores. There are around 20 shops alone on the row, which comes to life in May during the Falk Art Forum (www.falkart.hu). The event turns antique shopping into a street party with exhibitions, culinary bites and performances.

Any fashion fiend would do well to head to **Deák Ferenc utca.** Between Váci utca and Deák Ferenc tér, this small street is replete with luxury boutiques from international designers like Hugo Boss, Tommy Hilfiger, Lacoste, and Massimo Dutti. The street is also lined with luxury hotels and bistros.

MARKETS
While Central Market Hall is the most famous out of Budapest's markets, there are plenty of others to explore, whether you're looking for antiques or artisanal cheese.

Jewish Quarter
GOZSDU COURT
Gozsdu Court (Gozsdu udvar) is a set of interconnected courtyards lined with restaurants and bars that fill up with a hip, young crowd in the evenings, but on the weekends, it turns into a curious market with antiques, work from local designers, and more. You can find communist badges and soldiers' helmets on one table, prints from local artists on another, jewelry made out of cut-out 100-year-old letters, or necklaces made out of tiny globes of glass filled with copper wire. It can be hard to deal with the crowds to look at the stalls, but if you do get tired, fortunately there are plenty of cafés offering refuge.

KLAUZÁL SQUARE MARKET
Klauzál tér 11, tel. 06/1-785-4770, daily 7am-10pm
At the heart of the Jewish Quarter, Klauzál tér market reopened in 2015 following a renovation. On Sundays, this old red-brick building turns into an antique market (http://antikplacc.hu) with a difference—you can not only find classic antiques, but also those that have been given a revamp by local designers. You'll find repainted and upholstered

Best Souvenirs

Uniquely Hungarian items are known as Hungaricum, and some make great gifts. You can pick up food and drinks to take home, or folk art, porcelain or antiques.

FOOD AND DRINKS

- **Paprika:** You can find packs of powdered paprika from Szeged (a Hungarian town in the south) in places like the Central Market Hall, or in smaller souvenir shops or open-air markets, like the farmer's market at Szimpla Kert on Sunday morning. Hungarian paprika comes in two varieties: sweet (*édes*) and hot (*erős*). If you can pick up a pack of paprika in a cute embroidered or patterned cheese cloth bag, these make great gifts. Bags can range between HUF 1,500 to 3,700 depending on the size and if any extras are included, like wooden serving spoons.

- **Pálinka:** This strong fruit brandy can be found in most wine shops, but a good place to pick up a bottle is the Magyar Pálinka Háza. You can get this fruit brandy in a variety of flavors: plum, apple, pear, apricot, cherry, grape, and rarer types like raspberry and elderflower. I personally like the Rézangyal Brand (HUF 3,590-6,490), but you can always ask for recommendations when you go to a specialist shop.

- **Unicum:** a bitter herbal liquor that makes a good gift if you want something uniquely Hungarian. You can find Unicum (HUF 3,199-5,000 depending on the size) pretty much everywhere, including supermarkets and cigarette shops. If you want to take home a bottle that is less bitter, try the Unicum Szilva (HUF 3,199-5,000 depending on the size), which has been aged on a bed of dried plums.

- **Wine:** Hungary is gaining recognition for its wine, so why not take home a bottle? You can get wine at all price ranges, from HUF 500 to bottles that cost HUF 10,000s, but you can find something in between that makes the perfect gift. Head to a wine shop like Tasting Table where the staff can help you find something quality. If you want something special, pick up a bottle of Tokaj; if you're partial to reds then a good bottle of Egri Bikavér is the way to go.

ART AND DESIGN

- **Herend porcelain:** Herend porcelain stands out because of its delicate motifs, whether in a tea set, tableware with birds and flowers, or hand-painted figures of carnival workers or horses. You can get Herend porcelain for anywhere between 20,000 and 85,000 HUF, although there are rarer pieces that can cost hundreds (if not thousands) of dollars. Do note that there are a lot of fakes on the market, so be careful where you buy. To ensure authenticity, head to one of the Herend Porcelain stores (Szentháromság utca 5).

- **Zsolnay ceramics:** This is a unique type of porcelain that originated in the Hungarian town of Pécs. Zsolnay doesn't just produce architectural ceramics—they also create vases and dinnerware. What make Zsolnay different from Herend are the vibrant colors, and almost metallic hues and unique designs. There are a few Zsolnay stores (Rákoczi út 4-6) in Budapest, with prices ranging from as low as 8,000 HUF for small figurines to thousands for larger, rarer items.

- **Folk Art:** Embroidery makes a wonderful gift, whether on a tablecloth or stitched onto a shirt. You can find unique folk art in the Central Market Hall in the form of embroidery and lacework. Expect to pay around HUF 10-15,000 for quality items, and considerably less for smaller items like doilies.

- **Antiques:** Antiques are great gifts if you're looking to take a piece of history home, whether you pick up some Communist memorabilia from Ecseri Market or something more valuable on Falk Miksa utca, like a painting, an elegant dinner set or a wall mirror.

furniture, old watches fitted with new straps, or restrung jewelry.

SZIMPLA FARMERS' MARKET

Szimpla Kert may be best known as a ruin bar, but every Sunday morning till 2pm it turns into an extravagant farmers' market with artisanal cheeses, loaves of spelt bread, and seasonal vegetables—and you can listen to live jazz or Hungarian folk music. There is also a charity cookoff in the back of the bar. For a donation, you can get some freshly cooked gulyás (a spicy beef-paprika soup) or stew.

South Pest
ECSERI MARKET

Nagykőrösi út 150, tel. 06/1-348-3200, Mon-Fri 8am-4pm, Sat 5am-3pm, Sun 8am-1pm

Getting to Ecseri Market is an adventure that requires a long bus ride out into the suburbs. Then you have to cross the bridge over the highway—but once you're here, this fascinating antiques market is a sight. It's a labyrinth of curiosities, from grand serpentine fountains taken from Buda villas to vintage porcelain, old cameras, gramophones, and portraits of communist political leaders. Even if you're not looking to buy, it's worth visiting just for the experience.

DESIGN SHOPS
Castle District
FIAN KONCEPT DESIGN

Fortuna utca 18 and Úri utca 26-28, daily 10am-6pm

You'll find the FIAN Koncept design shops in the Castle District between the colorful houses on Úri utca and Fortuna utca 18. Both spaces are open-concept and modern, with exposed brick and all-white shelving, which is different from other souvenir shops filled with bags of embroidered paprika and postcards. Look for pieces by Romani Design (http://romani.hu), founded by two Roma sisters who wanted to incorporate traditional Romani designs into contemporary fashion.

Inner City and Around Parliament
RODODENDRON

Semmelweis utca 19, tel. 06/70-419-5329, www.rododendronart.com, Mon-Fri 10am-7pm, Sat 10am-5pm, Sun 11am-3pm

Rododendron Art and Design showcases work from around 30 local designers in its ground floor shop split between Semmelweis utca and Röser courtyard. The main focus is on art and jewelry, but you'll find other bits and pieces in its changing collection.

BOMOART

Régiposta utca 14, tel. 06/20-594-2223, www. bomoart.hu, Mon-Fri 10am-6:30pm, Sat 10am-6pm

BomoArt is a must for anyone who loves stationary. Their handbound diaries and notebooks with leather and prints displaying vintage hot air balloons, aviaries, and old-fashioned pictures of Budapest make unique souvenirs. They have a second location at the Castle Garden Bazaar, and you can find their products in many shops across town.

Jewish Quarter
PRINTA

Rumbach Sebestyén utca 10, tel. 06/30-292-0329, https://printa.hu, Mon-Sat 11am-7pm

Printa is a shop that doubles as a gallery and coffeeshop. This trendy silkscreen print studio also carries its own eco-friendly clothing made out of upcycled material. Many of their products also feature Budapest in some way. If you want a silkscreen print to take home or a trendy bag, Printa is your place.

SZIMPLA DESIGN

Kazinczy utca 14, Wed-Sat midday-7pm

Szimpla Design is set in the front of its namesake ruin bar. It's an Aladdin's Cave of items, with purses, postcards, and handwoven beanie dolls amongst curious pieces of antiques and upcycled items. It embodies the aesthetic of the ruin bar next door, but it offers you the chance to bring home a little of the Budapest ruin chic aesthetic.

South Pest
FLATLAB

Baross utca 3, bell 14, tel. 06/30-949-4286,
www.flatlab.hu, Mon-Fri 10am-8pm

Flatlab is an atelier set in a private apartment located in the city center, and it serves both as a workshop and a place where you can come to look around and buy pieces from the designers, such as urban cycling gear, bags made from plant-based material, stationary, and porcelain.

FOOD AND WINE

Hungarian food and wine can make good souvenirs, so why not take a packet of paprika or a bottle of Hungarian wine home with you? While somewhere like Central Market Hall is the obvious choice, you can pick up some bites to take home in these shops, too. You can also pick up some Hungarian products from local chain stores like Príma or Spar, but the quality and packaging may not make them ideal for gifts.

Inner City and Around Parliament
SZAMOS

Deák Ferenc utca 5, tel. 06/30-570-5973,
https://szamos.hu, Mon-Sun 10am-9pm

Nothing makes a better souvenir than a box of marzipan chocolates. You'll find Szamos shops and patisseries all over the city, but you'll find the most beautiful is on Vörösmarty tér. You can also buy decadent cakes (although these probably won't last the flight home), so why not treat yourself to a Dobos cake (a chocolate cake topped with hardened caramel) and a coffee in the café before perusing the boxes of chocolates with pictures of the city or Hungarian embroidery to take home?

Bródy Sándor utca 9, tel. 06/30-720-8197,
http://tastehungary.com/venue/, daily midday-8pm

For great Hungarian wines, head to Tasting Table. If you want to try before you buy, they organize a few wine tastings. You can book these for 3pm or 6pm daily via the website ($39-$54 per person). The people in the shop are friendly, speak English, and can help you find the right bottle. You can find a great selection of Tokaj wines here. For something special, try a bottle from Oremus (prices can range from HUF 4,800 for wines from 2010 to 150,000 for rare vintages from the 1950s). You'll also find other wines from Hungary and surrounding regions like Egri Bikavér (Bulls Blood), or sparkling wine from Somló near Lake Balaton.

MAGYAR PÁLINKA HÁZA

Rákóczi út 17, tel. 06/30-421-5463,
www.magyarpalinkahaza.hu, Mon-Sat 9am-7pm

Magyar Pálinka Háza, which translates as the "Hungarian House of *Pálinka*," offers a vast selection of this Hungarian spirit, not only in the type of fruit available but also its distilleries. This large shop stocks up hundreds of bottles, so deciding may be difficult. You can't taste before you buy, but the staff will help you make the right choice. Most locals will pick up a bottle from the supermarket (or make their own *pálinka*), the vast selection appeals to connoisseurs of the fiery fruit brandy and tourists looking for a special souvenir.

CLOTHING AND ACCESSORIES
Inner City and Around Parliament
NANUSHKA

Bécsi utca 3, tel. 06/70-394-1954,
www.nanushka.com, Mon-Sat 10am-8pm

Nanushka is perhaps Hungary's best-known fashion brand, with boutiques in over 30 countries. However, the headquarters can be found in downtown Budapest. Nanushka's

---

1 Ecseri flea market in the suburbs of Pest is a treasure trove of antiques and odd items. **2** Printa is one of the most popular design shops in Budapest selling alternative design souvenirs centered around Budapest.

designs are characterized by lush fabrics and playful cuts designed for the urban woman. Prices are on the high side, with most clothes costing a few hundred euros, but still priced less than international designers.

PALOMA
Kossuth Lajos utca 14, tel. 06/20-961-9160, Mon-Fri 11am-7pm, Sat 11am-3p

Paloma is a collective of designers hidden away in a Budapest courtyard in the Inner City. The series of shops on the first floor up from the winged courtyard staircase showcase work from 40 local, young, up-and-coming designers, with jewelry, bags, clothing, and shoes.

Jewish Quarter
SZPUTNYIK
Dohány utca 20, tel. 06/1-321-3730, https://szputnyikshop.hu, Mon-Sat 10am-8pm, Sun 10am-6pm

Szputnyik mixes up a large range of vintage clothing and accessories with newer, quirky bags, shoes, clothing and jewelry, as well as altered and revamped vintage items. It's a

popular shop for fashion-forward, trendy Hungarians skewing more to the alternative, boho crowd. Prices won't break a midrange budget.

RETROCK
Anker köz 2-4, tel. 06/30-472-3636, http://retrock. com, Mon-Sat 11am-9pm, Sun 11am-8pm

Pick out unique creations made by Hungarian and international designers from used and recycled materials, or secondhand items and accessories. Retrock is a treasure trove of bijoux and unusual fashion items, such as mountain man-style bags, gothic alien-inspired fashion lines and hand-made cycling accessories.

Around Andrássy Avenue
JAJCICA
Szondi utca 58, tel. 06/1-321-2081, Mon-Fri 10am-6pm, Sat 10am-2pm

Jajcica carries a huge collection of vintage clothes, shoes and accessories for both men and women. Whether you're looking for an '80s rock chick look, something from 1970s Saint-Tropez, or a biker's leather jacket, you can find it in this basement.

Food

Hungarian food is heavy. Portion sizes are large, meals center around meat, and of course, you'll get plenty of paprika accenting the dish to give it a slight kick. You won't leave a restaurant hungry, but if you're on a diet or vegetarian, you may want to visit an international or specialist restaurant.

Breakfast is usually a big deal. Hotels will ply you with cold cuts, chopped vegetables and plenty of bread in the morning. Fried eggs with bacon or sausage is a typical Hungarian breakfast.

CASTLE DISTRICT
Hungarian
21 MAGYAR VENDÉGLŐ
Fortuna utca 21, tel. 06/1-202-2113, www.21restaurant.hu, daily 11am-midnight, 3,680-5,680 HUF

Magyar Vendéglő literally means "Hungarian restaurant," but this chic bistro up in the Castle District applies an innovative and lighter twist on traditional dishes, like its paprika chicken, made with a paprika reduction and served with homemade dumplings. You may want to try the roasted Mangalica pork chop with cabbage strudel. Beyond the creative cuisine, this restaurant stands out for friendly service. (Plus, they bottle their own wine.)

Hungarian Specialties

Paprika is a staple in the Hungarian kitchen, with locals reaching for bottles of sweet or spicy powdered paprika in place of pepper at times.

ENTREES

- *Gulyásleves* (Hungarian goulash): Hungarian goulash is known the world over, but it's a soup and not a stew as commonly believed. This rich beef soup made with chunks of potato and peppers is accented with quality red paprika powder, which gives the soup its crimson color.

- *Halászlé:* Similar to *gulyásleves*, but made with fish instead of meat (called *halászlé*). This fisherman's soup comes from the south of the country, around Szeged.

- Chicken *paprikás:* A creamy chicken dish made with oodles of powdered paprika (which gives it a salmon hue), served with thin dumplings called *galuska* or *nokedli* and a side of sour cucumber salad.

- Mangalica pork: Keep an eye out for mangalica on the menu. This unique Hungarian breed of pig is not only rare for its woolly coat (that kind of looks like a sheep), but it's dubbed to be the "kobe beef of pork." It's a fatty meat that's loved for its marbled texture and superb taste.

STREET FOOD

Lángos is a deep-fried savory dough similar in texture to a donut, which usually comes topped with cheese and sour cream. You'll find this calorific street treat sold in kiosks and food trucks, mainly in parks, festivals, street food courts, and around metro stations.

WINE

Wine plays a big part in Hungarian meals, as the Central European country is home to numerous wine regions (including the famous golden Tokaji dessert wines). Hungarians also like to sip spicy reds from the southern part of the country, such as Szekszárd and Villány, crisp whites from Lake Balaton's Badacsony region or nearby Somló, and the iconic Bikavér ("Bulls Blood") red cuvee from Eger.

SPIRITS

- *Pálinka:* A famous fruit brandy distilled from local fruits like plum, pear, apple, quince, and apricot, which is often drunk with heavy Hungarian meals. Locals swear *pálinka* is a cure for digestive problems, colds, stomach aches and even heart pains.

- Unicum: A bitter liqueur made from a secret recipe of 40 herbs and spices, which is said to help digestion.

MANDRAGORA

Kacsa utca 22, tel. 06/1-202-2165,
www.mandragorakavehaz.hu, Mon-Sat 11am-11:45pm,
3,100-4,500 HUF

Mandragóra (named after the Mandrake, a humanoid-looking root used in witchcraft in the past) evokes images of magic and the occult, but this family-run restaurant employs its magic in the kitchen with its contemporary, seasonal takes of Hungarian classics, like paprika pike perch served with cottage cheese noodles and crumbles of bacon, or creative additions like the salt glaze crust on top of a goose leg. However, what makes Mandragóra really stand out is the desserts, especially the homemade chocolate cake, which is so good that they sell the cake to order so you can take it home.

★ CSALOGÁNY 26

Csalogány utca 26, tel. 06/1-201-7892,
www.csalogany26.hu, Tue-Sat midday-3pm and
7pm-10pm, 2,400-6,000 HUF entrees or 16,000 HUF
tasting menu

Csalogány 26 offers inspiring dishes made from local ingredients—like a spiced peasant consommé with homemade udon noodles or cottage cheese mouse with sea buckthorn. Some say this restaurant run by a passionate father and son team is one of the best in Budapest. Go all- out with their lavish degustation menu, or try the 3-course budget-friendly lunch menu for just HUF 2500.

International

ZÓNA

Lánchíd utca 7-9, tel. 06/30-422-5981,
www.zonabudapest.com, Mon-Sat midday-midnight,
3,900-7,700 HUF

Zóna embraces a modern, urban aesthetic and prepares creatively executed international dishes. The menu offers an eclectic selection from gourmet burgers to an elegant degustation menu with guineafowl goulash and lamb rump served with sweet potato, kale and panna cotta (yes, the Italian dessert). For something different, try the wild duck with an accent of vanilla. Zóna focuses on international fusion, mixing up Italian-inspired dishes with street food, along with tastes from Israel and Hungary thrown in.

ARANY KAVIÁR

Ostrom utca 19, tel. 06/1-201-6737, www.aranykaviar.
hu, Tue-Sun midday-3pm and 6pm-midnight,
4,900-18,900 HUF

This Russian restaurant embodies the principles of fine dining in an intimate setting and with beautiful food presentation. If you're a fan of fish eggs, try their caviar menu (they have more than five types) accompanied by traditional Russian blinis and *Smetana* (sour cream). If you fancy a splurge, try their tasting menu (14,900-30,000 HUF), but their three-course lunch menu (5,900 HUF) gives you a chance to try their fine Russian dishes without breaking the bank. Apparently Brad and Angelina came here on a date night once, so you may want to people-watch if you visit.

Bistro and Brunch

★ PIERROT

Fortuna utca 14, tel. 06/1-375-6971, www.pierrot.hu,
daily 11am-midnight, 3,780-8,640 HUF

Pierrot is a stylish bistro on the site of a 13th-century bakery. Its kitchen homes in on

---

Baltazar Grill and Wine Bar occupies the ground floor of a boutique hotel up in the Castle District.

Austro-Hungarian cuisine, but it's been updated for the more adventurous tastes of the twenty-first century diner. Try their venison goulash or confit of duck baked into puff pastry.

BALTAZÁR GRILL AND WINE BAR
Országház utca 3, tel. 06/1-300-7050, www.baltazarbudapest.com, daily midday-11pm, 3,180-9,680 HUF

The bistro in this boutique hotel attracts locals and visitors. Baltazár Grill and Wine Bar serves up tantalizing brunches (including pastries), but they are best-known for their charcoal-grilled meats and burgers. They also have an extensive wine collection from all around the Carpathian Basin. Another nice touch is their interesting gin selection with tailored garnishes that go towards making the perfect gin and tonic.

Vegan and Vegetarian
ÉDENI VEGÁN
Iskola utca 31, tel. 06/20-337-7575, www.edenivegan.hu, daily 8am-8pm, 690-1,490 HUF

You can find Édeni Vegán at the base of Castle Hill, in an old townhouse just off Batthyányi Square. This vegan restaurant serves hearty dishes made with organic ingredients, from burgers to salads and raw desserts. Gluten- and sugar-free options are also available.

Cafés and Cake
RUSZWURM
Szentháromság utca 7, tel. 06/1-375-5284, www.ruszwurm.hu, Mon-Fri 10am-7pm, Sat-Sun 10am-6pm, 420-720 HUF

Ruszwurm, Budapest's oldest functioning café and confectionary dating back to 1827 is in a pistachio-green baroque-style house. The interior is minimal, and the cakes are displayed in a wooden apothecary-style cabinet. Try the café's signature cake, the Ruszwurm Cream Pastry, a custard and cream-based dessert topped with layers flaky dough. (In the high season, you may find it hard to find somewhere to sit!)

BUDAVÁRI RÉTESVÁR
Balta köz 4, tel. 06/70-408-8696, www.budavariretesvar.hu, daily 8am-7pm, 310 HUF

It might take a while to find the Budavári Rétesvár, a hole-in-the-wall discoverable under a dark archway in the Castle District, but worth the exploration just for the strudels. You can find variations of the Hungarian strudel, known as rétes, with fillings including sweet poppy seed, plum or apple, plus savory dill and cottage cheese.

INNER CITY AND AROUND PARLIAMENT
Hungarian
KARPÁTIA
Ferenciek tere 7-8, tel. 06/1-317-3596, www.karpatia.hu, Mon-Sat 11am-11pm, Sun 5pm-11pm, 3,400-7,900 HUF

Karpátia dates back to the late 19th century and is worth visiting for the frescoed interior that looks like something out of a museum. When it comes to food, Karpátia serves up classic Hungarian dishes with a range of spicy goulash soups and variations of paprika-laced meat stews made with chicken or beef. If you come in the evening, you can expect to dine while listening to *csárdás* (traditional Hungarian-Romani folk dance music).

★ ZELLER BISTRO
Hercegprímás utca 18, tel. 06/30-651-0880, www.zellerbistro.hu, Tue-Sun midday-midnight, 3,200-6,500 HUF

Zeller Bistro specializes in contemporary Hungarian cooking using fresh and seasonal ingredients from local farmers, producers, and small Hungarian wineries. The restaurant is in a cozy downtown setting, and blends rustic with industrial chic. I recommend the duck liver brûlée with carrot and mango or the daily fish that comes straight from the market with a side of risotto. The carrot cake is also one of the best you'll find in town.

Fine Dining
★ ONYX

Vörösmarty tér 7-8, tel. 06/30-508-0622, www.
onyxrestaurant.hu, Tue-Fri midday-2:30pm, Tue-Sat
6:30pm-11pm, 33,900 HUF for its tasting menus
Try the two Michelin-starred take on
Hungarian food at Onyx with its six- or
more course tasting menu that documents
the evolution of Hungarian cuisine with creative dishes like goose liver paired with coffee and almond, or catfish bacon fish soup.
You can also try their "Beyond Our Borders"
tasting menu with seasonal takes inspired
by continental European cooking, featuring dishes like saddle of lamb with summer truffles. Onyx is more than just a meal
out—it's a dining experience that can last
for hours. Opt for the simpler three or four-
course lunch menu (18,900-25,900 HUF), if
you just want a taste.

BORKONYHA

Sas utca 3, tel. 06/1-266-0835, www.borkonyha.
hu, Mon-Sat midday-4pm and 6pm-midnight,
3,500-7,950 HUF
The menu is always changing at this contemporary Hungarian restaurant headed by
Chef Ákos Sárközi. Borkonyha earned its
Michelin star for its innovative Hungarian
menu, drawing inspiration mostly from the
Transylvanian kitchen, while playing with
international ingredients and modern cooking techniques. Try the foie gras wrapped in
flaky pastry, and anything that is made with
Mangalica pork. If you go for a tasting menu,
it's worth investing in the wine pairing—there
is a reason why this restaurant is called "Wine
Kitchen" in Hungarian.

International
BARAKA

Dorottya utca 6, tel. 06/1-200-0817,
www.barakarestaurant.hu, Mon-Sat 11am-3pm and
6pm-11:30pm, 7,500-17,500 HUF
If you love fine dining and Asian and French
food, you'll love Baraka. Since Baraka opened
its doors and presented Asian-French fusion
with a fine dining slant and a Hungarian

accent, it's been a fine-dining hub for foodie
lovers. Seafood dominates the menu, with
creative dishes such as Bouillabaisse made
with steamed fish gyoza, capers and seaweed.
There are options for meat eaters and vegetarian diners here, with degustation menus
and á la carte options available. East-meets-
West flavors combine in dishes like togarashi
with beetroot, or Hungarian wild boar with
ume shiso.

DA MARIO

Vécsey utca 3, tel. 06/1-301-0967, www.damario.hu,
daily 11:30am-11pm, 2,000-7,000 HUF
For authentic Italian cuisine, Da Mario is the
place to go. This Italian-owned restaurant offers classic pasta and pizza, as well as seafood
and meat dishes made with the best ingredients sourced from Italy. Italian wines are offered on the menu. The atmosphere is relaxed
and friendly, and the setting is stylish.

Bistro and Brunch
★ SZIMPLY

Károly körút 22 Röser Udvar, www.szimply.com,
Mon-Fri 8am-4pm, Sat 9am-4pm, 1,800-2,900 HUF
It's hard to get a table in this small breakfast
bistro (which does not accept reservations),
but Szimply is worth it if you can grab a spot.
With a choice of savory and sweet seasonal
specials, you can be sure to get fresh and
beautifully presented breakfast dishes, from
favorites like avocado toast to more innovative dishes like zucchini pancakes.

KISPIAC

Hold utca 13, tel. 06/1-269-4231, Mon-Sat
midday-10pm, 2,300-3,950 HUF
Kispiac Bisztró can be found in one of the
shopfronts of the Belvárosi market hall, and
the staff serves up hearty Hungarian dishes
with generous portions. Ingredients come
straight from the market, so everything is
fresh, and even the preserved ingredients, like
jams, bread and picked vegetables are hand-
crafted by the restaurant. Each day they put
up six dishes to choose from, as well as regular
Hungarian specials. (Take note: This bistro

only seats 20, so you might have stiff competition for a table.)

Cafés and Cake
GERBEAUD
Vörösmarty tér 7-8, tel. 06/1-429-9001, www.
gerbeaud.hu, daily midday-10pm, 1,150-4,990 HUF
Gerbeaud is an institution in Budapest's café and confectionary culture. Founded in 1858, it eventually became the most fashionable spot in the city for the elite. Today, its palatial interior with rococo friezes, silk drapes, and crystal chandeliers invites guests to sit at the marble-topped tables to sip coffee and take bites from decadent cakes.

JEWISH QUARTER
Jewish
Jewish food in Budapest frequently overlaps Hungarian food, but there are some distinguishing markers. You won't find the pork-heavy recipes you'd get elsewhere. Instead, you'll find alternatives like beef, lamb, or chicken. Hungarian-Jewish dishes like *cholent* (a bean stew), or goose feature heavily on menus. Not all restaurants are kosher. The only one that gets kosher approval from the Orthodox community is Hanna (in the courtyard of the Kazinczy street synagogue), but is not the place to go if you want an outstanding culinary experience. Other Jewish restaurants also draw influences from Israeli dishes, like hummus and tabbouleh.

MAZEL TOV
Akácfa utca 47, https://mazeltov.hu,
tel. 06/70-626-4280, Mon.-Fri. 6pm-2am,
Sat.-Sun. midday-2am, 1,990-5,890 HUF
What started out as the next generation of ruin pubs has morphed into a popular restaurant where booking is almost mandatory. Mazel Tov serves up Israeli fusion, such as pulled lamb with eggplant, tabbouleh and tahini or classic hummus-centered dishes, and sizzling Middle Eastern grilled meat plates with spicy Moroccan sausages and marinated skewers of meat. The setting, with exposed brick, twinkling fairy lights

wrapped around the tree in the courtyard, and Mediterranean tiled-bar, pulls in the crowds as much as the food. Reservations are a must.

KŐLEVES
Kazinczy utca 37-41, tel. 06/20-213-5999,
www.kolevesvendeglo.hu, Mon-Fri 8am-1am,
Sat-Sun 9am-1am, 2,180-5,180 HUF
Kőleves ("Stone Soup") serves Jewish-inspired dishes, like cholent, a traditional Jewish bean stew served up with egg or goose egg, and goose broth with a matzo ball. There are also plenty of vegetarian options, like vegetarian gratin made with black lentils, gruyere and walnuts.

FRÖHLICH
Dob utca 22, tel. 06/20-913-2595, www.frohlich.hu,
Mon-Thu 9am-6pm, Fri 9am-2pm, Sun 10am-6pm,
140-950 HUF
This kosher café and cake shop is a Jewish staple in the heart of the VII District. Fröhlich is famous for its flódni, a layered Jewish cake with apple, walnut, and poppy seed, but it's also worth trying some of their other baked goods and sweets. The interior has a faded old-world charm to it, with deep red walls and wooden lattice tables.

Hungarian
FRICI PAPA
Király utca 55, tel. 06/1-351-0197, http://fricipapa.hu,
Mon-Sat 11am-11pm 430-1,000 HUF
For Hungarian food on a budget, Frici Papa is the place to go. Frici Papa serves up classic Hungarian dishes in generous portions at fair prices. Even though it's located in a downtown, touristy area, it's still popular with locals. Just note that all dishes are sold separately, from meat and mains to side dishes.

KÁDÁR
Klauzál tér 9, tel. 06/1-321-3622,
Tue-Sat 11:30am-3:30pm, 1,000-2,500 HUF
The gentrification of the Jewish District hasn't stopped Kádár from serving up classic retro dishes over the generations. It's a time

Hungarian Bakeries

Hungarians love their *cukrászda* (confectionaries serving decadent cakes and coffees). Café culture is a big part of local life and a popular tourist attraction in itself. Old Habsburg-era grand cafés serving dessert and cakes still line the boulevards of Budapest. The New York Café is cited as the most beautiful café in Europe—if not the world—with marble columns, gold-gilt mirrors, and rococo-style frescoes on the ceiling and crystal chandeliers. Other cafés, like Gerbeaud, Művész, Central and Astoria, also carry on the Austro-Hungarian coffee traditions. New wave cafés are also percolating on the scene, catering to hip and trendy crowds who love their flat whites and Chemex coffees.

Look for the following desserts behind the glass cabinets of the city's loved *cukrászdas*:

- *Dobostorta:* A chocolate cake topped with a hard caramel topping.

- *Eszterházy:* Cake made with walnuts and rum.

- *Somloi galuska:* A Hungarian-style tiramisu without the coffee.

- *Krémes:* A custard and cream cake set between layers of flaky pastry.

capsule with checkered tablecloths, antique seltzer bottles, and vintage photos of celebrities on the wall. Kádár dishes up traditional Hungarian-Jewish cooking for lunch only, with plenty of boiled beef and dishes like sólet (cholent, a Jewish bean stew) on their ever-changing menu. You need to keep tabs on what you've eaten and drunk (including the slices of bread and the water consumed from the seltzer bottle) as each item is charged individually, but prices are very budget-friendly.

BARACK & SZILVA

Klauzál utca 13, tel. 06/1-798-8285,
www.barackesszilva.hu, Mon-Sat 6pm-midnight,
3,100-5,500 HUF
Barack & Szilva ("Peach and Plum") is a small family-run bistro serving up Hungarian provincial food fused with influences from French, Italian and Jewish cuisine. You can go á la carte, or dive into the seasonal chef's offer with a delicious tasting menu with a wine pairing option.

M RESTAURANT

Kertész utca 48, tel. 06/1-322-3108, www.metterem.
hu, daily 6pm-midnight, 2,400-3,600 HUF
The menu at M Restaurant changes daily and features Hungarian specials, sometimes with

a French twist. It has a cozy feel in a compact setting with sketched brown paper on the walls. Reservations highly recommended.

Fine Dining
BOCK BISZTRÓ

Erzsébet körút 43-49, tel. 06/1-321-0340,
www.bockbisztropest.hu, Mon-Sat midday-midnight,
3,400-17,400 HUF
Located in the building belonging to the Corinthia Hotel, Bock Bisztró gives you the chance to try Hungarian delicacies inspired by Spanish tapas. One of the main draws is its excellent and extensive wine list—with over 200 to choose from. Chef Lajos Bíró is legendary in local culinary circles, drawing Hungarians and visitors alike to this elegant establishment.

Street Food
★ BORS GASZTRO BÁR

Kazinczy utca 10, tel. 06/70-935-3263, daily
11:30am-9pm, 600-1,000 HUF
You'll always see waiting crowds outside this pantry-sized street food bar. Bors Gasztro Bár elevates street food with a menu that changes daily and is based on fresh, seasonal ingredients. Dishes include soups, baguettes, stews, and pasta, with innovative options like coconut-chili pumpkin cream soup or their French

Lady baguette that combines Emmentaler cheese and spiced chicken breast, accented with rosemary red onion jam.

KARAVAN

Kazinczy utca 18, tel. 06/30-934-8013, Sun-Wed 11:30am-11pm, Thu-Sat 11:30am-1am, 750-2,500 HUF

If you want a bite to eat before grabbing drinks at Szimpla Kert, Karavan is a great choice. This open-air street food court serves up a range of snacks from its numerous food trucks, from Hungarian lángos (deep fried savory pastries topped with cheese), to sausages, fried cheese, and vegan burgers. Head in with friends, and you can each buy from a different truck and sit together.

Cafés and Cake

NEW YORK CAFÉ

Erzsébet körút 9-11, tel. 06/1-8866-167, www.newyorkcafe.hu, daily 9am-midnight 1,650-18,000 HUF

Some say the New York Café is the most beautiful café in the world, and with its curved marble columns, rococo-style balconies and friezes, and generous application of gold leaf, it's certainly a candidate for the most opulent. This is not a place you come to for the food (which could be better, to be honest). However, people do come here for the experience. Along with the coffee and tempting cakes, the café also serves up plenty of history, since it was once a popular hangout for artists, nobility, and writers. Some of the most influential newspapers around 1900 were edited up in the café gallery. One local legend has it that writer Ferenc Molnár stole the keys to the café and tossed them in the Danube so the restaurant would be forced to stay open 24/7. Although it also functions as a restaurant, most come here to have a coffee and admire the scenery. But if coffee is not your thing, try the lemonade (which is based on a 19th-century recipe). Mornings are the best time to pop by, and if you're lucky, a cellist might even serenade you. You'll find the café inside the New York Palace Boscolo Budapest Hotel right on Grand Boulevard.

MY LITTLE MELBOURNE

Madács Imre út 3, tel. 06/70-394-7002, http://mylittlemelbourne.hu, Mon-Fri 7am-6pm, Sat-Sun 8:30am-6pm, 400-950 HUF

My Little Melbourne was one of the first new-wave coffee bars that opened in Budapest. Get quality espressos and flat whites in their tiny mezzanine café, or head next door to My Little Brew Bar, where you can treat yourself to a chemical lab's worth of drip coffees, from Chemex to syphon-made coffees.

AROUND ANDRÁSSY AVENUE

Hungarian

MENZA

Ferenc tér 2, tel. 06/1-413-1382, www.menzaetterem.hu, daily 10am-midnight 1,690-4,290 HUF

Menza combines retro interior design with Hungarian food classics adapted to the modern palate, like gulyás soup. They also offer more contemporary dishes, like duck burgers. The menu changes weekly. For a great bargain, come at lunch time during the week for quality food for only 1,290 HUF.

International

INDIGO

Jókai utca 13, tel. 06/1-428-2187, www.indigo-restaurant.hu, daily midday-11pm 1,200-4,900 HUF

Anyone from the local Indian community will recommend Indigo as the go-to Indian restaurant in Budapest. The menu focuses mostly on North Indian cuisine, cooked up by the best Indian chefs in the city. You'll find dishes from tandoor-cooked charred meats to creamy vegetarian curries. It's best to book in advance, but just in case you can't get a table at their Pest restaurant, they have another location in Buda (Fény utca 16).

Bistro and Brunch

KÉT SZERECSEN

Nagymező utca 14, tel. 06/1-434-1984, www.ketszerecsen.hu, Mon-Fri 8am-midnight, Sat-Sun 9am-midnight, 2,390-5,990 HUF

This cozy bistro serves up an eclectic menu,

with brunch classics such as eggs benedict and international dishes like Moroccan lamb shoulder and Thai curries. Két Szerecsen combines the classic coffeehouse vibe with a Parisian bistro environment. In the summer, there is a very nice terrace area just next to the café.

Vegetarian, Vegan and Gluten-free
DROP
Hajós utca 27, tel. 06/1-235-0468, http://droprestaurant.com, daily 8am-midnight 2,350-7,490 HUF
At Drop, there's a range of tasty gluten-free dishes to try, from salads and cheese plates to pasta dishes Hungarian specialties. It's also worth popping by for breakfast, especially if you want some gluten-free bread and baked goods. Lactose-free and vegetarian dishes are also available. (Great news for those who are gluten-intolerant or allergic—everything on the menu is gluten-free.)

KOZMOSZ
Hunyadi tér 11, tel. 06/20-514-6663, http:// vegankozmosz.hu, Tue-Fri 11:30am-3pm, 6pm-10pm, Sat-Sun 11:30am-10pm, 1,090-1,790 HUF
This small cellar restaurant on Hunyadi square offers vegan takes on classic Hungarian cuisine, like bean goulash and seitan paprika stew with traditional dumplings. Vegan burgers, BBQ seitan, and desserts are also available.

Street Food
PIZZICA
Nagymező utca 21, tel. 06/70-554-1227, Mon-Thu 11am-midnight, Fri-Sat 11am-3am, 190-490 HUF
For great Italian street food pizza, you can't beat Pizzica. The pizza here comes on the perfect thin base, with toppings like buffalo mozzarella or truffle cream. Slices are cut with scissors and served up on wooden boards. In the mezzanine, local art is usually on display.

Cafés and Cake
MŰVÉSZ
Andrássy út 29, tel. 06/70-333-2116, www.muveszkavehaz.hu, Mon-Sat 9am-10pm, Sun 10am-10pm, 550-890 HUF
A classic on the Hungarian cake and café scene since the 19th century, Művész is known for its cakes, with staples like custard cream and chocolate alongside seasonal specials. Try the house special—the Művész kocka—a layered cake with nuts, chocolate mousse, cream, and sheets of dark chocolate. The café interior captures a fading old-world decadence, with silk wallpaper, marble tables and crystal chandeliers. The Művész's proximity to the opera house and the theaters on Nagymező utca make it a good pre-theater hangout.

CITY PARK AND AROUND
Hungarian
BAGOLYVÁR
Károly út 4, tel. 06/1-468-3110, www.bagolyvar.com, daily midday-midnight 2,500-4,900 HUF
This family restaurant located next to the zoo offers good food at a reasonable cost. Bagolyvár ("Owl Castle"), named for its former avian residents, is the sister restaurant of the fancier, fine-dining Gundel restaurant next door. Bagolyvár serves up innovative cuisine inspired by chef Károly Gundel, but in a more relaxed atmosphere—and without the Gundel prices.

Fine Dining
★ GUNDEL
Gundel Károly út 4, https://gundel.hu, Tel. 1-889-8111, Daily noon-midnight, 5,500-39,000 HUF
Gundel is an institution whose founder is considered the Escoffier of Hungarian cuisine. Try the piquant goulash soup made from an in-house recipe, and the walnut pancakes accented with rum, raisins, and lemon zest—and drizzled with bitter chocolate. The extremely popular crepe-like Gundel pancake has inspired similar versions in restaurants across the country. If you want to try Gundel

Home Cooking

Eat&Meet (Danubius utca 14, tel. 06/30-517-5180, http://eatmeet-hungary.com scheduled dinners, see website, 11,000 HUF for a three-course meal including drinks) is no ordinary restaurant. Set in a private apartment in the XIII District (and in a garden house just outside Budapest in the summer), this unique pop-up restaurant runs regular dinners for those wanting to try authentic Hungarian food as you would have it at home. Zsuzska Goldbach, a young Hungarian woman who speaks both English and Italian, began Eat&Meet with her parents as a passion project to showcase true Hungrian home cooking you won't find in a restaurant. The three-course meal is seasonal, made with fresh, local ingredients, and dishes are paired with Hungarian wines. Zsuzska explains everything in detail, from specific ingredients to the wines and Hungarian culinary traditions. Guests are welcomed with the family's own aged *pálinka*. Dinners are scheduled on certain dates, so contact Eat&Meet to arrange when you'd like to come. You won't really find local Hungarians at Eat&Meet, but you feel like you're at an international dinner party where everyone is seated together. You may end the evening with a new friend or two. This restaurant is highly recommended if you're a solo traveler and fed up with dining alone. The food is fantastic and worth the price. It's made even more special by the Goldbach family's passion and attention to detail.

but it's out of your budget, head next door to the more affordable Bagolyvár.

International
ROBINSON
Városligeti tó, tel. 06/1-422-0222, www.robinsonrestaurant.hu, daily midday-3pm and 6pm-11pm, 3,500-6,200 HUF

On a small island in the heart of City Park, Robinson is all about the location. Robinson is in a two-story glass-paneled lake house, so when you're inside, it feels like you're dining on the water. Although you'll find Hungarian dishes like Hortobágy Pancakes (meat-filled pancakes topped with a creamy paprika sauce) on the menu, the focus is more on international cuisine (mostly French), along with grilled dishes and sizzling steaks.

Bistro and Brunch
VÁROSLIGET CAFÉ AND BAR
Olof Palme sétány 6, tel. 06/30-869-1426, www.varosligetcafe.hu, daily midday-10pm, 1,990-9,990 HUF

Városliget Cáfe and Bar overlooks Vajdahunyad Castle with views of the lake (or ice rink, depending on the season). It's in a beautiful 19th-century, neo-baroque pavilion. The food is a mix of international bistro cuisine with a few Hungarian specials

like paprika chicken, stuffed cabbage, and roasted goose leg. The restaurant prides itself on its Tányérhús, (slow-cooked boiled beef served over three courses, starting with beef broth, then the marrow on toast, and then finally the tender meat with sides like fried potatoes, cream of spinach and horseradish-spiked apple sauce), inspired by the Austrian Tafelspitz. Make sure you close the meal with their signature Liget Coffee, made with their in-house blend, roasted and ground on-premises.

MARGARET ISLAND AND AROUND
Hungarian
POZSONYI KISVENDÉGLŐ
Radnóti Miklós utca 38, tel. 06/1-787-4877, Mon-Fri 9am-midnight, Sat-Sun 10am-midnight, 1,100-3,050 HUF

Pozsonyi Kisvendéglő is popular with locals for its friendly, welcoming atmosphere. It's always full, and it can be a challenge to get a table, but with generous portions and budget-friendly prices, it's easy to see why. You'll find all the classic Hungarian dishes, and you may feel overwhelmed by the choices. Try the goulash or the roasted duck, or take advantage of the seasonal menu. Reservations highly recommended.

Cafés and Cake
SARKI FŰSZERES
Pozsonyi út 53-55, tel. 06/1-238-0600, 8am-8pm
Mon-Fri, 8am-3pm Sat, 790-2,300 HUF
This retro café is a great spot for a quick brunch or sandwich. Sarki Fűszeres is both a wine shop and a delicatessen selling platters of cheese and artisanal meat cuts. Whether you have a savory or sweet palate, you can be sure to find a snack to tempt you.

SOUTH BUDA
Bistro and Brunch
HADIK
Bartók Béla út 36, tel. 06/1-279-0290,
www.hadik.eu/, daily midday-1am, 1,600-3,600 HUF
Located on up-and-coming Bartók Béla út, Hadik delivers a mix of classic Hungarian and more experimental dishes. Hadik was once a hangout for the Buda literary elite, and it sports a more laid-back industrial chic look. Neighboring **Szatyor** (www.szatyorbar.com/home) offers the same menu and has an eclectic ruin-bar feel. Both places fill up quickly in the evenings, and during the day they make a great stop for coffee.

Vegetarian, Vegan and Gluten-free
VEGAN LOVE
Bartók Béla út 9, www.veganlove.hu;
daily 11am-9pm 1,590-1,990 HUF
For Budapest's best vegan burgers, head to Vegan Love. This street food bar offers delicious vegan options like sweet potato or BBQ tofu burgers and vegan chili dogs. The creations here are adventurous and flavorful, and they will also appeal to non-vegans.

Cafés and Cake
KELET
Bartók Béla út 29, tel. 06/20-456-5507, Mon-Fri
7:30am-11pm, Sat-Sun 9am-11pm, 350-1,850 HUF
This charming café, covered wall-to-wall with books, is popular with locals for its third-wave artisanal coffees and tempting snacks, like creative toasted sandwiches made with Indonesian-style peanut butter or exotic chutneys. Make sure you try their hot chocolates or drip coffees made from single origin beans.

SOUTH PEST
International
PATA NEGRA
Kálvin tér 8, tel. 06/1-215-5616, https://patanegra.hu,
daily 11am-midnight, 650-2,650 HUF
Share some tapas at Pata Negra, a Spanish tapas bar featuring classics like patatas bravas, croquetas, and jamón iberico. This restaurant is ideal to visit with a group so you can share different dishes and a jar of Sangria, or enjoy a glass of Spanish wine or sherry.

Fine Dining
★ COSTES
Ráday utca 4, tel. 06/1-219-0696, www.costes.hu,
Wed-Sun 6:30pm-midnight, 9,000-13,000 HUF
Costes was the first restaurant in Hungary to receive the much-coveted Michelin star. Chef de Cuisine Eszter Palágyi has created a fine dining experience that marries Hungarian family recipes with international trends. The restaurant features locally sourced fish dishes and more experimental signature recipes, like wild pigeon served with beetroot and Ethiopian coffee crumbs.

Bistro and Brunch
PÚDER
Ráday utca 8, tel. 06/1-210-7168, www.puderbar.hu,
daily midday-1am, 1,850-3,950 HUF
Púder is an eclectic bistro and bar with a decor that combines the look of ancient Pompeii with quirky local art and dilapidation. The menu mixes up light bites with more substantial bistro food, like pork knuckles with rosemary, or rosé duck breast with arugula mashed potato and cinnamon-plum red wine ragout.

CSIGA
Vásár utca 2, tel. 06/30-613-2046, daily
8am-11:45pm, 1,500-4,000 HUF
It's almost impossible to get a seat at Csiga, which attracts a local bohemian crowd of artists and VIII District creatives due to its

Running from the Liberty Bridge well into the XI District's Kelenföld Station, Bartók Béla Avenue is a lifeline on the Buda side of the river. The far end takes you past the concrete apartment blocks off the tourist route, and the first stretch until Móricz Zsigmond körtér Feneketlen tó (the "Bottomless Lake") is an exciting mixture of fin de siécle architecture, contemporary art galleries, alternative cultural centers, vegan street food, and vibrant café culture. The influx of visitors has turned the trendy Inner City areas into a tourist hub. Hip Hungarians now hang out on the other side of the river in cafés like booklined **Kelet** or historic **Hadik** (once the hangout for the Hungarian literary elite), which has recently undergone a makeover to embrace the trending industrial chic look. Bartók Béla Avenue is the new up-and-coming district, with new cafés and galleries popping up in art nouveau buildings each week.

The area around Bartók Béla Avenue is one of the most happening neighborhoods in Buda.

relaxed ambience. The menu includes soups, salads and modern takes on Hungarian dishes. It's a great choice for vegetarians, and if you want to eat lunch on a budget, take advantage of their lunch menu that changes weekly. (Call to make a reservation.)

Cafés and Cake
LUMEN
Horánszky utca 5, tel. 06/20-402-2393, Mon-Fri
8am-midnight, Sat-Sun 10am-midnight
Lumen is a café within the heart of the Palace District that draws in the local arts crowd with its laid-back atmosphere and exhibitions held on-site (focusing mostly on photography). This café has its own roastery. You can get some light bites if you're hungry, like soup and hummus, or daily specials on the lunch menu, like curried vegetable soup and lasagna.

ÓBUDA AND BUDA HILLS
Hungarian
★ NÁNCSI NÉNI
Ördögárok út 80, tel. 06/1-397-2742, http://
nancsineni.hu, daily midday-11pm, 2,350-4,780 HUF
Náncsi Néni is worth the journey into the leafy Hűvösvölgy area, especially in the summer.

It's noted for its exceptional Hungarian traditional classics (like your Hungarian grandmother would cook), but there are also more creative concoctions, like duck liver marinated in sherry and served with steamed grapes, as well as a number of freshwater fish dishes and steaks. Reservations highly recommended.

FÖLDES JÓZSI
Bécsi út 31, tel. 06/70-500-0222, http://
foldesjozsietterme.hu, Mon 11:30am-3:30pm,
Tue-Sun 11:30am-10pm, 2,250-4,800 HUF
This simple restaurant, established by hotel chef "Joe Earthy" (Földes Józsi) serves excellent Hungarian homestyle dishes, with a menu that changes seasonally. Földes Józsi is worth the visit if you find yourself on this side of Buda. Try their paprika chicken (or if in season, their goose specials).

International
OKUYAMA NO SUSHI
Kolosy tér 5, tel. 06/1-250-8256,
http://okuyamanosushi.uw.hu, Tue-Sun 1pm-10pm,
1,400-7,000 HUF
Although you can find sushi restaurants all over Budapest, this basement sushi restaurant

is favored by both Japanese expats and travelers, and always seems to be full. Okuyama No Sushi is led by Japanese sushi chef Sachi Okuyama, who many argue makes the best sushi in town. You can get all the usual maki rolls, as well as seasonal sashimi and grilled fish on the menu.

Bistro and Brunch
VILLA BAGATELLE
Németvölgyi út 17, tel. 06/30-359-6295, http://villa-bagatelle.com, Mon-Fri 8am-7pm,

Sat-Sun 9am-6pm, 890-3,990 HUF
In a beautiful bright villa in the Buda Hills, Villa Bagatelle is a special place to have brunch, and is worth the excursion out of town. Make sure you try their coffee, which is made with special care using beans from a local roaster. And try their salmon breakfast, where slices of wholegrain toast are topped with avocado, smoked salmon and a poached egg. Or go all out and indulge in the champagne breakfast.

Accommodations

Picking the right location really depends on what you are looking for. If you want to be in the heart of the action and just crawl into bed straight from the ruin bars, then stay in the Jewish Quarter. If you want a good night's sleep, avoid anything with "Party Hostel" in the name. If seclusion, nature and peace and quiet are what you desire, you might check into the Grand Hotel on Margaret Island. Hotels in the Inner City lean toward luxury. Budget options will lie further afield in neighborhoods such as the residential area around City Park or out in Óbuda, but will give you the chance to immerse yourself more fully in local life.

It's not unusual to find accommodation in formerly residential buildings (or occupying a floor in a still-residential building), which can provide a less-touristy atmosphere while you're in the city. Most hotels do offer breakfast, but some might charge for it, so double-check before booking.

CASTLE DISTRICT
Under €150
BALTAZAR
Országház utca 31, tel. 06/1-300-7051, http://baltazarbudapest.com, 95-135€ d
This family-owned boutique hotel, with just 11 rooms and suites, is located at the northern

end of Castle Hill. This hotel has a bohemian feel with quirky and colorful rooms and vintage furniture. It's noted for its bistro and grill and its wine bar downstairs.

PEST-BUDA DESIGN BOUTIQUE HOTEL
Fortuna utca 3, tel. 06/1-800-9213, www.pest-buda. com, 90-140€ d
One of the oldest hotels in Budapest, the Pest-Buda Design Boutique Hotel opened in 1696. The hotel was renovated in 2016, and now blends worn wood with a touch of industrial chic and vintage sketches in its 10 individually designed rooms and suites in a three-story house. (Note: There is no elevator, only stairs.) Continental breakfast is available in the popular ground-floor bistro.

€150-250
ART'OTEL
Bem rakpart 16-19, tel. 06/1-487-9487, www.artotels. com/budapest-hotel-hu-h-1011/hunbuart, 135-189€ d
This four-star hotel overlooking the Danube Bank exhibits 600 works by American artist Donald Sultan, and guests can join a free tour to learn more about the artist and his work. Art'otel occupies a modern seven-story building with a small baroque wing inside. The main draw of the hotel is its views,

some overlooking the Castle District up the hill, or overlooking the river. There are 75 rooms here, and the hotel offers disabled access and facilities.

MAISON BISTRO AND HOTEL

Országház utca 17, tel. 06/1-405-4980, http://maisonbudapest.hu, 149-179€ d

In a baroque house built upon 15th-century foundations, Maison Bistro and Hotel captures the historical essence of the Castle District. The 17 rooms and suites feature king-size beds, with twins available upon request. Some rooms come with a private garden terrace. Guests are treated to a welcome drink upon arrival.

Over €250
HILTON

Hess András tér 3, tel. 06/1-889-6600, www.danubiushotels.com/en/our-hotels-budapest/hilton-budapest, 280-450€ d d

The Hilton Budapest incorporates the ruins of a 13th-century Dominican monastery into its design. This Hilton is located by Fisherman's Bastion, and it has 298 rooms and 24 luxury suites, some with views over the Danube. The hotel has its own restaurant (ICON) serving Hungarian and international food, and there's a fitness center on-site. It is also accessible for travelers with disabilities.

INNER CITY AND AROUND PARLIAMENT
€150-250
KEMPINSKI

Erzsébet tér 7-8, tel. 06/1-429-3777, www.kempinski.com/en/budapest/hotel-corvinus/welcome/, 145-280€ d

The Hotel Kempinski is next door to the Ritz Carlton, but it sports a different aesthetic. This modern hotel with a Zen in-house spa and gastronomic quarter puts it on the map. There are 349 rooms, including 33 suites. On-site restaurants include Nobu, an avant-garde fusion of Japanese-Peruvian cuisine, and És Bisztró, serving contemporary

Austro-Hungarian cuisine, as well as the Living Room and the Blue Fox Bar.

HOTEL PRESIDENT

Hold utca 3, tel. 06/1-510-3400, www.hotelpresident.hu, 160-199€ d

With a rooftop terrace overlooking the Royal Postal Savings Bank and the Hungarian Parliament, Hotel President has some of the best views in the city. This four-star hotel has 106 rooms and two suites, as well as a wellness center with a jet stream pool. The highlight is its rooftop, which serves as a café and a restaurant in the summer, and becomes an ice rink in the winter (which is free for guests).

Over €250
★ FOUR SEASONS

Széchenyi István tér 5, Tel. 1-268-6000, www.fourseasons.com/budapest/, 440-640€ d

The Four Seasons Hotel Gresham Palace not only ticks the box for one of the best views in town (facing the Chain Bridge and Buda Castle head-on), but it's also one of the most beautiful art nouveau buildings on the Danube. This five-star hotel has 160 rooms (51 of which overlook the Danube) and 19 suites in a palette of cream and ivory. In addition, there's **Kollázs Brasserie & Bar**, its own fine-dining restaurant, and a rooftop spa.

★ ARIA

Hercegprímás utca 5, tel. 06/1-445-4055, www.ariahotelbudapest.com, 235-425€ d

There is a reason that the Aria Hotel tops numerous lists as one of the world's best hotels. This design hotel was built around an old Inner City townhouse, and has a musical theme throughout, from its piano key-decorated lobby to its 49 rooms, each of which is named after a musician or composer. Every room comes with its own balcony, and there's a wellness center in the basement. But the real piece de resistance is the rooftop bar overlooking St. Stephen's Basilica. Guests can also relax to live piano music in the lobby while sampling complimentary wine and cheese between 5pm and 7pm.

RITZ CARLTON
Erzsébet tér 9-10, tel. 06/1-429-5500,
www.ritzcarlton.com/en/hotels/europe/budapest,
390-490€ d

The Ritz Carlton Budapest attracts guests not only with its modern take on old-world luxury, but also with its central location close to Váci utca and the few minutes' walk to the Jewish Quarter. The hotel, occupying the former Adria Palace, emulates the tones of the Danube in a palette of blues and grays. The most beautiful feature in the hotel is the stained-glass dome under the Kupola Lounge. There are 170 rooms and 30 suites. In 2016, the hotel opened a new fitness and wellness center, including a naturally lit pool.

JEWISH QUARTER
Under €150
WOMBATS CITY HOSTEL BUDAPEST
Király utca 20, tel. 06/1-883-5005,
www.wombats-hostels.com, €20/dorm bed, €65 d

Wombats City Hostel Budapest is located in the heart of the action in the Jewish Quarter. You can either sleep in a dorm or take a private room in this modern, clean hostel. There is a 24-hour common kitchen and a laundry room, plus social areas. There is also a buffet breakfast on offer.

ROOMBACH HOTEL
Rumbach Sebestyén utca 17, tel. 06/1-413-0253,
https://roombach.accenthotels.com, 85-100€ d

Roombach Hotel stands right next to bustling Király utca and Gozsdu Court, but on a peaceful side street opposite the Rumbach Synagogue. This colorful, youthful hotel with en-suite rooms and geometric décor offers a lovely view of a quiet courtyard. This is a great budget option in the city center.

Over €250
★ CORINTHIA HOTEL BUDAPEST
Erzsébet körút 43-49, tel. 06/1-479-4000,
www.corinthia.com/en/hotels/budapest, 125-360€ d

Located on the Grand Boulevard, the Corinthia Hotel Budapest possesses a fascinating history. The original mirrored ballroom (as well as a spa) were forgotten for decades, until plans arose to build an underground parking lot. Stories abound in this grand hotel. Behind its original 19th-century façade, you'll find modern luxury, with over 400 rooms, as well as four restaurants, one bar, and a music club. Check out the placard in the marble lobby that lists the names of actors, musicians, and other well-known figures who have stayed in the hotel.

BOSCOLO BUDAPEST
Erzsébet körút 9-11, tel. 06/1-886-6118,
https://budapest.boscolohotels.com, 204-280€ d

The Boscolo Budapest, famous for its extravagant **New York Café,** is in an elegant 19th-century building on the Grand Boulevard. The hotel's 185 rooms are decorated in an Italian style, with soft, warm tones and lush fabrics. There is a wellness center on-site, with a steam bath and relaxation pool. There's also a fitness center.

AROUND ANDRÁSSY AVENUE
Under €150
KAPITAL INN
Aradi utca 40, tel. 06/30-915-2029,
www.kapitalinn.com, 89-149€ d d

This cute boutique hotel is on the third floor of a classic old apartment block just off Andrássy Avenue. It offers five luxurious rooms with a sleek, modern design. One of the main draws is the stunning rooftop terrace. Rooms go fast at this popular hotel. (Note that there is no lift in the building.)

€150-250
HOTEL MOMENTS

Andrássy út 8, tel. 06/1-611-7000,
http://hotelmomentsbudapest.hu, 199-244€ d

Just a few steps from the Hungarian State Opera House, Hotel Moments is centrally located within walking distance of main sights. This four-star hotel has 99 elegant rooms, as well as an on-site Hungarian bistro, where a buffet breakfast is served (which also includes gluten-free baked products).

CITY PARK AND AROUND
Under €150
MIRAGE MEDIC HOTEL

Dózsa György út 88, tel. 06/1-400-6158,
http://miragemedichotel.hu, 115-160€ d

The Mirage Medic Hotel is in a historic villa on the fringes of City Park. This hotel, owned by a Chinese doctor, offers in-house medical services and holistic remedies ranging from herbalism to acupuncture. The 37 rooms come with mattresses designed to work on pressure points and regulate body temperature. Disabled access rooms are also available.

This is not the usual wellness break (there are no saunas on-site), but if you book for more than two nights, you get a holistic diagnosis from the hotel's Chinese doctors. Even if you're not looking for anything to do with alternative medicine, the value and the location merits a stay.

BUDAPEST VILLE BED AND BREAKFAST

Damjanich utca 32, tel.06/1-791-9962,
www.budapestville.com, 45-80€ d

Budapest Ville Bed and Breakfast occupies a floor in a 19th-century apartment block. It features an arched double courtyard in a quiet neighborhood next to City Park. The design follows a vintage chic look, combining modern comforts with nostalgia in its four rooms.

€150-250
MAMAISON HOTEL ANDRASSY BUDAPEST

Andrássy út 11, tel. 06/1-462-2100,
www.mamaisonandrassy.com, 150-205€ d

Mamaison Hotel Andrassy Budapest is on the illustrious boulevard close to City Park. The hotel has 61 rooms and seven suites decorated in warm colors and a modern design to give it the feel of a boutique hotel. A buffet breakfast is served at the on-site La Perle Noire Restaurant for a surplus of €16.

MARGARET ISLAND AND AROUND
Under €150
DANUBIUS GRAND HOTEL MARGITSZIGET

Budapest-Margitsziget, tel. 06/1-889-4700,
www.danubiushotels.com/en/our-hotels-budapest/
danubius-grand-hotel-margitsziget, 85-130€ d

Margaret Island lies away from the bustle of the city, making sister hotels the Danubius Grand and Hotel Margitsziget relaxing places to stay. For a wellness getaway, guests can use the thermal water spa in the modern part of the hotel, and they can opt for treatments like the salt cave or doctor-prescribed health treatments.

The hotel is in two parts. The original Grand Hotel is a beautiful 19th-century hotel, one of the first in Budapest; the other is a more modern building constructed around the 1960s. The two parts are connected via an underground passage, giving guests easy access to the wellness center.

AVENTURA BOUTIQUE HOSTEL

Visegrádi utca 12, tel. 06/1-239-0782,
www.aventurahostelbudapest.com,
11-14€ dorms, 15-30€ d per person per night

This laid-back, family-run hostel takes guests around the world with its themed rooms including India, Africa, Japan (and outer space). The dorms sleep four to eight people. There are also private apartments available. The dorms link up with a common kitchen.

The hostel is in the quiet Újlipót district in Pest, close to Margaret Island and the Grand Boulevard. It's noted for being LGBTQ-friendly as well.

SOUTH BUDA
Under €150
SHANTEE HOUSE

Takács Menyhért utca 33, tel. 06/1-385-8946, www.backpackbudapest.hu, 10-16€ dorms, 13.50-26€ yurt, 39-52€ private room

This hostel located in the XI District welcomes visitors with its sense of community. Private rooms and dorms are available, as well as a yurt in the summer. There is a kitchen you can use, with free tea and coffee offered during your stay. There is also a small bar on-site, where you can pick up wine (€3 a bottle) chilled beer (€1.50 for a 500ml bottle), and smoke some shisha (€3.50) in the garden. Bicycles and skateboards are available for rent (€10 for 24 hours), and there are hammocks in the garden to relax in.

€150-250
GELLERT HOTEL

Szent Gellért tér 2, tel. 06/1-889-5500, www.danubiushotels.com/en/our-hotels-budapest/ danubius-hotel-gellert/, 65-250€ d

The Danubius Hotel Gellért opened its doors in 1918 and has since become an icon in the city—most notably for its baths. One of the main perks of staying in its 234 rooms and suites is one free entrance for guests to the baths. The Art Nouveau hotel has old-world charm. There are restaurants on-site, like the **Panoráma Restaurant** or the **Gellért Brasserie,** but its location close to Bartók Béla Avenue and transport connections to Pest make it a good base to explore other dining options nearby.

SOUTH PEST
Under €150
★ BRODY HOUSE

Bródy Sándor utca 10, tel. 06/1-266-1211, www.brody.land/brody-house, 80-130€ d

This illustrious townhouse in the Palace District started as an artists' studio and bohemian clubhouse before its owners converted it into a boutique hotel. There are 11 shabby-chic rooms featuring work by the artists who once painted there. Breakfast is available (€10), along with an honesty bar and other concierge services. Guests at the hotel get temporary membership to

the Tinei Room at bohemian boutique hotel Brody House

the Brody Studios members' club just off Andrássy Avenue.

HOTEL PALAZZO ZICHY

Lőrincz Pap tér, tel. 06/1-235-4000, www.hotel-palazzo-zichy.hu, 88-150€ d

Once the residence of Count Nándor Zichy, this 19th-century mansion blends rococo stuccos and wrought-iron balustrades with contemporary design—plus a glass pyramid roof. Guests can enjoy a complimentary lavish breakfast or beverages in the lobby bar. There are 80 rooms and a sauna and gym on-site.

BOHEM ART HOTEL

Molnár utca 35, tel. 06/1-327-9020, www.bohemarthotel.hu, 115-290€ d

The Bohem Art Hotel uses the concept of a local art gallery (featuring work by young Hungarian artists). Its 60 hotel rooms are each decorated by a different artist, and guests can choose a room based on the art they like in the building's public gallery. You can enjoy a full American breakfast here, served with sparkling wine.

ÓBUDA AND BUDA HILLS
Under €150

AQUINCUM HOTEL

Árpád Fejedelem útja 94, tel. 06/1-436-4100, www.aquincumhotel.com, 70-120€ d

Located close to the historic Baroque squares in Óbuda, the Hotel Aquincum stands right alongside the Danube overlooking Margaret Island. The hotel has a vast wellness center complex, which is complimentary for guests. It draws its therapeutic thermal water from Margaret Island. There are 310 guest rooms, along with various dining options on-site with a 15% discount for hotel guests.

WALTZER HOTEL

Németvölgyi út 110, tel. 06/1-319-1212, www.hotelwalzer.hu, 35-75€ d

This romantic hotel up in the Buda Hills offers the chance to get away from the busy streets of the Inner City, but it is still accessible to town. The hotel, surrounded by lush greenery and picturesque villas, resides in a castle-like building. Guests can dine on Hungarian food in its restaurant and take advantage of the sauna. There is also a wonderful garden on the property.

Information and Services

TOURIST INFORMATION

You can find **Budapestinfo** (Sütő utca 2, tel. 06/1-486-3300, www.budapestinfo.hu daily, 8am-8pm) Tourist Information Points in various locations in the city: in the Inner City, up at the airport terminal, and in the ice rink building at City Park. Pick up free publications and maps, buy tickets for sights, theater or opera productions, and get some help on navigating the city from the multilingual staff. These Budapestinfo tourism bureaus are also a good place to buy a **Budapest Card**.

BUSINESS HOURS

Most shops in Budapest open at 10am and close at 6pm. At one point, shops were required to close on Sundays, but due to popular demand, they reopened. (Note that opening hours may be shorter, and smaller shops and boutiques may not open on Sunday.) Budapest is not a city with seasonal opening hours, unless what you want to visit is an outdoor attraction, where you may find closing time correlates with the hours of sundown.

EMERGENCY NUMBERS

Hungary's emergency number is **112**. The average time to answer the phone is five seconds, and the operators speak English. However, it's not the only emergency number available. If you need an ambulance, call **104;** fire brigade **105;** police **107**. There is also a 24-hour English-speaking medical hotline called Falck's SOS: 06/1-2000-100.

CRIME

The main crime risks for tourists are **pickpockets** and **restaurant scams**. Take care with your belongings in busy, public spaces and on public transportation, and also ask for a menu with a price list when dining out. If you have any problems, you can call the **Tourist Police** (06/1-438-8080), a 24-hour hotline with English-speaking operators.

HOSPITALS AND PHARMACIES

There are dozens of hospitals in Budapest, usually one for each district. If you're looking for a private option, the **Medicover Health Center** (Teréz körút 55-57, tel. 06/1-435-3100, www.medicover.hu) has English-speaking doctors and a 24-hour receptionist. **FirstMed** Centers (Hattyú utca 14, tel. 06/1-224-9090, www.firstmedcenters.com) accepts some US insurance, and has an entirely English-speaking staff.

You can find pharmacies all over Budapest, denoted by a green cross and the word *gyógyszertár*. Most of them are open for regular shopping hours and close in the evenings and on Sundays, but there are a few that are open 24 hours, like Teréz körút 41 and Fővám tér 4 in the central areas in Pest.

FOREIGN CONSULATES

If you have an emergency (like losing your passport or you need consular help), the **United States Embassy** (Szabadság tér 12, tel. 06/1-475-4400) is located in the city center, close to the Hungarian Parliament. The **Canadian Embassy** (Ganz utca 12-14, tel.06/1-392-3360) can be found in Buda, along with the **British Embassy** (Füge utca 5-7, tel. 06/1-266-2888) and the South African Embassy (Gárdonyi Géza út 17, tel. 06/1-392-0999). There is no **Australian** (Mattiellistraße 2-4, Vienna, tel. +43-1-506-740) or **New Zealand Embassy** (Mattiellistraße 2-4, Vienna, tel. +43-1-505-3021) in Budapest, so you will have to go to Vienna.

Transportation

GETTING THERE
Air

Budapest has one international airport, the **Ferenc Liszt International Airport** (BUD, tel. 06/1-296-7000, www.bud.hu) sometimes known by its former name of Ferihegy Airport, located in the south-eastern suburbs. There are two terminals, but terminal 1 has been closed since 2012, so all flights go in and out of 2A and 2B.

Flights between Budapest and Vienna take 45 minutes and 1 hour 10 minutes for Prague (but once you factor in the time to check-in, getting to the airport, and so on, you're better off taking the train).

AIRPORT TRANSPORTATION

Getting to and from the airport is easy. For door-to-door service, the **miniBUD** (tel. 06/1-550-0000, www.minibud.hu, HUF 4900 one way to the city center) minibus service offers easy access to your hotel around the clock. miniBUD customer service counters can be found as soon as you exit arrivals. You may have to wait up to 30 minutes for a minibus; they will either call your name or your Budapest address. The journey time depends on your destination in the city, the traffic or the number of passengers with you (the bus stops door-to-door in the neighborhood), so account for around 30 minutes to an hour for the journey into town. You can get return tickets when you buy your ticket arrivals, or you can book online (latest—five hours before departure).

Another option is to take the **100E bus** (HUF 900) which will take you directly into the city center. The buses usually run on a half-hourly basis (from 4am to 11:30pm) and take 30 minutes to get downtown.

A **taxi** from the airport can cost HUF 5,500 to 7,000 and takes around 30 minutes to reach the city center.

Train

Budapest has four main train stations. **Keleti** (Eastern) Train Station (Metro 2 and 4) is the main one. The others are the **Nyugati** (Western) Train Station (Metro 3), **Déli** (Southern) Train Station (Metro 2) and **Kelenföld** (Metro 4). Except for Kelenföld, all are located in the city center with good transport connections by metro, trams and buses.

There are a number of trains that go to and from Budapest to other destinations in Hungary and abroad. You can buy tickets and check timetables from **MÁV** (www.mav.hu) for both international and domestic connections. There are regular trains going a few times a day to Vienna and Prague. If you buy an international train ticket from Budapest, you will get a code. If you buy the ticket online, you'll need to print it from the ticket machine, or you can go to the international desks at the Nyugati and Keleti Train Stations.

From Prague: Trains to Budapest run by **Ceske Drahy** (www.cd.cz), **Regiojet** (www.regiojet.com) or **Leo Express** (www.leoexpress.com/en) depart from Hlavní nádraží every 1-2 hours from about 6am to 4pm with a few late night options until midnight. The journey takes about 6.5 hours during the day and about 9-12 hours for an overnight train. Prices ranges roughly 600-1,500 CZK on different carriers and direct trains or transfers.

From Vienna: Trains run from Wien Hauptbahnhof every one to two hours to Budapest Keleti (2.5-3 hours, €13-30) either running with Austria's **ÖBB Railjet** (www.

oebb.at) or EuroCity trains that are run by various European train operators, like the Hungarian MÁV. However, do note that if you're leaving Vienna you cannot buy a ticket from the MÁV website as tickets need to be printed from the ticket machines in the Hungarian train stations—so unless you're starting in Budapest before you go onto Vienna you will need to buy tickets from ÖBB Railjet website or from the ticket offices at Wien Hauptbahnhof.

Bus

The main bus station for international journeys is Népliget Bus Station, which connects to Metro line 3. **Flixbus,** in collaboration with the domestic Volánbusz company (http://nemzetkozi.volanbusz.hu/en/) is the most reliable international bus service to other European destinations, including Vienna and Prague.

From Prague: Buses from Florenc to Budapest run almost every hour from around 5am to 5pm, and then once every 2-3 hours until midnight. The journey takes anywhere from 7-10 hours and ranges from 400-800 CZK with different carriers, including **Regiojet, Leo Express,** and **FlixBus** (www.flixbus.com).

From Vienna: FlixBus (www.flixbus.com) run regular bus services from Vienna Edberg to Budapest several times per day, operating hourly or even more frequently. The journey is around 3 hours and costs €9-14.

Car

There are five motorways and four main roads in Hungary, with eight starting from Budapest. If you're planning to drive on the motorway, you must buy a motorway sticker (HUF 3,000 for a 10-day sticker), available at the border crossing or gas stations. The **M1** motorway brings you into Budapest from Vienna or Prague, whereas the **M3** will take you out of the city towards Eger or Gödöllő and all the way to the Ukrainian border, and the **M7** heads toward Lake Balaton. The **M5** will head down towards the Serbian border. The Hungarian

Don't Forget To Validate!

Unless you have a Budapest Card or a 24-hour or longer pass, you will need to **validate your bus, metro, or tram ticket** by punching it in a slotted box. Find these boxes at metro entrances and onboard the tram and bus. Some older trams require you to put the ticket in vertically and pull it down hard so the ticket punches. **Double-check for the time stamp or punch marks,** as some machines may run out of ink and ticket validation won't be visible.

Ticket inspectors (sometimes in uniform, sometimes plain-clothed with a purple armband) check transport at random for tickets. **Keep your validated tickets with you at all times** as you can be inspected at any point—even when exiting the metro. If you are caught without a ticket, ticket inspectors can get unpleasant and charge a fine of HUF 8,000, which you can pay on the spot or at designated BKK Customer Service Centers (such as Rumbach Sebestyén utca 19-21 or Akácfa utca 22) within two days. You can also pay by bank transfer if you exceed the two-day threshold, but this will cost more (HUF 16,000).

There are a few "fake" ticket inspectors who may insist on a cash fine. If you are suspicious, insist on paying at the BKK Customer Service Centers. (Paying by transfer after two days is more expensive, but at least you'll know that you're not just giving money to someone taking advantage of the system.) If you can get to a customer service center as soon as possible, the fine should be the same as paying immediately.

If you have a pass and left it at the hotel, you can request a form and pay a reduced fine of HUF 2,000 at the BKK Customer Service Center when you prove you had a pass. Typically, inspectors will ask you for identification, and you may be asked to get off the tram/bus/metro if you don't have a validated ticket.

Highway Code (KRESZ) is similar to the rest of the EU, with speed limits within the cities at 50km/h and on the motorways at 130km/h. Front and rear seat belts are compulsory, and mobile phones must be used with a hands-free kit.

From Prague: The 325-mile drive can take 5-8 hours depending on traffic. Head south and east on the D1/E65 and D2/E65 highways and cross Slovakia to get to Hungary on the M1. There are tolls on parts of the route (CZK 350 in the Czech Republic, €10 in Slovakia for 10-day stickers).

From Vienna: Drive 150 miles southeast on the A4 and M1 highways to reach Budapest (tolls apply, in addition for the Hungarian motorway vignette, the Austrian one costs €9 for a 10-day sticker). The drive takes around 2.5 hours.

GETTING AROUND

Budapest is a relatively compact city that's easy to get around on foot or with public transport operated by Budapest's public transit network, the **Budapesti Közlekedési Központ**

(**BKK,** www.bkk.hu). You have plenty of modes to choose from: metro, bus, tram, and trolleybus. Just note that single use tickets are not valid for transfers—except on the metro.

Transit Passes

You can buy transit passes at the kiosk in the metro or from purple machines next to the bus, tram or metro. Passes can come in the 24-hour variety (1,650 HUF), 72 hours (4,150 HUF) or 7 days (4,950 HUF), and can be used on all forms of transport, except the BKK boat on weekends. Single tickets cost 350 HUF or 3,000 HUF for a block of 10.

Metro

Budapest has four metro lines denoted by numbers and colors. The **yellow metro line 1** runs from Vörösmarty tér, traversing the entire stretch of Andrássy Avenue to City Park. The **red metro line 2** passes under the Danube and the city center. The **blue line metro 3** runs from the suburbs in northern Pest into the city center and up towards the airport. The newest line, **green metro 4,** goes between the Keleti and Kelenföld Train Stations, crossing from Pest into South Buda. You can change between metro lines at Deák Ferenc tér (lines 1, 2, 3); Kálvin tér (lines 3 and 4), and Keleti pályaudvar (lines 2 and 4).

Metros operate between 4:30am and 11:30pm

Tram, Bus and Trolleybus

The tram is the easiest and quickest way to get around Budapest. Lines **4** and **6** running along the Grand Boulevard are the most efficient for getting from Buda to Pest and take you all the way around the center—and line 6 runs all night long (most trams run at the same time as the metro 4:30am-11:30pm). Other tram lines, like 2 or 41, are a scenic way of seeing the city. Buses and trolley buses are less attractive for travelers, but the buses are efficient and will take you further out of the city than the tram. The red trolley buses only really operate in Pest, and tend to take you out into the more residential areas.

Boat

In the summer, you can take BKK's public boat along the Danube, which is free during the week with a travel pass, or 750 HUF for a single ticket or on the weekends. There are docks all along the Danube, with some going as far as Rómaifürdő.

Taxi

Avoid hailing a taxi, as there are some rogue operators who take advantage of tourists. Instead, call a reputable taxi company, like **City Taxi** (tel. 06/1-211-1111), **Fő Taxi** (tel. 06/1-222-2222), **Taxi Plus** (tel. 06/1-888-8888), **Taxi 6x6** (tel. 06/1-666-6666) or use an app like **Taxify**.

Car

Budapest is a very pedestrian-friendly city, and it's easier and quicker to get around on public transport than by car. However, if you want to get out of the city, you can rent cars from international rental companies such as **Hertz** (tel. 06/1-296-0999 for local reservations, tel. 06/1-235-6008; for international reservations, www.hertz.hu), **Europecar** (tel. 06/1-421-8333, www.europcar.hu), and **Avis** (tel. 06/30-934-4050, www.avis.hu). You'll find all the above rental companies in the airport or in the Inner City.

Day Trips from Budapest

You can spend days, if not weeks, exploring Budapest, but there is more to Hungary than its capital. The good news is Hungary is a small country, which makes it easy to jaunt off for the day, whether you catch the train down to Lake Balaton—Central Europe's largest lake—ride a boat up the dramatic valleys of the Danube Bend, explore the colorful art colony of Szentendre, or taste the famed "Bull's Blood" wine in the Valley of Beautiful Women outside Eger.

PLANNING YOUR TIME

Popular day trips from Budapest include the village of Szentendre, which brings in the crowds all year round, accessible on the suburban train in just 40 minutes, or the Danube Bend, whose main towns are between 30 minutes to just over an hour away by train or bus.

Highlights

Look for ★ to find recommended sights, activities, dining, and lodging.

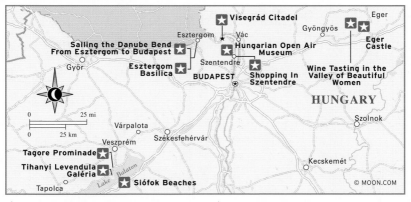

★ **Hungarian Open Air Museum:** For a taste of life in rural Hungary, visit this open-air museum divided into areas that represent different regions of the country (page 418).

★ **Shopping in Szentendre:** Szentendre, an artists' colony since the 1920s, is a wonderful place to shop for folk crafts and contemporary design alike (page 418).

★ **Visegrád Citadel:** The views from the top of this 13th century citadel are among the best in Hungary (page 424).

★ **Esztergom Basilica:** Walk around the dome of the largest church in Hungary for sweeping views across the Danube to Slovakia on the other side of the river (page 427).

★ **Sailing the Danube Bend from Esztergom to Budapest:** The slow boat back to Budapest is a leisurely float past Esztergom's basilica, the surrounding hills, and local wildlife. Plus, there's a bar on board (page 428).

★ **Tagore Promenade:** This tree-lined promenade in Balatonfüred makes for a beautiful walk along Lake Balaton (page 430).

★ **Tihanyi Levendula Galéria:** Tihany, one of the loveliest spots on Lake Balaton, is known for its fields of lavender. Shop for local lavender products in this quaint shop in the heart of town (page 433).

★ **Siófok Beaches:** Join the Budapest locals who escape the city to sunbathe on these golden beaches on the banks of Lake Balaton in summer (page 437).

★ **Eger Castle:** Explore the interior of this fortress-like castle along with the complex labyrinth of tunnels that snakes beneath it (page 439).

★ **Wine tasting in the Valley of the Beautiful Women:** This atmospheric valley outside Eger holds wine cellars ranging from simple to stunning, some of which are carved into the hillside. The cellars are conveniently next to one another (page 442).

Previous: the historic town of Eger **Above:** Esztergom at the Danube Bend; shopping in Tihany

Day Trips from Budapest

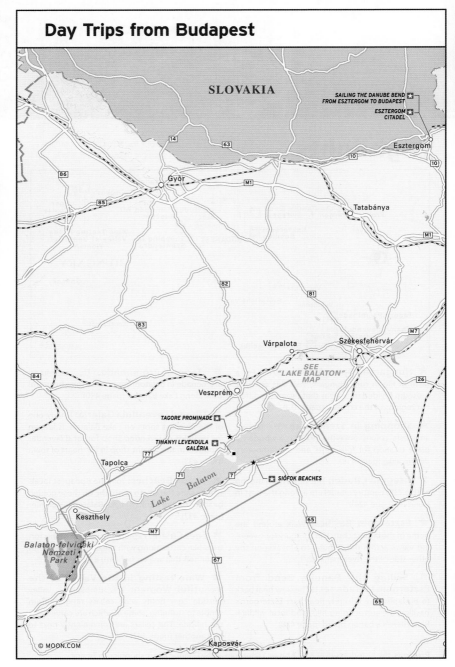

SLOVAKIA

SAILING THE DANUBE BEND
FROM ESZTERGOM TO BUDAPEST

ESZTERGOM
CITADEL

Esztergom

14

63

86

Győr

M1

85

Tatabánya

M1

82

81

83

M7

Várpalota

Székesfehérvár

84

26

SEE
"LAKE BALATON"
MAP

Veszprém

TAGORE PROMINADE

TIHANYI LEVENDULA
GALÉRIA

Tapolca

77

71

Balaton

7

SIÓFOK BEACHES

Keszthely

M7

65

Balaton-felvidéki
Nemzeti
Park

67

65

© MOON.COM

Kaposvár

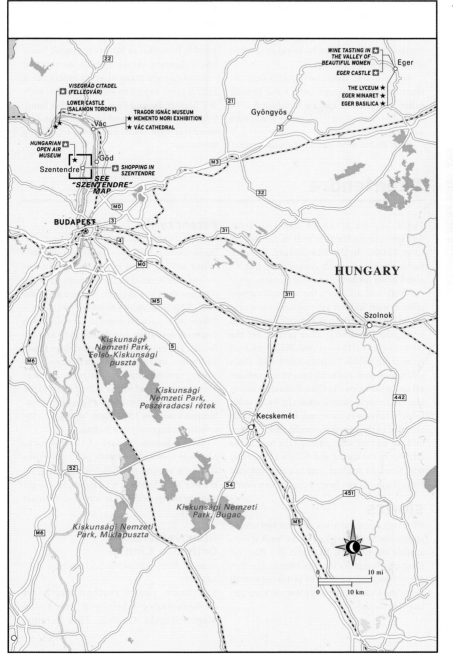

Others also opt to go further afield. Some destinations, such as Lake Balaton (1.5-3 hours from Budapest by train) or Eger (2 hours from Budapest by train), can be rewarding when done as an overnight trip.

You can also combine day-trip destinations that are geographically close to each other: Szentendre can be combined with other destinations on the Danube Bend, such as Visegrád.

Each destination has its seasonal appeal.

Lake Balaton is most popular in the summer months, but is still charming in spring and fall if the weather is good. The Danube Bend is beautiful to visit year-round, but if you're planning to take the boat, do note that connections are seasonal, so to experience it fully it's best to visit from late spring to early fall. Szentendre and Eger, on the other hand, buzz all year round, and can make good alternatives if you want to add a day trip during the winter.

Szentendre

For a low-maintenance day trip from Budapest, hop a train or boat to Szentendre (pop. 25,000). In the 18th century, the town had a thriving Serbian community, but it's also known for being an artists' colony since the 1920s and still sports the bohemian atmosphere, with hidden art and ceramic workshops tucked away in the town's courtyards and galleries. Shortly after getting off the train, or even off the boat, you'll find yourself wandering cobbled streets lined with stalls selling antiques and artists painting canvases set up on the sidewalk. Colorful houses undulate under white church towers in warm tones from honeydew to claret red. It can get a little crowded in the summer months when visitors look for an easy way to escape the heat in the city, but in the spring and fall it's a lovely day trip. Since it's so close, you can also just visit for half a day, if you fancy a change in scenery.

SIGHTS

Although Szentendre is a city you can simply appreciate by getting lost in the back streets around the Catholic **St. John the Baptist Church** (Templom tér, Vár Domb, Tue-Sun 10am-5pm) and its steps, or by taking a stroll along the Danube, there is plenty to keep you busy for the day.

Ferenczy Károly Museum

Kossuth Lajos utca 5, tel. 06/26-779-6657, www. muzeumicentrum.hu, Tue-Sun 10am-6pm, 1,200 HUF

When arriving by the local suburban train or by bus, the Ferenczy Károly Museum is the first museum you'll reach on your way into town. This 18th century mansion with canary-yellow walls once belonged to the Hungarian impressionist artist Károly Ferenczy and his family. The museum spreads over three floors and hones in on the local art history, with works from Ferenczy and other Szentendre-based artists. Head to the second floor to see work by the founders of the 1920s artists' settlement known as "The Eight," along with interesting temporary exhibitions.

This museum is part of the Ferenczy Museum Center, a network of 17 museums scattered around Szentendre, but being on the way into the town, it's a good place to get your bearings and figure out your own art itinerary.

Blagoveštenska Orthodox Church

Fő tér, tel. 06/26-310-554, Tue-Sun 10am-5pm, 400 HUF

You know you've reached the heart of Szentendre when you reach the Blagoveštenska Church. This baroque

Szentendre

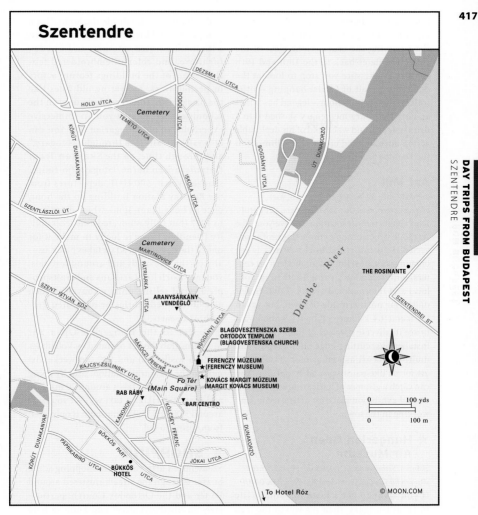

church looks like your average 18th century Hungarian church on the outside, but you'll find an ornate Serbian orthodox heart within. The church served the Serbian community residing in Szentendre between the 14th and 19th centuries, and its heritage shows through the wooden paneling varnished in black with accents of gold and traditional Eastern icons around the altar.

Serbian Ecclesiastical Art Museum

Pátriárka utca 5, tel. 06/26-312-399,
Tue-Sun 10am-6pm, 700 HUF

Explore Szentendre's Serbian heritage through its collection of sacred objects and icons on display at the Serbian Ecclesiastical Art Museum. It's a small private museum, made up of only two large rooms on two floors with an interesting display of iconography, including a 14th century glass painting depicting the crucifixion. Most of the collection dates back to the 18th and 19th century. Make sure you stop to look at the defaced portrait of Christ hanging on the wall on the upstairs floor—legend has it that an anti-Habsburg mercenary slashed it in a drunken rage, and when told of his deplorable action once sobered up, he threw himself in the Danube and drowned.

Art Mill

Bogdányi utca 32, tel. 06/20-779-6657, www. muzeumicentrum.hu, Tue-Sun 10am-6pm, 1,200 HUF

Don't let its remote location deceive you: The Art Mill, which occupies three floors of a converted 19th century red-brick saw mill, is one of Hungary's most important modern art centers, with temporary exhibitions from both local and international artists. You'll find it on the far northern side of town, but worth the scenic 1.4-kilometer (about 0.9 mile) walk to see its diverse displays of light and sound installations, cutting-edge photography, and multi-media art as well as more traditional art forms like paintings and sculptures. You can catch a glimpse of local art here, as it's the central exhibition place for artists living and working in the town.

★ Hungarian Open Air Museum

Skanzen, Sztaravodai út, tel. 06/26-502-537, http:// skanzen.hu Tue-Sun 10am-5pm Apr-Nov, 2,000 HUF

If you want to get a taste for village life in rural Hungary, then it's worth the trek up to the Hungarian Open Air Museum. The museum spreads out over 46 hectares, divided into areas representing different regions within Hungary, so you can take a trip from the Great Plains to a village in Transdanubia in just one afternoon. Wander by whitewashed farmhouses topped with thatched roofs and sweeping windmills, peppered with a few churches

and bell towers. Slip inside the houses for a glimpse of rural life, with rooms decked out with hand-painted ceramics and wooden furniture, and colorful embroidered fabrics. Some of the buildings feature actors in period dress, recreating old roles like the blacksmith, the store clerk, or even the school teacher, to give you an immersive experience in old Hungarian life. You can also take a train ride through "Hungary," and through time, on the **Skanzen Train** (http://skanzen.hu/hu/latogatas/jo-tudni/ skanzen-vonat, 500 HUF, departures from the Railway Station Building on the hour, once an hour 10am-4pm), which dates back to 1927 (but fully renovated and accessibility friendly). If you're lucky to make it for one of the days where a fair takes place, usually on the weekends and around festivals, you may catch local artisans and craftspeople around selling unique souvenirs such as embroidered fabrics or decorated gingerbread hearts.

To get to the Hungarian Open Air Museum, grab the bus operated by Volánbusz 878 (on weekdays) and 879 (on weekends) next to the local train station, usually going from bay 7. The bus takes around 20 minutes and costs 230 HUF. A taxi will set you back around 3,000 HUF. The museum is only open from spring to fall.

★ SHOPPING

Szentendre's arts and crafts shopping scene buzzes through the streets clustered around Fő tér and the Orthodox Church, particularly on Bogdányi street and Dumtsa Jenő road. Shops selling folk crafts, contemporary design, and fine art gather along these cobbled streets, and painters usually sit on the sidewalk putting their brush to the easel while stacks of their paintings stand propped against the yellow- or ochre-colored walls ready for you to buy one.

---

1 Souvenir shop in Szentendre. **2** Blagoveštenska Orthodox Church. **3** Stroll Szentendre's cobbled streets.

PALMETTA DESIGN GALLERY & SHOP

Bogdányi út 14, tel. 06/26-313-649,
www.palmettadesign.hu, daily 10am-6pm

Couple István and Anna Regős established the Palmetta Design Gallery back in 1998 in a 200-year-old wine cellar under their house at the heart of Szentendre. Their mission to create a space dedicated to Hungarian and international design lives 20 years on and locals and tourists flock through the doorway of their Baroque house and down the stone steps to visit their showroom. Pick up one of Anna Regős's hand-woven handbags or peruse curiosities from other designers such as FruFru's match boxes that double as fridge magnets featuring Hungarian landscapes, or notepads with updated motifs of Hungarian folk art.

PARTI MEDVE

Városház tér 4, tel. 06/20-254-3729,
Mon-Fri 7:45am-6:45pm

Parti Medve is the multitasking sanctuary in the Szentendre shopping scene, occupying a two-story Baroque town house opposite the City Hall, where you'll find a café, gallery, and bookshop on site. A great place to take the kids as you can find toys and books for adults and kids—in English, too—as well as art for sale. Grab a table on the terrace or wander up the spiral staircase to the indoor cafe for a cup of tea or coffee, before taking home a book, mug, bag, plushy toy, or a local piece of art.

OLD GOAT ART GALLERY

Dumtsa Jenő utca 15, tel. 06/30-523-9184,
daily 11am-6pm

This charming gallery run by an artist husband and wife pair, Hungarian Eszter Györy and American Osiris O'Connor, has a new-age vibe with colorful surreal paintings and "Soul Angels," angel-shaped statuettes made from alabaster sometimes decorated with paint, Swarovski stones, Bohemian crystals and Murano Glass. Each angel comes with a birth certificate and a number—their "adopter" gets to name them. You can also pick up hand crafted metal pendants and rings. Most of the art work and sculptures are created by the couple, who are happy to chat about their art when you visit the shop.

FOOD

ARANYSÁRKÁNY

Alkotmány utca 1/a, tel. 06/26-301-479,
www.aranysarkany.hu, daily midday-10pm,
2,500-5,900 HUF

The name Aranysárkány, meaning Golden Dragon, may evoke Chinese food, but actually carries usual Hungarian favorites like goulash soup to wild boar ragout, plus a few non-Hungarian wildcards, such as a few Serbian dishes. They have a fun variation of a personal Hungarian favorite, fried cheese, which uses breaded Port Salut, smoked and non-smoked Brie with cranberry jam and tartar sauce. Forgot your reading glasses and struggling with the menu? No worries, they have a selection of prescription glasses in an old tea box you can borrow! The atmosphere here is intimate and cozy, with rusty carpet weaves and vintage brass pots and pans decorating the walls.

MJAM

Városház tér 2, tel. 06/70-440-3700,
daily 11am-10pm, 2,500-4,750 HUF for entrees

You will find an abundance of paprika-laden restaurants scattered around Szentendre, but if you want something a little different that goes away from the violin music and goulash, then try Mjam. From the outside, it'll look like your typical baroque townhouse, but inside this breezy, minimalist restaurant you can tuck into a bold Caribbean fusion menu, with items such as duck breast smoked with tea leaves.

GETTING THERE

Szentendre is a popular day trip from Budapest since it's so easy to get to from the city center. The journey by train is the most comfortable. The boat is the slowest way to get there, but allows you to take in the scenery along the Danube, including Budapest's

Cycling up the Danube to Szentendre

Budapest's most popular cycling trail is the route on the Buda side of the river to Szentendre. This dedicated paved bike path skirts the banks of the river with amazing views and plenty of stop over opportunities on the way. It's mostly flat, so you won't need to worry about cycling up any hills. You can take the bikes back on the HÉV, the local suburban rail network back to town.

BIKING AND IMBIBING

It's a 17-mile ride from Budapest to Szentendre. If you're feeling ambitious, you can cycle all the way, or stop off at the **Római Part embankment,** popular for its Danube beaches, for a few fröccs (a white or rosé wine spritzer) at one of the many riverside bars, like the bike-friendly and stripy deck-chair-clad **Fellini Római Kultúrbisztró** (Kossuth Lajos üdülőpart 5, www. felliniromai.hu, Mon-Thu 2pm-11pm, Fri midday-midnight, Sun-Sat 10am-midnight) before returning to the city or heading onwards to Szentendre.

BIKE RENTAL

Yellow Zebra

Lázár utca 16, Budapest, www.yellowzebratours.com/yellow-zebra-szentendre-bike-tour.php, rental rates begin at 1,000 HUF per hour

Rent a bike from a company like Yellow Zebra, who also do private bike tours to Szentendre if you prefer to have someone to guide you.

Bike Base Budapest

Podmaniczky utca 19, http://bikebase.hu, rates begin from 2,200 HUF for 5 hours, Apr-Sep.

Bike Base Budapest is another option for rentals.

landmarks and the tree-covered Danube islands. Also, you can cut out all the walking from the train and bus station as the boat will put you down in the center.

Train

From Budapest, you can grab the H5 local suburban train operated by **BKK** (www. bkk.hu) from either Batthyány tér or under Margaret Bridge—just make sure you catch the one going all the way to Szentendre and buy a Suburban Railway Extension ticket that covers the region outside Budapest. (Note that this is sold by how many kilometers you go outside the city boundary, from the city to Szetendendre this would be a 15km ticket.) You can buy these from the ticket office in the metro station or from the purple ticket machines across town. If you only have a local ticket, the inspector who gets on at Békásmegyer can sell you an extension, usually for around 370 HUF extra.

The journey by train takes around 40 minutes. Tickets cost 760 HUF and trains run every 20 minutes (sometimes every 10 minutes in peak times) from 4am to 11:30pm. When you arrive in Szentendre, take the underpass just north of the station and then continue north along Kossuth Lajos utca. It will take around 10-15 minutes to reach the town center on foot.

Bus

You can take a bus 880, 889, 890 with Volánbusz (www.volanbusz.hu) from Újpest-Városkapu in Budapest, which is accessible with Metro line 3. The bus ride is only 25 minutes and costs 310 HUF, but considering you need to take a metro all the way out of the city, it's not the most convenient way to get to Szentendre, but it's a good alternative if you have issues getting the H5. Or if you miss the H5 coming back, the bus station is right next to the train station, so you have an alternative. Buses run every 20 minutes during the day (fewer services after 8pm) from 5:30am to 10:55pm.

Boat

In the summer, **Mahart Passnave** (www.mahartpassnave.hu) runs boat services from downtown Budapest, either at the Vigadó tér dock or the Batthyány tér, to go to Szentendre. It departs Budapest at 10:30am, getting to Szentendre around noon. There is also an afternoon line going at 2pm, getting there at 3:30pm. The journey back is much quicker, leaving at 7pm, taking only 50 minutes as you're going down stream. One way tickets cost 2,310 HUF, returns 3,470 HUF.

Car

Szentendre is only a 30-minute drive from Budapest city center. Take the road along the embankment on the Buda side of the city (the west side of the river) and drive due north and take route 11. The town is sign posted and you

won't need a motorway vignette on this route. Parking is strictly regulated in Szentendre and costs between 280-360 HUF per hour, depending on where you park. The highest parking rates are usually around the Danube promenade.

Getting Around

The best way to get around Szentendre is to walk, and apart from the Hungarian Open Air Museum, you won't need to get public transport to around town, however, while the walk to the center follows a straight line, it will take around 15 minutes to get there from the bus and the train station (which are located in the same place), so budget some extra time to walk back and forth.

If you want to get a taxi, you can call a couple of local companies, **Szentendre Taxi** (tel. 06/20-266-6662) or **Szentendre Taxi 8** Nagy István (tel. 06/26-314-314).

Danube Bend

North of Budapest, the Danube River threads through hills and valleys passing medieval castles, baroque towns and wild hillsides. If you're into scenery coupled with history and dramatic views, then the Danube Bend is the day trip for you. In the summer you can also grab a boat or a hydrofoil from Budapest or from one of the towns on the Danube Bend to really appreciate the scenery hugging the river.

The Danube Bend covers a vast area. You can either explore parts with the rental car, sail down the river and enjoy the scenery from the boat going to or from Budapest, or simply pick one or two of the destinations to visit.

VÁC

Vác (pop. 33,000) lies just 30 kilometers (about 19 miles) north of Budapest on the east

bank of the Danube. It's the perfect alternative to the more crowded Szentendre, as you can explore its historic cobbled streets with churches and baroque townhouses, or stroll along the Danube side promenade, away from the crowds that flock to the other side of the river. If you love history, you'll find plenty of it in Vác, which is one Hungary's oldest towns and once the local seat for the Catholic church.

It takes 10 minutes to walk from the train or bus station (which are next to each other) in Vác to the town center and the Danube, so the best way to explore this Baroque town is on foot. Just head south in the direction of the river. If you arrive by boat, this will put you down in the town center, only minutes away on foot.

Sights

TRAGOR IGNÁC MUSEUM–MEMENTO MORI EXHIBITION

Marcius 15 tér 19, tel. 06/30-555-3349, http://muzeumvac.hu, Tue-Sun 10am-6pm, 1,200 HUF

For something truly offbeat, head to the cellar under Március 15 tér 19 to discover the 18th century mummies and painted coffins found in a secret crypt that was walled up for 200 years. You can see some of the coffins as well as rosaries, crucifixes, icons, and coins excavated in the crypt at the permanent Memento Mori Exhibition in this cool cellar under the Tragor Ignác Museum. The museum also has other exhibitions, including the Ars Memorandi exhibition (included in the price), focusing on the history of the town from the liberation of Ottoman rule to the "Golden Age of Vác" at the end of the 18th century.

VÁC CATHEDRAL

Schuszter Konstantin tér 11, tel. 06/27-814-184, www.vaciegyhazmegye.hu, Mon-Sat 10am-midday and 2pm-5pm, 7:30am-7pm Sun Mar-Nov, free entry

The impressive Vác Cathedral is just a 5-minute walk away to the south east of the Tragor Ignác Museum. This neoclassical cathedral built in an awkwardly epic scale when compared to its more humble surroundings was built in the 18th century. Its grand entrance is marked by a gate of Corinthian columns leading into a surprisingly breezy interior with cream colored walls and a vibrant fresco painted by Franz Anton Maulbertsch on the vaulted dome.

Food

HEKK TERASZ

Sánc dűlő, tel. 06/70-252-7295, http://hekkterasz.hu Sun-Thu 11am-9pm, Fri-Sat 11am-10pm, 1,490-3,500 HUF entree

Grab some freshly caught and cooked fish at Hekk Terasz. This restaurant on the Danube is a little out of town on the bicycle route, but worth the 50-minute walk along the river for its fish dishes and riverside views. You'll want to book in advance if you plan to go, as it's very popular with locals and day trippers from Budapest. The fish is charged by the weight, so the price may vary depending on how big the fish is or on the type of fish, and if you're not sure what to go for then go for its namesake *hekk*, freshwater hake, that comes deep fried, and have some with fries and their homemade herb or mayonnaise based dips.

MIHÁLY PATISSERIE

Köztársaság út 21, tel 06/20-390-3367, http://mihalyipatisserie.com Tue-Sun 10am-6pm, 990-1,600 HUF for cakes

Mihály Patisserie may only have three tables, but its cakes are a work of art. Whether you want to just sit with a coffee and a cake or get a few macarons to go to savor by the riverside, you'll be glad you popped in for something sweet.

Getting There

From Budapest, the easiest way to get to Vác is by train from Nyugati train station (25-40 minutes, 650 HUF). Trains run every half an hour from 4:45am to 9:50pm.

In the summer, there is a hydrofoil with **Mahart Passnave** (www.mahartpassnave.hu) from the Vigadó dock in Budapest at 10am getting to Vác in 40 minutes (3,300 HUF).

If you're athletic, cycle the path up the Danube. The 40-kilometer (25-mile) route is a mix of regular roads and a paved bike path along the Pest side of the Danube. The good news is that this is relatively flat all the way, and this route is less crowded than the one to Szentendre (on the Buda side of the river), which is very popular in summer.

You can reach Vác by car by driving up Váci út in Budapest in Pest until you reach route 2. The journey by car will take an hour and parking in Vác costs around 300-400 HUF per hour.

VISEGRÁD

To really appreciate the beauty of the Danube Bend, head to Visegrád (pop. 1,800), a small town on the west bank of the river at the tightest point of the bend, and the only point where the Danube flows north. Most people pick

Visegrád for its medieval castle perched on the top of the hill that you can reach either by car or by hiking the foot-trodden paths through the woodland past the calvary, an open-air representation of the crucifixion of Jesus.

Sights
★ VISEGRÁD CITADEL (Fellegvár)

Várhegy, tel. 06/26-598-080, daily 9am-5pm Mar-Apr, Oct, 9am-6pm May-Sep, 9am-3pm Nov-Mar, 1,800 HUF

Towering over the valley, the Visegrád Citadel can be seen from miles away, whether you arrive by train or boat. It dates back to the 13th century and its ruined ramparts give it a romantic edge. From the top, get ready for some of the best views in Hungary, overlooking the most dramatic curve of the Danube Bend from above. The citadel itself is also a fascinating slice of history, and although it looks ruined from afar, part of it is still intact. You can still patrol the old walls, visit the armory, and even a mini-waxwork museum inside the citadel.

You can drive or take a taxi, which takes around 10 minutes from the center of the town to the citadel and costs around 1,000 HUF, or, if you're feeling athletic, you can hike up to the top, which will take around an hour. From the dock of the Nagymaros-Visegrád ferry, take the road going west up the hill, to the left turn up Magasköz utca and then take the path through the woods that will take you up to the calvary. Just follow the trail up the hill (it's very steep and rocky, so wear good shoes) and you will reach the Citadel in 20-40 minutes.

LOWER CASTLE (Salamon Torony)

Salamontorony utca, http://visegradmuzeum.hu, Wed-Sun 9am-5pm Apr-Sep, 700 HUF

The Lower Castle, located half way up the hill to the south of the town, is accessible by taking the stairs leading up from the boat jetty for the Budapest boat line. It was once a fortification system built in the 13th century that used to connect the Citadel with the Danube and once protected the vulnerable southern entrance. The highlight here is the Solomon Tower, a hexagonal tower that now houses a museum about the town. It gets its name from a local legend that Solomon was guarded in the tower after losing against King László and Géza in battle.

THE ROYAL PALACE

Fő utca 29, tel. 06/26-597-010, http:// visegradmuzeum.hu, Tue-Sun 9am-5pm 1,300 HUF

Before you leave, make sure you head over to the partly-reconstructed Renaissance palace used by King Matthias set on the river bank. This beautiful palace is easy to reach—no climbing required, just a 10-minute walk from the Nagymaros ferry—and is also accessible for people with disabilities, with ramps and lifts installed in the complex. The palace ruins are very beautiful, with the reconstructed buildings bringing the ruins to life, like the arched lion fountain made out of pink marble or the colonnaded 15th century courtyard surrounding the Matthias Fountain.

Food
RENAISSANCE RESTAURANT

Fő utca 11, tel. 06/26-398-081, https://renvisegrad.hu, Sun-Fri midday-10pm, Sat midday-11pm, 2,900-5,500 HUF entrees

This family-owned restaurant taps into Visegrád's historical spirit with a medieval feast served up in homemade crockery and locally supplied dishes. It's theatrical, but the food (Hungarian Renaissance dishes given a modern upgrade) is actually good—try the venison goulash or freshly grilled trout, all washed down with some Hungarian wine, of course. In the summer you can sit out on their terrace with full views of the river. You can even dress up for the part if you want, and if you don't you can just take a look at the period costumes hanging by the entrance waiting to be tried on.

PANORÁMA ÉTTEREM

Fekete-hegy Hotel Silvanus, tel. 06/26-398-311,
https://hotelsilvanus.hu/en/hotel/gastronomy/
panorama-restaurant, daily 7am-10pm,
2,390-5,790 HUF

Panoráma Étterem at the Hotel Silvanus has the most amazing terrace overlooking the bend in the Danube from above. The menu oscillates between Hungarian dishes mostly focused on game, like their goulash served in a mini cauldron, to more international flavors, like their gourmet venison burger. It's 3.5 kilometers outside the town, very close to the citadel, so you may want to either take a taxi or visit after your hike to the castle.

Accommodations

SILVANUS HOTEL

Feketehegy, tel. 06/26-398-311, https://hotelsilvanus.
hu, €112-260 dd per night

It's worth staying at the Silvanus just for the view. Set up on the top of the hill, just 300 meters (330 yards) from the Visegrád Citadel, the view over the Danube Bend is spectacular. The Silvanus also boasts a spa and wellness facility, with an outdoor pool with a view over the valley, as well as an indoor pool, saunas, and an aroma and salt chamber. Spa treatments on offer also include Ayurvedic treatments. The hotel has a retro hunting lodge feel with dark wood paneled walls and autumnal colors. Most price packages include breakfast and dinner.

Getting There

Bus is the most direct way to get to Visegrád, but in summer, boat is of course the best option.

BUS

The most direct way to get to Visegrád is to take the 880 bus from Újpest-Városkapu in Budapest (accessible on the line 3 metro), which takes 1 hour 15 minutes (around 750 HUF). Buses run once to twice an hour depending on the time of day (more frequent around 1pm to 4pm) beginning at 5:35am and running till 10:55pm.

You can also take local bus 880 or 882 from the Szentendre's train station, costing around 465 HUF.

TRAIN AND FERRY

You can grab a train run by **MÁV** (www.mavcsoport.hu) to Nagymaros from Nyugati train station in Budapest (40 minutes, 1120 HUF) and take the hourly ferry across the river. Trains go twice an hour beginning at 4:45am and ending 9:50pm. Once you get to Nagymaros, you need to walk 5 minutes westwards down Magyar utca to the ferry.

From Nagymaros, the first ferry leaves at 6:30am, then goes on the hour from 8am to 8pm. The journey across the river takes around 15 minutes and costs 450 HUF per person. You can also bring a car across for 1,550 HUF.

Ferries leave Visegrád 45 minutes past each hour from 7:45am till 7:45pm.

BOAT

In the summer the best way to get there is by hydrofoil run by **Mahart Pasnave** (www.mahartpassnave.hu) from Vigadó at 10am daily in the summer (returning from Visegrád at 6pm), which takes an hour to get to Visegrád (ticket 4,300 HUF, return 6,500 HUF).

There is also a slower boat route run by the same boat company that takes three and a half hours from Budapest, leaving Vigadó at 9am, with the return journey taking two and a half hours—faster as you're sailing downstream) leaving Visegrád at 5:40pm. Tickets cost 2,890 HUF one way, 4,330 HUF return. The dock for the Budapest boat is not in the same place as the ferry coming over from Nagymaros, but is set towards the north next to the Lower Castle.

CAR

It takes around 30 minutes to drive to Visegrád from Szentendre. There is one route that will take you through the Pilis Hills but this is complicated, so it's easier to follow route 11 along the Danube banks to the town. This

will also offer striking views along the river. From Vác things get a little more complicated as there are no bridges across the Danube in the area, so you will need to take a ferry in Vác to Tahitófalú (going once an hour, costing 1,500 HUF per car and 430 HUF per person) and then continue on route 11. This journey will take around an hour. Alternatively, you can drive back to Budapest and take the Megyeri Bridge across the Danube and join route 11. Another variation is to drive northwards 20 minutes to Nagymaros and take the ferry across, which also runs on the hour at the same rates. In Visegrád, parking costs around 300 HUF per hour.

Getting Around

The town itself is compact and takes minutes to get around on foot; however, getting up to the castle is a strenuous uphill hike. There's not too much in terms of public transportation. If you need a taxi while you're in town, call **Visegrád Taxi** (tel. 06/20-266-6662). You can also ask for a taxi at the Nagymaros-Visegrád ferry ticket office when you arrive in Visegrád, as they also manage the taxi service.

ESZTERGOM

The Danube Bend ends, or rather begins, at the Hungarian-Slovak border by the town of Esztergom (pop. 28,000). Many come to Esztergom for the photogenic view from Hungary's largest basilica, which looms over the river. Vác may have been once the center of Catholicism in Hungary, but that torch has been passed upstream to Esztergom, the hometown of Hungary's first king St. Stephen. In fact, Esztergom was the royal seat of the country from the 10th century to the mid-13th century, so you'll find plenty of history around the old castle walls and historic city streets to keep you busy once you've visited the main site.

1 start by sailing down the Danube Bend from Esztergom **2** The best way to see the Danube Bend is to hike up to Visegrád Castle.

Sights
★ ESZTERGOM BASILICA

Szent István tér 1, tel 06/33-402-354, www.bazilika-esztergom.hu, Mon-Sat 9am-7pm, Sun 9am-6pm May-Sep, daily 9am-6pm Sep-Oct and Apr, daily 9am-5pm Mar, daily 9am-4pm Oct-Jan, free entry for the church, 700 HUF dome, 1,500 HUF combined ticket to the crypt, dome, and treasury

If you thought St. Stephen's Basilica was impressive in Budapest, wait till you visit the Esztergom Basilica, which is the largest church in Hungary, rising 72 meters (236 feet) high to its dome! Entry is free for this impressive cathedral and it's open to visitors all year round, but if the weather is good (and you're not scared of heights) it's worth the climb up the numerous stairs to the dome. This will take you up to the panorama terrace first, a large hall with a window overlooking the river and a café half way up the church, then even more stairs up to the colonnaded corridor on the outside under the dome. You'll already be treated to wonderful views over the town, but wait in line to get right up to the top of the dome (numbers are restricted). You can walk all the way round for 360 degrees of the whole region overlooking the Danube, Slovakia (just on the other side of the river) and the hills leading further south down the Danube Bend. You can also visit the Cathedral Treasury and the crypt on your visit to this classical-style cathedral.

Food
PADLIZSÁN

Pázmány Péter utca 21, tel. 06/33-311-212, daily noon-10pm, 2,000-2,500 HUF entrees

Padlizsán, which translates as eggplant in English, lies at the base of the castle walls, looking up towards the Basilica in a small baroque townhouse. The food lives up to the view, with modern, seasonal Hungarian dishes from grilled pike perch from the Danube to autumnal chicken in wild mushroom sauce to vegetarian fried cheese served with cranberry sauce and apple compote.

PRÍMÁS PINCE

Szent István tér 4, tel. 06/33-541-965,
www.primaspince.hu, Mon-Thu 10am-9pm, Fri
10am-10pm, Sun 10am-5pm, 2,000-4,000 HUF
entrees; 20,000 HUF fixed price (see online menu
for details)

The Prímás Pince in the cellars below the basilica feels more like a museum than a restaurant, with high-vaulted ceilings and stone blocks. But if you're looking for great wine and food, Prímás delivers, as it carries 100 Hungarian wines—including rare varieties—and you'll find plenty of creative takes on Hungarian dishes on the menu. Try the aged wild boar tenderloin served with a sauce made from the famous Eger "Bull's Blood" red wine and plums. You can also pay a visit to the exhibition about wine, showing the history of the Hungarian church and winemaking in Hungary.

★ Sailing from Esztergom to Budapest

The best way to spend a day in Esztergom is to take the train up from Budapest, then spend a couple of hours exploring the Basilica and the area surrounding it before having lunch. Then take the 4pm slow boat back to Budapest for a leisurely 4-hour Danube cruise—you will also get the best views of the Basilica from the water. Just sit back, relax, and watch the landscape slip by as you pass the hills around Visegrád and then the marshy island around Szentendre dotted with storks and other wildlife at the golden hour—in the late spring the water here is filled with fallen acacia petals and smells divine! Unlike the faster hydrofoil, there is also a bar on this boat.

Getting There

TRAIN

There are regular trains from Nyugati train station in Budapest that take a little over an hour (1,120 HUF) to get to Esztergom, however these will still leave you about a 40-minute walk from the center. Trains run every half an hour beginning at 4am and finishing at 11:15pm. You can either take a taxi to town (around 1,000 HUF), or hop on a local bus, 1 or 11 (150 HUF) and get off at Bazilika.

BOAT

In the summer, the best way to reach Esztergom is by hydrofoil, operated by **Mahart Passnave** (www.mahartpassnave. hu), which departs at 10am from Vígadó in the summer, and takes 1 hour 30 minutes (5,300 HUF one way, 8,000 HUF return). The return ferry leaves at 5:30pm, getting back to Budapest at 7pm.

The slow ferry by the same company leaves Budapest at 9am (taking 5 hours 20 minutes) but leaves Esztergom at 4pm (taking 4 hours). A one-way ticket is 3,470 HUF, a return 5,200 HUF. I highly recommend taking the slow boat back in the summer for a scenic leisurely cruise.

CAR

It takes an hour to drive to Esztergom from Budapest. Take the route 10 from the Buda side of the river from Flórián tér in northern Buda and follow the signs till Esztergom. Parking costs around 300 HUF per hour.

GETTING AROUND

If you need a taxi in Esztergom, try **Esztergom Taxi** (tel. 06/30-634-0403) or **Taxi 1000** (tel. 06/20-622-1000).

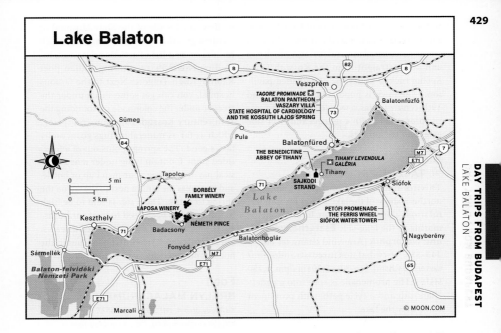

Lake Balaton

Lake Balaton

Lake Balaton, with its stretches of turquoise water dotted with yachts and sailboats, is perhaps the most memorable escape from Budapest. The largest lake in Central Europe, it's just a couple of hours from the capital. When the temperatures rise, it seems most of Budapest flees the city to find refuge along the beaches of the "Hungarian Sea."

You can think of Balaton as being split into north and south. The northern shore is more beautiful, with volcanic hills lined with vineyards and elegant resorts, while the south gets the golden beaches and lakeside party spots like Siófok. There is something for everyone, whether you want to hike up into the hills, take a plunge in the lake, just relax along the water on a summer's day sipping a glass of Kéknyelű, a white wine made from a local grape from Badacsony, or hit the bars in Siófok.

The area around Lake Balaton is vast, and

realistically you won't be able to hit all the listed towns in a day. Choose which town or area that interests you the most and focus your trip there. Balaton is a place locals come to escape the heat of the summer, so expect a relaxed, holiday vibe—the last thing you'll want to do is rush around from town to town. Take the train down and spend a relaxed day by the lake like a local.

BALATONFÜRED

Balatonfüred (pop. 13,000) is a historic resort on the northern shore of Balaton, where you'll find palatial hotels and villas once frequented by the artistic elite from Budapest overlooking the water. It's a couple of hours by train from Budapest, making it the perfect gateway.

Balatonfüred has an old-world appeal as a historic resort, and is a great choice for a quiet, yet elegant, day by the lake. More than just a lakeside town, artists and writers were drawn to the scenic northern shore of Lake Balaton for their health as well as the views. (The town sits on carbonated mineral springs, which you can drink straight from the Kossuth Lajos Spring tucked under the colonnaded pavilion.) The town is populated with 18th- and 19th-century villas, a wooded park, and a scenic promenade with a marina and river side cafes and restaurants.

Sights
★ TAGORE PROMENADE
This tree-lined promenade running along the northern shore of the lake makes for wonderful strolls along Lake Balaton. It runs from the marina to the lake-side **Eszterházy Beach and Waterpark** (Aranyhíd sétány, tel. 06/87-343-817, www.balatonfuredistrandok.hu/eszterhazy.html, Jun-Aug 8:30am-7pm, 1,250 HUF). The promenade is split into a pedestrian path and a cycle path, with prominent views over the lake.

BALATON PANTHEON
Gyógy tér, free entry
Tucked under the arches of the building on the northeastern side of Gyógy tér, there is an interesting pantheon featuring placards to the famous figures who came to Balatonfüred to take their cures, a kind of who's who of the town, before it stretches out into a woody parkland gently crawling up the hill.

VASZARY VILLA
Honvéd utca 2-4, tel. 06/87-950-876, http://kultura.balatonfured.hu, Tue-Sun 10am-6pm, 1,800 HUF
Step inside this beautiful late 19th century villa, the former home of the once prominent Vaszary family. The most famous of the family is impressionist Hungarian painter, János Vaszary, whose paintings are exhibited in the villa. The museum also has a delightful collection of art and artifacts from the 18th century.

STATE HOSPITAL OF CARDIOLOGY AND THE KOSSUTH LAJOS SPRING
Gyógy tér 2, (Free entry for the Kossuth Lajos Spring)
I personally love Gyógy tér around the whitewashed walls of the State Hospital of Cardiology—the largest in Hungary—which has drawn in a list of artistic celebrities, including Novel-Prize winning Indian poet Rabindranath Tragore. Next to the famous hospital, you can get some shade under the trees or under the colonnade surrounding the 19th century Kossuth Lajos mineral spring, which as far as mineral springs go, actually tastes good. The spring spouts out of a four-sided stone fountain lying under a neo-classical pavilion. Bring your own cup or bottle, and just press the button next to the tap on the spring to drink. The water is said to be high in iron and has been used to treat cardiovascular, digestive, and diabetes related diseases, but is also a good, free thirst quencher in the hot summer months.

Food
BRKLYN MALACKRUMPLI
Kisfaludy utca 4, tel. 06/30-636-5577, http://malackrumpli.hu, Tue-Sun midday-11pm, 2,690-3,690 entrees
Inspired by a food truck, BRKLYN Malackrumpli hones its niche on gourmet street food and trendy cocktails right, with specials like their Angus beef burger with coleslaw and fries. The fish and chips is also a good bet. The restaurant prides itself on its farm to table service. It's particularly nice in the summer when you can sit on the terrace under the colorful lights.

HORVÁTH HOUSE WINE GALLERY
Gyógy tér 3, tel. 06/30-458-7778, http://horvath-haz.hu, Sun-Thu midday-8pm, Fri-Sat midday-9pm, 3,690-5,690 HUF entrees
Horváth House Wine Gallery lies in the cellar of a prestigious 19th century villa, but despite external appearances, it has a modern interior that couples well with the old wine-making apparatuses you'll find on site. Although the beat is local wine from Balaton, make sure you

---

1 Balatonfüred is one of the easiest resorts on Lake Balaton to reach from Budapest. **2** The Tihany peninsula on Lake Balaton makes a magical escape from Budapest.

try their *pálinka* or, if you prefer to stay dry, their artisanal syrups. They have an excellent selection of game dishes like wild boar and venison, but you can also pick out some fish dishes to try.

Accommodations
ANNA GRAND HOTEL
Gyógy tér 1, tel. 06/87-581-200, https://annagrandhotel.hu, €126-220 dd per night including breakfast and dinner

More than 200 years old, this grand hotel captures the elegant spirit of Balatonfüred. Set right next to the Balaton Pantheon and the Kossuth Lajos spring, and only 100 meters (330 feet) from the lake, it has one of the best addresses in the city. There are more than 100 rooms and a 1,200 square meter (13,000 square feet) modern wellness department fully equipped with a pool, sauna, hot tub, and steam bath; there is also a bowling alley in the hotel. Foodies will love the homemade cakes based on 19th-century recipes made on the premises at the hotel café. Try to peek into the grand ballroom, which since 1824 has been hosting the famous Anna Ball, held once a year on a Saturday around the end of July.

PASTEL GUESTHOUSE
Eötvös Károly Köz 2, tel. 06/70-209-7521, www.pastelguesthouse.com/ €45-55 dd per night

Pastel is an elegant guest house decked out with a chic, vintage aesthetic in natural pastel shades of grey and light brown, with green and rustic chandeliers and vases filled with fresh flowers. There is a communal kitchen in the guest house, and the owners live upstairs ready to help should you need anything. This is a good choice for adults looking for a peaceful getaway, as it's a grown-up friendly environment and the hosts ask that guests do not bring children under 16. Free parking included at the property and the Pastel Guesthouse is only 10 minutes from the lake.

Getting There and Around

From Budapest, the easiest way to get to Balatonfüred is by train (2 hours, 2,725 HUF), serviced by MÁV (www.mavcsoport.hu) from Budapest Déli station. Direct trains run four times a day, starting at 8am, and the last train leaving Budapest departs at 3:55pm and the last train leaving Balatonfüred goes at 6pm. You can also take the number 4 metro line operated by the Budapest public transport system, BKK, in Budapest to the Budapest Kelenföld train station, located in the city's western suburbs.

The center of Balatonfüred is a good 15-20 minute walk southeast from the train station. Call **Taxi Balatonfüred** (tel. 06/30-751-7518) if you prefer not to walk, or take the local bus lines 1 (every 2 hours, even numbered hours), 1B (10 past the hour, every one to two hours), and 2 (every 2 hours, 30 past the hour for odd-numbered hours) and buy the ticket (310 HUF) from the driver.

The drive from Budapest to Balatonfüred takes around an hour and a half. Take the M7 southwest of the city. Parking in Balatonfüred ranges from 140 to 500 HUF per hour depending on the zone and the season.

TIHANY

Tihany (pop. 1,400) is a peninsula that sticks out into the middle of Lake Balaton. In my opinion, it is one of the most beautiful spots on the lake. The town rises high above the water, crowned with the baroque Benedictine Abbey bell towers. Although the main town lies perched on the hillside, you can hike to the shore down winding steps and paths slinking in and out of the woods, past flaking villas to the jetty, or you can even follow marked trails that guide you to secret beaches you can't get to by car. If you come in June, the lavender fields are in full bloom and you can pick your own bunches of lavender, but even off season you can still buy all kind of lavender products at the vintage-style shops scattered around Tihany.

Sights
THE BENEDICTINE ABBEY OF TIHANY
András tér 1, tel. 06/87-538-200,
www.tihanyiapatsag.hu, daily 9am-6pm Apr-Sep,
10am-5pm Oct, 10am-4pm Nov-Mar, 1,000 HUF
The ochre-colored Benedictine Abbey of Tihany with its twin bell towers rises above the town and the lake from the top of the volcanic hill. Entrance to the abbey includes the museum, which is accessed from the crypt of the church. The museum displays artifacts from the old abbey, manuscripts, and even contemporary art. Make sure you stop in the abbey shop on the way out and buy some of the craft beers brewed by the abbey monks.

Recreation
HIKING
There are two lakes on Tihany itself, the Inner Lake (Belső tó) and Outer Lake (Külső tó), both of which formed from the craters of two volcanoes that make up the peninsula. You get spectacular views on the walks around them.

The Inner Lake lies next to the town. Take the streets down the hill from the abbey due west—keep an eye out for Major utca which will bring you down to the lake side, or, instead, head north west from the abbey to Kiserdőtelep út and walk here till you see the trails marked.

Another popular route is the wood-dense trail up to the calvary, an open-air representation of the crucifixion of Jesus, with statues and crosses marking the trail up the hill, which winds through a forested valley to the medieval hermitage carved into the rocks by Greek Orthodox Hermits in the 11th century. Begin the hike at the calvary, just north to the monastery on Árpád utca, and walk up to the top. Make sure you turn around for amazing views of the abbey and Lake Balaton from the top of the hill. From here, you'll see signs marked to the hermitage (Barátlakások) and just follow the woodland trail. The hike will take around 40 minutes.

The tourist information center on Tihany (Kossuth Lajos utca 20, tel. 06/87-448-804, http://tourinform.hu, Mon-Fri 10am-4pm Jan-Apr, Sat 10am-3pm from mid-April, Mon-Fri 9am-5pm, Sat-Sun 10am-4pm May-Jun, Mon-Fri 9am-6pm, Sat-Sun 10am-6pm, Jun-Aug, Mon-Fri 9am-5pm, Sat-Sun 10am-4pm Sep) can provide detailed information on hiking trails.

Beaches
SAJKODI STRAND
Sajkodi Sor 22, tel. 06/70-380-0328, http://
sajkodistrand.hu, daily 8am-8pm May-Sep 400 HUF
The Sajkodi Beach lies on the Western end of the peninsula far away from the more popular and busier Tihany. It's a 50-minute walk or a 10-minute ride in a car (or a taxi). Compared to other beaches in Balaton, this beach is quiet and hidden—perfect if you want to escape the crowds. The grassy banks leading down to the lake, with steps leading into the water, give this beach a green and romantic look. The views from here are incredible—overlooking the western side of the lake, you can see the volcanic mountains of the northern shore in the distance. You can rent a sunbed for 500 HUF, and parking costs 1,200 HUF for the day. You can also rent water bicycles (2,000 HUF per hour, from the ticket office) or kayaks (600-2,000 HUF per hour).

Shopping
★ TIHANYI LEVENDULA GALÉRIA
Kossuth utca 41, tel. 07/366-3367,
http://levendulamanufaktura.hu, daily 10am-6pm
This little boutique in the heart of Tihany specializes in all things lavender. Whether you want to buy bundles of dried flowers artfully wrapped up, artisanal soaps, lavender based cosmetics, or even cute pastel floral pouches filled with the aromatic flower, you can find a charming gift from here. The shop feels inspired by rustic, vintage Provence, with faded white furniture, vintage ceramics and stone walls. There is another shop in the village on Batthyányi út.

Food
RÉGI IDŐK UDVARA ÉS SKANZEN

Batthyányi út 3, tel. 06/70-284-6705,
Tue-Sun midday-9pm, mains 3,150-5,200 HUF
This unique restaurant does more than just
serve up local specials, like Hungarian-style
fattened goose liver with a ratatouille of local
vegetables and egg barley or cold smoked trout
served simply with bread and gherkins. The
establishment doubles as an amateur ethno-
graphic museum with old farm equipment
hanging in the bar-terrace. It's worth walking around this peaceful garden and inside
the white washed interior of this traditional
Tihany farmhouse. Try the beer—which is
brewed on site.

★ REGE CÚKRÁSZDA

Kossuth Lajos utca 22, tel. 06/30-289-3647,
www.tihanyiapatsag.hu/Programok_vendegeinknek/
Apatsagi_Rege_Cukraszda.html, open daily 9am-6pm
May-Oct, cakes 850-1,200 HUF
Rege Cúkrászda is a magical little café and
confectionary set just besides the abbey. It's
worth the visit for its incredible terrace with
perfect views of Lake Balaton from 150 meters
(almost 500 feet) above the lake and extensive panoramas. They serve all kinds of local
delicacies such as craft beer made in the abbey
next door and lavender lemonade, but a must
try is their lavendula krémes, a layered custard
cake with lavender infused cream.

Accommodations
KÉK LILLIOM HÁZ

Visszhang 1, tel. 06/30-243-9369,
www.booking-tihany.com, €74-102 for an apartment
of 2 including breakfast
Kék Lilliom Ház is a magical farmhouse complex at the heart of Tihany. From the street it's
hidden but enter through the wooden gate and
climb up the stone steps, and you rise up into
an enchanted garden. Swallows nest under the
arches of the white-washed porch in the summer and kids splash about in the small garden pool. The old thatched-roofed farmhouse
has been split up into apartments catering for

two and also parties of four and five. Breakfast
is an elaborate spread of seasonal and local
specials, like in-season vegetables and local
cheeses, and if the weather is good enough you
can take it on the terrace, if not just sit in the
beamed dining room by the fire.

Getting There

To get to Tihany from Budapest, take the
train to Balatonfüred. Just next to the train
station you'll find a bus depot where you can
get the bus to Tihany (it's written on the front
of the bus). It will take about 30 minutes from
the train station, and you get a really scenic
bus ride thrown in. Buses are operated by
Volánbusz (www.volanbusz.hu) and go two
to three times an hour, up to 15 times a day,
and take 20-30 minutes to reach Tihany, tickets 310 HUF.

If you take the bus from Balatonfüred, this
will put you down at the heart of the small
town at the heart of the peninsula. From here
most sites, like the famous abbey, are a 5- to
10-minute walk.

The drive from Balatonfüred takes around
10 minutes. Just follow route 71 and the signs
to Tihany. Parking prices around the town
range from 120 to 250 HUF per hour, depending on the location.

BADACSONY

Badacsony (pop. 2,300), a famous wine region on Balaton's northern shore, is known
for its volcanic terroir and scenic vineyards.
Badacsony lies around a volcanic hill of the
same name that kind of looks like a plug—or
more appropriately a cork—and you may need
trek up the hill to reach the best vineyards, but
it'll be worth it for the view and the wine. The
downtown part of Badacsony is a little touristy, with a jetty, souvenir shops, a beach and
restaurants, kind of like what you'll find in
Balatonfüred and not really worth the extra
minutes on the train. Your best bet is to hit the
wineries—try some wine made from the local
Kéknyelű grape—on the slopes of the hill to
get the best out of Badacsony.

Wineries

The Badacsony wine region is spread out around the Badacsony Hill and is away from the bustle of the port-side town, usually a 20-30-minute walk northwards up the hill. To reach the wineries, it's best to walk or take a taxi (or drive if you have someone willing to be a designated driver).

BORBÉLY FAMILY WINERY

Káptalantóti út 19, tel. 06/30-927-1414, www.borbelypince.hu, open on demand, call to make an appointment for a tasting

Explore this beautiful winery—and drink wine—in the middle of a vineyard. It's worth coming in the summer to taste their wines on the terrace overlooking the surrounding countryside, but if the weather is off there is a cozy cellar, too. You will need to call in advance to register for tastings—you can call or reserve on their website—you can choose whether you want to try 6, 8, or 10 wines (3,000-6,000 HUF per person). Try their Tomaj Badacsonyi Rózsakő – Olaszrizling-Kéknyelű blend for a classic Badacsony white with mineral hints.

To reach this family-run vineyard, get off the train at the Badacsonytomaj train station instead of Badacsony, take Kert utca and continue up the hill due north. The walk is around 20 minutes and the winery is signposted.

NÉMETH PINCE

Római út 127, tel. 06/70-772-1102, www.nemethpince. hu, daily 11am-6pm May-Oct, appointment only Nov-Apr

This is one of Badacsony's smallest wineries, but its central location (it's a 10-minute walk from the Badacsony train station) and familial atmosphere make it worth the visit. The vineyard has been passed down through the Németh family over the generations, and specializes in late harvested grapes which makes their wines a little sweeter than the others in the region as the grapes retain more sugar. Another delightful detail is that their wines come in hand-painted bottles, and can be painted to order, so make the perfect gift.

Try the Kéknyelű (1,000 HUF for a glass) or the sweet ice wine—a dessert wine made from grapes that have been frozen on the vine (1,000 HUF).

LAPOSA WINERY

Római út 197, tel. 06/20-777-7133, www.bazaltbor.hu, Mon-Sun 11am-7pm

The Laposa Estate perches itself on the edge southern banks of Badacsony Hill overlooking Lake Balaton from above. Sip through a tasting selection of their quality wines from their terrace with amazing views. Wine tastings come with cold savory bites from local producers, but if you call in advance you can also request a meal prepared from one of the family recipes with local produce to go with the wines you want to try. You can choose to taste wines by the glass, or try a guided wine tasting of 6 to 9 wines (3,000-4,000 HUF per person). You can reach Laposa on foot, a 15-minute walk due north east from the train station or take a taxi.

Food

SZEREMLEY BORHÁZ

Kisfaludy Sándor utca 5, tel. 06/87-431-382, www.szeremleyborhaz.hu, Thu-Sat midday-10pm, 2,800-5,000 HUF entrees

Szeremley Borház wins when it comes to location, being high up on the hill overlooking Lake Balaton through the vines. Dine on local dishes and sip the wine from their vineyards under their vine-covered colonnade overlooking the lake from above. The menu changes on a seasonal basis, but if you can, try the catfish paprikás with homemade pasta served with cottage cheese, lardons and sour cream or the grilled zander fish served with a Kéknyelű wine sauce with sautééd vegetables and polenta.

KATICA

Egry sétány 8, http://katicavendeglo.hupont.hu, daily midday-10pm May-Sept, 1,790-5,400 HUF entrees

Katica is a family-owned restaurant in a wooden house between the vineyards and the town, great for families and hungry tummies.

You can't go wrong with goulash, fish soup, or any of the local fish dishes with fresh catch from the lake, and you can be sure you won't leave hungry. But note that the wines served are only table wines, so if you want to taste something fancy, this is not the place for you.

Accommodations
ÓBESTER PANZIÓ
Római út 203, tel. 06/30-213-0225, www.obester.hu, €60-77 dd including breakfast

This family-owned B&B resides in a 200-year-old building on the western side of the hill. It's a quiet sanctuary enveloped with walnut trees and vines, and has amazing views across to the lake. The center of Badacsony is a short walk away. The B&B has eight rooms and two apartments, and all come with private bathrooms, refrigerator, and air conditioning. The look of the hotel blends the old with the new, where heavy, dark wood beams, and pillars add character to the old farm house, whereas the décor is white, brightened up with colorful accents from the pillows and rugs, along with modern abstract art hanging on the walls.

HOTEL BONVINO
Park utca 22, tel. 06/87-532-210, https:// hotelbonvino.hu, €230-260 dd including breakfast and dinner

Hotel Bonvino brings you the two pleasures and pastimes on Lake Balaton: Wine and Wellness. Just 300 meters from the shores of the lake, this modern luxurious hotel has 48 uniquely designed rooms drawing inspirations from the surrounding wine region. There is a state of the art wellness area, with a stunning pool with an artificial waterfall, a Jacuzzi, Finnish and infra-sauna, and a steam room. The hotel restaurant serves up local dishes and snacks; try the locally sourced Mangalica ham or goats cheese, and there are more than 100 wines on the wine list.

Getting There
The easiest way to get to Badacsony is by train operated by MÁV from Déli train station in Budapest, in the direction of Tapolca. It's further that Balatonfüred, taking at least 2 hours 40 minutes from Budapest, but can be over 3 hours if you take a slower train. One-way train tickets cost 3,395 HUF and there are 4 trains per day, the first leaving Budapest at 8am, the last at 3:55pm. The last direct train leaves Badacsony at 5:15pm, but you can also come back later if you do not choose a direct train, such as the 8:30pm train going to Székesfehérvár, where you can change for trains to Budapest. Badacsony could be combined with Balatonfüred as there are direct train connections between the two (easier if you do this with a rental car), but unless you're spending the night, it's best to choose either Balatonfüred or Badacsony as you won't fit everything into one day.

From Balatonfüred the drive takes around 45 minutes along route 71, which is a scenic drive along the lake. Most wineries will have their own parking, but public parking in the center of the town close to the lakeside will cost around 280 HUF an hour.

To get around Badacsony, you can explore the area on foot or get a taxi, like **Badacsony Taxi** (06/20-544-4234).

SIÓFOK
Set on the southern shore of the lake, what Siófok (pop. 25,000) lacks in scenic hills of the north it makes up with atmosphere, earning its title as the "Capital of Lake Balaton." Budapest flocks to its golden lakeside beaches with its shallow water and its vibrant nightlife in the summer. Siófok has that "seaside" feel, with endless neon signs, cocktail happy hours, and a 40-meter-high (131-foot-high) Ferris wheel around the Petőfi Promenade. Scale the water tower built in 1912 for incredible views over the lake, where you'll find viewing platforms and chic bars.

Because Siófok lies on the southern shore of the lake, it's difficult to combine with the resorts of the northern shore unless you're planning to spend the night.

Sights
PETŐFI PROMENADE
Running parallel to Siófok Main Beach, the Petőfi Promenade is packed with people in shorts, slapping the sidewalk with flip flops as they walk along the mile-long stretch in summer. Tall trees, umbrella covered beach bars, restaurants, street food vendors and pop up shops in wooden huts line this road just south of the beach, filled with people. After 7pm, it becomes a pedestrian-only zone, and by night it becomes a happening spot clad in neon lighting and party goers staggering in and from the clubs and pubs. You will also find most of the hotels in the area immediately surrounding it.

THE FERRIS WHEEL
Petőfi Sétány, http://siofokoriaskerek.hu, Sun-Thu 4pm-midnight, Fri-Sat 4pm-1am Jun-Sep, 2000 HUF
Towering more than 60 feet tall, the Ferris wheel in Siófok is the very first Hungarian-made wheel. Not only that, during the 10-minute ride you can enjoy views over Central Europe's most famous lake from open-air pods that can fit 5-6 people. You can see all the way over to Tihany and even spot the twin towers of the famous abbey, as well as the volcanic hills on the northern shore of the lake.

SIÓFOK WATER TOWER
Fő tér 11, tel. 06/30-244-8888, www.viztorony. com, daily 9am-midnight Jun-Sep, Tue-Thu and Sun 10am-5pm, Fri 10am-9pm, Sat 10am-10pm Oct-May, 800 HUF
Since it was built in 1912, the Siófok Water Tower has become a symbol of the town. It rises up around 45 meters (150 feet), made out of reinforced concrete. This historic tower is now a huge tourist draw following its renovation in 2012. Now it has an open-air viewing platform with 360-degree views, the Water Tower Café & Oxygen Bar (same opening hours as above) and the Samsung Experience Center (same opening hours as above) are set inside the old tower. The Samsung Experience Center occupies the top floor on a rotating platform seated at a coffee table with interactive touch screen games.

★ Beaches
SIÓFIOK MAIN BEACH
Petőfi Sétány 3, tel. 06/84-310-327, daily 8am-6pm May-Sep, 1,000 HUF
Siófok's Main Beach is Balaton's largest beach, covering an area that's over 8 hectares, with a capacity for 13,500 people. This is not the beach for you if you want peace and quiet, but with its Bluewave Flag, indicating the water quality here is excellent, and along with its high services, you can still get that resort feel in Hungary even though it's a land-locked country. Although most of the beach area is covered with grass, the eastern part of the beach is sandy, popular for families with kids. Trendy young people head over to **Plázs** (http://plazssiofok.hu, free entry), a beach club with a huge sundeck, pool, terrace, and sun loungers.

SIÓFIOK GOLDEN COAST PUBLIC BEACH
Szent István Sétány, tel. 06/84-696-236, daily 8am-9pm, 200 HUF 8am-4pm, 100 HUF 4pm-6pm, free after 6pm
If you want an alternative to the main beach, head east of the Main Beach to Siófiok's Golden Coast Public Beach, which offers bathing on a budget. Tickets are less than a euro in peak times, and are free after 6pm, and you have plenty of places to set a towel down on the 4 kilometers-long (2.5-mile-long) grassy stretch. The views are wonderful at sunset, so worth staying here till the sun goes down, after which you can saunter back to the Petőfi Prominade for the evening.

Nightlife
PALACE DANCE CLUB
Deák Ferenc utca 2, tel. 06/30-200-8888, http://palace.hu, daily 10am-5am July-Aug, 2,000-2,500 HUF cover charge
The Palace Dance Club may only operate through July and August, but it's still one of

the hottest party spots on Lake Balaton, and most enduring, having been partying each summer since 1990. The club is split into indoor and outdoor sections, perfect for those hot summer nights—there is even a pool (sometimes there are pool parties organized, but good luck fitting in there as the club is always packed). The Palace Dance Club has such a legendary reputation, with big international DJs such as Carl Cox and DJ Tiesto having spun here. Expect big parties with foam or confetti here.

RENEGADE PUB

Petőfi Sétány 3, tel. 06/20-317-3304, http://renegadepub.hu, Mon-Sat 7pm-7am, Sun 7pm-midnight Jun-Sep, no cover charge

The party goes on till late in this wooden beamed pub on the busy Petőfi Sétány. Things can get a little out of hand when the live music or the DJ kicks off the party and the dance floor gets so cramped that party going hedonists will get on top of the tables to dance.

Food

CALVADOS

Erkel Ferenc utca 11, tel. 06/84-314-579, www.calvados.hu daily midday-10pm, 2500-5000 HUF entrees

Calvados serves up a selection of Hungarian dishes with international inspirations. Perched right next to the marina, you can't get more downtown than this. You can ask the server for recommendations, but you can fall back on the goose liver cooked in Tokaj wine sauce or any of their fish dishes from the local catch. Sit out on the terrace if you can get a table, but since there is a large indoor section, the restaurant is also open off-season.

MALA GARDEN RESTAURANT

Petőfi sétány 15/a, tel. 06/84-506-688, http:// en.malagarden.hu/restaurant/ daily 11am-10:30pm off-season, 11am-midnight peak season, 2,790-6,990 HUF entrees

Grab a table on the terrace at Mala Garden Restaurant overlooking the beach along the lake. The menu is eclectic, with modern takes on Hungarian favorites like paprika chicken and roasted pork cutlets, as well as some Mediterranean specials and South-East Asian noodle dishes. You can try a range of Hungarian wines from their extensive wine menu, but if you're feeling adventurous, make sure you have a shot of the celery *pálinka*!

Accommodations

MALA GARDEN HOTEL SUPERIOR

Petőfi sétány 15/a, tel. 06/84-506-688, http:// en.malagarden.hu, €82-125 dd including breakfast

Balaton may buzz with crowds on the beach by day and with its hedonistic nightlife by night, but Mala Garden offers an oasis of tranquility when you want some rest. The hotel backs onto the grassy banks of the Danube shore, with Deluxe Rooms overlooking the lake (although all rooms have their own balcony). The rooms are a globe-trotter's fantasy decorated with warm red walls, vintage kilims, hand-knotted Persian carpets, and handcrafted items from Bali. A luxurious Champagne breakfast is included in the price, as is the use of the wellness center.

Getting There

Siófok takes 1 hour 20 minutes from Déli station in the direction of Nagykanizsa. Train tickets cost 2,375 HUF and runs up to 9 times a day, starting at 6:30 am until 7:30pm. Siófok's main train station puts you right in the heart of the town, just a five-minute walk from the lake and the main sites, like the water tower.

The drive from Budapest takes just over an hour, if you take the M7 southwest and follow the signs to Siófok. Parking costs between 160-320 HUF per hour depending on the location and the season.

Eger

Eger (pop. 53,000) has gone down in Hungarian legend as a bastion that resisted the Ottoman occupation in the 16th century. The city paints a vibrant picture with baroque houses adorned with intricate ironwork, as well as the northernmost Ottoman minaret, and its impressive medieval castle famed for its siege is still a draw today. All of this makes perfect day trip for anyone who loves history. You can also come just for the wine. Eger is known for its spicy Bull's Blood wine—named partly for its deep red color, but also believed by the Turks to have given the Hungarians superhuman power during battle. Taste it in the wineries around the city, or head to the cellars embedded in the caves at the Valley of Beautiful Women.

Eger is a compact city that's easy to get around on foot. You can also take in the sights around the town on the little trackless train, (**Eger Városnéző Kisvonat,** begins Egészségház utca, https://kisvonatok.hu/eger, daily 10am-6pm, 1,000 HUF) that will take you out to the Valley of Beautiful Women. Otherwise I recommend making a beeline to the castle and then explore some of Eger's other sites before rounding up at the Valley of Beautiful Women for some wine.

SIGHTS
★ Eger Castle

Vár 1, tel. 06/36-312-744, www.egrivar.hu, Castle gate open 8am-6pm Nov-March, 8am-10pm Apr-Oct, exhibitions 10pm-4pm Nov-March, 10am-6pm Apr-Oct, 1,700 HUF for the museums, 850 HUF grounds

Eger Castle resides on 500 square meters (5,400 square feet) of land at the top of a hill and is built more like a fortress than a fairy tale castle. It was built up over several centuries—you'll even find foundations of a 12th century cathedral on site—but most of what you'll see dates to the 15th-16th centuries,

including the Gothic Bishop's Palace (mostly a 20th century reconstruction but still contains elements from the original 15th century palace) and the wood-turreted topped stone walls of the Bornemissza Bastion (1554) at the main gate.

It's worth walking along the path running parallel to the battlements just for views over the terracotta-hued rooftops, the minaret, and the towers of Baroque churches. High stone walls enclose the grounds housing a cluster of buildings, like the aforementioned the Bishop's Palace (housing a museum of the castle on the second floor) and modern buildings housing the Eger Art Gallery.

There is a complex labyrinth of tunnels and casemates carved into solid rock running underneath the castle, some going as far as 24 kilometers (15 miles) from the town, and although you can only visit about 300 meters (320 yards) with a guide, it's fascinating to catch a glimpse of Eger's intricate castle engineering—part of the secret why Eger held out against the Turks for such a long time. The price for the museums includes entrance to the casemates, whose entrance lies at the Dark Gate in the eastern part of the castle complex. When buying your ticket for the castle, you can ask about tours to the casemates (times vary, so call in advance; they usually leave every hour on the hour from the cash desk). Most tours are in Hungarian, but for an extra 800 HUF you can get an English language guide, but you may need to ask in advance. Tours last around 40 minutes.

The best way to reach Eger Castle is to walk up the castle path leading up from Tinódi Sebestyén tér at the foot of the castle, which will bring you up to the castle gate. The gentle 300 meter stroll up to the castle walls is worth it for the view alone. You'll see a panorama over the terracotta rooftops, church spires and even the minaret.

The Lyceum

Eszterházy tér 1, tel. 06/36-520-400, https://
uni-eszterhazy.hu, Tower and Astronomical Museum,
www.varazstorony.hu, Tue-Sun 9:30am-5:30pm
May-Aug, 9:30am-3:30pm Mar-Apr, Sep-Oct,
9:30am-1pm Fri-Sun Nov-Dec and Feb-Mar, 1,300
HUF; Library: Tue-Sun 9:30am-1:30pm Mar-Apr,
9:30am-3:30pm May-Sep 1,000 HUF

If you like beautiful old libraries, vintage observatories, and historic university buildings, then pay a visit to Eger's Lyceum, an 18th century college building that is a particularly fascinating landmark. The Lyceum towers above the city center, even taller than the church and basilica towers. Climb to the top of the tower to see one of the three camera obscuras in the world that's still operational today. On the way up, you can break your journey with an astronomical museum set in an old observatory with 18th century telescopes and curiosities, and there is also the "Magic Tower," an interactive physics laboratory that's fun for kids as well as adults. The highlight of the Lyceum, which began as a theological college in the 1700s, is the baroque, wood-clad library with beautiful frescoes on the first floor.

Eger Minaret

Knézich Károly utca, tel. 06/70-202-43-53,
www.minareteger.hu, daily 10am-6pm Apr-Sep,
10am-5pm Oct-Mar, 400 HUF

Eger may symbolize the Hungarian resistance against the Turks, but you'll find plenty of traces of the Ottomans embedded into the cityscape. Eger's minaret—the northernmost building from the Ottoman era in Europe—is quite the sight, rising 130 feet with 97 steps going up in a spiral to the top. The Turks built the minaret in 1596 following their victory. When the Habsburg army recaptured the town 91 years later, they tried to pull it down with 400 oxen, but the tower held out. The balcony at the top of the tower is worth it for the view, but it is rather narrow and you may feel dizzy or claustrophobic, since the stairway

up is also pretty tight. At the time of writing, the minaret was closed for renovations, but is scheduled to reopen in 2019.

Eger Basilica

Pyrker János tér 1, tel. 06/36-420-970,
www.eger-bazilika.plebania.hu, Mon-Sat 7am-7pm,
Sun 1pm-7pm

Eger Basilica is the third largest in Hungary, after Esztergom and Budapest. You'll find this neoclassical basilica facing the Lyceum, looking like an overwrought Roman temple with imposing Corinthian columns. It's worth taking a look inside (especially if you appreciate frescoes), and the murals that adorn the three huge domes in bright bold colors will impress any art lover. Music lovers should pay a visit to one of the daily organ half-hour concerts (Mon-Sat 11:30am-midday, Sun 12:45pm-1:15pm May-Oct, 800 HUF).

WINE CELLARS

Wine has got its tendrils into Eger like the vines climbing the terraces surrounding the town. Thanks to Eger's mild microclimate, you can find both excellent whites and reds in the region. Although you can get single varietal wines, particularly from the quality cellars, Eger is most famous for its cuvées. The spicy, blood-red Egri Bikavér, the Bull's Blood of Eger blends three to five grape types. If you're partial to whites, try the Egri Csillag—the Star of Eger—a dry, crisp white blend made from local grape types with floral and fruity notes.

There are some really good wine producers in Eger, where it's worth keeping an eye out for St. Andrea, Bolyki, or Orsolya. However, these wineries are located far out of town and require a car to get you there. If you want to taste some local wine, sample some Eger specials in the following cellar.

GÁL TIBOR FUSION

Csiki Sándor utca 10, tel. 06/20-852-5002,
www.galtibor.hu, Tue-Thu 10am-7pm, Fri-Sat
10am-11pm, Sun 10am-1pm

Wine maker Gál Tibor has 40 hectares of

---

1 Eger Castle 2 Eger is famous for its wine production. 3 historic town of Eger

Wine Tasting in the Valley of Beautiful Women

For quality wine, you may be better off going to a wine bar in Eger or a winery in the surrounding countryside, but if it's atmosphere you're looking for, the Valley of Beautiful Women (Szépasszony-völgy) has it in spades. There are dozens of legends behind the region's seductive name, by the way. One recounts the story about a beautiful Hungarian girl who escaped marriage to a Turk by giving him some Bull's Blood wine (he wasn't used to drinking wine) and another says the beautiful women were prehistoric goddesses who received sacrifices in the valley.

There are close to 200 cellars embedded in a crescent-shaped valley in the suburbs of Eger. Some of the cellars are stunning, completely carved into the hillside and look more like a church than a wine cellar. Others are more modest with just a few plastic chairs propped up against the bare cave walls. I love going from musty cellar to cellar, tasting wine straight from the barrel. The experience is best shared with friends and with a slice of *zsíros kenyér*—bread spread with goose or pork fat, raw onions and paprika (and, yes, it is more delicious than it sounds)—or a *pince lepény*, a kind of baked savory pancake with cheese and ham (these are usually extra and will set you back around 500 HUF).

WINES

The wines vary depending on the harvest and the winery, but you can find the famous red cuvee, **Bull's Blood,** and other wines like those from indigenous grapes like **Egri leányka** (a dry white wine made from an indigenous grape), **olaszrizling** (a white wine that can be sweet or dry) and **hárslevelű** (an aromatic sweet white). Should you like any of the wine, you can take some back in a plastic bottle (prices are by the liter and directly from the barrel will cost around 1,000 HUF), which is only a good idea if you plan to drink it before your flight home.

★ WINE CELLARS

Wine cellars in this area are informal, and most people come for the experience rather than to visit a specific cellar. However, the two following are worth seeking out:

Hagymási Pincészet

Szépasszony-völgy 19, tel. 06/20-326-4364, www.bormester.hu, daily 9am-11pm

Stepping inside this cellar feels more like you've entered a temple dedicated to wine. Set on two levels, this wine cellar fortified with bricks can fit up to 100 guests. Old wine-making equipment hangs on the stone walls, and a stone statue resides in the niche in the brick arch above the bar. You can try 18 wines here, as well as 2 types of *pálinka*. If you're hungry you must try their *pince lepény!*

---

vineyards around Eger, but the good news is you don't need to go far out of town to try these fantastic wines. In downtown Eger, Gál Tibor Fusion occupies a 1,400 square meter (15,000 square feet) complex, home to a 500-year-old wine cellar, as well as a bar and a wine tasting room that can seat 120 people. The building is worth the visit for its blend of modern design, with features like wireframe lampshades and chalkboard art, and the building's history. There is also a free museum dedicated to the history of Bull's Blood wine on the first floor. Try the zingy and floral Egri Csillag or the Pinot Noir Rosé with hints of strawberry.

FOOD

MACOK BISTRO AND WINE BAR

Tinódi Sebestyén tér 4, tel. 06/36-516-180, www. imolaudvarhaz.hu/en/the-macok-bisztro-wine-bar.

Eger, the Valley of Beautiful Women

Sike Tamás

Disznófősor 43, tel. 06/742-9024, http://sikeboraszat.hu, Mon-Thu 10:30am-9pm, Fri-Sat 10:30am-11pm, Sun 9am-7pm

This 100-meter-long cellar fits 120 people inside and 60 on the terrace. Wines are matured in oak barrels and bottles in the inner part of the cellar, and the great thing about this traditional cellar carved into the rock in the hillside is the staff on hand are happy to teach you about the wines you're drinking. Individuals and small groups can drop in for tastings, but do contact the cellar in advance if you're coming in a big group. Taste their Merlot or Syrah, or their blend of Egri Csillag if you prefer a white.

GETTING THERE

The cellars are a 20-minute walk from Eger's city center. You can also take the little dotto train to Szépasszony-völgy or a taxi (you can ask for Valley of Beautiful Women if you can't pronounce the Hungarian). The valley is compact and all the cellars lie right next to each other so just explore the area on foot.

html Sun-Thu midday-10pm, Fri-Sat midday-11pm, 2,950-7,900 HUF entrees

Just because Macok Bistro and Wine Bar lies by the entrance of the castle, doesn't make it a tourist trap. You'll find Hungarians and an international crowd at this eccentric restaurant that blends industrial chic with its own quirky style. But what's even better is its modern, adventurous kitchen, offering gourmet degustation menus at excellent prices. Creative dishes, such as duck liver brûlée served with homemade milk loaf and plum jam, or coconut and pumpkin soup with pumpkin seed mousse, are beautifully presented and use locally sourced ingredients. The wine list features Eger's best local wineries—try some spicy reds from St. Andrea, Gál Tibor, or Attila Pince.

1552

Eger Castle, tel. 06/30-869-6219, www.1552.hu,
daily 11am-10pm, 2,790-6,890 HUF entrees

1552 is the only restaurant in Eger Castle, but it has done something quite original, combining Hungarian cuisine, Turkish dishes (a nod to its Ottoman past), and cutting-edge culinary techniques. Daunted by the menu? Go for the game, as chef Mátyás Hegyi's specialty is wild boar. The décor inside is bold, with claret leatherette seating, exposed brick set against patterned peach wall paper, Turkish-style tiles, and bulbs handing inside birdcages. This is not a place to come when you're in a hurry, though, as the service can be a bit slow.

ACCOMMODATIONS

HOTEL EGER & PARK

Szálloda utca 3, tel. 06/522-222, https://
hotelegerpark.hu, €90-170 dd including breakfast

The Hotel Eger & Park are actually two hotels: The Park Hotel was Eger's first hotel, which opened in the 1929, and is built in a neo-baroque style, whereas the Hotel Eger was built at the end of the 20th century. Today the two hotels are joined by a connecting corridor, and guests from both hotels can use the state-of-the-art wellness facility and spa, with thermal water pools, swimming pools, infra sauna, aroma cabin and salt chamber. The Park Hotel is much smaller, with only 35 rooms, whereas the Hotel Eger has over 170 rooms. You can find the filling buffet breakfast in the elegant dining rooms in the Park Hotel.

SENATOR HOUSE HOTEL

Dobó tér 11, tel. 06/36-320-466, www.senatorhaz.hu,
€64-81 dd including breakfast

Senator House Hotel lies right at the heart of Eger in an 18th century inn. There are 11 cozy rooms on the upper floors decorated all in white with accents coming from brightly colored oil paintings, pillows, and flowers. The reception area, filled with curiosities and antiques, shares the ground floor with a restaurant. The best thing is really the location, as rooms either look out to Dobó square or one of the narrow side streets.

GETTING THERE

You can catch the train operated by MÁV to Eger from Keleti train station in Budapest (2 hours, 2,725 HUF). You can also get a direct bus with Volánbusz from the Stadion bus station in Budapest (2 hours, 2,725 HUF). There are 9 trains a day beginning at 5am until 7pm and buses run every half an hour from 8:15am-10:45pm. When you get arrive in Eger by bus, you will arrive in the city center (the bus station is a 3-minute walk from Eger Basilica). The train on the other hand puts you a 20-minute walk away in the south of the town. Local bus services are sporadic, so you may be better off taking a taxi (which will probably set you back around 1,000 HUF). Try City Taxi Eger (tel. 06/36-555-555) if you need a cab.

The drive by car takes around 1 hour 40 minutes from Budapest. Take the M3 north east and keep an eye out for signposts to Eger. Parking costs in Eger range between 200-360 HUF per hour.

Background

The Landscape

GEOGRAPHY

The landscape and climate throughout the Central European region are quite similar. At first glance you'll notice that the three cities are marked by their proximity to a major river, with one side with hills and the other flat. Winters are usually cold, sometimes freezing, and summers are hot and balmy with a breeze.

Prague

The Vltava River divides Prague into two distinct halves with the

hillside neighborhoods of Letná, Hradčany, and Petřín wrapping from north to west along the river bend and Malá Strana tucked into the shadow of the Prague Castle below. Across the water and on lower ground, Old Town and New Town lie on lower ground, spreading southeast from the riverbanks into the neighborhoods of Vinohrady, Vršovice, Žižkov, and Karlín. Vyšehrad hill marks the southern edge of where most tourists will venture and Vitkov Hill creates a large natural barrier between the grittier Žižkov area and Karlín's clean tree-lined streets on the east side of town. Prague covers about 115 square miles with elevation between 581 and 1,309 feet above sea level. The urban capital is punctuated with plenty of green space in the form of large parks in almost every neighborhood.

Vienna

Austria may evoke Alpine scenery, but the area around Vienna is mostly flat and mild. Vienna lies in what is known as the Vienna Basin, a level area stretching on a plateau beyond the Danube River. The suburbs of the city spreading south of the Danube stretch out into the Vienna Woods, a hilly area that resides in the foothills of the Alps. Vienna has a total area of 160 square miles with elevation ranging 495-1,778 feet above sea level. As a city, Vienna is very green with abundant parkland, woodland, vineyards, and also has a swampy water forest in the eastern fringes of the city known as the Lobau. Unlike Prague and Budapest, the river lies a little outside the city center with its north bank being entirely populated by modern builds, divided by the long Danube Island which stretches down the river for 13 miles.

Budapest

Just like Prague is split in two by the Vltava, Budapest centers around the Danube River. The west bank, in Buda, is hilly with the highest point stretching up to 1,729 feet above sea

level and some 200 caves underneath the hills once created by the thermal waters bubbling under the city, whereas Pest in the east spreads out on a flat plain. Budapest's unique geography comes from a fault line running along the bed of the Danube, which has caused some 80 geothermal springs to bubble up under the city. The river cuts through the city with three islands lying within the city limits: Margaret Island, Óbuda Island, and a part of Csepel Island.

CLIMATE
Prague

Prague weather is unpredictable. Snow has been known to start as early as October or as late as January, and either disappears after a week or blankets the city one last time in April depending on the year. Average winter temperatures dip below freezing (32°F/0°C) before rising to highs in the 30s F (-1°-5C) between December and February. Summers vary between pleasant and muggy days without much air conditioning available. Humidity often builds and breaks in summer thunderstorms, with temperatures ranging anywhere between 68-95°F (20-35°C) June-August. May and September are reliably mild and comfortable for sightseeing, but pack an umbrella and raincoat for almost every season to be on the safe side. Czechs (and most Europeans) operate on a Celsius scale and are not likely to relate to temperature discussions in Fahrenheit.

Vienna

Vienna has a mild climate, with warm summers in the ranges of 70-81°F (21-27°C) on average, although it can sometimes shoot up to 100°F (38°C). Winters are cold and usually quite dry, with temperatures hovering just above freezing. Snow rarely settles in the inner city, although it may pepper the hillsides. The mildest times in Vienna are the spring and fall, which are pleasantly warm without being too cold, although it can get rainy and gray,

---

Previous: Charles Bridge and the Prague Castle

so it's a good idea to bring a raincoat and an umbrella.

Budapest

Budapest is a city of contrasts when it comes to climate. In the winter, it can be brutally cold—so much so the Danube sometimes freezes over—with heavy snow or sleet. The temperature in the summer can rise above 100°F (38°C), but even if the temperatures are high, pack an umbrella as sudden heavy showers and thunderstorms often punctuate the summer skies and can even rain so much that parts of the city flood. The mildest times to come is fall and spring, where usually there is a little bit of rain and longer sunny days.

Architecture

Each Central European country has its own architectural DNA with a few crossovers. You will notice similarities as you stroll the streets of Prague, Vienna, and Budapest, but also the nuances that make them different. Prague adds drama to the skies with its gothic spires, Budapest carries a taste of the exotic with its Ottoman bathhouses and Asian inspired art nouveau, whereas Vienna mixes up baroque opulence with Secessionist styles and avant-garde, modern architecture.

GOTHIC

Piercing spires, dramatic buttresses, and soaring towers capture the spirit of Central European Gothic architecture. In the 14th century, Prague rose to become one of the greatest cities in Europe, and even today the Middle Ages set the foundations for the town with the stunning St. Vitus Cathedral, the Old Town Hall and its Astronomical Clock and the foundations of Charles Bridge. Vienna also has its share of Austrian gothic style, most notably St. Stephen's Cathedral with its jagged spires and vaulted arches—it is the most spectacular example of the style. Budapest, on the other hand, has very little left behind from the period—much of the Medieval architecture was destroyed over the various occupations—although you can catch a glimpse of Gothic art in the Budapest History Museum with its collections of gothic sculptures or the Hungarian National Gallery with its triptychs.

BAROQUE

Forget less-means-more when it comes to Baroque architecture, which you'll find in abundance throughout Central Europe dating back to the 17th and 18th centuries. Vienna has some of the most opulent examples, with winged palaces, lashings of marble and enough ornate gold leaf and fiddly friezes to tire your eyes out. Baroque architecture embodies grand cupolas, marble columns, and over the top frescoes, which you'll find in abundance in the Habsburg palaces and at Vienna's Karlskirche. Curved forms and elaborate details embody the Baroque style, which you'll see in Budapest and Prague, too. Architecture is a little more modest in the cities that were satellites to Vienna as the Habsburg Empire capital. Churches with copper-green domed bell towers dot the Central European cities and countryside, whereas pastel-colored townhouses with floral frieze details or statues also capture the style. And if you thought that Baroque was over the top—pay a visit to Maria Theresa's rooms in Schönbrunn Palace for its even fussier and more ornate successor: Rococo.

HISTORICISM AND ECLECTIC STYLE

In the 19th century, historical revival came into vogue in cities like Vienna and Budapest. All the neos— neo-classicism, neo-gothic, neo-orientalism, and neo-renaissance styles peppered the wide boulevards of Budapest and along Vienna's newly built Ringstraße. This eclectic style adds a richness to the cities of Central Europe and a new form of opulence that's more individual than the formulaic Baroque. If you ride on a tram along the Ringstraße, you'll spot buildings that resemble Greek Temples, Renaissance Palaces and even Flemish style gothic builds. Budapest, too, embraced this aesthetic in the prosperous years it joined hands as a dual capital with Vienna in the Austro-Hungarian Empire. Prague also took its architectural cues from Vienna's historicism, copying all the neo-styles, particularly neo-gothic.

ART NOUVEAU

Although art nouveau is a label you can slap on the three cities, each country has its own national interpretation of the style. Vienna's Secessionist style, led by artists like Gustav Klimt and architects such as Otto Wagner, focused more on floral motifs, sensual feminine forms, and lashings of gold, or stark modernism by Adolf Loos. Prague, as a contrast, has blended a more ornate Parisian style with Vienna's subdued art nouveau. Of course, much of what we think of as art nouveau in art has a heavy Czech influence thanks to Alphons Mucha. Budapest drew art nouveau inspiration from Hungarian folk art and orientalism loved by Ödön Lechner, whose colorful buildings resemble Gaudí more than Wagner's brand of architecture.

EARLY-MID 20TH CENTURY

The 20th century is perhaps the most diverse in style between each city. In the 1930s and 40s, Hungarian architects embraced the Bauhaus movement, which blended functionality with style. As Budapest expanded with new apartment blocks, many in the area outside the Grand Boulevard drew inspiration from Bauhaus with its elegant, simple curves and art deco accents. Vienna during this period also saw urban expansion in the interwar period, with the Werkbund Estates, social

housing built in the period known as "Red Vienna," when the Social Democrats were in power between 1918 and 1934. The Nazi era in Vienna left little concerning architecture, except for the imposing Flak Towers you can still see in recreational parks like the Augarten. Architecture in Prague moved away from the curves of Bauhaus and the simple lines of Red Vienna to cubism in architectural form. It never caught on outside the Czech Republic as a style of architecture, but you can find a few examples of this unique style in Prague, like the cubist street lamp or the House of the Black Madonna.

COMMUNIST FUNCTIONALITY AND SOCIALIST REALISM

Once Hungary and the Czech Republic fell under the communist regime, a new architectural style defined these two capitals. Budapest's "panel" houses (sizeable concrete apartment blocks) and Prague's functionalist and brutalist buildings may not be the most beautiful sites in the respective cities, but they are still a part of its history. For a taste of Socialist Realism, head out to Budapest's Memento Park, which has become a graveyard to communist statues, or Prague's former Hotel International.

MODERN

Many think of Prague, Vienna, and Budapest as historic cities, but scattered between the grand old buildings modern pieces of architecture pop. In Vienna, the Hundertwasserhaus by Friedensreich Hundertwasser brightens the streets close to the Danube Canal with bright colors and irregular forms, and the same can be said about the Dancing House in Prague by Vlado Milunic and Frank Gehry, where glass and steel melt into each other along the Vltava River. Budapest blends the old and the new with the "Whale," an undulating glass structure built on the foundations of the red brick warehouses set along the Danube. Vienna also combines history with modernity in the MuseumsQuartier, the former stables once belonging to the Habsburg rulers now transformed into a modern art hub. Modern art playfully invades the three cities. The twisted towers of the Dancing House embrace along the Vltava Riverbanks, whereas tiny micro statues that appear out of nowhere have become Easter eggs for observant pedestrians along the banks of the Danube in Budapest.

Government and Economy

PRAGUE
Politics and Government

The Czech Republic is a parliamentary democracy with both a Prime Minister, who holds more political power, and a president who often resides in the Prague Castle. The president acts as more of a ceremonial state figurehead but also holds some important political responsibilities, such as appointing the Prime Minister. The Czech Republic is a multi-party system often built on coalitions between multiple parties.

The current 74-year-old President Miloš Zeman was re-elected in 2018 and is often referred to as the "Czech Donald Trump" for his nationalist, anti-immigrant beliefs and blunt statements. Zeman is also notorious for being (allegedly) intoxicated at most official events. Prime Minister and 64-year-old media magnate Andrej Babiš is one of the country's wealthiest men and owns the two local newspapers. The current Czech Parliament is divided between ANO 2011, a populist party founded by Andrej Babiš in 2011; the liberal-conservative ODS party; the new pro-transparency Czech Pirate Party; the anti-immigrant, anti-EU SPD party (ironically, founded by a Japanese-Czech immigrant); and a handful of smaller groups including the Communist and Green parties.

Mentioning politics to many Czechs will be met with eye rolls and complaints of corruption, but many citizens remain politically active. Wenceslas Square still fills with crowds for both political protests (as recently as May 2018) as well as patriotic celebrations of historical anniversaries.

Economy

The Czech Republic may not have the highest salaries in the EU (quite the opposite, in fact, ranking 20th out of 28 countries) but it can claim one of the lowest rates of income inequality in Europe. The local economy has traditionally centered on manufacturing industries like automotive parts and diesel engines, but Prague's tourism and service sectors are rapidly gaining percentage points. EU Commission reports show that GDP has continued to rise in recent years, and an innovative startup scene has produced success stories like booking agent Kiwi.com (formerly Skypicker) and local rideshare app Liftago.

VIENNA
Politics and Government

Austria is a federal republic with a parliamentary democracy made up of nine independent federal states. Each state has its own provincial government, but on the whole, the federal legislation comes from the Nationalrat, the national council, together with the Bundesrat, the Upper House of Parliament. Austria is a member of the European Union, and has been a republic since the fall of the Habsburgs in 1918, and then again following World War II. Since the war, the power has been shared between the Social Democratic Party (SPÖ) and the conservative People's Party (ÖVP). Other parties, like the nationalist Freedom Party (FPÖ) and the Green Party, have risen over the past few years in popularity. Austria has a president, which is a mostly ceremonial position, with Alexander van der Bellen—a Green

Party politician who ran independently—elected in December 2016. The head of the Austrian government is the federal chancellor, Sebastian Kurz who became the youngest head of government in December 2017. Kurz heads up the People's Party, and formed a coalition with the Freedom Party, making it the only country in Western Europe with a far-right presence in government. .

Economy

Vienna is one of the wealthiest cities in the European Union, and ranks highly as one of the most livable cities in the world and made it to number nine on the list as one of the most economically powerful cities in 2015. Vienna's most important economic division is the service sector, followed by industry and commerce. Trade, scientific and technological services, and real estate are also a core part of Vienna's economy. Research and development play a significant role in the local sector, along with tourism, too.

BUDAPEST
Politics and Government

Hungarian politics reside in a framework of a parliamentary democratic republic, with Budapest as the seat of the Hungarian government. Like Austria, Hungary has a President (currently János Áder) who acts in a mostly ceremonial position as head of state, and a Prime Minister who is the head of government in a multi-party system. Multiple parties can run for office, but the main parties in Hungary are the ruling conservative Fidesz party, headed up by Prime Minister Viktor Orbán, and two considerable oppositions, the Hungarian Socialist Party (MSZP) and far-right Jobbik. There are a few other smaller parties who have gained more traction in the 2018 elections, such as Politics Can Be Different (LMP), Democratic Coalition (DK), Dialogue for Hungary (PM) and Together (Együtt), among others. Hungary is criticized by some as being a "flawed democracy."

Economy

Budapest is the epicenter of Hungary's economic world, being home to major corporations and banks. Beyond Hungarian companies, the capital is an international hub with international offices from big-name companies who hold branches in the city. Most of Budapest's income comes from retail, construction materials, schools, and food processing. It's also become a hub for the start-up and tech scene in recent years, with businesses like Prezi and LogMeln springing up from the capital. Tourism is another booming area of Budapest's economy.

People and Culture

The first rule of Central Europe is you do not confuse it with Eastern Europe. Vienna seems to get away without the "East" label, but if you say either Prague, Budapest, or Bratislava are in Eastern Europe you will lose any new friends you've made on your travels pretty quickly. Central Europe lies at Europe's geographic heart whose countries both share a common past—having mostly been part of the Austro-Hungarian Empire under the rule of the Habsburgs—and yet are divided by their political and economic history—where one part lay behind the Iron Curtain as communist satellite states to the Soviet Union, such as Hungary, Czech Republic, Slovakia, Poland, Slovenia, and East Germany, while the other side resided in the affluent West, like Austria, West Germany, Switzerland and Liechtenstein. This economic divide is still apparent today, as the countries in the eastern

1 The Art Nouveau Museum of Applied Arts in Budapest 2 Gothic cathedral in Prague 3 The Belvedere castle 4 Gellert Thermal Bath in Budapest

part of Central Europe are trying to catch up with their wealthy neighbors after shaking off their communist past and are also quite "new" countries, geopolitically speaking.

PRAGUE
Demographics

The population of Prague hovers around 1.3 million people, which is more than triple the size of the second-largest city of Brno. While more than 7 million tourists diversify the city each year, the resident population remains largely homogenous with around 85-90 percent of the population sticking close to their Czech roots. The 10-15 percent of transplants to the Czech capital come largely from Ukraine (around 50,000), Slovakia (around 30,000), Russia (around 22,000), with roughly 6,000 Americans coming in fifth.

A significant Vietnamese minority—roughly 80,000 in the Czech Republic and around 12,000 in Prague—has lived alongside Czechs since the 1960s, largely due to a guest worker and study program under the Communist government that also allowed for an escape from the Vietnam War. This influence is most visible to visitors in the number of Vietnamese restaurants as well as the local habit of referring to convenience stores and small grocer's often run by this community as "Vietnamese shops."

Religion

The Czech Republic is a largely atheist or agnostic country—a 2017 Pew Research study found that 72 percent of Czechs do not identify with a specific religious group—but the country overall remains fairly tolerant towards many religions. (There is, however, definitely some strong anti-Islamic sentiment among segments of the population.) Spiritual beliefs are largely seen as a private matter in Prague. Holidays like Christmas and Easter are treated as cultural celebrations with religious and pagan rituals mixed together rather than sacred holy days for devoted churchgoers.

There are practicing communities of Catholic, Protestant, and Jewish faiths in the Czech capital. The local sense of humor is also known to arise when asked about religion. Over 15,000 residents embraced the Force and wrote "Jedi" under religious affiliation in the last census.

Language

There is less English signage in Prague than in many European capitals. You can certainly expect some English-speaking information at major tourist attractions, but public transport and street signs are often limited to Czech, even in the city center. Smaller shops and restaurant menus in the surrounding neighborhoods may or may not have English translations or staff members able to understand questions. Basically, the more "local" an experience you want to have, the less likely it is to include English.

With that said, the language landscape is rapidly changing. English is much more prevalent among younger generations. Older residents, shopkeepers, or salespeople in places like the train station or post office may speak limited English, may try German or Russian to communicate, or may simply refuse to interact. Learning a few basic phrases or numbers in Czech can help, but the locals are also not used to foreigners speaking their language and may have trouble with anything less than native pronunciation.

On the bright side, Czech is a phonetic language, so you can pronounce words the way they are written. You may also be pleasantly surprised by how much communication is actually possible when approached with politeness, patience, and a willingness to use body language to get your point across.

VIENNA
Demographics

As of January 2018, Vienna's population clocked in at 1.889 million. It's a city that continues to grow with a diverse community that comes from a migration background.

Once the heart of the Habsburg Empire, Vienna has been a cosmopolitan city for centuries. Today this international legacy shows in the demographics, where 50 percent of Viennese have a migration background, either having been born abroad or has at least one parent who has. Most of Vienna's international population come from the surrounding countries like the Czech Republic, Hungary, and Slovakia, with significant people from the Balkans and Germany. There is also a significant Asian and Turkish population within Vienna.

Religion

Austria is a majority Catholic country, but its capital Vienna has seen a significant decrease in practicing Catholics. Since 2001, the number of Roman Catholics in the capital has declined from around 50 percent to 35 percent in 2016. Those with no religion increased from 26 to 30 percent in 15 years, and other religions like Orthodox Christianity and Islam have risen in correlation with the growing migrant populations. Vienna used to be a city with one of the largest Jewish communities in Europe, but ever since the Holocaust, the city's Jews fell into a marginal minority. The 2001 census only listed 6,988 Jews living in Vienna.

Language

Vienna may be a city of immigrants, but German is still the primary language you'll encounter in the Austrian capital. The local government runs free German language courses to help foster integration into the local community. Austrian German is a variety of Standard German and differs with the German spoken in Germany the same way British English and American English do, with minor differences in word usage, grammar, spelling, and pronunciation. Although German is the official language, being a cosmopolitan capital, you'll find plenty of people who speak English as a second language, as well as native languages being spoken. For example, you'll probably hear Hungarian, Czech, or Turkish being spoken by locals with migrant backgrounds.

BUDAPEST
Demographics

In 2017 Budapest's population reached 1.779 million in the city, with over 3 million in the metropolitan area. Over 30 percent of the Hungarian population lives in the vicinity of the capital in commuting distance. The makeup of Budapest's population is less diverse than nearby Vienna. Many ethnic Hungarians born outside today's borders of Hungary (following the Treaty of Trianon) earned the right to Hungarian nationality, and many Hungarians from Romania and Slovakia crossed the border and made Budapest their home, or at least for the time being. There is also a growing Chinese community in Budapest, where there are even an Asian market and a "Chinatown" area in the suburbs.

Within Budapest, the main minority groups are the Jews and the Romani. Budapest is home to one of the largest Jewish communities in Europe, which unlike Vienna, bounced back the decades following the Holocaust and World War II. The Romani population is the most substantial minority in the country, whose origins are believed to stem from North India and first appeared in Hungary in the 14th-15th centuries, and there is a sizable population—around 1 percent—living in Budapest. There are still issues with discrimination against the Romani, many of whom fall below the poverty line in Hungary.

Religion

Hungary and its government like to cite that it's a Christian country. In Budapest, the religious composition is mostly Roman Catholic, numbering at 32 percent in 2015, with the Hungarian Reformed Church clocking up the numbers at 26.5 percent and the Evangelicals at 15.5 percent. There is also a minority Eastern Orthodox number at 1 percent. Budapest has a 2 percent Jewish population, with those citing no religion or Atheist at 23 percent.

Language

Hungary has one of the most curious languages in Europe, as it's not part of the Indo-European group and has little to nothing in common with those spoken in neighboring countries. It is part of the Finno-Ugric language family, which also includes Finnish and Estonian, and is supposed to originate from the Uralic regions in Russia with a few Siberian languages having similarities with Hungarian. Hungarian has a few words it's picked up over the centuries from Turkish, Slavic, and German, but the chances are even if you speak German or any Slavic language there would be very little you would recognize. Fortunately, Hungarian uses a Latin script so you can read the signs and metro station names easily enough. In Budapest, there are a lot of people who speak English, some who speak German, and some of the older generations speak Russian.

Some languages, like Romanian and Slovakian area, also spoken among migrants from the neighboring countries, and the Romani population, although they speak Hungarian, have their own language, too. If you're strolling around the Jewish Quarter, don't be surprised if you spot Hebrew script on some of the doors or signs around the synagogues.

Essentials

Getting There

Travelers arriving via air have the option to fly into Prague's **Vaclav Havel International Airport** (Aviatická, www.prg.aero), **Vienna International Airport** (VIE, tel. 01/700-722-233, www.viennaairport. com), or Budapest's **Ferenc Liszt International Airport** (BUD, tel. 06/1-296-7000, www.bud.hu).

FROM THE UNITED STATES
Prague
Finding a direct flight into Prague from anywhere in the US is tough.

You can find sporadic non-stop service from Newark on **United Airlines** (www.united.com), from Philadelphia on **American Airlines** (www.aa.com), or from New York (JFK) on **Delta Airlines** (www.delta.com), with flight times around 8.5 hours. Otherwise, transferring in a major hub like London, Amsterdam, or Frankfurt is more common.

Vienna

Reaching Vienna from the US is easy. **Austrian Airlines** (www.austrian.com) runs direct flights to Vienna International Airport from Chicago, Los Angeles, New York, and Miami. Direct Flights from the East Coast will take around 8.5 hours, whereas flights from the West Coast have a flight time of just under 12 hours.

Budapest

Until recently, Budapest had no direct flight connections from the US. If you flew in from any of the major US cities, you would need to change planes in somewhere like London, Frankfurt, Munich, or even Reykjavik. At the time of writing this, **LOT Airlines** (www.lot.com) just launched new routes from Budapest Liszt Ferenc Airport with direct flights between New York and Chicago with flight times lasting around 10-11 hours.

FROM EUROPE

The great thing about traveling in Central Europe is you have an abundant selection when it comes to which mode of transport to pick. You can go by bus, train, car, plane, or in some instances by ferry.

By Air

Low-cost airlines are also an option if you're traveling from further afield, like the UK. Airlines like **EasyJet** (www.easyjet.com), **WizzAir** (www.wizzair.com), and **Ryanair** (www.ryanair.com) offer inexpensive flights to the main airports of Prague, Vienna, and Budapest from many European destinations. Ryanair also flies into Bratislava. It takes between 2 to 2.5 hours to reach Central Europe from London by plane.

By Train

Traveling by train through Europe is a pleasure. You get to see the landscape change as you do. If you're heading to Hungary or Austria from Western Europe, chances are you're in for a ride through the Alps. You can plan your train itinerary on the website **Bahn.de,** which shows plenty of train timetables and connections to destinations like Prague, Vienna, and Budapest so you can prepare more efficiently.

If you're feeling adventurous—or simply hate flying—you also have the option of traveling to Central Europe by train. You can take the **Eurostar** (www.eurostar.com) to Brussels (train tickets for this leg only are usually around €100-200), which go every two hours from London St. Pancras Station. However, from Brussels you will need to go to either Frankfurt or Cologne and change trains again to journey onto Vienna and Prague (Budapest will require another change at Vienna) with the total journey time (with the fewest connections) lasting between 14.5-19 hours. Tickets for onward journeys from Brussels could also cost an extra €150-250. This is not the most budget nor the most time friendly way to travel, but definitely the most adventurous!

By Bus

Buses can be the cheaper option, and although they may not be as comfortable as a train, buses like **Eurolines** (www.eurolines.eu) and **FlixBus** (www.flixbus.com) are quite comfortable, usually having toilets on board and operate across Europe. Taking the bus is quite the Odyssey across Europe and I would recommend doing it only if you really want

---

Previous: Praha Hlavní Nádraží, the main Prague train station

to save money traveling overland—and with low cost airlines offering frequent flights to Europe, you're not really saving that much.

You have the option to take a bus from London. Flixbus runs weekly direct buses going from London to Vienna, which will take 25 hours and cost €100 going Sunday night. **RegioJet** (www.regiojet.com) operates daily bus services to Prague, taking around 18.5 hours costing €50-70. There are no direct buses from London to Budapest.

By Ferry

If you want to move between countries in Central Europe, your best bet is to go on a river cruise—some even go as far as coming from Amsterdam all the way down to Budapest connection to the Danube via canals. **AMA Waterways** (www.amawaterways. com) and **Viking River Cruises** (www. vikingrivercruises.co.uk) run river cruises from Amsterdam to Budapest (and vice-versa), which take around 15 days.

By Car

Europe has a well-connected highway network, so depending on how far you're planning to drive, it's relatively easy to reach Central Europe. Highways are smooth and well maintained throughout the region, but you may find some roads in the countryside, in Hungary especially, in poorer condition. Most roads are well lit and well maintained but do note that you must use winter tires during the winter if you're planning to drive across Central Europe as the roads—especially in the mountains in Austria—can get icy and slippery.

ROAD RULES

Driving laws vary throughout the region. In Hungary the minimum driving age is 17, whereas the Czech Republic and Austria both have minimum ages of 18. Blood alcohol levels permitted while driving in Austria are 50mg in 100 milliliters of blood, whereas in Hungary there is zero tolerance for any alcohol detected in the blood. There is one road

rule the countries of continental Europe do have in common: You must drive on the right side of the road.

All the countries covered in this guide require a vignette for the country you're in where most main roads have tolls. You can usually buy these from gas stations, at the border, or online (www.asfinag.at/toll/vignette for Austria; www.hungary-vignette.eu for Hungary; eznamka.sk/selfcare/purchase for Slovakia, you cannot buy vignettes online for the Czech Republic) for some countries. These will need to be displayed in the window of your car unless it's an electronic one tied to your number plate.

While traveling, you'll need your passport and driver's license. If you're from the US or Canada, it may be a good idea also to get an **International Driving Permit** (IDP). This is an official translation of your license from back home, and although you won't need it in all countries, it's a good idea if you're planning on driving in Austria, Hungary, Poland, Croatia, Greece, Slovenia or Slovakia. You can get a permit from the American Automobile Association (AAA.com) or the Canadian Automobile Association Office (CCA.ca) for $20.

BORDER CROSSINGS

Ever since the Schengen Agreement removed border controls between the members of the EU states, traveling by car throughout Europe has got easier. Some countries though may check at the border at random, so always have your papers—like your passport or ID, license (International Drivers Permit, if applicable), registration, insurance papers—to hand over. Peak seasons may lead to queues at the border.

SAFETY

In the winter, mountain passes may be slow, or even closed off if the weather is bad. If you're driving through the Alps, it's best to keep an eye on the news and drive through smaller roads at low speeds. You must also fit your car with winter tires or all-season tires between the months of November and April. Speaking of winter driving conditions, you should also carry snow chains with you this season. Winter conditions tend to be the worst from December to February, but it's not impossible to have snow hit as late as early November, late March or even early April. Winter controls are enforced at control points, especially in Austria. And—all year round—if you're planning on driving through Germany note that some highways won't have speed limits so expect some crazy road runners.

CAR RENTALS

If you want to head out on an epic road trip from one European country to another with a rental car, you'll want to pick a company like **Europcar** (www.europcar.com), **Sixt** (www.sixt.com), or **Hertz** (www.hertz.com), who have offices in other countries that allow you just to drop the car off, but these will include a "drop fee" which is an extra added charge to return the car to another office. Talk to your rental company about your itinerary. You can find the best rental deal with price comparison sites like **Skyscanner** (www.skyscanner.com) or **Kayak** (www.kayak.com). The minimum age to rent a car in Prague and Budapest is 21; it's 19 in Vienna. Some companies require you to be at least 25 years of age, so confirm with your rental car company.

Should you prefer to cross Europe by car, but don't drive yourself or prefer not to drive, you can also try the car-sharing service **Bla Bla Car** (www.blablacar.com) a carpooling service that matches up drivers and passengers at reasonable prices.

FROM AUSTRALIA AND NEW ZEALAND

There are no direct flights from Australia and New Zealand to Central Europe. The quickest and most direct route is to connect through Bangkok, Doha, Dubai, or Shanghai. **Emirates** (www.emirates.com) and **Qatar** (www.qatarairways.com) serve most of the flights from Australia and New Zealand, which take around 22 hours or more, including transfers. **Air China** (www.airchina.com) and **Thai Airways** (www.thaiairways.com) also have services connecting the region to Oceania.

FROM SOUTH AFRICA

There are no direct flights from South Africa to Prague, Vienna, or Budapest. The easiest way is to fly with **Emirates** or **Qatar Airways** and change in Dubai or Doha. Flights take around 15 to 18 hours or more. Some routes also go through Paris Charles de Gaulle with Air France or Zurich with Swiss Airlines on route from Johannesburg.

Getting Around

CITY TRANSPORT

One thing Central European cities have in common is excellent **public transport.** Each city has a well-connected subway service, a vast network of tram lines, and of course, buses. Each of the three cities' public transit systems are operated by one managing entity, so you use the same passes on multiple forms of transit, such as bus and metro. All three cities have passes that are sold in chunks of time, so you can get a pass for 24 hours, 48 hours, etc. (In Budapest and

Vienna, it's also possible to purchase single-ride tickets.)

You can also get around each city by **bike,** as all three have bike sharing systems. Budapest and Vienna are bike friendly cities, with designated bicycle lanes and paths all across the city. Prague is not quite as bike-friendly inside the city, and drivers are not always known for giving way or stopping for crosswalks, but there are numerous cycling paths once you get into the countryside (see www.czechtrails.com for details).

Validating Transit Tickets

Another thing each municipality shares is the loyalty system when it comes to enforcing public transit tickets. It works like this: you buy a ticket or a pass, and you validate it and keep it with you. Most of the time, there are no ticket inspectors, but if there are and you don't have a valid ticket prepare for trouble. Ticket inspectors are usually in civilian dress, so until the armband comes on or the ID gets put out from under the shirt you won't know, and they take no prisoners nor excuses. If your ticket is not validated or valid, you will get fined—and the experience can ruin your trip. You can usually buy tickets from automated machines, tobacconists, or ticket offices. You typically need to validate them when you enter the metro or get on the tram or bus. Look out for the validation boxes and double check the validation mark shows. Sometimes, passes won't need validating—in Budapest passes are issued from the date you request—but in Vienna, for example, you will need to validate the pass the first time you use it.

GETTING AROUND CENTRAL EUROPE

Getting between Prague, Vienna, and Budapest, the easiest way is to go by train or by bus. Each city has direct connections.

The main rail companies running in Central Europe are **ÖBB Railjet** (www.oebb.at), **MÁV** (www.mavcsoport.hu), **České Dráhy** (www.cd.cz), **RegioJet** (www.regiojet.com) and **Deutsche Bahn** (www.bahn.de). You can check timetables for all continental European connections on Deutsche Bahn's website (www.bahn.de). There are also regular buses operated by companies like **Flixbus** (www.flixbus.com) and **Eurolines** (www.eurolines.eu).

You also have the option to fly between the cities, but unless you're flying between Budapest and Prague with **Czech Airlines** (www.csa.cz), which operates flights three times a day for €75-300 one way taking an hour and a half, you won't actually save much time once you've checked in and gone through security. Trains and buses are fast, efficient and much cheaper than flying, so it makes more sense to travel between Budapest and Vienna, or Prague and Vienna overland. If you really have to take a plane, **Austrian Airlines** (www.austrian.com) does connect Vienna with both cities.

In the past, you could take the ferry between Vienna and Budapest, but unfortunately, the route has been canceled. You can travel between Vienna and Bratislava by boat if you wish.

Visas and Officialdom

Austria, Czech Republic, Hungary, and Slovakia all reside within the EU and the Schengen Zone.

U.S. TRAVELERS

As a US citizen, you will not need an entry permit (visa) to enter any of the countries. You can come to Austria, Czech Republic, and Hungary as a tourist for up to 90 days in any 180-day period. However, you do require a passport that is valid for at least three months after your departure from the European Union.

EU/SCHENGEN TRAVELERS

If you're from another EU state, you do not need a visa to enter any of the Schengen countries, like Austria, Czech Republic, or Hungary. When you travel from one Schengen country to another, chances are you won't even have your passport or ID checked, although it's a good idea to keep it on you as some borders still check IDs, such as the train from Budapest to Vienna. UK travelers should check for new regulations post-Brexit.

TRAVELERS FROM AUSTRALIA AND NEW ZEALAND

Australians and New Zealanders can come to Austria, Czech Republic, and Hungary visa-free for a maximum period of 90 days in any 180-day period without taking up employment. Your passport must be valid for three months beyond the planned date of departure from the Schengen area.

TRAVELERS FROM SOUTH AFRICA

South Africans require a visa to enter the Schengen Area. You can obtain a Schengen visa from any of the Schengen Area member countries, which will allow for free movement between the whole Schengen zone. It's best to apply for the country you're planning to visit first, for example, if you're flying into Austria, apply for a tourist visa from the Austrian Embassy, but make sure it's a Uniform Schengen Visa (USV) if you're planning on traveling onto Budapest, Prague, or even Bratislava. This visa will grant entry for 90 days in a 180-day period.

For Austria, visa applications should be submitted at the Austria Visa Application Center in Johannesburg, Cape Town, or Durban. These will be assessed by the Embassy of Austria in Pretoria.

If your first country is Hungary, then you can apply for your Schengen Visa from the Embassy of Hungary in Pretoria, or apply at the consulates in Durban or Cape Town.

Travelers beginning their journey in Prague should apply for the Schengen Visa at the Embassy of the Czech Republic in Pretoria.

Festivals and Events

JANUARY

New Year's Day Concerts (Vienna and Budapest) are a local tradition, especially in Vienna. The Musikverein hosts the most famous New Year's Day concert, which is broadcast globally. Although Vienna takes the spotlight, Budapest also has its fair share of classical concerts to ring in the New Year.

FEBRUARY

Opera Ball (Vienna) is the most important event on the Viennese social calendar. Out of some 300 balls held in the season of January and February, Vienna's Opera Ball is the most lavish and anticipated.

MARCH

March 15 (Budapest) is a huge national holiday in Hungary to remember the revolution of 1848 against the Habsburg rule.

APRIL

Vienna Easter Markets (Vienna) take place at Schönbrunn Palace, exhibiting Easter decorations and Austrian crafts.

Čarodejnice ("Witches Day") (Prague) marks the end of winter. Families gather in parks to prepare bonfires topped with wooden figures dressed in witch's clothes.

MAY

Prague Spring Festival (Prague) brings music to the city's concert halls, with everyone from symphony orchestras to young musicians competing for prizes.

Budapest 100 (Budapest) gets you a behind-the-scenes look inside private residential buildings which are normally closed to the public.

Falk Art Forum (Budapest) opens up the streets around 50 Budapest galleries for festivities, performances, music, theater, and food.

Prague Fringe Festival (Prague) brings nine days of comedy, cabaret, music, dance, and theater to the city.

JUNE

Donauinselfest (Vienna) is a free music festival held on the Danube Island. It lasts for three days and is the largest festival of its kind.

Regenbogenparade (Vienna) is a massive gay and lesbian festival attracting over 150,000 people to the Ringstraße.

Karlovy Vary International Film Festival (Czech Republic) runs for eight days in early June or late July, and screens films all over town.

JULY

Jazz Fest Wien (Vienna) bring jazz, blues, and soul to Vienna's large and small venues, from the Staatsoper to small clubs.

Formula 1 Grand Prix (Budapest) is one the most important events in motorsports, bringing thousands to Budapest each year for the races.

Identities (Vienna) is an International Queer Film Festival that takes place every other year in June.

AUGUST

Sziget Festival (Budapest) is one of Europe's largest music festivals, taking place on Óbuda Island. The week-long festival pulls thousands in from around Europe.

SEPTEMBER

Budapest Wine Festival (Budapest) gets the best Hungarian winemakers up to Buda Castle. Sip and taste wines from the region with fantastic views over the river.

OCTOBER

Budapest Design Week (Budapest) takes over the city during the first half of October. Exhibits of Hungarian contemporary fashion, art, and design are scattered throughout Budapest, and most events are free.

Prague Signal Festival (Prague) is a celebration of light installations and video shows, often projected onto Prague's architecturally attractive buildings.

Art Market Budapest (Budapest) takes place every October and is the leading art fair of Central and Eastern Europe. All manner of art is showcased here, to view and to buy, and there is a different guest country participant every year.

NOVEMBER

Saint Martin's Day (Prague) celebrates Saint Martin's bringing of the first snow of the season. The first taste of Svatomartinské young wine is poured on November 11th.

DECEMBER

Christmas Markets in all three cities set up shop from the end of November till the end of December, and are a considerable draw to the region.

New Year (Vienna and Budapest) is an epic party in any city, and in the center of Vienna and Budapest, it becomes quite the street party. In Vienna, the Grand Ball takes place at the Hofburg and gives you the chance to see in the New Year in style.

Paying Your Bar Tab in Prague

Servers often keep a tally of the drinks on a piece of paper at your table in a traditional pub or an automated system in other venues. Separate checks are expected, but it is the responsibility of the patrons to remember what they had and tell the server which food or drinks they want to pay for at the end of the night—something to note if you're the last one of your group to pay the bill! Credit cards are accepted in maybe 65 percent of venues, but many systems don't allow tips on cards, so carrying cash in the local currency is always a good backup plan. Euros may be accepted in some touristy pubs around the center, but usually at an abysmal exchange rate.

Food and Nightlife

Food in Central Europe is dominated by meat, particularly pork. Starchy ingredients like potatoes and dumplings also make up the base for food in this part of the world, and vegetables—especially in Hungary and the Czech Republic—tend to come in pickled form.

MEALTIMES

PRAGUE
Breakfast in Prague is often small—a quick pastry on the go—and the lunch hour starts early around 11am, with daily lunch specials usually served until 2pm. You can usually expect dinner service to last until at least 10pm

VIENNA
Breakfast is eaten between 7am and 10am and is usually a lavish affair with a roll, a boiled egg, jam and butter, some juice at the minimum—and a coffee, naturally. Meal times in Austria are similar to the rest of Central Europe, with lunch taking place between midday and 2pm, dinner 7pm-9pm.

BUDAPEST
Hungary shares similar meal times with Austria. Most people will have breakfast between 7am and 10pm, with lunch usually taking place at 12-1:30pm, dinner around 7pm, but can be as early as 6pm or late as 8:30pm.

TIPPING
Tipping is not required, but is customary for good service. The general rule is to round up for small amounts (e.g. 50 CZK for a 42 CZK beer) or around 10% for a nice meal. You should tell your server how much you want to pay on the spot, when handing them cash or your card (e.g. Server: "That's 565 crowns." You: "600, please.") Don't leave cash on the table and your credit card slip will not come with a line to add the tip. In Hungary especially, if you give a note over and say "thank you," the waiter will assume that includes tip and you won't get change.

DIETARY RESTRICTIONS
Central Europe's vegetarian scene is slowly improving, with lots of raw and vegan restaurants opening in recent years in all three cities—and there is even a vegetarian Michelin star restaurant in Vienna. However, in many Czech, Austrian and Hungarian restaurants, the meat-free menu is still limited to fried cheese (*smažený sýr* in Czech, *rántott sajt* in Hungarian, and *Gebackener Käse* in German) and vegans may struggle to find anything suitable outside of restaurants that specifically cater to their diet. Seafood, ham, bacon, lard, and even rabbit have been known to pop up on vegetarian sections in village pubs, so double-check with your server to be 100% sure.

Some restaurants are better than others when it comes to dairy or gluten sensitivity. Requests to leave out certain ingredients are usually honored when possible, but substitutions or asking for ingredients on the side is not common practice and will likely be met with confusion or annoyance—especially in rural areas. Restaurants are required to list certain allergens on their menus. For severe allergies, printing a list of the specific words in Czech, German, or Hungarian may help communicate your needs.

Accommodations

HOTELS

Hotels in Central Europe get graded on a star system running from one to five stars. Just how many stars a hotel will have depends on factors like the services and facilities available in the hotel, the infrastructure, and quality. Five-star hotels will offer luxury, like the Four Seasons Gresham Palace or the Hotel Sacher. There will usually be a spa and fine dining options. Three-star hotels are generally comfortable for most travelers. The term boutique hotel will pop up while traveling. This usually refers to a smaller hotel with 10 to 100 rooms, and may even have a design twist, that gives it a unique selling point for visitors. Most hotels will have en suite bathrooms—especially for hotels three stars and above—but it's best to check before booking if you're uncertain. Basic toiletries will always be provided, like soap and shampoo, for hotels over 3 stars.

Hotels will ask for your ID or passport upon arrival and may also want to photocopy your documents. Sometimes a city tax will be added to your bill on top of your hotel fee, and check to make sure breakfast is included in the price of the room. Many hotels include a complimentary breakfast in the price in Hungary but in Austria and the Czech Republic it's pretty common to charge extra for breakfast, especially in four or five star hotels. When it comes to tipping hotel staff, it's enough to give a bellhop or porter a couple of euros or 500 HUF per bag. If you're happy with the cleaning service, then you can leave a similar gratuity on the bed each night for the housekeeper. Tipping hotel staff in the Czech Republic is not expected, but 20 CZK per bag or 100-200 CZK per stay for the cleaning staff is still a nice way to express gratitude.

BED AND BREAKFASTS

Bed and Breakfasts are usually smaller than a hotel and independently owned. Breakfast is often included in the price, and often cooked by the owner. If you're looking for a place with a familial feel, then a B&B is a good choice. Rates are usually much lower than in a larger hotel, and you will get a more authentic feel in the area.

Do note though that some B&Bs occupy old residential apartments and houses, so bathrooms and toilets may not be located in the room and are down the hall. You can usually request en suite when booking the B&B.

HOSTELS

Young travelers, backpackers, and those on a budget will love hostels. Most hostels offer rooms in 6- to 8-bed dorms, but some may have single or double rooms at budget prices too, however bathrooms and toilets will usually be shared and located outside the room. Some travelers also love hostels for the community spirit, as they usually come with a common room or a shared kitchen which provides an excellent opportunity for travelers to meet and mingle. Breakfast is usually extra, if offered by the hostel. However, if peace, quiet, and a good night's sleep is what you're after, steer clear of the Party Hostels, with their regular happy hours, in-house bars or clubs. However, if you want to get to see the city's nightlife or make friends with other travelers, they can be great.

APARTMENT RENTALS

If you prefer to self-cater or have the experience of living like a local in the city you're visiting, then an apartment rental may be the option for you. The most popular way of doing this is Airbnb, but this has caused significant controversy for pushing up the rents of locals, especially in cities like Budapest and Prague.

Booking.com also rents out apartments. Just note in some apartment rentals, the toilet may be shared and located out in the hall—even in Vienna—so do your research before you book one. Also, note that with the independence an apartment will give you, you won't have the support concerning tourist information and orientation that you would have with a hotel.

Conduct and Customs

LOCAL HABITS

Hungary, Austria, and the Czech Republic share some habits, but they also have their differences. Austrians tend to be more formal than their Bohemian and Hungarian neighbors, and you'll find there is more formality than in Anglo-Saxon countries in all the Central European countries. You may even notice that people won't smile at you all the time like back home. Don't expect service with a smile in Central Europe. Some places have friendly staff, but as a rule, most waitstaff, especially classic cafes, will be on the surly side. Although smiles are not mandatory, politeness is. Always say hello or good day in the local language if you can whenever you go into a shop or a cafe, stand on the right of the escalator in the metro and give up your seat to the elderly on the bus. When it comes to tipping, it's best to say how much you'd like to pay in total when paying rather than leaving change on the table.

GREETINGS

Greetings are especially important in Central Europe. It's expected you say good day when you enter a shop. Even if you've brushed up on your German, don't use the classic German "Guten Tag," but instead go with the local greeting of "Grüß Gott"—pronounced "gruess got." In Hungary, you can say "Jó napot

kívanok," pronounced "your nap-ot kee-van-ok," and in the Czech Republic you would say "dobrý den" pronounced "dough-bree-den"

It's also considered polite to say goodbye when leaving.

Greeting one another with a couple of kisses on the cheek is also common in Central Europe, but this usually happens between men-women, women-women. In some cases such as close family or older men you may see the men do it, too. Kisses are generally exchanged at the beginning and the end of most social encounters. In business settings or between two men, a handshake is often the norm.

ALCOHOL

Alcohol rules in Central Europe are more relaxed than in the States, with the legal drinking age being 18 in the Czech Republic and Hungary. Austria is more relaxed in parts of the country, with the drinking age in Vienna (it varies based on the province between 16 and 18) being 16. However, despite the more liberal attitude to alcohol, getting very drunk in public in Vienna is more frowned upon than in countries like the UK, and there are fines for anti-social behavior while drunk. In Hungary, particularly in the countryside, don't be surprised to see locals doing a shot first thing in the morning, and in the Czech Republic, you may be surprised to find that the beer can be cheaper than water most of the time.

There are restrictions on the sale of alcohol at certain times. In Budapest, for example, certain districts put a cap on late night shops

---

1 *chlebíčky* (open-faced sandwiches) are popular Czech snacks 2 European dessert in Salzburg 3 traditional Hungarian fried bread *lángos*

selling alcohol after 11pm. And don't think of driving even if you've had one beer—drinking and driving is taken very seriously and can incur punishment if any shows up in a test.

SMOKING

Smoking is legal from the age of 18, and the laws will vary between the countries. In Hungary, you can only buy cigarettes from National Tobacco Shops (Nemzeti Dohány Bolt), which have brown signs and an 18 logo inside a red circle and the colors of the Hungarian flag—red, white, green. A lot of Hungarians smoke, but it's not allowed inside and only in designated areas outside in restaurants and cafes, and the Czech Republic is the same. (Up until May 2017, ashtrays were an essential part of most pubs in Prague, but the recent smoking ban has restricted cigarettes to only outdoor dining areas.) Austria is very relaxed when it comes to smoking. Don't be surprised to find restaurants and cafes with smoking sections indoors. Keep an eye out for the smoking and no smoking signs on the doors when you go out to eat or drink.

DRUGS

The Central European region has never had a reputation as being a drug hotbed, but dealing still happens around train stations and transport hubs. Hungary has stricter drug laws than the Czech Republic, where cannabis is entirely illegal, whereas in the Czech Republic personal possession of marijuana has been decriminalized and medical cannabis is also legal. Austria has also relaxed its cannabis laws, allowing for it to be used for medicinal purposes, and decriminalized small quantities, but it's still discouraged to smoke marijuana in public places. Other drugs are illegal in all three countries, and possession can lead to up to two years imprisonment in Hungary and up to six months in Austria. It's best to play it safe while traveling and avoid consuming or possessing drugs—even in small quantities.

PROSTITUTION

Prostitution in Austria is legal and regulated, however while sex work is not forbidden, prostitutes must be registered and work from licensed brothels. Legal prostitution operates around the northern Gürtel, Naschmarkt, and in Leopoldstadt.

Although prostitution has been legalized in Hungary and sex workers pay tax, there is no official red light district in Budapest, and in the Czech Republic the line is even more blurred. Despite being legal, Czech laws prohibit organized prostitution and sex work is not regulated. There are some 200 brothels in Prague alone but their operations are not quite legal thanks to ambiguously written laws.

DRESS

Hungary and the Czech Republic have a more relaxed dress code. You'll see people walking around in jeans and t-shirts in Prague and Budapest, where most restaurants—unless we're talking somewhere elite—won't enforce a strict dress code. On the other hand, in Vienna, especially in the I District, you'll notice the locals tend to be elegantly dressed in smart casual attire. For high-class restaurants or a night at the opera, formal wear is preferred, which also applies to Prague. Although with the opera, you may notice some people in jeans and casual attire in the last-minute standing seats. In most churches, women will be expected to cover shoulders and wear skirts below the knee.

Health and Safety

EMERGENCY NUMBERS

The number to dial in an emergency is the same throughout continental Europe: **112.**

CRIME AND THEFT

Crime and theft in Central Europe are moderate. When it comes to violent crime, Vienna, Prague, and Budapest are generally safe cities. Pickpockets perhaps present the primary risk in crowded places like the metro or festivals, so keep an eye out for your belongings when out and about. Scams are another thing to be aware of, like the classic Budapest scam when young, attractive women approach you (if you are male) on Váci utca asking for directions and then invite you to a drink—and take you to bar with no menus that will fleece you for as much money as you have. In Prague, avoid changing money on the street or you'll likely end up with a currency that isn't Czech Koruna. It's important not to let your guard down, but with a little common sense and avoiding areas with a bad reputation—such as the train stations—you should be fine.

MEDICAL SERVICES

Vaccines are not required for any of the countries in Central Europe, but if you're traveling in the window between November to March, you may want to invest in a flu shot. Also, if you're planning to head out into nature, you may want to get a Tick-Borne Encephalitis vaccine as ticks are a growing risk in Central Europe. You can also pick up bug spray in local pharmacies that is good to ward of mosquitos and ticks, so if you haven't been vaccinated, it's a good idea to take precautions when in parks or wooded areas—even within the city.

Medical care in Austria is excellent, but in Hungary, standards will vary depending on the hospital, with some being better than others. Public health services in Hungary are understaffed and overburdened. The Czech Republic falls somewhere in between the two countries.

DRINKING WATER

The water is not only safe to drink in all three cities, but it's actually pretty good—especially in Vienna—so go ahead and feel free to bottle some tap water.

PHARMACIES

Pharmacies in Central Europe can help you pick up any medications, vitamins, or herbal supplements you may need while traveling. Drugs like ibuprofen and paracetamol (acetaminophen), won't require a prescription in European pharmacies, but some drugs will require a local prescription from a doctor of that country, like antibiotics or sedatives. European pharmacies also sell more than just medication, but you can also buy skincare products and toiletries developed by dermatologists (if you've heard about beauty bloggers rave about French pharmacy skin care products the good news is you can find the same French brands like La Roche-Posay and Nuxe in larger Central European pharmacies). You may also find European pharmacies sell alternative medicines like homeopathy as well.

You can spot a pharmacy in each country by the bright green cross symbol. You can find a pharmacy that's open any time of day or night, either in an assigned all night pharmacy like those in Budapest, or rotating with the schedule printed on the door of each pharmacy as in Vienna.

SECURITY

Prague and Budapest to date have not seen any terrorist attacks; Vienna, however, has had instances of lone wolf knife attacks, and Austria is the most likely out of the three countries to be at risk from terrorism. Just like any city in Europe, it's best to be vigilant and consult your embassy for travel advice. Also, if offered, register your travel with your embassy before traveling so that you're entitled to consular help.

Practical Details

WHAT TO PACK

When it comes to packing, the best bet is to pack smart-casual attire and plenty of layers. The climate in the region is changeable, so keep a jacket or a cardigan in your bag for those days when the cooler evening chill sets in.

Expect to do a lot of walking in each city so pack a pair of **comfortable shoes.** The old towns in Prague, Vienna, and Budapest have cobbles so bear that in mind when considering footwear. Since the climate is changeable—in the summer you can go from blazing heat to flash storms—pack layers and an umbrella or a raincoat to hand. If you're going in the winter, pack warm clothes as the temperatures can plummet below zero.

It's a good idea to bring **swimwear** if you're traveling to Budapest or Vienna since Budapest has its famous thermal baths and Vienna also has some stunning pools worth taking a dip in.

If you're coming from the UK or the States, make sure you pack an **adapter** so you can use your electronics in Continental Europe. Plugs in Central Europe use two round prongs with a voltage of 220V. You will definitely want a camera or at least a good quality phone to snap pics, but bring extra memory cards, because you will need them!

Finally, **earbuds or headphones** can be useful for accessing museum audio guides that you can download onto your phone.

BUDGETING

One thing you will notice is that prices between the three cities will vary. Vienna is by far the most expensive city out of the three, and Prague the cheapest. A cup of coffee in Vienna can cost between $3.40-6.50, whereas in Prague and Budapest you'd pay $2. A beer in Vienna would set you back $3.60-4.60, $2.60 in Budapest and in Prague under $2. A 24-hour ticket in Vienna will cost $9.30, $6.50 in Budapest and $5.30 in Prague. If you're planning a budget for the three cities, allocate a higher threshold for Vienna. You may want to balance things out by going for more budget accommodation or self-catering in Vienna while living it up in Budapest or Prague.

MONEY

The EU is generally great to travel in since you usually have a single currency, but in the case of Prague, Vienna, and Budapest, we're sorry to say that only Austria is in the Eurozone—however if you want to pop over to Slovakia for the day, the good news is they also use the euro. The Czech Republic uses the Czech Koruna, and Hungary the Hungarian Forint.

You'll find that **ATMs** will take foreign cards and most shops (fewer in Prague) will take Visa, Mastercard, or Maestro. Some won't take American Express, so best to check before ordering. If you prefer, you can also change money at official money changers, either in banks or official changers (they usually have a Western Union sign outside, too).

Some restaurants and shops will only take **cash;** most markets are cash only. It's a good idea to carry some smaller bills with you if you're planning on paying in cash. Most large supermarkets and restaurants will break larger notes, but you might get a few irritated servers or sellers if you try to pay with a 20,000 HUF note, 1,000 CZK, or a €100 bill in a smaller venue. It's a good idea to keep some small change on you at all times, especially for public toilets (some in Vienna are automated, for example and will only take 50 cent coins).

Sightseeing without the Crowds

When it comes to finding a quiet moment in tourist hot spots, the common refrain among photographers is to arrive before sunrise. The most famous sights can be pretty crowded from morning to evening during summer and Christmas seasons. Saving these sights for weekdays instead of weekends, arriving first thing in the morning, or waiting until nighttime can give you a different experience with fewer crowds. Otherwise, just be patient and take your time at the sights you choose to visit. Wait for the crowds to rise and disperse around you and watch for the moment to get a good view or picture as you immerse yourself in the moment.

OPENING HOURS

Shops usually open around 9am or 10am and close around 6pm, perhaps later in large shopping malls, Mondays to Saturdays. On Sundays, the case will vary between cities. In Vienna, most shops close on Sundays, whereas in Budapest shops in the city center will open for shorter hours on Sunday, and in Prague, large stores or supermarkets may stay open on Sundays, but others will close. Sometimes, smaller stores will close for lunch hours.

Museums, in general, tend to close on Mondays, but check the opening times of any place you're interested in visiting—some popular attractions open every day of the week, others may have a rest day on Tuesday or Sunday.

PUBLIC HOLIDAYS

During high holidays, like Christmas and New Year's Day, most shops and attractions will be closed. Businesses also tend to close for religious holidays, but also national holidays, like October 23, March 15, and August 20 in Hungary; and in Austria October 26; in the Czech Republic May 8 and September 28, to name a few.

COMMUNICATIONS
Phones and Cell Phones

The country codes for Austria is 43, for Hungary 36 and the Czech Republic 420. If you're calling from the US, dial the international access code 011, from a US or Canadian landline, or use the plus sign, and add the country code, then dial the number (drop the 0 before calling). From the UK, just dial 00 and then the country code.

Within each country, just dial the number without dropping the 0, if there is one. For long distance calls within Hungary, dial 06. Don't get nervous if phone numbers seem irregular in number. Standards are a little harder to predict. Mobile phone numbers can come with their own prefixes, and sometimes landline number length will also vary.

To call out of the country, dial 00 or the plus sign and the country code. For US and Canada this is 1 and then add in the phone number with the area code.

Most smartphones will work in Central Europe with a US, UK, or Canadian SIM card, but talk to your provider to make sure you don't rattle up any unwanted roaming charges when you go abroad.

Internet Access

You should find it easy to get online in any of the cities. You should find WiFi access in your hotel, but most cafes, malls, and even hotspots in the city center should get you connected online for free. Some free WiFi services may ask you to register with an email and click on their terms and conditions.

Shipping and Postal

If you're looking only to post a card, then you may want to skip the queues at the post office and buy a stamp at the tobacconist (Austria) or newsagent (Hungary, Czech Republic). Should you go to a post office, some require you press a button and take a number for the queue. Postcards to the US will cost around € 1 to 2 to post.

Traveler Advice

ACCESS FOR TRAVELERS WITH DISABILITIES

With its cobbled streets, stairways leading up from one lane to another, and old metro stations, Central Europe can be a challenge for disabled travelers. Out of the three cities, Vienna is the most accessible. Ramps leading into buildings are generally standard, as are elevators in the U-Bahn, and buses and trams have spaces allocated for wheelchairs. You can request an Accessible Vienna pamphlet from the Tourist Info Wien for a list of places catering to visitors with specific needs. Even if you go further afield in Austria, ÖBB, the Austrian rail network has the option for Accessible Booking, but make sure you order 24 hours in advance for domestic services. Prague and Budapest are a little behind when it comes to catering to disabled travelers. Historic buildings may not have a lift, and some of the older metro stations may be stairs only. It's best to do some additional research, contact either the **Hungarian Federation of Disabled Persons' Associations** (www. meosz.hu/en) for Hungary or the **Prague Wheelchair Users Organisation** (www. pov.cz/en) for the Czech Republic.

TRAVELING WITH CHILDREN

Whether you want to visit Europe's oldest zoo, ride a railway staffed by children, or picnic Petřín Hill overlooking Prague, Central Europe offers something for all the family. Kids get discounts on public transport and museums, and some restaurants even offer a children's menu. There's plenty to keep the little ones busy when traveling Central Europe. Some tourist offices will provide brochures with family-friendly ideas. It's worth researching museums to see if any have play areas for children—for example, in Vienna's MuseumsQuartier, ZOOM is a museum with interactive programs that can keep the kids occupied while you pay a visit to the Leopold or mumok.

WOMEN TRAVELING ALONE

Prague, Vienna, and Budapest are relatively safe cities for solo female travelers, but exercise the same caution as you would in any other European city. Most downtown areas are okay to explore your own, even at night. However, if you feel anxious walking down quiet streets after dark, then try to pick accommodations on a main road, since all three cities will have side streets that may unnerve you after dark. Taxis can be a great option to get back if you don't like taking public transport late night, or there are no services to where you're staying, but make sure you take a licensed operator. And should you go to a bar, take care never to leave your drink unattended.

SENIOR TRAVELERS

Senior travelers may struggle with the cobbled streets and the less accessible sites in Central Europe, but on the whole, it's a region that's great for older travelers. The thermal baths in Budapest, Prague's historical sites, or Vienna's world-class museums all attract travelers of all ages, including older ones. Most museums have lifts and benches, and of course, discounts for senior citizens. Public transport is either free—in the case of Budapest, it's free for EU citizens aged 65 and over—or at a discount. Just take care not to book a hotel in the heart of a party district, such as Budapest's Jewish Quarter, if you're looking for a peaceful night's sleep.

GAY AND LESBIAN

Austria, Hungary, and the Czech Republic are quite varied when it comes to welcoming gay and lesbian travelers. Hungary has conservative views, but attitudes are changing, especially in Budapest, as the number grows in Pride each year with more and more allies joining the march. There have been some violent demonstrations from the far-right in the city, but beyond the noise, there is an increasing amount of gay-friendly spaces in the city center. Vienna is tolerant towards gays and lesbian travelers, and like Budapest more so in the capital than in the rest of Austria. Prague has a vibrant gay scene, mostly concentrated in the Vinohrady area.

When traveling outside the cities, members of the LGBTQ community may feel a little uncomfortable in rural areas. Austria is a predominantly Catholic country; however same sex marriage became legal in January 2019. LGBTQ travelers in rural Austria should feel as safe as they would be in Western European countries. In rural Hungary—and even in Budapest—members of the LGBTQ community tend to remain invisible, and public displays of affection are not seen, the Czech Republic on the other hand has a more liberal stance but public displays of affection, especially in smaller villages, may still draw looks. The **Spartacus International Gay Guide** (spartacus. gayguide.travel/gayguide) offers a lot of useful information for LGBTQ travelers for all the countries listed in this book.

TRAVELERS OF COLOR

Vienna is an incredibly cosmopolitan city, and travelers of color should feel comfortable in the city. Prague and Budapest may present more challenges for a traveler of color. Travelers from some ethnic or religious backgrounds, particularly those with darker skin, may experience xenophobic attitudes and unwanted attention.

You'll notice most of the population is quite homogeneous so travelers of color may get stared at in Hungary and the Czech Republic, where neither country has the best reputation when it comes to racism and discrimination, especially Hungary with its anti-migrant campaigns following the recent refugee crisis. Austria has also leant towards the right in the past years. However, the capital cities tend to be more liberal and open-minded, and you should not experience anything more than a few curious stares.

However, anti-immigrant or anti-Muslim marches are usually met with an equal or larger march in support of diverse societies, but this is a divisive political issue.

Outside of the cities, travelers of color may be met with stares from locals—especially in rural regions—but there is no need to be concerned about safety when visiting the daytrips recommended in this book. These are all popular with visitors from across the world, and welcome travelers of color.

Resources

Glossary

CZECH

autobus: bus
cukrárna: sweet shop
divadlo: theater
dům: house or building
heslo: password
hospoda: pub
hrad: castle
jízdenka: public transit ticket
kavárna: café/ coffee shop
Kč: Czech crown (also abbreviated CZK)
klimatizace: air conditioning
kostel: church
kreditní karta: credit card
lékárna: pharmacy
město: town
most: bridge
muži: men (or men's room)
nádraží: train station
náměstí: town/public square
nástupiště: platform
obchod: shop
odlety (airport)/odjezdy (train or bus station): departures
ostrov: island
pivo: beer
pokladna: ticket office
potraviny: mini-market
přílety (airport); příjezdy (train or bus station): arrivals
řáda: row
sedadlo: seat
ulice: street
vinárna/vinoteka: wine bar
vlak: train
(vyhlídková) věž: (observation) tower
zámek: chateau
zastávka: bus, tram, or train stop
ženy: Women (or women's room)

GERMAN

Abfahrt: departure
Ankunft: arrival
Anschluss: connection (transport)
Apotheke: pharmacy
Ausfahrt: exit
Auto: car
Bäckerei: bakery
Badezimmer: bathroom
Bahnhof: station
Beisl: inn/Austrian bistro
Bett: bed
Briefmarke: stamp
Brücke: bridge
Dom: cathedral
Einbahnstraße: one way street
Eingang: entrance
Eisenbahn: railway
Fahrkarte: rail or bus ticket
Fahrkartenschalter: ticket office (railway)
Flughafen: airport
frei: free
Gasse: alley
Gebäude: building
Gegend: neighborhood
Geld: cash
geschlossen: closed
gut: good
heiß: hot
Herberge: hostel
Hilfe: assistance
Kassa: ticket office (theater)/checkout

Kassierer: cashier
Kellner: waiter
Kirche: church
Kleingeld: small change
klimatisiert: air-conditioned
Konditorei: pastry shop
Konsulat: consulate
Kreditkarte: credit card
Laden: shop
Lebensmittelmarkt: grocery store
Markt: market
nicht alkoholisch: nonalcoholic
Ober: waiter
Offnen: open
Parkplatz: parking lot
Platz: square
Polizei: police
Reservierung: reservation
Strand: beach
Straße: road/street
Straßenbahnhaltestelle: tram stop
Tabak: tobacco shop
Turm: tower
U-Bahn: subway
U-Bahn Haltestelle: U-bahn stop
Vorspeise: appetizer
Ziel: destination
Zeitplan: timetable
Zimmer: room
Zoll: customs
Zug: train

HUNGARIAN

ágy: bed
alkohol: alcohol
alkoholmentes: nonalcoholic
állomás: station
ár: price
autó: car
bejárat: entrance
borozó: wine bar
busz: bus
célállomás: destination
csatlakozást: connection (transport)
cukrászda: pastry shop
dohánybolt: tobacco shop
élelmiszerbolt: grocery store
előétel: appetizer

emlékmű/műemlék: monument
épület: building
érkezés: arrival
étterem: restaurant
fasor: avenue
foglalás: reservation
forró: hot
gyógyszertár: pharmacy
híd: bridge
hitelkártya: credit card
indulás: departure
ingyenes: free
jegy: ticket
jegypénztár: ticket office
készpénz: cash
kijárat: exit
konzulátus: consulate
légkondicionált: air-conditioned
liget: park
menetrend: timetable
metró: subway
metrómegálló: subway stop
mosdó: bathroom
nagykövetség: embassy
nyitva: open
országút: highway
parkoló: parking lot
pékség: bakery
pénztáros: cashier
pénzdarab: coin
piac: market
pincér: waiter
rendőrség: police
repülőtér: airport
segítség: assistance
strand: beach
szálló/hostel: hostel
szálloda: hotel
székesegyház: cathedral
szoba: room
templom: church
tér: square
torony: tower
újságos: newsstand
út: road
utca: street
üzlet/bolt: shop
vám: customs

vasút: railway
villamos megálló: tram stop

vonat: train
zárva: closed

Czech Phrasebook

Czech is quite a difficult language—four genders (neuter, feminine, masculine animate, and masculine inanimate), seven cases that change word endings, formal and informal phrases—plus it includes one sound, the vicious ř, that many schoolchildren need speech therapy to master! On the bright side, the language is phonetic so you can say what you see. Some quirky letters pronounced differently than English include: au, c, č, ď, j, ř, š, ť, ž, and any vowel with an accent mark.

Some locals are delighted by foreigners speaking their language, while others quickly lose patience and get frustrated if you don't understand their responses in Czech. Asking a question in Czech will likely receive an answer in Czech, and most locals are not used to simplifying their own language for foreigners. Some Czechs in the service sector will switch to English to ensure accuracy and efficiency. In many cases, simplicity (e.g. "Liberec?" while pointing to the bus) is easier to facilitate communication. This also makes it easier for the locals to understand than the unavoidable mispronunciation of their own language or small grammatical errors that can change meanings. However, do feel free to try some Czech phrases when you have the time and a willing native speaker.

a as in "father"
á longer as in "ahhhh"
au like "ow" as in "how"
c "ts" always a soft c as in "patience" (never hard like "ck")
č "ch" as in "change"
ch like an "h" but in the back of your throat like the composer "Bach"
ď a "dy" sound
e as in "egg"
é like "ai" as in "fair"
ě like adding a "y" before the "e" as in "yes"

i as in "fit"
í like "ee" as in "free"
j like "y" in "yes"
ň like "ny" as in "menu"
o as in "oh"
ó longer "oh" as in "oooooh"
ř no English equivalent; in Czech it combines saying "ž" plus a rolled "r" simultaneously, as in the composer's name Dvořák; English speakers can get by with just saying "ž" like the "s" in "pleasure"
š "sh" as in "shampoo"
ť a "ty" sound as in "architecture"
u as in "soup"
ú or ů like a long "u" as in "true"; the character ú is used at the beginning of a word while ů is used in the middle
y like a short "i" as in "bit"
ý like a long "e" as in "me"
ž like "s" in "measure"

ESSENTIAL PHRASES

Hello *Dobrý den* (formal, for strangers and acquaintances; used anytime you enter a shop or restaurant)
Hi / Bye *Ahoj* or *Čau* (informal, used somewhat interchangeably but only for close friends and family)
Good morning *Dobré ráno*
Good evening *Dobrý večer*
Good night *Dobrou noc*
Goodbye *Na shledanou* (used anytime you leave a shop or restaurant)
Where are you from? *Odkud jste?*
I am from the US / England / … *Jsem z USA / Jsem z Anglii …*
Nice to meet you *Těší mě*
Please/You're welcome *Prosím*
Excuse me *Pardon* or *Promiňte*
Sorry *Promiňte*
Thank you *Děkuji*

Excuse me, do you speak English?
Promiňte, nemluvíte* Anglicky ? (* In Czech
the more polite sentence structure is similar
to "Don't you speak English?")

Is there WIFI? *Nemáte* WIFI?* (* In Czech the
more polite sentence structure is similar to
"Don't you have WIFI?")

What's the WIFI password? *Jaké je heslo
na WIFI?*

Yes *Ano* (formal, and often shortened to *"no"*
so be careful because *"'no"* in Czech means
"Yes!")

No *Ne*

TRANSPORTATION

bus station *autobusové nádraží*
train station *vlakové nádraží*
Where is…? *Kde je…?*
How far is it to…? *Jak daleko je…. odsud?*
Is there a bus to Liberec / Brno / …? *Je
autobus do Liberce* / Brna* / …?* (* Almost
all Czech words, including place names,
change depending on the sentence.)
Is this the bus to…? *Je to autobus na …?*
What time does the bus/train leave?
V kolik hodin autobus / vlak odjíždí?
Where is the subway station? *Kde je
stanice metra?*
Where's the ticket office? *Kde je
pokladna?*
A round-trip/single ticket to… Zpáteční
/ jízdenku na…

FOOD

Can I make a reservation, please? *Mohu
si udělat rezervaci, prosím?*
A reservation for one/two… *Rezervace
za jednu osobu / dvě osoby*
Two people at 2pm *dva lidé v dvě
odpoledne*
Do you have a reservation? *Máte
rezervaci?*
Do you have an English menu? *Nemáte
anglické menu?*
Are you ready to order? *Máte vybráno?*
**Excuse me, may I order,
please?** *Promiňte můžu objednat, prosím?*

I'm vegetarian. *jsem vegetarian* (male) /
jsem vegetarianka (female).
I'll have… please. *Dám si….prosím.*
Is everything okay? *Všechno pořádku?*
**I would like to pay / We would like to
pay, please.** *Zaplatím / Zaplatíme, prosím.*
Cash or card? *Hotově nebo kartou?*
breakfast *snídaně*
beer *pivo*
lunch *oběd*
dinner *večeře*
menu *jídelní lístek*
wine *vino*
water *voda*
coffee *káva*
tea *čaj*
(soy / almond) milk *(sójové / mandlové)
mléko*
gluten / gluten-free *lepek / bezlepkový*
fruit *ovoce*
bread *chléb*
meat *maso*
fish *ryby*

SHOPPING

money *peníze*
How much does it cost? *Kolik to stojí?*
I'm just looking around. *Jen se rozhlížím.*

HEALTH

drugstore *drogérie*
pharmacy *lékárna*
It hurts here. *Bolí mě tady.*
I have a fever. *Mám horečku.*
I have a headache. *Bolí mě hlava.*
I have a stomach ache. *Bolí mě břicho.*
I have a toothache. *Bolí mě zub.*
I feel nauseated. *Je mi nevolno.*
to vomit *zvracet*
medicine *lékařství*
antibiotic *antibiotika*
pill/tablet *pilulka / tabletka*
I need a doctor *Potřebuji lékaře*
To the hospital, please. *Do nemocnice,
prosím.*
I am diabetic / pregnant. *Jsem diabetik
/ těhotná*

I take birth control pills. *Užívám antikoncepci.*
I am allergic to... penicillin. *Jsem alergický (male) / alergická (female) na... penicilín.*
blood type *krevní skupina*

NUMBERS

0 *nula*
1 *jeden (m.) / jedna (f.) / jedno (n.)*
2 *dva / dvě*
3 *tři*
4 *čtyři*
5 *pět*
6 *šest*
7 *sedm*
8 *osm*
9 *devět*
10 *deset*
11 *jedenáct*
12 *dvanáct*
13 *třináct*
14 *čtrnáct*
15 *patnáct*
16 *šestnáct*
17 *sedmnáct*
18 *osmnáct*
19 *devatenáct*
20 *dvacet*
21 *dvacet jedna*
30 *třicet*
40 *čtyřicet*
50 *padesát*
60 *šedesát*
70 *sedmdesát*
80 *osmdesát*
90 *devadesát*
100 *sto*
200 *dvě stě*
300 / 400 *tři / čtyři sta*
500 / 600 / 700 / 800 / 900 *pět / šest / sedm / osm / devět set*

1,000 *tisíc*
2,000 *dva tisíce*

TIME

What time is it? *Kolik je hodin?*
It's 1am / 3pm (15:00) *Je jedna hodina / Je patnáct hodin*
noon/midday *poledne*
midnight *půlnoc*
morning (early, before leaving the house) *ráno*
morning (before noon) *dopoledne*
afternoon *odpoledne*
evening *večer*
yesterday *včera*
today *dnes / dneska*
tomorrow *zítra*
now *ted'*

DAYS AND MONTHS

week *týden*
month *měsíc*
Monday *pondělí*
Tuesday *úterý*
Wednesday *středa*
Thursday *čtvrtek*
Friday *pátek*
Saturday *sobota*
Sunday *neděle*
January *leden*
February *únor*
March *březen*
April *duben*
May *květen*
June *červen*
July *červenec*
August *srpen*
September *září*
October *říjen*
November *listopad*
December *prosinec*

German Phrasebook

German is the national language in Austria, and although there are some regional differences between Austrian German and the standard German you had learned at school (if you studied German, that is), you can still communicate without any issues. German shares a lot of words with English and much of the pronunciation is similar to English words, making it perhaps the easiest language to decipher in the three countries. A couple of phonetic things to note:

ch is pronounced kh (think the ch in the composer Bach's name)

r comes from the back of the throat

ß is a double s

sch is like our sh

tsch is like our ch

ö kind of sounds like er, but think of it as going to say o but changing to an a

ä is like a sort e, like in bet

ü make your lips form the shape they would take if you would say o but try to say e instead.

ESSENTIAL PHRASES

Hello *Grüss Gott/Servus*

Good morning *Guten morgen*

Good evening *Grüss Gott/Guten abend*

Good night *Guten nacht*

Good bye *Auf Wiedersehen*

Nice to meet you *Es ist schon, Sie kennen zu lemen*

Thank you *Danke*

You're welcome *Bitte*

Please *Bitte*

Excuse me *Entschuldigung*

Sorry *Entschuldigung*

Do you speak English? *Sprechen Sie Englisch?*

I don't understand *Ich verstehe nicht.*

Yes *Ja*

No *Nein*

TRANSPORTATION

Where is...? *Wo ist...?*

How far is...? *Wie weit ist...?*

Is there a bus to...? *Gibt es einen Bus nach...?*

Does this bus go to...? *Fährt dieser Bus nach...?*

Where do I get off? *Wo muss ich aussteigen?*

What time does the bus/train leave? *Wann fährt der Bus/Zug ab/?*

Where is the nearest subway station? *Wo ist die nächste U-Bahn Station?*

Where's the ticket office? *Wo ist der Ticketschalter?*

A round-trip ticket/single ticket to... *Eine Rückfahrkarte/einfache Fahrkarte nach...*

FOOD

A table for one person/two people... *Ein Tisch für eine Person/zwei Personen, bitte.*

Do you have a menu in English? *Gibt es eine Speisekarte auf Englisch?*

What is the dish of the day? *Was ist das Tagesgericht?*

I'm ready to order. *Ich möchte bestellen.*

I'm vegetarian. *Ich bin Vegetarier/ Vegetarierin (m/f).*

May I have... *Kann ich... haben?*

The check, please. *Zahlen, bitte.*

beer *Bier*

breakfast *Frühstück*

cash *Bar geld/bar*

check *Rechnung*

coffee *Kaffee*

dinner *Abendessen*

glass *Glas*

hors d'oeuvre *Vorspeise*

ice *Eis*

ice cream *Eis*

lunch *Mittagessen*

restaurant *Restaurant*

snack *Snack*

waiter *Ober/Kellner*
water *Wasser*
wine *Wein*

SHOPPING

money *Geld*
shop *Laden*
What time do the shops close? *Wann schließen die Läden?*
How much is this? *Was kostet das?*
I'm just looking. *Ich sehe mich nur um.*

HEALTH

drugstore *Apotheke*
pain *Schmerz*
fever *Fieber*
headache *Kopfschmerzen*
stomach ache *Magenschmerzen*
toothache *Zahnschmerzen*
burn *Brandwunde*
cramp *Krampf*
nausea *Übelkeit*
vomiting *Erbrechen*
medicine *Medizin*
antibiotic *Antibiotikum*
pill/tablet *Pille/Tablette*
aspirin *Aspirin*
I need a doctor *Ich brauche einen Arzt.*
Please take me to the hospital *Bringen Sie mich bitte ins Krankenhaus.*
I have a pain here... *Es tut hier weh...*
I am diabetic/pregnant. *Ich bin zuckerkrank/schwanger.*
I am allergic to penicillin/cortisone. *Ich bin gegen Penicillin/Kortison allergisch.*
My blood group is... positive/ negative. *Ich habe Blutgruppe... positiv/ negativ.*

NUMBERS

0 *zero*
1 *eins*
2 *zwei*
3 *drei*
4 *vier*
5 *funf*
6 *sechs*
7 *sieben*
8 *acht*
9 *neun*
10 *zehn*
11 *elf*
12 *zwölf*
13 *dreizehn*
14 *vierzehn*
15 *funfzehn*
16 *sechszehn*
17 *seibzehn*
18 *achtzehn*
19 *neunzehn*
20 *zwanzig*
21 *einundzwanzig*
30 *dreißig*
40 *vierzig*
50 *funfzig*
60 *sechzig*
70 *siebzig*
80 *achtzig*
90 *neunzig*
100 *hundert*
101 *einhundertundeins*
200 *zweihundert*
500 *funfhundert*
1,000 *tausend*
10,000 *zehntausend*
100,000 *hunderttausend*
1,000,000 *million*

TIME

What time is it? *Wie spät ist es?*
It's one/three o'clock. *Es ist ein/drei Uhr.*
midday *Mittag*
midnight *Midnacht*
morning *Morgen*
afternoon *Nachmittag*
evening *Abend*
night *Nacht*
yesterday *Gestern*
today *Heute*
tomorrow *Morgen*

DAYS AND MONTHS

week *Woche*
month *Monat*
Monday *Montag*
Tuesday *Dienstag*

Wednesday *Mittwoch*
Thursday *Donnerstag*
Friday *Freitag*
Saturday *Samstag*
Sunday *Sonntag*
January *Januar*
February *Februar*
March *März*
April *April*

May *Mai*
June *Juni*
July *Juli*
August *August*
September *September*
October *October*
November *November*
December *Dezember*

Hungarian Phrasebook

Hungarian is a language that has nothing in common with its Slavic, Germanic, and Latin neighbors around. The good thing is Hungarian is in Latin script, so you should be able to read signs and the basics, but the bad news is apart from borrowed words from English there won't be much you'll understand. Hungarian is quite tricky for English speakers to pronounce, but here are a few basics to help:

s   is pronounced sh
sz   is what we think is an s
ny   is easiest explained as sounding like the
     Spanish ñ, but if you don't speak Spanish
     think of it like the ny in the singer's name
     Enya.
gy   is more like d'ya, the g is very soft
ő   is like a long o and an e put together
ű   resembles a long e and u together
dzs is like our j
j   is like a y
ó   sounds like or, as in Eeyore
é   is a long e
í   is a long i
á   is like a sigh of relief, aah
ú   sounds like oo
ö   is a short and rounded o
ü   is a short and rounded u

ESSENTIAL PHRASES

Hello *Szervusz/Szia* (informal)
Good morning *Jó reggelt*
Good afternoon *Jó napot*
Good evening *Jó estét*

Good night *Jó éjszakát*
Good bye *Viszontlátásra*
Nice to meet you *Örvendek*
Thank you *Köszönöm*
You're welcome *Szívesen*
Please *Kérem*
Do you speak English? *Beszél angolul?*
I don't understand. *Nem értem.*
Yes *Igen*
No *Nem*

TRANSPORTATION

Where is...? *Hol van...?*
How far is...? *Milyen messze van...?*
Is there a bus to...? *Van egy busz...?*
Does this bus go to...? *Ez a busz megy...?*
Where do I get off? *Hol kell leszállni?*
What time does the bus/train
    leave? *Mikor indul a busz/vonat?*
Where is the nearest subway
    station? *Hol van a legközelebbi metró?*
Where can I buy a ticket? *Hol tudok jegyet
venni?*
A round-trip ticket/single ticket
    to... *Egy menettérti jegyet/jegy...*

FOOD

A table for one/two... *Egy ember/két
ember számára kérek asztalt*
Do you have a menu in English? *Van
angol menü?*
What is the dish of the day? *Mi a napi
étel?*
We're ready to order. *Szeretnénk rendelni.*

I'm vegetarian. *Vegetáriánus vagyok.*
I would like to order a... *Szeretnék rendelni egy...*
The check, please. *A számlát, kérem.*
beer *sör*
breakfast *reggeli*
cash *készpénz*
check *számla*
coffee *kávé*
dinner *vacsora*
glass *pohár*
hors d'oeuvre *előétel*
ice *jég*
ice cream *jégkrém*
lunch *ebéd*
restaurant *étterem*
sandwich *szendvics*
snack *falatozás*
waiter *pincér*
water *víz*
wine *bor*

SHOPPING

money *pénz*
shop *bolt/üzlet*
What time do the shops close? *Mikor zárnak a boltok?*
How much is it? *Mennyibe kerül*
I'm just looking. *Csak nézelődök.*
Is there a local specialty? *Van egy helyi specialitás?*

HEALTH

drugstore *gyógyszertár*
pain *fájdalom*
fever *láz*
headache *fejfájás*
stomach ache *hasfájás*
toothache *fogfájás*
burn *égés*
cramp *görcs*
nausea *hányinger*
vomiting *hányás*
medicine *gyógyszer*
antibiotic *antibiotikum*
pill/tablet *tabletta*
aspirin *aszpirin*
I need a doctor. *Szükségem van egy orvosra.*

I need to go to the hospital. *Kórházba kell mennem.*
I have a pain here... *Fájdalom van itt ...*
She/he has been stung/bitten. *Elcsípett/ megharapott.*
I am diabetic/pregnant. *Cukorbeteg/ Terhes vagyok*
I am allergic to penicillin/ cortisone. *Allergiás vagyok a penicillinre / kortizonra.*
My blood group is... positive/ negative. *A vércsoportom... pozitív/ negatív.*

NUMBERS

0 *nulla*
1 *egy*
2 *kettő*
3 *három*
4 *négy*
5 *öt*
6 *hat*
7 *hét*
8 *nyolc*
9 *kilenc*
10 *tíz*
11 *tizenegy*
12 *tizenkettő*
13 *tizenhárom*
14 *tizennégy*
15 *tizenöt*
16 *tizenhat*
17 *tizenhét*
18 *tizennyolc*
19 *tizenkilenc*
20 *húsz*
21 *huszonegy*
30 *harminc*
40 *negyven*
50 *ötven*
60 *hatvan*
70 *hetven*
80 *nyolcvan*
90 *kilencven*
100 *száz*
101 *száz és egy*
200 *kétszáz*
500 *ötszáz*

1,000 ezer	month hónap
10,000 tízezer	Monday Hétfő
100,000 százezer	Tuesday Kedd
1,000,000 millió	Wednesday Szerda
	Thursday Csütörtök

TIME

What time is it? Mennyi az idő?	Friday Péntek
	Saturday Szombat
It's one/three o'clock Egy/Három óra van	Sunday Vasárnap
midday dél	January Január
midnight éjfél	February Február
morning reggel	March Március
afternoon délután	April Április
evening este	May Május
night éjszaka	June Június
yesterday tegnap	July Július
today ma	August Augusztus
tomorrow holnap	September Szeptember
	October Oktober

DAYS AND MONTHS

November November

week hét

December December

Suggested Reading

PRAGUE

Nonfiction

Prague: A Cultural History. Richard D. Burton. An in-depth, academic look at Czech history, architecture, and culture organized into easy-to-follow sections. The expanded listings on popular monuments and their connections to history add additional context and background for visitors.

The Czechs In a Nutshell. Terje B. Englund. This tongue-in-cheek description of Czech culture by a Norwegian man is a sarcastic encyclopedia-style overview on subjects like beer, beauty pageants, and the Battle of White Mountain. A few observations (from 2004) have changed over time, but the light-hearted tone is a good primer on Czech history, quirks, and cultural differences.

Believe in People: The Essential Karel Čapek. Czech novelist Karel Čapek is best known for inventing the word "robot" in his 1920

sci-fi play *RUR.* This collection of his translated journalistic works and letters to his wife, Olga, paints a picture of early 21st-century Czech life through the interesting observations of a local literary legend.

Prague Winter. Madeline Albright. The former US Secretary of State offers a touching story of discovering her Czech roots later in life. Personal memories from a uniquely political perspective inform her observations of WWII, the rise of Communism, and the Cold War.

Fiction

The Good Soldier Švejk. Jaroslav Hašek. Czech literature is full of anti-heroes and ironic humor and "Svejk" is their most famous archetype. Follow the smartest man in the room (or the luckiest bumbling idiot, depending on your interpretation) as he navigates the Austro-Hungarian army and bureaucracy in general during WWI.

I Served the King of England. Bohumil Hrabal. Another great example of Czech satire, this historical novel is set during WWII and the subsequent Communist occupation. A man named Dítě (meaning "child" in Czech) narrates his life, dreams, and aspirations in the hospitality industry.

HHhH. Laurent Binet & Sam Taylor. Those four Hs stand for Nazi leader Heinrich Himmler and his "brain" ("hirn" in German) Reinhard Heydrich, AKA the "butcher of Prague". A historical tale based on true events, this novel follows Heydrich through his time in the Third Reich to his eventual execution by a young team of Czechs. This story is also available in film form in the movie *Anthropoid* (see below) and provides context for the real-life memorial to the Czech soldiers located in New Town.

The Book of Laughter and Forgetting. Milan Kundera. Kundera's first major international success weaves together politics, philosophy, surrealism, and banality through rumination on the challenges of life in communist Czechoslovakia. In seven different narratives, Kundera explores the theme of forgetting and what that means for relationships both between people and between a government and its subjects.

Me, Myself, & Prague. Rachael Weiss. A single, 40-year-old Australian woman decides to move to Prague, write a novel, and discover her Czech roots. Obviously things don't go as smoothly as planned. Weiss' self-deprecating, semi-biographical recounting offers a relatable read through the eyes of an outsider discovering the Czech capital.

Czech Fairytales. Božena Němcová & Karel Jaromír Erben. Kings, queens, witches, and magic are essential elements of Czech children's literature and ingrained in much of the culture. Want proof? Fairy tales are shown non-stop on television from morning to night on December 24th as part of the Christmas festivities. This collection makes for great bedtime reading in the weeks leading up to your trip.

VIENNA
Nonfiction

Vienna: A Cultural and Literary History. Nicholas T. Parsons. A comprehensive introduction to Vienna's history from prehistory through to the modern day. Great to orientate yourself in the city's history and people and get some background understanding into the city.

Fin de Siecle Vienna. Carl Emil Schorske. The Fin de Siecle marked Vienna in many ways, and this collection of essays offers a comprehensive analysis of the city's politics, art, architecture, and the birth of psychoanalysis.

The World of Yesterday. Stefan Zweig. This beautiful, biographical book chronicles the history of the early 20th century Europe from through the decline of the Habsburg Empire and the World Wars. The evocative prose by Zweig inspired Wes Anderson's *Grand Budapest Hotel*.

Wittgenstein's Vienna. Alan Janik. Follow in the steps of the philosopher Ludwig Wittgenstein across Vienna in a unique portrait of the pre-war city.

Only in Vienna. Duncan J.D. Smith. Go off the beaten track in Vienna with this alternative guide to all the quirky and unique places you can only find in the Austrian capital.

The Habsburgs: The History of a Dynasty. Benjamin Curtis. Get some background on the Habsburg family with this in-depth account of Central Europe's most important family.

Hitler's Vienna: A Dictator's Apprenticeship. Brigitte Hamann. Hitler spent his formative years in Vienna, and this book paints a portrait of the terrible dictator who would tear Europe apart.

The Spell of the Vienna Woods: Inspiration and Influence from Beethoven to Kafka. Paul Hofmann. Discover why the Vienna Woods are so iconic for the Viennese with stories and anecdotes about the artists and musicians who found inspiration in the woods, threaded into their history.

Fiction

The Radetzky March. Joseph Roth. This epic tale chronicles four generations of an aristocratic family who lived during the decline and fall of the Habsburg Empire.

The Man Without Qualities. Robert Musil. A modernist door-stopper, this book tells the tale of the morally ambiguous Ulrich, a man with a complicated history as an ex-soldier, mathematician, and seducer. The novel charts the twilight days of the Habsburg Empire at the beginning of World War I.

Dream Story. Arthur Schnitzler. If you've seen Stanley Kubrick's *Eyes Wide Shut*, the plot of this pocket-sized book will seem familiar (it was the original source material). Arthur Schnitzler's novelette is a throwback to a decadent Vienna, wrapped inside a masked psycho-sexual drama that is very Viennese.

The Piano Teacher. Elfriede Jelinek. A high-octane drama set in 1960s Vienna that's not for everyone. Intense, highly sexual, and violent, the story traces the neurotic fantasies of Erika Kohut as she tries to escape her controlling mother's clutches by descending into the dark world of voyeurism, self-harm, and sadomasochism.

BUDAPEST
Nonfiction

Budapest 1900. John Lukacs. This fascinating historical account about Budapest's golden age around the turn of the 20th-century is a fun read that gives you context about the history of the city.

Budapest: A Critical Guide. András Toörök. Although it's a guidebook with walking tours, Török's voice and anecdotes take you deeper into the city's history and culture, offering excellent local insight into the city.

Hungarian Wine: A Tasting Trip to the New Old World. Robert Smyth. Get acquainted with Hungarian wine, its varieties, and vineyards if you're interested in knowing what to taste on your trip.

Enemies of the People. Kati Marton. If you're curious about life behind the Iron Curtain, this book exposing life under Communism told from the author's point of view, and the story of her family offers insight into life under Soviet eyes.

Journey to a Revolution: A Personal Memoir and History of the Hungarian Revolution of 1956. Michael Korda. Korda's book blends memoir with the history of the 1956 revolution as he returns to his father's homeland.

A Guest in My Own Country: A Hungarian Life. George Konrád. Konrád takes readers back through his life and the turbulent history of mid-20th century Budapest's. After narrowly escaping the Jewish deportations in his hometown in the countryside, Konrád survives the Siege of Budapest and the revolution of 1956; this memoir offers a personal take of the city's history.

Jewish Budapest: Monuments, Rites, History. Kinga Frojimovics, Geza Komoroczy, Viktoria Pusztai, Andrea Strbik. A comprehensive guide to Budapest's Jewish history from the city's grand monuments to the daily life of the city's Jewish community.

Fiction

Fatelessness. Imre Kertész. This semi-autobiographical novel by Nobel Prize-winning author Imre Kertész tells the story of a 14-year-old Hungarian-Jewish boy who is sent to Auschwitz.

Prague. Arthur Phillips. Don't let the title fool you, this is a novel about expat life in post-communist Budapest, where the whining residents feel they don't have it as good as their fellow Americans in Prague.

The Paul Street Boys. Ferenc Molnár. Despite being a book for young adults, the Paul Street Boys is an exciting piece of classic Hungarian literature capturing the spirit of Budapest's VIII District in the early 20th century.

The Door. Magda Szabó. Visceral, moving, and beautiful, this character-based novel based in Budapest tells the story of a writer and her mysterious cleaning lady.

The Baron's Sons. Mór Jókai. If you want something set during the Hungarian Revolution of 1848 and the War of Independence that followed, this family saga surrounding the Baradlay family and the Hungarian revolution.

Suggested Films and Television

PRAGUE

Anthropoid. This painstakingly researched film tells the story of a small, brave team of Czech soldiers and citizens who pulled off an assassination of a top Nazi general during WWII. It's great for adding context before visiting the New Town memorial to their lives.

Palach. Czech student Jan Palach stood at the top of Wenceslas Square in 1969 and set himself on fire to protest the Russian occupation of Prague. This biography examines the last six months of his life.

Masaryk. Not all of Czech history follows its greatest heroes. *Masaryk* takes a complicated look at Jan Masaryk, the son of the first Czechoslovak president, Tomáš Garrigue Masaryk, and his political role in the events of the mid-20th century.

Outlander (Season 2). Fans of the Scottish time-traveling romance series may recognize the streets of Malá Strana standing in for Paris in the second season of this cult cable television favorite

Spiderman: Far From Home. At the time of writing, the next installment of this Hollywood superhero saga was filming in both Prague and Liberec.

VIENNA

The Third Man. This iconic film noir starring Orson Welles was filmed on location in 1940s post-war Vienna. If there is one movie you watch before going to Vienna, make it this one - then you can follow in its footsteps.

Before Sunrise. A romantic classic from the 1990s starring Julie Delpy and Ethan Hawke, this delightful movie takes you on a journey through Vienna from the Prater to the Cemetery of the Nameless.

Sissi. This Austrian classic, starring Romy Schneider, is about the life of Empress Elizabeth and her marriage to Emperor Franz Joseph I.

Amadeus. Although filmed in Prague, *Amadeus* is a delightful romp through Mozart's life and his alleged rivalry against Salieri.

Museum Hours. Get in the mood for a visit to the Kunsthistorisches Museum with this tale of a Canadian tourist and museum steward bonding over the work of art in the museum.

A Dangerous Method. Delve into the friendship and the rift between Sigmund Freud and Carl Jung in this film starring Viggo Mortensen and Michael Fassbender.

BUDAPEST

Kontroll. Filmed entirely on the Budapest subway system, this Hungarian surreal dark comedy about ticket inspectors and a mysteriously hooded murderer makes curious watching.

Son of Saul. This Holocaust drama set in Auschwitz put Hungarian cinema on the map when it won an Oscar in 2015.

The Witness. This 1960s black comedy was banned under the communist regime and went on to become a cult classic. It tells the tale of Pelikan, a simple man who mysteriously moves up the ranks with the communist big guys as they try to bribe him to become a false witness.

Sunshine. Starring Ralph Fiennes, *Sunshine* tells the story of an aristocratic Jewish family in Budapest from the turn of the 20th century through to the Holocaust and under communism.

White God. White God takes place in a world when mixed breeds of dogs are outlawed, and tells the story of 13-year-old Lily and her dog, Hagen. Once Lily is separated from her dog, chaos ensues when 250 dogs follow Hagen on a rampage through the city.

Internet and Digital Resources

PRAGUE
General Information
www.prague.eu/en
Prague City Tourism's website offers tons of basic info and object histories of the most popular tourist sights.

www.czechtourism.com/home/
Turn to the country's official website to discover a "Land of Stories" with photos and basic info about both Prague and destinations across the country.

www.youtube.com/c/honestguide
Straightforward, funny advice for tourists on how to avoid scams and tourist traps from a

pair of young Czech guys turned YouTube sensations.

www.socialismrealised.eu/
An accessible, English-friendly look as the Communist era through a catalog of artifacts, videos, and texts with educational support.

www.expats.cz/
Pop culture news, events, and commentary on life as a foreigner in the Czech Republic.

www.tasteofprague.com/
Gorgeous food photography and the latest in Prague's gastronomy scene from two passionate Czech foodies.

www.duolingo.com/
An easy language-learning app to pick up some useful Czech vocabulary through five-minute lessons before your visit

Transport
www.dpp.cz/en/
The official website for Prague's transport authority offers updated info on construction plus ticket info and maps.

www.cd.cz/en/default.htm
Check train schedules and purchase tickets through the official state-run railway website.

www.regiojet.com/
This local coach and train company offers comfortable, affordable service, plus tickets that you can modify or cancel up to 15 or 30 minutes before your departure (check booking details for confirmation) either online or through their smartphone app.

www.liftago.com/
Local rideshare app with great customer service and an English interface.

VIENNA
General Information
www.wien.info/
This comprehensive website from Vienna's Tourism Board has all the basic information you need.

www.viennawurstelstand.com/
An English-language magazine about Viennese life and what's going on about the town.

www.austria.info
Similar to wien.info, but good if you're planning a day trip or anything further afield.

www.wien.gv.at
The city of Vienna's government site.

Transport
www.wienerlinien.at/
Vienna's official public transport website

Qando App
Download the Qando app to get public transport information in real time.

Wiener Linien
Another app from Wiener Linien, where you can buy and download transport tickets onto your smartphone.

www.oebb.at/
Purchase tickets and checks the train times for national and international departures.

National Parks
www.donauauen.at
Find all the information you need for the Donau-Auen National Park including the Lobau.

www.bpww.at/
Discover all the information about the Vienna Woods Biosphere Reserve surrounding the city.

BUDAPEST
General Information
https://hellohungary.com/
The website of the official Hungarian Tourism Agency, with information on Budapest and beyond.

www.welovebudapest.com
Find out all the latest places that have opened, news about events and general information.

https://funzine.hu/en/
Keep up to date with all the most recent developments and news in the city with this online English-language magazine.

https://ruinpubs.com
Your go-to directory for information on all the best ruin bars in town.

www.spasbudapest.com/
Everything you need to know about Budapest's thermal baths.

Transport
https://bkk.hu/
Find out everything you need to know about Budapest's public transport on the official website for the BKK.

BKK App
Download the app to know when the next tram or metro is due in real time.

www.mavcsoport.hu/
Buy tickets and check the timetables for national and international trains.

Index

A

accommodation: Budapest: 402–407; general information: 463–465; Prague: 128–134; Vienna: 273–280; see also specific place

air travel: Budapest: 408–409, 455–456; general information: 22–23, 28, 458, 459; Prague: 136, 455–456; Vienna: 281–282, 455–456

Albertina: 202

Alfons Mucha Museum: 47, 60–61

Alsergrund and Josefstadt (9th, 8th Districts): 190; accommodation: 279; bars and nightlife: 239, 241–242, 243; food: 271–272; maps: 224–225; sights: 229–230

amusement parks: 223

Anděl: 48, 91, 98, 115, 121

Andrassy Avenue (VI District): 324–325; accommodation: 404–405; bars and nightlife in: 371, 372–373, 374; food: 397–398; performing arts: 375–377; shopping: 390; sights: 345–347

animals: Budapest: 347; Prague: 107; Vienna: 234

Anker Clock: 199

Anthropoid mission: 64

Aquincum: 319, 361–362

architecture: 148; Budapest: 35–36, 447–449; general information: 9, 447–449; Prague: 32–33, 37, 447–449, 451; Vienna: 33, 35, 447–449

Architecture Center: 210

Art Market Budapest: 377

Art Mill: 418

art nouveau architecture: 148

Art Nouveau Museum of Applied Arts: 450

Artstetten Castle: 201, 299–300

Astronomical Clock: 6, 51, 53, 55

Augarten: 248, 251

Augarten Porcelain Manufactory and Museum: 228

Aurelius, Marcus: 361–362

Austrian National Library: 204

Austro-Hungarian Empire: 7, 42, 183, 221, 321, 322

B

Badacsony: 434–436

Baden bei Wien: accommodation: 296; food: 295–296; parks: 295; sights: 293–294; transportation: 296–297

Baden Casino: 294

Balatonfüred: 28, 429–432

Balaton Pantheon: 430

Bálna: 358, 359

Baroque architecture: 447

Baroque Theater: 163

bars and nightlife: Budapest: 11, 17, 29, 31, 318, 322, 369–375, 386, 391; general information: 29, 31, 465–466; LGBT travelers: 29; Prague: 15, 29, 38, 42, 43, 47, 50, 77, 80, 82, 89–100, 94, 112–113; Vienna: 17, 25, 26, 29, 31, 236–244, 261; see also specific place

Bartók Béla Avenue: 401

Basilica of Sts. Peter & Paul: 32, 80, 82

beach bars: 29, 31, 237

beaches: Budapest: 379–381; Siófok: 413, 437; Tihany: 433; Vienna: 252

Bear Moat: 161

Becherovka Museum & Factory: 159

beer and breweries: Budapest: 373; Prague: 15, 29, 38, 47, 50, 80, 92, 94, 96; Vienna: 242

Beethoven, Ludwig van: 230, 294–295

Beethoven Frieze: 212

Beethoven House: 294–295

Beethoven Pasqualatihaus: 230

Belvedere Palace area: 27, 182, 221–222; accommodation: 278; Belvedere Palace: 182, 217–220, 451; food: 260, 268–270; shopping: 255

Belvedere Palace Gardens: 220

Benedictine Abbey of Tihany: 28, 433

Biedermeier: 211

biking: see cycling

Blagoveštenska Orthodox Church: 416–417, 419

Blue Church: 35, 286, 312

boat: Bratislava: 315; Budapest: 332–333, 383, 411, 457; Danube Bend: 413, 426; Esztergom: 428; general information: 457; Szentendre: 421; Vienna: 252; Vienna Woods: 30; Visegrád: 30; Wachau Valley: 26, 30, 286, 298

Bohemian Paradise: accommodation: 156; castles: 153–154, 155; food: 155; hiking: 153–155, 158; transportation: 156

bone church: see Sedlec Ossuary

Borromeo, Charles: 214

Bratislava: 30, 285; accommodation: 314–315; Blue Church in: 35, 286, 312; food: 313–314; Old Town: 286, 311; sights: 311–313; transportation: 315–316

Bratislava Castle: 312

breweries: see beer and breweries

Brno: accommodation: 172; bars and nightlife: 170; food: 170–172; map: 168; sights: 167–170; transportation: 172–173

Buda Arboretum: 355

Buda Castle: 27, 318, 330, 332

List of Maps

Photo Credits

Title page photo: view of St. Nicolas Church from Charles bridge, Prague © martinmolcan | dreamstime.com. Page 2 © samot | dreamstime.com; page 3 © irinasen | dreamstime.com; page 6 © (top left) manfredxy | dreamstime.com; (top right) tomas1111 | dreamstime.com; (bottom) alyssand | dreamstime.com; page 7 © (bottom right) jennifer walker; (top) bogdan | dreamstime.com; pages 8-9 © Janoka82 | Dreamstime. com; page 10 © (top) tevfikmg | dreamstime.com (bottom) pytyczech | dreamstime.com; page 11 © (top) holman77177 | dreamstime.com; (middle) aiciagm | dreamstime.com; (bottom) gerasimovvv | dreamstime. com; pages 12-13 © (top) mikecphoto | dreamstime.com (bottom) gtsichlis | dreamstime.com; page 14 © mikepax | dreamstime.com; page 15 © (middle) kunsthistorisches museum; page 16 © (top) café central at palais ferstel, vienna; (bottom) josefkrcil | dreamstime.com; page 17 © (top) alexmu | dreamstime.com (middle) romanple | dreamstime.com (bottom) daliu80 | dreamstime.com; page 19 © pigprox | dreamstime. com; page 20 © elenakirey | dreamstime.com; page 22 © tanyarozhnovskaya | dreamstime.com; page 23 © toxawww | dreamstime.com; page 24 © kirillm | dreamstime.com; page 25 © (left) auburn scallon; (right) danielschreurs | dreamstime.com; page 26 © forgiss | dreamstime.com; serawood3 | dreamstime.com; page 27 © (top) rosshelen | dreamstime.com; (bottom) emicristea | dreamstime.com; page 28 © jennifer walker; skovalsky | dreamstime.com; page 30 © basiczto | dreamstime.com; page 31 © jennifer walker; page 32 © ysk1954 | dreamstime.com; byvalet | dreamstime.com; page 33 © markovskiy | dreamstime.com; katerinalin | dreamstime.com; page 35 © jennifer walker; page 36 © jennifer walker; page 37 © olgacov | dreamstime.com; page 44 © scanrail | dreamstime.com; page 55 © (top left) auburn scallon; (top right) charles stewart; (bottom) mapics | dreamstime.com; page 59 © (top) felker | dreamstime.com; (left middle) auburn scallon; (right middle) auburn scallon; (bottom) nomadbeg | dreamstime.com; page 64 © auburn scallon; page 65 © sazonoff | dreamstime.com; page 66 © zhu_zhu | dreamstime.com; page 69 © (top left) auburn scallon; (top right) dimbar76 | dreamstime.com; (bottom) pytyczech | dreamstime.com; page 76 © (top) dimbar76 | dreamstime.com; (right middle)samurkas | dreamstime.com; (bottom) lefpap | dreamstime.com; page 79 © (top left) gonewiththewind | dreamstime.com; (top right) auburn scallon; (bottom left) auburn scallon; (bottom right) mariangarai | dreamstime.com; page 83 © auburn scallon; page 84 © (top) florinseitan | dreamstime.com; (bottom) auburn scallon; page 87 © auburn scallon; page 88 © auburn scallon; page 93 © auburn scallon; page 94 © auburn scallon; page 96 © auburn scallon; page 97 © (top left) auburn scallon; (top right) auburn scallon; (bottom) auburn scallon; page 101 © (top) auburn scallon; (bottom) pytyczech | dreamstime.com; page 107 © auburn scallon; page 109 © (top left) auburn scallon; (top right) auburn scallon; (bottom) auburn scallon; page 115 © auburn scallon; page 119 © auburn scallon; page 126 © (top left) auburn scallon; (top right) auburn scallon; (bottom left) auburn scallon; (bottom right) auburn scallon; page 140 © auburn scallon; page 142 © elenajs | dreamstime.com; page 143 © (left) auburn scallon (right) smokon | dreamstime.com; page 148 © (top) auburn scallon; (left middle) auburn scallon; (right middle) auburn scallon; (bottom) zhu_zhu | dreamstime.com; page 153 © auburn scallon; page 158 © (top left) auburn scallon; (top right) xantana | dreamstime.com; (bottom left) auburn scallon; (bottom right) auburn scallon; page 165 © (top) smokon | dreamstime.com; (bottom) poooow | dreamstime.com; page 176 © (top) graphiapl | dreamstime.com; (left middle) auburn scallon; (right middle) rostislav_sedlacek | dreamstime.com; (bottom) milangonda | dreamstime.com; page 181 © dezign80 | dreamstime.com; page 182 © (left) digitalpress | dreamstime.com; (right) travelwitness | dreamstime. com; page 188 © jennifer walker; page 198 © (top) mila103 | dreamstime.com; (left middle) tanjakrstevska | dreamstime.com; (right middle) Jennifer Walker (bottom) svetlana195 | dreamstime.com; page 200 © jennifer walker; page 203 © jennifer walker; page 206 © (top) kunsthistorisches museum; (bottom) kunsthistorisches museum; page 210 © jennifer walker; page 213 © jennifer walker; page 215 © (top left) vvoevale | dreamstime.com; (top right) jennifer walker; (bottom) jennifer walker; page 218 © (top left) mtree555 | dreamstime.com; (top right) belvedere, wien; (bottom) minnystock | dreamstime.com; page 221 © jennifer walker; page 226 © (top) jennifer walker; (top right) jennifer walker; (left middle) jennifer walker; (right middle) jennifer walker; (bottom) jennifer walker; page 232 © jennifer walker; page 233 © jennifer walker; page 235 © jennifer walker; page 247 © deepbluero | dreamstime.com; page 249 © jennifer walker; page 251 © (top left) jennifer walker; (top right) jennifer walker; (bottom left) bwagner656 | dreamstime.com; (bottom right) jennifer walker; page 257 © (top) jennifer walker; (bottom) jennifer walker; page 263 © jennifer walker; page 276 © jennifer walker; page 277 © hotel imperial vienna; page 285 © tomas1111 | dreamstime.

MOON
CAMINO DE SANTIAGO

SACRED SITES,
HISTORIC VILLAGES,
LOCAL FOOD & WINE

BEEBE BAHRAMI

Embark on an epic journey along the historic Camino de Santiago, stroll the most popular European cities, or chase the northern lights in Norway with Moon Travel Guides!

MOON
AMALFI COAST
With Capri, Naples & Pompeii
LAURA THAYER

MOON
BARCELONA & MADRID
JESSICA JONES

MOON
CROATIA & SLOVENIA
SHANN FOUNTAIN ALIPOUR

MOON
EDINBURGH, GLASGOW & THE ISLE OF SKYE

MOON
ICELAND
JENNA GOTTLIEB

MOON
IRELAND
CAMILLE DeANGELIS

MOON
NORMANDY & BRITTANY
With Mont-Saint-Michel
CHRIS NEWENS

MOON
NORWAY
DAVID NIKEL

MOON
PORTUGAL
CARRIE-MARIE BRATLEY

MOON
PRAGUE, VIENNA & BUDAPEST

MOON
PROVENCE

MOON
ROME, FLORENCE & VENICE
ALEXEI J. COHEN

GO BIG AND GO BEYOND!

These savvy city guides include strategies to help you see the top sights and find adventure beyond the tourist crowds.

OR TAKE THINGS ONE STEP AT A TIME

Stunning Sights Around the World

- BELIZE
- COSTA RICA
- FIJI
- MACHU PICCHU — TRIP OF A LIFETIME
- MOROCCO
- NORWAY
- PATAGONIA — TRIP OF A LIFETIME
- ROME, FLORENCE & VENICE

Guides for Urban Adventure

- BUENOS AIRES
- LISBON
- MEXICO CITY
- MONTRÉAL
- NEW YORK CITY
- OSLO
- VANCOUVER
- WASHINGTON DC

MAP SYMBOLS

Expressway	○ City/Town	✈ Airport	Golf Course
Primary Road	◉ State Capital	Airfield	P Parking Area
Secondary Road	⊛ National Capital	▲ Mountain	Archaeological Site
Unpaved Road	★ Point of Interest	✛ Unique Natural Feature	Church
Feature Trail	• Accommodation	Waterfall	Gas Station
Other Trail	▼ Restaurant/Bar	▲ Park	Glacier
Ferry	■ Other Location	⊓ Trailhead	Mangrove
Pedestrian Walkway		Skiing Area	Reef
Stairs	⋀ Campground		Swamp

CONVERSION TABLES

°C = (°F - 32) / 1.8
°F = (°C x 1.8) + 32
1 inch = 2.54 centimeters (cm)
1 foot = 0.304 meters (m)
1 yard = 0.914 meters
1 mile = 1.6093 kilometers (km)
1 km = 0.6214 miles
1 fathom = 1.8288 m
1 chain = 20.1168 m
1 furlong = 201.168 m
1 acre = 0.4047 hectares
1 sq km = 100 hectares
1 sq mile = 2.59 square km
1 ounce = 28.35 grams
1 pound = 0.4536 kilograms
1 short ton = 0.90718 metric ton
1 short ton = 2,000 pounds
1 long ton = 1.016 metric tons
1 long ton = 2,240 pounds
1 metric ton = 1,000 kilograms
1 quart = 0.94635 liters
1 US gallon = 3.7854 liters
1 Imperial gallon = 4.5459 liters
1 nautical mile = 1.852 km

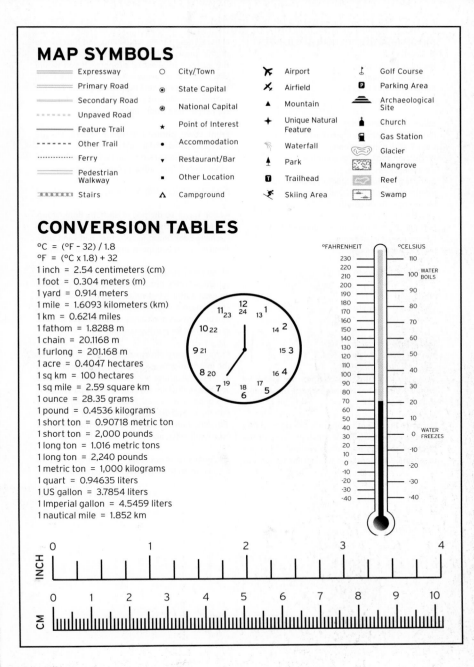

MOON PRAGUE, VIENNA & BUDAPEST

Avalon Travel
Hachette Book Group
1700 Fourth Street
Berkeley, CA 94710, USA
www.moon.com

Editor: Nikki Ioakimedes
Project Management: Marco Pavia
Copy Editor: Kammy Wood
Production and Graphics Coordinator:
  Lucie Ericksen
Cover Design: Faceout Studios, Charles Brock
Interior Design: Domini Dragoone
Moon Logo: Tim McGrath
Map Editor: Kat Bennett
Cartographers: Karin Dahl, Kat Bennett
Proofreader: Rachel Aubin
Indexer: Arc Indexing, Inc.

ISBN-13: 978-1-64049-011-6

Printing History
1st Edition — July 2019
5 4 3 2 1